Pipe Flow: Research and Applications

Pipe Flow: Research and Applications

Guest Editors

Leonardo Di G. Sigalotti
Carlos Enrique Alvarado-Rodríguez

MDPI

Basel • Beijing • Wuhan • Barcelona • Belgrade • Novi Sad • Cluj • Manchester

Guest Editors
Leonardo Di G. Sigalotti
Department of Basic Sciences
Metropolitan Autonomous
University-Azcapotzalco
Campus
Mexico City
Mexico

Carlos Enrique
Alvarado-Rodríguez
Department of Chemical
Engineering
University of Guanajuato
Guanajuato
Mexico

Editorial Office
MDPI AG
Grosspeteranlage 5
4052 Basel, Switzerland

This is a reprint of the Special Issue, published open access by the journal *Fluids* (ISSN 2311-5521), freely accessible at: https://www.mdpi.com/journal/fluids/special_issues/KAQ4MJ43E6.

For citation purposes, cite each article independently as indicated on the article page online and as indicated below:

Lastname, A.A.; Lastname, B.B. Article Title. *Journal Name* **Year**, *Volume Number*, Page Range.

ISBN 978-3-7258-4436-4 (Hbk)
ISBN 978-3-7258-4435-7 (PDF)
https://doi.org/10.3390/books978-3-7258-4435-7

Contents

About the Editors

Leonardo Di G. Sigalotti

Dr. Leonardo Di G. Sigalotti is a professor in the Area of Physics of Irreversible Processes at the Department of Basic Sciences, Universidad Autónoma Metropolitana (UAM) Azcapotzalco, Mexico City. Born on May 10, 1961, in Udine, Italy, he earned his B.Sc. in Physics from the Universidad de Los Andes in Mérida, Venezuela, and both his M.Sc. and Ph.D. in Theoretical Astrophysics from the Scuola Internazionale Superiore di Studi Avanzati (SISSA) in Trieste, Italy, under the guidance of Professors Dennis W. Sciama and Fernando de Felice. He subsequently held a postdoctoral position at the International Centre for Theoretical Physics (ICTP) in Trieste. In 2000, he joined the Physics Center of the Venezuelan Institute for Scientific Research (IVIC) in Caracas as a permanent researcher. In 2014, he was invited to UAM Azcapotzalco to hold the Francisco Medina Nicolau Chair in the Area of Physics of Irreversible Processes. His research interests encompass star formation processes, flow dynamics in pipes and channels, drop and bubble dynamics, the numerical analysis of particle methods, and multiphase and multicomponent fluid flows. He has authored and co-authored numerous research articles and book chapters in these areas and has edited several volumes on fluid dynamics. He is also co-author of the books *Time Series Analysis in Seismology* and *Air Turbulence and its Methods of Detection*.

Carlos Enrique Alvarado-Rodríguez

Carlos E. Alvarado-Rodríguez is a Mexican researcher specializing in chemical engineering, currently affiliated with the Department of Chemical Engineering at the University of Guanajuato.

His academic background includes undergraduate, master's, and doctoral studies at the same institution, where he also completed a postdoctoral fellowship in 2018.

His research focuses on biochemical engineering, with an emphasis on numerical simulation and modeling of industrial processes. He has published over 40 scientific articles, with more than 4,000 reads and approximately 140 academic citations.

Alvarado-Rodríguez has contributed to studies involving flow simulation in porous media using the Smoothed-Particle Hydrodynamic (SPH) technique, as well as research on the dispersion and adsorption of hexavalent chromium in corn stalk biomass.

In addition to his research work, he has co-edited academic books on continuous improvement in education and governance in upper secondary education, highlighting his commitment to academic outreach and development in his field.

Preface

The transport of fluids through pipes is a cornerstone of modern infrastructure, enabling the delivery of water, oil, gas, chemicals and other critical resources across vast distances. Despite its apparent simplicity, pipe flow continues to present complex challenges, especially as demands for efficiency, sustainability and resilience increase. The interplay of fundamental fluid mechanics, advanced materials, computational modeling and innovative engineering solutions continues to drive this field forward.

This Special Issue, "Pipe Flow: Research and Applications", brings together cutting-edge contributions from researchers and practitioners around the world. It highlights recent advances in both theoretical and applied aspects of pipe flow, ranging from turbulence modeling and multiphase flows to smart pipeline systems and field-scale implementations. The aim is to provide a comprehensive overview of the latest research while fostering dialogue between academia and industry.

We are pleased to feature studies that not only deepen our understanding of classical flow regimes but also address emerging challenges such as flow assurance in extreme environments, energy-efficient transport and the integration of real-time monitoring technologies. Several contributions also demonstrate how modern numerical tools and data-driven approaches are reshaping the way we design, monitor, and optimize pipeline systems.

We extend our sincere gratitude to all the authors for their high-quality submissions, the reviewers for their thoughtful evaluations and the editorial team for their support throughout the process. We hope that this Special Issue will serve as a valuable resource for researchers, engineers and policy-makers engaged in the science and practice of pipe flow.

Leonardo Di G. Sigalotti and Carlos Enrique Alvarado-Rodríguez
Guest Editors

fluids

MDPI

Editorial

Special Issue: Pipe Flow: Research and Applications, First Edition

Leonardo Di G. Sigalotti

Departamento de Ciencias Básicas, Universidad Autónoma Metropolitana, Unidad Azcapotzalco (UAM-A), Av. San Pablo 420, Colonia Nueva el Rosario, Alcaldía Azcapotzalco, Ciudad de México 02128, Mexico; leonardo.sigalotti@gmail.com

The transport of fluids through pipes and channels is a foundational topic in fluid mechanics, with direct applications spanning many branches of science and engineering. Whether delivering potable water across urban areas [1,2], transporting hydrocarbons through continental pipelines [3,4], or optimizing coolant flow in nuclear reactors [5,6], pipe flow remains at the heart of countless real-world systems. In recent years, new computational techniques, novel experimental diagnostics, and increasing environmental concerns have reinvigorated research in this classical field [7–10].

The first edition of this Special Issue on Pipe Flow: Research and Applications aims to highlight the breadth and depth of ongoing innovations and challenges in pipe flow research. The contributions in this Special Issue reflect the state of the art in both fundamental and applied aspects of the discipline. They include advances in various topics dealing with fluid transport in pipes. Authors from both academia and industry have provided insights that bridge theoretical developments and practical implementations, demonstrating the real-world value of research in this field. The cross-disciplinary nature of such studies underscores the versatility of pipe flow research and its adaptability to evolving technological landscapes. This Special Issue contains a collection of 13 papers, whose findings and significance are commented on as follows.

Benmbarek and Moujaes [11] performed computational fluid dynamics (CFD) simulations to investigate the heat transfer performance in a spirally corrugated tube [12,13]. They found that inserting a twisted plate into the tube significantly enhances heat transfer performance in heat exchangers and proposed a new insert geometry, which, apart from establishing a foundation for further innovation, is promoting the design of the next generation of heat exchangers.

In hydraulic engineering, the investigation of air–water interactions in pipelines is crucial for enhancing the efficiency and longevity of water supply systems [14–17]. In this line of research, Bonilla-Correa et al. [18] provided a numerical solution to the complex problem of entrapped air pockets in pipelines. The application of their model will be of great practical use to engineers working in collapse prevention and risk reduction in both the interruption and shortage of the water service.

Enhanced accuracy without significant computational costs continues to be a challenge in the art of mathematical modeling. This is especially important for real-time or large-scale simulations where three-dimensional CFD is largely impractical. Wiens [19] investigated a way to derive correction factors from CFD simulations that can be used by existing one-dimensional methods for an accurate flow description in curved pipes. This contribution is of great practical significance because by correcting for curvature, the models better reflect the real-world designs found in hydraulic systems, automotive, aerospace, and industrial machinery.

Understanding how non-Newtonian fluids interact with deformable microchannels provides valuable insight for industries working with complex biological or polymeric fluids [20–22]. Rubio Martinez et al. [23] developed a mathematical model to investigate how an elastic microchannel (made of polydimethylsiloxane) deforms under the flow of a power law (non-Newtonian) fluid. This model is applicable to emerging technologies like photonic crystals, microstructure analysis, and multiplexed diagnostics, all of which rely on accurate microfluidic control.

De la Cruz-Ávila et al. [24] performed CFD simulations to underscore the importance of turbulence model selection in accurately simulating cavitation in Venturi tubes. The cavitation number trends matched well with the experimental results, supporting the model's validity in capturing cavitation onset and intensity. Their findings enhance our understanding of how turbulence affects vapor cloud dynamics, which is critical for improving hydraulic machinery performance, erosion prediction, and cavitation mitigation strategies [25].

Using experimental data obtained from the multiphase flow loop at the National University of Singapore, Guzmán et al. [26] tested existing model correlations for air–oil pressure drop predictions, providing a novel insight into two-phase flow behavior under high flow conditions. This analysis has implications in our understanding of the process of crude oil transportation through pipelines, which is a critical aspect of the midstream petroleum industry [27].

The formation and localization of pipe structures in sedimentary basins, especially in fluid migration and expulsion processes, are of great geophysical relevance. Gay et al. [28] presented laboratory experiments for the simulation of fluid injection into water-saturated sands using a Hele-Shaw cell setup, focusing on bilayered sediments. Their study reveals that maximum surface deformation occurs only when the fine layer is fluidized, providing a mechanistic basis for predicting subsurface fluid behavior in geophysical settings.

The internal flow dynamics in submerged entry nozzles (SENs) under varying sliding-gate valve (SGV) conditions has direct implications for steel quality in continuous casting processes. In this line of work, Gonzalez-Trejo et al. [29] performed an experimental study of how the SGV modifies the structure and dynamic behavior of the outlet jets for flat-bottom and well-bottom bifurcated SENs used in continuous casting machines. An important practical implication of this study is that steel producers can use these findings to adjust SGV operation and SEN design to achieve the desired mold flow characteristics, enhancing slab uniformity and quality.

Kinra and Pal [30] investigated how suspensions of cellulose nanocrystals (CNCs) behave during pipeline flow, specifically examining how changes in concentration and pipe diameter affect the flow characteristics. CNC suspensions are industrially relevant because their flow behavior is critical for pumping, mixing, and processing design [31,32]. A key finding of this study is that at concentrations lower than 1 wt%, CNC suspensions behave as a Newtonian fluid, while at higher concentrations, the suspensions exhibit a non-Newtonian, power law behavior. The transition from Newtonian to non-Newtonian behavior with an increasing concentration has broader implications in the rheology and fluid mechanics of nanomaterials [33–35].

Krishnappa et al. [36] compares single-channel serpentine flow field (SCSFF) and cross-split serpentine flow field (CSSFF) geometries in an all-iron redox flow battery (AIRFB). This study contributes valuable data and modeling validation for improving the fluid dynamics and operational efficiency of redox flow batteries, which are key components in scalable, renewable energy storage solutions.

Valuable insights for improving the efficiency and safety of sluice gate operations in hydraulic engineering were provided by the study performed by Abbaszadeh et al. [37], who investigated the effects of gate openings and different sill widths on the sluice gate's energy dissipation and discharge coefficient. Most importantly, they provided non-linear polynomial relationships based on dimensionless parameters to predict the energy dissipation and outflow coefficient.

Rodríguez-Rivera et al. [38] performed CFD simulations to investigate the hydrodynamic performance of a novel pipe network using a Rhombic Tessellation Pattern (RTP) with allometric scaling, compared to a traditional Parallel Pipe Pattern. Their study reveals that the RTP provides a highly promising geometry for advanced fluid transport systems, especially where energy efficiency and flow control are critical [39,40].

This Special Issue closes with a comprehensive review of fluid flow in helical pipes [41]. In general, helically coiled pipes are relevant in industrial applications involving heat exchangers, steam generators, and chemical reactors [42–44]. This review addresses important fluid dynamics characteristics that are unique to helical pipes, such as the emergence of secondary flows, the delay of the laminar-to-turbulent transition compared to straight pipes, and turbulence stabilization effects. This review compiles and compares experimental and theoretical studies from the open literature, highlights areas that require further exploration, acts as a knowledge base for researchers and practitioners, and facilitates practical design and optimization in industry.

As the Guest Editor of this Special Issue, I am encouraged by the quality and diversity of the submissions. The articles selected for publication within this Special Issue not only reflect current advancements but also chart future directions for pipe flow research. I hope that this Special Issue will serve as a valuable resource for researchers, engineers, and policy-makers alike and fosters continued innovation and collaboration in the field.

In spite of recent effort, several challenges and future needs persist as systems become ever more complex and performance demands increase continuously [45–47]. Current challenges in pipe flow research include the following: the accurate prediction of turbulent flows under varied geometries and transient conditions, the development of better predictive tools for multiphase and multicomponent pipe flows, the derivation of better constitutive models for non-Newtonian and complex fluids, the development of in situ flow diagnostics for aging systems due to pipe corrosion, scaling and biofilm growth, and, last but not lease, the accurate prediction of the coupled fluid–structure interaction that can cause pipe damage and efficiency losses. Therefore, future research needs and directions must focus on the development of high-fidelity simulation tools and data-driven modeling for creating real-time digital representations of fluid networks, the use of advanced experimental techniques, such as high-speed imaging to capture detailed flow dynamics, optical fiber sensors, and ultrasound for real-time flow measurements inside pipes. Other needs require improving the energy efficiency and optimization of flow control strategies under variable demands and promoting research in emerging areas, such as micro- and nanoscale pipe flow, which are becoming increasingly more important for biomedical devices and microfluidics. In the near future, the rise of smart infrastructure will demand the integration of CFD modeling, experimental data, and machine learning to advance the field.

I express my sincere gratitude to all the authors, reviewers, and editorial staff whose efforts made this Special Issue possible. A very special thanks goes to Assistant Editor Ms. Cori Jia for all her help and assistance. I also look forward to the second edition of this Special Issue that will continue to capture the dynamism and relevance of pipe flow research in an ever-changing world.

Conflicts of Interest: The author declares no conflicts of interest.

References

1. Dawidowicz, J. Evaluation of a Pressure Head and Pressure Zones in Water Distribution Systems by Artificial Neural Networks. *Neural Comput. Appl.* **2018**, *30*, 2531–2538. [CrossRef] [PubMed]
2. Taiwo, R.; Yussif, A.-M.; Zayed, T. Making Waves: Generative Artificial Intelligence in Water Distribution Networks: Opportunities and Challenges. *Water Res. X* **2025**, *28*, 100316. [CrossRef]
3. Han, F.; Lan, Q.; Liu, Y.; Yin, G.; Ong, M.C.; Li, W.; Wang, Z. Unveiling Turbulent Flow Dynamics in Blind-Tee Pipelines Enhancing Fluid Mixing in Subsea Pipeline Systems. *J. Mar. Sci. Eng.* **2024**, *12*, 1199. [CrossRef]
4. Manzano-Ruiz, J.J.; Garballo, J.G. *Multiphase Transport of Hydrocarbons in Pipes*; John Wiley & Sons: Hoboken, NJ, USA, 2024.
5. Wang, H.; Zhu, Z.; Zhang, M.; Han, J. Numerical Investigation of the Large Over-Reading of Venturi Flow Rate in ARE of Nuclear Power Plant. *Nucl. Eng. Technol.* **2021**, *53*, 69–78. [CrossRef]
6. Xiao, H.; Yang, T.; Xie, A. CFD Study of Two-Phase Cross Flow and Heat Transfer in Subchannels of Pressurized Water Reactor Fuel Assemblies. *IOP Conf. Ser. Earth Environ. Sci.* **2023**, *1171*, 012012. [CrossRef]
7. Kalpakli Vester, A.; Örlü, R.; Alfredsson, P.H. Turbulent Flows in Curved Pipes: Recent Advances in Experiments and Simulations. *Appl. Mech.* **2016**, *68*, 050802. [CrossRef]
8. Kassim, M.S.; Sarow, S.A. Flows of Viscous Fluids in Food Processing Industries: A Review. *IOP Conf. Ser. Mater. Sci. Eng.* **2020**, *870*, 012032. [CrossRef]
9. Kavokine, N.; Netz, R.R.; Bocquet, L. Fluids at the Nanoscale: From Continuum to Subcontinuum Transport. *Annu. Rev. Fluid Mech.* **2021**, *53*, 377–410. [CrossRef]
10. Zhang, J.; Zou, Z.; Fu, C. A Review of the Complex Flow and Heat Transfer Characteristics in Microchannels. *Micromachines* **2023**, *14*, 1451. [CrossRef]
11. Benmbarek, M.M.; Moujaes, S.F. CFD Analysis of Heat Transfer Enhancement for Twisted Tape Inserted in Spirally Corrugated Tubes and Proposal of a New Vane-Inserted Geometry. *Fluids* **2025**, *10*, 73. [CrossRef]
12. Li, X.; Liu, S.; Mo, X.; Sun, Z.; Tian, G.; Xin, Y.; Zhu, D. Investigation on Convection Heat Transfer Augment in Spirally Corrugated Pipe. *Energies* **2023**, *16*, 1063. [CrossRef]
13. Yu, C.; Shao, M.; Zhang, W.; Huang, M.; Wang, G. Enhancing Heat Transfer Efficiency in Corrugated Tube Heat Exchangers: A Comprehensive Approach Through Structural Optimization and Field Synergy Analysis. *Heliyon* **2024**, *10*, e30113. [CrossRef] [PubMed]
14. Valero, D.; Felder, S.; Kramer, M.; Wang, H.; Carrillo, J.M.; Pfister, M. Air-Water Flows. *J. Hydraul. Res.* **2024**, *62*, 319–339. [CrossRef]
15. Zuo, J.; Qian, Y.; Zhu, D.Z.; Zhang, Z. Air-Water Interaction in a Partially Filled Circular Pipe. *Phys. Fluids* **2025**, *37*, 013315. [CrossRef]
16. Chen, Y.; Li, P.; Fei, Z.; Wang, R.; Zhang, H.; Zhu, D.Z.; Qian, S. Air-Water Interactions During Rapid Filling of a Closed Horizontal Pipe. *Phys. Fluids* **2025**, *37*, 043326. [CrossRef]
17. Paternina-Verona, D.A.; Coronado-Hernández, O.E.; Fuertes-Miquel, V.S.; Arrieta-Pastrana, A.; Ramos, H.M. Two-Dimensional Analysis of Air-Water Interaction in Actual Water Pipe-Filling Processes. *Water* **2025**, *17*, 146. [CrossRef]
18. Bonilla-Correa, D.M.; Coronado-Hernández, O.E.; Arrieta-Pastrana, A.; Pérez-Sánchez, M.; Ramos, H.M. Proposed Approach for Modelling the Thermodynamic Behaviour of Entrapped Air Pockets in Water Pipeline Start-Up. *Fluids* **2024**, *9*, 185. [CrossRef]
19. Wiens, T. Correction Factors for the Use of 1D Solution Methods for Dynamic Laminar Liquid Flow through Curved Tubes. *Fluids* **2024**, *9*, 138. [CrossRef]
20. Raj, M.K.; Chakraborty, J.; DasGupta, S.; Chakraborty, S. Flow-Induced Deformation in a Microchannel with a Non-Newtonian Fluid. *Biomicrofluidics* **2018**, *12*, 034116. [CrossRef]
21. Anand, V.; David, J., Jr.; Christov, I.C. Non-Newtonian Fluid-Structure Interactions: Static Response of a Microchannel Due to Internal Flow of a Power-Law Fluid. *J. Non-Newton. Fluid Mech.* **2019**, *264*, 62–72. [CrossRef]
22. Tanveer, A.; Salahuddin, T.; Khan, M.; Malik, M.Y.; Alqarni, M.S. Theoretical Analysis of Non-Newtonian Blood Flow in a Microchannel. *Comput. Methods Programs Biomed.* **2020**, *191*, 105280. [CrossRef] [PubMed]
23. Rubio Martinez, A.; Chávez Castellanos, A.E.; Noguez Méndez, N.A.; Aragón Rivera, F.; Pliego Díaz, M.; Sigalotti, L.D.G.; Vargas, C.A. Flow Modeling of a Non-Newtonian Viscous Fluid in Elastic-Wall Microchannels. *Fluids* **2024**, *9*, 77. [CrossRef]
24. De la Cruz-Ávila, M.; De León-Ruiz, J.E.; Carvajal-Mariscal, I.; Klapp, J. CFD Turbulence Models Assessment for the Cavitation Phenomenon in a Rectangular Profile Venturi Tube. *Fluids* **2024**, *9*, 71. [CrossRef]
25. Li, J.; Li, D.; Li, T. Progress in the Understanding and Modeling of Cavitation and Related Applications. *Fluid Dyn. Mater. Process.* **2025**, *21*, 445–470. [CrossRef]
26. Guzmán, E.; Hernández Pérez, V.; Aragón Rivera, F.; Klapp, J.; Sigalotti, L.D.G. Comparative Study of Air–Water and Air–Oil Frictional Pressure Drops in Horizontal Pipe Flow. *Fluids* **2024**, *9*, 67. [CrossRef]
27. Hamied, R.S.; Ali, A.N.M.; Sukkar, K.A. Enhancing Heavy Crude Oil Flow in Pipelines through Heating-Induced Viscosity Reduction in the Petroleum Industry. *Fluid Dyn. Mater. Process.* **2023**, *19*, 2027–2039. [CrossRef]

28. Gay, A.; Tangevelou, G.; Vidal, V. Pipe Formation by Fluid Focalization in Bilayered Sediments. *Fluids* **2024**, *9*, 66. [CrossRef]
29. Gonzalez-Trejo, J.; Miranda-Tello, R.; Gabbasov, R.; Real-Ramirez, C.A.; Cervantes-de- la-Torre, F. Experimental Analysis of the Influence of the Sliding-Gate Valve on Submerged Entry Nozzle Outlet Jets. *Fluids* **2024**, *9*, 30. [CrossRef]
30. Kinra, S.; Pal, R. Pipe Flow of Suspensions of Cellulose Nanocrystals. *Fluids* **2023**, *8*, 275. [CrossRef]
31. Shojaeiarani, J.; Bajwa, D.S.; Chanda, S. Cellulose Nanocrystal Based Composites: A Review. *Compos. Part C Open Access* **2021**, *5*, 100164. [CrossRef]
32. Xu, J.; Wang, P.; Yuan, B.; Zhang, H. Rheology of Cellulose Nanocrystal and Nanofibril Suspensions. *Carbohydr. Polym.* **2024**, *324*, 121527. [CrossRef] [PubMed]
33. Zhuang, Y.; Liu, Z.; Xu, W. Experimental Investigation on the Non-Newtonian to Newtonian Rheology Transition of Nanoparticles Enhanced Phase Change Material During Melting. *Colloids Surf. A Physicochem. Eng. Asp.* **2021**, *629*, 127432. [CrossRef]
34. Yan, Z.; Li, Z.; Cheng, S.; Wang, X.; Zhang, L.; Zheng, L.; Zhang, J. From Newtonian to Non-Newtonian Fluid: Insight into the Impact of Rheological Characteristics on Mineral Deposition in Urine Collection and Transportation. *Sci. Total Environ.* **2022**, *823*, 153532. [CrossRef] [PubMed]
35. Kaveh, K.; Malcherek, A. Enhancing Non-Newtonian Fluid Modeling. A Novel Extension of the Cross Flow Curve Model. *J. Hydro-Environ. Res.* **2024**, *56*, 17–27. [CrossRef]
36. Krishnappa, R.B.; Subramanya, S.G.; Deshpande, A.; Chakravarthi, B. Effect of Serpentine Flow Field Channel Dimensions and Electrode Intrusion on Flow Hydrodynamics in an All-Iron Redox Flow Battery. *Fluids* **2023**, *8*, 237. [CrossRef]
37. Abbaszadeh, H.; Norouzi, R.; Sume, V.; Kuriqi, A.; Daneshfaraz, R.; Abraham, J. Sill Role Effect on the Flow Characteristics (Experimental and Regression Model Analytical). *Fluids* **2023**, *8*, 235. [CrossRef]
38. Rodríguez-Rivera, R.; Carvajal-Mariscal, I.; Torres-Peña, H.; De la Cruz-Ávila, M.; De León-Ruiz, J.E. Numerical Evaluation of the Flow within a Rhomboid Tessellated Pipe Network with a 3 × 3 Allometric Branch Pattern for the Inlet and Outlet. *Fluids* **2023**, *8*, 221. [CrossRef]
39. Yu, H.; Li, T.; Zeng, X.; He, T.; Mao, N. A Critical Review on Geometric Improvements for Heat Transfer Augmentation of Microchannels. *Energies* **2022**, *15*, 9474. [CrossRef]
40. Agoua, W.; Favier, B.; Morales, J.; Bos, W.J.T. A critical Transition of Two-Dimensional Flow in Toroidal Geometry. *J. Fluid Mech.* **2024**, *988*, A33. [CrossRef]
41. Sigalotti, L.D.G.; Alvarado-Rodríguez, C.E.; Rendón, O. Fluid Flow in Helically Coiled Pipes. *Fluids* **2023**, *8*, 308. [CrossRef]
42. Hardik, B.K.; Prabhu, S.V. Heat Transfer Distribution in Helical Coil Flow Boiling System. *Int. J. Heat Mass Transf.* **2018**, *117*, 710–728. [CrossRef]
43. Çolak, A.B.; Akgul, D.; Mercan, H.; Dalkılıç, A.S.; Wongwises, S. Estimation of Heat Transfer Parameters of Shell and Helically Coiled Tube Heat Exchangers by Machine Learning. *Case Stud. Therm. Eng.* **2023**, *42*, 102713. [CrossRef]
44. Sahin, H.E.; Ozturk, H.K. A Novel Model for U-Tube Steam Generators for Pressurized Water Reactors. *Energies* **2025**, *1886*, 1506. [CrossRef]
45. Eckert, M. Pipe Flow: A Gateway to Turbulence. *Arch. Hist. Exact Sci.* **2021**, *75*, 249–282. [CrossRef]
46. Avila, M.; Barkley, D.; Hof, B. Transition to Turbulence in Pipe Flow. *Annu. Rev. Fluid Mech.* **2023**, *55*, 575–602. [CrossRef]
47. Mendes Quintino, A.; da Fonseca Junior, R.; Hernandez Rodriguez, O.M. Experimental Study of Liquid/Dense-Gas Pipe Flow. *Geoenergy Sci. Eng.* **2023**, *230*, 212179. [CrossRef]

fluids

MDPI

Article

CFD Analysis of Heat Transfer Enhancement for Twisted Tape Inserted in Spirally Corrugated Tubes and Proposal of a New Vane-Inserted Geometry

Mouhsine M. Benmbarek and Samir F. Moujaes *

Mechanical Engineering Department, University of Nevada Las Vegas, Las Vegas, NV 89154-4027, USA; benmbare@unlv.nevada.edu
* Correspondence: samir.moujaes@unlv.edu

Abstract: This research investigates the enhancement of heat transfer in a heat exchanger that is made of a corrugated tube which has a twisted plate inserted in it; the corrugation and twisted plate are expected to increase the amount of heat transfer since the plate is acting as a connection between the center of the flow and the edges of the tube. The turbulence will cause an increase in pressure drop along the channel length, so the investigation will try to find the best compromise between the gain in heat transfer and loss of hydraulic energy by using well-established metrics. A positive heat transfer gain is achieved if the metric indicates a value equal to or greater than 1. This CFD research will be compared with the experimental results found in previous studies cited in the text. After validating the CFD results, it is proposed to investigate a new insert geometry to further improve the efficiency of the heat exchanger. The computational fluid dynamics (CFD) simulation was conducted to investigate and validate the CFD model, which evaluates the heat transfer performance in a spirally corrugated tube that has a twisted tape inserted. The heat transfer was then compared to a simple corrugated tube without the twisted tape and to a smooth tube with no corrugations and no twisted tape.

Keywords: spirally corrugated tube; twisted tape; heat transfer enhancement; friction factor; Nusselt number; computational fluid dynamics (CFD); star CCM+

1. Introduction

The use and transfer of energy is necessary in our society today, but that does not come without drawbacks on our planet's environment and our economy. Natural resources are decreasing, as is their cost to produce and transfer. Creating ways to maximize the energy transfer process is extremely valuable, and one way to do so is to increase the performance of heat exchangers to reduce energy loss, costs, and materials [1]. One of the best methods to enhance heat transfer in heat exchangers is compound enhancement, which is when different enhancement techniques are used simultaneously. This field is promising for future development [2].

The heat transfer coefficient can be increased significantly using compound enhancement by inserting different devices into a modified tube [2]. The aim of this study is to create a CFD model that is reliable for future attempts at different geometries. Many researchers relied on experiments to develop these enhancements. Heat transfer is increased by corrugation in turbulent flow by increasing the turbulence level and breaking the boundary layer of the flow [3]. Many researchers started using computational methods since these have been developed over recent decades and different computational calculation

 https://doi.org/10.3390/fluids10030073

methods were created. Sparrow et al. (1983) [4] adopted a numerical simulation as early as the 1980s to simulate laminar flow in triangular corrugated tubes and study its heat transfer performance. These new methods allow researchers to save time and effort, as well as funds that would otherwise be needed to create experimental setups and structures [5].

Corrugated tubes are widely used in heat exchangers; Chorak et al. (2014) [6] used CFD to investigate the effect of pitch length over the heat transfer. The authors used different pitch distances ranging from 10 to 40 mm and an inlet velocity ranging from 0.5 to 2 m/s, with water as the working fluid. The grooves of the corrugation have a diameter of 1 mm, while the temperature on the walls of the tube is 58.6 °C. The authors pointed out that the diameter of the grooves plays a big role in the turbulence of the flow; the greater the diameter of the grooves is, the more turbulence is created, and hence more heat transfer. If the diameter decreases, the behavior of the flow looks like a smooth tube. The authors predict that the heat transfer is accomplished mainly by free convection when the ratio of the pitch and the groove decreases, while it is governed by forced convection when the opposite happens.

Rahimi et al. (2009) [7] discussed an experimental and computational fluid dynamics (CFD) investigation on the heat transfer and friction factor characteristics of a tube with modified twisted tape inserts. The study aimed to investigate the effect of different modified twisted tape inserts on heat transfer enhancement and friction factor characteristics. The experimental setup involved a horizontal test section with a heated tube and a modified twisted tape insert. The modified twisted tapes were made of aluminum and had various modifications to the geometrical parameters, such as tape width, twist ratio, and cut angles. The heat transfer coefficient and friction factor were measured experimentally, and CFD simulations were also carried out to validate the experimental results, which showed that the modified twisted tape inserts significantly enhanced the heat transfer coefficient and friction factor compared to the plain tube. Furthermore, the CFD simulations agreed well with the experimental data. The study also investigated the effect of different flow rates on the heat transfer and friction factor characteristics. It was found that increasing the flow rate increased the heat transfer coefficient and friction factor for all the modified twisted tape inserts. In conclusion, the study showed that the modified twisted tape inserts can significantly enhance the heat transfer coefficient and friction factor of a tube. The results can be useful for the design of heat exchangers and other thermal systems where heat transfer enhancement is important [8].

Lou et al. (2011) [9] conducted a simulation study of heat transfer tubes equipped with twisted tape inserts, which are commonly used in heat exchangers to enhance heat transfer. The simulations were conducted using computational fluid dynamics (CFD) techniques to investigate the effects of different twisted tape geometries on heat transfer and fluid flow characteristics. The study found that the twisted tape inserts significantly enhanced the heat transfer rate in the tubes, with the best results achieved using tapes with a twist ratio of 5 and a width ratio of 0.156. Additionally, the twisted tape inserts caused an increase in friction factor, which is a measure of the resistance to fluid flow. However, this increase was relatively small and considered a reasonable trade-off for the improved heat transfer performance. Overall, the study highlights the potential of twisted tape inserts as an effective method for enhancing heat transfer in heat exchangers and provides valuable insights into the optimal design of these inserts for different applications [10].

Salman et al. (2014) [11] ran experiments and numerical simulation to study the effects of the twist ratio and Reynolds number on the heat transfer distribution on a plate heat exchanger. Three twisted tapes were used with twist ratios of 2.93, 3.91, and 4.89. Reynolds numbers ranged from 4000 to 16,000. The authors conducted numerical simulations using k-omega and k-epsilon models. The k-omega model was more accurate relative to the experiment for a conventional jet, while the k-epsilon was more accurate for the jet with swirls. However, the heat transfer rate was more substantial in the conventional jet than in the jet with twisted tapes, but among the jet with a twisted tape group, the heat transfer was greater with a twist ratio of 4.89 than 2.93 and 3.91.

Amini et al. (2015) [12] investigated the effect of twisted tapes as well on the heat transfer of impinging jets. The authors focused on three parameters: Re ranging from 4000 to 16,000, the distance between the jet and the plate with ratios of 2, 4, 6, and 8, and the twist ratio of the twisted plate ranging from 3 to 6. The optimal conditions were found to be at a jet-to-plate interspace of 6 and 8 and twist ratio of 6. These conditions produced a maximum Nusselt number of just under 100 at a Reynolds number of 16,000. However, the authors did notice that the exit velocity dropped by more than half compared to the inlet velocity, which points to a high pressure drop, but no further investigation was conducted to evaluate the energy loss against the heat transfer gain.

Mat Lazim et al. (2014) [13] numerically investigated the impact of spiral corrugation features on overall thermal performance in their study using two-start spirally corrugated tubes. According to the findings, a shape with smooth spiral corrugations can greatly improve heat transmission at low and medium Reynolds numbers. While the rise in friction factor after Re of 700 is significantly more than the increase in heat transmission, the corrugation profile was found to be the master key for generating better heat transfer with the least amount of pressure drop, and it needed to be adjusted to create more heat transfer with the least amount of pumping power. The severity index u has a significant impact on heat transfer enhancement and friction factor, with heat gained accompanied by pressure loss, particularly at high Re. It was also discovered that this corrugation profile created harmony and ordered swirls in the secondary flow region, lowering pressure drop and saving pumping power.

Vahidifar and Banihashemi (2023) [14] studied a simple geometry of turbulators; a tube with the disc, ring, and O-ring turbulators with an area ratio equal to the cross-section of the turbulator to the pipe (40%) were assessed in different pitches. The effect of stimulating the main air flow in increasing the Nu and thermal performance was investigated. The Nu for the pipe in the presence of turbulators is much higher than that of the smooth pipe in turbulators, and heat transfer increases. By inserting a ring turbulator, the highest value of convection heat transfer coefficient is obtained.

The Nu increases between 2.59- and 3.21-fold at PR = 2 (PR is pitch ratio distancing) for ring, and as the Re increases, so does the heat transfer. The Nu value for the circular ring turbulator is higher than that for the O-ring turbulator, because the vortices' strength, number, and magnitude are important in transferring heat energy. The friction coefficient of the O-ring and circular ring turbulators decreases with the increase of Reynolds number, and the friction coefficient of the circular ring turbulator is higher than that of the O-ring turbulator due to the lack of a streamlined shape and the aerodynamic shape.

Various aspects of shell-and-tube heat exchangers were discussed in Su et al. (2022) [15], emphasizing the use of U-tube heat exchangers with one tube plate for disassembly convenience and suitability in high-temperature, high-pressure applications. This study introduces different baffle designs proposed by researchers, including quadrant helical baffles and circumferential overlap trisection helical baffles.

A new heat exchanger structure involving special-shaped hole or orifice baffles is also presented, aiming to reduce flow resistance, prevent vibration damage, and facilitate tube bundle cleaning. The experimental setup involves heat exchangers with replaceable tube bundle cores, and the testing system uses water in both sides with hot and cold water flowing in the shell-side and tube-side, respectively.

The text details the experimental apparatus, including the testing system, data measurement system, and data control system. It emphasizes the importance of experimental methods in validating simulation models for heat exchangers. The experimental data processing method involves determining fluid properties and analyzing uncertainty.

The performance evaluation section compares helical and segmental baffle schemes, highlighting higher heat transfer coefficients for helical designs. Orifice baffle schemes are shown to outperform segmental baffles, producing a jet effect for enhanced heat transfer. The comparison of different heat exchanger types concludes that helical and orifice baffle schemes exhibit superior overall and shell-side heat transfer coefficients compared to segmental schemes, with ladder helical schemes slightly outperforming orifice baffle schemes according to comprehensive indexes.

The text by Gu et al. (2020b) [16] discusses helical flow applications in heat exchangers, particularly focusing on twisted elliptical tube heat exchangers (TETHX). It emphasizes the advantages of TETHX over segmental baffle heat exchangers, highlighting better flow and heat transfer characteristics. Previous studies on TETHX, considering factors such as aspect ratio and twist pitch, are cited.

A new type of TETHX with alternating V-rows of coupling-vortices is proposed to improve heat transfer performance and energy utilization efficiency. The study involves constructing and simulating eleven geometric models, comparing a conventional parallel-vortex structure with the proposed coupling-vortex structure.

The physical model involves a unique tube layout configuration with 37 tubes of a fixed length of 1000 mm and a major axis fixed at 12.3 mm. The hydraulic diameter of the tube bundle is defined as the cross-sectional area on the shell side multiplied by four.

The simulation results are validated against experimental correlations, and the analysis includes velocity, pressure, and temperature fields. The unique coupling-vortex technology is proposed as an effective enhancement for TETHX without additional manufacturing costs.

Comprehensive performance analysis considers Nusselt number, friction factor, and a comprehensive index. The study concludes that the coupling-vortex schemes in TETHX exhibit higher heat transfer coefficients, slightly higher pressure drops, and more uniform temperature fields compared to parallel-vortex schemes. The mean values for the coupling-vortex schemes are reported as 7.8%, 8.7%, and 4.9% for heat transfer coefficients, pressure drops, and temperature field uniformity, respectively. The unique coupling-vortex technology is suggested as a promising enhancement for TETHX with improved thermal and hydraulic performance.

The study conducted by Li et al. (2021) [17] delves into the intricacies of shell-side convection heat transfer and hydraulic resistance in double tube heat exchangers (DTHEs) employing twisted oval tubes (TOTs). Notably, the research identifies Case 10 as yielding the highest comprehensive heat transport performance.

In the realm of double tube heat exchangers, renowned for their widespread application in diverse industries, the investigation concentrates on the deployment of twisted oval tubes (TOTs). This choice stems from the notable heat transfer performance exhibited by TOTs, prompting a departure from previous studies primarily focused on high Reynolds numbers. Instead, this research deliberately explores the dynamics at play in low Reynolds number flow scenarios.

The physical model under scrutiny involves DTHE configurations featuring coaxial TOTs and circular tubes (CTs). The investigation encompasses 14 distinct cases, each characterized by unique geometric dimensions. To facilitate clear communication, a nomenclature is introduced, aiding in the systematic description and differentiation of the various DTHE configurations.

Employing a sophisticated 3-D computational model, the study meticulously scrutinizes the heat transport and hydraulic resistance properties within the shell side of DTHEs. The turbulent regime is captured using the SST k-w turbulent model, and a comprehensive performance evaluation criterion (PEC) becomes the yardstick for assessing the multi-faceted performance metrics.

Prior to delving into the specifics of the investigation, the study ensures the independence of the computational grid and validates the numerical model. The SST k-w turbulent model emerged as the most fitting choice for capturing the nuanced behavior of twisted oval tubes. Validation exercises demonstrated a commendable alignment between numerical simulations and experimental data.

In conclusion, the study illuminates the substantial augmentation of heat transport performance achievable in DTHEs through the strategic integration of TOTs and CTs. The observed enhancements range from 24.0% to 39.0%, underscoring the potential of this configuration. Additionally, it becomes evident that manipulating the inner aspect ratio (Ai/Bi) exerts a more discernible influence on performance than variations in the outer aspect ratio (Ao/Bo).

Pirbastami and Moujaes (2016) [18] present a computational fluid dynamics (CFD) study on heat enhancement in helically grooved tubes. The study explores the impact of different groove dimensions on the thermal performance and pressure drop of water inside grooved tubes. The authors investigate three rectangular grooved tubes with varying groove width (w) and depth (e) and analyze the Reynolds number (Re) range of 4000–10,000. The results show that the highest performance is achieved with specific groove dimensions (w = 0.2 mm and e = 0.2 mm). Additionally, the study examines the influence of pitch size to tube diameter (p/D) ratios on Nusselt number (Nu) and friction factor (f). The findings indicate that increasing the p/D ratio leads to a decrease in both Nu and f values. The paper provides empirical correlations for Nu and f as functions of p/D and Re number, suggesting that incorporating internal grooves with specific dimensions can enhance heat exchanger performance.

2. Numerical Method and Procedure

2.1. Geometry and Grid Generation

Zimparov [2] investigated eight 1.2 m long copper spirally corrugated tubes, and Table 1 represents the dimensionless parameters of the tubes. Figure 1 shows the different geometrical parameters of the corrugations and twisted tape. Tubes whose last digit ends with 0 are corrugated tubes (i.e., 5030), while a last digit of 3, 4, or 5 means that the tube has a twisted plate inserted with the following dimensions: t = 0.8 mm; 3—H/Di = 7.6; 4—H/Di = 5.7, and 5—H/Di = 4.7. The focus of this study is on the tube 5035 because, during Zimparov's experiment, it had the best performance enhancement, and it is compared against a smooth tube and tube 5030. The smooth tube has a diameter of 16.0 mm with a wall thickness of 0.8 mm. Tube 5035 is 1.2 m long and has a diameter of 13.51 cm, a wall thickness of 2.2 mm, and the material is copper.

Table 1. Geometric parameters of tube 5030.

No	D_o mm	D_i mm	e mm	p mm	β deg	t mm	s mm	e/D_i	p/e	B*	Twisted Tape
5030	15.31	13.51	0.767	5.19	83.0	1.836	0.371	0.057	6.77	0.922	N/A
5035	15.31	13.51	0.767	5.19	83.0	1.836	0.371	0.057	6.77	0.922	H/Di = 4.7

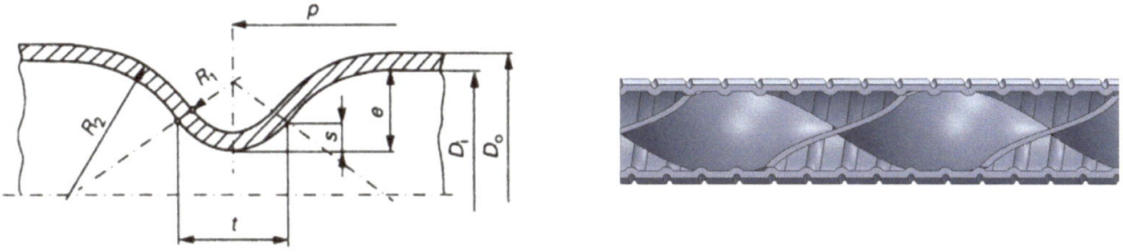

(a) (b)

Figure 1. (**a**,**b**) Pictures showing geometrical parameters presented in Table 1 [2].

The geometry was modeled using SOLIDWORKS 2022, then imported to STAR-CCM+ 2022.1 for simulation and analysis. A polyhedral mesh was used. Its main advantage is that each element has many adjacent cells, which helps reduce errors in gradients. Polyhedrons are also less susceptible to stretching than tetrahedrons, resulting in enhanced mesh quality and model numerical stability [6].

$$R_1 = 0.5s\,[1 + 0.25(t/s)2] - 0.8$$

$$R_2 = 0.5(e - s)[1 + 0.25(t/s)2] + 0.8$$

A prism layer was also used to make the mesh finer at the walls of the tube and make the twisted tape capture the change of the temperature gradient. Figure 2 shows the prism layer with a total thickness of 10% of the mesh size. The mesh size is 3 mm. It was found to be the best mesh supported by a grid independency study, which will be presented later.

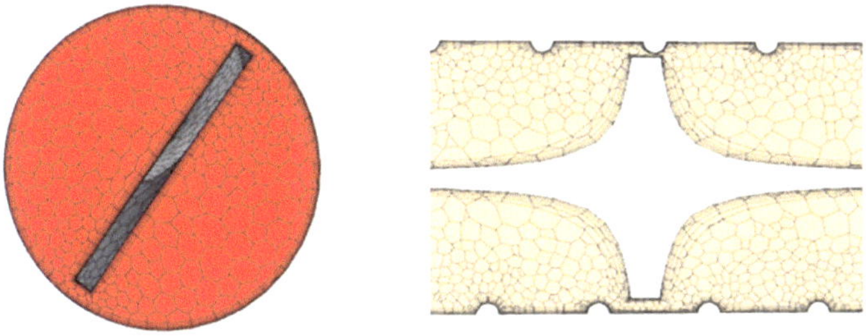

Figure 2. Volume mesh showing prism layer at solid boundaries.

2.2. Governing Equations and Turbulence Model

This study focuses on turbulent flow at a range of Reynolds number of $3.5 \times 10^3 < Re < 5.0 \times 10^4$, and the twisted plate mixes the flow and adds turbulence, as shown in Figure 3. The tubes are the same as the ones studied by Zimparov et al. (2012) [2].

The governing equations of this simulation are the incompressible Reynolds averaged Navier–Stokes equations, the energy equation, and the steady 3-D form of the continuity [7].

Conservation of mass:

$$\frac{\partial u}{\partial x} + \frac{\partial v}{\partial y} + \frac{\partial w}{\partial z} = 0. \quad (1)$$

Navier–Stokes equations:

$$\rho\left(\overline{u}\frac{\partial \overline{u}}{\partial x} + \overline{v}\frac{\partial \overline{u}}{\partial y} + \overline{w}\frac{\partial \overline{u}}{\partial z}\right) = -\frac{\partial \overline{p}}{\partial x} + \mu\nabla^2\overline{u} - \frac{\partial}{\partial x}\left(\rho\overline{u'u'}\right) - \frac{\partial}{\partial y}\left(\rho\overline{u'v'}\right) - \frac{\partial}{\partial z}\left(\rho\overline{u'w'}\right) \quad (2)$$

$$\rho\left(\overline{u}\frac{\partial\overline{v}}{\partial x}+\overline{v}\frac{\partial\overline{v}}{\partial y}+\overline{w}\frac{\partial\overline{v}}{\partial z}\right)=-\frac{\partial\overline{p}}{\partial y}+\mu\nabla^2\overline{v}-\frac{\partial}{\partial x}\left(\rho\overline{u'v'}\right)-\frac{\partial}{\partial y}\left(\rho\overline{v'v'}\right)-\frac{\partial}{\partial z}\left(\rho\overline{v'w'}\right) \quad (3)$$

$$\rho\left(\overline{u}\frac{\partial\overline{w}}{\partial x}+\overline{v}\frac{\partial\overline{w}}{\partial y}+\overline{w}\frac{\partial\overline{w}}{\partial z}\right)=-\frac{\partial\overline{p}}{\partial z}+\mu\nabla^2\overline{w}-\rho\left[\frac{\partial\overline{w'u'}}{\partial x}+\frac{\partial\overline{w'v'}}{\partial y}+\frac{\partial\overline{w'w'}}{\partial z}\right] \quad (4)$$

Conservation of energy:

$$\rho c_p\left(u\frac{\partial T}{\partial x}+v\frac{\partial T}{\partial y}+w\frac{\partial T}{\partial z}\right)=K\left(\frac{\partial^2 T}{\partial x^2}+\frac{\partial^2 T}{\partial y^2}+\frac{\partial^2 T}{\partial z^2}\right)-\frac{\partial}{\partial x}(\rho c_p u'T')-\frac{\partial}{\partial y}(\rho c_p v'T')-\frac{\partial}{\partial z}(\rho c_p w'T')+\overline{q} \quad (5)$$

Dissipation function:

$$\varphi=2\left[\left(\frac{\partial u}{\partial x}\right)^2+\left(\frac{\partial v}{\partial y}\right)^2+\left(\frac{\partial w}{\partial z}\right)^2\right]+\left(\frac{\partial u}{\partial y}+\frac{\partial v}{\partial x}\right)^2+\left(\frac{\partial v}{\partial z}+\frac{\partial w}{\partial y}\right)^2+\left(\frac{\partial w}{\partial x}+\frac{\partial u}{\partial z}\right)^2 \quad (6)$$

The CFD model used is the k-ε model [1,8,9]. In the k-ε two equation model, the velocity and length scale of turbulence are defined with two additional partial-differential equations: one for the turbulent kinetic energy k, the other for the dissipation rate ε, and an algebraic demonstration for the eddy viscosity [1,8,9] is also given as in Equation (9).

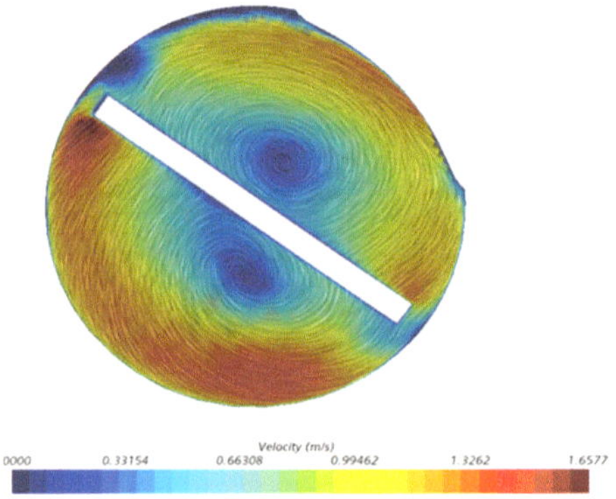

Figure 3. Scalar scene showing swirls created by the twisted plate.

Kinetic energy Equation k:

$$\rho\langle u_j\rangle\frac{\partial k}{\partial x_j}=2\mu_t\langle s_{ij}\rangle\frac{\partial\langle u_i\rangle}{\partial x_j}-\rho\varepsilon+\frac{\partial}{\partial x_j}\left[\left(\mu+\frac{\mu_t}{\sigma_k}\right)\frac{\partial k}{\partial x_j}\right] \quad (7)$$

Dissipation rate equation ε:

$$\rho\langle u_j\rangle\frac{\partial\varepsilon}{\partial x_j}=C_{\varepsilon1}P_k\frac{\varepsilon}{k}-C_{\varepsilon2}\rho\frac{\varepsilon^2}{k}+\frac{\partial}{\partial x_j}\left[\left(\mu+\frac{\mu_t}{\sigma_\varepsilon}\right)\frac{\partial\varepsilon}{\partial x_j}\right] \quad (8)$$

Eddy viscosity:

$$\mu_t=C_\mu\rho\frac{k^2}{\varepsilon} \quad (9)$$

The k and ε equations are solved with the mean Navier–Stokes equations. STAR-CCM+ offers a choice of eight different k-ε turbulence models. The constant variables of k-ε were suggested by STARCCM+ 2022.1 as follows [1]: C_μ = 0.09, $C_{\varepsilon1}$ = 1.44, $C_{\varepsilon2}$ = 1.92, σk = 1.3 and σε = 1.

Table 2, provided by Zimparov et al., represents the errors of the measured parameters, which will be useful to validate the CFD model, as the goal is to check that the CFD results fall within those margins of errors. The CFD simulation will not be concerned by the steam temperature, as the wall temperature is enough to be used as a boundary condition.

Table 2. Uncertainties of measured and calculated parameters [2].

Parameter	Uncertainty
Water and steam temperature, T_i, T_o, T_s	±0.1%
Mean tube wall temperature, T_w	±0.5%
Pressure drop, ΔP	±5.0%
Mass flow rate of water, $\dot{m}$	±2.0%
Fanning friction factor, f	±6.5%
Condensing heat transfer coefficient, h_o	±2.5%
Inside heat transfer coefficient, h_i	±(15–20)%

2.3. Flow and Boundary Conditions

As mentioned earlier, the flow has a Reynolds number that ranges between $3.5 \times 10^3 < Re < 5.0 \times 10^4$. The working fluid is water and the pipe wall (assumed copper) thickness is neglected in the CFD analysis. The justification for that is given is it was found that the pipe thickness thermal resistance is about 50 times smaller than that of the convection flow thermal resistance (h is calculated as an average along the length of the pipe as in Equation (11)) in the pipe. Hence, from this fact, the temperature drop across the inside and outside surface of the pipe was calculated as negligible compared to that of the flow. Therefore it is deduced that the temperature outside the pipe can be assumed to be that inside the pipe without loss of accuracy. A temperature T_w is applied directly on the fluid according to Zimparov's data.

The wall temperature ranged from 38 °C to 91.6 °C, the inlet temperature of the water ranged from 23.5 °C to 86.1 °C, and the inlet velocity of the water was calculated for each run from a given Re. A total of 16 runs were conducted for each tube. Tables 3 and 4 show the boundary conditions for each experiment.

Table 3. Boundary conditions for tube 5030 [2].

Run	R_e	V_i (m/s)	T_i (°C)	T_w (°C)
1	2590	0.170482	26	43.1
2	3540	0.233013	28.4	43.4
3	4400	0.289621	30.9	43.3
4	4750	0.312659	32.6	44
5	5900	0.388356	34.8	45.4
6	7030	0.462736	36.5	45.9
7	8440	0.555546	38.6	49.3
8	9420	0.620053	40.8	52
9	11,860	0.780661	43	52.7
10	14,340	0.943902	45.4	53.8
11	17,840	1.174283	47.9	54.9
12	21,090	1.388207	50.4	56.5
13	28,870	1.90031	58.4	64
14	33,010	2.172818	67	74.4
15	37,170	2.446641	76.4	83.6
16	42,060	2.768516	86	91.6

Table 4. Boundary conditions for tube 5035 [2].

Run	R_e	V_i (m/s)	T_i (°C)	T_w (°C)
1	2220	0.146111	23.5	38
2	3180	0.209294	27.7	41
3	4110	0.270502	30	41.4
4	4850	0.319206	32.8	43.2
5	5760	0.379098	35	44.1
6	4260	0.280375	37.3	45
7	8540	0.562066	39.6	47.55
8	10,500	0.691064	42.1	50.9
9	12,050	0.793079	44.4	52.1
10	14,560	0.958276	46.4	52.8
11	17,840	1.174151	48.8	55.1
12	21,540	1.417669	51.1	56.95
13	29,570	1.946169	60.1	63.5
14	34,280	2.256161	69.5	76.05
15	38,240	2.516791	78.5	84.62
16	41,620	2.739248	86.1	91.8

The water flow is considered incompressible, turbulent, three-dimensional, and at a steady state. A non-slip condition was considered for the walls, and the outlet pressure was the atmospheric pressure. The number of iterations needed to achieve convergence varied for each run as it got higher. As the Re number increased and the tube geometry changed, convergence ranged from 200 to 1500 iterations. Convergence was considered "achieved" when the energy equation residual reached 1×10^{-4} and the flow was thermally fully developed.

2.4. Parameters and Metric Definitions

The three parameters of interest in investigating in this study are the heat transfer coefficient and the friction factor. The inside heat transfer coefficient h_i is represented as a function of N_u with the following relation:

$$N_u = \frac{h_i Di}{k} \tag{10}$$

while h_i is:

$$h_i = \frac{\dot{Q}}{A_i \Delta T_m} \tag{11}$$

$\dot{Q}$ is the heat transfer in (W) and it was an output from STAR-CCM+, then Equation (11) is used to calculate h_i.

$$\Delta T_m = \frac{T_0 - T_i}{\ln\left(\frac{Tw,m - T_i}{Tw,m - T_0}\right)} \tag{12}$$

The same Equations (11)–(13) as Zimparov et al. [2] were used to maintain similarity. The accuracy of the temperature measurements was as follows: inlet and outlet water temperatures, steam temperature—0.1%, and mean tube wall temperature along the length—0.5%. The accuracy of the calculated heat transfer coefficients was estimated at 2.5% for the condensing heat transfer coefficient and at 15–20% for the inside heat transfer coefficient. All uncertainties of the measured quantities and calculated parameters are presented in Table 2 [1]. These uncertainties are used later to correlate between our CFD results and the experimental results.

The fanning friction factor is given by:

$$f = \frac{\rho \pi^2 D_i^5}{32L} \frac{\Delta P}{\dot{m}^2} \tag{13}$$

ΔP is the pressure drop. It is an output from STAR-CCM, then Equation (13) is used to calculate f. Coefficient (η) is introduced to evaluate the gain in heat transfer against the energy loss due to the increased pressure drop caused by the tubes' geometry (i.e., corrugations and twisted tape) [1].

$$\eta = \frac{\frac{Nu}{N_{us}}}{\frac{f}{f_s}} \tag{14}$$

N_u is the Nusselt number of a given tube and Nus is for the smooth tube. The same applies to the friction factor.

The ratios N_u/N_{us} and f/f_s are a dimensionless representation of the heat transfer and friction factor, respectively, that allows for the comparison of both properties. Other papers have used a similar factor, such as [13,14].

3. Results

3.1. Grid Independency Study

The grid independency study was conducted to achieve a 1–2% error between different mesh sizes, which helped to choose the right size that balances accuracy and computing time. Four grids were tested: grid 1: 1,250,789 elements; grid 2: 2,603,124 elements; grid 3: 3,762,700 elements; and grid 4: 5,341,023 elements. The approach to choose the most optimal grid is done by comparing the heat transfer parameters; in this case, axial velocity and temperature along the outlet diameter for all the grids (Figures 4 and 5). When the change in results becomes minimal as meshes becomes finer, then grid independency has been achieved and the grid with the smaller number of elements is chosen, after which the results do not change significantly. In this case, it was mesh 3.

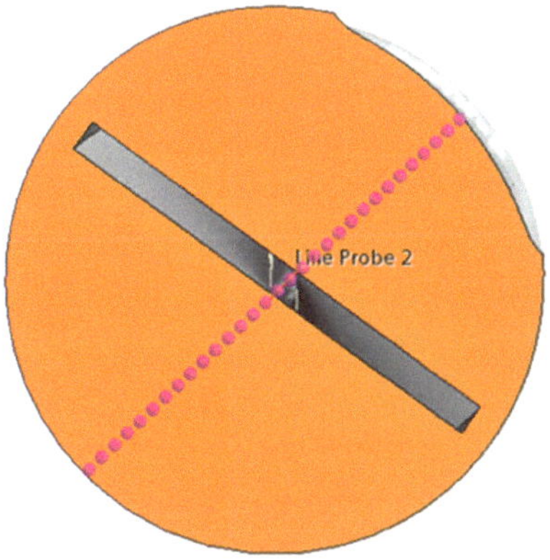

Figure 4. Probe line along outlet diameter for axial velocity and temperature results.

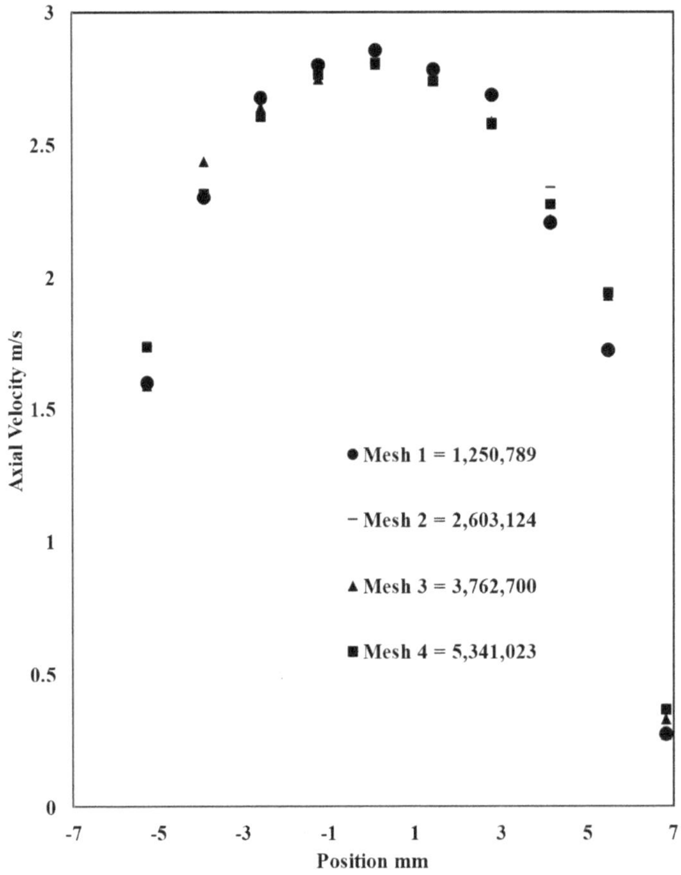

Figure 5. Axial velocity for four different meshes along outlet diameter of the pipe.

3.2. Experimental Data and CFD Validation

To make sure the CFD model is correct, comparing the simulation results against experimental data [1] is necessary before conducting any further studies. The uncertainties from experimental measurement are represented by error bars (Table 2). The same boundary conditions from the experiment were used in the CFD simulation, courtesy of Dr. Zimparov. The Nusselt number, friction factor, and heat transfer coefficient were calculated from Equations (10), (11) and (13), while the pressure drop ΔP and heat transfer $\dot{Q}$ were obtained from the CFD results. In [1], the heat transfer coefficient was presented as Nu*Pr-0.4. The CFD validation is done by comparing key parameters (i.e., heat transfer coefficient, friction factor and the Nusselt number). The purpose of this validation is to be able to use the same model parameters to confidently run other simulations with different geometries and expect reasonable accuracy.

The friction factor was calculated by implementing Equation (12) into the software, while the area, mass flow rate, and pressure drop were calculated automatically from STAR-CCM+.

The CFD results agree with the experimental results as shown in Figure 6 for tube 5035.

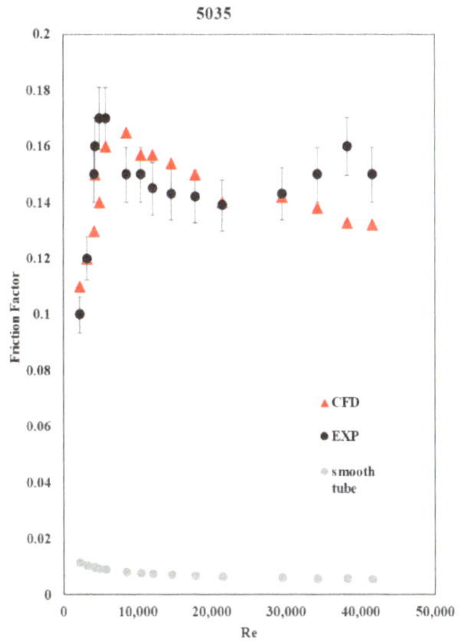

Figure 6. Comparison of friction factor obtained from CFD simulation with experimental data [2] for tube 5035.

As expected, the friction factor increased substantially in tube 5035 due to the added friction by the twisted plate. This means that there is an increase in head loss, which will require more pumping power to transfer the water from one end to another.

For tube 5035, the Nusselt number kept increasing with Re as shown in Figure 7. Zimparov et al. [2] represents the Nusselt number as $NuPr^{-0.4}$, where Pr is the Prandtl number for water, and Nu is calculated using Equation (10).

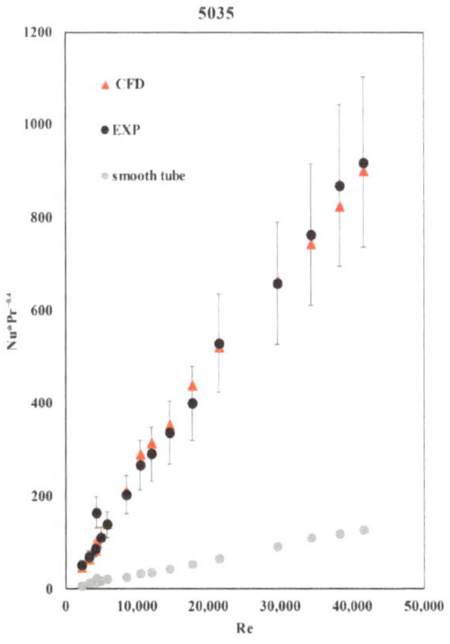

Figure 7. Comparison of Nusselt number obtained from CFD simulation with experimental data [2] for tube 5035 and smooth tube.

As mentioned before, there was an increase in the amount of heat conducted by the twisted plate, along with more friction caused by the plate's geometry, which resulted in head loss.

Our goal is to increase the heat transfer without increasing the pressure drop to a level where it is no longer beneficial due to the required pumping power.

The enhancement factor (Equation (14)) allows us to evaluate the gain in heat transfer against the energy loss where N_{u5}/N_{us} is the ratio of the Nusselt number of the smooth tube and tube 5035, and f_5/f_s is the ratio for the fanning factor.

If $\eta < 1$, that means that the friction factor is greater than the heat transfer, indicating that the tube's design is not efficient for transferring heat without increasing the cost of energy consumption required for pumping.

On the other hand, if $\eta \geq 1$, the tube design can be used for enhancement purposes.

The error bars represent the combined errors from the friction factor and the heat transfer coefficient, which is considered in the Nusselt number.

From Figure 8, the enhancement is beneficial when Re ranges from 10,000 to 28,000. Outside of this range, even though there is a greater heat transfer coefficient, the friction factor is high enough to require more energy to pump the water through the pipe, thus resulting in diminution of the η factor.

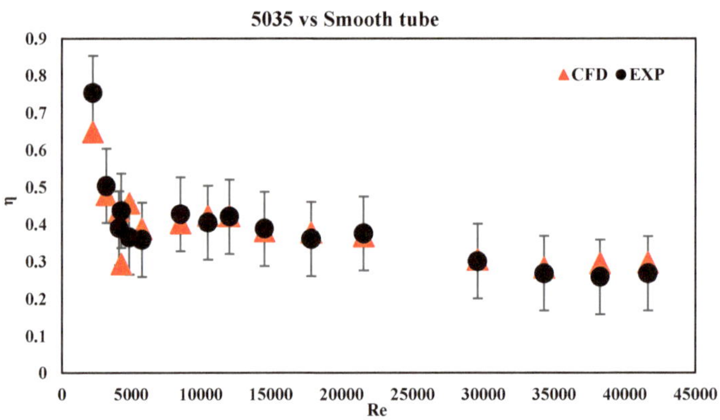

Figure 8. Enhancement factor η comparing the performance of tube 5035 with smooth tube.

3.3. Proposed Vane Geometries

The purpose of this section is to introduce a new geometry that will make use of the same enhancement technique which is compound enhancement. The principle behind this is similar to the geometry discussed above, as it will induce turbulence inside the tubes using a different insert.

This geometry attempted to increase the heat transfer at the same level of tube 5035 while trying to keep the pressure drop at a reasonable level to maximize the η factor.

The new geometry was made of 21 vanes mounted on a 1 m long shaft and inserted inside a simple tube of 12 mm diameter, with equal spacing between each set of vanes.

The geometry was modeled using SolidWorks. The vanes were angled at 135° with respect to the shaft axis. The vanes were equally spaced around the shaft at 45° between each vane. Each vane set was rotated by 15° from its precedent until eventually completing a full 360° rotation. Four variations were made of this with different spacing between each vane set: 5 cm, 7.5 cm, 10 cm and 12.5 cm.

Figures 9–11 show more details about the geometry of the vanes.

Figure 9. Front view of vane insert.

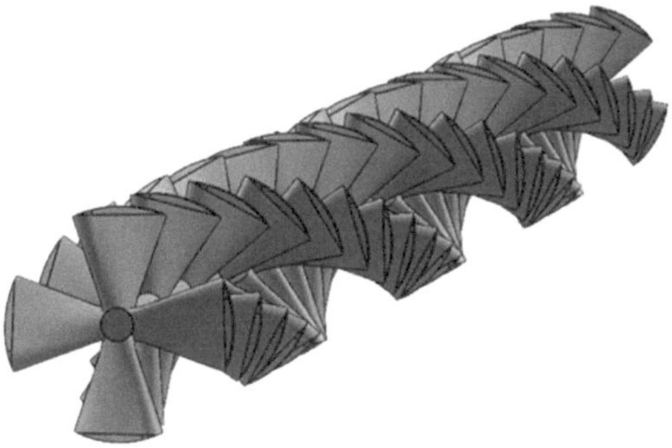

Figure 10. Isometric view of vane insert.

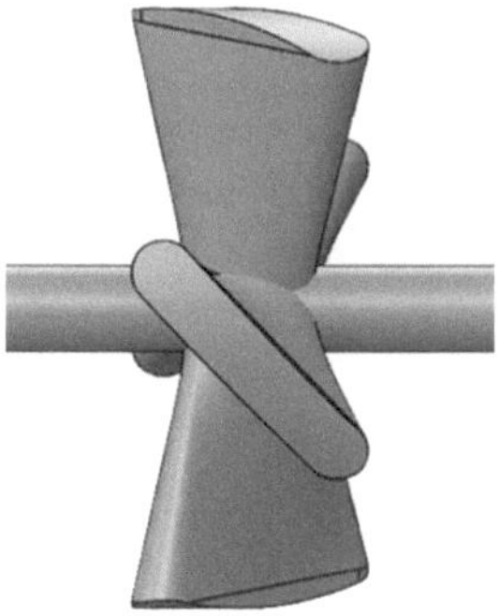

Figure 11. Side view of vanes.

Since the previous model was validated by the experimental data, the same mesh settings mentioned in Section 3.3 was used for this new geometry.

Figures 12 and 13 show the construction of mesh after using the same settings as the tube 5035 model. The prism layer can be noticed near the tube wall to capture the temperature gradient, it can be noticed as well that the mesh has an adaptive size; it becomes finer near the walls of the tube and the walls of the vanes to predict turbulence more accurately.

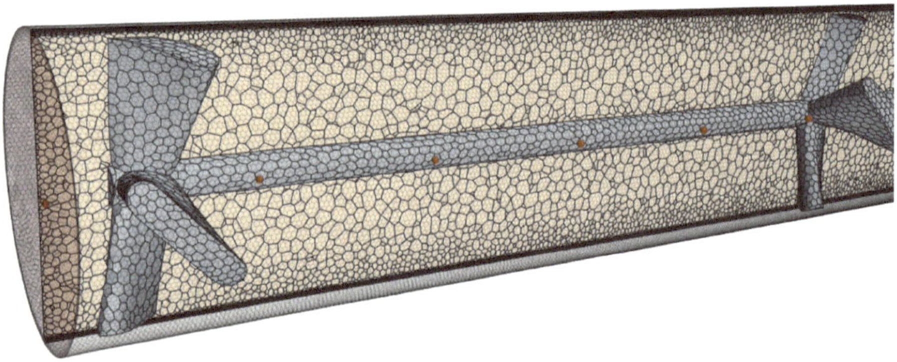

Figure 12. Isometric view of mesh.

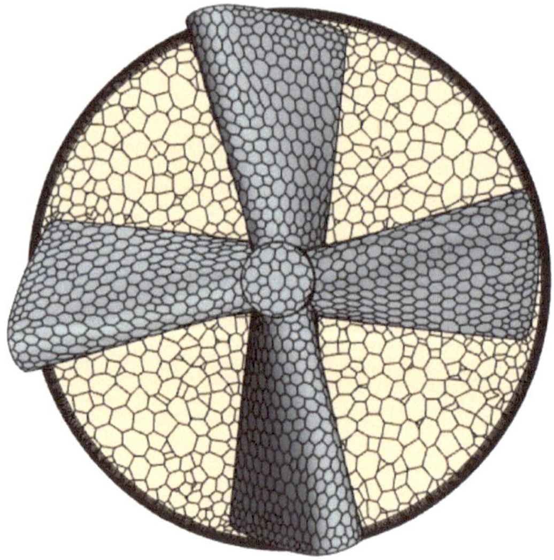

Figure 13. Front view of mesh.

To keep similarity for comparison purposes with the previous model and experimental data, the same boundary conditions presented in Section 2.3 were applied for the vane geometry.

Figures 14–17 show the different variations that were tested in this section.

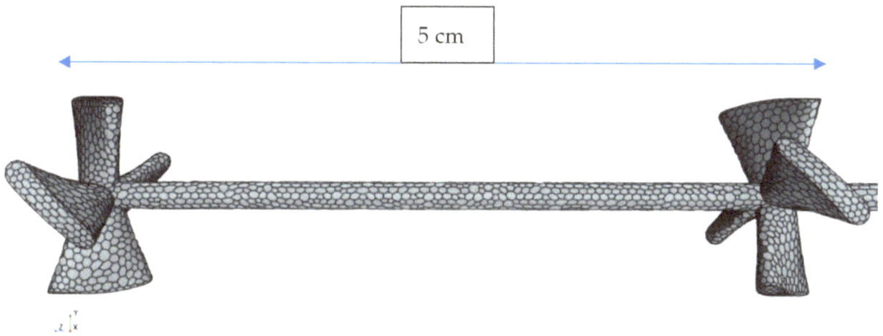

Figure 14. Vanes spaced at 5 cm.

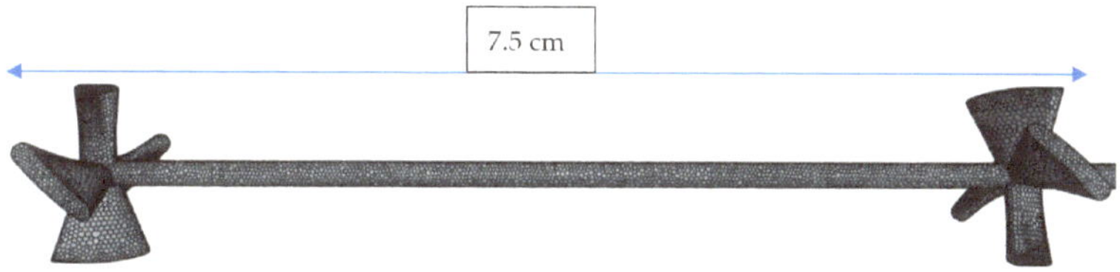

Figure 15. Vanes spaced at 7.5 cm.

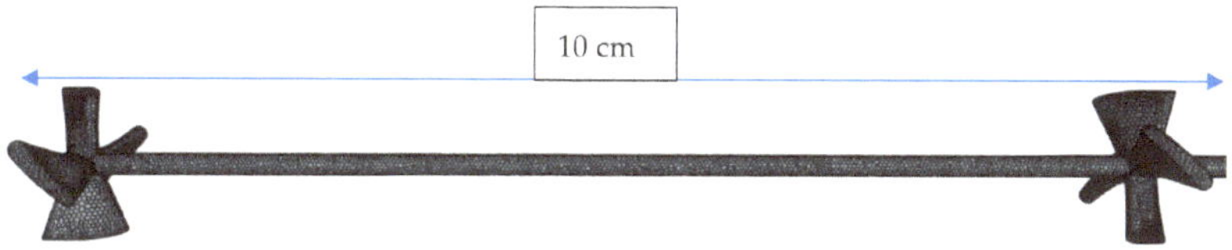

Figure 16. Vanes spaced at 10 cm.

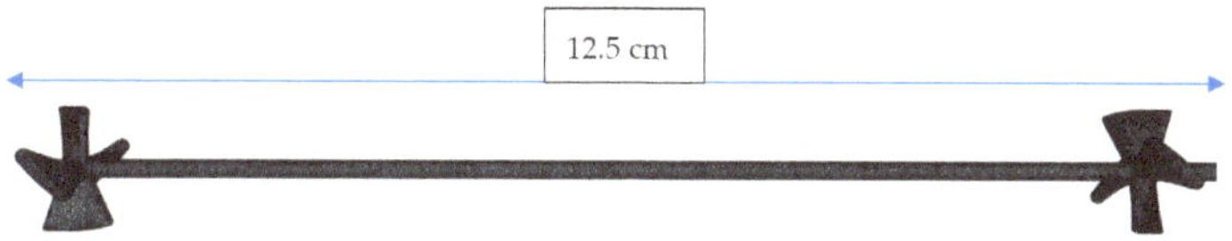

Figure 17. Vanes spaced at 12.5 cm.

From Figure 18a, it can be noticed that the vanes variations had slightly less heat transfer than tube 5035, which was expected since the vanes do not run continuously through the tube, hence the heat transfer through conduction is lesser.

The vane geometries had a considerably lower friction factor value than tube 5035. This was the attempted goal of these geometries, that by reducing material from the insert there will be less fluid friction and hence less hydro-mechanical losses.

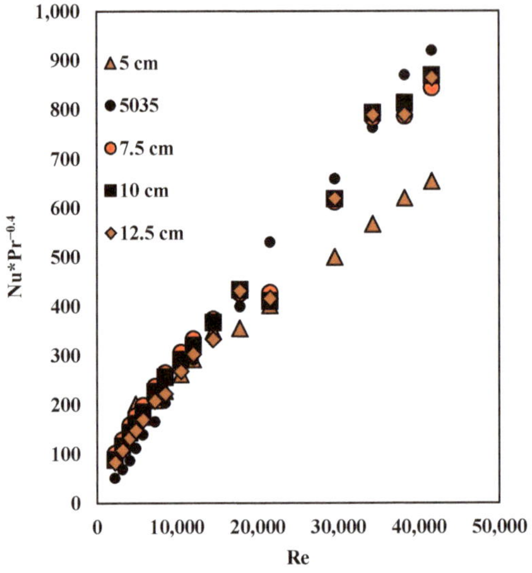

(a)

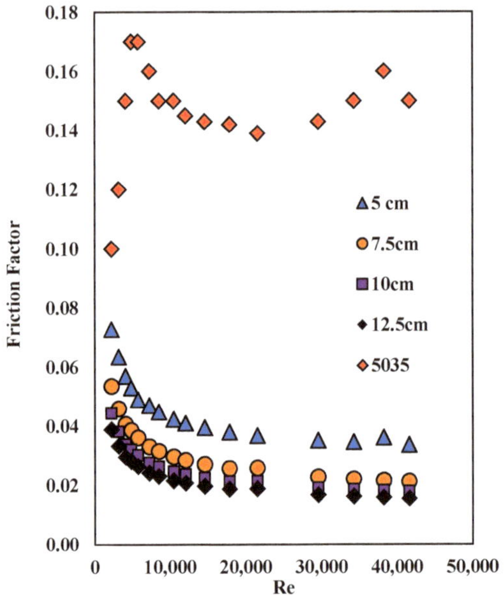

(b)

Figure 18. (**a**) Comparison of Nusselt number for vane variations and tube 5035. (**b**) Friction factor comparison of the vane geometries and tube 5035.

3.4. Thermal Performance

The factor η allows for a direct comparison between the characteristics mentioned above and the different types of geometries mentioned thus far in this study. Figure 19 shows the η factor calculated for the vane geometry with tube 5035 as reference. It can be noticed that the thermal performance ranges from 4 to around 9 for the different variations.

The 5 cm spaced vanes had the lowest increase. The 12.5 cm spaced vane geometry had the biggest enhancement in terms of the η factor. These results are mainly due to the significantly lower friction factor shown in Figure 18b, since the geometries with 7.5–10 and 12.5 cm had roughly the same heat transfer values.

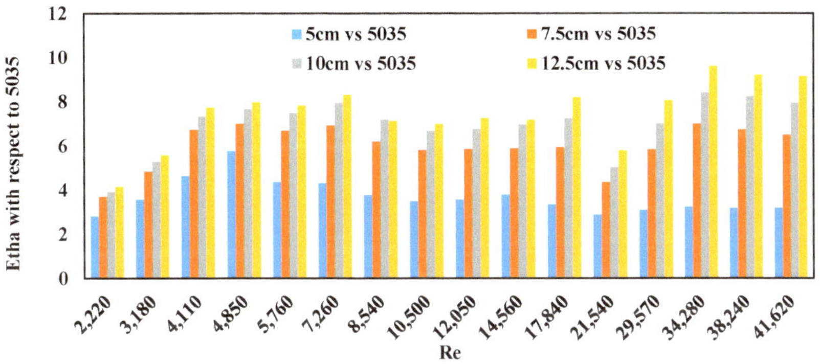

Figure 19. η factor using ratios of vane geometries and tube 5035.

4. Conclusions

The enhancement in heat transfer is undeniable in tubes with a twisted insert, but according to this study's CFD results, when the friction caused by the twisted plate is considered, the enhancement is optimal only for Re ranging from 10,000 to 28,000, where 39.6 C < T_i < 51.5 C, and 49.3 C < T_w < 91.8 C, where η > 1. For higher Re, the Nusselt number increased significantly due to the elevated turbulence, and thus an increased mixing of the flow in the transverse direction but with higher friction requires more power to pump the flow, where η < 1.

The CFD model accurately predicted the experimental data, and the parameters used in the model are appropriate and can be replicated in similar simulations.

Figures 11 and 12 show that the compound enhancement method has an undeniable positive effect on the heat transfer coefficient. Tube 5035 with both corrugations and the twisted insert had a heat transfer coefficient two to three times higher than tube 5030 with only corrugations at the same Re number range. A practical use of such heat exchangers can be in nuclear reactor cooling, automotive radiators, and other applications where tubular heat exchangers are used.

On the other hand, the pressure drop increased significantly as well. Figures 13 and 14 show that tube 5035 experienced more than two times the pressure drop when compared to tube 5030 at the same Re number range.

In this study, a new tubular heat exchanger geometry with vanes insert was proposed to enhance heat transfer while maintaining a reasonable pressure drop. The vanes were designed and modeled using SolidWorks, with 21 vanes mounted on a 1 m long shaft and inserted inside a 12 mm diameter tube.

CFD simulations were conducted to evaluate the thermal and hydrodynamic performance of the vane geometries. The Nusselt number was used to assess heat transfer, and it was found that the vanes insert achieved significantly higher Nusselt numbers compared to a smooth tube, up to nine times higher. However, the heat transfer of the vane geometries was slightly lower than a tube with continuous enhancement, such as the previously studied tube 5035.

Regarding the friction factor, the vane geometries exhibited higher values compared to a smooth tube, as expected due to increased flow obstruction. However, the friction factor of the vane geometries was considerably lower than the tube with continuous enhancement, indicating reduced hydro-mechanical losses.

The thermal performance, evaluated using the η factor, showed that the vane geometries achieved enhancement ratios ranging from 1 to around 3 for different variations. The 12.5 cm-spaced vane geometry demonstrated the highest η factor due to significantly lower friction factors which makes it the better option in this study.

Further analysis of the 5 cm-spaced vanes at high Reynolds numbers showed lower heat transfer coefficient and increased skin friction coefficient compared to the 12 cm-spaced vanes. This indicated that the closer spacing of the vanes resulted in lower overall performance.

Based on the findings of our study, it can be reasonably concluded that the implementation of vane inserts in the tubular heat exchanger demonstrates promise and effectiveness in enhancing heat transfer performance. These results suggest a potential avenue for further exploration and application in heat exchanger design and optimization. The 12 cm spacing between vanes appears to be a more favorable choice for achieving a balance between heat transfer enhancement and pressure drop. Further investigations and optimizations can be performed to refine the design and maximize the thermal performance of the vane geometries.

Overall, this study provides valuable insights into the potential of using vane inserts in tubular heat exchangers and lays the foundation for further research and development in this area.

Author Contributions: Conceptualization, S.F.M.; Methodology, S.F.M.; Validation, M.M.B.; Formal analysis, M.M.B. All authors have read and agreed to the published version of the manuscript.

Funding: This research received no external funding.

Data Availability Statement: The original contributions presented in the study are included in the article, further inquiries can be directed to the corresponding author.

Conflicts of Interest: The authors declare no conflict of interest.

Nomenclature

A	heat transfer surface area, m^2
D	tube diameter, m
R	corrugation radius, m
e	ridge height, m
f	fanning friction factor
H	pitch of the twisted tape in 360° twist, m
h	heat transfer coefficient, $W/(m^2 \cdot K)$
K	thermal conductivity, $W/(m \cdot K)$
k	turbulent kinetic energy, m^2/s^2
L	tube length, m
$\dot{m}$	mass flow rate in tube, kg/s
Nu	Nusselt number
p	pitch of ridging, m
Δp	pressure drop, Pa
Pr	Prandtl number
η	performance factor
q	heat transfer rate, W
Re	Reynolds number

s	cap height of the ridge, m
t	cap width of the ridge, m
ΔT	temperature difference, K
U	overall heat transfer coefficient, $W/(m^2 \cdot K)$
u, v, w	velocity components in x, y, z directions respectively, m/s
u′, v′, w′	instantaneous fluctuating components in x, y, z; m/s
β	helix angle of rib, deg
B*	$B^* = \beta/90$
φ	dissipation function
μ	dynamic viscosity, Pa·s
ρ	fluid density, kg/m^3
σ	surface tension, kg/s^2
Subscripts	
i	inside/inlet, or value at x = 0
m	mean value
o	outside/outlet, or value at x = L
s	smooth tube
w	wall
c	experimental constants

References

1. Pirbastami, S.; Moujaes, S.F.; Mol, S.G. Computational fluid dynamics simulation of heat enhancement in internally helical grooved tubes. *Int. Commun. Heat Mass Transf.* **2016**, *73*, 25–32. [CrossRef]
2. Zimparov, V.; Petkov, V.; Bergles, A. Performance characteristics of deep corrugated tubes with twisted-tape inserts. *J. Enhanc. Heat Transf.* **2012**, *19*, 1–11. [CrossRef]
3. Vicente, P.G.; Garcıa, A.; Viedma, A. Experimental investigation on heat transfer and frictional characteristics of spirally corrugated tubes in turbulent flow at different Prandtl numbers. *Int. J. Heat Mass Transf.* **2004**, *47*, 671–681. [CrossRef]
4. Sparrow, E.M.; Prata, A.T. Numerical solutions for laminar flow and heat transfer in a periodically converging-diverging tube, with experimental confirmation. *Numer. Heat Transf.* **1983**, *6*, 441–461. [CrossRef]
5. Yang, P.; Zhang, H.; Zheng, Y.; Fang, Z.; Shi, X.; Liu, Y. Investigation and optimization of heat transfer performance of a spirally corrugated tube using the Taguchi method. *Int. Commun. Heat Mass Transf.* **2021**, *127*, 105577. [CrossRef]
6. Chorak, A.; Ihringer, E.; Abdellah, A.B.; Dhimdi, S.; Essadiqi, E.H.; Bouya, M.; Faqir, M. Numerical evaluation of heat transfer in corrugated heat exchangers. In Proceedings of the 2014 International Renewable and Sustainable Energy Conference (IRSEC), Ouarzazate, Morocco, 17–19 October 2014.
7. Rahimi, M.; Shabanian, S.R.; Alsairafi, A.A. Experimental and CFD studies on heat transfer and friction factor characteristics of a tube equipped with modified twisted tape inserts. *Chem. Eng. Process. Process Intensif.* **2009**, *48*, 762–770. [CrossRef]
8. Sosnowski, M.; Krzywanski, J.; Grabowska, K.; Gnatowska, R. Polyhedral meshing in numerical analysis of conjugate heat transfer. *EPJ Web Conf.* **2018**, *180*, 02096. [CrossRef]
9. Lou, J.Z.; Li, J.P.; Dong, Y.J.; Wang, M. Study on Simulation of Heat Transfer Tubes with Twisted-Tape Inserted. *Appl. Mech. Mater.* **2011**, *66–68*, 1342. [CrossRef]
10. Jiji, L.M. *Heat Convection*, 2nd ed.; Springer: Berlin/Heidelberg, Germany, 2006; pp. 22–45.
11. Salman, S.D.; Kadhum, A.A.H.; Takriff, M.S.; Mohamad, A.B. Experimental and Numerical Investigations of Heat Transfer Characteristics for Impinging Swirl Flow. *Adv. Mech. Eng.* **2014**, *6*, 631081. [CrossRef]
12. Amini, Y.; Mokhtari, M.; Haghshenasfard, M.; Barzegar Gerdroodbary, M. Heat transfer of swirling impinging jets ejected from Nozzles with twisted tapes utilizing CFD technique. *Case Stud. Therm. Eng.* **2015**, *6*, 104–115. [CrossRef]
13. Mat Lazim, T.; S kareem, Z.; Mohd Jaafar, M.N.; Abdullah, S.; Abdulwahid, A. Heat Transfer Enhancement in Spirally Corrugated Tube. *Int. Rev. Model. Simul. IREMOS* **2014**, *7*, 970. [CrossRef]
14. Vahidifar, S.; Banihashemi, S. Experimental and numerical evaluation of heat transfer enhancement by internal flow excitation. *Int. J. Therm. Sci.* **2023**, *192*, 108395. [CrossRef]
15. Su, J.; Chen, Y.; Wu, J.; Fei, F.; Yang, S.; Gu, H. Experimental investigation on heat transfer performances in half-cylindrical shell space of different heat exchangers. *Int. J. Heat Mass Transf.* **2022**, *189*, 122684. [CrossRef]
16. Gu, H.; Chen, Y.; Wu, J.; Sunden, B. Performance investigation on twisted elliptical tube heat exchangers with coupling-vortex square tube layout. *Int. J. Heat Mass Transf.* **2020**, *151*, 119473. [CrossRef]

17. Li, X.; Wang, L.; Feng, R.; Wang, Z.; Liu, S.; Zhu, D. Study on shell side heat transport enhancement of double tube heat exchangers by twisted oval tubes. *Int. Commun. Heat Mass Transf.* **2021**, *124*, 105273. [CrossRef]
18. Pirbastami, S.; Moujaes, S. Effect of Groove Dimension on Thermal Performance of Turbulent Fluid Flow in Internally Grooved Tube. In Proceedings of the ASME 2016 International Mechanical Engineering Congress and Exposition, Phoenix, AZ, USA, 11–17 November 2016. [CrossRef]

fluids MDPI

Article

Proposed Approach for Modelling the Thermodynamic Behaviour of Entrapped Air Pockets in Water Pipeline Start-Up

Dalia M. Bonilla-Correa [1], Oscar E. Coronado-Hernández [2], Alfonso Arrieta-Pastrana [2], Modesto Pérez-Sánchez [3,*] and Helena M. Ramos [4]

1 Facultad de Ciencias Exactas y Naturales, Universidad de Cartagena, Cartagena 131001, Colombia
2 Instituto de Hidráulica y Saneamiento Ambiental, Universidad de Cartagena, Cartagena 131001, Colombia
3 Departamento de Ingeniería Hidráulica y Medio Ambiente, Universitat Politècnica de València, 46022 Valencia, Spain
4 Civil Engineering, Architecture and Environment Department, CERIS, Instituto Superior Técnico, University of Lisbon, 1049-001 Lisbon, Portugal; helena.ramos@tecnico.ulisboa.pt
* Correspondence: mopesan1@upv.es

Abstract: Water utilities are concerned about the issue of pipeline collapses, as service interruptions lead to water shortages. Pipeline collapses can occur during the maintenance phase when water columns compress entrapped air pockets, consequently increasing the pressure head. Analysing entrapped air pockets is complex due to the necessity of numerically solving a system of differential equations. Currently, water utilities need more tools to perform this analysis effectively. This research provides a numerical solution to the problem of entrapped air pockets in pipelines which can be utilised to predict filling operations. The study develops an analytical solution to examine the filling process. A practical application is shown, considering a 600 m long pipeline with an internal diameter of 400 mm. Compared with existing mathematical models, the results of the new analytical equations demonstrate their effectiveness as a new tool for computing the main hydraulic and thermodynamic variables involved in this issue.

Keywords: air pocket; analytical approach; start-up process; water distribution systems

1. Introduction

A pipeline start-up is an ordinary operation in water distribution systems that water utilities must conduct [1,2]. This operation represents a complex modelling problem, requiring an appropriate combination of thermodynamic and hydraulic formulations to describe the air and water phases [3,4]. Additionally, several pipeline ruptures have occurred due to the unsuitable performance of this operation. Ruptures can be provoked during this process's initial stages, since air pockets are rapidly compressed, increasing the air pocket pressure inside hydraulic installations [3,5].

The modelling of this problem has been approached using one-dimensional (1D), two-dimensional (2D), and three-dimensional (3D) numerical resolution schemes [6–9]. The elastic-column (ECM) and rigid-column (RCM) models have been extensively used to study the behaviour of water movement, employing a system composed of differential equations [10–12]. Both models provide similar results, since the elasticity of the air phase is much greater than the pipe wall's elasticity and the water phase's volumetric changes [3]. Several researchers have recently undertaken the formulation using these models.

Two-dimensional and three-dimensional models have been addressed using computational fluid dynamics (CFD), employing the commercial packages ANSYS and OpenFOAM [8,13]. These models have been primarily used to explore complex scenarios where 1D models have limitations related to the shapes of air-water interfaces [14]. One-dimensional, two-dimensional, and three-dimensional models provide similar water velocity, air pocket pressure, and the length of water column pulses when air–water interfaces coincide perpendicularly with the main direction of pipelines. However, when air–water interfaces tend towards the shape of bubble flow, plug, stratified wave, or stratified smooth flow, only 2D and 3D CFD models can adequately simulate the behaviour of the leading hydraulic and thermodynamic variables in water installations during this process.

During the occurrence of start-up processes, two instances are particularly relevant. The first corresponds to the process's end, as water utilities can compute the total duration for cleaning or maintenance manoeuvres on water installations. The investigation conducted by Bonilla-Correa et al. (2023) [15] provided an explicit formulation to compute the final time of this process. The second instance is marked by the peak value of an air pocket pressure pulse, which must be considered to determine if the pipe's resistance class is sufficient to prevent a rupture.

According to various investigations, this peak value usually occurs during the initial stages, as rapid compression of air pockets occurs at this time [3,5]. To compute this maximum value, a complex system of differential-algebraic equations needs to be solved, taking into account the momentum equation for modelling the water phase, the air–water interface formulation, and the air phase's polytropic formulation [12]. Water utilities require practical tools for rapidly computing these values, as they must analyse many water installations [16]. A semi-empirical equation has been previously proposed by Tijsseling et al. (2015) [17].

Although 1D models require less computational time than 2D and 3D CFD, they necessitate implementing a complex system of differential equations that must be formulated based on the specific water pipeline configurations. No commercial software is available to predict filling operations in water distribution systems.

This research demonstrates an analytical equation [18,19] for modelling the thermodynamic behaviour of air pockets in a single water pipeline start-up. The equation considers the physical equations governing the behaviour of this process. Engineers can use this equation to compute the maximum value in air pocket pressure in water pipelines during this hydraulic event. The demonstrated equation is valid until the instance of backflow occurrence. A practical application is conducted considering a pipe length of 600 m and an internal diameter of 400 mm.

The results show that the analytical equation provides a similar maximum value in air pocket pressure compared to the numerical resolution of the differential-algebraic equations system, confirming its adequacy for computing this maximum value. A sensitivity analysis using different mathematical approximations was conducted to demonstrate the robustness of the analytical approach.

2. Materials and Methods

Starting-up a water pipeline is a standard procedure for cleaning and maintenance by water utilities. This process begins with the pipeline at rest ($v = 0$) because the regulating valves are closed. When a valve operation begins, air pockets are compressed, increasing air pocket pressure. Ensuring that an air pocket pressure does not exceed a pipe's resistance class value is crucial if no air valves exist. Figure 1 shows the main hydraulic and thermodynamic variables involved when a system is at rest. L_0 corresponds to the initial length of a water column, x_0 is the initial air pocket size, p_0^* is the pressure supplied by a tank or a pumping station, and L_T is the total pipe length.

When a regulating valve is opened, a water column fills a hydraulic installation, causing the air–water interface to change over time. Since no air valve is located at the highest point of the water installation, the air pocket is rapidly compressed. At the end of the transient event, the air pocket remained inside the system.

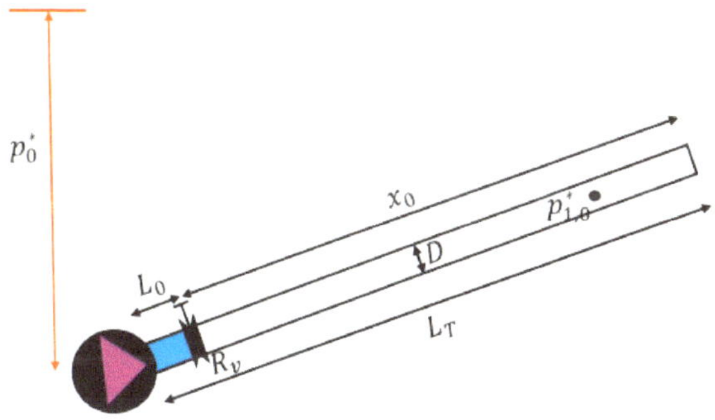

Figure 1. Water pipeline start-up scheme.

2.1. Current Mathematical Model

A system of differential equations has been defined to analyse the problem of filling processes in single pipelines. The ECM and RCM yield similar results because the pipe thickness and the volumetric changes of the water are not significant; the elasticity of the air phase is much higher in comparison. These models have been previously developed by Zhou et al. (2013) [20] and Coronado-Hernández at al. (2019) [21]. Both models assume that an air–water interface is perpendicular to the main direction of a pipe. The RCM is used for describing the movement of a water column in a filling pipe process, as follows:

- The air–water interface formulation assumes that this front is perpendicular to the main direction of a pipe system [1,16]:

$$\frac{dL}{dt} = v, \tag{1}$$

where v = water velocity, and L = length of a water column at time t.

- The polytropic law describes the air behaviour:

$$p_1^* x^k = p_{1,0}^* x_0^k, \tag{2}$$

where p_1^* = air pocket pressure, $p_{1,0}^*$ = initial air pocket pressure, x = air pocket size at time t, and k = polytropic coefficient. Considering that the air pocket size can be calculated as $x = L_T - L$, then the air pocket pressure at time t is providing by:

$$p_1^* = \frac{p_{1,0}^* x_0^k}{(L_T - L)^k}, \tag{3}$$

Usually, an air pocket pressure begins at atmospheric conditions ($p_{1,0}^* = p_{atm}^*$ = 101,325 Pa). The RCM can be used to describe the water phase movement [15,22].

$$\frac{dv}{dt} = \frac{p_0^* - p_1^*}{\rho L} + g\sin\theta - \frac{f}{2D} v|v| - \frac{R_v g A^2}{L} v|v|, \tag{4}$$

where f = friction factor, D = internal pipe diameter, θ = longitudinal slope, R_v = resistance coefficient of a regulating valve, g = gravitational acceleration, ρ = water density, and A = cross-sectional area of a pipe.

By plugging Equation (3) into Equation (4):

$$\frac{dv}{dt} = \frac{p_0^*}{\rho L} - \frac{p_{1,0}^* x_0^k}{\rho L (L_T - L)^k} + g\sin\theta - \frac{f}{2D} v|v| - \frac{R_v g A^2}{L} v|v|, \tag{5}$$

The initial conditions of a filling water process begin at rest which implies that $v(0) = 0$; $L(0) = L_0$; $p_1^*(0) = p_{atm}^*$; $x(0) = L_T - L(0) = x_0$.

2.2. Proposed Approach

This section presents the proposed approach developed in this research. The objective is to create a numerical-analytical solution that can be used for computing the maximum value of the air pocket pressure head without solving the complex system composed by Equations (1) and (5).

The assumptions underlying the proposed approach are outlined as follows:

- The pressure at the pipeline inlet is assumed to remain constant throughout filling operations.
- The air–water interface is analysed under the assumption of piston flow.
- The air phase's behaviour is modelled using the polytropic law.
- The RCM is utilised to describe the behaviour of the water phase.
- The operation of regulating valves is considered to be instantaneous.

2.2.1. Analytical Solution

Considering the chain rule for Equations (1) and (5), then $\frac{dv}{dL} = \frac{\frac{dv}{dt}}{\frac{dL}{dt}}$. Thus, it is possible to demonstrate that:

$$v\frac{dv}{dL} = \frac{p_0^*}{\rho L} - \frac{p_{atm}^* x_0^k}{\rho L(L_T - L)^k} + g\, sin\, \theta - \frac{f}{2D}v|v| - \frac{R_v g A^2}{L}v|v|, \tag{6}$$

In this case, $\frac{d(v^2)}{dL} = 2v\frac{dv}{dL}$. Thus:

$$\frac{d(v^2)}{dL} = \frac{2p_0^*}{\rho L} - \frac{2p_{atm}^* x_0^k}{\rho L(L_T - L)^k} + 2g\, sin\, \theta - \frac{f}{D}v|v| - \frac{2R_v g A^2}{L}v|v|, \tag{7}$$

The maximum value of the air pocket pressure in a rapid filling process without air valves occurs when the movement of the water column reaches zero velocity during the transient event. In this sense, considering that $v \geq 0$, then:

$$\frac{d(v^2)}{dL} = \frac{2p_0^*}{\rho L} - \frac{2p_{atm}^* x_0^k}{\rho L(L_T - L)^k} + 2g\, sin\, \theta - \frac{f}{D}v^2 - \frac{2R_v g A^2}{L}v^2, \tag{8}$$

Using $z = v^2$ and reorganizing terms in Equation (8):

$$\frac{d(z)}{dL} + \left(\frac{f}{D} + \frac{2R_v g A^2}{L}\right)z = 2\frac{p_0^*}{\rho L} - \frac{2p_{atm}^* x_0^k}{\rho L(L_T - L)^k} + 2g\, sin\, \theta, \tag{9}$$

where z = square of v.

Equation (9) is a first-order linear formula that can be solved using the integrating factor $e^{h(L)} = e^{\frac{f}{D}L + 2R_v g A^2 (lnL)}$. $h(L)$ is a function of friction factor, internal pipe diameter, resistance coefficient of a regulating valve, gravitational acceleration, cross-sectional area, and the variable of integration (s). The value of $h(L) = \int \frac{f}{D} + \frac{2R_v g A^2}{s} ds$.

Multiplying the left and right sides of Equation (9) by the integrating factor, then:

$$e^{h(L)}\left(\frac{d(z)}{dL} + \left(\frac{f}{D} + \frac{2R_v g A^2}{L}\right)z\right) = \left(e^{\frac{f}{D}(L)}(L)^{2R_v g A^2}\right)\left(2\frac{p_0^*}{\rho L} - \frac{2p_{atm}^* x_0^k}{\rho L(L_T - L)^k} + 2g\, sin\, \theta\right), \tag{10}$$

By organising terms and simplifying, it is possible to obtain:

$$\frac{d\left(ze^{h(L)}\right)}{dL} = \left(e^{\frac{f}{D}(L)}(L)^{2R_v g A^2}\right)\left(2\frac{p_0^*}{\rho L} - \frac{2p_{atm}^* x_0^k}{\rho L(L_T - L)^k} + 2g\sin\theta\right), \tag{11}$$

By integrating Equation (11) with limits from L_0 and L, where $L \in (L_0, L_T)$, and $v(S) > 0$ for all $S \in (L_0, L]$, then:

$$ze^{h(L)} = \int_{L_0}^{L} \left(e^{\frac{f}{D}(S)}(S)^{2R_v g A^2}\right)\left(2\frac{p_0^*}{\rho S} - \frac{2p_{atm}^* x_0^k}{\rho S(L_T - S)^k} + 2g\sin\theta\right)dS, \tag{12}$$

By solving for z, thus:

$$z = \left(\frac{1}{e^{\frac{f}{D}L}\, L^{2R_v g A^2}}\right)\int_{L_0}^{L} \left(e^{\frac{f}{D}(S)}(S)^{2R_v g A^2}\right)\left(2\frac{p_0^*}{\rho S} - \frac{2p_{atm}^* x_0^k}{\rho S(L_T - S)^k} + 2g\sin\theta\right)dS, \tag{13}$$

The water velocity (v) is yielding by the expression, as follows:

$$v(L) = \sqrt{\left(e^{\frac{f}{D}L}\, L^{2R_v g A^2}\right)^{-1}\int_{L_0}^{L} \left(e^{\frac{f}{D}(S)}(S)^{2R_v g A^2}\right)\left(2\frac{p_0^*}{\rho S} - \frac{2p_{atm}^* x_0^k}{\rho S(L_T - S)^k} + 2g\sin\theta\right)dS}, \tag{14}$$

which is valid from values of $v(L) > 0$.

Equation (14) corresponds to an analytical resolution that involves an integral that must be solved numerically, as presented below.

2.2.2. Numerical Resolution

The analytical solution presented in Section 2.2.1 contains a term that must be solved numerically using Simpson's 1/3 rule. This simple method approximates the integrand with a quadratic polynomial function [23], yielding a fifth-order error. Its approximation is employed because a water velocity (v) in the $L - v$ plane is a smooth concave function, making the method suitable for quadratic functions. Additionally, Simpson's 3/8 rule can be used, as it employs cubic polynomials, but this method also has a fifth-order error and is more complex to implement.

To approximate the integral of a function f over an interval $[a, b]$, the interval is divided into n equal subintervals, each with a length of $h = \frac{b-a}{n}$. The endpoints of each division are provided by $l_i = a + ih$ with $i = 0, 1, \ldots, n$. For Simpson's 1/3 rule, n is an even number, and the integral of f can be expressed as:

$$\int_a^b f(s)ds = \int_a^{l_2} f(s)ds + \int_{l_2}^{l_4} f(s)ds + \ldots + \int_{l_{i-1}}^{l_{i+1}} f(s)ds + \ldots + \int_{l_{n-2}}^{b} f(s)ds, \tag{15}$$

where l = points inside the interval (a, b).

Thus, each integral can be computed as:

$$\int_{l_{i-1}}^{l_{i+1}} f(s)ds \approx \frac{1}{3}h(f(l_{i-1}) + 4f(l_i) + f(l_{i+1})) \tag{16}$$

The integral of f is yielded by:

$$\int_a^b f(s)ds \approx (b-a)\frac{f(l_0) + 4\sum_{i=0}^{\frac{n-2}{2}} f(l_{2i+1}) + 2\sum_{i=1}^{\frac{n-2}{2}} f(l_{2i}) + f(l_n)}{3n}, \tag{17}$$

Before applying Simpson's 1/3 rule, it is crucial to analyse the term $\left(e^{\frac{f}{D}(S)}(S)^{2R_v g A^2}\right)\left(2\frac{p_0^*}{\rho S} - \frac{2p_{atm}^* x_0^k}{\rho S(L_T - S)^k} + 2g\sin\theta\right)$ in Equation (14). The integrand in the interval $[L_0, L]$ has large values; therefore, when performing the integration, the numbers become substantial, potentially causing memory issues for computers. Equation (18) reflects this situation:

$$z = \int_{L_0}^{L} \left(e^{\frac{f}{D}(S)}(S)^{2R_v g A^2}\right)\left(2\frac{p_0^*}{\rho S} - \frac{2p_{atm}^* x_0^k}{\rho S(L_T - S)^k} + 2g\sin\theta\right) dS, \tag{18}$$

In this context, the integrand is formulated as:

$$z = \int_{L_0}^{L} \left(\frac{1}{e^{\frac{f}{D}L}\, L^{2R_v g A^2}}\right)\left(e^{\frac{f}{D}(S)}(S)^{2R_v g A^2}\right)\left(2\frac{p_0^*}{\rho S} - \frac{2p_{atm}^* x_0^k}{\rho S(L_T - S)^k} + 2g\sin\theta\right) dS, \tag{19}$$

By substituting Equation (17) into Equation (19) to find the value of z, thus:

$$\begin{aligned} z \cong \frac{f}{3nD}(L - L_0) \Bigg[& \left(\frac{1}{e^{\frac{f}{D}L}\, L^{2R_v g A^2}}\right)\left(e^{\frac{f}{D}(L_0)}(L_0)^{2R_v g A^2}\right)\left(2\frac{p_0^*}{\rho L_0} - \frac{2p_{atm}^* x_0^k}{\rho L_0(L_T - L_0)^k} + 2g\sin\theta\right) \\ & + 4\sum_{i=0}^{(n-2)/2}\left(\frac{1}{e^{\frac{f}{D}L}\, L^{2R_v g A^2}}\right)\left(e^{\frac{f}{D}(l_{2i+1})}(l_{2i+1})^{2R_v g A^2}\right)\left(2\frac{p_0^*}{\rho l_{2i+1}} - \frac{2p_{atm}^* x_0^k}{\rho l_{2i+1}(L_T - l_{2i+1})^k} + 2g\sin\theta\right) \\ & + 2\sum_{i=1}^{(n-2)/2}\left(\frac{1}{e^{\frac{f}{D}L}\, L^{2R_v g A^2}}\right)\left(e^{\frac{f}{D}(l_{2i})}(l_{2i})^{2R_v g A^2}\right)\left(2\frac{p_0^*}{\rho l_{2i}} - \frac{2p_{atm}^* x_0^k}{\rho l_{2i}(L_T - l_{2i})^k} + 2g\sin\theta\right) \\ & + \left(\frac{1}{e^{\frac{f}{D}L}\, L^{2R_v g A^2}}\right)\left(e^{\frac{f}{D}(L)}(S)^{2R_v g A^2}\right)\left(2\frac{p_0^*}{\rho L} - \frac{2p_{atm}^* x_0^k}{\rho S(L_T - L)^k} + 2g\sin\theta\right)\Bigg] \end{aligned} \tag{20}$$

where n refers to the number of parts of the interval $[a, b]$.

The complete resolution of the system is provided by Equations (14) and (19).

2.3. Methodology

This section outlines the methodology this research uses, structured into five steps, as depicted in Figure 2. The input data pertain to practical applications of a water pipeline start-up typically conducted by water utilities. This initial step requires topological characteristics of pipelines and initial conditions of hydraulic and thermodynamic variables (such as water velocity, air pocket pressure, and water column length).

The case study is modelled using two formulations: (i) the mathematical model simulating the filling process through the RCM, the polytropic law, and the piston formula and (ii) the proposed approach developed in this research, which simplifies the current mathematical model. The numerical resolution was carried out using Octave v7.1.0 software, with the ODE45 function (Runge–Kutta method) employed to solve the proposed approach's numerical and analytical aspects. A sensitivity analysis of parameters is conducted to observe their influence on the responses of the proposed approach. Similarly, the results from the proposed approach are compared with those from the mathematical model. Finally, the section concludes with a discussion of the results obtained.

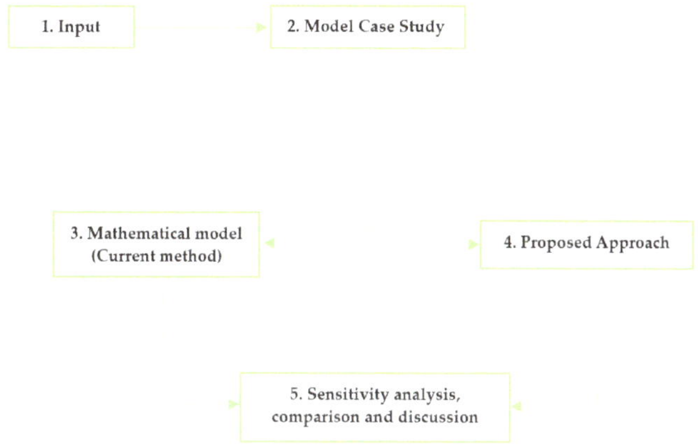

Figure 2. Research methodology employed.

3. Analysis of Results

This section presents the application of the proposed approach to a case study involving a filling process. The data for the case study are as follows: an initial air pocket size (x_0) of 400 m, an internal pipe diameter (D) of 0.4 m, a total length (L_T) of 600 m, a constant friction factor (f) of 0.018, an intermediate condition of polytropic evolution ($k = 1.2$), a longitudinal slope (θ) of 0.019 rad, and an initial pressure (p_0^*) of 202,650 Pa. This case study is referred to as the "baseline solution" in the following sections.

Figure 3 shows the results of the filling operation based on the proposed approach. This procedure is only applicable until the process reaches the first instance of zero water velocity, corresponding to when the air pocket pressure reaches its maximum value in this transient event. The proposed approach can be used to compute the maximum values of extreme variables (water velocity, air pocket pressure, and length of a water column). In this scenario, the initial size of the water column is 200 m when the system is at rest. The maximum water velocity is 4.77 m/s, which occurs when the water column length is 251.78 m. The highest peak in the air pocket pressure head is 33.59 m, which occurs when the water column length is 450.29 m. This is crucial, since the proposed approach can compute the extreme value during this process, which must be considered when selecting a suitable pipe resistance class.

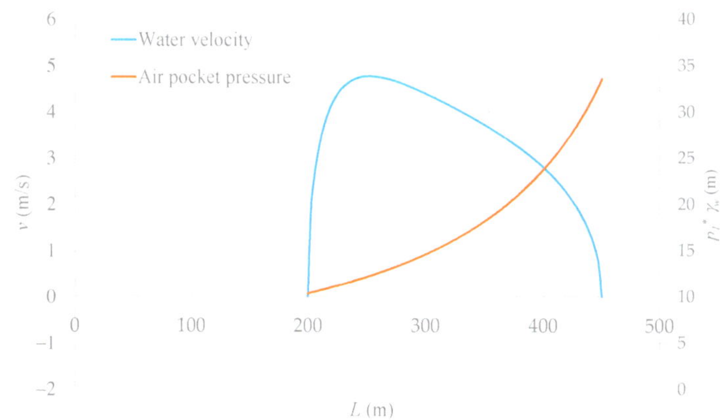

Figure 3. Results of the filling operation using the proposed approach.

Some parameters' influences were analysed to observe the responses of the proposed approach. Table 1 shows the range of variation in the analysed parameters.

Table 1. The range of parameters analysed.

Parameter	Units	Range	
		From	To
Internal pipe diameter (D)	m	0.2	0.5
Friction factor (f)	(-)	0.010	0.022
Longitudinal slope (θ)	rad	0.010	0.050
Polytropic coefficient (k)	(-)	1.0	1.4
Air pocket size (x_0)	m	200	500

The variation in parameters is analysed based on the results presented in Figure 3. Figure 4 illustrates the influence of internal pipe diameter, friction factor, and longitudinal slope. These variables exhibit a similar trend; therefore, the maximum value of the air pocket pressure head is analysed.

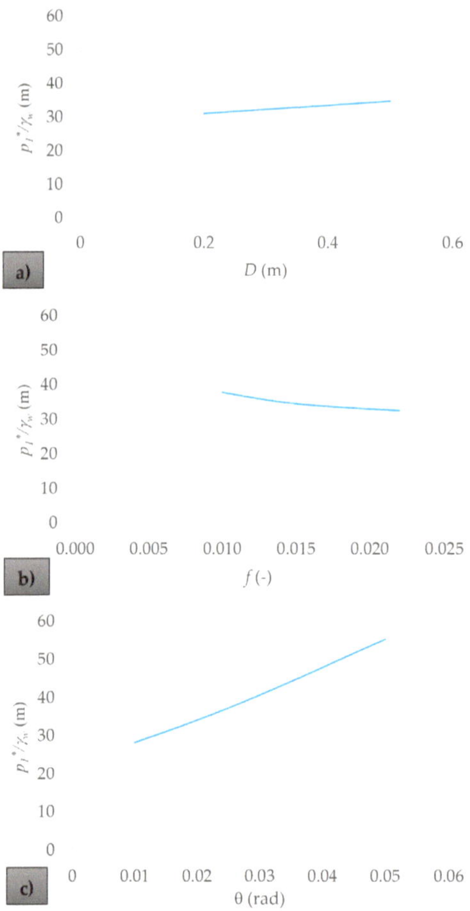

Figure 4. Influence of hydraulic and thermodynamic variables on maximum values in air pocket pressure head: (**a**) internal pipe diameter; (**b**) friction factor; and (**c**) longitudinal slope.

The internal pipe diameter varied from 0.2 to 0.5 m. As the pipe diameter increases, the air pocket pressure head rises due to the greater water volume in the system, as shown in Figure 4a. The air pocket pressure head varies from 31.15 to 34.85 m.

The friction factor is analysed from 0.010 to 0.022 (Table 1). The results indicate that a higher friction factor produces a lower air pocket pressure head (see Figure 4b). For instance, with a friction factor of 0.010, an air pocket pressure head peak of 37.86 m is achieved, while with a friction factor of 0.022, a value of 32.69 m is observed.

Another critical parameter is the longitudinal pipe slope. Its influence is analysed as shown in Figure 4c. The higher the longitudinal pipe slope, the greater the values in air pocket pressure attained. Air pocket pressure heads vary from 28.35 to 55.38 m for longitudinal slopes of 0.010 and 0.050 radians, respectively.

The transient event is analysed considering the variation in the air pocket size and polytropic coefficient, as shown in Figure 5. An isothermal evolution ($\boldsymbol{k} = 1.0$) shows greater values compared to adiabatic ($k = 1.4$) and intermediate ($k = 1.2$) behaviours. The maximum value of the air pocket pressure head during the transient event for an isothermal evolution is 34.28 m, while for adiabatic behaviour, 33.17 m is computed (see Figure 5a). Figure 5b presents the air pocket pressure graph versus the water column length, considering air pocket sizes of 200, 300, 400, and 500 m. As expected, the smaller the air pocket size, the higher the peak in air pocket pressure attained according to the polytropic law. Specifically, for an initial air pocket size of 200 m, a maximum air pocket pressure head of 41.26 m is reached. In comparison, for an initial air pocket size of 500 m, the maximum value is 31.51 m. Figure 5b shows the results when the air pocket size is varied.

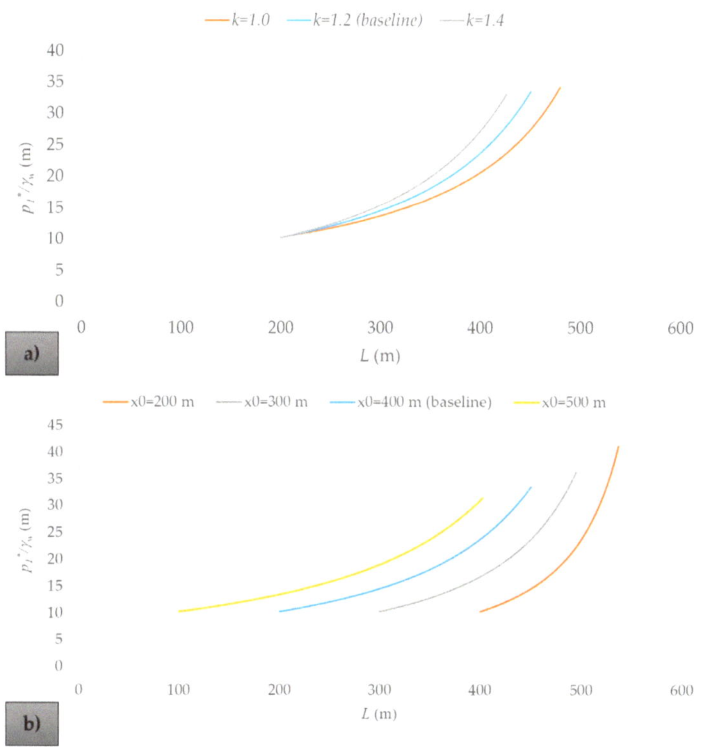

Figure 5. Analysis of hydraulic transient: (**a**) polytropic coefficient and (**b**) air pocket size.

4. Discussion

4.1. Comparison with a 1D Mathematical Model

The proposed approach can be applied from the beginning of the transient flow until the water velocity first reaches a null value. At this point, the maximum value of the air pocket pressure is achieved. Figure 6 presents the complete resolution (mathematical model) of the water pipeline start-up, considering Equations (1), (3), and (4), compared to the solution provided by the proposed approach. The mathematical model (grey and green lines) is suitable for simulating the complete transient event, as shown in Figure 6. Although the proposed approach (blue and orange lines) only presents the simulation until the water velocity reaches 0 m/s, it is sufficient for practical application, since the maximum peak in air pocket pressure is reached. Based on this value, engineers and designers can select an appropriate pipe resistance class. The proposed approach can reproduce the maximum value in air pocket pressure head of 33.59 m and the maximum value of water velocity of 4.77 m/s. These results coincide with the mathematical model, as presented in Figure 6.

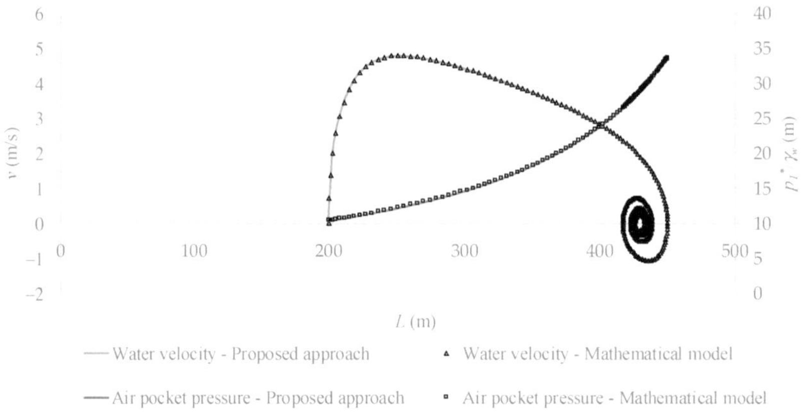

Figure 6. Comparison between the complete numerical resolution and the proposed approach.

4.2. Analysis of the Number of Intervals in the Proposed Approach

The number of intervals (n) for integrating the integral I was analysed, considering both even and odd numbers, as presented in Figure 7. Figure 7a shows the solution for even numbers 2, 6, 10, and 30. The case study was conducted with $n = 30$. The results indicate that the proposed approach achieves better accuracy as the number of intervals increases. For instance, with $n = 2$, the proposed approach tends to find the maximum value of the air pocket pressure head. Additionally, the maximum value of water velocity is adequately computed by the proposed approach using $n = 2$.

When an odd number of intervals is used, the proposed approach can compute the final value of the air pocket pressure head (33.59 m). However, it is not suitable for accurately representing the evolution of the transient event, as shown in Figure 7b, where n takes values of 5, 7, and 30 (baseline). This suggests that implementing the proposed approach should be carried out using an even number of intervals, as Simpson's 1/3 rule is defined under this condition.

Figure 8 shows the results of the integrand ***I*** considering Equations (18) and (19). For the case study, the reformulated equation to compute the integrand (Equation (19)) ensures appropriate values for evaluating the integral, avoiding large numbers. Implementing Equation (18) yields values of magnitude greater than -10^7.

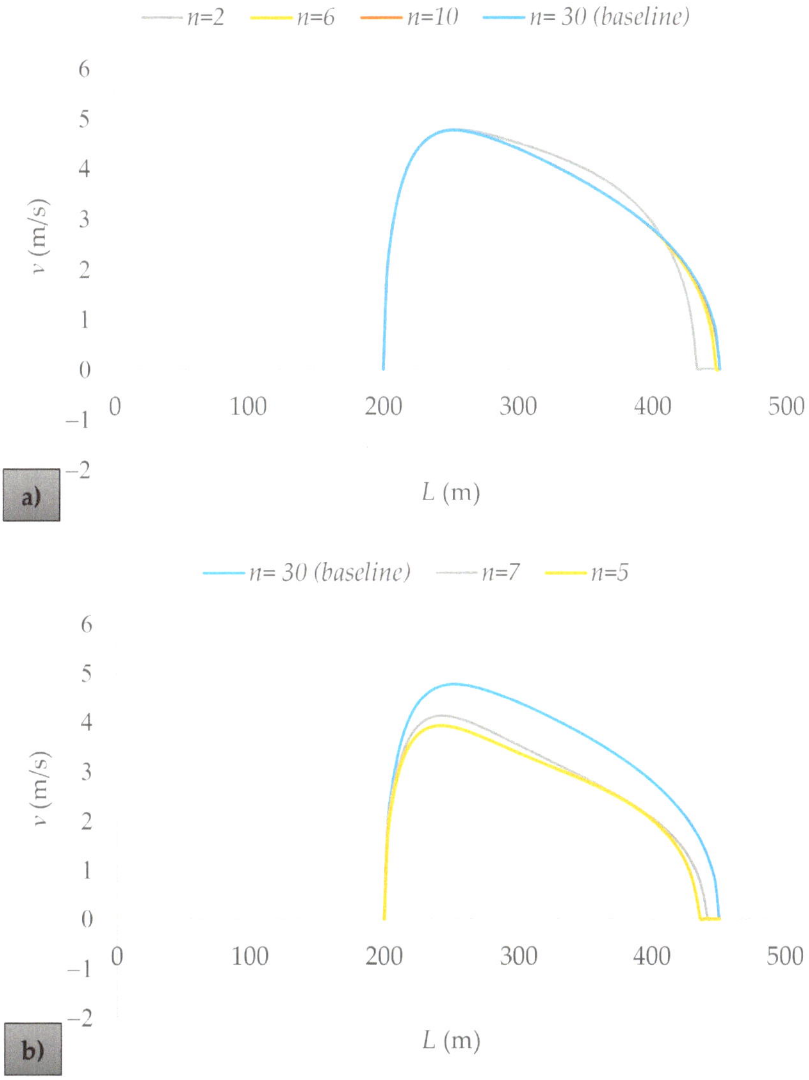

Figure 7. Analysis of the number of intervals (***n***) to integrate ***I***: (**a**) using an even number of intervals and (**b**) using an odd number of intervals.

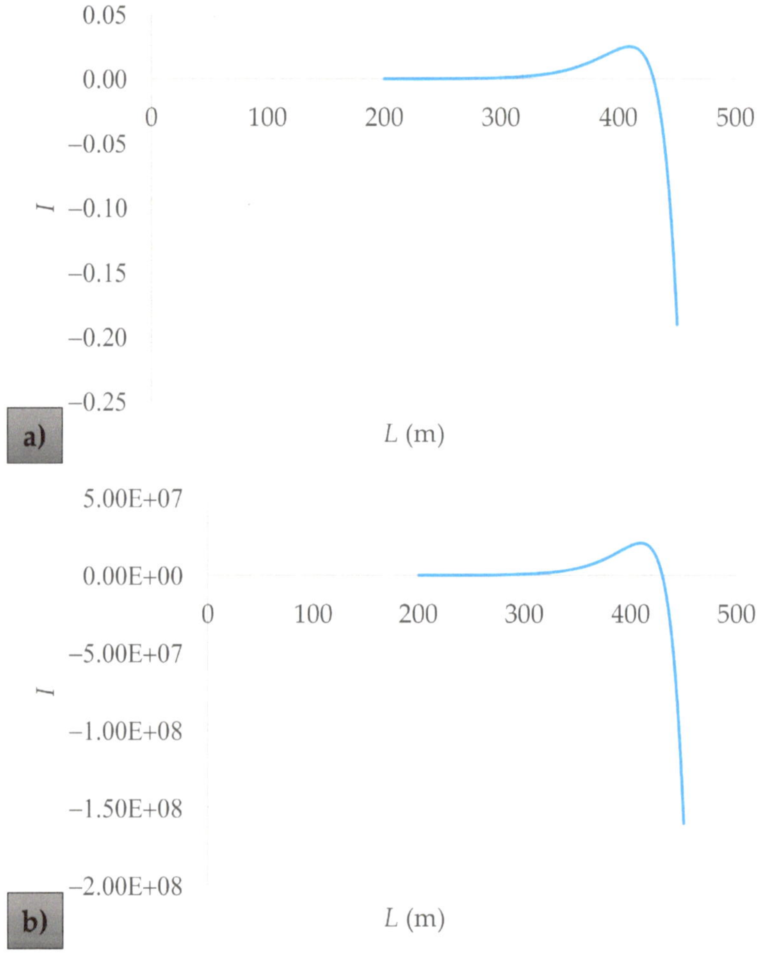

Figure 8. Analysis of integrand ***I*** using: (**a**) Equation (19) and (**b**) Equation (18).

4.3. Validation

The proposed approach is derived from the mathematical model presented in Section 2. Moreover, as illustrated in Figure 6, both models produce identical results for an instantaneous opening of regulating valves. The primary advantage of the proposed method is its ability to enable water utilities to calculate the maximum air pocket pressure in water pipelines rapidly. The proposed approach assumes an instantaneous valve opening, expected to yield higher values than scenarios involving gradual valve openings. In this context, the authors utilised the experimental data provided by Bonilla-Correa et al. (2023) [15]. The experimental setup consists of a 7.36 m long inclined pipeline with a nominal diameter of 63 mm and a pipe slope of 30°. The resistance coefficient (R_v) for a fully open valve was 17,000 ms^2/m^6. For the analysis, two air pockets (x_0) of 0.96 and 1.36 m were considered, with the initial pressure head (p_0^*) varying between 1.75 and 2.25 bar. Table 2 presents the experimental measurements.

Table 2. Experimental tests.

Test No.	p_0^*(bar)	x_0 (m)
1	1.75	0.96
2	1.75	1.36
3	2.25	0.96
4	2.25	1.36

The proposed approach was tested using the experimental measurements presented in Table 2. Figure 9 compares the computed and measured maximum air pocket pressure head for the tests analysed. The proposed approach is expected to yield higher air pocket pressure values than the exact solution, as the experimental tests involved a gradual manoeuvre. An electro-pneumatic valve with a 0.2-s aperture was used during the experiments.

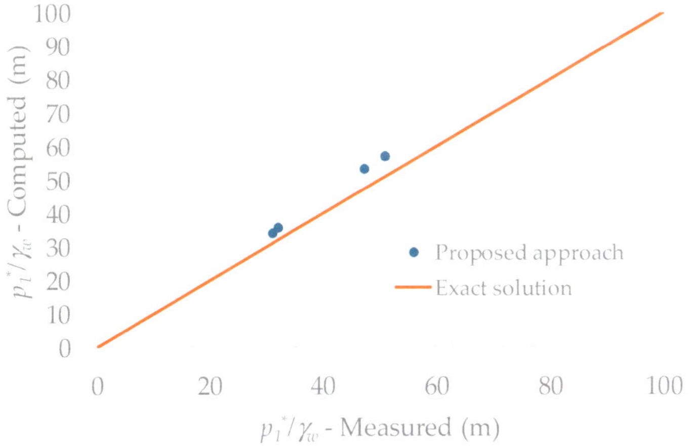

Figure 9. Comparison between computed and measured maximum air pocket pressure.

To assess the accuracy of the proposed approach, the root mean square error (*RMSE*) and the correlation coefficient (R^2) were calculated as follows:

$$RMSE = \sqrt{\frac{1}{N}\sum_{j=1}^{N}\left(p^*_{1,computed,j} - p^*_{1,measured,j}\right)^2}, \quad (21)$$

where $p^*_{1,computed}$ = air pocket pressure computed by the proposed approach, $p^*_{1,measured}$ = measured air pocket pressure, and N = total number of tests analysed.

$$R^2 = \frac{\sum_{j=1}^{N}\left(p^*_{1,computed,j} - \overline{p^*_{1,computed}}\right)\left(p^*_{1,measured,j} - \overline{p^*_{1,measured}}\right)}{\sqrt{\sum_{j=1}^{N}\left(p^*_{1,computed,j} - \overline{p^*_{1,computed}}\right)^2}\sqrt{\sum_{j=1}^{N}\left(p^*_{1,measured,j} - \overline{p^*_{1,measured}}\right)^2}}, \quad (22)$$

Based on the results presented in Figure 9, the RMSE and R^2 values are 4.72 m and 0.99, respectively. This indicates that the proposed approach is well suited for application in water utilities, as it closely aligns with the experimental results, even when not accounting for a gradual manoeuvre.

4.4. Comparison with Previous Models

Water utilities can utilise the proposed approach to calculate the maximum air pocket pressure during filling operations, particularly when considering an instantaneous valve-opening manoeuvre. This scenario is more critical, as it produces the highest pressure surges. The proposed approach can yield results comparable to 1D, 2D, and 3D models [3]. Implementing 1D models is complex, necessitating the numerical solution of partial and ordinary differential equations when formulating the elastic and rigid water models [15,20]. These models are well suited for capturing both rapid and slow valve-opening manoeuvres. The 2D and 3D CFD models provide a more intricate solution, allowing for detailed consideration of thermodynamic and hydraulic variables [3,24]. However, these models demand significantly higher computational resources than 1D models and the proposed approach.

5. Conclusions

This paper introduces an approach for computing water pipeline start-ups involving entrapped air pockets. The proposed approach simplifies an existing 1D mathematical model developed by the authors which incorporates the rigid column model, the polytropic law, and the piston flow equation to simulate the air–water interface. It is valid until the system reaches zero water velocity during the transient event.

The proposed approach is beneficial for determining the maximum value of an air pocket pressure head during a filling operation. It is paramount, as the proposed approach represents the sole analytical-numerical equation developed from physical equations in the current literature. The results of the proposed approach can be used to verify whether the pipe resistance class was appropriately selected, enhancing system feasibility. It is a practical tool that can be used for water utilities to evaluate extreme pressure with entrapped air pockets in pipelines. Its implementation is more accessible than rigid- and elastic-column models. The proposed approach is based on an analytical resolution, which includes an integrand that needs to be solved numerically using Simpson's 1/3 rule.

A practical application was tested using a 600 m long pipeline with an internal diameter of 400 mm. A sensitivity analysis of varying parameters such as pipe diameter, friction factor, longitudinal slope, polytropic coefficient, and air pocket size was conducted. The proposed approach yielded values consistent with the current mathematical model.

Furthermore, the proposed model was compared with the 1D mathematical model, demonstrating that both models accurately predict extreme air pocket pressure heads. This confirms that the proposed approach can be considered reliable for selecting the pipe resistance class. A sensitivity analysis was also performed on Simpson's 1/3 rule, showing that the proposed approach maintains good accuracy under the specified assumptions.

The proposed approach involves an instantaneous opening manoeuvre in regulating valves, enabling the computation of the maximum air pocket pressure. Water utilities can use this information to select the appropriate pipe resistance class for pipelines. The approach was validated using experimental measurements conducted on a 7.36 m long pipeline with a nominal diameter of 63 mm.

The proposed approach should be tested on more complex pipeline networks for future work. Additionally, its implementation should be incorporated into commercial software packages for filling operations.

Author Contributions: Conceptualization, D.M.B.-C. and O.E.C.-H.; methodology, D.M.B.-C., O.E.C.-H., and M.P.-S.; formal analysis, D.M.B.-C., A.A.-P., O.E.C.-H., and H.M.R.; writing—original draft preparation, A.A.-P. and O.E.C.-H.; supervision, A.A.-P. and H.M.R. All authors have read and agreed to the published version of the manuscript.

Funding: This work was supported by project HY4RES (Hybrid Solutions for Renewable Energy Systems) EAPA_0001/2022 from the ERDF INTERREG ATLANTIC AREA PROGRAMME 2021–2027.

Data Availability Statement: The original contributions presented in the study are included in the article, further inquiries can be directed to the corresponding author.

Acknowledgments: The research was carried out during Modesto Pérez-Sánchez's stay at the CERIS-IST research centre, named "Incorporation of New Water Resources in Irrigation Systems through the Use of Sustainable Technologies and Computational Tools to Mitigate Water Scarcity".

Conflicts of Interest: The authors declare no conflicts of interest.

Nomenclature

The following abbreviations were used in this manuscript:

Variables	
A:	cross-sectional area of a pipe (m^2)
D:	internal pipe diameter (m)
g :	gravitational acceleration (m/s^2)
$h(L)$:	function that depends on some variables (-)
k :	polytropic coefficient (-)
I:	integral
L:	length of a water column (m)
l:	points inside the interval (a, b) (-)
L_T:	pipe length (m)
n:	refers to the number of parts of an interval $[a, b]$ (-).
p_0^*:	pressure provides by an energy source (Pa)
p_{atm}^*:	atmospheric pressure (101,325 Pa)
p_1^*:	air pocket pressure (Pa)
R_v :	resistance coefficient of a regulating valve (ms^2/m^6)
s:	variable of integration
v:	water velocity (m/s)
x:	air pocket size (m)
z:	water velocity square (m^2/s^2)
θ :	longitudinal slope (rad)
ρ:	water density (kg/m^3)
γ_w:	water unit weight (N/m^3)
Subscripts	
0:	refers to an initial condition
Acronyms	
ECM	elastic-column model
RCM	rigid-column model

References

1. Izquierdo, J.; Fuertes, V.S.; Cabrera, E.; Iglesias, P.L.; Garcia-Serra, J. Pipeline Start-up with Entrapped Air. *J. Hydraul. Res.* **1999**, *37*, 579–590. [CrossRef]
2. Li, H.; Bai, C.; Wang, J. Experiments and Numerical Analysis of the Dynamic Flow Characteristics of a Pump−pipeline System with Entrapped Air during Start-Up. *Eng. Appl. Comput. Fluid Mech.* **2023**, *17*, 2238853. [CrossRef]
3. Fuertes-Miquel, V.S.; Coronado-Hernández, O.E.; Mora-Meliá, D.; Iglesias-Rey, P.L. Hydraulic Modeling during Filling and Emptying Processes in Pressurized Pipelines: A Literature Review. *Urban Water J.* **2019**, *16*, 299–311. [CrossRef]
4. Vasconcelos, J.G.; Wright, S.J. Investigation of Rapid Filling of Poorly Ventilated Stormwater Storage Tunnels. *J. Hydraul. Res.* **2009**, *47*, 547–558. [CrossRef]
5. Zhou, F.; Hicks, F.E.; Steffler, P.M. Transient Flow in a Rapidly Filling Horizontal Pipe Containing Trapped Air. *J. Hydraul. Eng.* **2002**, *128*, 625–634. [CrossRef]
6. Tijsseling, A.S.; Hou, Q.; Bozkuş, Z.; Laanearu, J. Improved One-Dimensional Models for Rapid Emptying and Filling of Pipelines. *J. Press. Vessel Technol.* **2015**, *138*, 031301. [CrossRef]
7. Zhou, L.; Liu, D.; Ou, C. Simulation of Flow Transients in a Water Filling Pipe Containing Entrapped Air Pocket with VOF Model. *Eng. Appl. Comput. Fluid Mech.* **2011**, *5*, 127–140. [CrossRef]
8. He, J.; Hou, Q.; Lian, J.; Tijsseling, A.S.; Bozkus, Z.; Laanearu, J.; Lin, L. Three-Dimensional CFD Analysis of Liquid Slug Acceleration and Impact in a Voided Pipeline with End Orifice. *Eng. Appl. Comput. Fluid Mech.* **2022**, *16*, 1444–1463. [CrossRef]
9. Malekpour, A.; Karney, B.W.; Nault, J. Physical Understanding of Sudden Pressurization of Pipe Systems with Entrapped Air: Energy Auditing Approach. *J. Hydraul. Eng.* **2016**, *142*, 04015044. [CrossRef]
10. Abreu, J.; Cabrera, E.; Izquierdo, J.; García-Serra, J. Flow Modeling in Pressurized Systems Revisited. *J. Hydraul. Eng.* **1999**, *125*, 1154–1169. [CrossRef]

11. Wan, W.; Zhang, B.; Chen, X. Investigation on Water Hammer Control of Centrifugal Pumps in Water Supply Pipeline Systems. *Energies* **2019**, *12*, 108. [CrossRef]
12. Biao, H.; Zhu, Z.D. Rigid-Column Model for Rapid Filling in a Partially Filled Horizontal Pipe. *J. Hydraul. Eng.* **2021**, *147*, 06020018. [CrossRef]
13. Paternina-Verona, D.A.; Coronado-Hernández, O.E.; Espinoza-Román, H.G.; Arrieta-Pastrana, A.; Tasca, E.; Fuertes-Miquel, V.S.; Ramos, H.M. Attenuation of Pipeline Filling Over-Pressures through Trapped Air. *Urban Water J.* **2024**, *21*, 698–710. [CrossRef]
14. Wang, J.; Vasconcelos, J.G. Investigation of Manhole Cover Displacement during Rapid Filling of Stormwater Systems. *J. Hydraul. Eng.* **2020**, *146*, 4020022. [CrossRef]
15. Bonilla-Correa, D.M.; Coronado-Hernández, Ó.E.; Fuertes-Miquel, V.S.; Besharat, M.; Ramos, H.M. Application of Newton–Raphson Method for Computing the Final Air–Water Interface Location in a Pipe Water Filling. *Water* **2023**, *15*, 1304. [CrossRef]
16. Zhou, L.; Liu, D.; Karney, B.; Zhang, Q. Influence of Entrapped Air Pockets on Hydraulic Transients in Water Pipelines. *J. Hydraul. Eng.* **2011**, *137*, 1686–1692. [CrossRef]
17. Ferras, D.; Manso, P.A.; Schleiss, A.J.; Covas, D.I. One-dimensional fluid–structure interaction models in pressurized fluid-filled pipes: A review. *Appl. Sci.* **2018**, *8*, 1844. [CrossRef]
18. Feng, Y.; Yi, H.; Liu, R. Analytical Solution for Transient Electroosmotic and Pressure-Driven Flows in Microtubes. *Fluids* **2024**, *9*, 140. [CrossRef]
19. Tijsseling, A.S.; Hou, Q.; Bozkuş, Z. Rapid Liquid Filling of a Pipe With Venting Entrapped Gas: Analytical and Numerical Solutions. *J. Press. Vessel Technol.* **2019**, *141*, 041301. [CrossRef]
20. Zhou, L.; Liu, D.; Karney, B.; Wang, P. Phenomenon of White Mist in Pipelines Rapidly Filling with Water with Entrapped Air Pockets. *J. Hydraul. Eng.* **2013**, *139*, 1041–1051. [CrossRef]
21. Coronado-Hernández, Ó.E.; Besharat, M.; Fuertes-Miquel, V.S.; Ramos, H.M. Effect of a Commercial Air Valve on the Rapid Filling of a Single Pipeline: A Numerical and Experimental Analysis. *Water* **2019**, *11*, 1814. [CrossRef]
22. Martin, C.S. Entrapped Air in Pipelines. 1977.
23. Budak, H.; Hezenci, F.; Kara, H.; Sarikaya, M.Z. Bounds for the Error in Approximating a Fractional Integral by Simpson's Rule. *Mathematics* **2023**, *11*, 2282. [CrossRef]
24. Huang, B.; Fan, M.; Liu, J.; Zhu, D.Z. CFD Simulation of Air–Water Interactions in Rapidly Filling Horizontal Pipe with Entrapped Air. In Proceedings of the World Environmental and Water Resources Congress, Virtual, 7–11 June 2021; pp. 495–507. [CrossRef]

fluids

MDPI

Article

Correction Factors for the Use of 1D Solution Methods for Dynamic Laminar Liquid Flow through Curved Tubes

Travis Wiens

Department of Mechanical Engineering, University of Saskatchewan, Saskatoon, SK S7N 5A9, Canada; t.wiens@usask.ca

Abstract: The modeling of transient flows of liquids through tubes is required for studies in water hammer, switched inertance hydraulic converters, and noise reduction in hydraulic equipment. While 3D gridded computational fluid dynamics (CFD) methods exist for the prediction of dynamic flows and pressures in these applications, they are computationally costly, and it is more common to use 1D methods such as the method of characteristics (MOC), transmission line method (TLM), or frequency domain methods. These 1D methods give good approximations of results but require many orders of magnitude less computation time. While these tubes are typically curved or coiled in practical applications, existing 1D solution methods assume straight tubes, often with unknown deviation from the curved tube solution. This paper uses CFD simulations to determine the correction factors that can be used for existing 1D methods with curved tubes. The paper also presents information that can be used to help evaluate the expected errors resulting from this approximation.

Keywords: transient flow; laminar flow; pipe flow; curved; CFD

1. Introduction

Modeling of fluid flows through curving pipes has a long history, both as examples of theoretical calculus solution methods as well as for practical engineering. The interested reader is referred to two review papers [1,2] for details, but a brief overview is presented here. Consider the curved tube shown in Figure 1, with the radius of curvature defined as r_b, the inner radius of the circular cross-section of the rigid tube as r, and the curve angle is θ. Boundary conditions include the pressure, $p(t)$, and volumetric flow rate, $q(t)$, at the inlet and outlet (denoted with subscripts A and B, respectively). The pressure is assumed to be constant across the inlet or outlet. Given the initial pressure and velocity fields within the tube and two of these four transient boundary conditions, the problem is to determine the other two boundary conditions.

Although others had previously noted the effect of curved passageways on an open channel flow and air through pipes, steady-state solutions to this problem typically start with the 1927 works of Dean [3], who established much of the theoretical groundwork and nomenclature used in the subsequent research, including this paper. He defined what would become known as the Dean Number, as

$$D = Re\left(\frac{r}{r_b}\right)^{\frac{1}{2}} \tag{1}$$

where Re is the Reynolds number and r/r_b is the curvature ratio. This number characterizes the nature of the flow via the ratio of the square root of the product of the inertial and centrifugal forces to the viscous forces [2].

The steady-state flow solution results in a secondary vortex flow perpendicular to the main streamwise flow, with the strength and number of these vortices related to the Dean number. It has also been noted that these vortices can have a significant effect on the flow for some distance downstream of the pipe bend [2]. For the sake of this paper, we will not concern ourselves with the internal details of the flow pattern but will concentrate on the inlet and outlet flows.

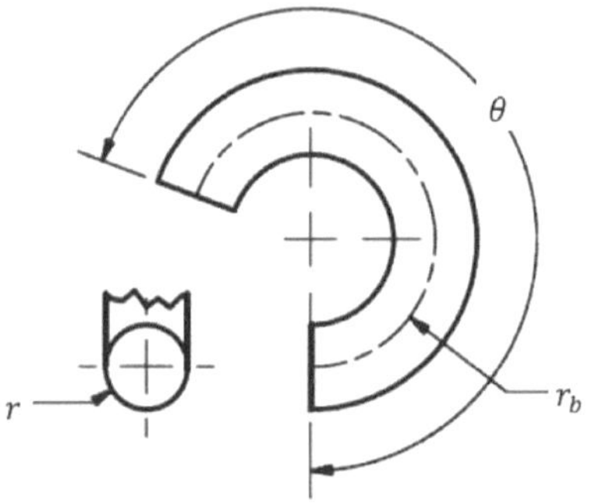

Figure 1. Geometry and nomenclature for a curved tube, showing the curved tube in plan view and also the cross-section. The radius of the cross-section is defined as r, the bend radius as r_b, and the bend angle as θ.

Although theoretical solutions exist for some simplified situations, the most reliable relations come from empirical correlations. The early part of the 20th century resulted in much of the careful experimental data still in use today. This includes references [4,5], which resulted in Hasson's empirical correlation for steady-state flow, formulated as

$$\frac{\lambda}{\lambda_s} \approx 0.0969(2D)^{\frac{1}{2}} + 0.556 \tag{2}$$

where λ/λ_s is the ratio of the steady-state resistance to the flow of a curved pipe relative to the resistance of a straight pipe with the same parameters ([6] via [2]). Note that the solution for the laminar flow through a straight pipe is the classical Poiseuille flow solution:

$$\lambda_s = \frac{p_A - p_B}{q_A} = \frac{p_A - p_B}{q_B} = \frac{8\pi\mu L}{\pi r^2} \tag{3}$$

where μ is the fluid dynamic viscosity and L is the tube length. Refer to [1] for a more comprehensive list of suitable correlations for various situations. The above correlation is for laminar flow, noting that transition to turbulent flow has been observed to occur at higher Reynold numbers than for straight pipes.

While the steady-state solution for the flow through curved pipes is relatively well understood, the dynamic response due to wave propagation under the influence of viscous friction is much less studied. Starting with straight tubes, analytical solutions taking into account the frequency-dependent nature of viscous friction exist in the frequency domain [7–9]. These solutions can be calculated very quickly at a very low computational cost but are only applicable for problems where the entire system is linear and time is invariant. In situations where there are other parts of the system model that require nonlinear dynamic models (common in hydraulic system design), it is common to use either the method of characteristics (MOC) or the transmission line method (TLM). The method of characteristics [10–12] divides the tube into an evenly spaced 1D grid along its length. The flow and pressure at any grid point can then be calculated, moving forward through time with a time step selected so that the propagating wave moves exactly one spatial grid distance in each time step. This method is somewhat more computationally expensive than the frequency-domain method, but allows for parameters that change in time, as well as along the length of the tube, and also may be connected to arbitrary dynamic models at its inlet and outlet. However, the required equations have not yet been developed for curved pipelines, and it appears that this may not be theoretically possible.

Another method of modeling dynamic responses is using the transmission line method. Developed by a number of researchers over recent years [13–15], this method uses a four-port model (flow and pressure at inlet and outlet) and applies a number of parameterized linear transfer functions and delays to connect the four ports, ignoring the internal pressures and flows. The parameters of these transfer functions are selected to give the desired overall input–output characteristics, typically to minimize the error with respect to an analytical solution. This is an approximate method, but the errors can be small, and it has the advantages of being relatively computationally efficient and integrating well with dynamic modeling software packages such as Simulink [16], Hopsan [17], etc. This method was originally designed for simple, straight, rigid-walled tubes, but the author of the present paper has collaborated with others to expand the concept to allow for straight tapered tubes, tubes with elastic pipe walls with varying thickness, as well as arbitrary cross-sections [18,19].

There has been relatively little work carried out, either experimentally or theoretically, on the dynamic response of general flow through curved tubes. One series of experimental results is available [20–22], but the apparatus had a very large bend radius and was designed to accentuate fluid–structure interactions, so it is difficult to separate this effect from the purely fluid response. Some work has been performed on specific applications, such as blood flow through the circulatory system [23], but these results are sufficiently specialized with respect to the pressure signal limitations and fluid properties to be inapplicable in most other general applications.

Some recent works have also used 3D computational fluid dynamics (CFD) to solve the transient flow of fluids through curved and other complex geometries, such as [24–28]. Unfortunately, these methods can be unstable and require many orders of magnitude more computation time and resources to complete than 1D methods.

The main objective of the present paper is to invest time in CFD results to determine the correlation for correction factors that will enable the use of high-speed 1D solution methods for curved tubes. This paper will also present information related to the expected errors when using these methods with or without these correction factors.

2. Materials and Methods

The objective of this paper is to provide correction factors so that existing 1D solution methods for transient pipe flows may be used to approximate the flows in curved pipes. The solution for a straight, rigid pipe with a laminar flow of Newtonian fluid and with a constant wave speed can be entirely defined by three parameters: the characteristic impedance, dissipation number, and time scale. The shape of the overall response is controlled by the dissipation number, while the scaling of the magnitude of the flow–pressure relationship is set by the characteristic impedance, and the scaling in time is controlled by the time scale. In this section, CFD methods are used to establish the factors required to correct these values for use with flow through curved tubes.

For the purpose of this paper, assume a laminar flow through a smooth, rigid tube. This ensures no structure–fluid interactions or compliance in the tube wall and ensures a linear, time-invariant dynamic system. Assume that the sonic speed of the fluid is large relative to the fluid velocities and assume small changes in pressure, which will allow for the wave propagation solutions to be superimposed over a variety of mean flows and to be calculated for arbitrary boundary conditions. The pressure distribution is constrained to be constant across the inlet and outlet, but the pressure distribution within the tube is not constrained, nor is the velocity profile constrained at any point.

2.1. Characteristic Impedance

The characteristic impedance of a tube is the ratio of the magnitude of a pressure wave traveling through a tube to the magnitude of the resultant flow wave. For a lossless straight tube, this is related to the ratio of the inertia per unit length to the compliance per unit length and is defined as

$$Z_{cs} = \frac{\rho c}{A} \quad (4)$$

where ρ is the fluid density, c is the wave speed, and $A = \pi r^2$ is the cross-sectional area of the tube (a subscript "s" is used to refer to quantities related to a reference straight tube in order to differentiate them from an arbitrarily curved tube under consideration). Note that this value is only related to the properties of the fluid and of the cross-section; there is no dependence on the length of the tube. This impedance would be measurable at the inlet of a tube of infinite length or at the inlet of a tube of finite length for the initial part of the response prior to the influence of returning reflected waves. This is shown in Figure 2 for a Method of Characteristics solution for the inlet flow, q_A, in a straight tube of finite length subjected to a step in inlet pressure of Δp_A. The ratio $q_A Z_c / \Delta p_A$ is equal to 1 in the middle portion (around $t = L/c$) of this plot for a lossless tube (small dissipation number β). A similar method is used to measure the characteristic impedance of curved tubes, using response calculated using a CFD simulation.

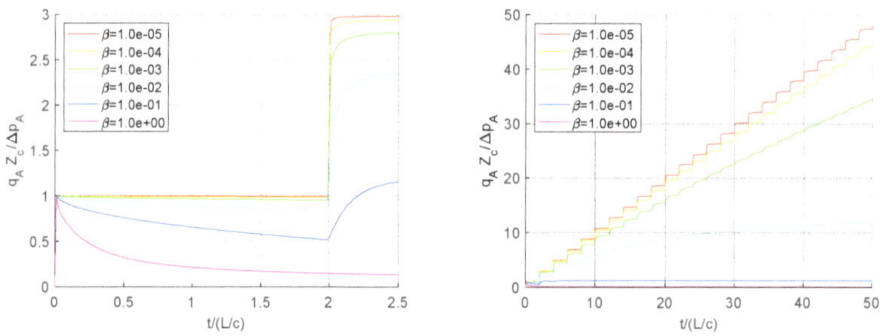

Figure 2. Inlet flow responses to a step in inlet pressure for a straight tube with an open (constant pressure) outlet for varying dissipation numbers. The (**left**) and (**right**) plots show the same data at different time-scale zoom levels. For straight tubes, this response is totally defined by the dissipation number, β, the characteristic impedance, Z_c, and the time scale L/c, where L is the length and c is the wave speed.

The CFD responses are calculated using the OpenFOAM CFD package [29]. The "sonicLiquidFoam" solver was used, which is a compressible flow solver intended for studies of wave propagation in liquids with laminar flows. It uses an equation of state with a density described by

$$\rho = \rho_0 + \psi(p - p_0) \quad (5)$$

where subscripts 0 denote reference conditions and $\psi = 1/c^2$ is the (constant) derivative of density with respect to pressure. The default finite volume discretization of Gaussian integration is used.

The tube was meshed with the grid, shown in Figure 3, for half of the pipe (symmetry along the central plane is exploited to reduce the solution size). Following a similar study by Fries [25–27], the pipe's cross-section is divided into a central core with equal cell spacing, while the outer 2/3 of the radius is graded, with smaller cells toward the pipe walls to allow for better resolution of near-wall effects. In each cross-section, there are a total of 290 cells. This cross-section is then extruded in either a straight line of total length L_s or revolved about an axis over an angle of θ (with a centerline length of $L_s = \theta r_b$). The cells in the axial direction are spaced with a 1 mm spacing along the center line of the tube (approximately equal to the spacing in the radial and circumferential directions at the edge of the central core). OpenFOAM's data structures are only concerned with the connections between cells, which permits the situation of $\theta > 2\pi$, which is physically impossible as the rotations would overlap in space, but allows for a longer length of tube and therefore more accurate solutions that minimize inlet effects. This can also be thought of as a helical coil in the limit as the helical pitch approaches zero. The baseline parameters for simulations are shown in Table 1.

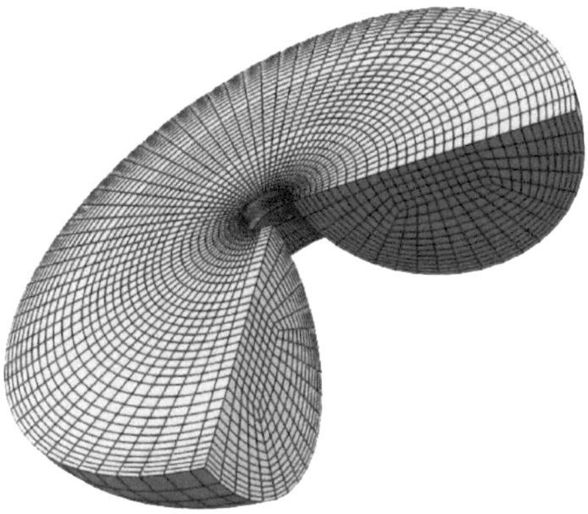

Figure 3. Example meshing for a portion of a tube with an extreme bend radius. Note the inner core with equal grid spacing and the outer section with cells graded toward the outer wall. A symmetry plane bisects the tube.

Table 1. Baseline simulation parameters.

r	Tube inner radius	10 mm
r_b	Bend radius	20 mm
L_s	Centerline length	1 m
μ	Dynamic viscosity	1 Pa s
ρ	Density	1000 kg/m^3
c	Wave propagation velocity	1000 m/s

The above tube was initialized with zero velocity and an initial pressure of 100 kPa. Boundary conditions were applied with a constant pressure of 100 kPa at the outlet and 200 kPa at the inlet, corresponding to an inlet pressure step of ΔP_A = 100 kPa. A no-slip boundary condition was applied to the pipe walls and a symmetry plane boundary condition along the central plane. It should be noted that one could instead apply a flow boundary condition to the inlet, which can improve solution stability but would require some other method to determine the non-parabolic velocity profile of the inlet velocity.

The solution was then solved with a time step of 5×10^{-7} s for a period of 5 ms. This was selected as a time that would allow for the sonic wave to traverse the length of the straight tube approximately five times. (The change in the effective length of the curved tube will change the number of times that the wave actually transits the tube).

The volumetric flow was calculated by integrating the normal velocity over the plane of the inlet and outlet (and doubled to take into account the other symmetric half of the tube). The characteristic impedance was then calculated as the inlet pressure step divided by the flow, measured at the first time that the outlet flow equals the inlet flow (t_1 in Figure 4). The characteristic impedance correction factor is defined as

$$K_{Zc} = \frac{Z_c}{Z_{cs}} \quad (6)$$

where Z_{cs} is the geometrical characteristic impedance (Equation (4)) and Z_c is the impedance measured from the CFD results. The above was then repeated for a range of curve radii.

These calculations were performed on a desktop computer with two Xeon 4114 processors (a total 20 physical cores) with 128 GB of RAM. ESI OpenFOAM version v2312 was used, running on Ubuntu Linux 22.04.4.

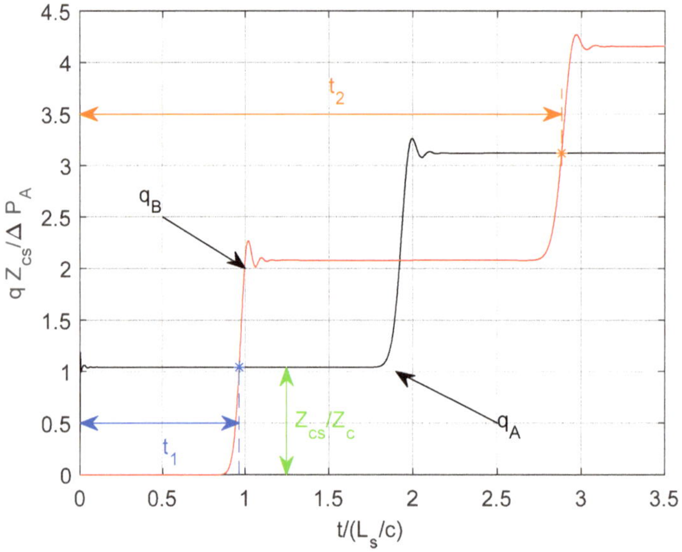

Figure 4. Sample CFD flow responses for inlet (q_A) and outlet (q_B), showing points used to measure K_{Zc} and K_L.

2.2. *Time Scale*

The second parameter required for the use of 1D solution methods is the time scale L/c. In this case, it is assumed that the wave propagation speed, c, is constant and assumed that changes in the response are due to changes in the effective length L. This change can be explained by the fact that some wave energy may preferentially travel from inlet to outlet following the shorter path length along the inside of the curve.

The same CFD results from Section 2.1 were used to determine this effect. In this case, we identify the time it takes for a wave to travel the length of the tube, reflect off the open boundary, and return. As shown in Figure 4, for a sample waveform, t_1 is defined as the first time that the outlet flow, q_B, exceeds the inlet flow, q_A. t_2 is defined as the first time that the outlet flow exceeds the inlet flow after $t = 2\,L_s/c$. The effective length can then be calculated using

$$L = \frac{(t_2 - t_1)c}{2} \tag{7}$$

and the correction factor is defined as

$$K_L = \frac{L}{L_s} \tag{8}$$

where $L_s = \theta r_b$ is the centerline length.

2.3. *Dissipation Number*

The dissipation number for a tube reflects the damping induced by the fluid viscosity. This is analogous to the damping ratio of a dynamic system: a dissipation number near unity will reach the steady-state value with little overshoot, while a system with a low dissipation number will take many oscillations before reaching steady-state, as shown in Figure 2, for MOC solutions for varying dissipation numbers.

For a straight tube, the dissipation number is defined as

$$\beta_s = \frac{\nu L}{c r^2} \tag{9}$$

which is equal to

$$\beta = \frac{\lambda}{8 Z_c} \tag{10}$$

where λ is the steady-state laminar resistance of the tube; this second equation applies to curved tubes as well as straight tubes.

The estimate for the effective dissipation number of a curved tube is determined by using the same CFD model as described in Section 2.1, but with the end time extended to 10 L_s/c. As before, the dynamic flow response to a step in pressure is calculated. The dissipation for a method of characteristics (MOC) solution (available for download from [12]) was determined for a straight tube that best fits this response. The characteristic impedance and effective length relations developed in the previous sections were used to compensate for these effects. The iterative, non-derivative global optimization scheme fminsearch, provided with the Matlab 2023a software package, was used to minimize the error between the MOC straight tube response and the CFD curved tube response by varying the MOC dissipation number. The normalized root mean squared error between the straight tube MOC solution, q_{Bs}, and the curved tube CFD solution, q_B, was minimized, and defined as

$$E = \frac{Z_{cs}}{\Delta P_A} \left[\frac{1}{t_{end}} \int_0^{t=t_{end}} (q_B - q_{Bs})^2 \, dt \right]^{1/2} \tag{11}$$

where $t_{end} = 10\ L_s/c$. The effective dissipation number correction factor can then be defined as

$$K_\beta = \frac{\beta}{\beta_s}. \tag{12}$$

where β is the effective dissipation number and β_s is the dissipation number for a straight tube of the same centerline length (Equation (9)).

3. Results

3.1. Validation

In order to have some confidence in the CFD solution, the CFD solution for a straight pipe was calculated with parameters in Table 1, which can be compared to the validated method of characteristics and frequency domain solutions. These results are shown in Figure 5, along with varied viscosity solutions to show the effect of dissipation number. The results have good general agreement. One area with some differences is during the rapid change in flow around $t/(L/c) = 1, 2, 3$, and 4 as the wave fronts are reaching the reflective boundaries. This may be due to the assumption in the 1D solutions that the tube is narrow with no waves moving in the radial direction. Since the 3D CFD solution allows some wave energy to move diagonally through the pipe, some energy will arrive later, leading to the wave front's arrival being less sharp.

A mesh invariance test was also performed to ensure that the mesh had been selected appropriately. The mesh size was halved in each dimension, along with halving the time step to ensure a constant Courant number. The results are shown in Figure 6. The Courant number was also checked by maintaining the original grid spacing while reducing the time step, as shown in Figure 6. Again, there is good agreement, and one can have confidence in the time and spatial mesh.

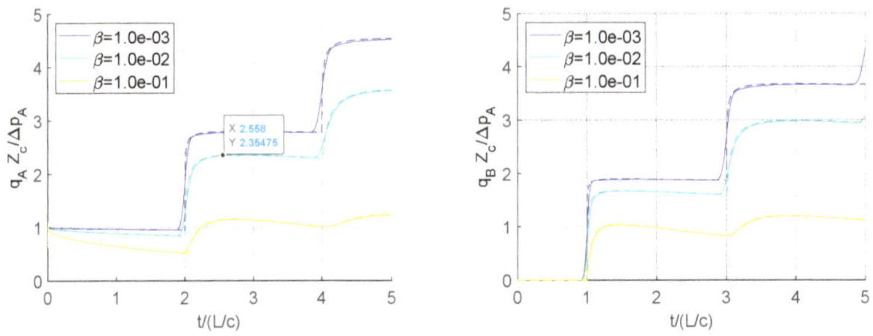

Figure 5. Comparison of flow responses (inlet flow at **left** and outlet at **right**) for straight tubes for CFD (solid lines) and MOC (dashed lines).

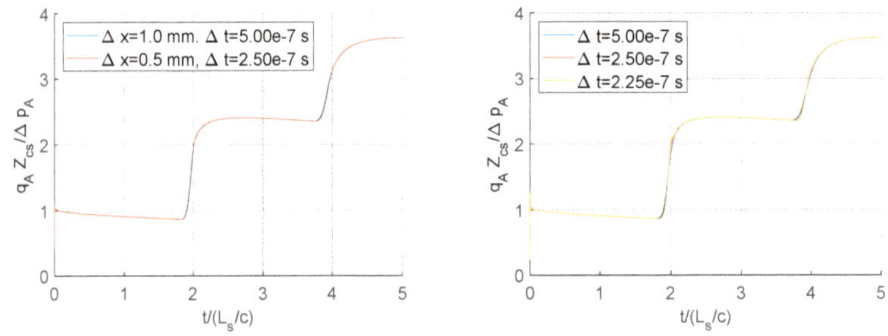

Figure 6. Mesh invariance test (**left**), showing little effect when the spatial mesh spacing is halved in each dimension while also halving the time step to maintain the same Courant number. (**Right**) the minimal effect of the Courant number is shown by reducing the time step (while maintaining a consistent spatial mesh).

Finally, the linearity of the transient solution was verified by doubling the driving pressure step magnitude, Δp_A. As shown in Figure 7 for curved tubes, the resulting flow doubles, but the shape is nearly exactly the same, with deviations only noticeable for extreme bend ratios and low dissipation numbers. This validates the linearity assumption and demonstrates that the solution does not rely on the Dean number (as it would for static solutions). The nonlinear static solution would be important for very large pressure waves, but the results presented here can be viewed as accurate for small variations about an operating point.

3.2. Characteristic Impedance

Examples of inlet flow wave forms for varying bend radii are shown in Figure 8. Note that as $r/r_b \to 1$ (more extreme bends), the magnitude of the flow between the steps increases, meaning the characteristic impedance decreases. There is also a change in the timing of the steps, which will be addressed in the next section. The associated calculated characteristic impedance correction factors are shown in Figure 9. Data for double the tube radius is also included, which is nearly identical, demonstrating that the curve for the characteristic impedance correction factor is a function of the bend radius *ratio*, not the radius itself. This curve can be approximated by a fit of

$$K_{Zc} = \frac{Z_c}{Z_{cs}} \approx 1 - 0.2239\left(\frac{r}{r_b}\right)^{3.276}. \tag{13}$$

For better accuracy, a higher order polynomial could be fit to the data in Table A1.

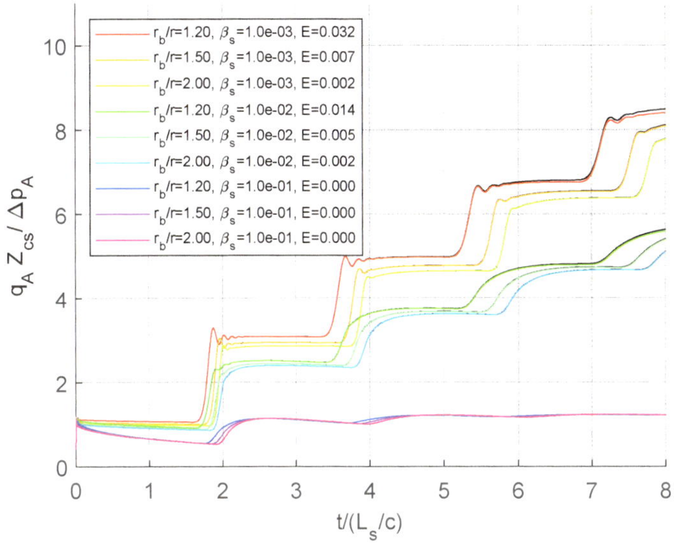

Figure 7. Linearity test, showing the CFD flow response for a variety of bend ratios and dissipation numbers for the base case of Δp_A = 100 kPa (black), and for the case of Δp_A = 200 kPa (colored). The results are very similar and overlap for almost all cases. The only visible difference is for extreme bend ratios and small dissipation numbers (top right of the plot). The error between the two solutions, E, is calculated using Equation (11).

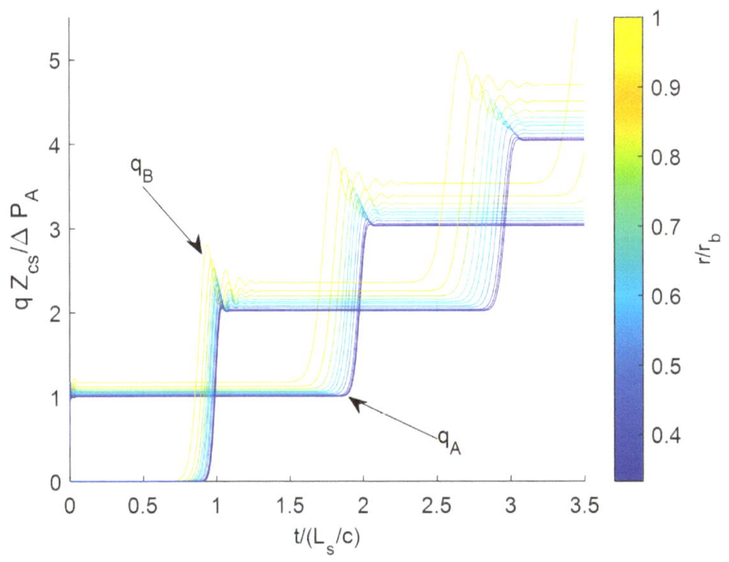

Figure 8. Flow responses to a step in inlet pressure for $\beta = 0$, while varying bend ratio.

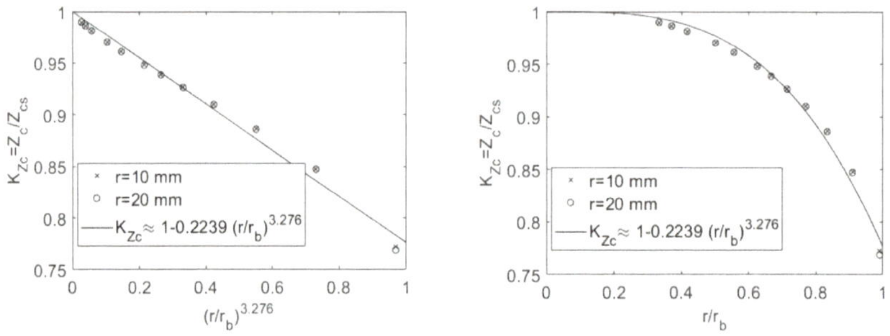

Figure 9. Characteristic impedance correction factor for a curved tube relative to a straight tube of the same dimensions and wave speed. The same data is plotted in each graph, with the exponent applied to the left plot's x-axis to show linearity.

3.3. *Effective Length*

As shown in Figure 8, the curve ratio clearly affects the arrival time of the steps in flow (after they have traveled the length of the tube). The calculated effective length correction factor is shown in Figure 10, which is very similar to the correction factor for characteristic impedance. The correlation was fit to a similar form:

$$K_L = \frac{L}{L_s} \approx 1 - 0.2095\left(\frac{r}{r_b}\right)^{2.965} \quad (14)$$

It is unclear at present whether the difference in values in this equation should be assumed to be due to simulation error and taken as identical to Equation (13) or whether this difference exists in reality.

It should be noted that the K_L correction factor is not equal to the change attributable to following the shortest path length through the inside of the curve, indicating that the wave traveling along this shortest path is "pulled back" by the neighboring waves traveling longer paths.

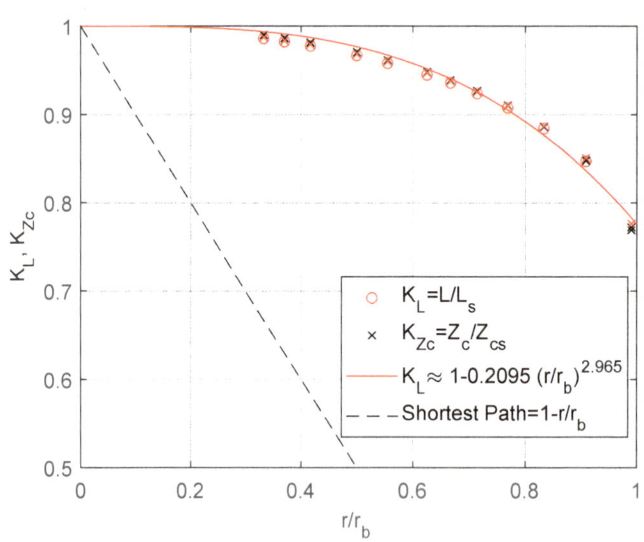

Figure 10. Effective length correction factor for a curved tube relative to a straight tube of the same dimensions. This also shows the same K_{Zc} data as Figure 9 for comparison.

3.4. Dissipation Number

Examples of the inlet flow responses are shown in Figures 11–13 for a range of bend ratios and dissipation numbers, along with the associated 1D MOC solutions with the best-fit dissipation number. These demonstrate a relatively good fit, especially for the parts of the response between the steps with moderate rates of change and also for moderate bend ratios and dissipation numbers. The more extreme bend ratios exhibit an oscillation in the volumetric flow as the wave fronts reflect at the boundary. There is no fluid experimental data available to validate this effect for large bend ratios, but these oscillations are visible in some data from curved microwave antennas [30], which are governed by similar wave propagation equations. This may be due to the nonplanar wavefronts that are generated in the strongly curved tubes. An example of this nonplanar wave front is shown in Figure 14, with the white contour line showing that the wave has progressed faster in the middle of the tube than along the outer bend radius. Figure 15 shows a plot of the pressure distribution along a radial line. This shows that the assumption of constant pressure across the cross-section that is commonly made for straight tubes is not applicable here. It also shows the fact that constructive interference has occurred with the maximum pressure considerably above the inlet's driving pressure.

The calculated dissipation number correction factor is plotted in Figures 16 and 17, along with the RMS error in Figure 18. As shown in Figure 17, the correction factor can be significant for strongly curved tubes, especially if the dissipation number is low. In most cases, the corrected response provides a usefully accurate estimation of the flow, although it does not capture the oscillations immediately after each step for strongly curved tubes.

To provide an indication of the relative computation time required for the CFD and MOC solutions, the typical time required to calculate a single response in this section was 1600 s for CFD and 190 ms for the MOC, a speedup of over 8000 times. In addition, the CFD fully utilized the 20 cores of the computer, while the MOC code was not parallelized and ran on a single core, with associated speed improvements expected, it was to run on multiple cores.

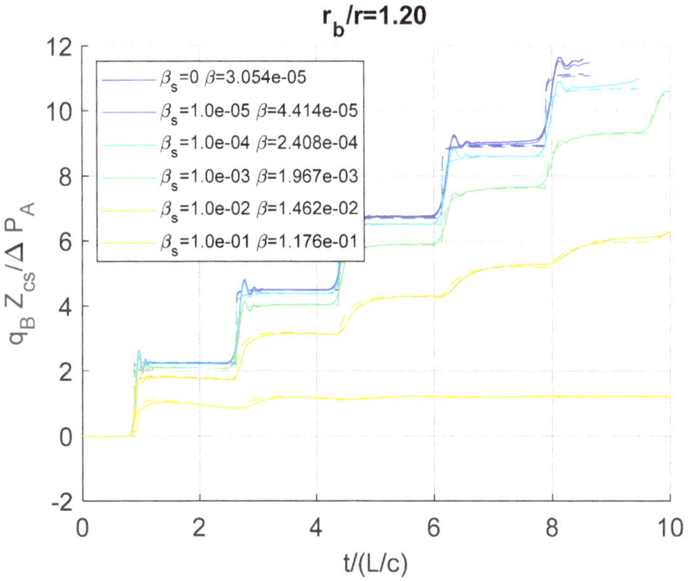

Figure 11. CFD (solid lines) and best-fit MOC (dashed lines) solutions for r_b/r = 1.20.

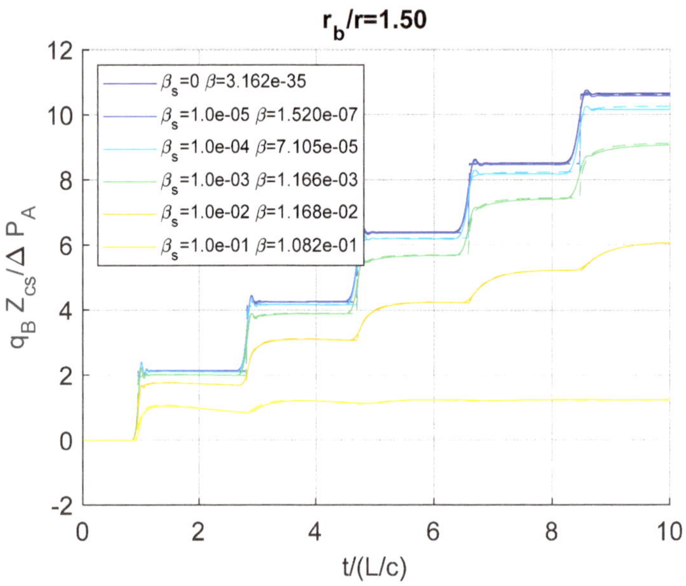

Figure 12. CFD (solid lines) and best-fit MOC (dashed lines) solutions for r_b/r = 1.50.

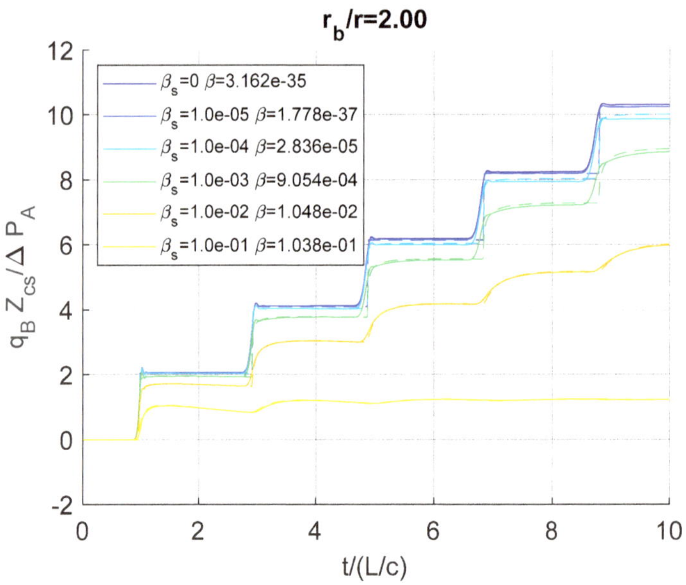

Figure 13. CFD (solid lines) and best-fit MOC (dashed lines) solutions for r_b/r = 2.00.

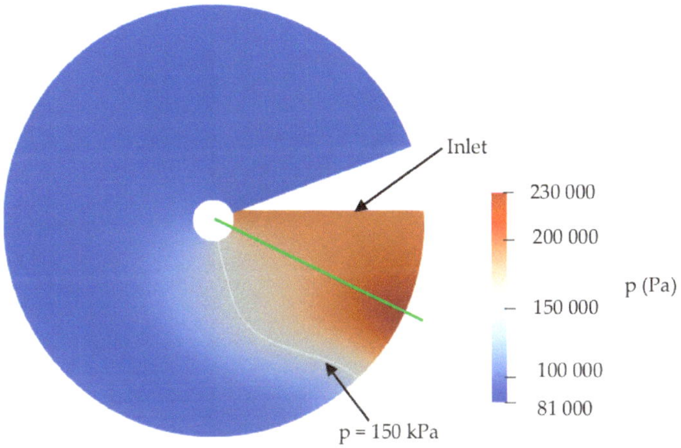

Figure 14. Example of the pressure distribution on the central plane after the wave has traveled clockwise from the inlet for 15 μs, for an extreme bend radius of $r_b/r = 1.2$ and $\beta_s = 0.1$. Note the nonplanar wave front, denoted by the white pressure contour at 150 kPa. Also, note the overpressure above the inlet pressure of 200 kPa, plotted along the green line in Figure 18.

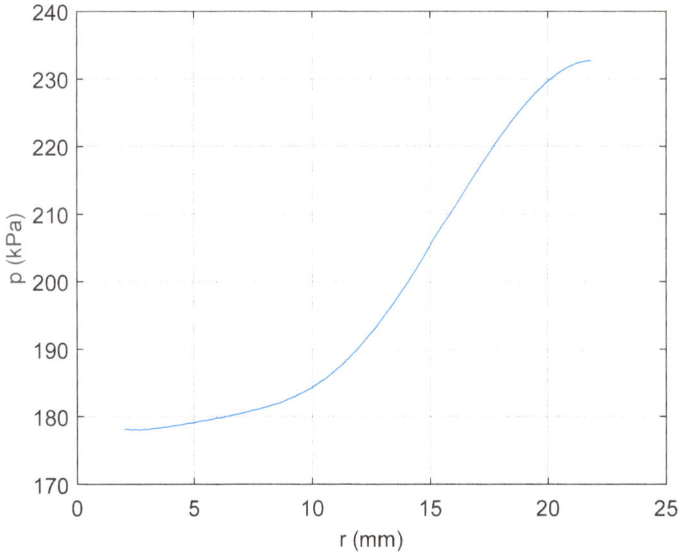

Figure 15. The plot of the pressure distribution along the green line in Figure 17, showing the non-constant pressure distribution across the cross-section, which exceeds the inlet pressure of 200 kPa.

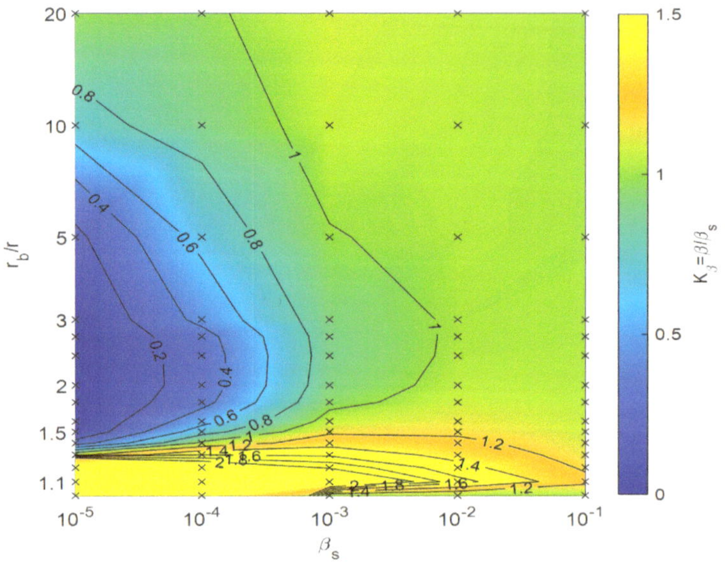

Figure 16. Measured dissipation number relative to the straight pipe dissipation number. Each "X" indicates a CFD simulation location.

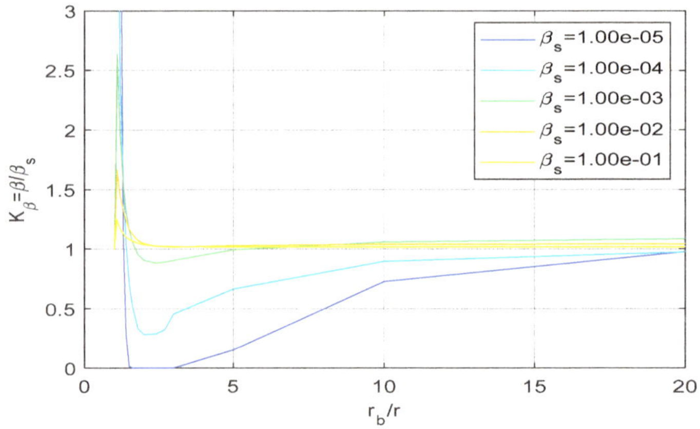

Figure 17. Calculated effective dissipation number correction factor (relative to the straight pipe dissipation number).

3.5. Overall Effect

One additional piece of useful information is how much of an overall effect a curved tube has, and under what conditions a straight tube approximation can be used without correction factors. In this case, one can calculate the error between the CFD-calculated responses for curved and straight tubes with the same cross-section and centerline length. The resultant normalized root mean squared (RMS) error is shown in Figure 19. As one can see from this plot, it is possible to make the straight tube simplifying assumption for more extreme bends if the dissipation number is large. For example, for zero viscosity, the relative error reaches 1% at r_b/r = 16.2, while for $\beta_s = 0.1$ the same error can be achieved with the more extreme bend ratio of r_b/r = 3.5. Another feature that can noted from this graph is that the dissipation number makes little difference for β_s less than 1×10^{-4}, which is similar to the effect in straight tubes for most applications of interest.

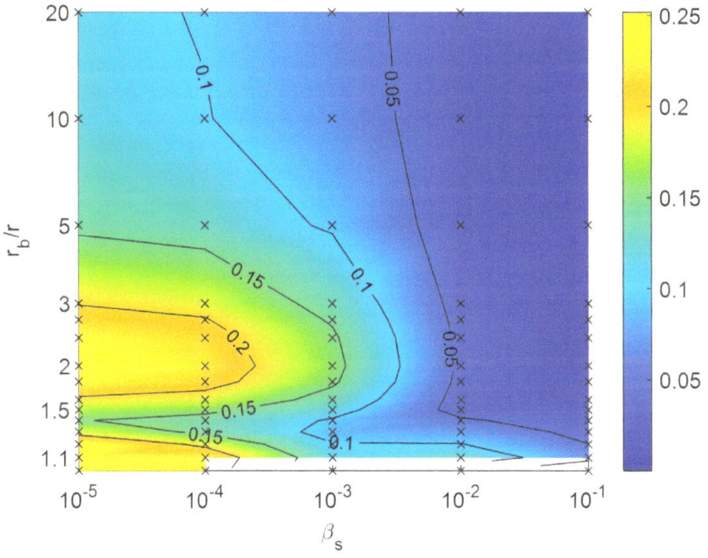

Figure 18. Residual error between corrected MOC solution and CFD solution after optimizing the dissipation number.

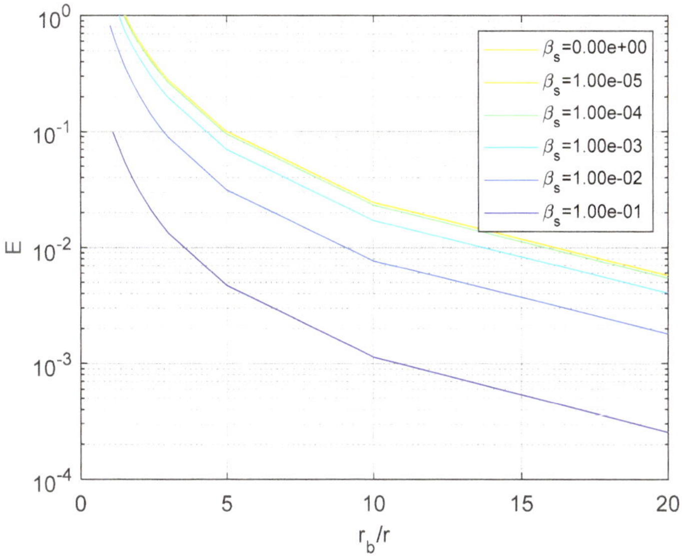

Figure 19. Error between the straight and curved CFD flow solutions for a range of dissipation numbers and bend ratios.

4. Conclusions

The results in the previous section can be used to provide guidance with regard to a number of important questions that may be relevant to those employing 1D models to speed up transient flow calculations relative to CFD solutions. The first is whether the curvature of the tube in a particular application can be ignored and safely modeled as a straight tube. This can be evaluated by referencing the error calculated in Figure 19, quantifying this effect for a range of curve ratios and dissipation numbers.

If it is determined that this level of error is unacceptable, one can then use the presented information to obtain better approximations using correction factors. In particular, the characteristic impedance can be corrected using Equation (13), the effective length corrected using Equation (14), and the dissipation number corrected using Figure 14 or Figure 15.

While these results are applicable for small pressure changes and laminar flows, it is left to future work to establish the exact bounds of applicability with regard to these factors and establish additional methods of operating outside of these bounds. It is also left to future work to experimentally verify the presented results.

Funding: This research received no external funding.

Data Availability Statement: The original contributions presented in the study are included in the article, further inquiries can be directed to the corresponding author.

Conflicts of Interest: The authors declare no conflict of interest.

Nomenclature

c	wave propagation velocity
D	Dean number
E	normalized root mean squared error
K_L	length correction factor
K_{Zc}	characteristic impedance correction factor
K_β	dissipation number correction factor
L	length of pipe (or effective length)—subscript "s" for a straight pipe
p	pressure. Subscript A for inlet, B for outlet
q	volumetric flow—subscript A for inlet, B for outlet
r	tube inner radius
r_b	bend radius
Re	Reynolds number
t	time—subscripts 1 and 2 denote times in Figure 4
Z_c	characteristic impedance—subscript "s" for a straight tube with the same dimensions
β	dissipation number—subscript "s" for a straight tube with the same dimensions
θ	bend angle
λ	resistance to flow—subscript "s" for a curved pipe with the same centerline length
μ	dynamic viscosity
v	kinematic viscosity
ρ	density
ψ	derivative of density with respect to pressure

Appendix A. Results Tables

Table A1. Results for the characteristic impedance correction factor, as plotted in Figure 9.

r_b/r	K_{Zc}	
	r = 10 mm	r = 20 mm
1.01	0.7723	0.7689
1.1	0.8477	0.8473
1.2	0.8865	0.8860
1.3	0.9102	0.9098
1.4	0.9267	0.9263
1.5	0.9388	0.9386

Table A1. *Cont.*

r_b/r	K_{Zc}	
	r = 10 mm	r = 20 mm
1.6	0.9480	0.9478
1.8	0.9613	0.9612
2	0.9702	0.9702
2.4	0.9811	0.9813
2.7	0.9860	0.9864
3	0.9895	0.9899

Table A2. Results for the effective length correction factor, as plotted in Figure 10.

r_b/r	K_L	
	r = 10 mm	r = 20 mm
1.01	N/A	0.7765
1.1	0.8470	0.8505
1.2	0.8845	0.8870
1.3	0.9080	0.9098
1.4	0.9240	0.9255
1.5	0.9360	0.9377
1.6	0.9452	0.9472
1.8	0.9582	0.9600
2	0.9670	0.9683
2.4	0.9777	0.9790
2.7	0.9828	0.9835
3	0.9863	0.9870

References

1. Sigalotti, L.D.G.; Alvarado-Rodríguez, C.E.; Rendón, O. Fluid Flow in Helically Coiled Pipes. *Fluids* **2023**, *8*, 308. [CrossRef]
2. Berger, S.A.; Talbot, L.; Yao, L.S. Flow in Curved Pipes. *Annu. Rev. Fluid Mech.* **1983**, *15*, 461–512. [CrossRef]
3. Dean, W.R. XVI. Note on the Motion of Fluid in a Curved Pipe. *Lond. Edinb. Dublin Philos. Mag. J. Sci.* **1927**, *4*, 208–223. [CrossRef]
4. White, C.M.; Appleton, E.V. Streamline Flow through Curved Pipes. *Proc. R. Soc. Lond. Ser. A Contain. Pap. A Math. Phys. Charact.* **1929**, *123*, 645–663.
5. Adler, M. Strömung in Gekrümmten Rohren. *ZAMM-J. Appl. Math. Mech. Z. Angew. Math. Mech.* **1934**, *14*, 257–275. [CrossRef]
6. Hasson, D. Streamline Flow Resistance in Coils. *Res. Corresp.* **1955**, *1*, 81.
7. Muto, T.; Kinoshita, Y.; Yoneda, R. Dynamic Response of Tapered Fluid Lines: 1st Report, Transfer Matrix and Frequency Response. *Bull. JSME* **1981**, *24*, 809–815. [CrossRef]
8. Tahmeen, M.; Muto, T.; Yamada, H. Simulation of Dynamic Responses of Tapered Fluid Lines. *JSME Int. J. Ser. B Fluids Therm. Eng.* **2001**, *44*, 247–254. [CrossRef]
9. Zielke, W. Frequency-Dependent Friction in Transient Pipe Flow. *J. Basic Eng.* **1968**, *90*, 109–115. [CrossRef]
10. Vítkovský, J.; Lambert, M.; Simpson, A.; Bergant, A. Advances in Unsteady Friction Modelling in Transient Pipe Flow. In Proceedings of the 8th International Conference on Pressure Surges, The Hague, The Netherlands, 12–14 April 2000; BHR Group: Bedford, UK, 2000; pp. 471–482.
11. Trikha, A. An Efficient Method for Simulating Frequency-Dependent Friction in Transient Liquid Flow. *J. Fluids Eng.* **1975**, *97*, 97–105. [CrossRef]
12. Wiens, T. Method of Characteristics Solver for Transmission Lines. 2020. Available online: https://github.com/tkw954/MOC_solver (accessed on 10 May 2024).
13. Krus, P.; Weddfelt, K.; Palmberg, J.-O. Fast Pipeline Models for Simulation of Hydraulic Systems. *J. Dyn. Syst. Meas. Control* **1994**, *116*, 132–136. [CrossRef]

14. Johnston, N. The Transmission Line Method for Modelling Laminar Flow of Liquid in Pipelines. *Proc. Inst. Mech. Eng. Part I J. Syst. Control Eng.* **2012**, *226*, 586–597. [CrossRef]
15. Johnston, N.; Pan, M.; Kudzma, S. An Enhanced Transmission Line Method for Modelling Laminar Flow of Liquid in Pipelines. *Proc. Inst. Mech. Eng. Part I J. Syst. Control Eng.* **2014**, *228*, 193–206. [CrossRef]
16. Wiens, T.; van der Buhs, J. Transmission Line Models. 2020. Available online: https://github.com/tkw954/usask_tlm (accessed on 10 May 2024).
17. Braun, R.; Krus, P. Multi-Threaded Distributed System Simulations Using the Transmission Line Element Method. *Simulation* **2016**, *92*, 921–930. [CrossRef]
18. Wiens, T. Transmission Line Modeling of Laminar Liquid Wave Propagation in Tapered Tubes. *J. Fluids Eng.* **2019**, *141*, 101103. [CrossRef]
19. Wiens, T. Modeling Arbitrarily Shaped Liquid Pipelines Using a Segmented Transmission Line Model. *J. Dyn. Syst. Meas. Control* **2020**, *142*, 064502. [CrossRef]
20. Ferras, D.; Manso, P.A.; Schleiss, A.J.; Covas, D.I.C. Hydraulic Transients in Straight and Coil Pipe Rigs. In Proceedings of the 12th International Conference on Pressure Surges, Dublin, Ireland, 18–20 November 2015.
21. Ferras, D. Fluid-Structure-Interaction in Pipe Coils During Hydraulic Transients: Numerical And Experimental Analysis. In Proceedings of the 36th IAHR World Congress, The Hague, The Netherlands, 8 June–3 July 2015.
22. Ferras, D.; Manso, P.A.; Covas, D.I.C.; Schleiss, A.J. Fluid–Structure Interaction in Pipe Coils during Hydraulic Transients. *J. Hydraul. Res.* **2017**, *55*, 491–505. [CrossRef]
23. Gijsen, F.J.H.; Allanic, E. The Influence of the Non-Newtonian Properties of Blood on the Flow in Large Arteries: Unsteady Flow in a 903 Curved Tube. *J. Biomech.* **1999**, *32*, 705–713. [CrossRef] [PubMed]
24. Azhdari, M.; Riasi, A.; Tazraei, P. Numerical Analysis of Fluid Hammer in Helical Pipes Considering Non-Newtonian Fluids. *Int. J. Press. Vessel. Pip.* **2020**, *181*, 104068. [CrossRef]
25. Fries, C.; Manhartsgruber, B. Dynamics of Transmission Line Junctions: Comparison of CFD Results Against Measurements. In Proceedings of the 8th FPNI Ph.D Symposium on Fluid Power, Lappeenranta, Finland, 11–13 June 2014; American Society of Mechanical Engineers: Lappeenranta, Finland, 2014; p. V001T02A003.
26. Fries, C.; Manhartsgruber, B. CFD Based Modeling of Wave Propagation in Liquid Transmission Line Junctions. In *Volume 1A, Symposia: Advances in Fluids Engineering Education; Advances in Numerical Modeling for Turbomachinery Flow Optimization; Applications in CFD; Bio-Inspired Fluid Mechanics; CFD Verification and Validation; Development and Applications of Immersed Boundary Methods; DNS, LES, and Hybrid RANS/LES Methods*; American Society of Mechanical Engineers: Incline Village, NV, USA, 2013; p. V01AT03A025.
27. Fries, C. Coupling of Liquid Transmission Line Models with 3-Dimensional CFD in OpenFOAM. Ph.D. Thesis, Johannes Kepler Univsitat Linz, Linz, Austria, 2016.
28. Riedelmeier, S.; Becker, S.; Schlücker, E. *3D CFD Simulation of Water Hammer Through a 90° Bend: Applicability of URANS, 3D Effects and Unsteady Friction*; Volume 4: Fluid-Structure Interaction, American Society of Mechanical Engineers: Anaheim, CA, USA, 2014; p. V004T04A094.
29. Chen, G.; Xiong, Q.; Morris, P.J.; Paterson, E.G.; Sergeev, A.; Wang, Y. OpenFOAM for Computational Fluid Dynamics. *Not. AMS* **2014**, *61*, 354–363. [CrossRef]
30. Thomann, W.; Isele, B.; Russer, P. Characterization of a 90 Degrees Curved Microstrip Transmission Line in the Time-Domain and Frequency-Domain with 3D-TLM-Method and Measurements. In Proceedings of the IEEE Antennas and Propagation Society International Symposium 1992 Digest, Chicago, IL, USA, 18–25 June 1992; Volume 2, pp. 658–661.

fluids

MDPI

Article

Flow Modeling of a Non-Newtonian Viscous Fluid in Elastic-Wall Microchannels

A. Rubio Martínez [1,2], A. E. Chávez Castellanos [2], N. A. Noguez Méndez [3], F. Aragón Rivera [4,*], M. Pliego Díaz [1], L. Di G. Sigalotti [5,*] and C. A. Vargas [5]

1 Tecnológico Nacional de México, Campus Querétaro, Av. Tecnológico s/n esq. Mariano Escobedo, Centro Histórico, Querétaro 7600, Mexico; alejandro.rm@queretaro.tecnm.mx (A.R.M.); mpliego@mail.edu.mx (M.P.D.)
2 Facultad de Química, Universidad Nacional Autónoma de México, Ciudad Universitaria, Ciudad de México 04510, Mexico; ae.chavezcastellanos@gmail.com
3 Departamento de Sistemas Biológicos, Universidad Autónoma Metropolitana, Unidad Xochimilco, Calzada del Hueso No. 1100, Villa Quietud, Ciudad de México 04960, Mexico; nanoguez@correo.xoc.uam.mx
4 Departamento de Energía, Universidad Autónoma Metropolitana, Unidad Azcapotzalco (UAM-A), Av. San Pablo 420, Colonia Nueva el Rosario, Alcaldía Azcapotzalco, Ciudad de México 02128, Mexico
5 Departamento de Ciencias Básicas, Universidad Autónoma Metropolitana, Unidad Azcapotzalco (UAM-A), Av. San Pablo 420, Colonia Nueva el Rosario, Alcaldía Azcapotzalco, Ciudad de México 02128, Mexico; carlovax@gmail.com
* Correspondence: micme2003@yahoo.com.mx (F.A.R.); leonardo.sigalotti@gmail.com (L.D.G.S.); Tel.: +52-55-21761287 (F.A.R. & L.D.G.S.)

Abstract: The use of polymer microspheres is becoming increasingly widespread. Along with their most common applications, they are beginning to be used in the synthesis of photonic crystals, microstructure analysis and multiplexed diagnostics for disease control purposes. This paper presents a simple mathematical model that allows us to study the transport mechanisms involved in the deformation of an elastic microchannel under the flow stream of a power-law fluid. In particular, we analyze the momentum transfer to a non-Newtonian fluid (Polydimethylsiloxane, PDMS) due to the deformation of the elastic ceiling of a rectangular microchannel. Hooke's law is used to represent the stress–deformation relationship of the PDMS channel ceiling. Stop-flow lithography is modeled, and the pressure exerted by the deformed PDMS ceiling on the fluid when the microchannel returns to its original form is taken into account. It is found that the response time of the elastic ceiling deformation increases with the channel width and length and decreases with the channel height independently of the power-law exponent of the injected fluid. However, an increase in the power-law exponent beyond unity causes an increase in the wall-deformation response time and the maximum deformation of the channel height compared to a Newtonian fluid.

Keywords: intermittent-flow lithography; microchannel; lubrication approximations; power-law fluids

1. Introduction

The use of polymer and colloid microparticles is becoming increasingly widespread. In addition to more common applications [1], such as paints, coatings and fractionating columns, emerging applications like optical devices [2], controlled-release drug delivery systems [3,4] and disease diagnosis systems [5] are gaining more and more strength, and while microspheres have been used extensively, non-spherical particles with predetermined anisotropic features are paving the way for the development of new technologies. These technologies include the synthesis of photonic crystals [4] and multiplexed diagnostics microlabs for disease control [6,7]. However, synthesizing these particles is not a simple task. The emulsion polymerization and suspension polymerization processes based on traditional approaches, which are commonly used to synthesize polymer particles, do not ensure a proper control over morphology and anisotropy, which are crucial aspects in the design of non-spherical particles.

Ideally, synthesis processes of such complex particles produce large numbers of monodispersed particles with predetermined anisotropic shapes and properties. In addition, the process allows for the use of functionalizable and biocompatible materials depending on the application requirements. In recent years, various processes focusing on microflows to synthesize particles have been reported in the literature [8]. These methods involve the convergence of two substances of different phases flowing into synthesizing devices, typically T-shaped cylindrical tubes [9,10] or other converging geometrical shapes [11,12]. This setup enables the formation of a large number of monodispersed droplets [9,13] of a precursor monomer for the desired polymer. The next step involves light or thermally induced polymerization into solid droplets [14,15]. However, these methods are significantly limited in terms of the shapes obtained, which typically comprise spheres or sphere-like shapes such as discs [16,17], half-spheres, core-shell spheres [18] and obloids [19–21].

New techniques are currently being explored to enhance resolution without compromising the number of synthesized particles. In particular, stop-flow lithography (SFL) is one such technique. This method induces particle formation between two monomer flows, which are brought to a stop within the PDMS microchannel before being flushed out, and this process is repeated cyclically. The efficiency of SFL is closely related to the response of the microflow system to pressure changes, enabling control over the flow frequency in each cycle. One approach employed to control the frequency uses pulsed compressed airflows instead of syringe pumps, thus shortening the response times. Nevertheless, the response time is not instantaneous due to the deformation caused by the airflow pressure on the PDMS elastomer (microchannel) walls. Given the increased use of PDMS in constructing microfluidic channels, it becomes imperative to study the effect of wall deformation on the monomer flow pattern.

The effects of wall deformation in a steady-state rectangular microchannel on the monomer flow profile have been extensively studied [22–30]. However, the effects on the flow profile of a non-Newtonian monomer due to the dynamic behavior of the walls and the geometry of the PDMS microchannel when subject to external pressure pulses have not been thoroughly addressed. Therefore, it is important to study this behavior in a cyclic process and determine the time required to reach a steady-state condition for the full cycle. In our study, we use a power-law model to describe the effect of the PDMS elastomer walls of a rectangular microchannel on the flow profile of a viscous non-Newtonian fluid in an SFL process (see Figure 1).

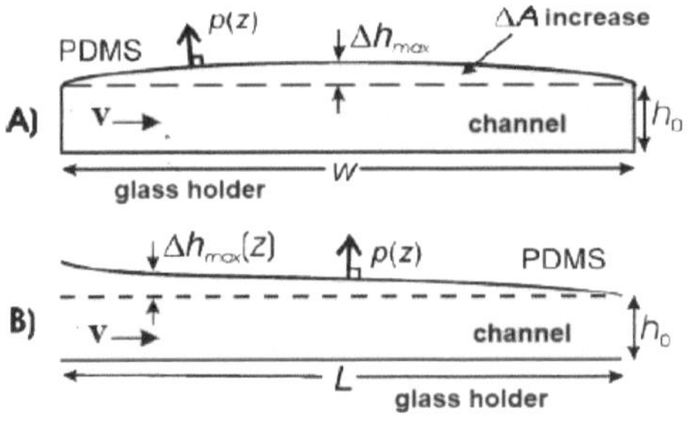

Figure 1. Schematic representation of the deformation of the rectangular microchannel as a result of a given flow. (**A**) Frontal cross-sectional view and (**B**) lateral view of the microchannel.

Stop-Flow Lithography (SLF) System

Microflow devices usually utilize syringe pumps to inject an incompressible fluid into the device. Inflow through the needle causes flow transitions that may last several minutes in the case of systems on a micrometric scale [27]. Therefore, when a rapid dynamic response is desired, the use of compressed air to inject the fluids into the device is preferable [28]. Even though compressed airflow devices eliminate the pulse pressure gradient transition, there are still finite transitions associated with the PDMS wall deformation.

Three cyclic stages are identified in stop-flow lithography, namely flow interruption, polymerization and fluid flow. During the first stage, thrust pressure on the oligomer stream through the device is stopped, transitioning from a specified entry pressure determined by the compressed air device to atmospheric pressure. The flow takes a finite time to stop, which is a function of the time required for the PDMS channel to retract due to deformation and then regain its non-deformed rectangular cross-section and flush the fluid out of the device. During the second stage, oligomer particles are polymerized during the flow stop, exposing them to UV light by briefly opening (during 0.3 to 1 s) the lamp shutter. During the third stage, the parent particle flows due to the opening of the three-way valve, causing the pressure to change from atmospheric pressure to that of the specified entry pressure. Three specific times can be characterized in this process: the time of flow residence in the channel (t_{stop}), i.e., the time when flow is stopped (where t_{stop} > time of wall response t_r), the time required to begin particle polymerization (i.e., the shutter time $t_{shutter}$) and the time required to flush the particles out, t_f. While $t_{shutter}$ and t_f are easily determined, t_{stop} can only be determined after the first estimation of t_{rp} that works as a lower bound for the stop time.

2. Flow of a Viscous Non-Newtonian Fluid Through a Microchannel with Elastic Walls

The mathematical model described here is based on a theoretical methodology developed by Dendukuri et al. [24] for Newtonian fluids. Here, a generalization of Dendukuri et al.'s [24] model is developed for power-law fluids.

2.1. Microchannel Geometry

The system under study is a microchannel of height H (before the deformation caused by the circulating flow), length L and width W. The microchannel floor is made of glass lined with a very thin film of PDMS with a Young modulus $E = 62$ GPa, while the ceiling is made of PDMS that is several millimeters thick with $E = 1$ MPa. The PDMS characteristics used here were taken from Dendukuri et al. [24]. In addition, this choice represents a good example to determine the characteristic parameters of the system and test new copolymers that are being synthesized in the Polymer Synthesis Laboratory of the Xochimilco Campus of the Autonomous Metropolitan University in Mexico City, which will then be used to replace the PDMS. Thus, the deformation of the channel floor is negligible compared to that of the ceiling. Figure 2 shows a schematic drawing of the cross section of the deformed rectangular channel after a pressure pulse. The flow is from left to right and maximum height deformation in the channel occurs at the entrance and then decreases gradually until it becomes negligible at the exit.

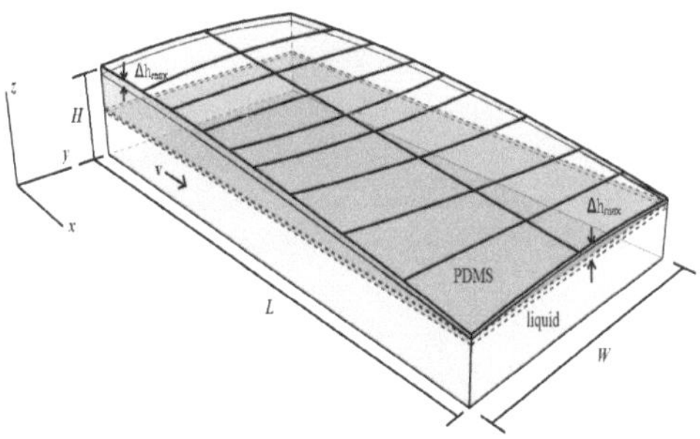

Figure 2. Schematic representation of the deformed channel under a circulating flow.

2.2. PDMS Elasticity Modeling

Hooke's law is used to represent the stress-deformation relationship of the PDMS channel ceiling, which is given by $\xi = \sigma/E$, where ξ is the deformation, σ is the stress applied to produce the deformation, and E is the PDMS Young modulus [23]. The stress to which the device is subjected is proportional to the external pressure applied.

2.2.1. Fluid Flow Modeling

To describe the fluid flow under study, we specify the power-law constitutive equation that relates the applied stresses to the resulting deformations. In the present case, the dependent variables are the time-dependent flow velocity **v** and pressure p. The flow is represented in Cartesian coordinates (x, y, z) and the mainstream flow velocity is directed along the x-axis (see Figure 2). In this way, the velocity vector field is

$$\mathbf{v} = (v_x, v_y, v_z) = [v_x(x,z), 0, v_z(x)]. \tag{1}$$

For a steady-state, incompressible fluid, the continuity equation reduces to

$$\frac{\partial v_x}{\partial x} + \frac{\partial v_z}{\partial z} = 0. \tag{2}$$

The total stress tensor for this case study will take the following form:

$$\mathbb{T} = -p\mathbb{I} + \underline{\underline{\sigma}}, \tag{3}$$

where $\mathbb{I}$ is the identity tensor, and $\underline{\underline{\sigma}}$ is the shear stress tensor. According to the established velocity field, where movement occurs predominantly along the x-direction and the variations are along the z-direction, the shear stress tensor takes the form

$$\underline{\underline{\sigma}} = \begin{pmatrix} 0 & 0 & \sigma_{xz} \\ 0 & 0 & 0 \\ \sigma_{zx} & 0 & 0 \end{pmatrix}, \tag{4}$$

from which Cauchy's equation in rectangular coordinates reduces to

$$\frac{d\sigma_{xz}}{dz} = -\frac{dp}{dx}, \tag{5}$$

where $h(x) = H + \Delta h$, and $\sigma_{zx} = \sigma_{xz}$. Moreover, the pressure gradient is assumed to be constant along the x-direction, and hence,

$$\sigma_{xz} = -\frac{dp}{dx}z + \frac{dp}{dx}\frac{h(x)}{2}. \tag{6}$$

If $\sigma_{xz} = 0$, then from Equation (6), it follows that $z = h(x)/2$.

Substitution of the constitutive equation for a power-law fluid

$$\sigma_{xz} = -k\left(\frac{\partial v_x}{\partial z}\right)^n$$

into Equation (5) yields

$$\left(\frac{\partial v_x}{\partial z}\right)^n = \frac{1}{k}\frac{dp}{dx}\left(z - \frac{h(x)}{2}\right), \tag{7}$$

where k and n are the power-law constant and exponent, respectively. Under the boundary condition $v_x = 0$ for $z = 0$, integration of the above equation gives the following expression for the mainstream flow velocity

$$v_x(x,z) = \left[\frac{1}{k}\frac{dp}{dx}\right]^{q-1}\left(\frac{1}{q}\right)\left[\left(z - \frac{h(x)}{2}\right)^q - \left(\frac{h(x)}{2}\right)^q\right], \tag{8}$$

where the parameter $q = (n+1)/n$. This equation describes the flow of a power-law fluid in a rectangular microchannel. If n is an odd number, then Equation (8) describes only real solutions for the flow velocity. In particular, future experiments will be conducted to study the behavior of synthesized copolymers and the power-law fluid model employed here, in addition to approximately describing the behavior of non-Newtonian fluids, allows mathematical prediction to be made more easily and to correlate the experimental data.

Since $v_x = v_x(x,z)$, it follows from the continuity Equation (2) that

$$v_z(x) = -\frac{h(x)^q}{2^q q}\left(\frac{1}{k}\frac{E}{W}\right)^{q-1}\left[\frac{h(x)}{q+1}\left(\frac{\partial^q h(x)}{\partial x^q}\right) + \left(\frac{\partial h(x)}{\partial x}\right)^q\right] \tag{9}$$

for the z-component of the velocity field. If the above equation is solved for $z = h(x)$, it results in a non-linear differential equation for the instantaneous deformation of the microchannel ceiling $h = h(x,t)$.

A solution to the momentum balance equations for the flow of a power-law fluid in a rectangular channel with an elastic ceiling and rigid floor is here obtained using the lubrication approximations. For this purpose, (i) a system of characteristic variables is specified, (ii) an order-of-magnitude analysis is performed for the balance equations, and (iii) reasonable assumptions based on the physical nature of the phenomenon are made to simplify the equations and allow an analytical mathematical treatment. This allows for an objective description of the system and estimation of analytical results to be compared with previous analytical and/or experimental results.

A PDMS fluid can be considered to be a semi-infinite medium, where the deformations disappear throughout the channel since the PDMS is several millimeters thick, while the channel has a height of only a few micrometers (see Figure 2). Thus, the appropriate length scale to determine the deformation along the z-axis is given by the channel width W, while the deformation of the channel ceiling will be proportional to the ratios of the height increase, $\Delta h(x)$, over the channel width, W, and the applied local pressure, p, over the Young modulus, E, [23,26], that is

$$\Omega \sim \frac{\Delta h(x)}{W} \sim \frac{p}{E}. \tag{10}$$

Under the above approximations, the height deformation is then proportional to the local pressure as can be inferred from Equation (10). When the pressure decreases along the length of the channel, the deformation also decreases along the same direction. The maximum deformation is therefore observed at the entrance of the channel and is given by

$$\Delta h_{\mathrm{max}} \approx \frac{pW}{E}. \tag{11}$$

Since the height, H, of the microchannel is much smaller than its width, W, i.e., $H/W \ll 1$, the deformation of the PDMS-ceiling is negligible along the width. As a consequence, the three-dimensional problem of the fluid flow through the rectangular cross-section reduces to a two-dimensional problem if the height of the deformed channel $h(x,y)$ is averaged over the channel width (i.e., along the y-axis), so that the cross-longitudinal section deformation of the device is given by $h(x)$. In addition, if the flow is due to drag (Re $\ll 1$, where Re is the Reynolds number) as is indeed the case here, the equation describing the dynamics of the flow will be given by Equation (6). In passing, it is also important to assume that the PDMS-ceiling curvature is small in relation to the device length.

2.2.2. Coupling between the Elastic Wall and the Flow

When an external pressure is applied to the rectangular cross-section, the device deforms, causing the ceiling to bulge and then return to its original form when the pressure is removed. This in turn gives rise to a compression flow that regulates the flow present in the device. This type of flow is asymmetric in the sense that the flow at the entrance of the channel is greater than that at the exit, with the flow being sustained until the excess fluid is flushed from the device. This process is associated with a characteristic time, which is a function of the properties of the elastic-wall material (PDMS in this case), the fluid (oligomer), the channel geometry and the pressure applied. In this elastohydrodynamic problem, the deformed PDMS ceiling exerts a pressure on the fluid when the microchannel returns to its original form [27,29].

For small deformations, the pressure exerted on the fluid throughout the channel can be considered to be proportional to the deformation of the elastic PDMS wall, according to Equation (11). The length scale for the stress is the channel width, W, so that the pressure along the channel is given by

$$p(x) = \frac{E\Delta h(x)}{W} = E\left(\frac{h(x) - H}{W}\right), \tag{12}$$

where, as it was previously mentioned, H is the height of the non-deformed channel. Thus, its variation as a function of x will be

$$\frac{\partial p}{\partial x} = \frac{E}{W}\frac{\partial h}{\partial x}. \tag{13}$$

The scale analysis reveals important features of the problem. Since the channel deformation is small compared to the height of the channel, then

$$H \gg \frac{pW}{E}. \tag{14}$$

Also $h \sim H$, which means that the deformation can be approximated as $\Delta h \sim PW/E$, the length as $x \sim L$ and the time as $t \sim t_r$ (where t_r is the response time of the elastic wall of the device and must be determined for each of the partial derivatives of the equation describing the deformation velocity for the microchannel elastic ceiling). Hence, the velocity along the z-axis becomes

$$v_z = \frac{\partial h}{\partial t} \sim \frac{pW}{Et_r}, \tag{15}$$

while

$$\left(\frac{\partial h(x)}{\partial x}\right)^q \sim \left(\frac{pW}{EL}\right)^q, \tag{16}$$

and

$$h\left(\frac{\partial^q h}{\partial x^q}\right) \sim \left(\frac{HpW}{EL^q}\right). \tag{17}$$

Substitution of Equations (15)–(17) into Equation (9) gives the following relation

$$\frac{pW}{Et_r} \sim \frac{H^q}{2^q q}\left(\frac{E}{KW}\right)^{q-1}\left[\frac{1}{q+1}\left(\frac{HpW}{EL^q}\right) + \left(\frac{pW}{EL}\right)^q\right]. \tag{18}$$

Furthermore, since $H \gg pW/E$, the second term inside the brackets in the above equation can be neglected, so that

$$t_r \sim \frac{2^q q(q+1)L^q}{H^{q+1}}\left(\frac{KW}{E}\right)^{q+1}. \tag{19}$$

From this equation, two important conclusions can be drawn. First, the response time is independent of the pressure, and second, it is inversely proportional to the Young modulus (E) as long as the applied pressure does not cause a deformation of the channel height.

In order to calculate the height deformation along the channel, two dimensionless variables are defined, namely $\Theta = h(x)/H$ and $\epsilon = x/L$, where $h(x)$ is the variable height of the channel induced by the pressure gradient, H is the height of the non-deformed channel, x denotes any position along the channel, and L is the channel length. Thus, Equation (19) is recast in the form

$$\left[\frac{h(x)}{\Theta}\right]^{q+1} \sim 2^q q(q+1)\frac{1}{t_r}\left(\frac{x}{\epsilon}\right)^q\left(\frac{KW}{E}\right)^{q-1}. \tag{20}$$

A clear limitation of the present method is the use of a power-law model to describe the behavior of non-Newtonian fluids, which does not take into account rheological properties that may appear in the system under consideration, as could be the case of thixotropic fluids, which, being highly viscous, can become more liquid in a time-dependent fashion when subjected to shear forces, and rheopectic fluids, whose viscosity, on the contrary, increases with stress over time.

3. Results

For the case of a Newtonian ($n = 1$) fluid, the solution is compared with the experimental data provided by Dendukuri et al. [24] for an oligomer consisting of Poly(ethylene glycol) diacrylate PEG-DA with viscosity $\mu = 5.6 \times 10^{-8}$ mPa s. The case with $n = 0.554$ and $n = 0.716$, corresponding to pseudoplastic fluids, is compared with data reported by Bird et. al. [25] for carboxymethyl cellulose at 1.5 and 0.67% weight/volume in water at 25 °C with $k = 31.3$ and $k = 3.04$ dyn s^n cm^{-2}, respectively. Finally, for $n = 1.2$, corresponding to a dilatant fluid, the results are compared with data obtained from the Molecular Pharmacy and Controlled Release Laboratory (Internal Technical Report) of the Autonomous Metropolitan University, Xochimilco Campus, for a glucose solution at 6%, 25 °C and $k = 0.0064$ dyn s^n cm^{-2}.

The approximate solution provided by Equations (15)–(20) allows for a direct estimation of the effects of the channel height, width and length on the response time along with the dependence of the response time of the channel elastic wall on fluid pressure at the entrance of the channel. In addition, the results obtained show the effects of each of these variables separately. This is possible because of the lubrication approximation technique used, which, on the other hand, provides a simple model for the qualitative description of all factors involved.

The results of the present model for $n = 1$ (Newtonian fluid) and different channel widths ($W = 50, 200, 500$ and 1000 µm) as compared with the experimental data obtained by Dendukuri et al. [24] (filled dots) are depicted in Figure 3. The model fits qualitatively well with the linear trend of the experimental data and predicts the response time. In terms of the root-mean-square error (RMSE), the experimental measurements are predicted with an error close to 6.4%. As the channel width is increased, the pressure applied due to deformation of the channel elastic wall decreases, which in turn causes an increase in the response time.

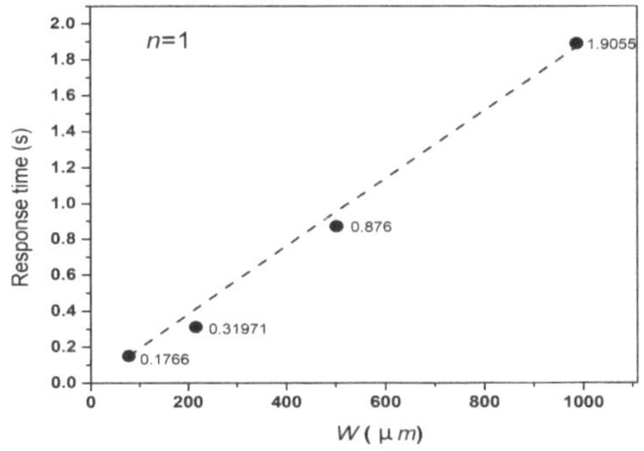

Figure 3. Predicted wall response time for the $n = 1$ fluid as a function of the channel width for a constant pressure of 3 psi, channel length of 1 cm and channel height of 200 µm (dashed line) as compared with Dendukuri et al.'s [24] experimental measurements (filled dots).

Figure 4 shows the dependence of the response time on channel height for $n = 1$ as predicted by the model (dashed line). The results are compared with Dendukuri et al.'s [24] experimental data for $H = 2$, 10, 20 and 40 μm (filled dots). The model reproduces the experimental linear trend with a 3 s μm^{-1} slope. Increasing the channel width causes a reduction in the recovery stress of the channel elastic wall, with a consequent increase in the response time. In this case, the model prediction matches the experimental data with a RMSE of less than about 10%. The response times for the pseudoplastic and dilatant fluids as predicted by the model are also depicted (solid lines). As for the $n = 1$ case, the response time also decreases with H for a power-law fluid. In particular, for the dilatant case ($n = 1.2$) the linear decrease closely follows a 3 s μm^{-1} slope, while for the pseudoplastic fluids ($n = 0.554$ and 0.716), the linear decrease follows a 2.82 s μm^{-1} slope. However, compared to the Newtonian and dilatant power-law fluids, the response time for the $n = 0.554$ pseudoplastic fluid is reduced by about four orders of magnitude, while for the $n = 0.716$ case, the reduction is approximately of an order of magnitude. In passing, we note that the response time experienced by the dilatant fluid is only slightly longer than the one experienced by the Newtonian ($n = 1$) fluid. As the channel height is reduced, the response time of the system increases. This occurs because in channels of a smaller height, there is a greater flow resistance that the fluid must overcome when it is flushed away from the channel.

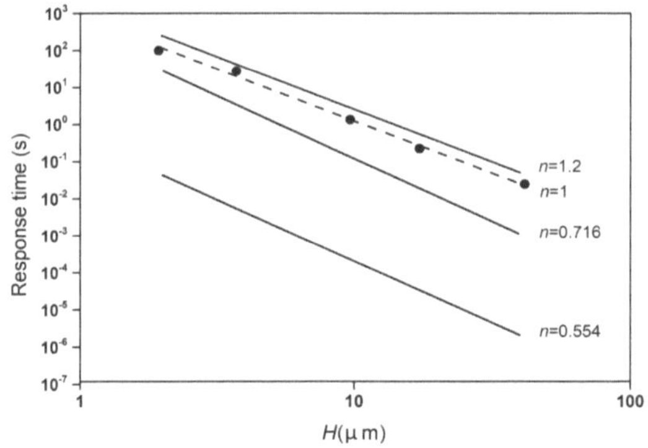

Figure 4. Dependence of the wall response time on the channel height for a constant pressure of 3 psi, a channel length of 1 cm and a channel width of 200 μm. The dashed line describes the tendency of the Newtonian case, which is compared with the experimental data of Dendukuri et al. [24] for $n = 1$. The solid lines depict the dependence of the $n = 1.2$, 0.716 and 0.554 power-law fluids.

The effects of the channel length on the wall response time are displayed in Figure 5. For $n = 1$, the response times also fit the experimental data for varying channel lengths (i.e., 0.25, 0.5, 1 and 1.2 cm), all with a constant channel width of 200 μm, height of 10 μm and pressure 3 psi. The response time for both the Newtoninan and the dilatant fluid increases linearly following a 2 s μm^{-1} slope. No difference is actually observed between both trends. In contrast, for the pseudoplastic fluids, the response time also increases linearly but this time with a 3.25 s μm^{-1} slope for $n = 0.716$ and 3 s μm^{-1} for $n = 0.554$. Moreover, compared to the Newtonian and dilatant fluids, the response times for the pseudoplastic fluids are an order of magnitude smaller than for the former cases. As expected, the response time is always seen to increase with the length of the channel. The shorter wall response times shown by the pseudoplastic fluids ($n = 0.554$ and 0.716) in Figures 4 and 5 compared to the Newtonian ($n = 1$) and dilatant fluids ($n = 1.2$) may be due to the fact that the former fluids lower their viscosity when subjected to large shear rates.

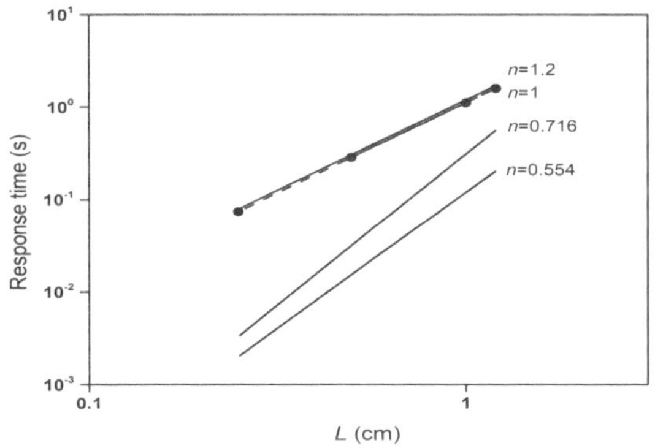

Figure 5. Dependence of the wall response time on the channel length for a constant pressure of 3 psi, a channel height of 10 μm and a channel width of 200 μm. The dashed line describes the dependence of the Newtonian case, which is compared with the experimental data of Dendukuri et al. [24] for $n = 1$. The solid lines depict the dependence of the $n = 1.2$, 0.716 and 0.554 power-law fluids.

The dependence of the response time on the applied pressure at the entrance of the channel for the Newtonian fluid (dashed line) as compared with the experimental data of Dendukuri et al. [24] (filled dots) is shown in the top-left frame of Figure 6. In fair agreement with the experimental measurements, the response time is almost invariant to changes in the applied pressure. The experimental data exhibit scattered values of the response time about the predicted line with small departures from it. Despite the scatter of the experimental data, the actual RMSE distance between the predicted values and the experimental measurements is less than $\sim 1\%$. This also evidences an approximate invariance with the applied pressure. In general, this behavior is expected in situations where the height deformation is small. However, a pressure increase above 15 psi causes significant deformation in the channel walls, which in turn causes an increase in the channel wall recovery elastic stress. This elastic stress increase is compensated when a larger liquid volume is expelled. The balance between elastic and viscous forces causes the response time to be pressure-independent for small deformations. Finally, the response time changes as a function of the μ/E-ratio associated with the visco-elastic characteristics of the system. This means that if an oligomer of low viscosity is used, or a more rigid PDMS device is built, the response time will be consequently smaller.

The top-right, bottom-left and bottom-right frames of Figure 6 show the wall response time as a function of the applied pressure at the entrance of the channel for the $n = 1.2$ (dilatant) and the $n = 0.716$ and 0.554 (pseudoplastic) fluids, respectively. In particular, the response time for the dilatant fluid decreases as the pressure is increased and is about an order of magnitude higher than that experienced by the Newtonian fluid at low pressures. For the pseudoplastic fluids ($n = 0.716$ and 0.554), the response time is from two to five orders of magnitude shorter than for the Newtonian case. The response time follows a trend similar to that displayed by the dilatant fluid, with larger values at low pressures. However, the differences between low and high pressures is so small that in general the response time for these fluids can be considered to remain almost invariant with pressure.

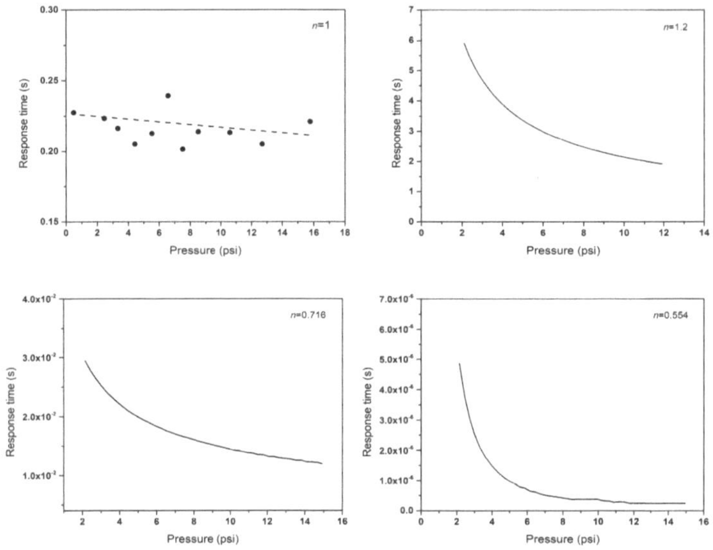

Figure 6. Dependence of the wall response time on the applied pressure at the entrance of the channel for the $n = 1$ (**top left**), $n = 1.2$ (**top right**), $n = 0.716$ (**bottom left**) and $n = 0.554$ (**bottom right**) fluids for constant channel height, width and length of 10 μm, 200 μm and 1 cm, respectively. The dots displayed in the top-left frame corresponds to Dendukuri et al.'s [24] experimental data.

The predicted response time per unit applied pressure as a function of the exponent of the power-law fluid model (solid line) is shown in Figure 7. The predicted values match very well with the experimental data for $n < 1$ with negligible relative errors. For $n = 1$, the predicted value differs from the experimental measurement by a relative error of $\sim 19\%$. The worst case occurs for $n = 1.2$, where the error grows to $\sim 66\%$. The response time increases exponentially for power-law fluids with $n > 1$ and is very sensitive to changes in the fluid viscosity. On the other hand, Figure 8 shows the functional dependence of the response time on the channel width to height ratio, W/H. In general, the response time increases linearly with increasing the W/H ratio. In all cases, the linear increase has an approximate 2.5 s slope as a result of the reduction in the deformation curvature of the channel rectangular area. The response times of the Newtonian and dilatant fluids are similar and converge to the same values at high values of the W/H ratio. For the pseudoplastic fluids, however, the response times are about four ($n = 0.716$) and six ($n = 0.554$) orders of magnitude lower than those of the Newtonian and dilatant fluids. Moreover, the functional dependence of the model computed response time per unit W/H ratio on the exponent of the power-law fluid (solid line) is shown in Figure 9 as compared with experimental data from Dendukuri et al. [24] for $n = 1$, Bird et al. [25] for $n < 1$ and present authors for $n = 1.2$. Sharp variations for more than seven orders of magnitude occurs when the exponent changes from 0.554 (for a pseudoplastic fluid) to 1.2 (for a dilatant fluid). The best fit of the numerical data deviates from the model prediction by a RMSE of ≈ 0.016, i.e., by approximately 1.6%.

Figure 10 shows the degree of deformation of the dimensionless channel height as a function of the dimensionless channel length for the power-law fluids analyzed for response times of 0.01 and 0.1 s and W/H ratios of 2.5 and 10. In particular, the top-left, top-right, bottom-left and bottom-right frames show the variation in the channel height for the $n = 1$, $n = 1.2$, $n = 0.716$ and $n = 0.554$ fluids, respectively. The model predicts a maximum deformation of 20% when the response time is 0.01 s and $W/H = 10$, which is in line with Dendukuri et al.'s [24] and Gervais et al.'s [23] experimental data.

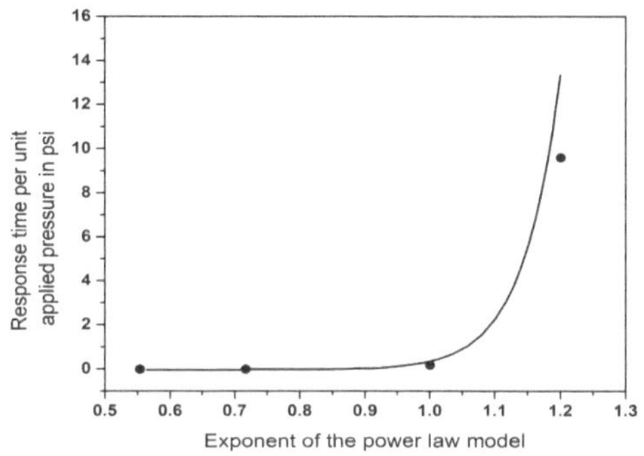

Figure 7. Predicted response time per unit applied pressure (in psi) as a function of the exponent of the power-law fluid model (solid line) as compared with experimental data obtained from Dendukuri et al. [24] for $n = 1$, Bird et al. [25] for $n = 0554$ and 0.716 and present authors for $n = 1.2$ (filled dots).

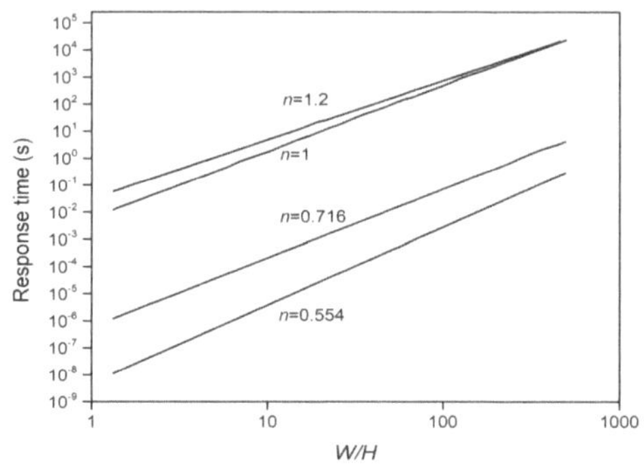

Figure 8. Wall response time against the channel width to height ratio for all power-law fluid models considered.

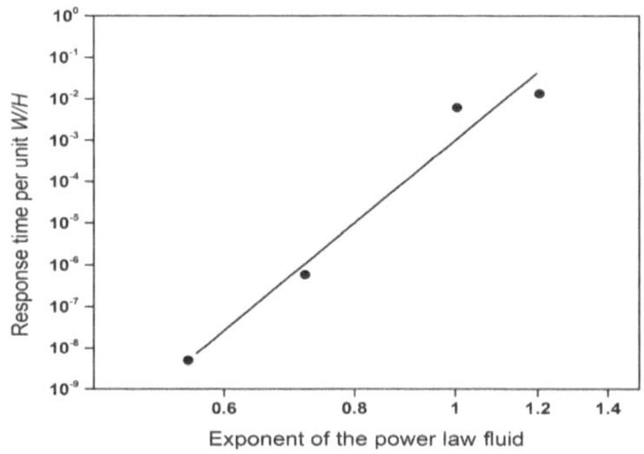

Figure 9. Predicted wall response time per unit W/H ratio against the exponent of the power-law fluid model (solid line) as compared with experimental data from Dendukuri et al. [24] (for $n = 1$), Bird et al. [25] (for $n < 1$) and present authors (for $n = 1.2$) (filled dots).

The variation in the deformation of the channel height with the W/H ratio is displayed in Figure 11 for all fluids analyzed and two different response times ($t = 0.01$ and 0.1 s). In general, the height deformation decreases with increasing W/H ratios. Evidently, as the deformation area increases, the maximum channel deformation is reduced. Furthermore, the level of deformation increases with the response time. The model also predicts a dependence of the maximum deformation on the exponent of the power-law fluid. In particular, the dilatant ($n = 1.2$) fluid causes a deformation, Δh, from 2.5 to 3 times the non-deformed height, H, of the channel. On the other hand, the deformation for the Newtonian and pseudoplastic ($n = 0.716$) fluids is from 0.2 to 0.8 times H, while for the $n = 0.554$ pseudoplastic fluid, the change is only from 0.12 to 0.6 times H. As opposed to pseudoplastic fluids, dilatant fluids become more viscous as more shear is applied. Therefore, they may cause an increase in the response time as they move slowly across the channel, thereby inducing a larger channel deformation. This could explain why the maximum height deformation is considerably larger for $n > 1$.

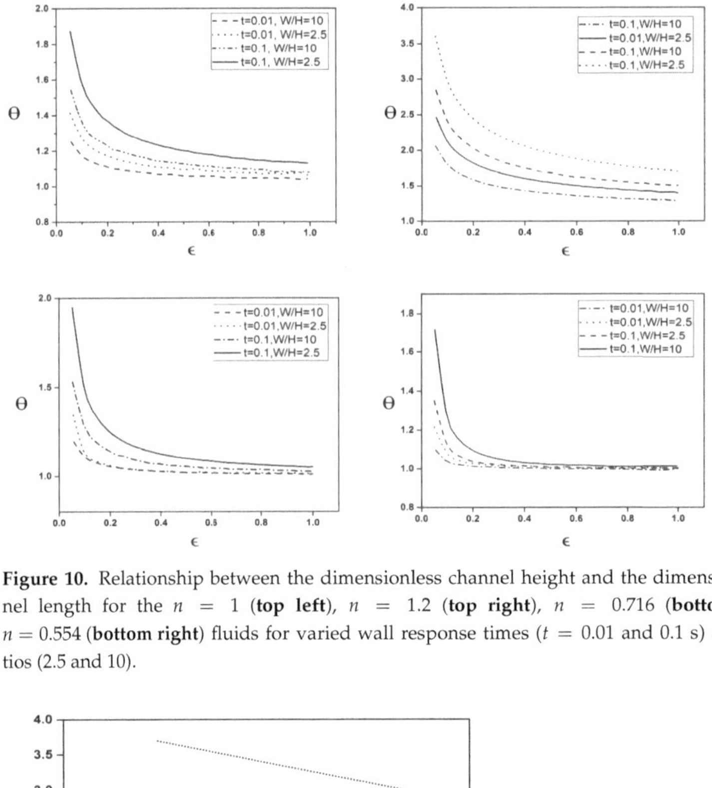

Figure 10. Relationship between the dimensionless channel height and the dimensionless channel length for the $n = 1$ (**top left**), $n = 1.2$ (**top right**), $n = 0.716$ (**bottom left**) and $n = 0.554$ (**bottom right**) fluids for varied wall response times ($t = 0.01$ and 0.1 s) and W/H ratios (2.5 and 10).

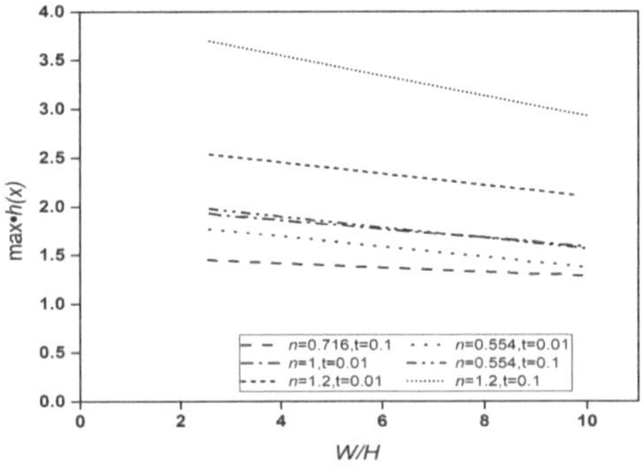

Figure 11. Maximum height deformation of the channel as a function of the W/H ratio for all fluids analyzed and two different response times (i.e., $t = 0.01$ and 0.1 s).

4. Discussion

When analyzing separately the effects of the channel dimensions on the response time for different power-law fluids, we found that as the channel height increases, with all other geometric variables remaining constant, the response time decreases for all power-law fluids analyzed. However, the response time as a function of the type of fluid varies up to four orders of magnitude. This is due to changes in the flow resistance that must be overcome by the fluid when flushed out from the channel. This effect is better evidenced by the behavior of the response time as a function of the W/H ratio. As this ratio increases, the maximum height deformation decreases, causing the response time to increase.

It was also found that for power-law fluids with $n \leq 1$, the maximum channel deformations were of 16–80% of the initial height, while for fluids with $n > 1$, the model-predicted deformation falls to between 2.5 and 3 times greater than the channel initial height. This is due to the influence of the fluid characteristics on the behavior of the fluid.

An increase in the exponent of the power-law fluid to $n > 1$ causes an increase in the response time as well as an increase in the maximum deformation of the channel height compared with a Newtonian fluid ($n = 1$). This is because fluids with $n > 1$ move more slowly across the channel, thereby causing the response time and the stress of the fluid on the elastic wall of the channel to increase.

Finally, it is important to mention that the balance between the elastic forces on the wall and the viscous forces of the fluid ensures that the response time is independent of the stress applied to the fluid at the entrance of the channel, especially when the deformations are small so that the response time varies as a function of the W/H ratio. Rigid PDMS devices will allow making changes in the response time so as to reduce it to a minimum. This favors the use of channels with shorter lengths and larger flow stresses at the entrance (within mechanical stability limits). These are optimal characteristics to obtain a fast and dynamic response in the operation and design of a stop-flow lithography device. Therefore, the present results have practical implications in the development of pharmaceutical microfluidic devices. Other practical applications of these microfluidic systems may include nanoparticle preparation, drug encapsulation and delivery, culture and development of stem cells as well as cell analysis and diagnosis. In the biomedical field they can be used as micro-heat pumps and sinks, in DNA analysis, Lab-on-a-chip, urinary analysis and droplet generation among many other applications, while in chemical engineering, they are used as microreactors and in the synthesis of functional materials. Many other potential applications can be found in other fields such as, for example, medicine, food engineering, biology and chemistry.

5. Concluding Remarks

In this work, we have presented a simple model for the flow of power-law fluids in a rectangular channel with elastic ceiling. The model relies on momentum balance equations that can easily be analyzed using the lubrication approximation. Furthermore, this study allows us to assess separately the impact of the fluid type, the channel dimensions and the fluid stress at the entrance of the channel on the response time of deformation of the elastic ceiling of the rectangular channel.

The main results can be summarized as follows:

- For a Newtonian fluid (with a power-law exponent $n = 1$), the model predicts the experimentally measured response times of wall channel deformation for different channel widths, heights and lengths with root-mean-square errors (RMSEs) less than $\sim$10%.
- For pseudoplastic fluids ($n < 1$), the deformation response times are from one to several orders of magnitude shorter than for Newtonian ($n = 1$) and dilatant ($n > 1$) fluids.
- The maximum channel deformation and the time of flow residence are largely determined by the fluid power-law order and the width-to-height ratio of the elastic channel.
- As a function of the channel width-to-height ratio, the largest maximum wall deformations are observed for the $n = 1.2$ fluid.

- The solution methodology implemented here provides a lower bound to the non-linear problem and the results can be interpreted as a limiting case given by the lubrication approximation.
- In spite of its simplicity, the present model can be used to study the behavior of non-Newtonian power-law fluids applied to the development of novel pharmaceutical microfluidic devices.

Author Contributions: Conceptualization, A.R.M., A.E.C.C. and N.A.N.M.; methodology, A.E.C.C. and M.P.D.; formal analysis, A.R.M. and M.P.D.; investigation, F.A.R. and C.A.V.; writing—original draft preparation, L.D.G.S. and A.R.M.; writing—review and editing, L.D.G.S.; visualization, F.A.R.; funding acquisition, C.A.V. All authors have read and agreed to the published version of the manuscript.

Funding: This research received no external funding.

Data Availability Statement: The data presented in this study are available on request from the corresponding author.

Acknowledgments: We acknowledge the Department of Basic Sciences of the Autonomous Metropolitan University, Azcapotzalco Campus for financial and technical support.

Conflicts of Interest: The authors declare no conflicts of interest.

Abbreviations

The following abbreviations are used in this manuscript:

H	Microchannel height (μm)
L	Microchannel length (cm)
W	Microchannel width (μm)
E	Young modulus (MPa and GPa)
Re	Reynolds number (dimensionless)
$\mathbf{v}$	Fluid velocity vector (m s^{-1})
v_x, v_y, v_z	Fluid velocity components (cm s^{-1})
p	Pressure (psi)
x, y, z	Cartesian coordinates (μm)
$\mathbb{T}$	Stress tensor (kg m^{-1} s^{-2})
$\mathbb{I}$	Identity tensor (dimensionless)
n	Power-law exponent (dimensionless)
k	Power-law constant (dyn s^n cm^{-2})
q	Dimensionless parameter
$h(x,t)$	Deformation function of the microchannel ceiling (μm)
Δh	Height increase of microchannel ceiling (μm)
$\Delta h_{\max}$	Maximum height increase (μm)
t_{stop}	Time of flow residence in the channel (s)
t_{r}	Time of wall response (s)
t_{shutter}	Time to begin particle polymerization (s)
t_{f}	Time required to flush the particles out (s)
t_{rp}	Lower bound for the stop time (s)
Greek letters	
μ	Viscosity (mPa s)
σ	Stress applied to produce the deformation (MPa)
$\xi = \sigma/E$	Applied deformation (dimensionless)
$\underline{\underline{\sigma}}$	Shear stress tensor (kg m^{-1} s^{-2})
$\Omega = p/E$	Deformation of the channel ceiling (dimensionless)
$\Theta = h(x)/H$	Normalized deformation function (dimensionless)
$\epsilon = x/L$	Normalized position along the channel (dimensionless)

References

1. Urban, D.; Takamura, K. (Eds.) *Polymer Dispersions and Their Industrial Applications*; Wiley-VCH: Hoboken, NJ, USA, 2002.
2. Lu, Y.; Yin, Y.; Xia, Y. Three-dimensional photonic crystals with non-spherical colloids as building blocks. *Adv. Mater.* **2001**, *13*, 415–420. [CrossRef]
3. Langer, R.; Tirrell, D.A. Designing materials for biology and medicine. *Nature* **2004**, *428*, 487–492. [CrossRef] [PubMed]
4. Finkel, N.H.; Lou, X.; Wang, C.; He, L. Peer reviewed: Barcoding the microworld. *Anal. Chem.* **2004**, *76*, 352A–359A. [CrossRef] [PubMed]
5. Pregibon, D.C.; Toner, M.; Doyle, P.S. Multifunctional encoded particles for high-throughput biomolecule analysis. *Science* **2007**, *315*, 1393–1396. [CrossRef] [PubMed]
6. Steinbacher, J.L.; McQuade, D.T. Polymer chemistry in flow: New polymers, beads, capsules, and fibers. *J. Polym. Sci. Part A Polym. Chem.* **2006**, *44*, 6505–6533. [CrossRef]
7. Kawakatsu, T.; Kikuchi, Y.; Nakajima, M. Regular-sized cell creation in microchannel emulsification by visual microprocessing method. *J. Am. Oil Chem. Soc.* **1997**, *74*, 317–321. [CrossRef]
8. Thorsen, T.; Roberts, R.W.; Arnold, F.H.; Quake, S.R. Dynamic pattern formation in a vesicle-generating microfluidic device. *Phys. Rev. Lett.* **2001**, *86*, 4163–4166. [CrossRef]
9. Shelley, A.L.; Bontoux, N.; Stone, H.A. Formation of dispersions using "flow focusing" in microchannels. *Appl. Phys. Lett.* **2003**, *82*, 364–366.
10. Okushima, S.; Nisisako, T.; Torii, T.; Higuchi, T. Controlled production of monodisperse double emulsions by two-step droplet breakup in microfluidic devices. *Langmuir* **2004**, *20*, 9905–9908. [CrossRef]
11. Utada, A.S.; Lorenceau, E.; Link, D.R.; Kaplan, P.D.; Stone, H.A.; Weitz, D.A. Monodisperse double emulsions generated from a microcapillary device. *Science* **2005**, *308*, 537–541. [CrossRef]
12. Sugiura, S.; Nakajima, M.; Tong, J.; Nabetani, H.; Seki, M. Preparation of monodispersed solid lipid microspheres using a microchannel emulsification technique. *J. Colloid Interface Sci.* **2000**, *227*, 95–103. [CrossRef]
13. Nisisako, T.; Torii, T.; Higuchi, T. Novel microreactors for functional polymer beads. *Chem. Eng. J.* **2004**, *101*, 23–29. [CrossRef]
14. Dendukuri, D.; Tsoi, K.; Hatton, T.A.; Doyle, P.S. Controlled synthesis of nonspherical microparticles using microfluidics. *Langmuir* **2005**, *21*, 2113–2116. [CrossRef]
15. Xu, S.; Nie, Z.; Seo, M.; Lewis, P.; Kumacheva, E.; Stone, H.A.; Garstecki, P.; Weibel, D.B.; Gitlin, I.; Whitesides, G.M. Generation of monodisperse particles by using microfluidics: Control over size, shape, and composition. *Angew. Chem.* **2005**, *44*, 724–728. [CrossRef]
16. Nie, Z.; Xu, S.; Seo, M.; Lewis, P.C.; Kumacheva, E. Polymer particles with various shapes and morphologies produced in continuous microfluidic reactors. *J. Am. Chem. Soc.* **2005**, *127*, 8058–8063. [CrossRef]
17. Nisisako, T.; Torii, T.; Takahashi, T.; Takizawa, Y. Synthesis of monodisperse bicolored Janus particles with electrical anisotropy using a microfluidic Co-Flow system. *Adv. Mater.* **2006**, *18*, 1152–1156. [CrossRef]
18. Shepherd, R.F.; Conrad, J.C.; Rhodes, S.K.; Link, D.R.; Marquez, M.; Weitz, D.A.; Lewis, J.A. Microfluidic assembly of homogeneous and Janus colloid-filled hydrogel granules. *Langmuir* **2006**, *22*, 8618–8622. [CrossRef] [PubMed]
19. Dendukuri, D.; Hatton, T.A.; Doyle, P.S. Synthesis and self-assembly of amphiphilic polymeric microparticles. *Langmuir* **2007**, *23*, 4669–4674. [CrossRef] [PubMed]
20. Decker, C.; Jenkins, A.D. Kinetic approach of oxygen inhibition in ultraviolet-and laser-induced polymerizations. *Macromolecules* **1985**, *18*, 1241–1244. [CrossRef]
21. Glotzer, S.C. Some assembly required. *Science* **2004**, *306*, 419–420. [CrossRef] [PubMed]
22. Dendukuri, D.; Pregibon, D.C.; Collins, J.; Hatton, T.A.; Doyle, P.S. Continuous-flow lithography for high-throughput microparticle synthesis. *Nat. Mater.* **2006**, *5*, 365–369. [CrossRef] [PubMed]
23. Gervais, T.; El-Ali, J.; Günther, A.; Jensen, K.F. Flow-induced deformation of shallow microfluidic channels. *Lab Chip* **2006**, *6*, 500–507. [CrossRef] [PubMed]
24. Dendukuri, D.; Gu, S.S.; Pregibon, D.C.; Hatton, T.A.; Doyle, P.S. Stop-flow lithography in a microfluidic device. *Lab Chip* **2007**, *7*, 818–828. [CrossRef]
25. Bird, R.B.; Steward, W.E.; Lightfoot, E.N. *Transport Phenomena*; Wiley: Hoboken, NJ, USA, 2006.
26. Hayes, R.E.; Dannelongue, H.H.; Tanguy, P.A. Numerical simulation of mold filling in reaction injection molding. *Polym. Eng. Sci.* **1991**, *31*, 842–848. [CrossRef]
27. Anand, V.; Christov, I.C. Revisiting steady viscous flow of a generalized Newtonian fluid through a slender elastic tube using shell theory. *J. Appl. Math. Mech./Z. Angew. Math. Mech.* **2021**, *101*, e201900309. [CrossRef]
28. Inamdar, T.C.; Wang, X.; Christov, I.C. Unsteady fluid–structure interactions in a soft-walled microchannel: A one-dimensional lubrication model for finite Reynolds number. *Phys. Rev. Fluids* **2020**, *5*, 064101. [CrossRef]

29. Anand, V.; David, J.; Christov, I.C. Non-Newtonian fluid–structure interactions: Static response of a microchannel due to internal flow of a power-law fluid. *J. Non-Newton. Fluid Mech.* **2019**, *264*, 62–72. [CrossRef]
30. Skotheim, J.M.; Mahadevan, L. Soft lubrication. *Phys. Rev. Lett.* **2004**, *92*, 245509. [CrossRef]

fluids MDPI

Article

Comparative Study of Air–Water and Air–Oil Frictional Pressure Drops in Horizontal Pipe Flow

Enrique Guzmán [1], Valente Hernández Pérez [2,†], Fernando Aragón Rivera [3,†], Jaime Klapp [4,*] and Leonardo Sigalotti [5]

1 Instituto de Ingeniería UNAM, Circuito Escolar S/N, Ciudad Universitaria, Ciudad de México 04510, Mexico; jguzmanv@iingen.unam.mx
2 Tecnológico Nacional de México, Pachuca de Soto 42080, Mexico; valente.hp@pachuca.tecnm.mx
3 Departamento de Energía, Universidad Autónoma Metropolitana, Unidad Azcapotzalco (UAM-A), Ciudad de México 02128, Mexico; micme2003@yahoo.com.mx
4 Departamento de Física, Instituto Nacional de Investigaciones Nucleares (ININ), Estado de México Ocoyoacac 52750, Mexico
5 Departamento de Ciencias Básicas, Universidad Autónoma Metropolitana, Unidad Azcapotzalco (UAM-A), Ciudad de México 02128, Mexico; leonardo.sigalotti@gmail.com
* Correspondence: jaime.klapp@inin.gob.mx; Tel.: +52-55-3040-3724
† These authors contributed equally to this work.

Abstract: Experimental data for frictional pressure drop using both air–water and air–oil mixtures are reported, compared and used to evaluate predictive methods. The data were gathered using the 2-inch (54.8 mm) flow loop of the multiphase flow facility at the National University of Singapore. Experiments were carried out over a wide range of flow conditions of superficial liquid and gas velocities that were varied from 0.05 to 1.5 m/s and 2 to 23 m/s, respectively. Pressure drops were measured using pressure transducers and a differential pressure (DP) cell. A hitherto unreported finding was achieved, as the pressure drop in air–oil flow can be lower than that in air–water flow for the higher range of flow conditions. Using flow visualization to explain this phenomenon, it was found that it is related to the higher liquid holdup that occurs in the case of air–oil around the annular flow transition and the resulting interfacial friction. This additional key finding can have applications in flow assurance to improve the efficiency of oil and gas transportation in pipelines. Models and correlations from the open literature were tested against the present data.

Keywords: pipe flow; air–water flow; air–oil flow; two-phase flow; pressure drop; friction factor

1. Introduction

Pressure drop prediction remains a challenge within the multiphase flow community. There is an extensive body of work in this area that spans over six decades. Comprehensive reviews have been provided recently by Xu et al. [1] and Mekisso [2], regarding correlations and experimental data of two-phase frictional pressure drop in isothermal horizontal flow. However, most experimental work has been carried out with air–water mixtures, in small facilities, and most papers have focused on the evaluation of models for pressure drop calculation, some of them from a third-party point of view (see, for instance, Dukler et al. [3], Idsinga et al. [4], Ferguson and Spedding [5], Tribbe and Müller-Steinhagen [6], Garcia et al. [7] and Xu et al. [1]). Several different correlations have been suggested for use by different authors. In particular, Dukler et al. [3] found that the Lockhart–Martinelli correlation, the oldest of the five correlations tested, shows the best agreement with a set of carefully culled experimental data on pressure drop, which seems reasonable since some theoretical bases for this correlation were derived later by Chisholm [8]. On the other hand, Xu et al. [1] concluded that the correlations developed by Müller-Steinhagen and Heck [9] and Sun and Mishima [10] fit the entire experimental data under varying conditions and are recommended for use in two-phase pipe flow. However, their database was collected from experiments with channels with inner diameters from 0.0695 to 14 mm. They, as well as other authors, have also concluded that an improvement of presently available correlations and the development of new correlations are needed for more accurate predictions of two-phase frictional pressure drop.

It is well known that the total pressure drop in two-phase flow in a pipe consists of three contributions due to acceleration, friction and gravitational effects. For horizontal flows, the frictional pressure gradient usually forms the most significant contribution to the overall two-phase pressure drop. According to Ferguson and Spedding [5], this is the case when the total mass velocity $G_r < 2700$ kg m^{-2} s^{-1}, as the accelerational pressure drop, due to density change, is negligible. For single-phase flows, the pressure drop is caused by shear stress at the wall, but for two-phase flows, the situation is by far more complex since it involves indefinitely deformable interfaces. Due to this complexity, there are diverse predictive approaches of the pressure drop. They can be classified into: direct empirical correlations, homogeneous model correlations, correlations based on a two-phase multiplier, flow-pattern-specific models and numerical or interfacial friction models.

In the homogeneous model, two-phase flow is treated as a pseudo single-phase flow with average properties. The slip ratio is equal to unity, as both liquid and gas phases move at the same velocity. The standard form of this model is based on the Darcy equation as follows:

$$\left(\frac{dP}{dL}\right)_f = \frac{2f\rho_m V_m^2}{d} \tag{1}$$

where ρ_m is the mixture density, V_m is the mixture velocity, d is the pipe diameter and f is the Fanning friction factor calculated from average mixture properties. For fully developed laminar flow (i.e., Re < 2000), the friction factor is given by 64/Re. For turbulent flow in smooth pipes, the Blasius equation can be used, which is given by $f = 0.079\text{Re}^{-0.25}$ in the range $3000 < \text{Re} < 10^5$. It should be noted that some references use the factor 0.316 instead of 0.079 in the Blasius equation because, in the former case, the pressure drop is divided by four. A model for the two-phase viscosity is needed to calculate the Reynolds number, as described by Awad and Muzychka [11]. The calculation of the friction factor is the main difference among the correlations of the homogeneous model group. Direct empirical correlations express the pressure drop directly as a function of known parameters, such as mass flux, mass quality or mixture density, by using curve fitting. Examples are the correlations developed by Beggs and Brill [12] and Müller-Steinhagen and Heck [9].

In the two-phase flow multiplier model, also called a separated model, the two-phase pressure drop is calculated from the single-phase pressure drop multiplied by a two-phase multiplier, based upon the concept that the pressure drop for the liquid phase must equal the pressure drop for the gas phase regardless of the flow pattern. Examples of these correlations are those developed by Lockhart and Martinelli [13] and Friedel [14]. They introduced the two-phase multiplier, Φ_F, to define the ratio between the two-phase pressure gradient and the pressure gradient of either the gas or liquid phase.

$$\left(\frac{dp}{dL}\right)_{TP} = \Phi_F^2\left(\frac{dp}{dL}\right)_L. \tag{2}$$

The ratio of the liquid phase to the gas phase pressure drop that would occur if either fluid were flowing alone in the pipe with the original flow rate of each phase are related to the parameter χ, known as the Lockhart and Martinelli parameter, as

$$\left(\frac{dp}{dL}\right)_L = \chi^2\left(\frac{dp}{dL}\right)_G. \tag{3}$$

The parameter χ is independent of the void fraction and is a measure of the degree to which the two-phase mixture is close to being a liquid, i.e., $\chi_u^2 \gg 1$, or to being a gas, i.e., $\chi_u^2 \ll 1$.

The subscript u is sometimes used to mean that both phases are turbulent. Chisholm [8] provided a convenient relationship in the form of

$$\Phi_{TP}^2 = 1 + \frac{C}{\chi} + \frac{1}{\chi^2}, \tag{4}$$

where C is the Chisholm coefficient, which is defined for four gas–liquid flow regimes as $C = 20$ (turbulent–turbulent), $C = 12$ (turbulent–viscous), $C = 10$ (viscous–turbulent) and $C = 5$ (viscous–viscous).

A more complex approach is the mechanistic modeling. The first stage of this method is the prediction of the flow pattern. Therefore, the success of a comprehensive unified mechanistic approach depends upon the accurate prediction of the specific flow pattern. In addition, improvements might be required in the closure equations to obtain a fully accurate prediction. For instance, in the study by Holt et al. [15], a drift flux model is employed for bubbly flow, while slug flow is treated with a mechanistic description invoking a separate section around and between the Taylor bubbles. For annular flow, a phenomenological approach is used, utilizing descriptions for the rates of entrainment, deposition and film thickness. The numerical (or interfacial) friction approach is based on the two-fluid model. For pipe flow, the flow is assumed to be one-dimensional (1D). The mass and momentum conservation equations for both gas and liquid are solved numerically using an iterative procedure, as described by Issa [16], which yields cross-sectional average values of phase velocities, pressure and phase fraction along the pipe. Auxiliary relations representing the interfacial and shear stress forces are used, while different closure models are formulated for momentum transfer for each flow regime. A disadvantage of the phenomenological approach is that in practical situations, where, for example, high pressures and/or large pipe diameters occur, the present flow regime is often unknown [17]. In addition, numerical methods for two-phase flows suffer from a difficulty in obtaining data for their validation [18]. Moreover, the development of physics-based models can be thought of as being less mature. Thus, the correlation approach is still preferred for practical purposes. Some of the correlations have been developed for particular scenarios, such as for micro- and mini-channels [10], evaporating flows [19] and refrigeration [20].

Of particular importance is the role that fluid properties play in oil/gas production, which can vary from one well to another. There is also a wide range of applications that use different fluids, such as in chemical, power, refrigeration, air conditioning, oil/gas production and oil refining plants. The simple change in fluid from one mixture to another can result in a variation in several important properties, such as viscosity, density and surface tension. In fact, the viscosities measured for different heavy oils can vary by orders of magnitude. Since most of the predictive correlations of pressure drop are based on experimental data with air–water mixtures, as was reported by Mekisso [2], the extrapolation of these predictive methods to more industry relevant fluids might not work. Thus, more experimental data are required for validation, particularly for air–oil mixtures at high Reynolds numbers. For instance, pressure drop experimental data in horizontal air–water flow were reported by Hernández-Pérez [21]. In a more recent work, Hamad et al. [22] reported data for three different pipe diameters using air–water mixtures. Due to the short length of their pipes (1 m), the flow pattern was created in such a way that it was always homogeneous. Not surprisingly, they concluded that the homogeneous model for the prediction of the pressure drop was the best.

As a matter of fact, according to the two latest comprehensive reviews, only two references have reported air–oil pressure drops, which were all cited by Mekisso [2] and ignored by Xu et al. [19]. In particular, Dukler et al. [3] and Tribbe and Müller-Steinhagen [6] include gas–oil data from the industry field in their reports, but they do not give details. Additional separate data sets can be found from other sources. For example, Mattar and Gregory [23] investigated air–oil slug flow in a pipe slightly inclined upwards, including slug velocity, holdup and pressure gradient. On the other hand, Badie et al. [24] reported data of two-phase gas–liquid pressure gradient measurements for extremely low liquid, while Gokcal et al. [25] investigated experimentally the effects of oil with high viscosity on the flow pattern, pressure gradient and liquid holdup. Oil viscosities from 0.181 to 0.587 Pa s were obtained by changing the oil temperature. Their experiments were performed on a flow loop with a test section of 50.8 mm ID and 18.9 m long horizontal pipe. Superficial liquid and gas velocities varied from 0.01 to 1.75 m s^{-1} and from 0.1 to 20 m s^{-1}, respectively. They found that the pressure drop increases with the viscosity. A further experimental investigation on two-phase air/high-viscosity oil flow in a horizontal pipe was presented by Foletti et al. [26]. Similarly, Zhao et al. [27] found that the flow characteristics of high-viscosity oil and gas flow show several significant differences with those of low-viscosity liquid by experimenting with a pipe diameter of 26 mm and liquid superficial and gas velocities < 0.5 and 12 m s^{-1}, respectively. More recently, Farsetti et al. [28] investigated air–oil flow for different pipe inclinations, including the horizontal case. They obtained several parameters, including pressure drops for high-viscosity oil. However, the air superficial velocities were limited to only 1.5 m s^{-1}. Similarly, Abdulkadir et al. [29] reported pressure drop data using air–silicon oil within a limited range of superficial velocities.

Owing to the diversity of multiphase flow scenarios, other studies, such as those by Hernández-Pérez et al. [30] and Szalinski et al. [31], have compared air–water and air–oil flow, but only for vertical pipe flow, and no pressure drop data were reported, as they focused on Taylor bubble and phase distribution, respectively. Similarly, Foletti et al. [26] presented a comparison of flow pattern maps using air–water and air–viscous oil flow. A survey of the open literature shows that no comparison of the pressure drop between air–water and air–oil has been reported. Moreover, it can be observed that, despite their significance, gas–oil pressure drop data are scarce in the literature. A state-of-the-art multiphase flow loop facility is available at the National University of Singapore. Thus, the main objective of this work is to report unique experimental data of two-phase pressure drop from this facility for both air–water and oil–water mixtures. Since the general trend is to improve the accuracy of predictive models, a comparison is made of the present data with selected models in the literature. In addition, the physics behind the flow behavior under different fluids has been studied visually to understand and explain the results at a fundamental level.

2. Experimental Description

The overall operation of the flow loop facility has been previously described by Loh et al. [32]. The three-phase (air–water–oil) flow loop is equipped with a manifold into three different diameters of seamless, standard stainless-steel pipe (2, 4 and 6 inches), schedule 10. For the present work, the 2-inch (54.8 mm) line of the flow loop was selected. A schematic diagram of the facility is illustrated in the "supervisory control and data acquisition interface" shown in Figure 1.

A diagram of the test section is shown in Figure 2. It has a total length of 40 m and follows a rectangular shape. Measurements were taken after 14 m (i.e., pipe length over pipe diameter, $L/D \sim 280$) from the inlet. As described by Loh et al. [32], the two-phase flow mixtures are created by mixing air with water and air with oil. Air is supplied by two compressors connected in parallel to a receiver tank. Water and oil are supplied from a separator tank using a water and oil pump, respectively. Individual flow rates of air, water and oil are measured prior to the mixing section. The air is measured with a vortex-type flow meter, whereas both oil and water are measured with Coriolis-type flow meters. The mixing section consists of a concentric 2-inch pipe of air joining a 4-inch 90° bend with liquid in a mixing bend configuration, as shown in Figure 2. Check valves are used to prevent liquid going into the air line and vice versa. The air flow is calculated based on the test section pressure (2-inch P4 in Figure 1), which is in the loop itself at 14 m from the inlet. The calculation is carried out using an ideal gas equation. Since the facility is also being used as a reference to test the performance of third-party multiphase flow meters, the gas and liquid flow meters have been optimized for accuracy. The vortex gas flow meter used in the present experiments has a measurement uncertainty of 1% of the indicated value, while the Coriolis liquid flow meters have a measurement uncertainty of ±0.3% of the indicated value. The flow is controlled automatically from the computer control system using a PID algorithm implemented in the NI LabVIEW software (version 2013).

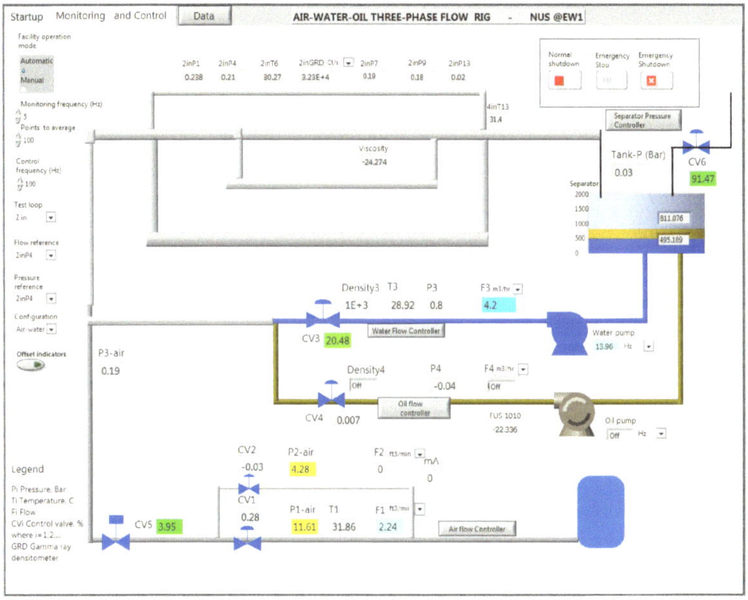

Figure 1. Monitoring, control and data acquisition system interface of the experimental setup.

After travelling across the flow loop, the mixture goes into a three-phase separator that also serves as a storage tank. After separation, the liquid is recycled, while air is released into the atmosphere through the control valve and a silencer. The separator tank volume is 16 m^3 and it holds 5 m^3 of water and 5 m^3 of oil. Efficient phase separation in the three-phase flow separator is confirmed by the density readings from the Coriolis flow meters.

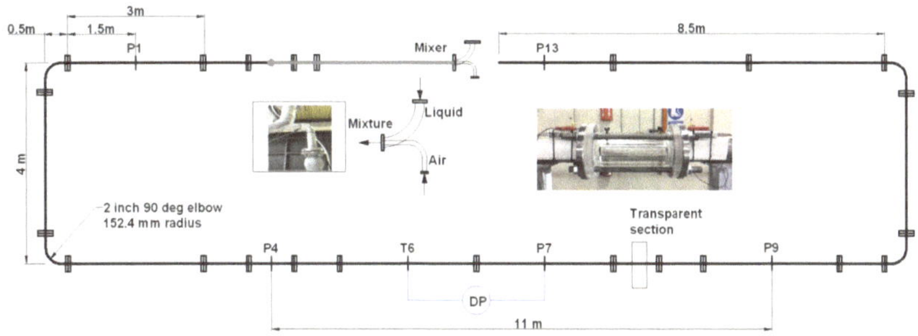

Figure 2. Top view of the physical configuration of the 2-inch test loop, mixing section and instrumentation.

2.1. Pressure Drop Measurement

Pressure and temperature sensors were placed at different axial locations along the test section, as shown in Figures 1 and 2. In addition, a DP cell was needed and used to read the lower pressure range (0–300 Pa m^{-1}). For the high range, the pressure drop was measured using two pressure sensors over a distance of 11 m of the straight pipe. All pressure taps were mounted flush in the tube wall. All sensors are factory calibrated and were tested on site. Pressure sensors have a measurement uncertainty of 0.05% of the scale (16 Bar). Due to the high values of pressure drop for these flow conditions, in this large-scale facility, these kinds of pressure sensors are adequate. They may be advantageous as opposed to the case of the DP cell, where care must be taken to ensure that air is not present in the pressure line that would distort the measured value. However, this is hard to maintain under intermittent flow conditions. Other researchers, such as, for example, Moreno-Quiben and Thome [33], Ortiz-Vidal et al. [34] and Talley et al. [35], have also successfully obtained pressure drop measurements from absolute pressure sensors. The measurement locations were chosen to minimize the inlet and outlet effects while maintaining a total development length of at least 200 diameters. The measurements were used to determine the differential pressure between 280 and 400, 400 and 500 and 280 and 500 diameters downstream of the inlet, respectively.

A comparison between the DP cell and the gauge pressure differential measurements is depicted in Figure 3 for both air–water and air–oil mixtures. This comparison shows that the agreement is good and gets better as the pressure drop increases. For the DP cell, the accuracy is higher as based on specifications. It is a differential pressure transducer (Siemens Sitrans P DS III) with an operational range of 0 to 1000 Pa and an accuracy of 0.075% of the full range, whose pressure tapings are 3 m apart. Taking this as a reference, we can estimate that, in the worst-case scenario, the pressure drops from the gauge pressure transducers have an uncertainty within or better than 10% (in the lower range), which comes mainly as a result of the uncertainty propagation. In the world of multiphase flows, this level of uncertainty is not uncommon. In their review, Dukler et al. [3] found that, for apparently similar test conditions, pressure drop data from different investigators vary by 30 to 60%. Ortiz-Vidal et al. [34] reported pressure drop data with uncertainty within ±8.5% depending on the flow conditions. Hamad et al. [22] compared single-phase pressure drop data with the Blasius equation and determined that the error associated with the pressure drop measurements is within the range (±10%). This shows the importance of reliable experimental data in improving the performance of prediction methods.

The pressure in the flow loop was kept close to atmospheric by fully opening the control valve (CV6) on the separator (see Figure 1). At very high liquid and gas flow rates, the pressure reaches nearly 2 Bars due to the pressure drop downstream the test section. The temperature was in the range between 29 and 31 °C. Once the flow stabilized, data from all instruments were recorded simultaneously at a sampling frequency of 10 Hz over a time interval of 180 s. The measurements were supplemented using a high-speed video camera to visualize the flow in some runs. The fluid properties are listed in Table 1. The same oil has been previously used by Loh and Premanadhan [32]. This oil is considered as light oil due to its properties, and its viscosity was measured using an HAAKE MARS III Rheometer.

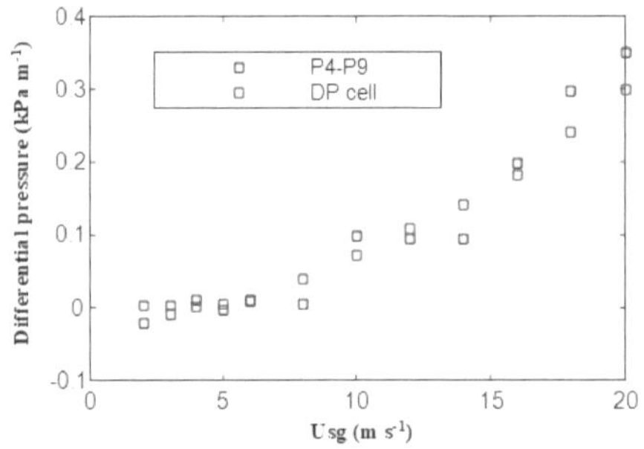

Figure 3. Comparison between pressure drop data from two gauge pressure sensors (P4−P9) and the DP cell.

Table 1. Physical fluid properties.

Fluid	Density (kg m^{-3})	Viscosity (kg m^{-1} s^{-1})	Surface Tension (N m^{-1})
Air	1.224	0.000018	0.072
Tap water	1000	0.001	
AP process oil	845	0.030	0.037

2.2. Single Phase Measurements

Since the pressure drop depends also on the inner surface roughness of the pipe material, ε, single-phase measurements were performed to verify the pipe friction coefficient, as displayed in Figure 4. A comparison with the standard value for smooth pipes shows a fairly good agreement when plotted against the Re number. Therefore, Blasius-type power-law expressions for the wall shear stresses can be used in the prediction models. These measurements show that the relative roughness, ε/D, is in the range of 1 to 2×10^{-5}. It can be seen that, according to the Blasius equation, the single-phase friction factor for oil is bigger than for water as it has a lower Reynolds number.

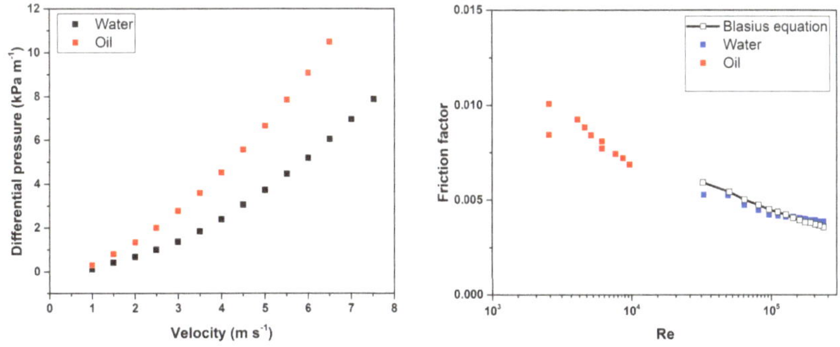

Figure 4. Single−phase pressure drop (**left**) and pipe friction coefficient (**right**) for oil and water.

3. Results and Discussion

A total of 254 data points were acquired and analyzed. The same flow conditions were set for both the air–water and air–oil mixtures. These flow conditions are similar to the ones commonly found in the oil and gas industry. In fact, similar flow rates in this flow loop have been used to test the performance of industrial multiphase flow meters for independent companies. They are also within the range where accelerational pressure drop can be neglected (see Ferguson and Spedding [5]). Thus, the measurements obtained correspond directly to the frictional pressure drop.

To investigate the pressure profiles along the pipeline, the measurements were made at axial locations of 280, 400 and 500 pipe diameters downstream of the inlet. The change in gauge pressure along the length of the test section is shown in Figure 5. It can be seen that the pressure gradient is fairly linear. Thus, the results obtained from P4–P7, P7–P9 and P4–P9 are consistent. Similar pressure profiles were obtained by Mattar and Gregory [23] for air–oil flow using differential pressure transducers whose low-pressure ports were joined together. Unfortunately, the gauge pressure P7 was not taken for all runs, as a DP cell was installed instead for low pressure drops at low superficial velocities using the same analog input channel in the data acquisition.

The automatic feature of the control system allows us to specify the gas and liquid superficial velocities directly during run time and based on the test section. However, the values of the gas superficial velocities are corrected with the pressure at the midpoint between the pressure taps by linearly interpolating the pressure from the P4 using the pressure gradient. Figure 6 shows a comparison of the pressure drops obtained by three different combinations of subtraction, namely P4–P7, P7–P9 and P4–P9. It can be observed that the values are quite similar, which gives confidence in the results. The value of P4–P9 is taken as the ultimate result for further analysis. Since the pressure drop is no more than 5 kPa m^{-1}, the pressure change is less than 5%. In passing, we note that the pressure drop for the air–oil mixtures behaves differently from that for the air–water mixtures. This difference can be explained partially in terms of the relative viscosities for both liquid phases. The oil under consideration has a viscosity ten times higher than that of the tap water used in the experiments. From a dynamical point of view, all gas–liquid interactions take place at the interface, where the local stress state varies according to the flow conditions there. When the apparent velocities are large, this stress state may become sufficiently large to induce K-H instabilities. In this case, the intefacial flow enters what Andritsos et al. [36] refer to as the K-H subregime. It follows that the shearing effects lead to significant distortions in the interface, which ultimately change the properties of the flow itself (a coupled effect). This is due to the exacerbated exchange of momentum in all directions promoted by the thickening and undulation of the interface. The 'off-axis' exchange of momentum manifests itself in the overall pressure registered by the instruments installed along the pipe.

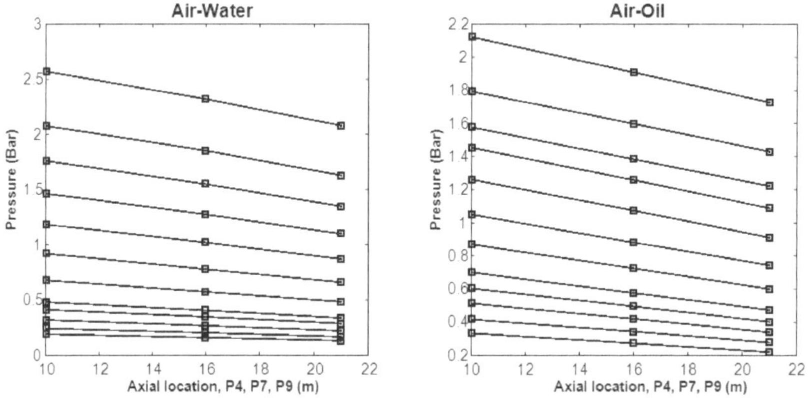

Figure 5. Example of typical pressure profiles for air–water (**left**) and air–oil (**right**) along the test section for different fixed flow conditions.

Figure 7 shows the pressure gradient as a function of the gas superficial velocity for varying values of the liquid superficial velocity. This allows other researchers to easily use these data and check if the pressure drop measurements are within the realistic range of values having consistent trends with neighbouring points. Compared to the air–water case, the air–oil flow exhibits a different pressure drop behavior, which is more evident in the intermediate velocity range between 0.25 and 1.5 m s^{-1}. It appears that the oil viscosity is such that a thicker layer of fluid remains adhered to the inner wall of the pipe after passage of a slug. At low liquid velocities, the interfacial stresses prevent the K-H instability from developing unsteadily, resulting only in a small undulating interface. However, as the liquid flow velocity increases, the interfacial stresses also increase, the effective cross-section is reduced as the layer becomes thicker and the K-H instability has more chances to develop. This results in a severe deformation of the thick oil layer around the wall, which, in turn, promotes flow separation and severe turbulence in the gaseous phase. These effects may induce adverse pressure gradients in the flow, resulting in an overall drastic reduction in the pressure drop along the pipe. In contrast, at high mixture velocities, the interfacial stresses are high enough to allow liquid removal from the layer. The removed fluid is dragged into the core of the flow, thereby leading to an effective reduction in the layer thickness. This marks a kind of transition where the overall pressure gradient is restored to a steady average value.

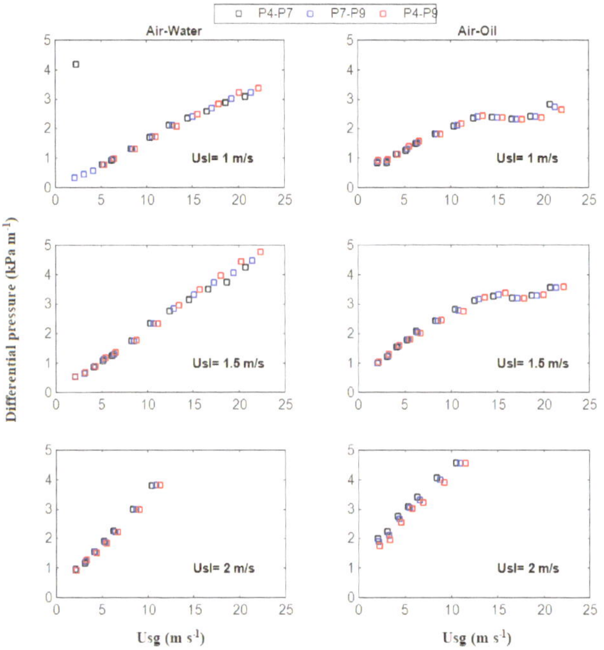

Figure 6. Comparison of pressure drop from P1–P7, P7–P9 and P4–P9 for air–water (**left**) and air–oil flows (**right**) in 2–inch line at different flow conditions of gas and liquid superficial velocities.

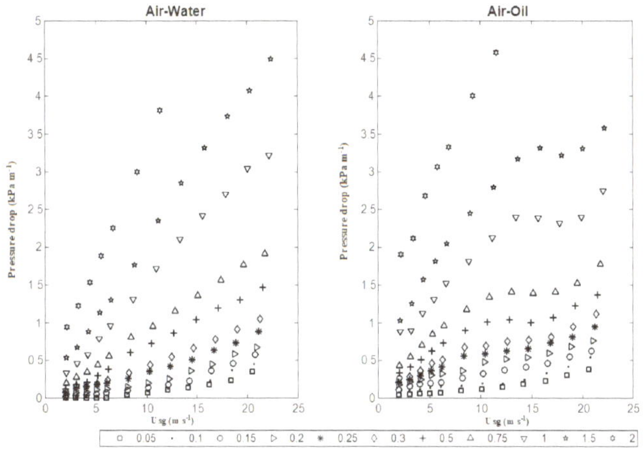

Figure 7. Pressure drop results for air–water (**left**) and air–oil flows (**right**) in 2–inch line at different flow conditions of gas and liquid superficial velocities.

In general, the effect of increasing the gas and liquid superficial velocities is to increase the pressure gradient. Also, for gas superficial velocities lower than around 10 m s^{-1}, as expected, the pressure drop is generally higher for the air-oil flow, since it is more viscous than water. Surface tension and density are less relevant due to the relatively big pipe diameter and horizontal pipe orientation. However, it can be noted that, for superficial velocities beyond around 10 m s^{-1}, the pressure drop in air–oil flow can be lower than that in air–water flow. This is interesting because, as the viscosity increases, the pressure drop normally increases, as was reported by Gokcal et al. [25]. An effort was devoted to ensure the correctness of this result. Figure 8 shows a side-by-side comparison between the air–oil and air–water pressure drop, whereas Figure 9 shows a comparison with pressure drop data provided by Gokcal et al. [25], where the effects of viscosity can be appreciated. To explain this, we resort to flow visualization with a high-speed video camera and the use of a transparent section. In addition, other literature data were used for comparison. The experimental data reported in Figure 9 differ from those of Gokcal et al. [25] because both data sequences correspond to different viscosities. In the present work, the viscosity was 0.03 Pa s against 0.181 Pa s in the study by Gokcal et al. [25].

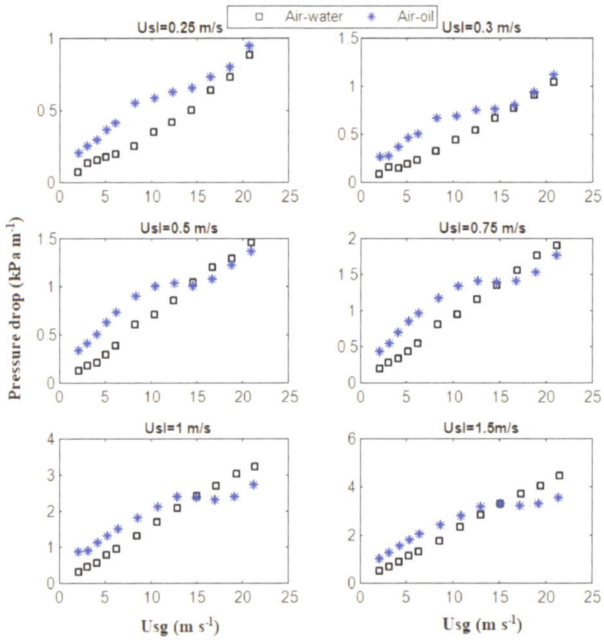

Figure 8. Comparison of pressure drop between air—water and air—oil flow for different liquid and gas superficial velocities.

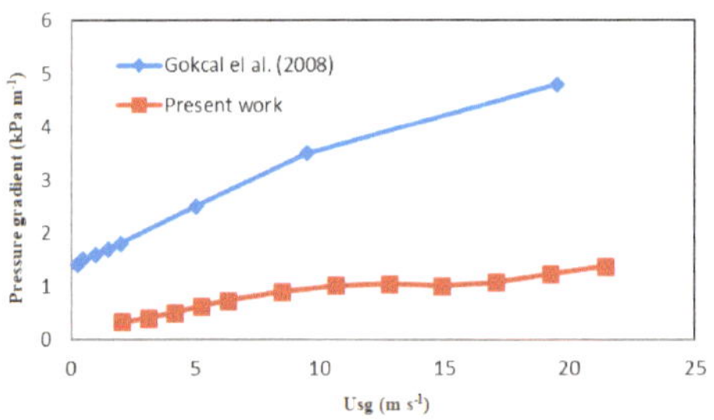

Figure 9. Comparison between Gokcal et al.'s [25] pressure drop measurements for air—oil flow with oil viscosity of 0.181 Pa s and present work. The data plotted correspond to a liquid superficial velocity of 0.5 m s^{-1}.

3.1. Flow Visualization

Figure 10 shows snapshots from the videos taken at a liquid superficial velocity of 0.5 m s^{-1} with the high-speed camera at 250 fps. The full videos are available as complimentary material in the appendix. The videos show that these conditions correspond to intermittent flow. However, we focus on the section of the stratified liquid layer to explain the results of the pressure drop comparison. The picture for air–water (on the left column) shows that the interface appears more blurred due to the highly disturbed flow. For air–oil (on the right column), the interface is smooth with a greater height and the film around the pipe wall is visibly thicker. Similar observations are described by Andritsos and Hanratty [37] for a viscosity of 80 cp, although no clear pictures were provided. The wavier interface suggests that there is a bigger interfacial friction factor in the air–water interface. The presence of waves at the interface can cause the interfacial shear stress to be much greater than the one that would be observed if the interface were smooth [36]. The presence of fully developed roll waves was also found to increase interfacial friction at the gas–liquid interface [38]. The friction at the interface is often represented as a function of the wall friction of the gas, $fi = \varphi fg$. Andritsos et al. [36] proposed empirical correlations for the ratio fi/fg for the 2D wave and Kelvin–Helmholtz (K-H) wave stratified sub-regimes. These regimes are characterized by significant distortions in the gas–liquid interface. Typically, these distortions correspond to wave flow patterns, which are promoted by the increased interfacial stresses caused by the increased slip velocity at the interface. According to Andritsos et al. [36], the interfacial friction factor can be up to 10x that of the gas phase in the K-H wave region. In the present experiments, the flow pattern reaches the annular flow region. As a result, larger pressure drops and lower liquid holdups are expected for the air–water case. Visual observations from the corresponding videos, with tiny bubbles trapped, reveal that the fluid in the stratified liquid layer seems to travel at a lower velocity for the case of oil compared to the air–water case. This explains the lower pressure drop obtained for the air–oil flow because the pressure drop depends on both the velocity and interfacial friction factor.

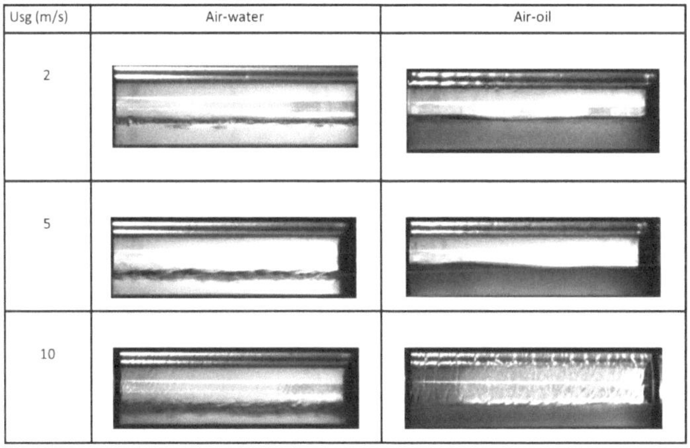

Figure 10. Visual comparison between the stratified liquid layers of air−water (**left column**) and air−oil flows (**right column**) for different gas superficial velocities of 2, 5 and 10 m s^{-1}. The liquid superficial velocity is 0.5 m s^{-1}.

On the other hand, Cohen and Hanratty [39] have proposed that the waves receive their energy from the gas through the work of pressure and shear stress perturbations induced by the waves. According to them, knowledge of the physical processes responsible for the generation of these waves is needed if one is to understand many of the phenomena that are observed in two-phase flow systems. However, most interfacial friction correlations consider knowledge of the liquid layer height instead of the fluid properties, which limits their predicting capabilities. The air–oil region shows a greater viscous sub-layer thickness, implying that more regions of the flow are affected by viscous dissipation. The pressure disturbances caused by the shearing action of the gas over the liquid do not penetrate deeper into the fluid film for oil flow, due to the viscous dissipational effects. Hence, a smoother interface prevails in comparison to the disturbed interface in air–water flow.

The modeling of the interfacial momentum transfer is considered to be the crucial issue in gas–liquid stratified flows [40]. Andritsos and Hanratty [37] developed a model for the interfacial friction factor. A more rigorous analytical description is beyond the scope of this work and might be the subject of a separate future paper. It can be concluded from the visualization that the observed flow behavior is consistent with the pressure drop measurements. The visual observations suggest that, for low gas velocities, the oil wall friction overcomes the interfacial friction in the water. As the gas flow rate increases, the water interfacial friction eventually overcomes the wall friction of oil flow. This happens in the intermediate region between the annular and slug flows. Consequently, two different trends of the pressure drop versus the gas superficial velocity can be obtained for low and high gas superficial velocity. Footage was taken for different flow conditions for both the air–water and air–oil flows. The liquid stratified layer is consistently thicker for oil across the stratified and intermittent flow patterns. This suggests that, during intermittent flow, the flow characteristics, such as the slug translational velocity and frequency, might also be different. This information can be obtained from the recorded footage of the flow. To look into this, an image processing algorithm was used, similar to that of Loh et al. [32]. The algorithm tracks the gas–liquid interface from the footage to obtain the time trace of the liquid layer height. The time series was obtained at 250 Hz and then a low-pass filter was applied to eliminate the noise. Since this technique is tedious, only a handful of data points are indeed presented.

To calculate the frequency, a slug-counting algorithm was developed. The power spectral density (PSD) technique did not work very well because the slugs were nonuniform and/or not periodic. Therefore, several different values of the frequency would result from this technique. For the translational velocity, the cross-correlation velocity was applied, which works because the time traces of the liquid layer height are strongly correlated. The results are shown in Figures 11 and 12. It can be noted that the slug frequency is higher for the air–oil flow compared to the air–water flow, whereas the translational velocity is roughly the same for both flows. The time series of the average liquid holdup at a cross-sectional area of the pipe were obtained using image processing techniques. The side-view images were obtained with a time resolution of 0.004 s. The quality of the image will then determine the accuracy of the results. For example, high-quality images allow the algorithm to identify the gas–liquid interface clearly due to the color contrast. This has been attained using proper illumination on the transparent test section. Due to the complex nature of the flow patterns, it is not always possible to obtain very clear images and so we only apply the algorithm to flow conditions for which the interface can be identified.

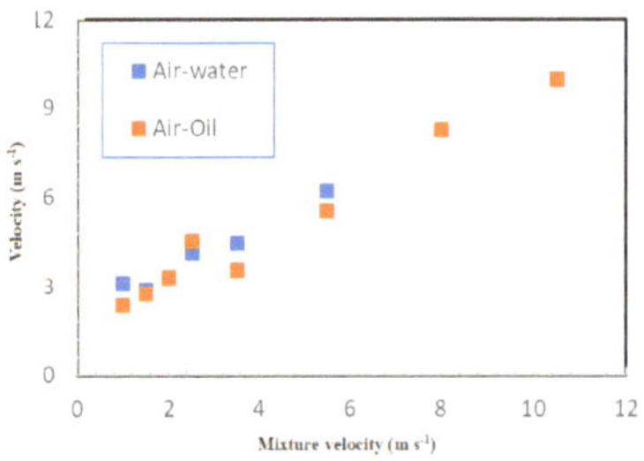

Figure 11. Comparison of the slug translational velocity between air—water and air—oil flows. The liquid superficial velocity is 0.5 m s^{-1}.

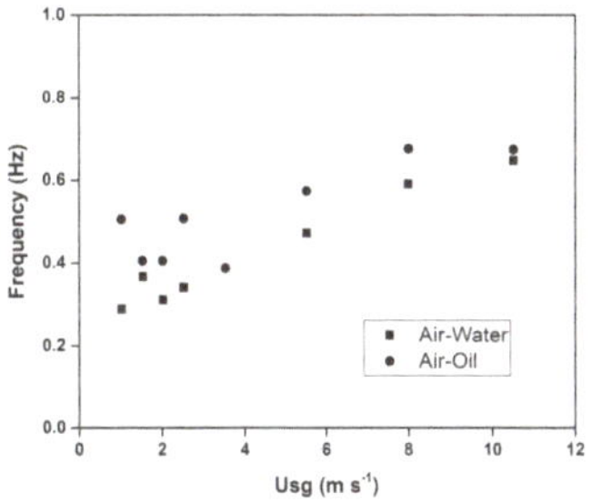

Figure 12. Comparison of the slug frequency between air–water and air–oil flows. The liquid superficial velocity is 0.5 m s^{-1}.

3.2. Comparison with Literature Data

As was mentioned in the introduction, pressure drop data for air–oil two-phase flows are scarce. Nevertheless, owing to industrial demands, the research community has preferred to investigate three-phase flows. Although three-phase flows are beyond the scope of this work, some scenarios can be used to compare our results on two-phase flows. This is because the air–oil flow is a particular case of three-phase flow in which the water cut (fraction by volume of water in the liquid phase) is 0%, and it is 100% for air–water. A comparison of the present data against independent relevant data compiled from the open literature is displayed in Figures 13 and 14).

Hewitt [41] reported some results for three-phase flows obtained on the Imperial College WASP facility for high and low gas velocities (see upper two frames of Figure 13). These results include the pressure drop as a function of the input water cut. A keen look at his data for high gas velocities indicates that a 100% water cut would produce a higher pressure drop than a 0% water cut. However, for low gas velocities, this is not observed. The oil used in these experiments was a lubricating oil with a density of 860 kg m^{-3} and a viscosity of around 40 cP (mPa s). The test section in this facility was a stainless steel pipe that was 38 m long and had a 77.92 mm internal diameter.

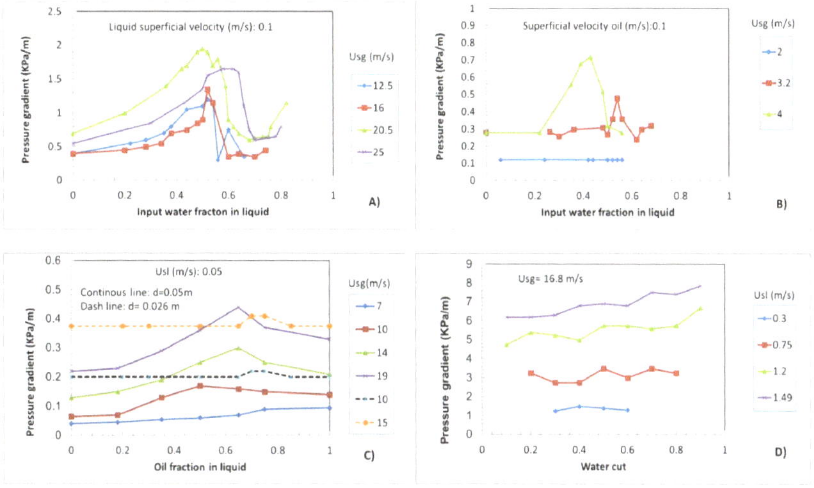

Figure 13. Experimental pressure drop data from three–phase flow experiments. The plots were reproduced from data reported by Hewitt [41] (**A**,**B**), by Spedding et al. [42] (**C**) and by Al-Hadhrami et al. [43] (**D**).

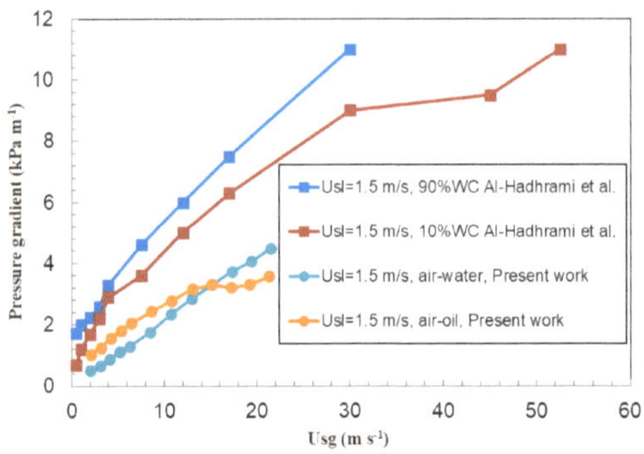

Figure 14. Pressure gradient as a function of the gas superficial velocity for the air−water and air−oil flow as compared with Al-Hadhrami et al.'s [43] experimental data for three−phase flow. In all cases, the liquid superficial veolocity is 1.5 m s^{-1}.

A further study was reported by Spedding et al. [42] (see bottom-left frame of Figure 13). The oil properties for the 0.0259 m ID facility were $\rho_0 = 828.5$ kg m^{-3} and $\mu_0 = 0.0122$ kg m^{-1} s^{-1}, while, for the 0.0501 m ID apparatus, they were $\rho_0 = 854.2$ kg m^{-3} and $\mu_0 = 0.0395$ kg m^{-1} s^{-1}, all at 24 °C. However, their results do not show the phenomenon observed in the present work, where the pressure drop for the air–water flow is higher than for the air–oil flow. In contrast, their liquid superficial velocities are limited to the low range compared to ours. In this range, we have also found a similar trend to theirs. In addition, what is interesting is that, for their 1-inch pipe diameter, the pressure drop is about the same for the mixture with a 0 and 100% water cut. Recently, Al-Hadhrami et al. [43] reported data for three-phase flow in a horizontal pipe at different water cuts, using Safrasol D80 oil with a density of 800 kg m^{-3} and dynamic viscosity of 1.77 cp, tap water with a dynamic viscosity of 1 cp and density of 1000 kg m^{-3} and air at standard conditions. Their section was an acrylic pipe of diameter equal to 22.5 mm. From the bottom-right frame of Figure 13, it can be seen that there is a clear trend of the pressure drop increasing with the water cut and the liquid superficial velocity.

Figure 14 compares the pressure gradient as a function of the gas superficial velocity of Al-Hadhrami et al.'s [43] data for a 10 and 90% water cut with present work for air–water and air–oil flow. Although Al-Hadhrami et al. [43] did not report data for pure air–oil and air–water flows, their data clearly show that the pressure drop is higher for a high water cut at high liquid superficial velocities in the whole range of gas superficial velocities. There is an agreement that the data for water show a higher pressure drop than the data for oil. It is worth noting that their oil viscosity is very low. However, their corresponding higher values can be attributed to their smaller pipe diameter. The difference with Al-Hadhrami et al.'s [43] data can be attributed to the fact that they used three-phase mixtures with different water cuts. Therefore, when the water content is bigger, the pressure is correspondingly higher. However, both data sequences predict an increase in the pressure gradient with the surface gas velocity, which indicates that our results are consistent.

From a comparison with experimental data available in the open literature, it can be concluded that there is implicitly enough independent evidence that the pressure drop for air–oil flows is lower than for air–water flows. However, from Gokcal et al.'s [25] data, it follows that, for high-viscosity oil, the lower pressure drop in air–oil flow might or might not happen at higher velocities. This apparently occurs because the wall friction in the high-viscosity oil is already too large to be overcome by the interfacial friction at the air–water interface. Furthermore, as shown in Figure 8, the pressure drop increases with increasing liquid superficial velocity because of the bigger interfacial area associated with a higher liquid stratified layer. This demonstrate the extreme complexity of multiphase flows and the need for a more basic understanding of them. This feature has important implications for oil and gas pipelines with high throughput, where three-phase (i.e., gas–water–oil) mixtures are normally handled. For instance, separating the water from the gas and oil may result not only in an overall operating cost saving but also in facilitating the transport of the gas–oil mixture.

3.3. Comparison of Correlations

The performance of the pressure drop correlations for two-phase flows, such as those that were reported in the introduction, were compared against the experimental database plotted in Figure 4. There are many correlations available in the literature. However, a selection has been made here of the most widely used and accepted models. Nine different pressure drop calculation methods were selected. The methods selected were compared by determining the deviation between predicted and measured pressure drops. The models and correlations for the prediction of the pressure drop are summarized in Table 2 and the results of the comparison are presented in Figures 15–17.

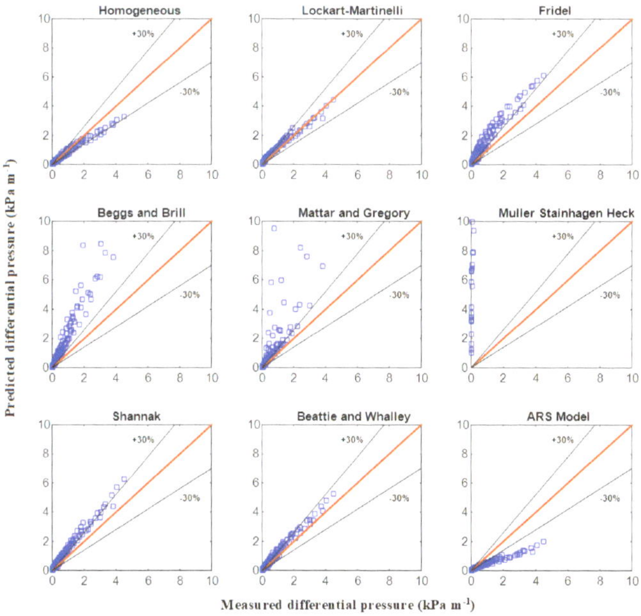

Figure 15. Comparison of the measured pressure drop data with the predictions of different correlations from the literature for air–water two–phase flow.

Owing to its simplicity, it is worth testing the homogeneous model given by Equation (1). One limitation in computing the two-phase frictional pressure gradient using the homogeneous modeling approach is the definition of the two-phase viscosity. It can be seen from Figure 15 that it underestimates the pressure drop for air-water, while, as shown in Figure 16, it overestimates the pressure drop for air-oil in the higher range. On the other hand, the Lockhart-Martinelli correlation, given by Equations (2)–(4), was developed based on experimental data in small-diameter pipes and including different two-phase mixtures consisting of air with benzene, kerosene, water and several oils. This correlation is limited by the viscosity, which will only affect the Reynolds number and consequently the value of the coefficient C. However, there are only two possible values of C as a function of the liquid Re. It follows from Figure 15 that, for air-water mixtures, the predictions are around the right place, while, for air-oil mixtures, the Lockhart-Martinelli correlation overpredicts the experimental data by up to 100%.

Table 2. Selected frictional pressure drop models and correlations.

Model Correlation	Equations
Homogeneous	Equation (1)
Lockhart-Martinelli (1949) [13]	Equations (2)–(4)
Friedel (1979) [14]	$\left(\frac{dp}{dL}\right)_{TP} = \phi_F^2\left(\frac{dp}{dL}\right)_L; \phi_F^2 = E + \frac{3.24FH}{\mathrm{Fr}_H^{0.045}\mathrm{We}_L^{0.035}}; \mathrm{Fr}_H = \frac{M^2}{gd\rho_H^2}$ $E = (1-x)^2 + x^2\frac{\rho_l f_g}{\rho_g f_l}; F = x^{0.78}(1-x)^{0.224}$ $H = \left(\frac{\rho_l}{\rho_g}\right)^{0.91}\left(\frac{\mu_g}{\mu_l}\right)^{0.19}\left(1-\frac{\mu_g}{\mu_l}\right)^{0.7}; \mathrm{We} = \frac{M^2 d}{\sigma\rho_H}$
Beggs and Brill (1973) [12]	$\left(\frac{dP}{dL}\right)_f = \frac{2f_m\rho_{ns}U_m^2}{d}; \rho_{ns} = H_L\rho_L + (1-H_L)\rho_G;$ $\mu_{ns} = \lambda\mu_L + (1-\lambda)\mu_G; f_m = f_{ns}e^s; \Re_{ns} = \frac{dU_m\rho_{ns}}{\mu_{ns}}$ $L1 = \exp(-4.62 - 3.757X - 0.481X^2 - 0.0207X^3)$ $L2 =$ $\exp\left(1.061 - 4.602X - 1.609X^2 - 0.179X^3 + 0.635 * 10^{-3}X^5\right)$ $X = \ln\lambda; \lambda = \frac{U_{sl}}{U_{sl}+U_{sg}}; \mathrm{Fr} = \frac{U_m^2}{gd}$ $\mathrm{Fr} < L1 \mathrm{segregated} H_L = \frac{0.98\lambda^{0.4846}}{\mathrm{Fr}^{0.0868}}$ $L1 \leq \mathrm{Fr} \leq L2 \mathrm{Intermittent} H_L = \frac{0.98\lambda^{0.5351}}{\mathrm{Fr}^{0.0173}}$ $L2 \leq \mathrm{Fr} \mathrm{Distributed} H_L = \frac{0.98\lambda^{0.5824}}{\mathrm{Fr}^{0.0609}}$ $f_{ns} = \left[2\log\left(\frac{\Re_{ns}}{4.5223\log\Re_{ns} - 3.8215}\right)\right]^{-2}$ $s = \frac{\ln y}{-0.0523+3.182\ln y - 0.8725(\ln y)^2 + 0.01853(\ln y)^4}; y = \frac{\lambda}{H_L^2};$ $s = (\ln 2.2y - 1.2)$ if $1 < y < 1.2$
Mattar and Gregory (1974) [23]	$\left(\frac{dP}{dL}\right)_f = \frac{\rho_m g\sin\theta + (2f\rho_{mE}U_m^2)/d}{1-(\rho_m U_m U_{sg})/P}; \rho_{mE} = H_L\rho_L + (1-H_L)\rho_G$ $f = 0.0014 + \frac{0.125}{(\Re_{mE})^{0.32}}; E_L = 1 - \frac{U_{gs}}{1.3(U_{sg}+U_{sL})+0.7}$
Müller-Steinhagen and Heck (1986) [9]	$\left(\frac{dP}{dL}\right)_f = G(1-x)^{1/3} + Bx^3; G = A + 2(B-A)x$ $A = \left(\frac{dP}{dL}\right)_{fl} = \frac{f_l M^2}{2\rho_l d}$ $B = \left(\frac{dP}{dL}\right)_{fg} = \frac{f_g M^2}{2\rho_g d}$
Shannak (2008) [44]	$\left(\frac{dP}{dL}\right)_f = \frac{f_{TP}M^2}{2\rho_{tp}d}$ $\frac{1}{\sqrt{f_{tp}}} =$ $-2\log\left[\frac{1}{3.7065}\frac{\epsilon}{d} - \frac{4.0452}{\Re_{tp}}\log\left(\frac{1}{2.8257}\left(\frac{\epsilon}{d}\right)^{1.1098} + \frac{5.8506}{(\Re_{tp})^{0.8981}}\right)\right]$ $\Re_{tp} = \frac{F_{lg}+F_{lf}}{F_{vg}+F_{vl}}; F_{lg} = \rho_g v_g^2 d^2; F_{lf} = \rho_f v_f^2 d^2; F_{vg} = \rho_g v_g^2 d^2;$ $F_{vf} = \rho_f v_f^2 d^2$
Beattie and Whalley (1982) [45]	$\left(\frac{dP}{dL}\right)_f = \frac{f_{TP}M^2}{2\rho_{tp}d}; \Re = \frac{Gd}{\mu}; \mu = \mu_l(1-\beta)(1+2.5\beta) + \mu_g\beta;$ $\beta = \frac{\rho_l x}{\rho_l x + \rho_g(1-x)}$
Apparent rough surface (ARS) model, Hart et al. (1989) [17]	$\frac{H_L}{1-H_L} = \frac{Usl}{Usg}\left\{1 + \left[10.4 + \Re_{sl}^{-0.363}\left(\frac{\rho_l}{\rho_g}\right)^{1/2}\right]\right\}; u_l = \frac{Usl}{H_L};$ $u_g = \frac{Usg}{1-H_L};$ $\mathrm{Fr} = \frac{u_l^2\rho_l}{gD\Delta\rho}; \Re_g = \frac{du_g\rho_g}{\mu_g}$ $\theta = \theta_0 + 0.26\mathrm{Fr}^{0.58}; \theta_0 = 0.52 + 0.26H_L^{0.374}; \frac{k}{d} = 2.3\frac{H_L}{4\theta}$ $f_i = \frac{0.0625}{\left[\log_{10}\left(\frac{15}{\Re_g} + \frac{kg}{3.715d}\right)\right]^2}; f_g = \frac{0.07725}{\left[\log_{10}\left(\frac{\Re_g}{7}\right)\right]^2};$ $f_{TP} = (1-\theta)f_g + \theta f_i$ $\left(\frac{dP}{dL}\right)_{TP} = \frac{1}{1-H_L}\left[4f_{TP}\left(\frac{1}{2d}\right)\rho_g u_g^2 - 4\theta f_i\left(\frac{1}{2d}\right)\rho_g(2u_g u_l - u_l^2)\right]$

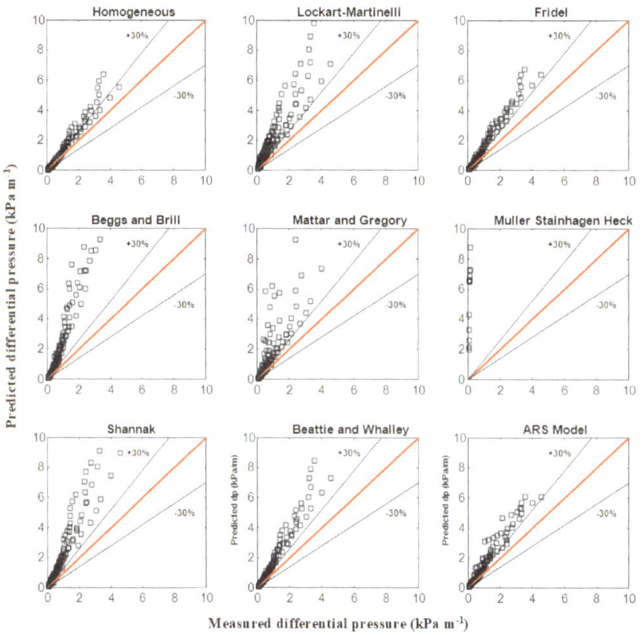

Figure 16. Comparison of the measured pressure drop data with the predictions of different correlations from the literature for air—oil two—phase flow.

An alternative method of calculating the two-phase flow multiplier is employed in the Friedel [14] correlation, which is based on one of the biggest data banks in the literature (16,000 data points). These include a wide range of two-phase systems (single and two components), mass fluxes, mass flow rates, density ratios, viscosity ratios, surface tension and hydraulic diameters of circular, rectangular and annular tubes, as well as horizontal flows, vertical up and down flows and, in particular, exhaustive air–oil data. With both the Chisholm [8] and Friedel [14] multipliers, the separated flow model appears to give reasonable results, particularly in the low pressure drop range, where the superficial velocities also happen to be the lowest. The reason for this could be attributed to the fact that, in this situation, the models seem to be more sensitive to small changes in some of the parameters involved in the overall calculation. For instance, in this case, the Lockhart–Martinelli parameter becomes very small and the two-phase multiplier increases, which gives as a result a higher predicted pressure drop. The way that the friction factor is calculated can also have an effect.

The Beggs and Brill correlation [12] was developed for inclined pipes based on air–water mixtures. Zhao et al. [27] found good agreement using pipes of 26 mm diameter at low viscosity. However, as can be observed from Figures 15 and 16, the Beggs and Brill correlation fails by quite a bit and is also too complicated. It overpredicts the pressure drop by about 100–300% even for air–water flows. However, it predicts reasonably well the pressure drop for inclined flow with high liquid holdups, especially in pipes of 38 mm diameter. Moreover, the correlation developed by Mattar and Gregory [23] seems to work reasonably well in the range of superficial velocities below 10 m s^{-1}. Beyond that limit, it yields randomly scattered values differing by several orders of magnitude (not shown here). This can be attributed to the fact that this correlation was developed based on the concept of the drift flux model for intermittent flow (slug and plug flows) and tested by the authors using only air-flow data.

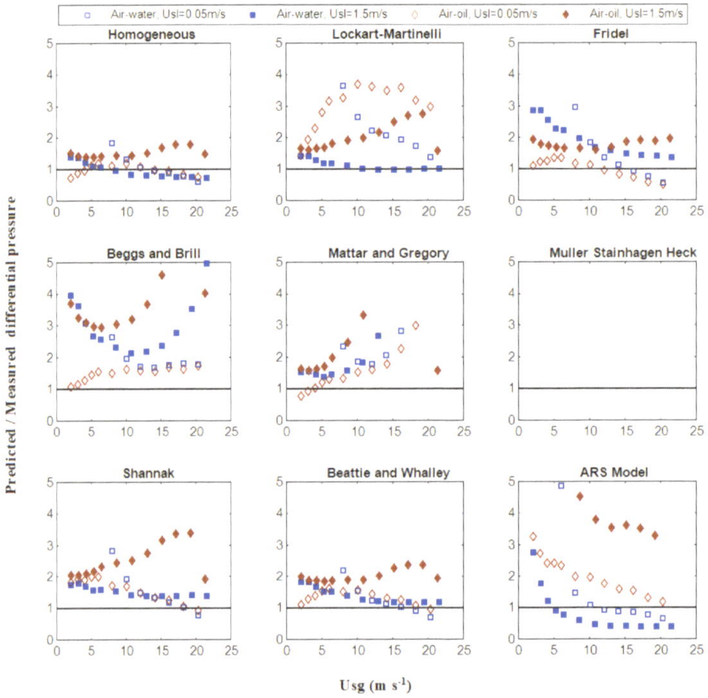

Figure 17. Effect of the gas superficial velocity on the ratio of predicted to experimentally measured pressure drops for different correlations.

As was stated by the authors, the correlation of Muller-Steinhagen and Heck [9] can be used only as long as the frictional pressure drop in the gas flow is higher than the frictional pressure drop in the liquid flow. Therefore, it is not applicable in the range spanning the present data. It was included here for the sake of completeness. It has been highly recommended by Xu et al. [19] and other authors, whose database was limited to pipe diameters of less than 14 mm and no oil data were included. As shown in Figures 15 and 16, this correlation fails to predict the correct pressure drops by several orders of magnitude. In passing, we note that one difference between small and large diameters might be the accelerational contribution to the pressure drop. A further correlation that is worth testing is the Shannak [44] correlation, which, in addition to being based on a simple concept, has been tested favorably against Friedel's database. According to Figures 15 and 16, this correlation overestimates the pressure drop in air–water flows by 30% and in air–oil flows by about 50%. In a particular way, it follows a similar trend to that of Friedel's [14] correlation for the case of air–water flow. The large errors exhibited by the different correlation models are expected because the experimental setup used in this work and the experimental conditions employed by the different authors are not the same. Even slight variations in the setup conditions may alter the nature of the flow since flow pattern transitions may occur at different operating points. For instance, the errors for the air–oil flows are far more significant than those for the air–water flows, while most correlations are approximately valid in the limit of low viscosities. This implies that viscosity plays a fundamental role in bringing about such discrepancies and that perhaps the inclusion of a correction factor to account for higher viscosities may help in reducing the errors. However, we do not have enough information at hand to recommend any improvements of this kind.

A further simple correlation was proposed by Beattie and Whalley [45] in which the flow pattern dependence is allowed in an implicit manner. This correlation is of a homogeneous type that uses a hybrid model to define the viscosity. Also, it uses the same equation for all values of the Reynolds number. From an inspection of Figures 15 and 16, the overall performance of this model is only second to the standard homogeneous model. Finally, the apparent rough surface (ARS) model developed by Hart et al. [17] was designed for very low liquid holdups. This model performs predictions of the pressure drop in horizontal pipe flows by using a modified expression for the pressure drop in the gas phase. As expected, it provides fairly good predictions only at flow conditions of low liquid and high gas superficial velocities. A quantitative assessment of the correlations plotted in Figures 15 and 16 is given in Table 3 in terms of the average relative error (ARE)

$$\mathfrak{R} = \frac{1}{n}\sum^{n}\left|\frac{(dp/dL)_{\text{pred}} - (dp/dL)_{\text{exp}}}{(dp/dL)_{\text{exp}}}\right| \times 100. \quad (5)$$

The prediction errors within 20 and 50% are also included in Table 3. In this case, the higher the value, the better the prediction performance. It follows that the homogeneous model gives the best overall results. However, if a particular scenario is considered, the result is slightly different. For air–water flows, the predictions of the Lockhart–Martinelli correlation is the best, while, for air–oil flows, the homogeneous correlation performs better. For low liquid at high gas superficial velocities, the ARS model is better. In general, for air–oil flows, the correlations tested perform worse than for air–water flows.

Table 3. Performance of pressure drop correlations.

Model	**Overall**			**Air–Water ARE (%)**	**Air–Oil ARE (%)**
	ARE (%)	**ARE (%) <20%**	**ARE (%) <50%**		
Homogeneous	54.59	47.43	84.98	84.79	24.14
Lockhart–Martinelli (1949) [13]	143.19	12.25	36.36	163.99	122.22
Friedel (1979) [14]	149.43	10.67	45.45	254.38	43.64
Beggs and Brill (1973) [12]	180.63	0.79	7.51	219.56	141.39
Mattar and Gregory (1974) [23]	607.88	13.83	35.57	314.93	903.16
Muller-Steinhagen and Heck (1986) [9]	16,891.84	0.00	0.00	17,872.55	15,903.34
Shannak (2008) [44]	157.42	3.16	18.58	193.21	121.34
Beattie and Whalley (1982) [45]	91.92	15.42	45.85	120.43	63.18
Apparent rough surface ARS model Hart et al. (1989) [17]	228.44	11.07	33.20	82.19	375.86

As was pointed out by Dukler et al. [3], the standard deviation is a completely descriptive measure of the spread between predicted and measured values only if the population of points follows a normal distribution. Furthermore, the results are biased if the data are not equally distributed. Therefore, the correlation performance is dependent on the experimental database. For instance, we can see that, for the case of air–water flow, the ARS model has the second best performance, which is due to the fact that more points were taken at low liquid and high gas superficial velocities.

On the other hand, if the predicted pressure drop is plotted against the experimental data, the errors are seen to grow at a higher pressure drop. However, it is not easy to see under which flow conditions the discrepancies happen. Figure 17 shows the ratio of predicted to experimental pressure drops as a function of the gas superficial velocity for both air–water and air–oil flows and all correlations listed in Tables 2 and 3. In general, for air–oil flows, the discrepancy between the predicted and experimental data grows as the gas superficial velocity increases. Note that only values of the ratio of predicted to experimental pressure drops up to 5 have been plotted in Figure 17. It is interesting to see that the correlation developed by Lockhart–Martinelli has a better performance than newer correlations.

Tribbe and Müller-Steinhagen [9] have shown that the precision and accuracy of phenomenological models are almost the same as those of empirical methods. However, because of their nature, the physically based models have more potential in the long term. Usually, when a new correlation or model is proposed, it is usually claimed to be superior to others. However, the present work, along with other independent test analyses, appears to not confirm this. In general, the experimental data also carry uncertainties, which are then transmitted to the proposed correlation. The degree of uncertainty may also depend on the measurement setup. In addition, since most correlations require information on the void fraction or flow pattern as input, errors in the void fraction accuracy and/or in the identification of the correct flow pattern are carried forward to the pressure drop prediction.

4. Conclusions

A comparative study of pressure drop in horizontal pipe flows has been carried out. A set of experimental data for air–water and air–oil mixtures has been reported. Based on these data, an evaluation of different models and correlations available in the open literature was performed. Flow visualization was also invoked to understand the results. The following conclusions can be drawn:

- The pressure drop increases as a function of the liquid and gas superficial velocities. This is particularly true for gas superficial velocities higher than 2 m s^{-1} because, in these cases, the pressure drop is dominated by the frictional component.
- The pressure drop in air–oil flows can be lower than that in air–water flows. Using flow visualization to explain this phenomenon, it was observed that this is due to the higher interfacial friction that occurs in the case of air–water around the annular flow transition. This also results in a greater height of the stratified liquid layer for the oil.
- Independent data from the open literature implicitly agree with the above findings.
- The phenomenon observed has important implications for flow assurance in oil and gas pipelines with high throughput, where three-phase (i.e., gas–water–oil) mixtures are normally handled. This is true because separating the water may result either in an overall operating cost saving or even facilitate the transport of the gas–oil mixture.
- Within the experimental range considered in this work, it is interesting to see that the Lockhart–Martinelli [13] correlation performed better in general than newer correlations. However, the homogeneous model performed better than all other more complex correlations.
- In general, the correlations tested were seen to perform worse for air–oil flows than for air–water flows.

Author Contributions: Conceptualization, E.G. and V.H.P.; methodology, E.G. and V.H.P.; software, F.A.R.; formal analysis, V.H.P.; investigation, F.A.R.; resources, E.G.; data curation, L.S.; writing—original draft preparation, V.H.P.; writing—review and editing, L.S.; visualization, F.A.R.; supervision, J.K.; project administration, E.G.; funding acquisition, J.K. All authors have read and agreed to the published version of the manuscript.

Funding: This research was funded by the European Union's Horizon 2020 Programme under the ENERXICO Project under grant number 828947 and by the Mexican CONAHCYT-SENER-Hidrocarburos Programme under grant number B-S-69926.

Data Availability Statement: The data presented in this study are available on request from the corresponding author.

Acknowledgments: We acknowledge support given by the Laboratorio de Flujos Multifásicos IIUNAM.

Conflicts of Interest: The authors declare no conflict of interest.

Abbreviations

Nomenclature	
A	Area, m^2
C	Chisholm coefficient
d	Diameter, m
dP/dL	Pressure drop per unit of length, Pa/m
E	In situ phase volume fraction
f	Friction factor
Fr	Froud number
g	Gravity acceleration, m/s^2
G	Mass flux, $kgm^{-2}s^{-1}$
HL	Liquid holdup
k	Average roughness of the tube wall
$L1$	Correlation boundary
$L2$	Correlation boundary
M	Mass flow rate, kg/s
Re	Reynolds number
u	Average phase velocity, m/s
Um	Mixture velocity, m/s
Usg	Superficial velocity of gas, m/s
Usl	Superficial velocity of liquid, m/s
We	Weber number
x	Quality
Subscripts	
f	Friction
g	Gas
i	Interface
l	Liquid
m	Mixture
ns	No-slip
T	Total
TP	Two-phase

References

1. Xu, Y.; Fang, X.; Su, X.; Zhou, Z.; Chen, W. Evaluation of frictional pressure drop correlations for two-phase flow in pipes. *Nucl. Eng. Des.* **2012**, *253*, 86–97. [CrossRef]
2. Mekisso, H.M. Comparison of Frictional Pressure Drop Correlations for Isothermal Two-Phase Horizontal Flow. Master's Thesis, Bahir Dar University, Bahir Dar, Ethiopia, 2013.
3. Dukler, A.E.; Wicks, M., III; Cleveland, R.G. Frictional pressure drop in two-phase flow: A. A comparison of existing correlations for pressure loss and holdup. *AIChE J.* **1964**, *10*, 38–43. [CrossRef]
4. Idsinga, W.; Todreas, N.; Bowring, R. An assessment of two-phase pressure drop correlations for steam-water systems. *Int. J. Multiph. Flow* **1977**, *3*, 401–413. [CrossRef]
5. Ferguson, M.E.; Spedding, P.L. Measurement and prediction of pressure drop in two-phase flow. *J. Chem. Technol. Biotechnol.* **1995**, *63*, 262–278. [CrossRef]
6. Tribbe, C.; Müller-Steinhagen, H.M. An evaluation of the performance of phenomenological models for predicting pressure gradient during gas–liquid flow in horizontal pipelines. *Int. J. Multiph. Flow* **2000**, *26*, 1019–1036. [CrossRef]
7. García, F.; García, R.; Padrino, J.C.; Mata, C.; Trallero, J.L.; Joseph, D.D. Power law composite power law friction factor correlations for laminar turbulent gas-liquid flow in horizontal pipelines. *Int. J. Multiph. Flow* **2003**, *29*, 1605–1624. [CrossRef]
8. Chisholm, D. A theoretical basis for the Lockhart–Martinelli correlation for two-phase flow. *Int. J. Heat Mass Transf.* **1967**, *10*, 1767–1778. [CrossRef]
9. Müller-Steinhagen, H.; Heck, K. A simple friction pressure drop correlation for two-phase flow in pipes. *Chem. Eng. Process. Process. Intensif.* **1986**, *20*, 297–308. [CrossRef]
10. Sun, L.; Mishima, K. Evaluation analysis of prediction methods for two-phase flow pressure drop in mini-channels. *Int. J. Multiph. Flow* **2009**, *35*, 47–54. [CrossRef]
11. Awad, M.M.; Muzychka, Y.S. Effective property models for homogeneous two-phase flows. *Exp. Therm. Fluid Sci.* **2008**, *33*, 106–113. [CrossRef]
12. Beggs, D.H.; Brill, J.P.A. A study of two-phase flow in inclined pipes. *J. Pet. Technol.* **1973**, *25*, 607–617. [CrossRef]

13. Lockhart, W.R. Proposed correlation of data for isothermal two-phase, two-component flow in pipes. *Chem. Eng. Prog.* **1949**, *45*, 39–48.
14. Friedel, L. Improved friction pressure drop correlations for horizontal and vertical two-phase pipe flow. *Rohre Rohrleitungsbau Rohrleitungstransport Int.* **1979**, *18*, 485–491.
15. Holt, A.J.; Azzopardi, B.J.; Biddulph, M.W. Calculation of two-phase pressure drop for vertical upflow in narrow passages by means of a flow pattern specific model. *Chem. Eng. Res. Des.* **1999**, *77*, 7–15. [CrossRef]
16. Issa, R.I.; Kempf, M.H.W. Simulation of slug flow in horizontal and nearly horizontal pipes with the two-fluid model. *Int. J. Multiph. Flow* **2003**, *29*, 69–95. [CrossRef]
17. Hart, J.; Hamersma, P.J.; Fortuin, J.M.H. Correlations predicting frictional pressure drop and liquid holdup during horizontal gas-liquid pipe flow with a small liquid holdup. *Int. J. Multiph. Flow* **1989**, *15*, 947–964. [CrossRef]
18. Quibén, J.M.; Thome, J.R. Flow pattern based two-phase frictional pressure drop model for horizontal tubes, Part II: New phenomenological model. *Int. J. Heat Fluid Flow* **2007**, *28*, 1060–1072. [CrossRef]
19. Xu, Y.; Fang, X. A new correlation of two-phase frictional pressure drop for evaporating flow in pipes. *Int. J. Refrig.* **2012**, *35*, 2039–2050. [CrossRef]
20. Didi, M.O.; Kattan, N.; Thome, J.R. Prediction of two-phase pressure gradients of refrigerants in horizontal tubes. *Int. J. Refrig.* **2002**, *25*, 935–947. [CrossRef]
21. Hernandez-Perez, V. Gas-Liquid Two-Phase Flow in Inclined Pipes. Ph.D. Thesis, University of Nottingham, Nottingham, UK, 2007.
22. Hamad, F.A.; Faraji, F.; Santim, C.G.S.; Basha, N.; Ali, Z. Investigation of pressure drop in horizontal pipes with different diameters. *Int. J. Multiph. Flow* **2017**, *91*, 120–129. [CrossRef]
23. Mattar, L.; Gregory, G.A. Air-oil slug flow in an upward-inclined pipe-I: Slug velocity, holdup and pressure gradient. *J. Can. Pet. Technol.* **1974**, *13*, PETSOC-74-01-07. [CrossRef]
24. Badie, S.; Hale, C.P.; Lawrence, G.F.; Hewitt, G.F. Pressure gradient and holdup in horizontal two-phase gas-liquid flows with low liquid loading. *Int. J. Multiph. Flow* **2000**, *26*, 1525–1543. [CrossRef]
25. Gokcal, B.; Wang, Q.; Zhang, H.Q.; Sarica, C. Effects of high oil viscosity on oil/gas flow behavior in horizontal pipes. *SPE Proj. Facil. Constr.* **2008**, *3*, 1–11. [CrossRef]
26. Foletti, C.; Farisè, S.; Grassi, B.; Strazza, D.; Lancini, M.; Poesio, P. Experimental investigation on two-phase air/high-viscosity-oil flow in a horizontal pipe. *Chem. Eng. Sci.* **2011**, *66*, 5968–5975. [CrossRef]
27. Zhao, Y.; Yeung, H.; Zorgani, E.E.; Archibong, A.E.; Lao, L. High viscosity effects on characteristics of oil and gas two-phase flow in horizontal pipes. *Chem. Eng. Sci.* **2013**, *95*, 343–352. [CrossRef]
28. Farsetti, S.; Farisè, S.; Poesio, P. Experimental investigation of high viscosity oil–air intermittent flow. *Exp. Therm. Fluid Sci.* **2014**, *57*, 285–292. [CrossRef]
29. Abdulkadir, M.; Hernández-Pérez, V.; Lowndes, I.S.; Azzopardi, B.J.; Sam-Mbomah, E. Experimental study of the hydrodynamic behaviour of slug flow in a horizontal pipe. *Chem. Eng. Sci.* **2016**, *156*, 147–161. [CrossRef]
30. Hernandez-Perez, V.; Abdulkareem, L.A.; Azzopardi, B.J. Effects of physical properties on the behaviour of Taylor bubbles. *WIT Trans. Eng. Sci.* **2009**, *63*, 355–366.
31. Szalinski, L.; Abdulkareem, L.A.; Da Silva, M.J.; Thiele, S.; Beyer, M.; Lucas, D.; Hernandez Perez, V.; Hampel, U.; Azzopardi, B.J. Comparative study of gas–oil and gas–water two-phase flow in a vertical pipe. *Chem. Eng. Sci.* **2010**, *65*, 3836–3848. [CrossRef]
32. Loh, W.L.; Premanadhan, V.K. Experimental investigation of viscous oil-water flows in pipeline. *J. Pet. Sci. Eng.* **2016**, *147*, 87–97. [CrossRef]
33. Quibén, J.M.; Thome, J.R. Flow pattern based two-phase frictional pressure drop model for horizontal tubes. Part I: Diabatic and adiabatic experimental study. *Int. J. Heat Fluid Flow* **2007**, *28*, 1049–1059. [CrossRef]
34. Ortiz-Vidal, L.E.; Mureithi, N.; Rodriguez, O.M.H. Two-phase friction factor in gas-liquid pipe flow. *Rev. Eng. Térmica* **2014**, *13*, 81–88. [CrossRef]
35. Talley, J.D.; Worosz, T.; Kim, S. Characterization of horizontal air–water two-phase flow in a round pipe part II: Measurement of local two-phase parameters in bubbly flow. *Int. J. Multiph. Flow* **2015**, *76*, 223–236. [CrossRef]
36. Andritsos, N.; Tzotzi, C.; Hanratty, T.J. Interfacial shear stress in wavy stratified gas-liquid two-phase flow. In Proceedings of the 5th European Thermal-Sciences Conference, Eindhoven, The Netherlands, 18–22 May 2008; p. 9.
37. Andritsos, N.; Hanratty, T.J. Influence of interfacial waves on hold-up and frictional pressure drop in stratified gas-liquid flows. *AIChE J.* **1987**, *33*, 444–454. [CrossRef]
38. Johnson, G.W.; Bertelsen, A.F.; Nossen, J. An experimental investigation of roll waves in high pressure two-phase inclined pipe flows. *Int. J. Multiph. Flow* **2009**, *35*, 924–932. [CrossRef]
39. Cohen, L.S.; Hanratty, T.J. Generation of waves in the concurrent flow of air and a liquid. *AIChE J.* **1965**, *11*, 138–144. [CrossRef]
40. Ullmann, A.; Brauner, N. Closure relations for two-fluid models for two-phase stratified smooth and stratified wavy flows. *Int. J. Multiph. Flow* **2006**, *32*, 82–105. [CrossRef]
41. Hewitt, G.F. Three-phase gas–liquid–liquid flows in the steady and transient states. *Nucl. Eng. Des.* **2005**, **235**, 1303–1316. [CrossRef]
42. Spedding, P.L.; Murphy, A.; Donnelly, G.F.; Benard, E.; Doherty, A.P. Pressure drop in three-phase oil–water–gas horizontal co-current flow: Experimental data and development of prediction models. *Asia-Pac. J. Chem. Eng.* **2008**, *3*, 531–543. [CrossRef]

43. Al-Hadhrami, L.M.; Shaahid, S.M.; Tunde, L.O.; Al-Sarkhi, A. Experimental study on the flow regimes and pressure gradients of air-oil-water three-phase flow in horizontal pipes. *Sci. World J.* **2014**, *2014*, 810527. [CrossRef]
44. Shannak, B.A. Frictional pressure drop of gas liquid two-phase flow in pipes. *Nucl. Eng. Des.* **2008**, *238*, 3277–3284. [CrossRef]
45. Beattie, D.R.H.; Whalley, P.B. Simple two-phase frictional pressure drop calculation method. *Int. J. Multiph. Flow* **1982**, *8*, 83–87. [CrossRef]

fluids

MDPI

Article

CFD Turbulence Models Assessment for the Cavitation Phenomenon in a Rectangular Profile Venturi Tube

Mauricio De la Cruz-Ávila [1,2,*], Jorge E. De León-Ruiz [3], Ignacio Carvajal-Mariscal [4] and Jaime Klapp [1,*]

1 Instituto Nacional de Investigaciones Nucleares, ININ, Carretera México Toluca-La Marquesa s/n, Ocoyoacac 52750, Mexico
2 Centro de Investigación y de Estudios Avanzados, CINVESTAV, Instituto Politécnico Nacional 2508, San Pedro Zacatenco, Mexico City 07360, Mexico
3 Centro de Investigación en Materiales Avanzados, S.C., CIMAV, Complejo Industrial Chihuahua, Miguel de Cervantes 120, Chihuahua 31136, Mexico; jedeleonr@gmail.com
4 Instituto Politécnico Nacional, ESIME—UPALM, Mexico City 07738, Mexico; icarvajal@ipn.mx
* Correspondence: mauriciodlca1@gmail.com (M.D.l.C.-Á.); jaime.klapp@inin.gob.mx (J.K.)

Abstract: This study investigates cavitation in a rectangular-profile Venturi tube using numerical simulations and four turbulence models. The unsteady Reynolds-averaged Navier–Stokes technique is employed to simulate vapor cloud formation and compared against experimental data. κ-ε realizable, κ-ε RNG, κ-ω SST, and κ-ω GEKO models are evaluated. The simulation results are analyzed for pressure, turbulence, and vapor cloud formation. Discrepancies in cavitation cloud formation among turbulence models are attributed to turbulence and vapor cloud interactions. RNG and SST models exhibit closer alignment with the experimental data, with RNG showing a superior performance. Key findings include significant vapor cloud shape differences across turbulence models. The RNG model best predicts velocity at the throat exit with an error of 4.145%. Static pressure predictions include an error of 4.47%. The vapor cloud length predictions show variation among models, with the RNG model having a 0.386% error for the minimum length and 4.9845% for the maximum length. The SST model exhibits 4.907% and 13.33% errors for minimum and maximum lengths, respectively. Analysis of the cavitation number reveals agreement with the experimental data and sensitivity to cavitation onset. Different turbulence models yield diverse cloud shapes and detachment points. Weber number contours illustrate the variation in the cavitation cloud behavior under different turbulence models.

Keywords: turbulence model κ-ε RNG; κ-ε realizable; κ-ω SST; κ-ω GEKO; cavitation; Venturi tube; vapor cloud

1. Introduction

The formation of vapor bubbles in a liquid due to a pressure drop is known as the cavitation phenomenon. This is a hydrodynamic phenomenon that occurs when the fluid pressure decreases enough to create vapor bubbles. These bubbles can rapidly collapse and create shock waves that damage the surrounding surfaces. It is a common problem in industrial and engineering applications, and can cause a loss of efficiency, increased noise, and equipment damage.

Many hydrodynamic applications, hydraulic systems, and turbo-machinery exhibit this behavior. They are classified as external or internal flow, as well as total or partial cavitation. For internal flow, such as hydro turbines [1], diesel injectors [2,3], or sudden contraction pipes [4], partial cavitation [5,6] is connected with a periodic shedding of significant vapor clouds [7], which causes erosion [8]. The most commonly observed form is partial cavitation, which occurs when the cavity closes on the surfaces of a flow obstruction. It eventually causes structural damage and affects the surface performance of the equipment. Such implications have motivated the analysis of different forms of cavitation, and great efforts have been made to understand the dynamics of partial cavitation in particular. These cavitation pockets are characterized by an oscillating closure zone [9], which causes cavity length oscillations [10,11] and vapor structure shedding [12]. Depending on the flow in the cavity closure zone, the partial cavity [13] can take one of two forms: a closed or quasi-stable cavity and an open cavity or cloud cavitation. With a relatively steady cavity length, a quasi-stable cavity exhibits only minor shedding near its closure zone. A cavitation cloud, on the other hand, is a very unstable event with a periodically fluctuating length linked with massive vapor cloud shedding [14]. This variety of cavities has been examined experimentally [15–18] and computationally [7,19,20] in order to understand the physical process, internal cavity structure, and turbulence–cavitation interaction, as well as to study the transition from quasi-stable to a cavitation cloud.

Numerical simulations based on the Navier–Stokes framework are widely used to predict cavitation. These simulations model the fluid dynamics and incorporate turbulence models to predict the formation and collapse of cavitation bubbles. Turbulence models, based on the Reynolds-averaged Navier–Stokes (RANS) technique, are particularly common for predicting cavitation. The accuracy and efficiency of these simulations depend significantly on the selection of a suitable turbulence model. The RANS models are widely accepted and computationally efficient for simulating industrial flows. They solve for time-averaged flow variables and rely on a turbulence closure model to account for turbulence fluctuations. The proper selection of turbulence models is crucial for accurate prediction of flow field, pressure distribution, and cavitation behavior.

Various RANS turbulence models have been employed to simulate the cavitation phenomenon, each with its own advantages and limitations. The most prominent models include the standard $k-\varepsilon$ [21,22], the $k-\varepsilon$ realizable [23,24], the $k-\varepsilon$ renormalization group (RNG) [25], the $k-\omega$ shear stress transport (SST) [26,27], and the $k-\omega$ generalized (GEKO) [28]. The standard $k-\varepsilon$ model is the simplest and most widely used turbulence model, but it has limitations in capturing complex flow features, such as separation, recirculation, and swirling flow. The $k-\varepsilon$ realizable improves upon the $k-\varepsilon$ standard model by accounting for the effects of streamline curvature and pressure-strain, but it is still limited in complex flow cases. The $k-\varepsilon$ RNG further improves upon the realizable by incorporating an extra term for anisotropy and enhancing the turbulence transport. The $k-\omega$ model is another commonly used turbulence model, which has a better prediction capability in near-wall regions and complex flows. The $k-\omega$ SST combines the benefits of the $k-\omega$ and $k-\varepsilon$ models and has been widely used in simulating turbulent flows with separation and recirculation. The $k-\omega$ GEKO is a relatively new turbulence model, which has shown promising results in simulating high-speed flows and cavitation. The RNG model is useful for predicting cavitation, which uses renormalization theory to account for turbulence effects at different scales. This model has the ability to predict both the formation and collapse of cavitation bubbles and can also predict the transition from a turbulent boundary layer to a laminar boundary layer, which is important for predicting bubble formation in the cavitation region. However, it has been observed that the RNG model may have lower accuracy in predicting flows with separation and recirculation.

On the other hand, the RLZ model uses a transport equation for turbulent stress that takes into account physical constraints and can accurately predict the boundary layer separation. However, the model may underestimate turbulence production and does not account for the presence of cavitation bubbles in the simulation.

The SST model uses two different equations for the turbulent kinematic viscosity in the boundary layer and in the core of the flow, allowing for accurate prediction of the transition from a laminar to a turbulent boundary layer. Additionally, the SST model is capable of predicting boundary layer separation and can be used in a wide range of applications. However, the model may be less accurate in predicting highly turbulent flows and may underestimate turbulence production.

Finally, the GEKO model uses a transport equation for kinematic turbulence and a transport equation for turbulent stress, allowing a better representation of boundary layer turbulence. Additionally, this model has an adjustment parameter that allows a more precise adaptation of the wall slope, making it more suitable for solving problems that require a high degree of detail in the boundary layer. However, a significant disadvantage is its complexity. Due to the inclusion of an additional transport equation for turbulent stress, the GEKO model requires more computational resources than the other turbulence models. Additionally, the choice of the adjustment parameter can be complicated and may require careful calibration to obtain accurate results. Therefore, the GEKO model may not be the best choice in situations where fast simulation is required or where limited computational resources are available.

Coutier-Delgosha et al. [29] carried out a study on the unsteady effects associated with cavitation by conducting 2D numerical simulations in three different cavitating systems. Various turbulence models were compared, and it was found that both the $k-\varepsilon$ RNG and $k-\omega$ turbulence models, with corrections for compressibility effects, were consistent with the available experimental data. The ability of the proposed physical cavitation model, associated with either of these two turbulence models, to predict the unsteady behavior of cavitation sheets was confirmed through two complementary test cases. However, their findings were limited by the fact that the simulations were in 2D, due to the high computational demand of calculation.

The performance of the $k-\omega$ SST and $k-\varepsilon$ turbulence models in simulating cavitation in a Venturi tube was evaluated by Chebli et al. [30]. The authors found that the $k-\omega$ SST model produced more accurate results than the $k-\varepsilon$ model, particularly in predicting the location of cavitation inception. They noted that the $k-\omega$ SST model was better suited for simulating the cavitation phenomenon in a Venturi tube due to its ability to model the effects of turbulence on the formation of the sheet cavity. Subsequently, Chebli et al. [31] compared the performance of different turbulence models, such as the $k-\varepsilon$ RNG and $k-\omega$ SST models, for predicting cavitating flows in hydrofoils. The results showed that both the $k-\omega$ SST and $k-\varepsilon$ RNG models provided good agreement with the experimental data. Additionally, an adapted modification of the turbulent viscosity produced even better cavity results. The study concluded that the $k-\omega$ SST model is the most suitable turbulence model for simulating cavitating flows in hydrofoils.

In a recent study [32], the performance of the $k-\omega$ SST, $k-\ell$, and Spalart–Allmaras [33] turbulence models was compared in simulating cavitation in a Venturi tube. The authors found that a four-equation adaption for any model produced the most accurate results when compared to experimental data. They noted that the Spalart–Allmaras model was not suitable for simulating cavitation in a Venturi tube due to its inability to accurately model turbulence. In fact, the results are not quite precise to represent a 3D model due to this formulation being developed for 2D simulation models.

Fadaei-Roodi and Pasandidehfard [34] conducted a numerical study on the cavitating flow around cylindrical projectiles with flat or hemispherical heads. Four turbulence models were used in combination with the Zwart cavitation model: $k-\varepsilon$ realizable, $k-\omega$ standard, $k-\omega$ SST, and GEKO. The aim was to predict the cavity dimensions, pressure distribution, and flow dynamics inside and around the cavity, specifically at the closing point. They concluded that the GEKO turbulence model outperforms other turbulence models, $k-\omega$ SST, $k-\omega$ standard, and $k-\varepsilon$ realizable, for predicting the cavitating flows around cylinders of flat and round heads. The study shows that the GEKO model predicts the results much better, especially for higher cavitation number values, and is considered the most suitable turbulence model for numerical simulation.

He and Bai's research [35] focused on the study of wet gas measurement using a circular profile Venturi meter, in which five turbulence models were analyzed, finding that the standard $k-\varepsilon$ model was the most accurate. As an additional recommendation, it is suggested to extend the length of the throat and decrease the convergent angle in the design of the Venturi tube to reduce adverse effects on the overmeasurement of wet gas. This note highlights the importance of selecting the correct turbulence model, as well as a compatible geometry for the cavitation zone.

The studies conducted have shown that the $k-\varepsilon$ RNG model is a reliable and accurate turbulence model for simulating partial cavitation in Venturi tubes and nozzles. Specifically, the $k-\varepsilon$ RNG model is better at predicting cavity size, location, and shape than the $k-\varepsilon$ standard and $k-\omega$ SST models. Additionally, the discussed studies suggest that the $k-\omega$ SST turbulence model is also accurate and suitable for simulating cavitation in a Venturi tube. However, the $k-\varepsilon$ RNG model is computationally more efficient and may be a good alternative for engineers. Nonetheless, the choice of turbulence model depends on the specific flow conditions and geometry being simulated, and it may be necessary to test multiple models to determine the most appropriate one for a given application.

Unfortunately, no conclusive study exists due to the scarcity of articles that specifically compare these four turbulence models. Moreover, existing studies are predominantly focused on analyzing airfoils or circular-profile Venturi tubes. Currently, very few investigations examine rectangular-profile Venturi tubes. In fact, the existing studies are conflicting regarding which turbulence model is most suitable or considered superior for various characteristics, including the oscillation frequency of the vapor cloud or bubble, incipient cavitation, or the interaction of vortices with the cavitation bubble.

This presents a significant challenge in selecting the appropriate turbulence model for more accurately modeling specific characteristics. Furthermore, achieving a unification of features that can be best represented by a single suitable turbulence model poses challenges. Compounded by the lack of studies on coupled models, incorporating factors such as compressibility coupled with interfacial tracking of the vapor cloud, vortex–vapor cloud interactions, and the adjustment of viscosity within these coupled phenomena, a more refined calculation methodology is attainable through the enhancement of turbulent viscosity limiting functions and the subsequent correction of mathematical formulations.

It is imperative to establish a systematic framework in order to effectively employ these numerical techniques, particularly when applied to rectangular-profile Venturi tubes. This approach mitigates the risk of utilizing an ill-suited model, thereby promoting a more reliable representation of complex flow phenomena.

Aim and Scope

The main objective of this research is to carry out a detailed comparison of different turbulence models for the numerical simulation of cavitation in a rectangular profile Venturi tube using the RANS framework. These simulations were carried out to generate a cavitation zone, and the results obtained were compared with the experimental data obtained previously. In particular, to assess the accuracy of the four most widely used turbulence models: the $k-\varepsilon$ RNG, the $k-\varepsilon$ realizable, the $k-\omega$ SST, and the most recent $k-\omega$ GEKO, the shape and size of the cavitation zone, vapor pressure, velocity distribution, and other relevant parameters were analyzed and compared.

The scope of this research includes numerical simulations using the aforementioned turbulence models to predict partial cavitation and the produced steam cloud. It is expected that the results of this investigation provide a basis for future studies that can extend the comparison to other turbulence models. This research contributes to the current knowledge of turbulence models for the numerical simulation of cavitation in rectangular-profile Venturi tubes using the URANS technique. Moreover, this study emphasizes the limitations of turbulence models in capturing the complex cavitation phenomenon within these configurations. By elucidating the challenges faced when using turbulence models to depict cavitation in such setups, this investigation provides a platform for future research aimed at refining mathematical formulations. This systematic approach holds the potential to greatly improve the accuracy of numerical simulations, bringing computational results into closer alignment with real-world observations. The information provided for the selection of the most adequate turbulence model to simulate cavitation in this type of pipe can contribute to improving the design and performance of hydraulic equipment and systems. The findings of this research might be useful regarding the design and optimization of industrial systems that involve the phenomenon of cavitation. In addition, this study can lay the foundation for future research focused on the design and optimization of Venturi tubes for industrial and engineering applications.

2. Experimental Setup

Figure 1 displays the complete scheme of the experimental setup employed. This experimental rig was constructed to identify possible pipe failures caused by thermal and/or mechanical stress, as well as pipe plausible surface damage such as fractures and/or erosion caused by corrosive fluids.

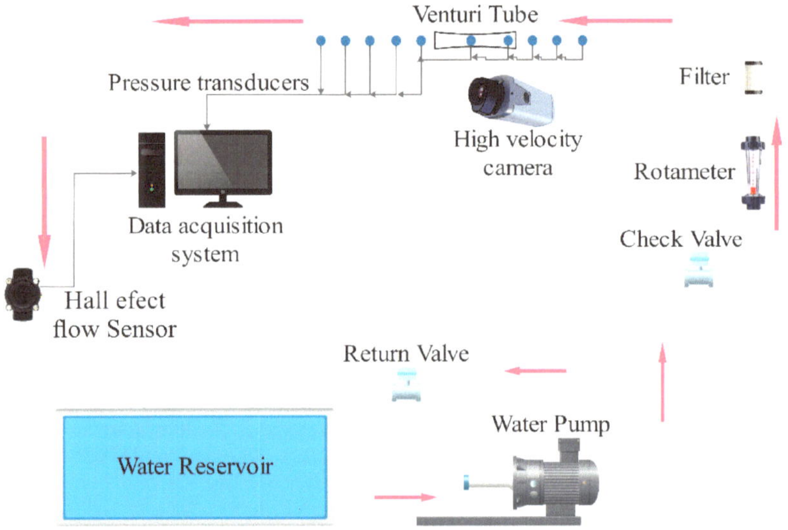

Figure 1. Complete experimental rig setup scheme, the red arrow is the flow direction.

For the experimental setup, water, selected as the working fluid, was contained in a 62 L storage tank. To facilitate fluid transportation, a centrifugal water pump with a maximum volumetric displacement of 60 L/min and a power rating of 1.5 HP was employed. The water flow was accurately measured using two different flowmeters. At the inlet flange, a Dwyer polysulfone flowmeter MOD UV-5112, with an accuracy of ±2% F.S., was fitted before a filter, and a YF-DN50 hall effect flowmeter, with an accuracy of ±3% F.S., was installed at the outlet flange, positioned after the Venturi tube as seen in Figure 1. To regulate the flow within the devised hydraulic loop, a pressure-regulation diaphragm valve was fitted at the pump discharge, leading to the storage tank. This recirculation internal loop, controlled by a posterior globe valve, serves the purpose of relieving pump pressure; preventing cavitation of the diaphragm valve when it is nearly closed. Finally, an array of pressure transducers, specifically the Setra Model 522 with a ±0.25% F.S. accuracy, was fitted over the Venturi tube. The data obtained from this measurement were utilized to numerically replicate the Venturi flow characteristics. The complete rundown of the experimental equipment and its configuration are described in detail in [36,37]. The obtained data were utilized to numerically replicate the Venturi flow characteristics. For these numerical simulations, the geometry or computational domain was specifically discretized for a rectangular-section Venturi tube. The system is focused on the Venturi throat zone to take advantage of computer resources for fluid development progression.

The assessment of uncertainty was conducted following the methodology established in the guide to the expression of uncertainty in measurement (GUM) [38], utilizing the Type A uncertainty approach. This process involved a statistical analysis using the Kolmogorov–Smirnov test to verify the normality of the distribution. As an additional note of the experimentation, the standard uncertainty was determined to be 0.911, with a coverage factor of 2 to maintain a 95% confidence interval. This resulted in an expanded uncertainty of 1.82, equivalent to a relative uncertainty of 12.64% with respect to the pressure variable. This value was derived from performing 14 tests per treatment. It is important to highlight that of the total treatments carried out, only a single set of values in this study is reported for volumetric flow and constant temperature in relation to a specific pressure value.

3. Numerical Setup

3.1. Case Study

A Venturi tube with a rectangular profile was selected for the construction of the numerical domain. The inlet large side of the rectangle profile, L_{in}, is 25 mm and the short one, l_{in}, is 6.35 mm with a total Venturi tube length, L, of 350 mm. The convergent zone (throat) measures $6 \times 6 \times 6.35$ mm per side, respectively. The Venturi tube includes a convergent inlet of 30° and a divergent outlet of 10° measured from the upper to the bottom wall of the rectangle profile. Additionally, the flow direction is as illustrated in Figure 2. The corresponding equivalent hydraulic diameters are: inlet diameter, $D_{eq} = 10.1276$ mm, and throat diameter, $d_{thro} = 6.17$ mm.

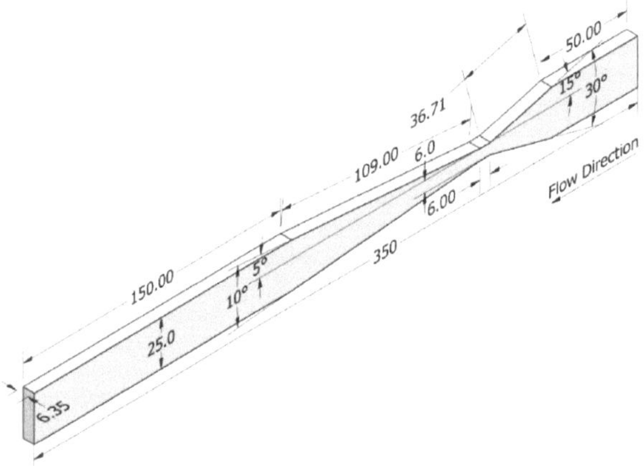

Figure 2. Scheme of the square Venturi tube virtual domain with dimensions in [mm]. Isometric left view.

In this study, the volumetric flow of the continuous phase was 32 L/min $= 5.33 \times 10^{-4} \left[m^3/s\right] = 0.548$ [kg/s], as well as a maximum inlet velocity of 3.46 [m/s]. The virtual fluids are water as the primary or transport phase and water vapor as the disperse phase. The thermodynamic properties are listed in Table 1. All numerical simulations were performed under the reference conditions as referred to in [37] of 298.15 K of constant temperature, 101,325 [Pa] of pressure. The saturation pressure $P_{sat} = 3178.75$ [Pa], water inlet static pressure $P_{I-Stc} = 48,336$ [Pa], water inlet total pressure $P_{tot} = 54,336.5$ [Pa], and water outlet static pressure $P_{O-Stc} = 13454.72$ [Pa] were used as the boundary conditions. ANSYS Fluent CFD commercial software [39] in a Xeon 32 cores workstation and two high-performance GPUs, a Nvidia Quadro 6000, and a Tesla C2075 to accelerate calculation were used as an ensemble to run the two-phase water-vapor 3D cavitation simulations.

Table 1. Thermodynamic fluids properties.

Phase	Temperature T [K]	Density ρ $\left[kg/m^3\right]$	Dynamic Viscosity μ [Pa·s]	Surface Tension σ [N/m]
Water liquid	298.15	998.048	8.91×10^{-4}	0.0725
Water vapor		0.023	9.87×10^{-6}	

3.2. Numerical Domain Details

The computational domain grid was generated by combining advancing-front meshing [40] and the cut-cell methodology [41]. The advancing-front method has numerous benefits on regular grids, such as the ability to adjust the mesh density and assist tessellation in geometrically complex domains. Whenever these two approaches are implemented, a consistent rise of thin layers and cells from the tube walls to the domain's center is created, resulting in an accurate simulation of the physical cavitation phenomena, especially when high-order discretization schemes are used.

As boundary conditions in the simulations, adiabatic and non-slip enhanced near wall functions treatment [42] were used to minimize any miscalculation. A generalized $Y^+ \approx 1.5$ was selected for the initial cell length because a desirable range is below 5 where an optimum value is in the range from 1 to 2 [43]. Moreover, this value is important in these sorts of simulations, which are heavily influenced by flow viscosity, to improve the created meshes. This Y^+ was also considered before the development of the cavitation cloud, where water is the transport liquid phase. To finish 10 thin layers, the first grid length on the walls is 0.000015 [m] with a 15% increase. Given that the differential pressure is gauged via pressure taps located along the Venturi tube's wall, the accurate representation of the near-wall region in numerical simulations holds relevant significance. The inflation technique has been employed to generate the near-wall mesh. Calculations of the first layer thickness for the inflation configuration have been conducted for each test case, aligned with Y^+ set at 1.5, chosen as the optimal thickness for the selected test cases. This meticulous selection ensures a finer resolution of the near-wall dynamics, crucial for precise numerical representation.

For the water supply, a mass flow input condition was used along with a gauge pressure gradient to ensure the correct inlet pressure. The far-outflow boundary occurs at an atmospheric pressure of 101,325 [Pa] and a temperature of 293 K. Figure 3 shows a right view of the numerical domain to facilitate the appreciation of the upper wall cells of the calculation domain. On the other hand, it provides a close-up view to appreciate the growth of the mesh layers in the throat area.

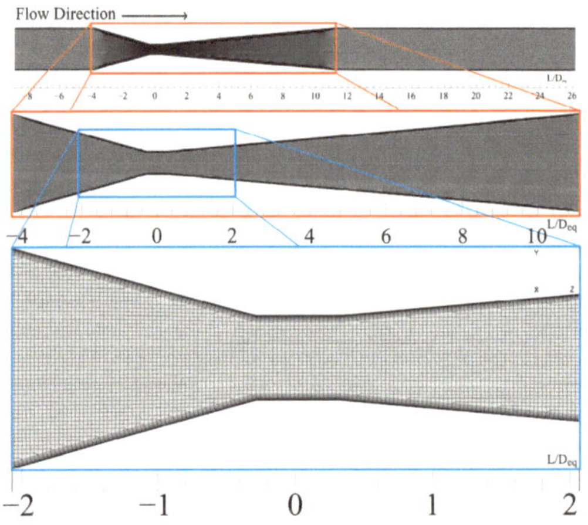

Figure 3. Structured cut−cell hexahedral mesh for the 3D Venturi tube numerical domain over the convergent zone in the YZ lateral plane view.

It is worth mentioning that the mesh within the domain is homogeneous because in the initial and boundary conditions it is necessary to add a small−scale symbolic numerical diffusion so that the turbulence, cavitation, and interface tracking models are better coupled. This means that another type of mesh is not considered as in those cases where the refinement is only located in the area of the convergent−divergent zone. Such a mesh would result in an extremely high numerical diffusion from the start, thus making the approximations and results inaccurate and ultimately increasing the total computation time.

3.3. Wall Function

In general, the ideal value of Y^+ depends on several factors, such as flow velocity, wall surface roughness, and mesh resolution. For cavitation simulations, it is generally recommended that the value of Y^+ be less than 5 to ensure adequate boundary layer resolution and avoid inaccurate estimation of the velocity gradient at the wall. However, the optimal value of Y^+ can vary depending on the turbulence model used and the flow regime in use [43]. Therefore, a careful and detailed evaluation of the specific simulation conditions must be performed to determine the appropriate Y^+ value for cavitation simulations in a particular micro rectangular profile Venturi tube throat.

The wall shear stress, τ_w, is determined by iterating on the product of Y^+ and U^+ obtained from the analytical velocity profile. A two-layer wall law is utilized at the wall as:

$$\begin{array}{ll} U^+ = Y^+ & if\, Y^+ < 11.13, \\ U^+ = \frac{1}{\kappa} ln Y^+ + 5.25 & if\, Y^+ > 11.13, \\ U^+ = \frac{u}{U_\tau};\ Y^+ = \frac{yU_\tau}{\nu_w}; & U_\tau = \sqrt{\frac{\tau_w}{\rho_w}}, \end{array} \quad (1)$$

in particular, the von Karman constant $\kappa = 0.41$, while the subscript w denotes wall values. It is assumed that the wall functions hold similarity in both single-phase and two-phase flows. The validity of this assumption was presented by Durbin et al. [44] and in the context of Venturi cavitation flows by Charrière et al. [32]. In the case of non-stationary boundary layers, a wall law is considered to hold at each instant. The efficacy of this approach was verified through comparisons with the thin boundary layer equations, which demonstrated its strong performance.

3.4. Numerical Discretization

There are a number of schemes for pressure and momentum discretization, each with its own advantages and disadvantages. The simulation studies were discretized in the following order.

The PISO stands for the pressure-implicit with splitting-operations [45] pressure–velocity coupling technique, which is part of the SIMPLE segregated algorithm family, and is based on a higher degree of approximation between the pressure and velocity correction. One of the constraints is that after solving the pressure correction equation, the new velocities and related fluxes do not fulfil the momentum balance. As a result, the computation must be repeated until the balance is achieved. This method applies two extra adjustments to increase the efficiency of the calculation: neighbor [45] and skewness correction [46]. For this case study, the liquid phase velocity is higher than the generated vapor phase, and even though it can handle this disparity, convergence usually takes much more time. This leaves, as an option, the use of the next high-accuracy scheme with a substantial improvement in the saving of calculation time.

The PRESTO! (pressure-staggering option [47]) scheme uses the discrete continuity balance for a "staggered" control volume about the face to compute the "staggered" pressure. This procedure is similar in spirit to the staggered-grid schemes used with structured meshes. Therefore, this scheme is more suitable for the convergent–divergent computational domain that represents the Venturi tube with a structured mesh.

Leonard's third-order quadratic upstream interpolation for convective kinematics (QUICK) [48] uses a quadratic fit through two upwind nodes and one downwind cell center. To find the exact location of the next upwind cell nodes increases the geometrical complexity and consumes relatively more memory and CPU time. If the notion of the truncation error is based on approximating the spatial derivative at cell centers in the linear convection equation, then this approach is second-order correct. The QUICK method becomes third-order accurate in accordance with other truncation error definitions made by other scholars [49,50]. Consequently, this variation in the precision of the scheme suppresses the valorization for use in the cavitation phenomena. For this reason, for the momentum solution, the third-order MUSCL (monotonic upstream-centered scheme for conservation laws [51]) was utilized, and for volume fraction reconstruction, the modified HRIC (high-resolution interface capturing [52,53]) was applied. This resulted in the development of a fully linked methodology for the pressure–velocity solution technique.

The findings show that the high-order MUSCL scheme substantially reduces numerical diffusion when compared to first-order techniques, achieving higher two-phase flow resolution. Additionally, the PRESTO! and HRIC with the pressure–velocity fully coupled working array demonstrate superior convergence when compared to alternative solutions.

Furthermore, a flexible step size was employed in this type of two-phase analysis for the numerical simulations to ensure that the time-step was appropriate for the fluid flow development. The time interval should be short enough to solve time-dependent features and provide convergence within the given timeframe. The time step is calculated using the following equation:

$$\Delta \mathrm{t} = \frac{\text{Typical Cell Size}}{\text{Characteristic Flow Velocity}}, \tag{2}$$

and the simulations take into account values in the order of $4 \times 10^{-6} < \Delta t < 6 \times 10^{-6}$.

3.5. *Vapor Cloud Tracking*

Because of the hydrodynamics of the water/vapor-cloud flow considered in this work, the volume of fluid (VoF, or surface-tracking approach) [54] is the best performance model for monitoring the surface of the two-phase fluids.

There are a few things to keep in mind before using the VoF model to ensure a good numerical description. That is, the sum of the volume fractions of all phases in each control volume must be one. The phases share all variable and attribute fields, which represent volume-averaged values as long as the volume fraction of either phase is identified per region. As a natural outcome, depending on the volume fraction values, the variables and features in any given cell are either solely reflective of one of the qth-phases, or indicative of the phases' conjunction.

$$\alpha_q = \begin{Bmatrix} 0 \rightarrow Cell\ is\ empty\ of\ the\ q^{th}\ fluid \\ 1 \rightarrow Cell\ is\ full\ of\ the\ q^{th}\ fluid \end{Bmatrix} \tag{3}$$

$$0 < \alpha_q < 1 \rightarrow The\ cell\ contains\ the\ interface. \tag{4}$$

Based on the local value of the phase α_q, the appropriate properties and variables will be assigned to each control volume within the domain. In this study, the primary phase is water, α_w.

3.6. *Interfacial and Surface Tension Treatment*

The VoF technique provides a piecewise-linear method to build the interface between the fluids. Within each cell, the interface between two fluids is assumed to have a linear slope. This linear form is used by the system to compute the fluid advection via the cell faces. The volume fraction and derivative values in each cell are used in the initial stage of interface reconstruction to determine the location of the linear interface with respect to the center of each partially filled cell. The fluid advection across each face is then recalculated using the resulting linear interface approximation and data about the face's both normal and tangential velocity profiles. Finally, the volume flux in each cell is calculated using the previous stage's flux balance.

Furthermore, the VoF approach considers interfacial tension at the phase contact. The model defines the contact angle between the phases and the wall, and the surface tension coefficient is assumed to be constant. To do this, the surface tension model use the continuous surface force model [55]. When surface tension is employed in the VoF computation, a source term, F, appears in the momentum equation, and the pressure drop over the surface may be estimated using the surface tension coefficient, σ. Then, the curvature of the surface can be estimated using the Young–Laplace equation and two radii in orthogonal directions, $R1$ and $R2$, can be defined as $P_2 - P_1 = \sigma(1/R_1 + 1/R_2)$. As a result, the pressure drop across the surface may be used to describe the surface tension. The source term for the two phases is going to be used in Equation (8) and written as:

$$F = \sigma\kappa \frac{\rho \nabla \alpha_g}{\frac{1}{2}(\rho_g - \rho_w)} . \tag{5}$$

The interface curvature κ is defined in terms of the divergence of the unit normal, $\hat{\mathbf{n}}$, as: $\kappa = \nabla \cdot \hat{\mathbf{n}}$, where $\hat{\mathbf{n}} = \mathbf{n}/|n|$. Here, the surface normal is $\mathbf{n} = \nabla \alpha_g$. The surface curvature is calculated based on the local gradient of the vector normal to the interface, defined as the gradient of the volume fraction of oil α_g. When using the implicit VoF formulation, which is the case, numerical diffusion caused by turbulent effects must be added. This added diffusion increases the solution stability and has desirable interpenetrating effects on the phases' virtual interface.

3.7. Cavitation Number

The cavitation number also known as the Thoma number, σ, serves as a dimensionless parameter of critical significance for characterizing flow regimes conducive or inhibitory to cavitation. It facilitates the distinction between conditions that lead to cavitation inception and those that suppress it. The cavitation number ς within a Venturi tube can be calculated employing the subsequent equation:

$$\varsigma = \frac{P_{abs} - P_v}{\left(\frac{1}{2}\rho u^2\right)} . \tag{6}$$

Here, P_{abs} represents the absolute pressure within the venturi throat which is calculated through numerical simulations, P_v signifies the absolute vapor pressure of water. It is crucial to note that P_v equals the saturation pressure P_{sat} of the liquid at the operational temperature. Additionally, u corresponds to the water velocity magnitude at the venturi throat, and ρ stands for the density of the liquid phase. Essentially, the cavitation number quantifies the interrelation between the pressure difference across the liquid in the Venturi throat and its saturation pressure, relative to the fluid's kinetic energy at the Venturi throat.

Throughout all conducted investigations presented in the state-of-the-art introduction section, the cavitation number's significance has been rigorously acknowledged. It has been consistently confirmed that when ($\varsigma > 1$), cavitation remains absent within the Venturi tube. Conversely, when ($\varsigma < 1$), the presence of cavitation phenomena is highly probable. This understanding holds paramount importance in predicting and managing cavitation in such hydrodynamic configurations.

3.8. Governing Equations

The solution of the continuity equation for the phase volume fraction allows the tracking of the interface between the phases and is given by:

$$\frac{\partial \rho}{\partial t} + \nabla \cdot \rho \vec{v} = \sum_n S_n , \tag{7}$$

where ρ is the density, $\vec{v}$ the velocity vector, t time, and $S = 0$ due to the no-mass-transfer assumption at the initial time. For the interfacial tracking, vapor gas as the secondary phase, α_g, is achieved by finding the solution of the Equation (6) for α_g; thus,

$$\frac{\partial(\rho_g \alpha_g)}{\partial t} + \nabla \cdot \rho_g \alpha_g \vec{v} = 0 . \tag{8}$$

Therefore, from the aforementioned considerations, the volume fraction of α_w is computed from the relation $\alpha_w + \alpha_g = 1$.

Because the resultant velocity field is shared by all phases, just one momentum equation is solved for the whole computational domain, which is determined by the volume fractions of all phases through ρ and μ,

$$\frac{\partial}{\partial t}\left(\rho\vec{v}\right) + \nabla\cdot\left(\rho\vec{v}\vec{v}\right) = -\nabla p + \nabla\cdot\left[\mu\left(\nabla\vec{v} + \nabla\vec{v}^{T}\right)\right] + \rho g + F, \quad (9)$$

where, ρ, $\vec{v}$, p, μ, g, and F are the density, velocity, pressure in the flow field, viscosity, acceleration due to gravity, and the body force, respectively. On the other hand, p and μ are estimated by using $\rho = \sum_1^p \rho_q\alpha_q$ and $\mu = \sum_1^p \mu_q\alpha_q$.

3.9. Turbulence Models

In this work, four turbulence models were compared to achieve better results of the cavitation phenomenon modelling. These include the $k-\varepsilon$ RNG [25], the $k-\varepsilon$ RLZ [23], the $k-\omega$ SST [27], and the modified $k-\omega$ GEKO [28]. All of them are based on the RANS framework and extended to the URANS technique.

3.9.1. k − ε RNG Turbulence Model

The RNG has shown substantial improvements where the flow features include strong streamline curvature, vortices, and rotation. The model is formulated by;

$$\frac{\partial}{\partial t}(\rho\kappa) + \frac{\partial}{\partial x_i}(\rho\kappa u_i) = \frac{\partial}{\partial x_j}\left[\alpha_\kappa\mu_{eff}\frac{\partial\kappa}{\partial x_j}\right] + G_\kappa + G_b - \rho\varepsilon - Y_M + S_\kappa, \quad (10)$$

$$\frac{\partial}{\partial t}(\rho\varepsilon) + \frac{\partial}{\partial x_i}(\rho\varepsilon u_i) = \frac{\partial}{\partial x_j}\left[\alpha_\varepsilon\mu_{eff}\frac{\partial\varepsilon}{\partial x_j}\right] + C_{1\varepsilon}\frac{\varepsilon}{\kappa}(G_\kappa + C_{3\varepsilon}G_b) - C_{2\varepsilon}\rho\frac{\varepsilon^2}{\kappa} - R_\varepsilon + S_\varepsilon, \quad (11)$$

where $C_{1\varepsilon} = 1.42$, $C_{2\varepsilon} = 1.68$, and $C_\mu = 0.0845$ and these values are derived analytically by the RNG theory. G_κ is computed from Equation (14) and μ_{eff} is similar to Equation (15). The quantities α_κ and α_ε are the inverse effective Prandtl numbers for κ and ε, respectively.

3.9.2. k − ε RLZ Turbulence Model

The $k-\varepsilon$ RLZ differs in two important ways. That is, it contains an alternative formulation for the turbulent viscosity, and a modified transport equation for the dissipation rate is derived from an exact equation for the transport of the mean-square vorticity fluctuation. The formulation is:

$$\frac{\partial}{\partial t}(\rho\kappa) + \frac{\partial}{\partial x_j}(\rho\kappa u_i) = \frac{\partial}{\partial x_j}\left[\left(\mu + \frac{\mu_t}{\sigma_k}\right)\frac{\partial\kappa}{\partial x_j}\right] + G_\kappa + G_b - \rho\varepsilon - Y_M + S_\kappa, \quad (12)$$

$$\frac{\partial}{\partial t}(\rho\varepsilon) + \frac{\partial}{\partial x_j}(\rho\varepsilon u_j) = \frac{\partial}{\partial x_j}\left[\left(\mu + \frac{\mu_t}{\sigma_\varepsilon}\right)\frac{\partial\varepsilon}{\partial x_j}\right] + \rho C_1 S\varepsilon - \rho C_2\frac{\varepsilon^2}{\kappa + \sqrt{\nu\varepsilon}} + C_{1\varepsilon}\frac{\varepsilon}{\kappa}C_{3\varepsilon}G_b + S_\varepsilon,$$

where $C_1 = max\left[0.43, \frac{\eta}{\eta+5}\right], \eta = S\frac{\kappa}{\varepsilon}, S = \sqrt{2S_{ij}S_{ij}}$.

In these equations, G_κ represents the production of turbulence kinetic energy due to the mean velocity gradients, and it is modelled identically for the standard, RNG, and RLZ:

$$G_\kappa = -\rho\overline{u_i'u_j'}\frac{\partial u_j}{\partial x_i}. \quad (14)$$

To evaluate G_κ in a consistent manner with the Bussinesq hypothesis $G_\kappa = \mu_t S^2$, where S is the modulus of the mean rate-of-strain tensor. G_b is the generation of turbulence kinetic energy due to buoyancy. Y_M represents the contribution of the fluctuating dilatation in compressible turbulence to the overall dissipation rate. C_2 and $C_{1\varepsilon}$ are constants. σ_k and σ_ε are the turbulent Prandtl numbers for κ and ε, respectively. S_κ and S_κ are source terms. The eddy viscosity is computed from:

$$\mu_t = \rho C_\mu \frac{\kappa^2}{\varepsilon}. \tag{15}$$

The difference from the RNG is that C_μ is no longer constant and $C_{1\varepsilon} = 1.44$, $C_2 = 1.9$, $\sigma_k = 1.0$, and $\sigma_\varepsilon = 1.2$.

3.9.3. k − ω SST Turbulence Model

Specifically, the $k - \omega$ SST is used to make the onset estimation and degree of flow separation under adverse pressure gradients easier by including transport effects into the eddy-viscosity approximation over the $k - \varepsilon$ turbulence models. The model is given by,

$$\frac{\partial}{\partial t}(\rho\kappa) + \frac{\partial}{\partial x_i}(\rho\kappa u_i) = \frac{\partial}{\partial x_j}\left(\Gamma_\kappa \frac{\partial \kappa}{\partial x_j}\right) + G_\kappa - Y_\kappa + S_\kappa + G_b\ , \tag{16}$$

$$\frac{\partial}{\partial t}(\rho\omega) + \frac{\partial}{\partial x_i}(\rho\omega u_j) = \frac{\partial}{\partial x_j}\left(\Gamma_\omega \frac{\partial \omega}{\partial x_j}\right) + G_\omega - Y_\omega + S_\omega + G_{\omega b}\ . \tag{17}$$

The term G_κ represents the production of turbulence kinetic energy due to mean velocity gradients; G_ω is the generation of ω: $\Gamma_\kappa = \mu + (\mu_t/\sigma_k)$ and $\Gamma_\omega = \mu + (\mu_t/\sigma_\omega)$ are the effective diffusivity of κ and ω; σ_k and σ_ω are the turbulent Prandtl numbers for κ and ω; Y_κ and Y_ω are the dissipation of κ and ω due to turbulence, respectively; $D_{\omega b}$ is the cross-diffusion term; S_κ and S_ω are user-defined source terms. The effective diffusivities for $k - \omega$ are the same as in the $k - \omega$ standard model.

3.9.4. k − ω GEKO Turbulence Model

The generalized $k - \omega$ GEKO, is a two-equation model that is based on the $k - \omega$ model formulation but has the flexibility to adapt the model over a wide variety of flow conditions. The key to such a technique is the availability of free parameters that may be altered for certain sorts of applications without affecting the model's core calibration. In other words, rather than suitable modification with flexibility through a plethora of distinct models, the present model tries to provide a single framework with multiple coefficients to cover various application fields.

However, the default parameter values have been calibrated to be equivalent to the SST model, which is a typical model applicable to many industries, and hence no parameter change is required. In place of the vast list of prior turbulence models, the GEKO model was designed and modified to be an all-inclusive turbulence model that can be utilized in virtually any application. The starting point for the formulation is:

$$\frac{\partial}{\partial t}(\rho\kappa) + \frac{\partial}{\partial x_j}(\rho\kappa u_j) = -\tau_{ij}\frac{\partial u_i}{\partial x_j} - C_\mu \rho\kappa\omega + \frac{\partial}{\partial x_j}\left[\left(\mu + \frac{\mu_t}{\sigma_k}\right)\frac{\partial \kappa}{\partial x_i}\right], \tag{18}$$

$$\frac{\partial}{\partial t}(\rho\omega) + \frac{\partial}{\partial x_j}(\rho\omega u) = C_{\omega 1}F_1\frac{\omega}{\kappa} - \tau_{ij}\frac{\partial u_i}{\partial x_j} - C_{\omega 2}F_2\rho\omega^2 + \rho F_3 CD + \frac{\partial}{\partial x_j}\left[\left(\mu + \frac{\mu_t}{\sigma_\omega}\right)\frac{\partial \omega}{\partial x_i}\right], \tag{19}$$

$$\mu_t = \rho v_t = \rho\frac{\kappa}{max(\omega, S/C_{Realize})};\ v_t = min\left(\frac{\kappa}{\omega}, C_{Realize}\frac{\kappa}{s}\right);\ S = \sqrt{2S_{ij}S_{ij}}\ ; \tag{20}$$

$$C_{Realize} = \frac{1}{\sqrt{3}}\ ; \tag{21}$$

$$CD = \frac{2}{\sigma_\omega} \frac{1}{\omega} \frac{\partial \kappa}{\partial x_j} \frac{\partial \omega}{\partial x_j} \ . \tag{22}$$

The free coefficients of the GEKO model are implemented through the functions (F_1, F_2, F_3) which can be tuned to achieve different goals in different parts of the simulation domain.

3.10. Eddy Viscosity Limitation

The presence of high turbulent viscosity, denoted as μ_t, in turbulence models, typically leads to the generation of stable cavities. This intense turbulent viscosity within the cavities acts as a deterrent for the development of reentrant jets and inhibits the formation of instabilities. However, a comprehensive understanding of the correlation between compressibility effects on turbulence and cavitation is still lacking. The intricate mechanisms governing the interaction between turbulent flows and cavitation have not been fully revealed, particularly in the context of small-scale phenomena.

To limit turbulent viscosity in the mixing region, an eddy viscosity limiter can be employed. One of the most renowned limiters is the one proposed by Reboud et al. [56], which has demonstrated its effectiveness in simulating sheet cavities. The implementation of this limiter has shown promising results in restricting turbulent viscosity and ensuring a more accurate representation of flow and cavitation phenomena in these configurations. As such, this limiter has become an important reference in the field of sheet cavity simulation and has been widely embraced by the scientific community due to its effectiveness [57,58]. The use of eddy viscosity limiters in modeling turbulent flows with sheet cavities is crucial for preventing the overestimation of turbulent viscosity and capturing the effects of turbulence more accurately in cavity formation and evolution. These viscosity limiter approaches are essential for enhancing reliability and accuracy in numerical simulations in such cases. The Reboud correction is proposed as an arbitrary limiter by introducing a function $f(\rho)$ in the computation of the turbulent viscosity for the two equations turbulence models as:

$$\mu_t = f(\rho) C_\mu \frac{\kappa^2}{\varepsilon} \ , \tag{23}$$

with

$$f(\rho) = \rho_v + (1-a)^n (\rho_l - \rho_v), \tag{24}$$

where the suffix l for liquid, v for vapor, with n a fixed parameter between 6 and 10 and a is the void ratio given by:

$$a = \frac{\rho - \rho_l^{sat}}{\rho_v^{sat} - \rho_l^{sat}} \tag{25}$$

This correction can be extended to other turbulence models with the same function $f(\rho)$. This approach will allow to trace more effectively the liquid-vapor interface as it evolves in the domain through the VoF model, where the volume fraction is used to identify the regions occupied by the liquid and vapor giving closure to the numerical models' implementations. This limiter was combined with all turbulence models analyzed in this study.

3.11. Cavitation Model

The Schnerr–Sauer cavitation model [59] applied to this numerical evaluation, which is based on the Rayleigh–Plesset equation [60], is a function of the radius of the bubble and the number of bubbles in the unit volume.

A simple two-phase cavitation model applied to the multiphase cavitation modelling technique consists of using conventional viscous flow equations governing the transport of phases and a turbulence model. The vapor transport equation governs the liquid-vapor mass transfer (evaporation and condensation) in cavitation:

$$\frac{\partial}{\partial t}(\alpha \rho_v) + \nabla \cdot \left(\alpha \rho_v \vec{V_v} \right) = R_e - R_c \tag{26}$$

where v is the vapor phase, α the vapor volume fraction, ρ_v the vapor density, $\overrightarrow{V_v}$ the vapor phase velocity, and R_e and R_c the mass transfer source term connected to the growth and collapse of the vapor bubbles, respectively.

$$R_e = F_{vap}\frac{\rho_v \rho_l}{\rho}\alpha(1-\alpha)\frac{3}{\mathcal{R}_B}\sqrt{\frac{2}{3}\frac{(P_v - P_l)}{\rho_l}}, P_v \geq P_l \tag{27}$$

$$R_c = F_{cond}\frac{\rho_v \rho_l}{\rho}\alpha(1-\alpha)\frac{3}{\mathcal{R}_B}\sqrt{\frac{2}{3}\frac{(P_l - P_v)}{\rho_l}}, P_v \leq P_l \tag{28}$$

where $\mathcal{R}_B$ which is the bubble radius and $\mathcal{R}_B = \left[\frac{3\alpha}{4\mu n_B(1-\alpha)}\right]^{1/3}$ was assumed to be a function of the vapor volume fraction, $n_B = 1 \times 10^{-13}\text{m}^3$ is the bubble number density. P_l is the fully recovered downstream pressure, and $P_l = P_{sat} = 3178.75$ [Pa] is the saturation vapor pressure under the operating conditions.

The Equations (7) and (8) govern the global system, driven by the liquid phase at both the domain inlet and outlet. During flow development, a computational pressure condition triggers fluid phase change, computed by the cavitation model. Thus, this model calculates vaporization and condensation, employing Equation (26) managing phase change events consistently within the global system. To maintain numerical stability, the volume fraction is determined for each phase, and the range is established through the cavitation model, reaching a P_{sat} value. Coupled with the VoF model, this approach avoids divergence by returning to a single-phase state post-calculation.

3.12. Sensitivity Analysis and Validation

For this part of the analysis, the already well-known $k-\varepsilon$ standard turbulence model [22,61] was used, as it is a versatile model for many simulations because it delivers good results despite its shortcomings for certain types of phenomena such as high swirl flows. This sensitivity study was designed to compare the outcomes of various turbulence models. Specifically, for the $k-\varepsilon$ standard model, results with maximum discrepancies of 10% are obtained. This implies that the refinement-based mesh will serve as the foundation for achieving more accurate results by incorporating each of the other turbulence models. This is because these models have specific adjustments compared to the $k-\varepsilon$ standard model.

It should be noted that the $k-\varepsilon$ standard model was used because when comparing results from different turbulence models, selecting a particular model in advance would mean selecting the mesh based on that model and its results. Consequently, the obtained results would be a direct function of that model rather than the mesh. The comparison would be influenced, and the error of defining the mesh as solely and exclusively related to that model would be made. A direct repercussion of this is that the outcomes would have a considerable bias and would almost certainly be unfavorable for any of the other turbulence models.

Mesh refinement was carried out using an automatic algorithm embedded in the software, guided by a condition based on a user-defined percentage. Initially, mesh construction was constrained to be structured dismissing the use of an irregular polyhedral to adjust the cell count and adapt to the computational domain. The first mesh is generated with specific parameters and conditions, such as satisfying the Y^+ parameter. This preliminary wall-mesh remains unchanged in terms of the number of layers towards the interior of the computational domain but adjusts in the remaining directions. Subsequent mesh construction is based on the current number of cells, utilizing the predefined percentage increase. It is worth noting that manual cell-increase construction in one direction would result in rectangular parallelepipeds instead of hexahedra. All meshes in this study are hexahedral, offering the advantage of mitigating numerical diffusion. The number of cells in Meshes 1 to 4 follows an increment of 25%, Meshes 5 and 6 follow an increment of 50%, and Mesh 7 an increment of 75%. To conduct the sensitivity analysis, mesh refinement was adapted to allow for the selection of an appropriate mesh. Table 2 gathers the characteristics of the constructed meshes.

Table 2. Mesh characteristics.

Mesh	Number of Cells	Computing Time in Hours.
1	458,880	≈3
2	585,816	≈5
3	757,008	≈16
4	992,953	≈27
5	1,859,552	≈68
6	2,860,602	≈127
7	3,577,320	≈187

Analysis of the Variables

In order to obtain numerical results that were not dependent on the mesh, seven mesh variants were created. Figure 4 depicts the outcome variations for each mesh version. The sensitivity analysis data were gathered from the data retrieved by using a central line or central marker of the pressure gradient along the calculation domain.

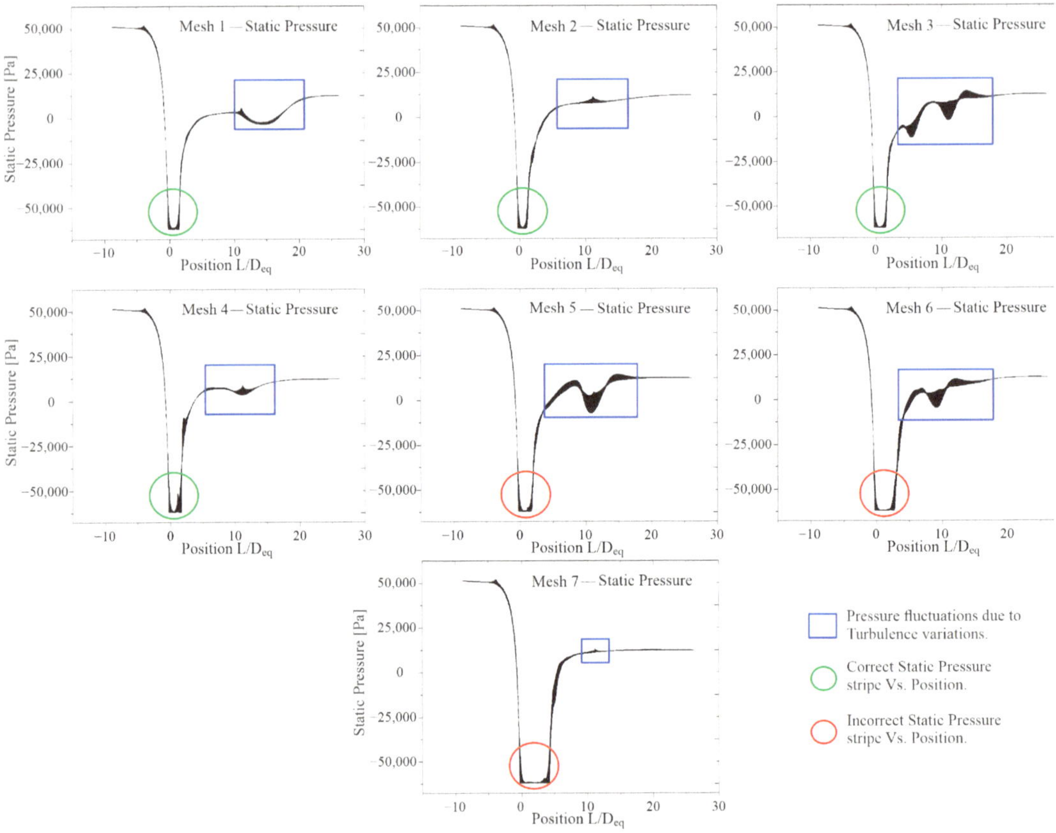

Figure 4. Mesh comparison: static pressure values of the $k - \varepsilon$ standard model.

At first glance, it is possible to determine that the static pressure, P_{I-Stc}, from the inlet zone located at $-8.63\ L/D_{eq}$ to the entrance of the convergent zone or throat at $-0.296\ L/D_{eq}$, does not vary with respect to the results obtained by the numerical simulations with the different meshes. These results are compatible with those obtained experimentally [37] and analytically. When comparing the P_{I-Stc} results after this zone in the multiple constructed meshes, two areas of interest stand out. The first and most interesting is the convergent zone, also known as the throat, which is located at the position $0\ L/D_{eq}$. The pressure must be within the throat length observed in this type of convergent–divergent configuration within this stripe. Similar findings have been reported by Tang, P. et al. [15].

These numerical results are stable and consistent in Meshes 1 to 4; however, when the number of cells increases significantly, or when Mesh 4′s cells are doubled, the location of P_{I-Stc} values is overestimated. This is because the calculation takes vaporization or phase change into account. Mass transfer in too-fine meshes usually results in insignificant differences. However, it is not possible to conclude that the difference between Mesh 4 and 5 is as large as twice the error. This is generally attributed to the turbulence model used, because not only must the equation solutions be coupled for each phase but the very abrupt change in viscosity is a factor that must be considered in advance: in this case, for the cavitation phenomenon. The $k-\varepsilon$ standard model does not account for these changes, but it does indicate that an adjustment in that zone is required. Each of the remaining models considered here makes the necessary adjustments to broaden the numerical representation of a wide range of phenomena. As stated in previous sections, each model has its own method of calculating the turbulent viscosity μ_t.

The expectation that the $k-\varepsilon$ standard model will yield good results is subject to specific conditions. As long as the geometry complies with a cross-sectional area greater than the value of Y^+ and U^+ for cavitation simulations, that is, it is not compromised by an extremely small size, it can be used as a reference framework. On the one hand, d_{thro} should be within the range of $0.30 < d_{thro} < 0.75$ of the diameter ratio $\beta = d_{thro}/D_{eq}$ [35,62]. On the other hand, according to Furness [62], the discharge coefficients of Venturi tubes are independent of the diameter ratio β, and their influence strictly depends on the Reynolds number within the range $2 \times 10^5 < Re < 2 \times 10^7$. However, for this study case with $Re = 2.0731 \times 10^4$, the Venturi tube discharge coefficient varies between 0.9 and 0.99, which depends on the β ratio and $Re < 2 \times 10^5$.

Based on the aforementioned points, it can be said that the mesh independence analysis will be accurate for the use of a mesh for the other turbulence models since each of them has substantial improvements, such as the calculation of the turbulent viscosity, μ_T, and it will avoid the results for each of them being dependent on the quantity or size of cells.

Furthermore, an analysis of the most representative variables for the cavitation phenomenon was carried out to provide greater certainty, which are the velocity behavior, the turbulence resultant, and the determination of the cavitation cloud size as shown in Figure 5.

With the $k-\varepsilon$ standard model, the values tend to stabilize when the mesh is sufficiently fine to capture the vapor cloud, in addition to the effects of the model itself when calculating μ_T. This implies, on the one hand, that the turbulence model must have adjustments for the calculation of μ_T because it overestimates the velocity variation, which is not dependent on the mesh, as increasing the number of cells repeats the maximum value of ≈ 15.443 [m/s]. On the other hand, it means that mesh independence has been achieved. The experimental results yield an average maximum velocity of ≈ 13.99 [m/s] [37], in comparison to the numerical result value which is a 10.38% overestimation, and it is within the acceptable range for this type of simulations.

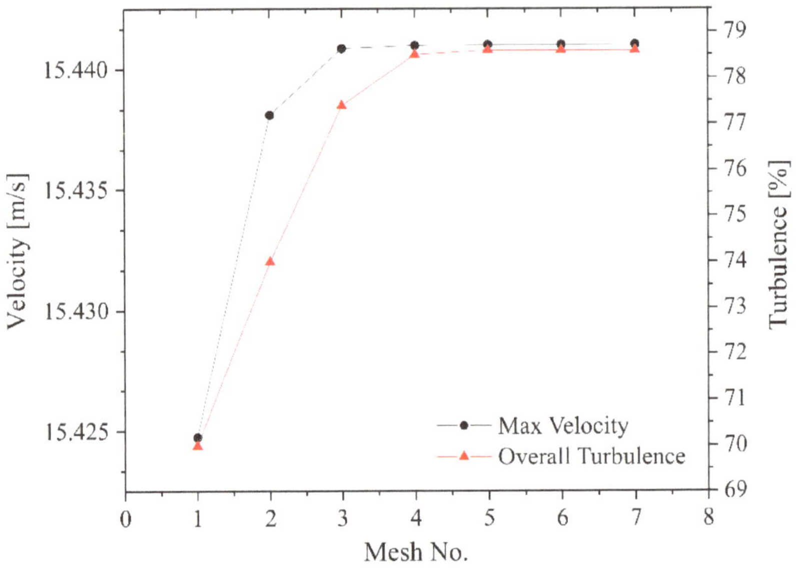

Figure 5. Velocity and turbulence intensity scatterplot for the $k - \varepsilon$ standard model.

To achieve mesh independence in other turbulence models, a mesh containing a minimum of 992,953 cells of Mesh 4 is required for the variables calculation results to be independent of mesh resolution. The calculation of velocity is a faithful representation of mesh independence in the absence of cavitation. However, when simulating the phase change from liquid to vapor, it is necessary to determine whether the turbulence model accurately represents the variable for which it was constructed, namely the calculation of turbulence intensity. It is worth noting that turbulence intensity is a measure of the magnitude of velocity fluctuations in a turbulent flow compared to the flow's mean velocity. It is used to quantify the strength or aggressiveness of turbulence within a flow field, and it is typically expressed as a percentage defined as:

$$Turbulence\ Intensity\ (\%) = (RMS\ velocity / Mean\ velocity) \times 100 \quad (29)$$

where *RMS velocity* is the square root of the mean square of velocity fluctuations in a particular direction and *Mean velocity* is the average velocity in the same direction.

Unfortunately, non-intrusive measurement devices do not exist for experimental data on turbulence intensity, as their use involves sensitive property intervention and alteration. For this reason, experimental data on turbulence intensity cannot be collected. Nevertheless, numerical results can be used for detailed analyses, provided that the turbulence model used is suitable for this task. Figure 5 shows the turbulence intensity in contrast to its maximum velocity for each mesh used. Similar to velocity calculation, the turbulence intensity tends to stabilize from Mesh 4 onwards, demonstrating the independence of the mesh for such a sensitive variable. Therefore, Mesh 4 contains the minimum number of cells necessary to conclude that it is suitable for the use of turbulence models in this particular study.

Furthermore, the variation in the length of the vapor cloud was also included in this analysis of mesh independence. The $k - \varepsilon$ standard model predicts a length consistent with the experimental data. When using different turbulence models, they must have a minimum tolerance range with respect to the length of the vapor cloud, as despite the severe deficiencies of the $k - \varepsilon$ standard model mentioned earlier, it is consistent with the experimental results. As a consequence, other models, with adjustments to their equation calculations, should be more precise and their results should not be prone to mesh dependence.

Figure 6 compares the length of the vapor cloud, l_{vc}, generated by the $k-\varepsilon$ standard model. Due to the highly unstable nature of the vapor cloud generation process, an average of the maximum length of the vapor cloud was obtained. As a result, a minimum value of ≈ 25.88 [mm] and a maximum value of ≈ 27 [mm] were achieved. In comparison with the turbulence model, a range of $26.82 < l_{vc} < 28.55$ [mm] was obtained. The percentage error for the minimum length is $\approx 3.5\%$, and for the maximum length, it is $\approx 5.7\%$.

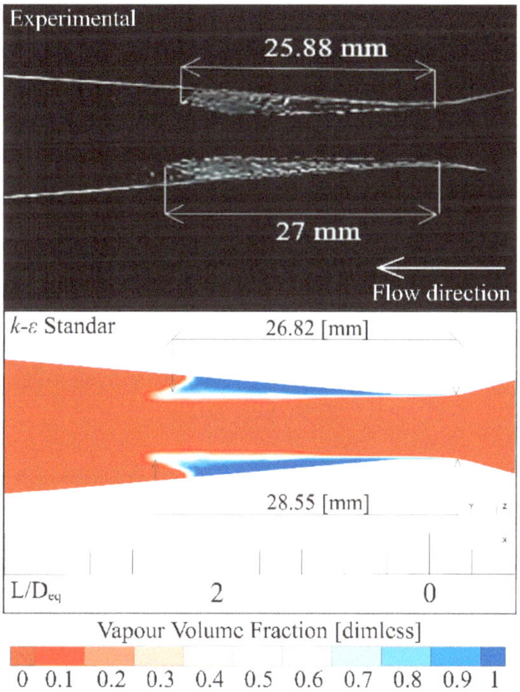

Figure 6. Experimental results of the l_{vc} vs. numerical results of the $k-\varepsilon$ standard model.

It is noteworthy that the $k-\varepsilon$ standard model is quite accurate in predicting the generation of the vapor cloud and its length, despite its deficiencies. Therefore, for the other turbulence models, the results should be close to these values and not be dependent on the mesh used.

The meshes from 1 to 3 are not quite accurate even for the $k-\varepsilon$ standard model when any variable is analyzed because the result of these are sub-estimated. On the other hand, for the meshes from 5 to 7, the results are overestimates resulting in a wrong representation of the cavitation phenomenon; therefore, these are inaccurate data. From this point onwards, Mesh 4 was used for the other turbulence models due to its balance between the results close to the experimental data, resolution time, and computational resources.

It is of particular interest that several articles [19,30,32,43,63] employ a lower cell density relative to the geometry size. This practice implies that computations relying on the analysis of a single variable against experimental comparison may lack representativeness in elucidating a robust sensitivity analysis. As a result, the chosen turbulence model, despite achieving convergence, might exhibit a higher error deviation compared to other variables. This substantial concern has served as a primary impetus for augmenting the data density presented in this section.

Conversely, this study underscores the insufficiency of solely possessing an experimentally-represented variable for various turbulence models. It emphasizes that a comprehensive approach entails the inclusion of every variable of interest prior to experimental design, thus rendering it an essential consideration for numerical modeling. Such inclusion ensures compatibility between the selected turbulence model's modeling capabilities and the targeted variables. This approach is pivotal for averting potential misinterpretations, overestimations, or underestimations in outcomes, thereby mitigating the impact of numerical diffusion-induced errors to a minimum.

4. Results and Analysis

The simulation of the cavitation phenomenon depends on both the flow rate and the velocity of the fluid. The flow velocity is especially important because an increase can lead to pressure values below the liquid's vapor pressure, affect the formation and collapse of the cavitation cloud, and influence the pressure distribution, turbulence intensity, and the formation of vortices. Generally, the higher the flow rate, the higher the turbulence intensity and the greater the cavitation probability. The relationship between the flow rate and the cross-sectional area of the tube is also important, as a section that is too large or too small may reduce the probability of cavitation bubble formation.

4.1. Basic Variables Analysis

Regarding the velocity contours, similarities can be seen in the total development of the fluid. Figure 7 shows a comparison of the velocity contours, as well as the static and absolute pressure, for the different turbulence models used.

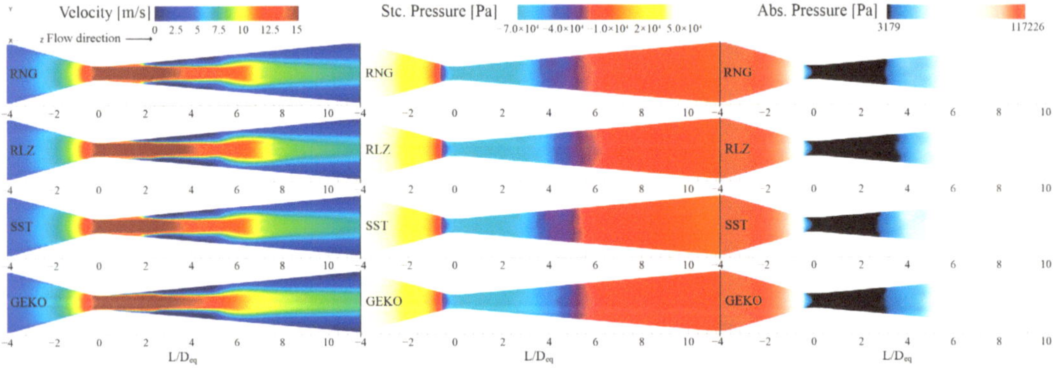

Figure 7. Velocity, static pressure, and absolute pressure contours comparison for the distinct turbulence models. YZ lateral plane view of the Venturi tube throat.

The RLZ model shows that the main fluid presents an early separation or detachment from the wall in a zone very close to the throat. This is because the RLZ model couples the calculation of the kinetic energy k and its dissipation ε with the momentum equation from a calculated value of μ_T. This is performed in order to improve calculations in geometries with prominent separation or separated flow from walls, such as geometries with steps or vena contracta [64], but it is not specifically designed to correct the effects of these regions on the calculation of turbulent viscosity as in the cavitation phenomenon. For these reasons, in a Venturi tube where there is an opening angle from the throat to the outlet, the calculation is overestimated because the RLZ model is programmed to obtain the result of fluid detachment from the hydrodynamic boundary layer, leading to a misconception of the result. Firstly, this occurs because the fluid will detach smoothly from the walls, meaning that the hydrodynamic layer will grow in that area, maintaining a laminar zone of greater amplitude. Secondly, even though the cavitation phenomenon is not present, the hydrodynamic boundary layer is a critical factor in the simulation, since in this zone, the flow decelerates due to friction and viscosity, generating a pressure drop.

Even though the opening from the throat to the outlet can influence the flow development, it is generally considered that the flow in this region is fully developed and is modelled by the mass and momentum conservation equations. For this reason, it can be observed that the length of the high-velocity contour strip extends up to $\approx 7.5\ L/D_{eq}$, compared to the other cases. On the other hand, the maximum velocity calculated is ≈ 15.42 [m/s], which is the highest compared to the other turbulence models, with a percentage error of 10.2%. Therefore, it is assumed that there is an overestimation of the velocity calculation when using the RLZ model.

Upon observing the results of the velocity calculation using the GEKO model, it can be noted that the detachment also occurs, but in an earlier location than in the RLZ model. This detachment occurs in a strip of $\approx 0.296\ L/D_{eq}$, which is a zone immediately after the throat exit: that is incorrect. The maximum calculated velocity, which is approximately 14.87 [m/s], is still within an acceptable range with a percentage error of 6.3% compared to the experimental data.

Due to the distinct formulation of the GEKO model compared to the standard, RNG, and RZL models, it employs the specific dissipation rate of turbulent energy ω. Thus, this model is mainly used for transonic or supersonic flows, in which compressibility is the most important factor. Although it is capable of accurately predicting separated and transitional flow regions and considers the effects of compressibility on turbulence, it has the same limitation in calculating turbulent viscosity. This μ_T calculation is based on an algebraic relationship between turbulent viscosity and the rate of turbulent energy dissipation. Therefore, it is essential to adjust the μ_T calculation for both RLZ and GEKO models in the context of Venturi tubes.

Upon comparing all of the models, it is possible to appreciate that both the RNG and SST models do not show discrepancies in modelling the flow development but do show differences in the calculated maximum velocity values. For RNG, it is approximately 14.57 [m/s], while for SST, it is $\approx$ 15.01 [m/s], with a percentage error of 4.14% and 7.3%, respectively.

The flow velocity is especially important as its increase can lead to pressure values below the liquid's vapor pressure, causing vapor bubble formation. Moreover, flow velocity also influences the turbulence intensity, affecting the formation and collapse of the cavitation cloud. Therefore, the RNG model is the best model for calculating the velocity at the throat exit.

By analyzing the static pressure contours of the numerical results from each turbulence model, the following points can be highlighted. The overall calculation of static pressure matches the experimental data [37] with a global percentage error of approximately 1.1% for all four models. This result is consistent in demonstrating that at least all analyzed turbulence models can make a hydrodynamic representation of the cavitation phenomenon in the constriction zone. However, a more detailed analysis shows that the value of static pressure in the throat, $P_{thro-Stc}$, has a severe discrepancy from one model to another. In particular, the value of pressure in the throat varies drastically. For example, the RLZ model presents a higher overestimation, followed by the SST, GEKO, and finally, the RNG, which is closer to the experimental value. This is mainly due to how the relationship between μ_T and ε or ω is represented according to the model used, specifically how the flow behavior is modelled when calculating μ_T for different turbulence models. As the static pressure in the Venturi tube is a function of flow velocity, the distribution of pressures and velocities along the tube also varies with the resolution of μ_T from each turbulence model.

When analyzing the absolute pressure contours, the discrepancies between the models become even more evident. Although all models correctly calculate the value of saturation pressure, $P_{sat} = 3179$ [Pa], the location, length, and shape of this zone differ between models. In Table 3, the results for velocity, static pressure, and absolute pressure are summarized along with their respective percentage errors.

Table 3. Velocity, static pressure, absolute pressure values, saturation pressure length, and error percent.

Model	Velocity [m/s]	Error %	$P_{thro-Stc}$ [Pa]	Error %	P_{Abs} [Pa]	Error %	$L_{P_{sat}}$ $[L/D_{eq}]$
RNG	14.57	4.145	−53,496.72	4.47	50,134.62	2.066	3.2
RLZ	15.42	10.221	−63,012.03	23.05	38,726.00	24.352	3.8
SST	15.01	7.290	−61,212.44	19.53	40,961.49	19.985	2.8
GEKO	14.87	6.290	−58,654.57	14.54	43,595.32	14.840	3.2
Experimental [37]	13.99		−51,207.22		51,192.77		N/A

4.2. Extended Variables Analysis

As mentioned in the previous section, the values of eddy viscosity, μ, refer to the effective viscosity developed in turbulence. In simple terms, it describes how turbulence affects the viscosity of the fluid and how this influences the formation and collapse of the cavitation cloud. It is important to highlight the following: turbulent viscosity is a property of turbulent flow that represents the resistance to movement caused by the interaction of eddies in the flow, which is a measure of the transfer of momentum from the larger scale of flow to smaller scales. On the other hand, eddy viscosity is a way of modelling turbulent viscosity in the Navier–Stokes equations, which describe the movement of fluids. Eddy viscosity is a coefficient used to approximate the effect of turbulence on the momentum transfer, and it is related to the turbulent diffusion of momentum in the flow.

In order to investigate the factors contributing to the creation of vortices and turbulence intensity, an extended analysis of variables has been conducted at this stage. This analysis includes an examination of μ, as well as an evaluation of the sources of these phenomena through an analysis of kinetic energy, k, values.

Figure 8 shows the contours of μ, turbulence intensity, and k. With the RLZ model, there are values of μ at the entrance of the calculation domain, indicating that the effect of turbulence on the momentum is being calculated from the beginning of flow development before entering the throat. This method may be efficient in other simulations where cavitation is not considered, but not in a Venturi tube where the turbulence intensity and cavitation cloud are directly related and dependent on each other. Additionally, it can be observed that μ values are obtained from the entrance of the throat, which implies a calculation of turbulence intensity, not due to the formation of the cavitation cloud, but due to the modelling of the turbulence equations a priori of mass transfer. This explains the difference in the values of the analyzed variables in the previous section. At the throat exit, these values are normalized and consistent with other turbulence models.

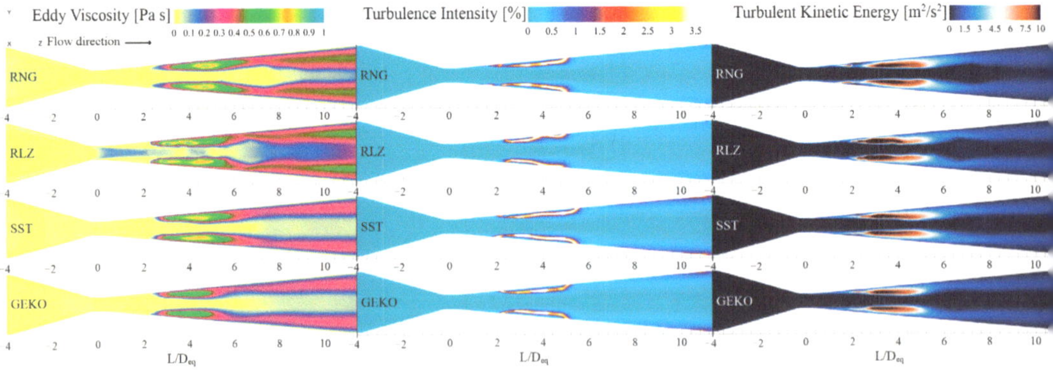

Figure 8. Eddy viscosity, turbulence intensity, and turbulent kinetic energy contours.

Since the RNG model also belongs to the $k-\varepsilon$ models, its behavior at the entrance of the calculation domain is similar to that of RLZ. It also obtains values of μ which, although not particularly representative with a value less than 0.1 [Pa s], require a more exhaustive and extensive analysis, both of the entrance of the calculation domain and of the particular turbulence model, which will not be addressed in this study.

As for the SST and GEKO models, due to their different formulations, there are no noticeable differences between them. However, when analyzing the lengths of μ development, there are variations that can be discussed. The RNG model has a μ range from 3.2 L/D_{eq} to 6.8 L/D_{eq}; the RLZ model has a range from 2.4 L/D_{eq} to 6 L/D_{eq}; the SST model has a range from 2.8 L/D_{eq} to 6.4 L/D_{eq}; and the GEKO model has a range from 2.9 L/D_{eq} to 5.2 L/D_{eq}.

It is worth noting that μ does not produce the vortices itself, but rather it is a measure of the influence that vortices or eddies have on the fluid motion. In simple terms, μ describes how turbulence affects the viscosity of the fluid and how this influences the formation and collapse of cavitation bubbles. For this reason, its correct representation is important in this study.

Now, turbulence plays a critical role in the formation and collapse of the vapor cloud, as well as in the intensity of cavitation in a Venturi tube. This chaotic flow state is characterized by random movements in all directions, where velocity and pressure fluctuate in time and space. These pressure fluctuations can generate regions of low pressure, increasing the likelihood of vapor cloud formation. In addition, turbulence can influence local pressure and vortex formation, which can affect the creation and collapse of cavitation voids.

It is important to highlight the length of the development of turbulence intensity and k to determine, within the cavitation zone, the length of the generated vapor cloud. For the RNG model, 1.2 $L/D_{eq} < l_{TI} <$ 5.1 L/D_{eq}; RLZ, 2.4 $L/D_{eq} < l_{TI} <$ 5 L/D_{eq}; SST, 1.8 $L/D_{eq} < l_{TI} <$ 5.6 L/D_{eq}; and GEKO, 2 $L/D_{eq} < l_{TI} <$ 5.2 L/D_{eq}. Regarding k, it can be expressed for the length values, l_{tke}, as follows. RNG, 1.2 $L/D_{eq} < l_{tke} <$ 5.3 L/D_{eq}; RLZ, 1.2 $L/D_{eq} < l_{tke} <$ 5.3 L/D_{eq}; SST, 1.2 $L/D_{eq} < l_{tke} <$ 5.8L/D_{eq}; and GEKO, 1.2 $L/D_{eq} < l_{tke} <$ 5 L/D_{eq}.

This is how the relation between the three variables analyzed in this point is presented: "Eddy viscosity", "Turbulence intensity", and "Turbulent kinetic energy". First and foremost, it is important to highlight that if k increases in a certain region of the tube, it may indicate the presence of a recirculation zone, vortices, or flow separation. As is known, μ is responsible for increasing vortices in the flow inside the Venturi tube. Furthermore, the formation of vortices [65] can generate regions of low pressure, which can lead to the formation of vapor bubbles. When vapor bubbles form in regions of high turbulence, they can collapse violently, and the energy released during the collapse can cause the implosion of the vapor bubble, generating shock waves and damaging the surfaces of the Venturi tube.

It is known that turbulence intensity can influence the mixing of the flow, which can affect the pressure distribution and the formation of cavitation bubbles. It can also generate regions of low pressure and affect the formation of vortices that influence the intensity of cavitation. Since the formation of vapor bubbles or a vapor cloud is a complex process, it can significantly influence the flow dynamics. This process can reduce k in the cavitation zone, as the energy dissipates in the formation and collapse of vapor bubbles. However, it is also possible that cavitation increases k in the region close to the cavitation zone. This is because the vapor bubbles that form in the cavitation zone can be carried by the flow towards the nearby region, where they collapse and generate additional turbulence. The way cavitation affects k depends on the magnitude and duration of cavitation, as well as the interaction between vapor bubbles and turbulent flow.

Figure 9 depicts the general behavior of velocity, static pressure, absolute pressure, and turbulence intensity. This figure shows the results obtained with the simulations in comparison with the experimental data. In general, it can be seen that, in the case of velocity, the RNG model fits excellently in both zones: the throat and the vapor cloud formation. As for the other models, these fit better with the values obtained at the throat exit after the cavitation zone. In the case of static pressure, the model that best predicts the pressure drop in the throat zone is the RNG model followed by the GEKO, SST, and finally the RLZ. After the cavitation zone and vapor cloud, all the models fit with the experimental data in practically similar ways. Regarding the results of the absolute pressure, again, the RNG model stands out in its approach and prediction of the values in relation to the experimental data.

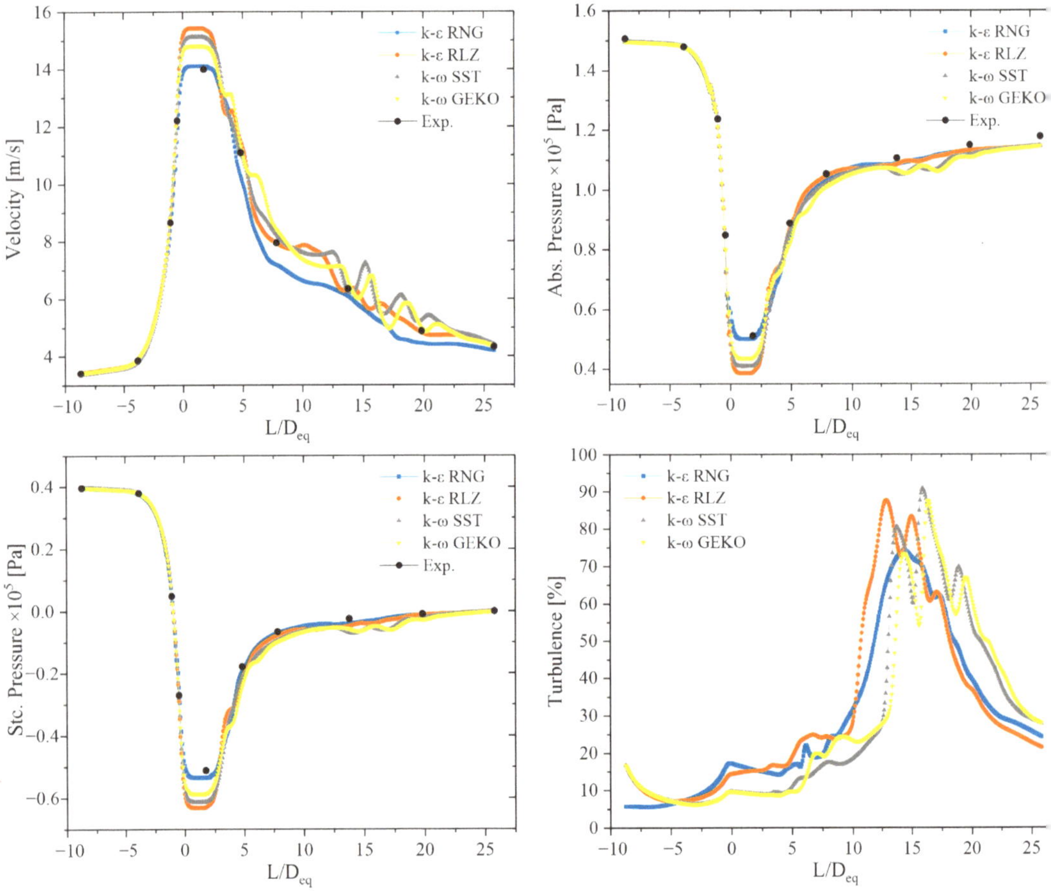

Figure 9. Scatterplots for velocity, static pressure, absolute pressure, and turbulence intensity along the Venturi tube.

Finally, each one of the models predicts the values of the turbulence intensity in a different way and according to the formulation of the closure of their respective equations. Although the RNG model indisputably fits well to the experimental values of other variables, it fails to accurately capture the fluctuations arising from the cavitation cloud, as well as the RLZ. Therefore, the interactions arising from the relationship between μ, k, and the generation of vortices may not be adequate to represent the fluctuations and frequency of the generation of the vapor cloud associated with the cavitation phenomenon. However, and due to the formulation of the models based on $k - \omega$, they do manage to make a slightly more accurate representation of the turbulence intensity and, consequently, could be better adapted to the oscillations of the vapor cloud due to cavitation.

It should be noted that, to make a precise evaluation of the vapor cloud and all its characteristics for a complete analysis, an extension to the study is presupposed with the inclusion of more advanced models and different techniques such as large eddy simulations, detached eddy simulations, or scale-adaptive simulations and which, in turn, make use of an adaptation by filtering the equations of the turbulence models of the RANS technique. However, these models, although they are not new, require a higher level of computational resources.

Figure 10 shows the cavitation vapor cloud length predicted by the distinct turbulence models. At first glance, there are no severe discrepancies between the values of the experimentally obtained measurements and the numerical results. However, when comparing the lengths of the vapor cloud, the shape of the cloud can be observed to vary, as well as the location of detachment and to a lesser extent the total length.

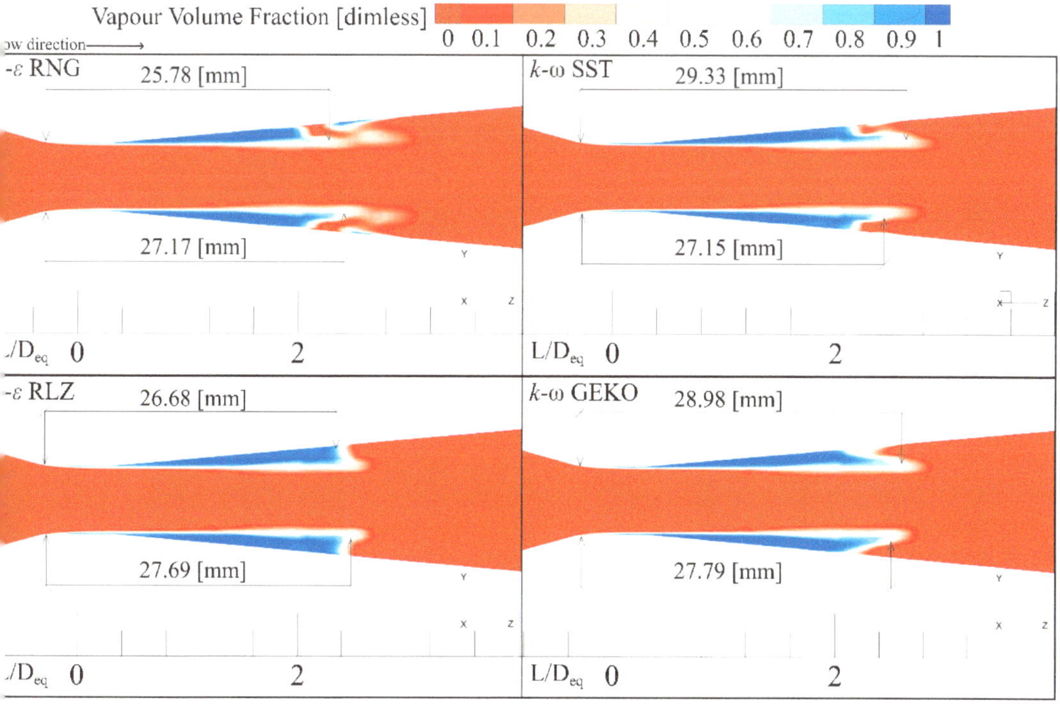

Figure 10. Comparison of the cavitation vapor cloud length calculated by the different turbulence models.

Regarding the shape and detachment of the vapor cloud from the walls, it is noteworthy that both the RNG and SST models obtain similar results. The cloud detaches in the form of a cavity with some bubbles still attached to the wall. This implies a direct relationship in how μ_T is calculated in these two models. In comparison, the RLZ and GEKO models detach the cloud in a U-shape mainly due to the RANS averaging technique. These results may be less accurate if a qualitative analysis is carried out and the focus is more on the shape than the length characteristic. However, the size results are consistent. Table 4 summarizes the values of the vapor cloud length with their respective percentage of error compared to the experimental data.

Table 4. Vapor cloud length values.

Model	l_{vc} Min	Error %	l_{vc} Max	Error %	Average l_{vc}	Deviation %	We
RNG	25.78	0.386	27.17	4.9845	26.475	2.299	53,014.4
RLZ	26.68	3.091	27.69	6.993	27.185	5.042	56,720.8
SST	27.15	4.907	29.33	13.330	28.24	9.119	46,495.9
GEKO	27.79	7.380	28.79	11.244	28.29	9.312	48,348.9
Experimental [37]	25.88		27		26.44		

4.3. Dimensionless Analysis

In flowing liquids, local pressure gradients arise due to variations in their velocity. Velocity changes occur within constrictions or branches; within regions of low pressure, the fluid phase transitions into the vapor phase, giving rise to vapor bubbles. These bubbles are generated from boiling nuclei which are recognized as pockets or cavities, and perturbations at the wall surface of the tube. Stable cavitation zones primarily form at downstream corners of the throat's outlet points. The flow has the potential to entrain these bubbles. Subsequently, these bubbles undergo collapse within regions of increasing pressure. This description encompasses the fundamental dynamics of cavitation inception and development in fluid flow scenarios. The generation, transport, and eventual collapse of vapor bubbles play a pivotal role in understanding the complex phenomenon of cavitation.

Figure 11 depicts contours representing the variation in ς as a function of the water vapor phase during the fluid development within the Venturi tube throat. Notably, in all cases, the maximum value of ς approximately equals 0.478 along the central axial line of the Venturi tube, aligning well with experimental findings [37]. Furthermore, apparent instabilities in the previously analyzed contours of the distinct features just downstream of the Venturi throat exit are exhibited with greater clarity. The vapor cloud collapse is represented through a ς value exceeding 0.478. This observation is of particular significance due to ς's remarkable sensitivity to abrupt pressure changes, evident from the contours in Figure 11 displaying a sharp transition to higher ς values.

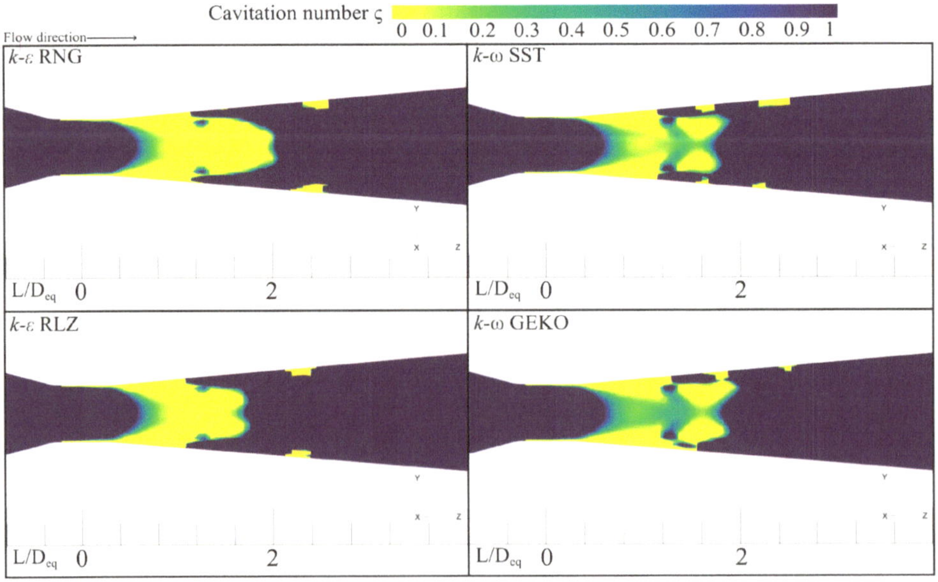

Figure 11. Comparison of ς during cavitation vapor cloud calculated by the different turbulence models.

Cavitation number ς sensitivity serves as a distinctive indicator for the onset of cavitation-related phenomena. Values of ς near 0 directly imply cavitation, encompassing phase transition, development, or dispersion processes. Conversely, higher ς values (>5 for these particular case study) conclusively signify inadequate pressure conditions for vapor cloud formation, indicating either a liquid phase presence, vapor cloud collapse, or liquid re-entrainment jet. The comprehensive analysis of ς and its correlation with vapor behavior adds depth to our understanding of cavitation dynamics within the Venturi tube. This analysis not only validates experimental findings but also offers insights into the nuanced interplay between pressure, phase transitions, and cavitation onset.

Considering the variations in vapor cloud shapes across different turbulence models, this additional analysis arises. The reentrant jet flow occurs at the downstream end of a cavity, where the external flow reattaches to the wall. The flow over the cavity takes the form of a liquid jet impinging obliquely on the wall, which then splits into two parts: the reentrant jet and the flow that causes the reattachment to the wall. The reentrant jet moves upstream, triggering the cavity detachment, while the other part leads to flow reattachment to the wall as previously shown in Figure 10 in the cavitation cloud shape. This phenomenon is governed by inertia, with periods of reentrant jet development followed by periods of emptying and entrainment of the two-phase mixture. The oscillation frequency of the reentrant jet instability is on the order of the product of the cavity length and velocity. The specific analysis of the oscillation frequency of the vapor cloud appearance and collapse is reserved for a forthcoming study.

The reentrant jet is a key factor in initiating cloud cavitation, and its development is influenced by the adverse pressure gradient in the flow as previously shown in Figure 10 in the cavitation cloud shape. The thickness of the reentrant jet is influenced by the pressure gradient and cavity thickness [66]. The reentrant jet is reflected in an inclined cavity closure line, resulting in a component along the jet velocity extent in three-dimensional configurations. The closure line of the cavity lip often takes on a convex shape, indicating the presence of three-dimensional effects.

The reentrant jet flow is characterized by the impinging liquid jet splitting into two flows: the reentrant jet and the concurrent mainstream flow. The reentrant jet and the incident stream flow along the cavity at constant pressure, while the downstream pressure is higher due to an adverse pressure gradient. The velocity profiles in the jets are assumed to be uniform, and the adverse pressure gradient is modeled by a global tangential force applied to the upper boundary of the flow.

A more insightful understanding of this comprehensive representation can be gleaned through analysis of the Weber number. The numerical model must consistently provide information on this topic to be considered the most viable option for modeling cavitation phenomena, as demonstrated later.

The comparison of the cavitation cloud through the contours of the water vapor volumetric fraction against variations in the Weber number during the fluid development within the Venturi tube throat is illustrated in Figure 12. The cavitation cloud undergoes a phase of dispersion after detaching from the walls, and subsequent to reaching its maximum length, it manifests regions with bubble formation near the tube's central axis. This phenomenon is observed exclusively in turbulence models based on the turbulent dissipation ε. The cloud primarily continues to disperse within the central region, which assumes a U-shape across all turbulence models. Near the walls, a portion of the cavitation cloud recedes as the general dispersion phase concludes. Notably, distinct interfacial deformation occurs between the ε-based models compared to the ω-based ones. The variation in the thickness and length of the cavitation cloud's base is also evident when analyzing the Weber number contours. Higher kinetic energy values associated with larger Weber numbers lead to an increased maximum dispersion size, as evident in the ω-based turbulence models.

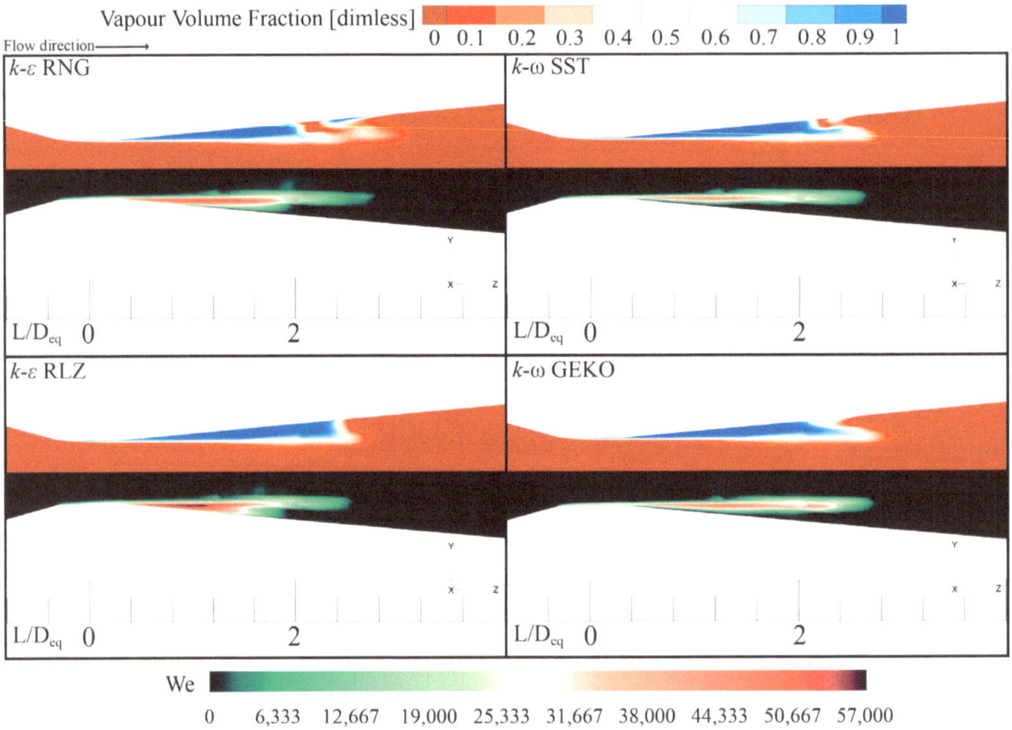

Figure 12. Comparison of the Weber number, We, during a cavitation vapor cloud calculated by the different turbulence models.

The extent of length damping achieved during the cavitation cloud's dispersion is notably distinct due to how the turbulence models handle kinetic energy dissipation, regardless of the Weber number magnitude. This behavior can be attributed to increased viscous dissipation and specific numerical modelling formulations. These findings provide valuable insights into the intricate dynamics of cavitation cloud dispersion and the differentiating impact of turbulence models on its manifestation and behavior.

5. Conclusions

This study provides valuable insights into dynamics of cavitation in the Venturi tube and highlights the importance of selecting appropriate turbulence models for accurate numerical simulations. Four turbulence models were selected including $k-\varepsilon$ RNG, $k-\varepsilon$ realizable, $k-\omega$ SST, and $k-\omega$ GEKO.

One of the fundamental reasons why the $k-\varepsilon$ RNG model proves to be suitable for simulating cavitating flows lies in its specific design to handle highly accelerated flows. This model has been conceived in such a way that its mathematical components can be replaced by specific functions for the calculation of turbulent viscosity, as applied in the present study through the Reboud correction. Specifically, the transport equations of the model incorporate additional terms for the production of turbulent kinetic energy that take into account the energy generated by cavitation, making it more suitable for simulating this phenomenon. Consequently, the $k-\varepsilon$ RNG model effectively benefits from this correction compared to other models, thanks to the intrinsic nature of the renormalized group. The combination of this feature with the implementation of the Reboud correction results in a particularly outstanding performance in simulating cavitation phenomena.

Another advantage of the $k - \varepsilon$ RNG model is its filtering technique based on the renormalization group theory. This technique allows the model to effectively deal with turbulence anisotropy, which is especially important for simulating highly accelerated and complex turbulent flows, such as those that occur in cavitation. The model's filtering technique also helps to reduce the model's sensitivity to the choice of diffusivity constant, which can be a problem in other turbulence models.

In addition, the $k - \varepsilon$ RNG model uses a fine mesh discretization for numerical resolution, making it more accurate than other turbulence models in simulating cavitation flows. This is especially relevant in cavitation, where high rates of deformation and time-scale variations occur, requiring precise numerical resolution to ensure accurate results.

Compared to other turbulence models, the $k - \varepsilon$ RNG model stands out in simulating cavitation flows due to its unique features. The $k - \varepsilon$ RLZ model, for example, is a variant of the standard $k - \varepsilon$ model that includes additional correction terms but is not specifically designed for simulating cavitation flows. On the other hand, the $k - \omega$ SST model and the $k - \omega$ GEKO model are suitable for simulating complex turbulent flows in general but do not have the specific corrections for cavitating flows.

Furthermore, the $k - \omega$ SST model and the $k - \omega$ GEKO model are based on a combination of the turbulent kinetic energy transport equation k and the energy dissipation ω transport equation, making them more suitable for simulating swirling flows in general and not necessarily specific to cavitation. The $k - \varepsilon$ RNG model, on the other hand, uses only the turbulent kinetic energy transport equation, but with specific corrections suitable for cavitation.

Of the four turbulence models mentioned, the $k - \varepsilon$ RNG model followed by the $k - \omega$ SST model are good prospects for simulating cavitation. However, because the rectangular-profile Venturi tube is a device with a specific geometry, it is desirable that a turbulence model designed specifically for tubes or ducts, such as the $k - \varepsilon$ RNG turbulence model, be more suitable for its simulation. Indeed, the choice of turbulence model plays a crucial role in the accuracy and efficiency of numerical simulations of cavitating flows, particularly in Venturi tubes.

Finally, the findings of this research show that for all the four models compared it is necessary to make a modification more sophisticated to how μ_T is calculated in the Venturi tube, extend to the compression modification, and take into account the vapor cloud oscillation and fluctuation attenuation context.

Author Contributions: Conceptualization, M.D.l.C.-Á. and J.E.D.L.-R.; methodology, M.D.l.C.-Á.; software, M.D.l.C.-Á. and I.C.-M.; validation, M.D.l.C.-Á. and J.E.D.L.-R.; formal analysis, M.D.l.C.-Á.; investigation, M.D.l.C.-Á. and J.E.D.L.-R.; resources M.D.l.C.-Á.; data curation, M.D.l.C.-Á.; writing—original draft preparation, M.D.l.C.-Á.; writing—review and editing, M.D.l.C.-Á., J.E.D.L.-R., and I.C.-M.; visualization, M.D.l.C.-Á.; supervision, J.K. and I.C.-M.; project administration, J.K.; funding acquisition, J.K. All authors have read and agreed to the published version of the manuscript.

Funding: The research work described in this paper was funded by European Union's Horizon 2020 Programme under the ENERXICO Project (Grant Agreement No. 828947) and under the Mexican CONACYT-SENER-Hidrocarburos (Grant Agreement No. B-S-69926).

Data Availability Statement: The data that support the findings of this study are available within the article.

Acknowledgments: The authors of this paper are grateful to the Laboratory of Applied Thermal and Hydraulic Engineering (LABINTHAP) at the National Polytechnic Institute of Mexico for their valuable contributions and provision of computational resources. Additionally, the assistance of Abimelec Moreno, from LABINTHAP, National Polytechnic Institute of Mexico, in providing the experimental data is sincerely appreciated.

Conflicts of Interest: The authors state that there are no conflicts to disclose. The funders had no role in the design of the study; in the collection of data; or the analyses.

References

1. Kumar, P.; Saini, R.P. Study of cavitation in hydro turbines—A review. *Renew. Sustain. Energy Rev.* **2010**, *14*, 374–383. [Cross
2. Sun, Y.; Guan, Z.; Hooman, K. Cavitation in Diesel Fuel Injector Nozzles and its Influence on Atomization and Spray. *Chem. Technol.* **2019**, *42*, 6–29. [CrossRef]
3. Balz, R.; IG, N.; Weisser, G.; Sedarsky, D. Experimental and numerical investigation of cavitation in marine Diesel injectors. *J. Heat Mass Transf.* **2021**, *169*, 120933. [CrossRef]
4. Li, R.; Xu, W.L.; Luo, J.; Yuan, H.; Zhao, W.Y. A Study on Aeration to Alleviate Cavitation Erosion in the Contraction Sectio Pressure Flow. *J. Fluids Eng. Trans. ASME* **2019**, *141*, 091108. [CrossRef]
5. Gouin, C.; Junqueira-Junior, C.; Goncalves Da Silva, E.; Robinet, J.C. Numerical investigation of three-dimensional par cavitation in a Venturi geometry. *Phys. Fluids* **2021**, *33*, 063312. [CrossRef]
6. Jahangir, S.; Wagner, E.C.; Mudde, R.F.; Poelma, C. Void fraction measurements in partial cavitation regimes by X-ray compu tomography. *Int. J. Multiph. Flow* **2019**, *120*, 103085. [CrossRef]
7. Charrière, B.; Goncalves, E. Numerical investigation of periodic cavitation shedding in a Venturi. *Int. J. Heat Fluid Flow* **2017** 41–54. [CrossRef]
8. Petkovšek, M.; Dular, M. Simultaneous observation of cavitation structures and cavitation erosion. *Wear* **2013**, *300*, 55- [CrossRef]
9. Podbevšek, D.; Petkovšek, M.; Ohl, C.D.; Dular, M. Kelvin-Helmholtz instability governs the cavitation cloud shedding in Ven microchannel. *Int. J. Multiph. Flow* **2021**, *142*, 103700. [CrossRef]
10. Dular, M.; Khlifa, I.; Fuzier, S.; Adama Maiga, M.; Coutier-Delgosha, O. Scale effect on unsteady cloud cavitation. *Exp. Fl* **2012**, *53*, 1233–1250. [CrossRef]
11. Long, X.; Zhang, J.; Wang, J.; Xu, M.; Lyu, Q.; Ji, B. Experimental investigation of the global cavitation dynamic behavior venturi tube with special emphasis on the cavity length variation. *Int. J. Multiph. Flow* **2017**, *89*, 290–298. [CrossRef]
12. Liu, Y.; Fan, H.; Wu, D.; Chen, H.; Feng, K.; Zhao, C.; Wu, D. Experimental investigation of the dynamic cavitation behavior wall static pressure characteristics through convergence-divergence venturis with various divergence angles. *Sci. Rep.* **2020** 14172. [CrossRef] [PubMed]
13. Mäkiharju, S.A.; Ganesh, H.; Ceccio, S.L. The dynamics of partial cavity formation, shedding and the influence of dissolved injected non-condensable gas. *J. Fluid Mech.* **2017**, *829*, 420–458. [CrossRef]
14. Brunhart, M.; Soteriou, C.; Gavaises, M.; Karathanassis, I.; Koukouvinis, P.; Jahangir, S.; Poelma, C. Investigation of cavita and vapor shedding mechanisms in a Venturi nozzle. *Phys. Fluids* **2020**, *32*, 083306. [CrossRef]
15. Tang, P.; Juárez, J.M.; Li, H. Investigation on the effect of structural parameters on cavitation characteristics for the venturi t using the CFD method. *Water* **2019**, *11*, 2194. [CrossRef]
16. Tomov, P.; Khelladi, S.; Ravelet, F.; Sarraf, C.; Bakir, F.; Vertenoeuil, P. Experimental study of aerated cavitation in a horizo venturi nozzle. *Exp. Therm. Fluid Sci.* **2016**, *70*, 85–95. [CrossRef]
17. Barre, S.; Rolland, J.; Boitel, G.; Goncalves, E.; Patella, R.F. Experiments and modeling of cavitating flows in venturi: Attac sheet cavitation. *Eur. J. Mech. B/Fluids* **2009**, *28*, 444–464. [CrossRef]
18. Jahangir, S.; Hogendoorn, W.; Poelma, C. Dynamics of partial cavitation in an axisymmetric converging-diverging nozzle. *I Multiph. Flow* **2018**, *106*, 34–45. [CrossRef]
19. Jain, T.; Carpenter, J.; Saharan, V.K. CFD Analysis and Optimization of Circular and Slit Venturi for Cavitational Activity. *J. M Sci. Mech. Eng.* **2014**, *1*, 28–33.
20. Hee Lee, G.; Ho Bae, J. CFD Simulation of Cavitation Flow inside a Cavitating Venturi using ANSYS CFX. In Proceedings of Transactions of the Korean Nuclear Society Virtual Spring Meeting, Virtual, 9–10 July 2020.
21. Launder, B.E.; Spalding, D.B. The numerical computation of turbulent flows. *Comput. Methods Appl. Mech. Eng.* **1974**, *3*, 269– [CrossRef]
22. Launder, B.E.; Spalding, D.B. *Lectures in Mathematical Models of Turbulence*; Academic Press, Inc: London, UK, 1975.
23. Shih, T.-H.; Liou, W.W.; Shabbir, A.; Yang, Z.; Zhu, J. A new k-ϵ eddy viscosity model for high reynolds number turbulent fl *Comput. Fluids* **1995**, *24*, 227–238. [CrossRef]
24. Shih, T.H.; Zhu, J.; Lumley, J.L. A new Reynolds stress algebraic equation model. *Comput. Methods Appl. Mech. Eng.* **1995**, 287–302. [CrossRef]
25. Yakhot, V.; Orszag, S.A. Renormalization group analysis of turbulence. I. Basic theory. *J. Sci. Comput.* **1986**, *1*, 3–51. [CrossR
26. Wilcox, D.C. *Turbulence Modelling for CFD*, 3rd ed.; DCW Industries, Inc.: San Diego, CA, USA, 2006.
27. Menter, F.R. Two-equation eddy-viscosity turbulence models for engineering applications. *AIAA J.* **1994**, *32*, 1598–1605. [Cross
28. Menter, F.; Lechner, R. *Best Practice: Generalized k-omega (GEKO) Two-Equation Turbulence Modeling in Ansys CFD*; ANSYS: Can Sburg, PA, USA, 2021; pp. 1–32.
29. Coutier-Delgosha, O.; Fortes-Patella, R.; Reboud, J.L. Simulation of unsteady cavitation with a two-equation turbulence m including compressibility effects. *J. Turbul.* **2002**, *3*, N58. [CrossRef]
30. Chebli, R.; Coutier-Delgosha, O.; Audebert, B. Numerical simulation of unsteady cavitating flows using a fractional step me preserving the minimum/maximum principle for the void fraction. *IOP Conf. Ser. Mater. Sci. Eng.* **2013**, *52*, 1–7. [CrossRef]
31. Chebli, R.; Audebert, B.; Zhang, G.; Coutier-Delgosha, O. Influence of the turbulence modeling on the simulation of unste cavitating flows. *Comput. Fluids* **2021**, *221*, 104898. [CrossRef]

Charrière, B.; Decaix, J.; Goncalvès, E. A comparative study of cavitation models in a Venturi flow. *Eur. J. Mech. B/Fluids* **2015**, *49*, 287–297. [CrossRef]
Spalart, P.R.; Allmaras, S.R. One-equation turbulence model for aerodynamic flows. *Rech. Aerosp.* **1994**, *1*, 5–21. [CrossRef]
Fadaeiroodi, R.; Pasandidehfard, M. Investigation of the New GEKO Turbulence Model For Flows with Cavitation Around Projectiles with Flat and Hemispherical Heads. *Fluid Mech. Aerodyn. J.* **2021**, *10*, 37–53.
He, D.; Bai, B. Numerical investigation of wet gas flow in Venturi meter. *Flow Meas. Instrum.* **2012**, *28*, 1–6. [CrossRef]
Moreno-García, A.; Rivera-López, J.E.; Arciniega-Nartinez, J.L. Experimental Characterization of the Flow Pattern in Different Cavitation and Liquid Temperature Regimens in a Rectangular Section Venturi. *Rev. Multidisc. Av. Invest. REMAI* **2018**, *4*, 31–39. (In Spanish)
Moreno-García, A. Numerical-Experimental Study of the Cloud of Cavitation Bubbles in a Venturi Tube. Master's Thesis, IPN, Mexico City, Mexico, 2021; p. 128. (In Spanish). Available online: http://tesis.ipn.mx/handle/123456789/28792 (accessed on 12 April 2021).
JCGM 100:2008; Evaluation of Measurement Data—Guide to the Expression of Uncertainty in Measurement. 1st ed, BIPM: Sèvres, France, 2008; Volume 50. Available online: http://www.bipm.org/en/publications/guides/gum.html (accessed on 12 April 2021).
ANSYS Fluent. *ANSYS, Inc Release 13 Southpointe, 275 Technol Drive*; ANSYS Fluent: Canonsburg, PA, USA, 2013.
Seveno, E. *Towards an Adaptive Advancing Front Method*, 6th ed.; International Meshing Roundtable: London, UK, 1997; pp. 349–362.
Ingram, D.M.; Causon, D.M.; Mingham, C.G. Developments in Cartesian cut cell methods. *Math. Comput. Simul.* **2003**, *61*, 561–572. [CrossRef]
Kader, B.A. Temperature and concentration profiles in fully turbulent boundary layers. *Int. J. Heat Mass Transf.* **1981**, *24*, 1541–1544. [CrossRef]
Goncalves, E.; Decaix, J. Wall model and mesh influence study for partial cavities. *Eur. J. Mech. B/Fluids* **2012**, *31*, 12–29. [CrossRef]
Durbin, P.A.; Medic, G.; Seo, J.M.; Eaton, J.K.; Song, S. Rough Wall Modification of Two-Layer k—ε. *J. Fluids Eng. Trans. ASME* **2001**, *123*, 16–21. [CrossRef]
Issa, R.I. Solution of the implicitly discretised fluid flow equations by operator-splitting. *J. Comput. Phys.* **1986**, *62*, 40–65. [CrossRef]
Freiziger, J.H.; Períc, M.; Street, R. *Computational Methods for Fluid Flow*, 4th ed.; Springer Nature: Cham, Switzerland, 2020. [CrossRef]
Patankar, S.V. *Numerical Heat Transfer and Fluid Flow*; Hemisphere Publishing Corporation: New York, NY, USA, 1980. [CrossRef]
Leonard, B.P. A stable and accurate convective modelling procedure based on quadratic upstream interpolation. *Comput. Methods Appl. Mech. Eng.* **1979**, *19*, 59–98. [CrossRef]
Waterson, N.P.; Deconinck, H. A unified approach to the design and application of bounded higher-order convection schemes. In *Numerical Methods in Laminar and Turbulent Flow, Proceedings of the Third International Conference, Seattle, WA, USA, 8–11 August 1983*; Pineridge Press: Atlanta, GA, USA, 1995; pp. 10–14.
Gaskell, P.H.; Lau, A.K.C. Curvature-compensated convective transport: SMART, A new boundedness- preserving transport algorithm. *Int. J. Numer. Methods Fluids* **1988**, *8*, 617–641. [CrossRef]
van Leer, B. Towards the ultimate conservative difference scheme. V. A second-order sequel to Godunov's method. *J. Comput. Phys.* **1979**, *32*, 101–136. [CrossRef]
Muzaferija, S.; Peric, M.; Sames, P.; Schellin, T. A two-fluid Navier-Stokes solver to simulate water entry. In Proceedings of the 22nd Symp. Nav. Hydrodyn. The National Academies Press: Washington, DC, USA, 1998; pp. 638–651.
Waclawczyk, T.; Koronowicz, T. Comparison of cicsam and hric high-resolution schemes for interface capturing. *J. Theor. Appl. Mech.* **2008**, *46*, 325–345.
Nichols, B.D.; Hirt, C.W.; Hotchkiss, R.S. *SOLA-VOF: A Solution Algorithm for Transient Fluid Flow with Multiple Free Boundaries*; No. LA-8355; Los Alamos National Lab.(LANL): Los Alamos, NM, USA, 1980.
Brackbill, J.U.; Kothe, D.B.; Zemach, C. A continuum method for modeling surface tension. *J. Comput. Phys.* **1992**, *100*, 335–354. [CrossRef]
Reboud, J.-L.; Stutz, B.; Coutier, O. Two-phase flow structure of cavitation: Experiment and modelling of unsteady effects. In Proceedings of the 3rd International Symposium on Cavitation CAV1998, Grenoble, France, 7–10 April 1998; pp. 1–8.
Goncalvs, E. Numerical study of unsteady turbulent cavitating flows. *Eur. J. Mech. B/Fluids* **2011**, *30*, 26–40. [CrossRef]
Ahn, S.J.; Kwon, O.J. Numerical investigation of cavitating flows for marine propulsors using an unstructured mesh technique. *Int. J. Heat Fluid Flow* **2013**, *43*, 259–267. [CrossRef]
Sauer, J.; Schnerr, G.H. Unsteady cavitating flow—A new cavitation model based on a modified front capturing method and bubble dynamics. *Am. Soc. Mech. Eng. Fluids Eng. Div. FED* **2000**, *251*, 1073–1079.
Plesset, M.S. The Dynamics of Cavitation Bubbles. *J. Appl. Mech.* **1949**, *16*, 277–282. [CrossRef]
Zhou, Z.; Li, Q.; Liang, T.; Gong, S. The Numerical Simulation of Cavitation Phenomenon in a Venturi Tube. *J. Phys. Conf. Ser.* **2022**, *2364*, 012051. [CrossRef]
Furness, R.A. BS 7405: The principles of flowmeter selection. *Flow Meas. Instrum.* **1991**, *2*, 233–242. [CrossRef]
Yayla, S.; Yaseen, S.; Olcay, A.B. Numerical Investigation of Cavitation on Different Venturi Models. *J. Inst. Nat. Appl. Sci.* **2015**, *20*, 22–33.

64. Sridevi, T.; Shekhar, D.; Subrahmanyam, V. Comparison of Flow Analysis Through a Different Geometry of Flowmeters U Fluent Software. *Int. J. Res. Eng. Technol.* **2014**, *3*, 141–149. [CrossRef]
65. Huang, B.; Zhao, Y.; Wang, G. Large eddy simulation of turbulent vortex-cavitation interactions in transient sheet/cloud cavita flows. *Comput. Fluids* **2014**, *92*, 113–124. [CrossRef]
66. Callenaere, M.; Franc, J.-P.; Michel, J.-M.; Riondet, M. The cavitation instability induced by the development of a re-entrar *J. Fluid Mech.* **2001**, *444*, 223–256. [CrossRef]

fluids

MDPI

icle

ipe Formation by Fluid Focalization in Bilayered Sediments

rélien Gay [1,*], Ganesh Tangavelou [2] and Valérie Vidal [2,*]

1 Géosciences Montpellier, CNRS, Université de Montpellier, Université des Antilles, Place Eugène Bataillon, 34095 Montpellier, France
2 ENSL, CNRS, Laboratoire de Physique, F-69342 Lyon, France
* Correspondence: aurelien.gay@umontpellier.fr (A.G.); valerie.vidal@ens-lyon.fr (V.V.)

Abstract: Pipe structures are commonly encountered in the geophysical context, and in particular in sedimentary basins, where they are associated with fluid migration structures. We investigate pipe formation through laboratory experiments by injecting water locally at a constant flow rate at the base of water-saturated sands in a Hele–Shaw cell (30 cm high, 35 cm wide, gap 2.3 mm). The originality of this work is to quantify the effect of a discontinuity. More precisely, bilayered structures are considered, where a layer of fine grains overlaps a layer of coarser grains. Different invasion structures are reported, with fluidization of the bilayered sediment over its whole height or over the finer grains only. The height and area of the region affected by the fluidization display a non-monotonous evolution, which can be interpreted in terms of fluid focusing vs. scattering. Theoretical considerations can predict the critical coarse grains height for the invasion pattern transition, as well as the maximum topography at the sediment free surface in the regime in which only the overlapping finer grains fluidize. These results have crucial geophysical implications, as they demonstrate that invasion patterns and pipe formation dynamics may control the fluid expulsion extent and localization at the seafloor.

Keywords: granular media; underwater sediments; two-phase flows; fluid pipes; multi-layered systems; interfaces

1. Introduction

In the geophysical context, "pipes" refer to structures of upward fluid migration in sedimentary basins, followed by fluid expulsion at the seafloor [1–4]. They are easily recognizable in seismic profiles, where reflectors corresponding to the different sedimentary layers are locally disturbed by the fluid rise and exhibit a vertical chimney (Figure 1). On the seafloor, these structures display a topography anomaly ranging from tens of meters up to a few kilometers [5]. In recent decades, they have increasingly focused the attention of the geophysical community due to their risk potential. On the one hand, fluid expulsion at the seafloor may trigger slope instability and large submarine landslides; on the other hand, they represent strong geohazards for anthropic activities such as offshore resources, transoceanic telecom fibers and CO_2 sequestration. Lastly, massive greenhouse fluid emissions have been correlated to important climate changes in Earth's history [6–11].

Although pipes in sedimentary basins have been extensively characterized (see, among many other examples, [2,5,12–14]) and new technologies provide more and more extensive and high-quality geophysical data, images and measurements at the seafloor only provide a present-day picture of these processes. The challenge, therefore, is to obtain insights into their dynamics—either short or long term—to evaluate their risk potential [15]. To do so, many analogue experiments [16–25] and numerical models [4,13,22,25–28] have been proposed in the literature (see also [29] for a complementary review). However, these models mostly consider a homogeneous sedimentary bed and scarcely account for its complex structure. Sedimentary basins are characterized by successive deposits, which appear as multiple reflectors in the seismic profiles, making it look like a geological millefeuille, with multiple layers exhibiting different physical properties (Figure 1). To our knowledge, few studies in the literature consider the effect of discontinuities, i.e., interfaces between two layers of different properties, on sediment mobilization and fluid escape structures [16,19,30]. The few existing works mainly focus on the effect of cohesion of the covering layer. Therefore, there is a gap in the literature about fundamental studies of the effect of a discontinuity between two layers of different granulometry on upward fluid migration and pipe formation.

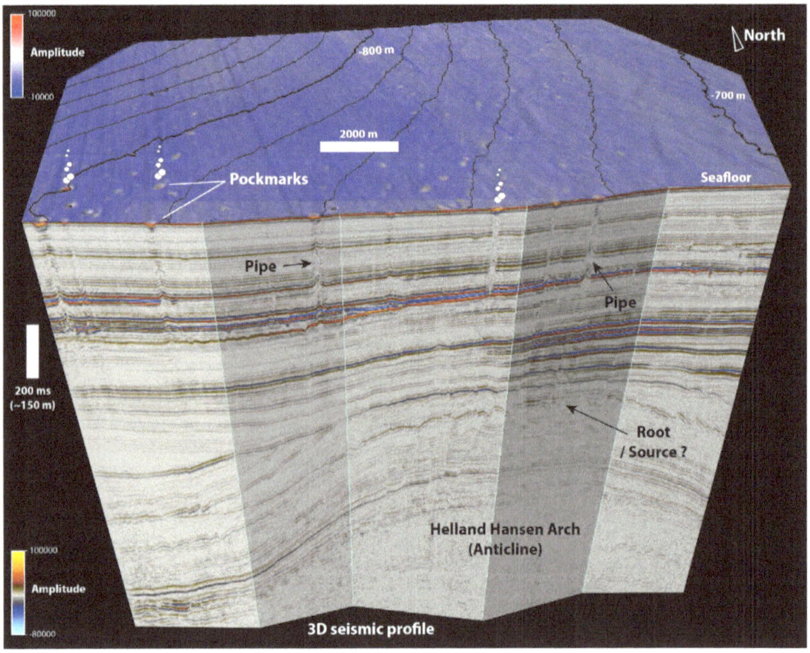

Figure 1. A 3D view of a fluid expulsion province in the Norway Basin (Helland Hansen Arch) [31]. Deep and shallow fluids migrate through a millefeuille of layers with different physical properties (porosity, permeability, cohesion, etc.) leading to focused fluid migration (pipes) and expulsion (pockmarks). These structures are identified on geophysical records as high-amplitude anomalies and/or dimming of reflectors. Even with the best resolution available, the root (or source) of fluids remains debated.

The present work aims at quantifying pipe formation and evolution in a bilayered sediment, considering non-cohesive granular materials. The goal here is to provide a precise quantification of the pipe dynamics in a non-cohesive sediment, in the presence of a discontinuity, to investigate its effect on the fluid focalization. To do so, we will consider a bilayer made of large grains at the bottom, and small grains overlaying the large grains. "Large grains" here refer to grains large enough so that without the smaller grains on their top, the fluid percolates through them—except for very thin monolayers. Conversely, a monolayer of "small grains" always displays fluidization in the range of parameters explored in this work. In the following, we present the materials and methods (Section 2). We then describe the formation of pipes, i.e., focalized fluid migration, in bilayered sediments, when varying the total sediment height or the ratio between the large and small grains height (Section 3). The results are finally discussed in Section 4.

2. Materials and Methods

2.1. Experimental Setup

The experimental setup (Figure 2) consists of a Hele–Shaw cell made of two glass plates (height 30 cm, width $W = 35$ cm) separated by a thin gap ($e = 2.3$ mm). This configuration makes it possible to visualize the migration pattern of the incoming fluid, which is otherwise impossible to see in opaque granular media. The cell is filled with a granular bed (see Section 2.2), initially immersed in clear distilled water (density $\rho_w = 1000$ kg.m^{-3}). At the beginning of the experiment, water at a constant flow rate Q is injected locally at the bottom center of the cell via a cylindrical nozzle (inner diameter 1.1 mm). The injected water is dyed in dark blue (food dye *Meilleur du Chef* E133, 0.6% vv.) so that it can be distinguished from the water in which the grains are initially deposited. It has been checked that the dye does not modify the physical properties of the liquid. The flow rate is imposed using a pump (Tuthill 7.11.468) coupled with a flow controller (Bronkhorst mini CORI-FLOW M14-AAD-22-0-S) and can be varied in the range of 2–100 mL/min. The water exits the system uniformly by the top cell aperture by overflow (Figure 2) and is collected using a gully surrounding the cell's top part.

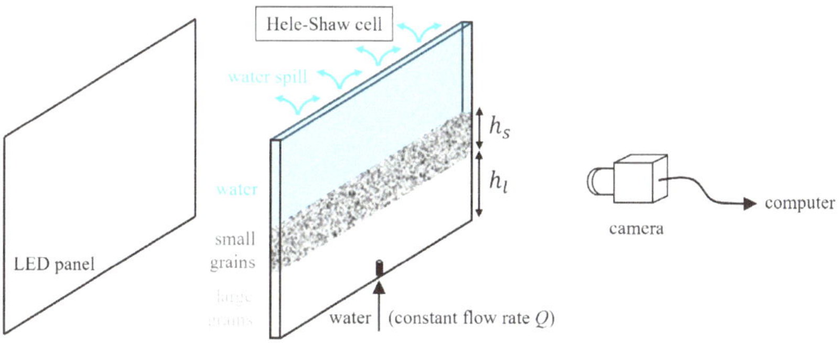

Figure 2. Experimental setup. The water spill system (by overflow) and the flow controller devices are not shown.

The cell is illuminated by transmission with a homogeneous light panel (Just Normlicht Classic Line) located behind the cell. Images are recorded with a camera (Basler monochrome, acA2040-90 µm, 2048 × 2048 pixels) mounted with a 16 mm or 25 mm lens, depending on the experiments. A calibration grid is used prior to each experiment to provide a precise conversion from pixels to mm. The acquisition frequency is set between 10 and 36 fps depending on the experiment. All experiments are performed at room temperature.

2.2. Granular Media

The grains used in the experiments are polydisperse spherical glass beads with a density $\rho_g = 2300$ kg.m^{-3}. Polydispersity is chosen on purpose; first, to avoid crystallization, a process that classically occurs in monodisperse spherical beads; and second, to mimick the polydispersity of natural sands. Two batches have been used to compose the bilayered sediment. The bottom layer (height h_l, Figure 2) is made of the larger grains (USF Matrasur, diameter $d_l = 425$–600 µm). The smaller grains (Wheelabrator, diameter $d_s = 106$–212 µm) are located in the top layer (height h_s, Figure 2), covering the sediments of a larger size. In the following, we will refer to these two batches as the "large grains" and "small grains", respectively. In the following, the total initial sediment height is $h_0 = h_l + h_s$.

The particle size distribution has been measured with a macroscope (Wild Makroskop M420 1.25×) mounted with a Makrozoom Leica 1:5 lens. Figure 3 displays the particle size distribution for the two grain batches.

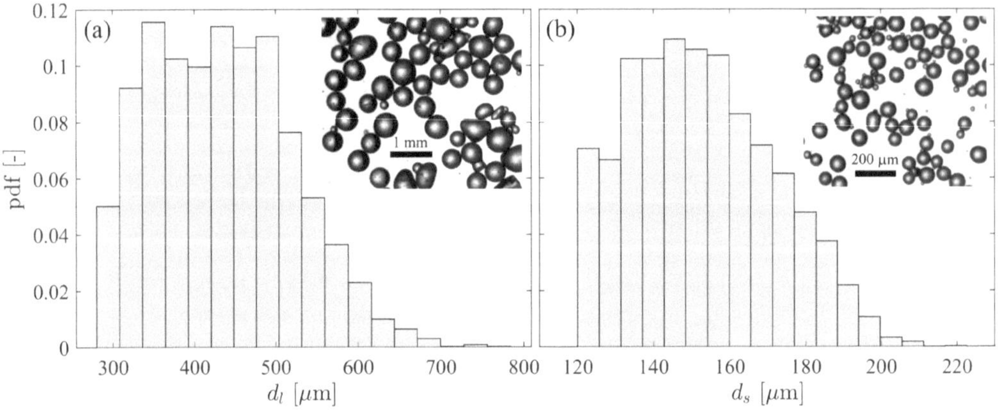

Figure 3. Particle size distribution (power density function) (**a**) for the large grains (d_l = 425–600 μm, over 3653 particles) and (**b**) the small grains (d_s = 106–212 μm, over 3333 particles).

3. Results

3.1. Invasion Regimes

Figure 4 displays the different invasion regimes for a constant total granular layer height (here, 11 cm) when varying the ratio between the large and small grains, h_l/h_s. As stated in the introduction, the "small grains" are chosen so that, in our experimental range, a monolayer of such grains always fluidizes (Figure 4a, Supplemental Video S1). The fluid penetrates the granular layer, forming a finger, which propagates upwards until reaching the granular free surface. At long times (Figure 4a, t = 98.52 s), the central fluidized zone has a specific shape well known in the geophysical context as the "stem and corolla" shape, with a vertical chimney topped by a flared area, also referred to as a "funnel and pipe" structure [5,32]. Note that the granular layer fluidization is coupled with percolation around the central zone since the initial invasion (Figure 4a, t = 3.24 s), and the lateral invasion due to this process increases in time (Figure 4a, t = 98.52 s).

Conversely, the "large grains" are chosen so that a monolayer of such grains, when high enough ($h_l \geq$ 3.5 cm), is in the percolation regime, i.e., the invading fluid will propagate through the pore network without moving the grains significantly. For very thin layers ($h_l <$ 3.5 cm), a "large-grain" monolayer exhibits fluidization. When introducing a small large-grain layer at the bottom of the experiment (Figure 4b, Supplemental Video S2), independently of the monolayer behavior, a percolation invasion regime always occurs at the first instant (Figure 4b, t = 1.96 s). However, when the invading fluid reaches the interface, it generates a horizontal decompaction zone (Figure 4b, t = 7.76 s, light region above the interface). This decompaction zone fluidizes the upper small-grain layer by generating, as in the above monolayer configuration, a finger that propagates upwards. In addition, it is capable of fluidizing the large grains layer, too, by entraining the particles above the injection nozzle.

An interesting change in the invasion regime appears when the ratio h_l/h_s reaches a critical value. Above this value, the flow-scattering due to the percolation process is strong enough that the effective flux crossing the interface is not able to entrain the large particles anymore, even at long times (Figure 4c,d, Supplemental Videos S3 and S4). Note that for our experimental parameters, the above small-grain layer is always fluidized. It is interesting to note that due to the fluid's incompressibility, the decompaction and fluidization above the interface starts before the dyed injected fluid reaches the interface (see, for instance, Figure 4c, t = 2.40 s). It therefore acts as a secondary source, located at the interface, with a spatial extent L_i given by the properties of the medium.

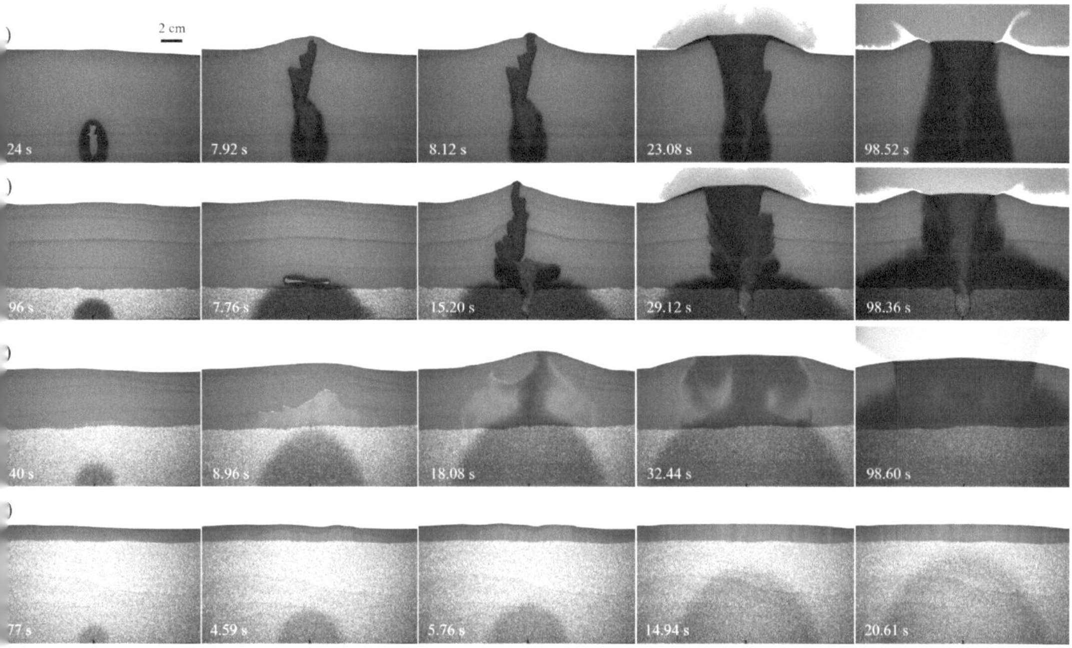

Figure 4. Different invasion regimes for a constant height when varying the large-to-small grain ratio [$Q = 30$ mL/min]. (**a**) Monolayer of small grains [$h_s = 11$ cm, Video S1]. (**b**) Fluidization of both layers of grains [$h_l = 3$ cm, $h_s = 8$ cm, Video S2]. (**c**) Percolation in the bottom layer, fluidization of the small grains [$h_l = 5.5$ cm, $h_s = 5.5$ cm, Video S3]. (**d**) Percolation in the bottom layer, fluidization of the small grains [$h_l = 10$ cm, $h_s = 1$ cm, Video S4].

Figure 5 summarizes the different invasion patterns when varying the total height of the sediments and the ratio between the large and small grains. The experimental points for a large or small-grain monolayer are reported in black with, as expected, percolation (black squares) or fluidization (black triangles), respectively. In the bilayer, the region where both layers fluidize (gray region, gray diamonds) can be clearly distinguished from the region where the invading fluid always percolates in the bottom (large-grain) layer, while it fluidizes the above (small-grain) layer (white region, white dots). Interestingly, the transition does not depend on h_s and seems controlled by a critical large-grain height, $h_l^c \approx 3.5$ cm. This constant value will be discussed in Section 4.1. Note that for this critical value, an intriguing behavior arises. Indeed, a monolayer of large grains with $h_l = h_l^c$ exhibits percolation. When adding a small-grain layer on top, the large grains still exhibit a percolation regime (white dots, Figure 5) until a critical load. When reaching $h_s = 9$ cm, the system exhibits fluidization in both layers. The reproducibility of such behavior has been checked by repeating the experiments (double symbols, Figure 5).

Next, in Section 3.2, we investigate the pipe formation dynamics. Unless otherwise stated, we will present results associated with a constant total sediment height, when varying the ratio h_l/h_s (Figure 5, dashed line).

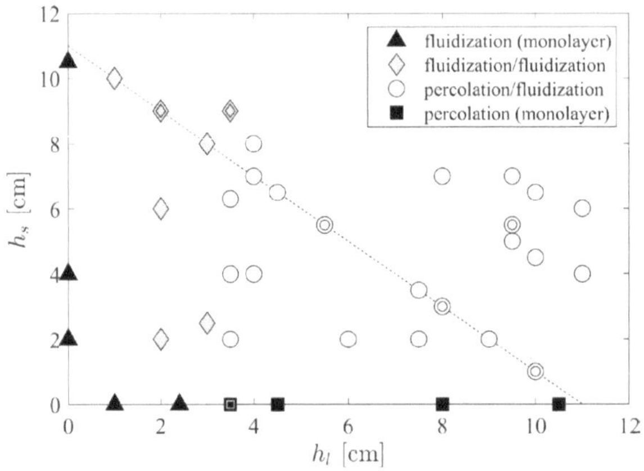

Figure 5. Regime diagram for the invasion patterns [$Q = 30$ mL/min]. For a monolayer, the system always fluidizes (small grains, black triangles) or percolates (large grains, black squares). Note that a large-grain monolayer may exhibit fluidization for a small height ($h_l < 3.5$ cm). For a bilayer, we report either fluidization of both layers (gray region, gray diamonds) or percolation in the large grains topped by fluidization of the above small grains layer (white region, white dots). The dashed line represents a constant total height $h_0 = 11$ cm, corresponding to the series of experiments most studied in this work. Double symbols indicate reproducibility check.

3.2. Pipe Formation Dynamics

3.2.1. Decompaction Front

As reported above, the pipe always initiates at the interface. Figure 6a displays a spatiotemporal diagram showing the dynamics of pipe initiation and formation. This diagram reports, for each time t, the intensity along a vertical line above the injection nozzle. This line, at $t = 0$, is characterized by the signature of the large-grain layer (white and dark pattern from $z = 0$ to 8 cm) and the small-grain layer (darker gray from $z = 8$ to 11 cm), topped with clear water (Figure 6a). Note here that although spatiotemporal diagrams are convenient to characterize the pipe dynamics, they have to be considered with caution. In particular, they can be interpreted only during the first stage of the pipe formation. Indeed, the pipe can later shift offline with respect to the vertical of the nozzle (see, for instance, Figure 4b, $t = 15.20$ s, left shift or Figure 4c, $t = 18.08$ s, right shift). If such a shift happens, the spatiotemporal diagram is not representative anymore of the topmost fluidized point, and the pipe dynamics may thus be misinterpreted. In particular, as the topmost fluidized point displays the fastest upward velocity, interpreting the spatiotemporal diagram in such a case may lead to an underestimation of the pipe front velocity.

At $t \geq 0$, the dyed water invades the large-grain layer from the bottom upwards (bottom dark region, Figure 6a). As the fluid migrates by percolation, the large grains do not move, resulting in fixed horizontal lines in the spatiotemporal diagram. After a time t_{front}, a decompaction front initiates at the interface, then grows and propagates upwards (light gray region in the small grains layer, Figure 6a). Figure 6b displays the altitude of this decompaction front, z_{front}, as a function of time from its initiation, t_{front}. At short times, it varies linearly in time, indicating a constant initiation velocity.

Figure 7 displays the decompaction front velocity as a function of the percentage of large grains, h_l/h_0, for a constant initial sediment height h_0. When introducing a small large grains layer at the bottom, the system, although exhibiting an initial percolation in the large grains layer, still fully fluidizes (gray diamonds, Figure 7), but the decompaction front velocity drops drastically—by almost two orders of magnitude for ~30% of large grains at the bottom. When increasing the large-to-small grains ratio, we enter the regime where the fluidization of the top small-grain layer is not able to entrain the large grains anymore. The bottom large-grain layer remains in the percolation regime, and the decompaction front velocity in the above layer exhibits an almost constant value (~0.1–0.2 cm/s, white dots, Figure 7).

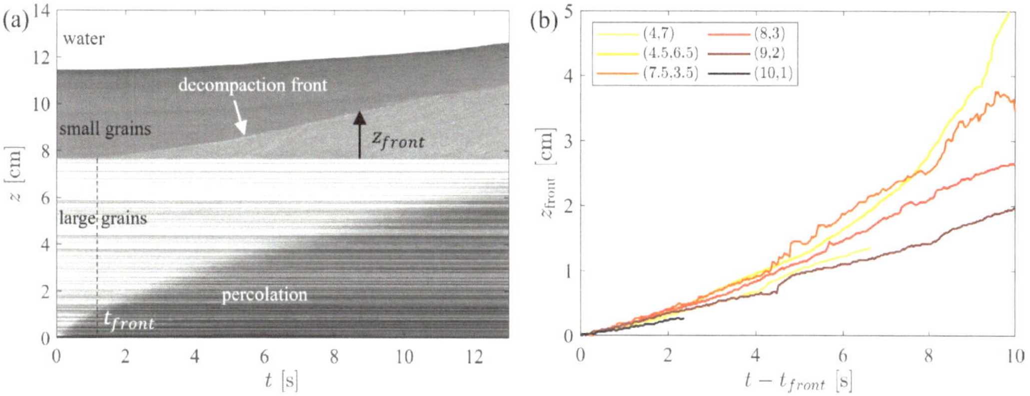

Figure 6. Dynamics of pipe initiation and formation. (**a**) Spatiotemporal diagram of the intensity along a vertical line above the injection nozzle [$h_l = 8$ cm, $h_s = 3$ cm, $Q = 30$ mL/min]. At time $t = 0$, the dyed water invades the large grains (percolation, bottom dark region). The fluidization starts at the interface at time t_{front}, via a decompaction front that propagates upwards (light gray region in the small-grain layer). (**b**) Decompaction front elevation from the interface, z_{front}, as a function of time counted from the decompaction front generation, $t - t_{front}$, for different granular layers (h_l, h_s) [cm] indicated in the legend. Note the linear behavior at short times.

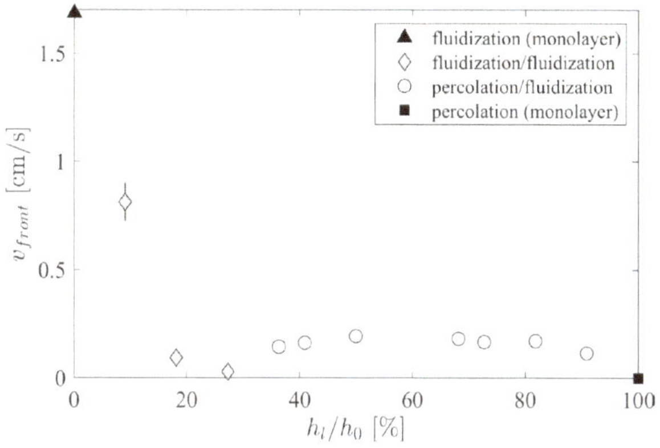

Figure 7. Decompaction front velocity v_{front} as a function of the large grain ratio h_l/h_0, in percents [$h_0 = 11$ cm, $Q = 30$ mL/min]. If not visible, the error bars are smaller than the symbol size. The white and gray regions indicate the invasion regimes (Figure 5).

The drastic drop in the decompaction front velocity is the consequence of the large-grain layer which acts as a scatterer for the incoming fluid. Even in the fluidization/fluidization regime, the fluid first invades the large-grain layer by percolation, before reaching the interface with the small grains and decompacting/fluidizing the whole system. Compared to a direct injection via the bottom nozzle, the fluid spread by the large grains reaches the small-grain layer with a much lower velocity, resulting henceforth in a slower decompaction process and a drastic drop in the decompaction front velocity.

3.2.2. Fluidization

After its formation, the decompaction front propagates upwards until reaching the free surface. We define the fluidization time, t_f, as the time between the start of injection, when the fluid first enters the system, until the time at which the fluidized region reaches the free surface of the sediment bilayer. Figure 8a displays the fluidization time as a function of the large-grain percentage, h_l/h_0. Experimental data are reported here for different initial sediment height h_0 (colorbar, Figure 8, right). In spite of different initial conditions (h_0 and h_l/h_0), the data are well organized into two distinct regions. The higher the large-grain percentage h_l/h_0 in the bilayer, the smaller the fluidization time at the transition between the two regimes (fluidization of both layers, diamonds, and fluidization of the top layer only, dots). This result may be surprising, as, when h_l/h_0 increases, one may think that the percolation will take longer to propagate up to the interface and then fluidize the smaller grains layer. However, it is important here to remember that, due to fluid incompressibility, as soon as the fluid is injected at the cell bottom, it propagates through the whole cell, including the small-grain layer, by percolation or fluidization.

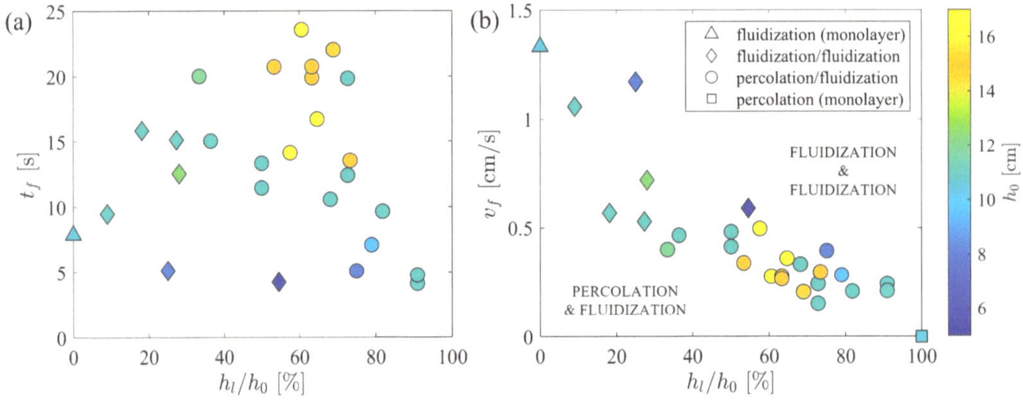

Figure 8. (**a**) Fluidization time t_f and (**b**) fluidization velocity $v_f = h_s/t_f$ as a function of the percentage of large grains, h_l/h_0 (see text). The error bars (~3 images at 36 fps corresponding to ~80 ms for t_f) are smaller than the symbol size. The symbols and white and gray regions indicate the invasion regimes (see Figure 5), while the colorbar (same for both figures) indicates the initial sediment height h_0 [$Q = 30$ mL/min].

To better understand the fluidization process, we report in Figure 8b the fluidization velocity, defined as $v_f = h_s/t_f$. It represents the average velocity of fluidization for the small-grain layer. Once again, all experimental data are grouped in two distinct regions, separating the two invasion regimes. This result makes it possible to define a critical fluidization velocity of about 0.5 cm/s, below which the flow is not able to entrain the large grains and fluidizes the small grains layer only. These results will be further discussed in Section 4.

3.3. *Height and Area of the Granular Bed*

When the sediment layer starts fluidizing, due to decompaction, we observe a deformation of the free surface. The free surface topography first increases, until the fluidized region reaches the surface (Figure 4), then decreases. In a similar way, the fluidized area increases, and then often decreases afterwards, due to the fluid focalization in the central region (see, for instance, Figure 4b). Let us denote δh the free surface topography elevation and δA the area increase at time t. Figure 9a displays an example of their temporal evolution. Their variation here is relative for δA to the initial bed area, $A_0 = Wh_0$ (Figure 9a), and for δh to the initial bed height, h_0 (Figure 9a, inset). Both the relative area and height variations show a similar behavior and exhibit a maximum named A_0^* and h_0^*, respectively (Figure 9a). Note that the maximum in the area and topography are reached at different times, indicated as t_A^* and t_h^*.

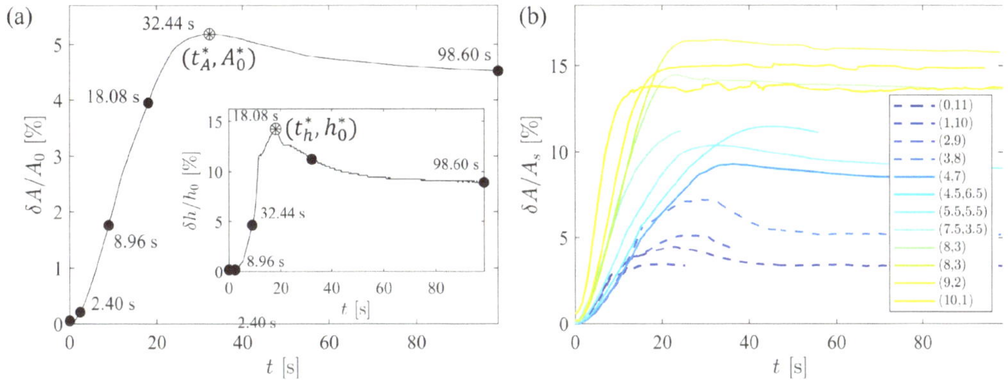

Figure 9. (**a**) Temporal evolution of the bed area (main plot) and bed height (inset) variations relative to the initial total bed area A_0 and total sediment height h_0, respectively (see text) [$h_l = 5.5$ cm, $h_s = 5.5$ cm, $Q = 30$ mL/min]. The times indicated for each dot for $t > 0$ correspond to the pictures shown in Figure 4c. A_0^* and h_0^* are the associated maxima reached at different times t_A^* and t_h^*, respectively. (**b**) Area variation relative to the initial small-grain area, $\delta A/A_s$, as a function of time, for different (h_l, h_s) [cm] [$h_0 = 11$ cm, $Q = 30$ mL/min].

Figure 9b reports the temporal variation of the bed area, δA, relative to the small-grain layer's initial area, $A_s = Wh_s$, for all experiments. This normalization was chosen for two reasons. First, the small-grain layer is the only one always fluidizing in all experiments, therefore contributing mainly to the topography and area variations. Second, the small-grain layer's height varies in the series with h_0 constant, and this variation has to be accounted for when normalizing the area variations. Applying this normalization displays an interesting ordering of the different experiments when varying (h_l, h_s) at constant total sediment height. Starting from a small-grain monolayer and increasing progressively the large grain ratio h_l/h_0, we observe a progressive increase in the maximum area which, at the same time, occurs later in time (Figure 9b, dark blue to light blue curves). After reaching an optimum both in the relative area $\delta A/A_s$ and in time t_A^*, both variables decrease. Note that if the times t_A^* and t_h^* do not vary depending on the normalization, the value of the maxima varies. For variables relative to the small-grain layer, we will denote the maxima in the area and height A_s^* and h_s^*, respectively.

Figure 10a displays the time t_A^* and t_h^* corresponding to the maximum in the bed area and height, respectively, as a function of the large-grain percentage, h_l/h_0. Both times follow the same trend. They increase while increasing the large-grain layer, until reaching the transition between the regime in which both layers are fluidized, and the percolating regime for the large-grain layer. After this transition, both times decrease. No point is available for $h_l/h_0 = 100\%$, as no fluidization occurs. The time to reach the maximum area is always larger than the time to reach the maximum sediment height. Figure 10b reports t_A^* as a function of t_h^*. Except close to the transition between the two regimes (larger times), which may be subjected to stronger fluctuations, a clear correlation appears between both times, with $t_A^* \approx 2t_h^*$ (dashed line, Figure 10b).

The maximum area and height relative to the initial sediment layer or the small-grain layer are represented in Figure 11 when varying the large-grain percentage. Similarly to their associated time to reach the maximum, A_0^* and h_0^* both display a non-monotonous behavior and a maximum value associated with the transition between the fluidization of both layers and the percolation regime for the large grains layer. The existence of this optimum can be interpreted as a focusing vs. scattering effect, which will be discussed in Section 4.2. Interestingly, when considering the area and height variations relative to the small-grain layer, A_s^* and h_s^*, no optimum is found, although the data variability strongly increases for large $h_l/h_0 \geq 40\%$. These results are further discussed in Section 4.3, wherein we propose a model to explain the decreasing area and height optimum in the percolation and fluidization regime (dashed line, Figure 11) and interpret the existence of an optimum in terms of fluid focusing vs. scattering.

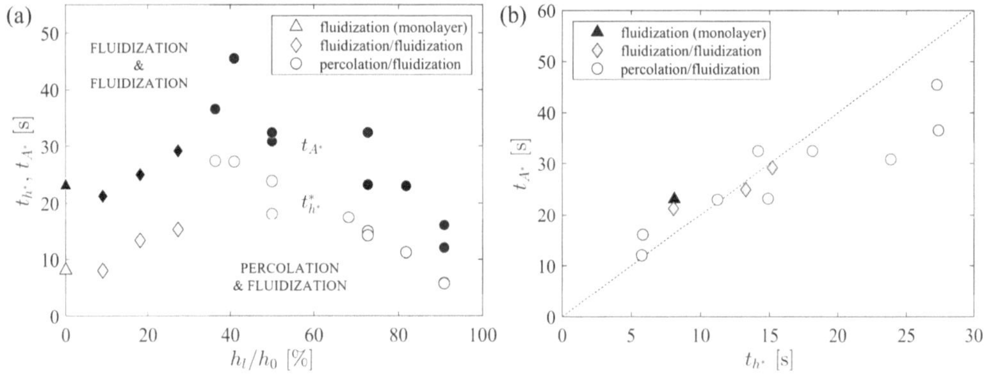

Figure 10. (**a**) Time to reach the maximum value of the bed area, t_A^* (black symbols), and height, t_h^* (white symbols), as a function of the large-grain percentage, h_l/h_0 [$h_0 = 11$ cm, $Q = 30$ mL/min]. (**b**) t_A^* vs. t_h^*. The dashed line indicates slope 2 (see text).

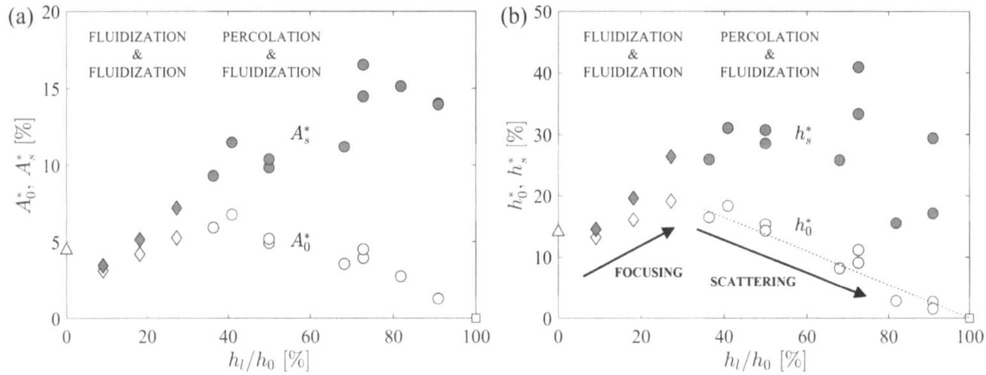

Figure 11. (**a**) Maximum bed area relative to the initial sediment height, A_0^* or to the small-grain area, A_s^*, as a function of the large grains ratio h_l/h_0. (**b**) Maximum bed height relative to the initial total sediment height, h_0^* or to the small-grain area, h_s^*, as a function of the ratio of large grains h_l/h_0. The symbols are identical to the ones in Figure 10a. The dashed line represents the model and the black arrows indicate the focusing vs. scattering effect (see Section 4.2) [$h_0 = 11$ cm, $Q = 30$ mL/min].

4. Discussion

4.1. Invasion Patterns: Transition from Percolation to Fluidization

In this section, we discuss the transition from percolation to fluidization reported for the large-grain layer when decreasing its height h_l (see Section 3.1). Experimentally, for $Q = 30$ mL/min, the critical height is $h_l^c \approx 3.5$ cm (Figure 5). The order of magnitude of h_l^c can be retrieved using a simple argument. Following previous erosion parameters introduced in the literature for soil or granular erosion threshold [33–36], we compare the fluid's upward velocity, u_f, to the particle settling velocity, u_p. Assuming that the interface between the two layers acts as a secondary source of length $L_i = \alpha h_l$, proportional to the large-grain layer height, the flow velocity at the interface is written as follows:

$$u_f = \frac{Q}{\alpha h_l e(1-\phi)} \tag{1}$$

where ϕ is the particle volume fraction. This velocity has to be compared to the particle settling velocity. In our experimental conditions, particles are in the inertial regime and their settling velocity is given by [37], as follows:

$$u_p = \sqrt{\frac{\Delta\rho}{\rho_g} g d_l} \tag{2}$$

where $\Delta\rho = \rho_g - \rho_w = 1300$ kg.m^{-3} is the difference between the particle and water density, $g = 9.81$ m.s^{-2} is the gravitational acceleration and d_l is the large grains' diameter. The flow at the interface manages to lift the large grains, i.e., to overcome the percolation-to-fluidization transition, when $u_f = u_p$, leading to the critical height:

$$h_l^c = \frac{Q}{\alpha e(1-\phi)} \left(\frac{\Delta\rho}{\rho_g} g d_l\right)^{-1/2} \tag{3}$$

This prediction can only provide a rough estimation, as the particles are strongly polydisperse (Figure 3), while a single particle diameter appears in Equation (3). As α is unknown in our system, we use Equation (3) with $h_l^c \approx 3.5$ cm to estimate its order of magnitude. The packing fraction of the large grains was measured by adding a known mass of grains into the cell, $\phi = 63.5 \pm 3.5\%$, and we consider the mean and standard deviation of the large grains' diameter from the particle size distribution (Figure 3a), $d_l = 430 \pm 85$ µm. This gives $\alpha \approx 0.19 - 0.28$. This range of values fits reasonably well with the experimental observations, with a secondary source at the interface always smaller than the initial bottom granular layer height. However, this approximation remains rough, as it is based on the settling velocity of a single particle, and considers neither polydispersity (except to infer the error on α) nor collective effects.

4.2. Fluid Focusing vs. Scattering

We discuss here the optimum found for the maximum area and height relative to the initial height, A_0^* and h_0^* (Figure 11). To do so, we compare the decompaction front velocity, v_{front}, to the fluidization velocity v_f (Figure 12). For a monolayer of small grains, which experiences full fluidization, the decompaction front initially propagates upwards at a speed *larger* than the average fluidization speed of the full layer (Figure 12, black triangle), meaning that the finger which propagates upwards (Figure 4a) decelerates before reaching the top. Introducing a small layer of large grains at the bottom of the system induces a drastic drop both in the decompaction front and in the total fluidization velocities. Whatever the percentage of large grains, as soon as h_l/h_0 is not null, the decompaction front at the interface exhibits an initial velocity that is lower than the full fluidization velocity (symbols below the dashed line, Figure 12). The decompaction front velocity almost drops to zero close to the transition between the regime in which both layers fluidize (gray region, Figure 12) and the regime in which the fluid always percolates in the large grains. In this second regime, v_f still decreases when h_l/h_0 increases, while v_{front} remains roughly constant.

We can interpret these results in terms of fluid propagation. Injecting fluid in a small grains monolayer leads to local fluidization close to the injection nozzle, resulting in the immediate formation of a finger (or "pipe") propagating upwards. The flow is then well focused up to the free surface. The introduction of a large grains layer at the cell bottom induces fluid percolation at short times in this layer, thus scattering the fluid in the granular matrix, before it meets the interface between both layers. This system can therefore be seen as a monolayer, with a larger effective source at its base (see Figure 4b). The resulting decompaction front propagates upwards and destabilizes to form a finger (pipe), which tends to refocus the flow. This focusing process tends to increase the maximum height and area of the granular bed (black upward arrow, Figure 11b). When the system is not able to fluidize both layers anymore (see Section 4.1), the scattering due to percolation in the large-grain layer and the resulting effective source at the interface becomes too large. The above small-grain layer is not able to refocus the fluid fully before reaching the free surface. The fluid may therefore pierce the free surface not at a single point, but over a wider area (see Figure 4d). The maximum height and area therefore decrease (black downward arrow, Figure 11b).

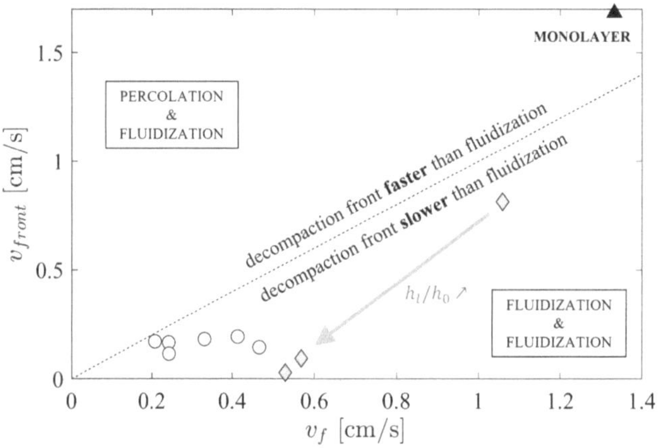

Figure 12. Decompaction front velocity v_{front} above the interface as a function of the fluidization velocity v_f of the small grains layer [$h_0 = 11$ cm, $Q = 30$ mL/min]. The symbols are identical to the ones in Figure 10.

4.3. Packing Fraction of the Fluidized Region

The decreasing behavior of h_0^* (black downward arrow, Figure 11b) can be modeled by considering a homogeneous packing fraction in the fluidized region, φ_f. Considering an initial packing fraction φ_0, it can be written as

$$\varphi_f = \left(\frac{h_s}{h_s + \delta h^*}\right)\varphi_0 \tag{4}$$

where δh^* is the maximum (absolute) topography variation.

Figure 13 displays the packing fraction in the fluidized region, φ_f, for all experiments. We have considered here $\varphi_0 = 65.2\%$, which has been measured directly in the experiments for small grains. In the regime in which only the small-grain layer fluidizes (white region, Figure 13), the packing fraction of the fluidized region remains almost constant, $\varphi_f \sim 51.2\%$. Extracting δh^* from Equation (4) and considering that $h_s = h_0\,(1 - h_l/h_0)$ gives

$$h_0^* = \frac{\delta h^*}{h_0} = \left(\frac{\varphi_0}{\varphi_f} - 1\right)\left(1 - \frac{h_l}{h_0}\right) \tag{5}$$

As φ_f is roughly constant, Equation (5) states that h_0^* varies as a decreasing linear function of h_l/h_0. Reporting this prediction without any adjustable parameter (dashed line, Figure 11b) provides a good estimation of the decreasing behavior of h_0^*, which is experimentally reported.

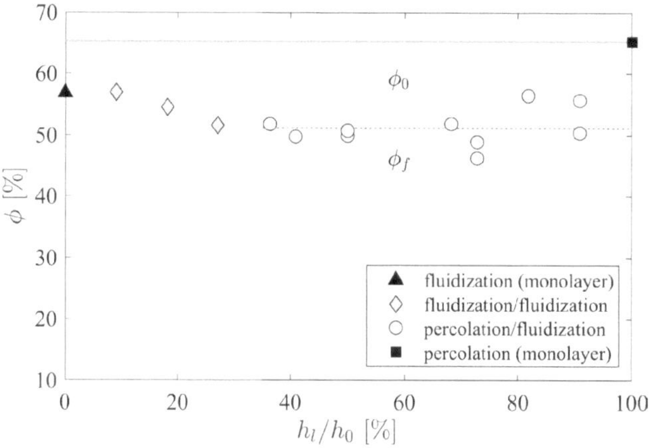

Figure 13. Packing fraction of the granular bed as a function of the percentage of large grains h_l/h_0. The initial packing fraction φ_0 is represented by the gray horizontal line (here $\varphi_0 = 65.2\%$, see text). The symbols represent the packing fraction computed in the small-grain fluidized region, φ_f, using Equation (4).

5. Conclusions

Geophysical pipes, which can be seen as focalized fluid migration structures, have been modeled in this work using laboratory experiments in which a fluid is injected at the bottom of a bilayered sediment. This study has demonstrated the drastic effect of the interface between the two sedimentary layers on the system dynamics. In particular, we have underlined the competition between fluid scattering in the bottom layer of coarse grains, due to percolation, and fluid focusing in the above small-grain layer, due to fluidization. The system displays a pipe formation when the focusing effect is stronger than the scattering effect, resulting in a single, localized fluid emission at the sediment's free surface. These "pipes" do not correspond here to the classical hydrodynamics or industrial definition of a rigid or deformable tube, but display a similar physics of fluid flow, either in a fixed geometry or, in the present case, in a geometry fixed by the system itself by fluid focalization.

The times associated with pipe formation (maximum height and area) exhibit a maximum for a percentage of large grains of about 35%, corresponding to the transition between the two invasion regimes (fluidization of both layers or percolation in the large grains and fluidization in the small-grain layer). This maximum can be interpreted as the largest scattering effect possible in the large grains layer in the regime where both layers fluidize. We cannot explain at present the ratio 2 between the time to reach the maximum area, and the time to reach the maximum height, and further theoretical arguments should be considered to understand this correlation.

The geophysical implications of this work are crucial. It is commonly believed that fluid expulsion at the seafloor is entirely controlled by faults acting as preferential paths for the fluid rising in the sedimentary layer. Here, we have demonstrated that invasion patterns and pipe formation dynamics control the fluid expulsion extent and localization at the seafloor without external driving factors. In addition, we have pointed out the utmost importance of sediments' composition. Indeed, sediments with a large-grain layer at their bottom, although of relatively small height, may act as a strong "scatterer" of the upward-moving fluid and slow down the pipe formation by decreasing its upward propagation velocity by one or two orders of magnitude. The perspectives for this work are to go further in the modeling of real sedimentary layers by considering multi-layered systems analogue to the geological millefeuille observed in sedimentary basins and introducing possible cohesive effects in the sediments.

Supplementary Materials: The following supporting information can be downloaded at: https://doi.org/10.5281/zenodo.10433274, Video S1: monolayer of small grains [h_s = 11 cm]; Video S2: fluidization of both layers of grains [h_l = 3 cm, h_s = 8 cm]; Video S3: percolation in the bottom layer, fluidization of the small grains [h_l = 5.5 cm, h_s = 5.5 cm]; Video S4: percolation in the bottom layer, fluidization of the small grains [h_l = 10 cm, h_s = 1 cm]. For all videos, Q = 30 mL/min (see Figure 4). Note that all movies start at $t < 0$, $t = 0$ being the time when the dyed fluid first invades the system.

Author Contributions: Conceptualization, A.G. and V.V.; investigation, G.T. and V.V.; methodology, V.V.; project administration, A.G. and V.V.; funding acquisition: A.G. and V.V.; resources, V.V.; software, G.T. and V.V.; supervision, A.G. and V.V.; validation, A.G., G.T. and V.V.; visualization, A.G. and V.V.; writing—original draft preparation, A.G. and V.V.; writing—review and editing, A.G., G.T. and V.V. All authors have read and agreed to the published version of the manuscript.

Funding: This research received no external funding.

Data Availability Statement: Data are contained within the article and Supplementary Materials.

Acknowledgments: The authors thank two anonymous referees for their pertinent comments which helped to increase the quality of the manuscript.

Conflicts of Interest: The authors declare no conflicts of interest.

References

1. Løseth, H.; Wensaas, L.; Arntsen, B.; Hanken, N.-M.; Basire, C.; Graue, K. 1000 m Long Gas Blow-out Pipes. *Mar. Pet. Geol.* **2** *28*, 1047–1060. [CrossRef]
2. Cartwright, J.; Santamarina, C. Seismic Characteristics of Fluid Escape Pipes in Sedimentary Basins: Implications for Pipe Gen *Mar. Pet. Geol.* **2015**, *65*, 126–140. [CrossRef]
3. Gay, A.; Migeon, S. Geological Fluid Flow in Sedimentary Basins. *Bull. Soc. Géol. Fr.* **2017**, *188*, E3. [CrossRef]
4. Räss, L.; Simon, N.S.C.; Podladchikov, Y.Y. Spontaneous Formation of Fluid Escape Pipes from Subsurface Reservoirs. *Sci.* **2018**, *8*, 11116. [CrossRef] [PubMed]
5. Gay, A.; Mourgues, R.; Berndt, C.; Bureau, D.; Planke, S.; Laurent, D.; Gautier, S.; Lauer, C.; Loggia, D. Anatomy of a Fluid Pip the Norway Basin: Initiation, Propagation and 3D Shape. *Mar. Geol.* **2012**, *332–334*, 75–88. [CrossRef]
6. Hovland, M.; Gardner, J.V.; Judd, A.G. The Significance of Pockmarks to Understanding Fluid Flow Processes and Geohaz *Geofluids* **2002**, *2*, 127–136. [CrossRef]
7. Svensen, H.; Planke, S.; Malthe-Sørenssen, A.; Jamtveit, B.; Myklebust, R.; Eidem, T.R.; Rey, S.S. Release of Methane fro Volcanic Basin as a Mechanism for Initial Eocene Global Warming. *Lett. Nat.* **2004**, *429*, 542–545. [CrossRef]
8. Svensen, H.; Planke, S.; Chevallier, L.; Malthe-Sørenssen, A.; Corfu, F.; Jamtveit, B. Hydrothermal Venting of Greenhouse G Triggering Early Jurassic Global Warming. *Earth Planet. Sci. Lett.* **2007**, *256*, 554–566. [CrossRef]
9. Olsen, J.E.; Skjetne, P. Current Understanding of Subsea Gas Release: A Review. *Can. J. Chem. Eng.* **2016**, *94*, 209–219. [Cross
10. Cardoso, S.S.S.; Cartwright, J.H.E. Increased Methane Emissions from Deep Osmotic and Buoyant Convection beneath Subma Seeps as Climate Warms. *Nat. Commun.* **2016**, *7*, 13266. [CrossRef] [PubMed]
11. Foschi, M.; Cartwright, J.A.; MacMinn, C.W.; Etiope, G. Evidence for Massive Emission of Methane from a Deep-water Gas F during the Pliocene. *Proc. Natl. Acad. Sci. USA* **2020**, *117*, 27869–27876. [CrossRef] [PubMed]
12. Gay, A.; Lopez, M.; Berndt, C.; Séranne, M. Geological Controls on Focused Fluid Flow Associated with Seafloor Seeps in Lower Congo Basin. *Mar. Geol.* **2007**, *244*, 68–92. [CrossRef]
13. Riboulot, V.; Sultan, N.; Imbert, P.; Ker, S. Initiation of Gas-Hydrate Pockmark in Deep-Water Nigeria: Geo-Mechanical Anal and Modelling. *Earth Planet. Sci. Lett.* **2016**, *434*, 252–263. [CrossRef]
14. Xu, C.; Xu, G.; Xing, J.; Sun, Z.; Wu, N. Research Progress of Seafloor Pockmarks in Spatio-Temporal Distribution and Classifica *J. Ocean. Univ. China* **2020**, *19*, 69–80. [CrossRef]
15. Vidal, V.; Gay, A. Future Challenges on Focused Fluid Migration in Sedimentary Basins: Insight from Field Data, Labora Experiments and Numerical Simulations. *Pap. Phys.* **2022**, *14*, 140011. [CrossRef]
16. Nichols, R.J.; Sparks, R.S.J.; Wilson, C.J.N. Experimental Studies of the Fluidization of Layered Sediments and the Formatio Fluid Escape Structures. *Sedimentology* **1994**, *41*, 233–253. [CrossRef]
17. Mourgues, R.; Cobbold, P.R. Some Tectonic Consequences of Fluid Overpressures and Seepage Forces as Demonstrate Sandbox Modelling. *Tectonophysics* **2003**, *376*, 75–97. [CrossRef]
18. Mörz, T.; Karlik, E.A.; Kreiter, S.; Kopf, A. An Experimental Setup for Fluid Venting in Unconsolidated Sediments: New Insi to Fluid Mechanics and Structures. *Sediment. Geol.* **2007**, *196*, 251–267. [CrossRef]
19. Mazzini, A.; Ivanov, M.K.; Nermoen, A.; Bahr, A.; Bohrmann, G.; Svensen, H.; Planke, S. Complex Plumbing Systems in the Subsurface: Geometries of Authigenic Carbonates from Dolgovskoy Mound (Black Sea) Constrained by Analogue Experim *Mar. Pet. Geol.* **2008**, *25*, 457–472. [CrossRef]

Nermoen, A.; Galland, O.; Jettestuen, E.; Fristad, K.; Podladchikov, Y.; Svensen, H.; Malthe-Sørenssen, A. Experimental and Analytic Modeling of Piercement Structures. *J. Geophys. Res.* **2010**, *115*, B10202. [CrossRef]
Mourgues, R.; Bureau, D.; Bodet, L.; Gay, A.; Gressier, J.B. Formation of Conical Fractures in Sedimentary Basins: Experiments Involving Pore Fluids and Implications for Sandstone Intrusion Mechanisms. *Earth Planet. Sci. Lett.* **2012**, *313–314*, 67–78. [CrossRef]
Luu, L.-H.; Noury, G.; Benseghier, Z.; Philippe, P. Hydro-Mechanical Modeling of Sinkhole Occurrence Processes in Covered Karst Terrains during a Flood. *Eng. Geol.* **2019**, *260*, 105249. [CrossRef]
May, F.; Warsitzka, M.; Kukowski, N. Analogue Modelling of Leakage Processes in Unconsolidated Sediments. *Int. J. Greenh. Gas Control* **2019**, *90*, 102805. [CrossRef]
Fu, X.; Jimenez-Martinez, J.; Nguyen, T.P.; Carey, J.W.; Viswanathan, H.; Cueto-Felgueroso, L.; Juanes, R. Crustal Fingering Facilitates Free-Gas Methane Migration through the Hydrate Stability Zone. *Proc. Natl. Acad. Sci. USA* **2020**, *117*, 31660–31664. [CrossRef]
Yarushina, V.M.; Makhnenko, R.Y.; Podladchikov, Y.Y.; Wang, L.H.; Räss, L. Viscous Behavior of Clay-Rich Rocks and Its Role in Focused Fluid Flow. *Geochem. Geophys. Geosyst.* **2021**, *22*, e2021GC009949. [CrossRef]
Montellà, E.P.; Toraldo, M.; Chareyre, B.; Sibille, L. Localized Fluidization in Granular Materials: Theoretical and Numerical Study. *Phys. Rev. E* **2016**, *94*, 052905. [CrossRef] [PubMed]
Yarushina, V.M.; Wang, L.H.; Connolly, D.; Kocsis, G.; Fæstø, I.; Polteau, S.; Lakhlifi, A. Focused Fluid-Flow Structures Potentially Caused by Solitary Porosity Waves. *Geology* **2022**, *50*, 179–183. [CrossRef]
Gupta, S.; Micallef, A. Modelling the Influence of Erosive Fluidization on the Morphology of Fluid Flow and Escape Structures. *Math. Geosci.* **2023**, *55*, 1101–1123. [CrossRef]
Werner, A.D.; Jazayeri, A.; Ramirez-Lagunas, M. Sediment Mobilisation and Release through Groundwater Discharge to the Land Surface: Review and Theoretical Development. *Sci. Total Environ.* **2020**, *714*, 136757. [CrossRef]
Warsitzka, M.; Kukowski, N.; May, F. Fluid-Overpressure Driven Sediment Mobilisation and Its Risk for the Integrity for CO_2 Storage Sites—An Analogue Modelling Approach. *Energy Procedia* **2017**, *114*, 3291–3304. [CrossRef]
Gay, A.; Berndt, C. Cessation/Reactivation of Polygonal Faulting and Effects on Fluid Flow in the Vøring Basin, Norwegian Margin. *J. Geol. Soc. Lond.* **2007**, *164*, 129–141. [CrossRef]
Gay, A.; Cavailhès, T.; Grauls, D.; Marsset, B.; Marsset, T. Repeated Fluid Expulsions during Events of Rapid Sea-Level Rise in the Gulf of Lion, Western Mediterranean Sea. *Bull. Soc. Géol. Fr.* **2017**, *188*, 24. [CrossRef]
Aderibigbe, O.O.; Rajaratnam, N. Erosion of Loose Beds by Submerged Circular Impinging Vertical Turbulent Jets. *J. Hydraul. Res.* **1996**, *34*, 19–33. [CrossRef]
Badr, S.; Gauthier, G.; Gondret, P. Erosion Threshold of a Liquid Immersed Granular Bed by an Impinging Plane Liquid Jet. *Phys. Fluids* **2014**, *26*, 023302. [CrossRef]
Vessaire, J.; Varas, G.; Joubaud, S.; Volk, R.; Bourgoin, M.; Vidal, V. Stability of a Liquid Jet Impinging on Confined Saturated Sand. *Phys. Rev. Lett.* **2020**, *124*, 224502. [CrossRef]
Alaoui, C.; Gay, A.; Vidal, V. Oscillations of a Particle-Laden Fountain. *Phys. Rev. E* **2022**, *106*, 024901. [CrossRef]
Clift, R.; Grace, J.R.; Weber, M.E. *Bubbles, Drops and Particles*; Academic Press: New York, NY, USA, 1978.

fluids

MDPI

Article

Experimental Analysis of the Influence of the Sliding-Gate Valve on Submerged Entry Nozzle Outlet Jets

Jesus Gonzalez-Trejo [1,*], Raul Miranda-Tello [2], Ruslan Gabbasov [1], Cesar A. Real-Ramirez [1] and Francisco Cervantes-de-la-Torre [1]

[1] Departamento de Sistemas, Universidad Autonoma Metropolitana, Mexico City 02200, Mexico; gabbasov@azc.uam.mx (R.G.); carr@azc.uam.mx (C.A.R.-R.); fcdt@azc.uam.mx (F.C.-d.-l.-T.)
[2] Departamento de Electronica, Universidad Autonoma Metropolitana, Mexico City 02200, Mexico; jrmt@azc.uam.mx
* Correspondence: gtji@azc.uam.mx; Tel.: +52-55-5318-9000 (ext. 2391)

Abstract: This work studies how the sliding-gate valve (SGV) modifies the features and the dynamic behavior of the outlet jets for flat-bottom and well-bottom bifurcated submerged entry nozzles (SENs) used in continuous casting machines. Three conditions for the SGV were studied: no obstruction, moderate obstruction, and severe obstruction. The experimental study used a scaled model, employing cold water as the working fluid. A high-frequency analysis of the flow inside the SEN's bore arriving at the outlet ports was performed by employing the particle image velocimetry (PIV) technique. Low-frequency measurements of the volumetric flow at the exit port were obtained by splitting the exit jet into four quadrants and employing digital flowmeters. It was observed that reducing the SGV clearance increases the turbulence of the flow inside the SEN bore, but the flow displays ordered rather than erratic fluctuations. Flowmeter measurements showed that, regardless of the level of obstruction in the SGV, the outlet jets on flat-bottom and the well-bottom SENs have dynamic behaviors and features with significant differences. This finding is relevant because the flow distribution inside the outlet ports is directly related to the jet's wideness, affecting the recirculation pattern inside the mold and, therefore, the quality of the finished steel slab.

Keywords: steel continuous casting; slab caster; submerged entry nozzle (SEN); sliding-gate valve

1. Introduction

Steel is a crucial material in the circular economy, a model of production and consumption that aims to minimize waste and promote the sustainable use of natural resources [1]. Recent works estimate that the global steel demand in 2050 will range from 2300 to 3000 million tons annually [2–4]. This colossal demand presents steelmakers with an enormous challenge, given that steel production generates around 7% of all CO_2 emissions [5]. Continuous casting is the world's predominant method for producing steel slabs [6,7]. Today, the industry uses at least three different types of continuous casting: conventional continuous casting (CCC), endless strip production (ESP), and thin slab caster (TSC). CCC remains the preferred method for producing the highest-quality steel sheet products [8]. In the CCC process, the quality of the finished steel slab depends on numerous factors which are intimately related to the fluid flow pattern inside the mold [9,10]. In turn, the hydrodynamic pattern within the mold depends strongly on the characteristics of the jets emerging from the exit ports on the submerged entry nozzle (SEN), whose design varies widely. The cylindrical-like external geometry of the SEN is the most common shape in CCC machines [11,12]. Typically, the shape of the SEN bore is also cylindrical [13]. The features of the SEN that have been employed to modify the hydrodynamic behavior inside the mold include the height of the inner bottom wall [13–15], and the number [16] and shape of the exit ports [17].

Besides modifying the geometric features of the SEN, an external device, the electromagnetic brake, has also been employed to impose a prescribed fluid flow pattern inside the mold [18–20]. Although this device has produced favorable results, recent works have shown that the magnetic field's features must be tuned carefully. Specifically, an undesirable hydrodynamic behavior inside the mold is obtained when the magnetic field is set incorrectly [21–23].

Finally, the device that controls the flow of the liquid steel from the tundish to the mold is an element that must be included in the process analysis [11,24–26]. Several investigations studying these devices' effects on the characteristics of the jets that emerge from the SEN are reported in the literature [25,27]. The results are phenomenologically consistent but have a level of uncertainty that is difficult to delimit. In addition, these investigations involve a complex methodology and expensive equipment [24]. Using numerical simulations, Bai and Thomas explained the features of SEN exit jets by splitting each of them into two parts: the upward and the downward jets [28]. Bai and Thomas report that, although the upward jet occupied around 30% of the exit port area, the volumetric flow fraction corresponding to this jet is considerably less than 30%. However, to the authors' knowledge, there are no works reported in the literature that, through physical simulations, fully corroborate or refute the assertions of Bai and Thomas.

Numerous works have employed numerical and physical simulations to design the shape of an SEN to enhance the steel quality. Based on similarity criteria, the hydrodynamic behavior of an actual steel CCC can be reproduced in a scaled model using cold water as the working fluid if the dimensions and operating conditions are set correctly [29]. This work is devoted to experimentally studying, in a scaled cold-water model, how the sliding-gate valve (SGV) modifies the hydrodynamic pattern inside the SEN and the characteristics of the jets emerging from it. The study included two variants of the bifurcated SEN, one with a flat bottom and another with a pool at the bottom. In addition, three "positions" or conditions of the SGV were studied: one where there is no flow obstruction, one with moderate obstruction, and another with severe obstruction. Based mainly on numerical simulations, previous works stated that the uneven distribution of the liquid flow across the SEN outlet largely determines the features of the exit jet [27,28]. The present work conducted experimental tests employing a modified SEN to divide each outlet into four quadrants and measure the volumetric flow crossing each. Our work confirms that the flow at the SEN outlet is distributed unevenly, and this distribution depends on the shape of the bottom of the SEN and the SGV clearance.

This work is organized as follows. The operating conditions of the scaled model of the SEN and its relationship with an actual CCC are presented in Section 2. The dimensions and the geometric features of the six SEN configurations studied in this work are also described and discussed in this section. Section 3 presents and analyzes the high-frequency, transient behavior of the fluid velocity field inside the SEN's bore in a zone above the exit ports obtained with the particle image velocimetry technique (PIV). The low-frequency, transient behavior of the SEN outlet jets is presented and analyzed in Section 4. In this case, each jet was divided into four quarters, and the volumetric flow that emerged from each quarter was measured using digital flowmeters. These temporal signals were subsequently analyzed. This section also discusses the adjustments made to the SEN to couple it with the flowmeters, and through numerical simulations, it is shown that these adjustments do not modify the fluid flow pattern inside the SEN. Finally, Section 5 presents some concluding remarks of this work and discusses its implications for actual CCC.

2. The CCC Process and the SEN Designs Studied in This Work

The molten steel with the specified composition is transported from the secondary refinement facility to the continuous casting section inside a ladle. There, the steel is discharged into the tundish, a container that distributes the molten steel into several casting lines. The molten steel is poured into the solidification mold through the SEN. The left-hand panel in Figure 1 shows a schematic of the casting section in a CCC machine for producing steel slabs. The solidification of the molten steel is initiated inside the mold, which is a water-cooled copper shell. The secondary cooling section is just below the mold, where, besides the steel slab being sprayed with cold water, the steel slab is pulled by withdrawal rollers. Typically, the mold width ranges from 800 to 1600 mm. When the slab width is above 1600 mm, it is considered a wide slab, and it is considered an ultra-wide slab when the width is close to 3000 mm [30]. The thickness of the mold ranges from 180 to 300 mm, and its length is around 1000 mm [31]. In CCC, the casting speed is the velocity at which the semi-solidified slab is drawn from the mold. Nowadays, most continuous casters work at speeds between 1000 and 2500 mm/min [7].

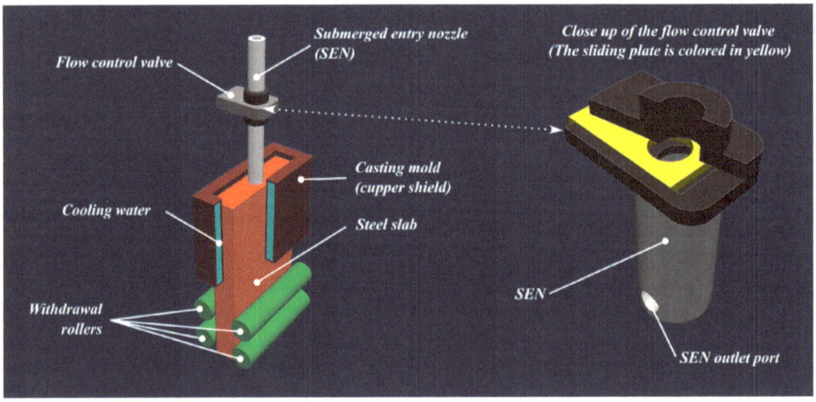

Figure 1. Schematic description of the casting section of a continuous casting machine for making steel slabs.

In actual CCC machines, each steelmaking company uses the SEN design that best meets its requirements, so its geometric characteristics can change [32,33]. The main design parameters for the SENs are the number, the shape, and the vertical tilt of the exit ports. Regarding the number, the preferred configuration is the bifurcated one with an SEN with two exit ports near the pipe's end. Each port is located on opposite sides of the SEN, so the exit ports' axis is perpendicular to the SEN's longitudinal axis. To minimize defects generated by an asymmetric fluid flow pattern inside the mold, the axis of the outlet ports of a bifurcated SEN must be parallel to the mold's wide walls. The most common shapes used for the exit ports are rectangular, circular, and oval [34]. In addition, the SEN could have outlet ports with a vertical tilt upwards, horizontally, or downwards [35–37]. In this work, the SEN designs have two outlet ports with a circular shape, and their vertical tilt is downward.

The flow entering the mold from the tundish is usually controlled by an SGV or a stopper rod (SR) [25,26,38–40]. However, this work will only consider the SGV as the flow-control device. The right-hand panel in Figure 1 shows a close-up of the SGV coupled with a bifurcated SEN. The SGV has an orifice in a plate that controls the steel's flow rate. The volumetric flow descending through the SEN depends on the height of the steel inside the tundish, which varies constantly. At the beginning of the cast, the tundish is filled to its maximum capacity, and the height of the molten steel decreases as the casting progresses until the tundish is filled again. So, to maintain a constant delivery of molten steel to the mold, the SGV plate's clearance is narrow at the beginning of the cast, increasing as the molten steel's height into the tundish decreases. An analysis of the transient reduction in the SGV plate's clearance is beyond the scope of the present work. Instead, three conditions of the SGV are studied: no flow obstruction, moderate flow obstruction, and severe flow obstruction.

Figure 2 shows three ways of coupling the SGV with the SEN. The coupling is named after the angle formed between the axis of the sliding plate, colored in yellow, and the SEN outlet ports: 0°, 45°, and 90°. Several works show that the 90° coupling induces less asymmetry in the fluid flow pattern inside the mold [27]. So, in all the SEN designs studied in this work, the axes of the sliding plate and the SEN outlet ports will be perpendicular to each other.

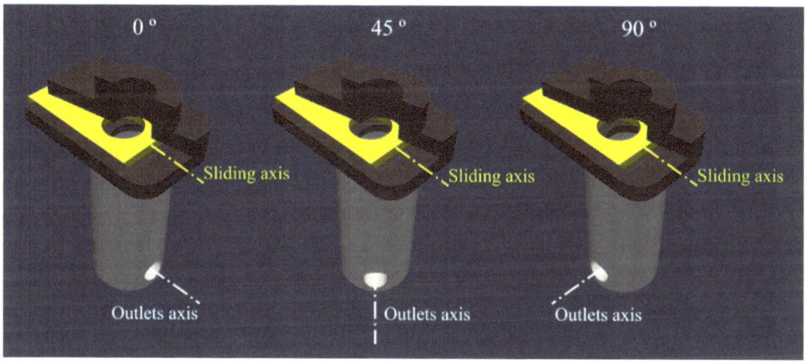

Figure 2. Typical arrangements of the tundish sliding-gate valve with respect to the axes of the exit ports of a bifurcated SEN.

Another design parameter for a bifurcated SEN is the height of the inner bottom wall relative to the height of outlet ports' inner lower edges. When the heights of the wall and the edges coincide, the design is labeled as a Flat-Bottom (FB) SEN. Otherwise, a pool or well emerges inside the SEN when the bottom wall height is below the ports' lower edges. Therefore, the design is called a Well-Bottom (WB) SEN. Figure 3 shows a conventional bifurcated SEN and the customized designs employed in this work. The customization relies on reducing the thickness of the walls to obtain SENs with extra-thin walls, so the sections colored in dark grey are removed. Therefore, the SENs employed in this work are composed only of the sections colored in light grey.

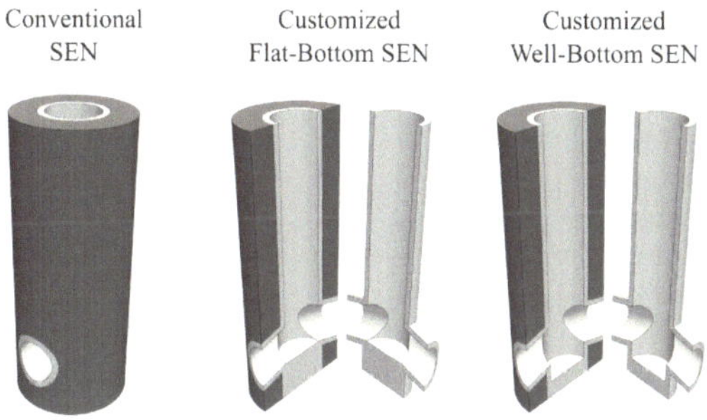

Figure 3. Conventional SEN and customized FB and WB SEN designs.

The kinematic viscosity of water at 25 °C and molten steel at 1550 °C are 0.893×10^{-6} and 0.784×10^{-6} m^2/s, respectively. Given that the kinematic viscosity of these two fluids is close enough, in 1972, Szekely and Yadoya showed that the hydrodynamic behavior inside a scaled model using water is similar to a CCC, ensuring the Froude number in both models is the same and that the liquid velocity in the scaled model is set correctly [29]. A scaled model ensuring thermal similarity with a CCC requires fulfilling other requirements. However, this work is restricted to studying the hydrodynamic behavior inside the SEN. Based on the previous discussion, the Froude similarity criterion between an actual CCC and the scaled model must be satisfied to specify the SEN dimensions and the operating conditions.

The left-hand panel in Figure 4 shows the dimensions of the customized SENs studied in this work based on a scale factor of 1 : 1/3. All the SENs have a bore diameter, D, of 26 mm; the outlet port inner diameter, *d*, is 20 mm; and their vertical tilt is 15° downwards. This panel also shows the width of the plate's clearance for the moderatep and severe-SGV-obstruction conditions, which are 15 and 10 mm, respectively. These obstruction degrees agree with those employed in actual CCC machines. The obstruction plate, shown in blue in this figure, is 300 mm above the outlet ports' upper edge. This positioning ensures that the plate's distance to the outlet ports is at least ten times the SEN's bore's diameter, D.

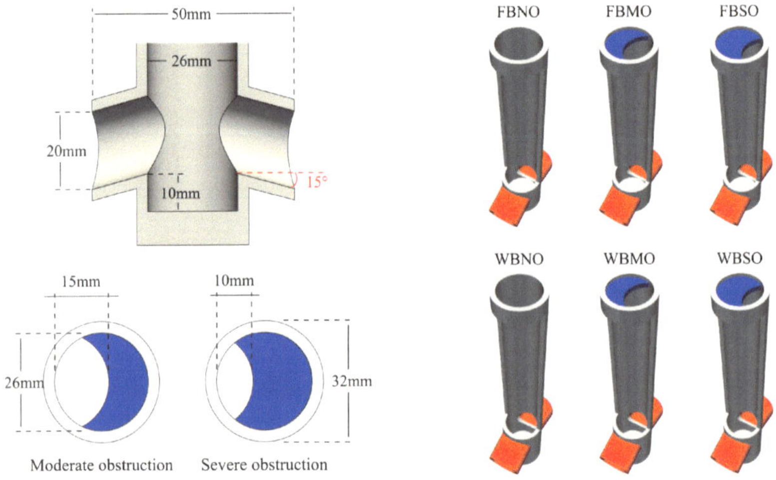

Figure 4. The left-hand panel shows the dimensions of SEN and the SGV clearance. The right-hand panel provides a 3D view of the six SEN configurations studied in this work.

The right-hand panel in Figure 4 depicts the six customized SEN designs studied in this work: flat-bottom with no obstruction (FBNO), flat-bottom with moderate obstruction (FBMO), flat-bottom with severe obstruction (FBSO), well-bottom with no obstruction (WBNO), well-bottom with moderate obstruction (WBMO), and well-bottom with severe obstruction (WBSO). The SEN's central long body was made with a Plexiglass pipe 3 mm in thickness. For the experiments presented in Section 3, the outlet ports, colored in red in Figure 4, were also made with Plexiglass pipes 3 mm in thickness. For convenience, in the experiments presented in Section 4, the SEN outlet ports were manufactured on a 3D printer with PLA filament, and their thicknesses were also 3 mm.

Regarding the operating conditions, all the experiments were conducted using the same water volumetric flow, 30 L/min. Recalling that the scale factor is 1:1/3 for an actual mold with a width of 1500 mm and a thickness of 210 mm, the casting speed in the cold-water scaled model with this volumetric flow is 857 mm/min. The measurements used in this analysis begin 30 s after the pump is turned on.

3. Transient Behavior of the Fluid Velocities Field inside the SEN's Bore

The transient behavior inside the SEN's bore is analyzed by calculating the fluid velocity field using the particle image velocimetry technique (PIV). The analysis is restricted to a central plane above but near the SEN's bottom zone. Figure 5 shows a schematic representation of the experimental rig employed for the PIV test, and a photo of the SEN used in these experiments. To allow us to see inside the SEN's bottom zone, at least partially, the camera's sensor and the laser sheet were not parallel. Notice that the entire SEN is made from Plexiglass pipes. The lower end of the central tube is closed using the stoppers (black), also shown in the figure. The stoppers' heights are different, allowing for both the FB and the WB SEN designs to be generated. After several attempts, the best video recordings were obtained when the SEN discharged the water jets directly into the air instead of submerging the SEN into a transparent receptacle filled with water. Therefore, two gadgets made of white PVC plumbing were attached to each outlet port, directing the water jets downward and avoiding excessive splashing. These gadgets are also shown in Figure 5. The device used to recreate the sliding plate under the severe obstruction condition is also shown in Figure 5. This device was manufactured with a 3D printer with PLA filament. The other device used to recreate the moderate obstruction condition is similar to this one.

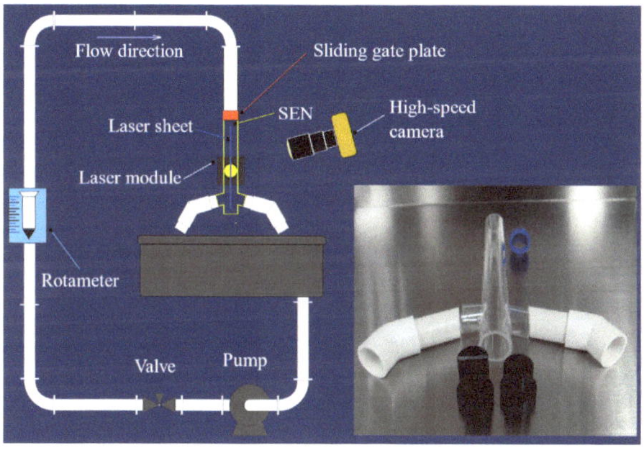

Figure 5. Schematic representation of the experimental rig employed for the PIV test. The inset shows a picture of the customized SEN and its associated devices.

The experimental tests reported and analyzed in this section were recorded using a monochromatic 9501AZ High-Speed Camera from AZ-Instruments Corp. (Taichung City, Taiwan), using a 6 − 60 mm, 720 p, F1.6, 1/3″ CS lens. Hollow glass spheres from Dantec Dynamics A/S (Skovlunde, Denmark), with diameters of 10 μm, were used as seeding particles to trace the fluid flow pattern. The SEN bore was illuminated using a 500 mW, 450 nm laser module, which generated a 1 mm thick lighting sheet. All the experimental tests were recorded at 835 frames per second, with a 640 × 480 image resolution. So, the elapsed time between each pair of consecutive images is 1.2 ms. This time gap is small enough because all the liquid velocities are expected to be below 1.6 m/s.

The left panel in Figure 6 shows a pair of consecutive images for the FBNO configuration to exemplify the recording results used for PIV analysis. Notice that the plane under study is perpendicular to the SEN outlet port's axis. The plane to be analyzed starts from the SEN's bottom zone and extends above the level of the exit ports to a height around twice the diameter of the SEN bore. The right panel in Figure 6 shows the flow pattern of the liquid in a zone just below the SVG. This image shows the path of reflective particles illuminated by a laser sheet. The particles' path becomes visible by setting the camera's exposure time high enough. The SGV creates two zones below it, the main flow and the recirculation zones, which are enclosed in red- and blue-colored rectangles, respectively. The importance of this flow separation will be highlighted below.

For the sake of space, the transient analysis of the velocities field inside the SEN bore will only be shown for the no-obstruction and severe-obstruction conditions. However, video files for the six SEN configurations are provided as Supplementary Materials. Figures 7 and 8 display the velocity fields for the FB and WB designs, respectively. Both figures have the same structure: The upper panels belong to the no-obstruction condition, whereas the lower panels were reported in the severe-obstruction condition. The flow patterns sketched on the right-hand side of Figures 7 and 8 were made based on the behavior observed in the high-speed recordings and the results of previous works reported in the literature.

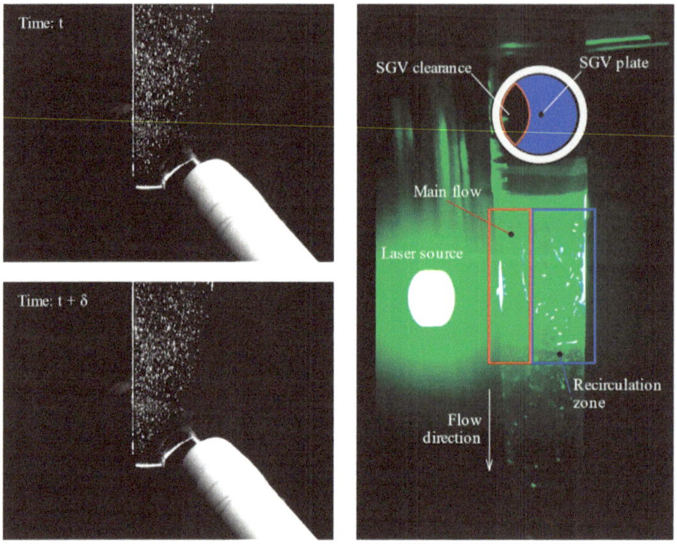

Figure 6. Left panel: A pair of consecutive images inside the SEN bore for the FBNO configuration. The image on the top was captured 1.2 ms after the one on the bottom. Right panel: Image showing the flow pattern inside the zone just below the SVG. The main flow and the recirculation zones are enclosed in red and blue colored rectangles, respectively.

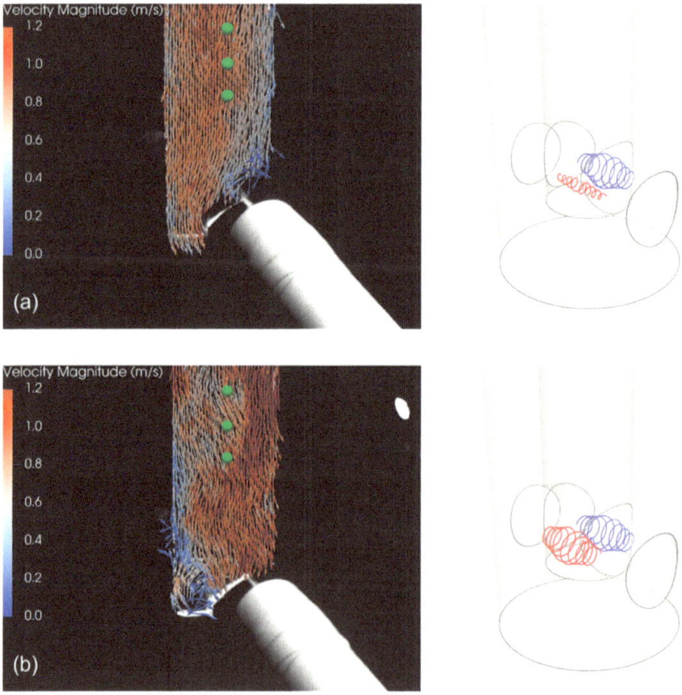

Figure 7. Left-hand panels: fluid velocity field for the FB design with no obstruction (**a**), and severe obstruction (**b**). The green dots are the measurements points. Right-hand panels: Red and blue lines outline the vortexes inside the SEN.

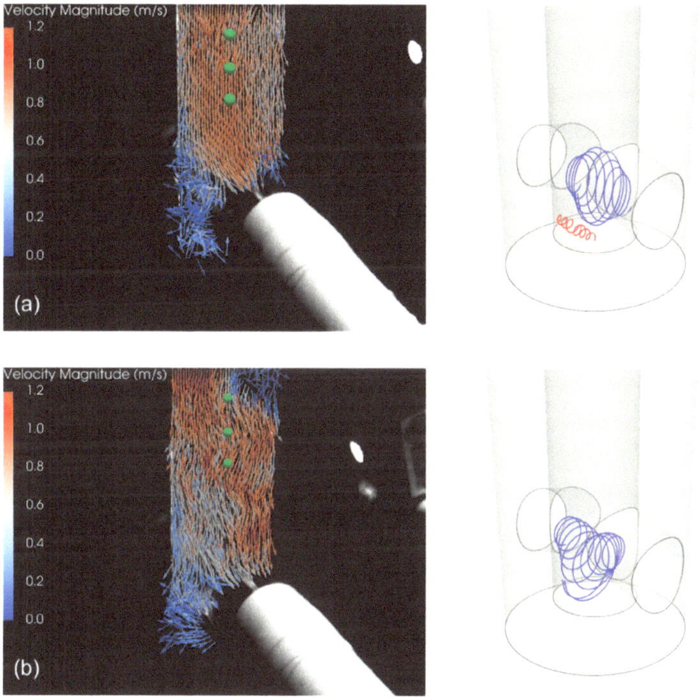

Figure 8. Left-hand panels: fluid velocity field for the WB design with no obstruction (**a**), and severe obstruction (**b**). The green dots are the measurements points. Right-hand panels: Red and blue lines outlinethe vortexes inside the SEN.

The upper panels in Figures 7 and 8 show that, for the no-obstruction condition and regardless of the SEN bottom shape, the liquid's flow pattern above the outlet ports zone resembles a fully developed turbulent flow. This flow pattern is distorted near the upper edges of the outlet ports. On the contrary, and as expected, the lower panels in Figures 7 and 8 show that the obstruction increases the intensity of the turbulence in the flow inside the SEN bore, but the flow displays ordered rather than erratic fluctuations. It can be noticed, in Figures 7 and 8, that the fluid-flow pattern is distorted differently when the liquid reaches the beginning of the outlet ports in the no-obstruction (panel a) and severe-obstruction conditions (panel b). We assume that this difference reflects a change in the flow pattern in the SEN's bottom zone.

For the FB design (Figure 7), it is well known that two counter-rotating vortexes characterize the flow pattern at the bottom of the SEN, and many works report that their sizes and intensities are the same [41,42]. However, recent studies have shown that the intensity of the vortexes can differ, and the small, weaker vortex can even disappear periodically. Precisely this behavior was observed for the no-obstruction condition [43–45]. On the other hand, for the severe-obstruction condition, the permanent presence of two vortexes with almost the same sizes and intensities was observed.

Concerning the WB design, several works have reported that the flow pattern at the bottom of the SEN is characterized by two counter-rotating vortexes, whose sizes and intensities differ enormously [45,46]. The biggest and strongest vortex occupies a significant fraction of the volume of the pool at the bottom of the SEN and extends to a height close to three-quarters of the height of the exit ports. On the contrary, the smallest and weaker vortex is inside the liquid pool, close to its bottom wall. This behavior coincides with that observed in experiments for the no-obstruction condition. However, for the severe-obstruction condition, the intensity of the biggest vortex increases, is pushed downwards, and sinks into the pool, occupying its volume almost entirely, and causing the weaker vortex to disappear. Additionally, it can be noticed that there is an increase in spreading in the stagnation zone above the ports and below the SGV plate clearance.

The analysis of the fluid transient velocity fields for each experiment was carried out using a set of 201 pairs of consecutive images. However, only the results at the locations marked with green spheres in Figures 7 and 8 are reported and analyzed, which were obtained from nodes of VTK files generated by PIVlab v2.62. Each location is named after its height: upper, middle, and lower. Figure 9 shows the evolution of the fluid velocity magnitude, v, over time for the four configurations and at the three locations. Figure 10 shows the evolution of the velocity vector vertical tilt, φ, over time. By observing the curves in these figures, the change in behavior under the no-obstruction and severe-obstruction conditions is evident. Table 1 summarizes the results of the quantitative analysis of the series shown in Figures 9 and 10 by calculating its arithmetic mean and standard deviation.

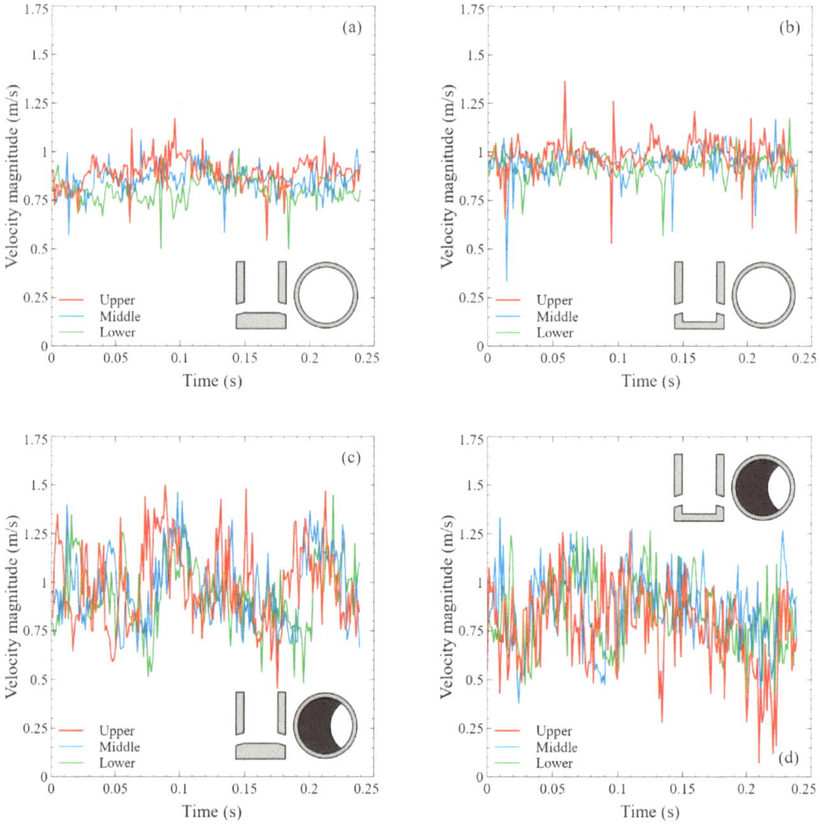

Figure 9. Time series of the velocity magnitude at the three positions marked in Figures 7 and 8 for the following SEN configurations: (**a**) FBNO; (**b**) WBNO; (**c**) FBSO; (**d**) WBSO. The SEN design and the SVG clearance are indicated on each panel with sketches.

Several conclusions can be drawn from Figure 9. The velocity magnitude analysis shows the following: The mean value decreases as the measurement height decreases for all the SEN configurations except at the upper position on the WBSO configuration. For the no-obstruction condition, the mean is lower for the FB design, but this trend reverses for the severe-obstruction condition.

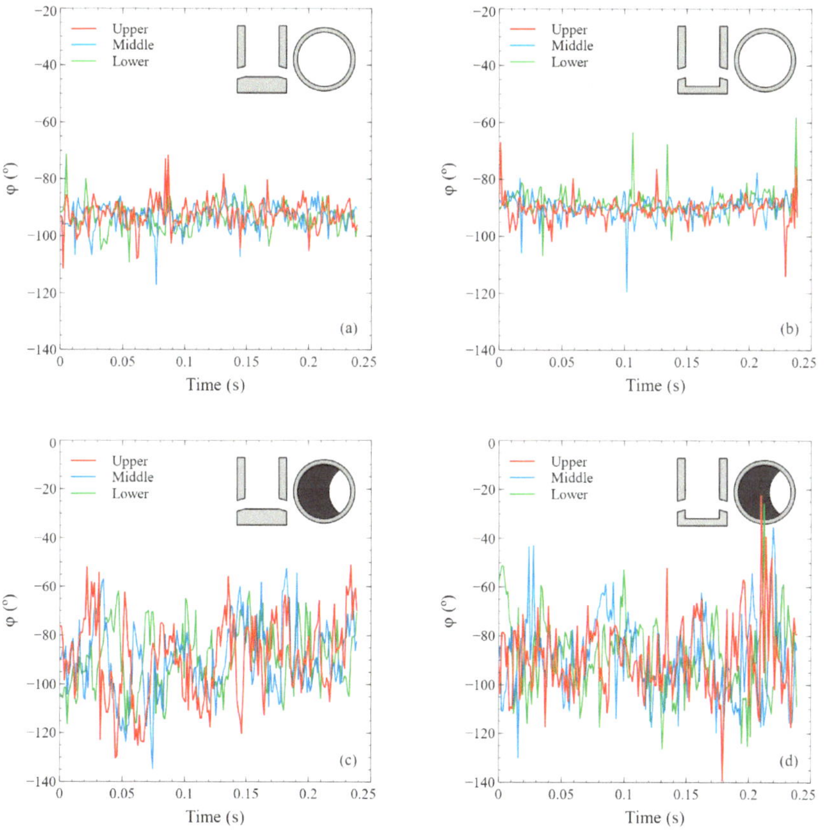

Figure 10. Time series of the velocity vector vertical tilt at the three positions marked in Figures 7 and 8 for the following SEN configurations: (**a**) FBNO; (**b**) WBNO; (**c**) FBSO; (**d**) WBSO. The SEN design and the SVG clearance are indicated on each panel with sketches.

Table 1. Arithmetic mean and standard deviation of the fluid velocity magnitude and the velocity vector tilt.

Property	**Measure Location**	**SEN Configuration**			
		FBNO	**WBNO**	**FBSO**	**WBSO**
$\overline{v}$ (m/s)	Upper	0.8933	0.9890	0.9841	0.7739
	Middle	0.8603	0.9706	0.9427	0.8660
	Lower	0.8027	0.9407	0.9283	0.8384
$\sigma_{\overline{v}}$ (m/s)	Upper	0.0797	0.2126	0.0934	0.2190
	Middle	0.0691	0.1830	0.0794	0.1923
	Lower	0.0672	0.1757	0.0664	0.1847
$\overline{\varphi}$ (°)	Upper	−92.1871	−89.5019	−90.4573	−89.0357
	Middle	−93.1295	−90.0346	−90.0301	−88.7205
	Lower	−93.5627	−89.7711	−88.2866	−88.7562
$\sigma_{\overline{\varphi}}$ (°)	Upper	4.9855	4.1513	16.6630	15.1172
	Middle	4.5028	3.9837	14.9233	16.1136
	Lower	4.7685	4.6367	12.8194	15.6815

The velocity magnitude standard deviation analysis is as follows: The trend observed in all the configurations is that the standard deviation decreases as the measurement height decreases. Notice that the FBNO and FBSO configurations have almost the same standard deviation. This similarity is also observed in the WBNO and WBSO configurations. On the contrary, the standard deviation for the WBNO configuration is around three times that of the FBNO configuration. A similar proportionality is observed between the WBSO and FBSO conditions.

In addition to the velocity magnitude, the deviation of the velocity vector from the downstream vertical axis was also calculated at the same locations. The mean value of the velocity vector's vertical tilt shows neither a specific trend nor proportionality between configurations. In addition, the difference among all the values is negligible. However, the standard deviation of the velocity vector's vertical tilt under the severe-obstruction condition is around three times the value for the same design under the no obstruction condition. The latter can be attributed to the large amount of fluid mixing occurring in the bore.

Along with the statistical analysis, a frequency analysis was also carried out. The power spectral density (PSD) was calculated using the corresponding function in the MATLAB R2023a package on the data shown in Figures 9 and 10. Again, for the sake of space, only the time series belonging to the velocity vector's vertical tilt at the lower height were analyzed. Figure 11 shows the estimated PSD vs. the frequency for the four SEN configurations. In the plots, near-zero frequency modes were excluded and the expected Nyquist frequency is 200 Hz. Note that the scales are different for the upper and lower panels. The shape of the PSD for the FBNO configuration (Figure 11a) suggests the presence of some periodic fluctuations. In contrast, the plot for the WBNO configuration (Figure 11b) resembles the behavior obtained from a white noise signal. On the other hand, the plots for the FBSO and WBSO configurations (Figure 11c,d) clearly show that the severe-obstruction condition reinforces some periodic behaviors present in the no-obstruction condition or creates new ones with high energy modes.

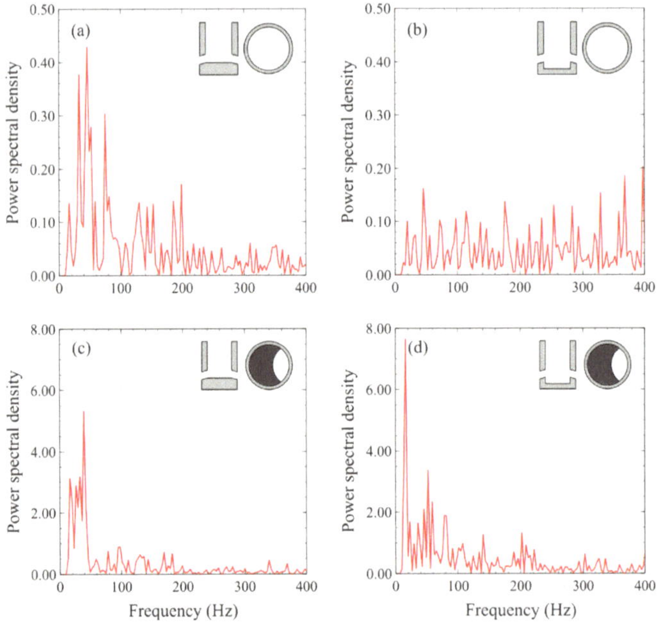

Figure 11. Frequency analysis of the velocity vector's tilt time series for the SEN configurations: (**a**) FBNO, (**b**) WBNO, (**c**) FBSO, and (**d**) WBSO. The SEN design and the SVG clearance are indicated on each panel with sketches.

In summary, the frequency analysis quantitatively corroborates the behavior observed in the high-speed recordings: the SGV increases the turbulence of the flow inside the SEN bore, but the flow displays ordered and periodic fluctuations rather than erratic behavior.

4. Transient Behavior of the SEN Outlet Jets

4.1. Adjustments Made to the SEN

Previous works have studied the control device's effect on the behavior of the SEN outlet jets by measuring the liquid velocity near the SEN outlets on scaled models using cold water as the working fluid [15,24,28,47]. In those works, the SEN was submerged in the water contained in the mold. The jet velocity was measured using PIV, ultrasonic Doppler velocimetry, and an impeller-velocity probe, among other techniques. The present work adopts a different approach. The SEN outlet jets' behavior is studied by analyzing transient measurements of the volumetric flow emerging from them. The main purpose of this analysis is not to determine the amount of flow emerging from the outlets but rather to characterize how the flow is distributed at the exit ports. Therefore, a set of customized devices was developed, which, besides dividing the flow emerging from the SEN, allows for coupling with digital flowmeters. Four pieces form this set, and they are shown in Figure 12. Notice that these devices divide the flow into four quarters. The two elements at each side of the SEN are glued together, and subsequently, the new body is glued to the corresponding SEN outlet port.

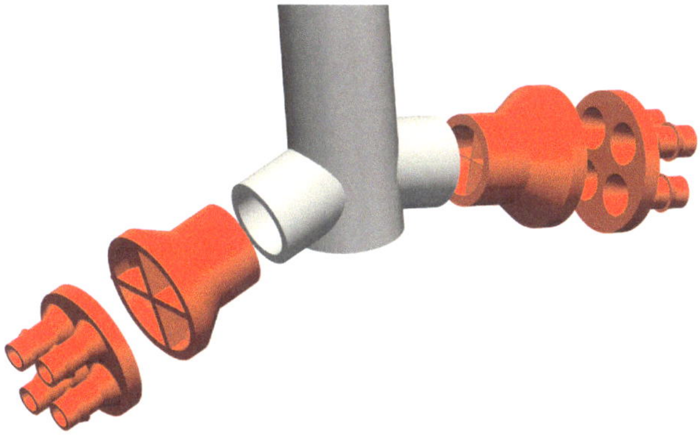

Figure 12. Customized devices employed for dividing the SEN emerging flow into four quadrants.

Figure 13 shows the experimental rig used for the tests reported in this section. The left panel shows the customized SEN with the devices described previously. As in Section 3, the lower end of the central tube is closed using stoppers with different heights, allowing for both the FB and the WB SEN designs to be generated. However, for convenience, the outlet ports and all the devices were manufactured using a 3D printer with a PLA filament, and their thicknesses were also 3 mm. This panel also shows how rubber pipes connect one coupler to four digital water flow sensors, GR-301 model, from GREDIA (China), shown in the panel on the left of Figure 13. Water exiting from the flow sensors freely falls into the container. The signals generated by the digital flowmeters were acquired using an *Arduino Mega* microcontroller board, also visible in the left panel of Figure 13.

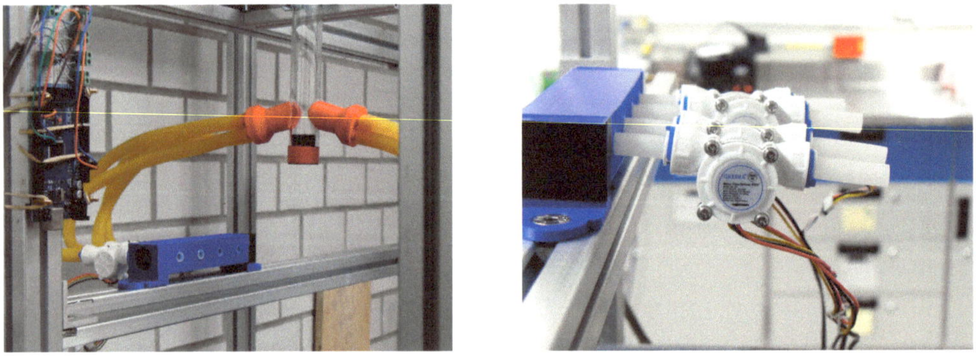

Figure 13. Experimental rig employed for measuring the volumetric flow at each quadrant and four digital rotational flow meters mounted on a horizontal hub.

The flow sensors employed in this work are turbine-like flowmeters. Therefore, the turbine's rotation speed is proportional to the volumetric flow rate. Additionally, given that the employed sensors belong to the Class I turbine flow meters (AWWA Standard C701 [48]), the sensors register 98–102% of the actual rate.

Each flowmeter was calibrated to obtain its characteristic proportionality constant. It was observed that the interval for counting the turbine's pulses must be at least two seconds to obtain reliable measurements. Thus, the acquisition rate for the volumetric flow signals was one measurement every two seconds. Furthermore, a moving average was applied to the volumetric flow time series to smooth out short-term fluctuations and highlight the longer-term trends.

4.2. Analysis of the Flowmeters Signals

This subsection presents and analyzes the volumetric flow time series obtained from the digital flowmeters using the six SEN configurations described in Figure 4. For clarity, these time series belong to only one of the outlet ports. Since each time series, $\{f_i\}$, represents the volumetric flow leaving the SEN through one of the outlet port's quadrants, it is crucial to specify the spatial relationship between the SGV plate clearance and the analyzed quadrant. Therefore, the SEN outlet ports quadrants are named after their cardinal direction: Northeast (NE), Northwest (NW), Southeast (SE), and Southwest (SW). The SGV plate's clearance was located directly above the NE and SE quadrants in all the configurations reported in this section.

Figures 14 and 15 show the transient measurements for the FB and WB SEN designs, respectively. Each panel on these figures uses drawings to indicate the SEN design and the outlet quadrant being studied. In addition, the line color distinguishes the specific SEN configuration. Notice that the scale of the vertical axis of the two graphs in the upper panels of both figures is the same. The same is true for the graphs in the bottom panels. By homogenizing the graph axes' scales, the time series in Figures 14 and 15 clearly outline the effect of the SGV clearance on how the volumetric flow distributes among each quadrant of the exit port. It is also visible that the effect of the SGV clearance on the SEN outlet jets changes substantially depending on the SEN bottom design.

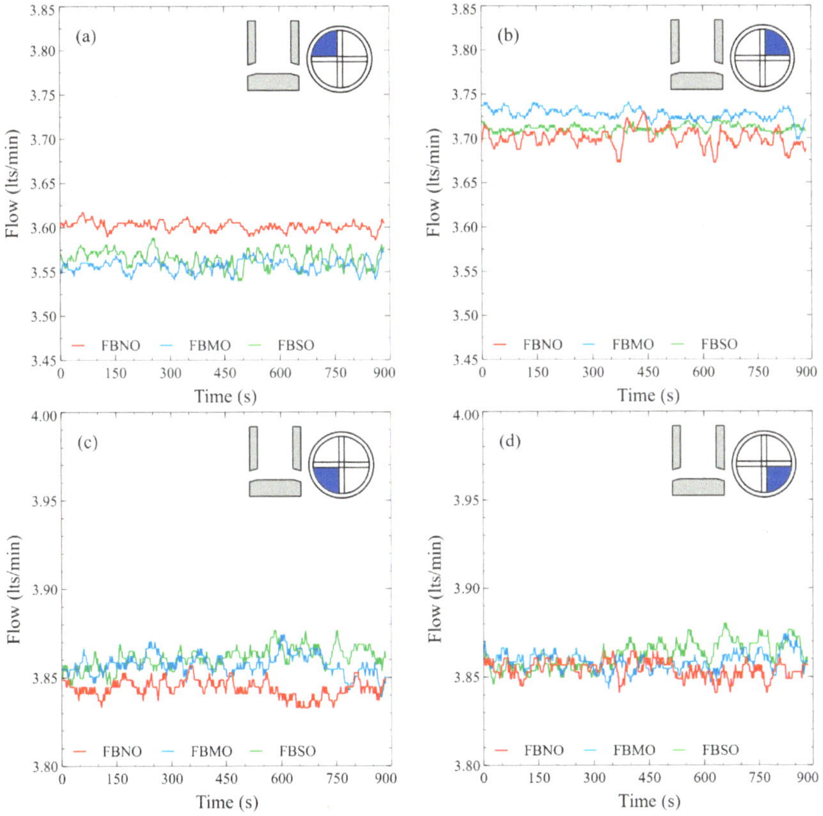

Figure 14. Time series of the volumetric flow at each quadrant for the FB design and the six SEN configurations. The SEN design and the port quadrant are indicated on each panel with sketches. (**a**) NW quadrant (**b**) NE quadrant (**c**) SW quadrant (**d**) SE quadrant.

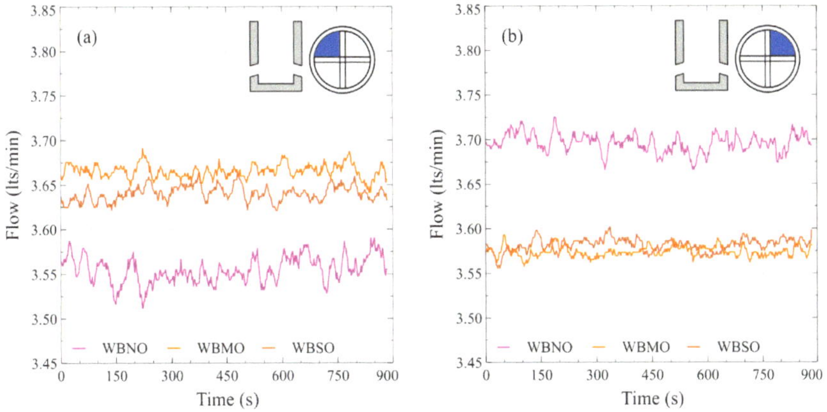

Figure 15. *Cont.*

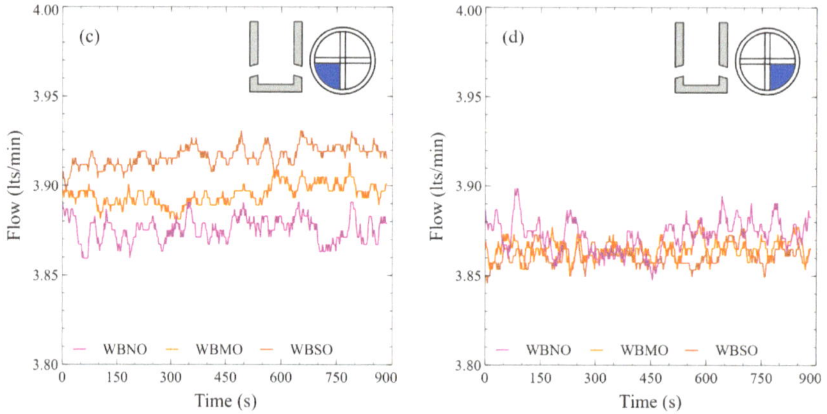

Figure 15. Time series of the volumetric flow at each quadrant for the WB design and the six SEN configurations. The SEN design and the port quadrant are indicated on each panel with sketches. (**a**) NW quadrant (**b**) NE quadrant (**c**) SW quadrant (**d**) SE quadrant.

To make the qualitatively observable behavior in Figures 14 and 15 quantifiable, let us construct a set of ad hoc statistics. Table 2 reports the arithmetic mean, $\bar{Q}$, the maximum, Q, and the minimum, q, of the flow rate for each time series, $\{f_i\}$. Equations (1)–(4) define the set of four ad hoc statistics, a_N, a_S, a_W, and a_E, employed to describe the behavior observed in Figures 14 and 15, and Table 3 reports the values of these statistics.

$$a_N = \left(\frac{\max(Q_{NW}, Q_{NE}) - \min(q_{NW}, q_{NE})}{\min(q_{NW}, q_{NE})} \right) \times 100\%, \tag{1}$$

$$a_S = \left(\frac{\max(Q_{SW}, Q_{SE}) - \min(q_{SW}, q_{SE})}{\min(q_{SW}, q_{SE})} \right) \times 100\%, \tag{2}$$

$$a_E = \left(\frac{\max(Q_{NE}, Q_{SE}) - \min(q_{NE}, q_{SE})}{\min(q_{NE}, q_{SE})} \right) \times 100\%, \tag{3}$$

$$a_W = \left(\frac{\max(Q_{NW}, Q_{SW}) - \min(q_{NW}, q_{SW})}{\min(q_{NW}, q_{SW})} \right) \times 100\%. \tag{4}$$

Table 2. Rank statistics of the volumetric flows time series.

Quadrant	Statistic (L/min)	SEN Configuration					
		FBNO	**FBMO**	**FBSO**	**WBNO**	**WBMO**	**WBSO**
NW	$\bar{Q}_{NW}$	3.602	3.557	3.565	3.555	3.666	3.641
	Q_{NW}	3.617	3.576	3.589	3.591	3.692	3.664
	q_{NW}	3.586	3.541	3.539	3.512	3.640	3.621
SW	$\bar{Q}_{SW}$	3.844	3.857	3.861	3.876	3.895	3.917
	Q_{SW}	3.857	3.874	3.877	3.891	3.913	3.931
	q_{SW}	3.833	3.839	3.846	3.859	3.881	3.896
SE	$\bar{Q}_{SE}$	3.854	3.859	3.863	3.873	3.865	3.861
	Q_{SE}	3.865	3.874	3.880	3.899	3.881	3.877
	q_{SE}	3.841	3.843	3.846	3.848	3.850	3.846
NE	$\bar{Q}_{NE}$	3.700	3.727	3.711	3.696	3.574	3.581
	Q_{NE}	3.731	3.741	3.723	3.725	3.593	3.602
	q_{NE}	3.672	3.698	3.696	3.666	3.558	3.555

Table 3. Customized statistics defined in Equations (1) through (4).

Statistic (%)	SEN Configuration					
	FBNO	FBMO	FBSO	WBNO	WBMO	WBSO
a_N	4.1	5.7	5.2	6.1	3.8	3.1
a_S	0.8	0.9	0.9	1.0	1.6	2.2
a_W	7.6	9.4	9.5	10.8	7.5	8.6
a_E	5.2	4.8	5.0	6.4	9.1	9.0

The statistic a_N expresses the difference between the flows leaving the SEN through the quadrants on the port's upper half. Similarly, a_S, a_W, and a_E represent the difference in the flows leaving the SEN through the quadrants on the lower half, the half on the left side, and the half on the right side, respectively.

Previous works devoted to the study of the influence of the bottom configuration on the spread of the jets emerging from SENs found that the WB design produces the broadest jets [45,46]. Those works attributed this feature to the difference between the flow patterns at the SEN's bottom zone. Based on the results of numerical simulations, they highlighted the difference between the halves on the left and right-hand sides of the jets emerging from the SEN outlet ports. With the data reported in Table 3, the sum of the statistics a_W and a_E for the FBNO configuration is 12.8 and 17.2 for the WBNO configuration. This calculation supports the premise raised in those works.

For the FB design, the data in Table 3 show that modifying the SGV plate's clearance has little influence on the differences in the outlet port's south and east halves. However, increasing the turbulence inside the SEN (by reducing the SGV plate clearance) increases the differences in the outlet port's north and west halves. This behavior can be explained as follows. Increasing turbulence inside the SEN promotes the constant presence of two counter-rotating vortexes in the SEN's bottom zone (lower panels of Figure 7). By increasing the turbulence, the vortexes' intensity increases too, but they do not become identical. Recall that the size of the vortex is directly related to the exit flow rate. This assertion is corroborated by the trend observed in Figure 14c,d.

The four statistics, a_N, a_S, a_W, and a_E, show changes in the WB design when the SGV plate clearance is reduced. The changes can be explained by recalling that, when the turbulence inside the bore increases, the intensity of the strongest vortex increases but is pushed downwards and sinks into the pool. The stagnation zone above the ports and below the SGV plate's clearance also increases its spread. Therefore, the streams flowing through the quadrants on the same half of the SGV plate's clearance reduce their volumetric flow while the streams on the other half increase their volumetric flow. Additionally, notice that a_N reduces its value by almost half, and the value of a_S increases to just over double. The frequency analysis of the volumetric flow signals was carried out in the same way as in the previous section, and the results are presented in Figures 16 and 17. Again, for clearness, only the analysis of time series belonging to no obstruction and severe obstruction is presented. The results for moderate obstruction are in between the presented extreme cases. Figures 16 and 17 both have the same structure and report the estimated PSD vs. the frequency for the FB and the WB designs, respectively. Notice that all the panels have the same scale for the PSD axis and the frequency range is limited by the Nyquist frequency. The red line displays the results for the no obstruction condition, while the blue line reports the results for the severe obstruction condition.

First, let us analyze the behavior for the no-obstruction condition. The dynamic fluctuations are weaker for the FB design than the WB design. For the FB design, the dynamic behavior in the lower quadrants is quite similar, contrasting with the behavior observed for the upper quadrants. The behavior in the lower quadrants resembles a white noise signal, that is, a quasi-steady-state dynamic behavior with weak random fluctuations. Figure 16 shows periodic fluctuations in both of the upper quadrants, but one has stronger fluctuations. Figure 17 shows periodic fluctuations in all the quadrants for the WB design.

Notice that, in this experimental test, the strongest fluctuations are in opposite quadrants, specifically NW and SE.

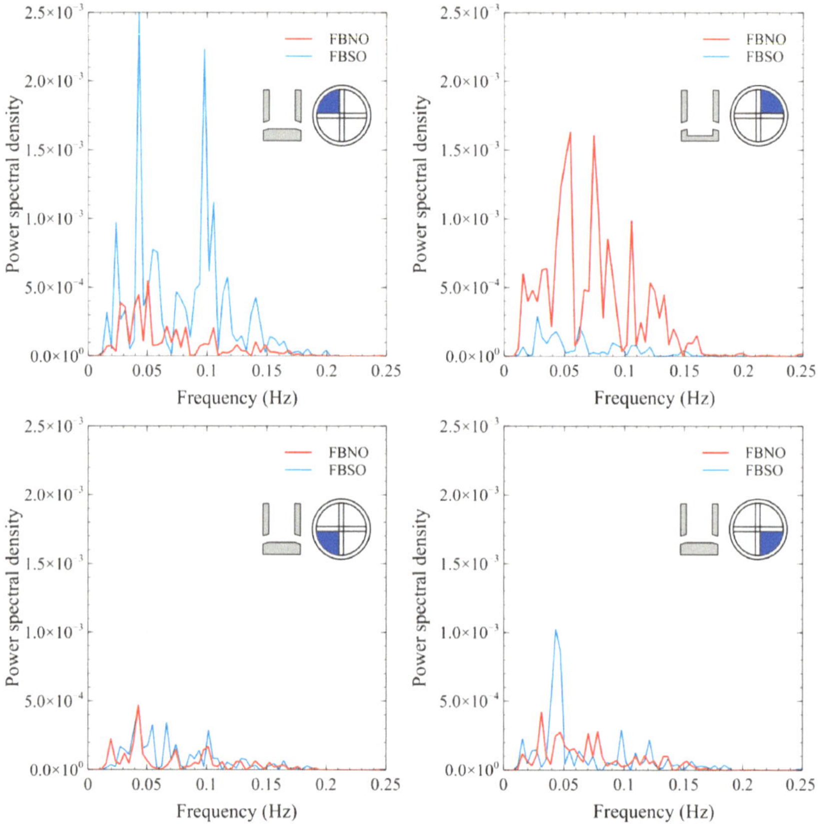

Figure 16. Frequency analysis of the volumetric flow time series at each quadrant for the FB design and the FBNO and FBSO configurations. The SEN design and the port quadrant are indicated on each panel with sketches.

Now, let us analyze the behavior for the severe-obstruction condition, but recall that the SGV clearance is above the NE and SE quadrants. For the FB design, Figure 16 shows that reducing the SGV clearance led to the following:

- The strength of the fluctuations in the lower quadrants increases, while for the SW it does not change;
- The strength of the fluctuations in the NE quadrant reduces significantly while periodic fluctuations considerably increase in the NW quadrant.

For the WB design, Figure 17 shows that reducing the SGV clearance has the following outcomes:

- The strength of the fluctuations in all the quadrants reduces, but it is much more noticeable in the southern quadrants;
- The strength of periodic fluctuations with specific frequencies increases, which is much more noticeable in the NE and SE quadrants.

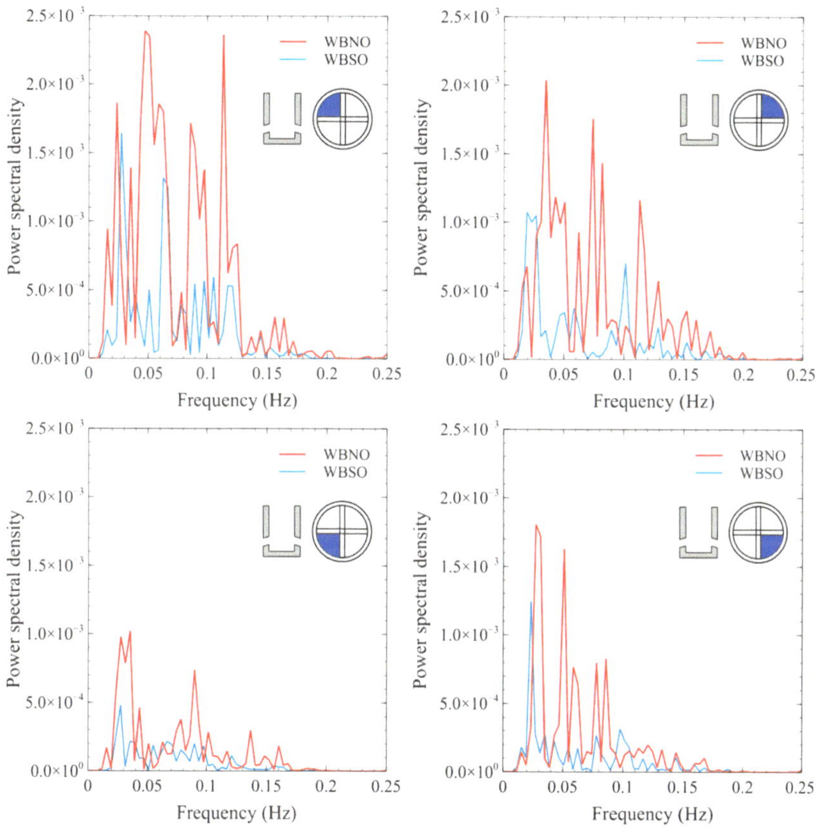

Figure 17. Frequency analysis of the volumetric flow time series at each quadrant for the WB design and the WBNO and WBSO configurations. The SEN design and the port quadrant are indicated on each panel with sketches.

The behavior observed in both designs can be understood by recalling that reducing the SGV clearance creates a stagnation zone above the quadrants on the same side of the clearance. This zone, in turn, increases the streams flowing through the quadrants on the opposite half. The overall effect of the SGV can be characterized as a suppression of multiple harmonics enhancing specific frequencies in the exit flow.

4.3. Analysis of the Conic Couplers Effect

The flowmeters mounted on each quadrant of the output ports allow us to measure their bulk flow rate and any slowly changing oscillations. The flowmeters introduce an additional pressure on the port where they are mounted which may lead to a bias in the discharge rate between the two ports. Although a constant pressure imposed on each outlet quadrant would change the total flow rate, this will not affect the measurements of differences in flow rates between quadrants. However, such bias may change the flow pattern inside the SEN's bore. Visual inspection of the high-speed recordings of the flow structure inside the bore when the flowmeters are mounted shows no qualitative difference with the case of freely discharging flow.

Moreover, the conical pipe couplers that divide the flow into four sections may change the flow pattern expected in the case of SEN without the couplers. The influence of the coupler cannot be readily determined from the experiments. For this reason, we performed numerical simulations using the SPH method. Previous works showed that SPH simulations of weakly compressible fluid satisfactorily reproduce the jet's structure and the SEN's internal vortices [15,16,49]. Details on the numerical parameters and the GPUSPH code are described in [50,51]. Here, we conduct two simulations of FBMO SEN: one without the couplers and one with couplers on both ports. In both cases, water enters through the inlet with a constant velocity $v = 1.0\ \mathrm{m/s}$. It further accelerates due to gravity and exists freely through the exit ports. The average number of fluid particles was 500,000 in both simulations. The geometry STL file of the SEN was meshed by unstructured triangular mesh with $\Delta x = 0.0005$ m and discretized with 500,000 (no couplers) and 600,000 (with couplers) particles.

To assess the vortex structure inside the SEN, we compare the velocity magnitudes of particles located in a thin slab in the YZ plane centered at $x = 0$. Figure 18 shows the velocity field inside the SEN captured after one second of evolution when the flow is roughly established. It is important to mention that it is expected that fully turbulent flow will settle after 8.0 s, as observed in experimental tests. However, due to excessive computational demand, only one-second numerical simulations were conducted, but we were looking for differences between the pattern with and without couplers. Notice that there is a very similar flow pattern in both cases. This similarity leads us to the conclusion that the fluid freely discharges through the exit ports with the conic couplers does not disrupt the flow pattern inside the SEN.

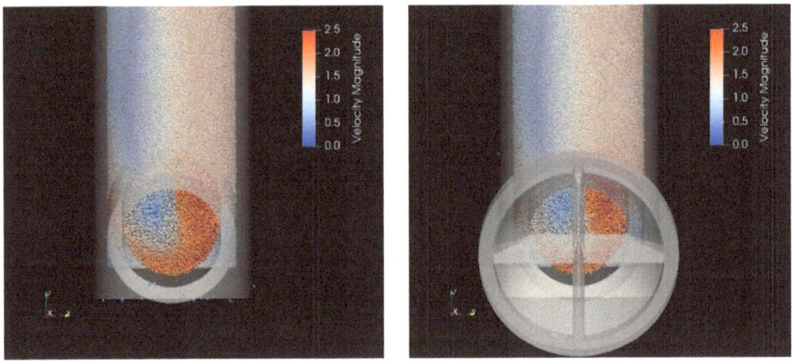

Figure 18. Velocity of particles along a thin slab centered at $x = 0$ for an exit port without (**left**) and with (**right**) conic coupler. Note that the SGV clearance is located on the right side of the bore leading to lower speed on the opposite side.

5. Concluding Remarks

This work analyzed how the SGV modifies the dynamic behavior of the fluid flow inside the bore and the SEN exit jets. Through several experimental tests, the frequency analysis of fluid flow fluctuations for six SEN configurations was carried out. For the sake of space, in some cases, only the no-obstruction and severe-obstruction SGV conditions were present. The observed behavior for the moderate-obstruction conditions is in between the presented cases, but the relationship is not linear. For interested readers, we include as Supplementary Material the raw high-speed videos of the flow inside the bore for all the six SEN configurations.

The high-frequency flow fluctuations inside the bore were determined by employing the PIV technique. Also, a low-frequency analysis of the SEN exit jets was carried out using digital flowmeter measurements. These two approaches confirm the observations previously reported for the SEN with no obstruction. Specifically, the WB design produces a dominant, strong vortex, which widens the SEN outlet jets. It was observed that reducing the SGV clearance increases the fluctuations' amplitude inside the bore, as expected, due to the asymmetry of the entering flow. Despite this, the flow inside the SEN bore displays ordered rather than erratic fluctuations. In addition, it was observed that a stagnation zone below the SGV clearance is formed, which increases the flow on the opposite side of the bore.

The effect of increasing the SGV obstruction is as follows. For the FB design, it promotes the permanent presence of two vortexes at the bottom of the SEN. For the WB design, the dominant vortex is pushed and sunk into the SEN pool, which increases the opening of the SEN outlet jets.

Our findings suggest that current strategies in which the walls of the SEN bore are modified by attaching flow modifiers are unnecessary because the dominant feature is the geometry of the SEN's bottom section, such as the bottom well. This statement is based on the rounded SEN exit ports used in this work. However, further studies employing ports with other shapes must be carried out.

Finally, several works have reported that the periodic fluctuations inside the mold are found in the 0.5–3.0 Hz frequency range. Our analysis does not cover this range. However, a further study with a new technique for measuring the SEN outlet jet fluctuations in this range is necessary for identifying possible resonant frequencies.

Supplementary Materials: The following supporting information can be downloaded at: https://www.mdpi.com/article/10.3390/fluids9010030/s1, Video S1: Flow pattern inside the bore for the FBNO configuration; Video S2: Flow pattern inside the bore for the FBMO configuration; Video S3: Flow pattern inside the bore for the FBSO configuration; Video S4: Flow pattern inside the bore for the WBNO configuration; Video S5: Flow pattern inside the bore for the WBMO configuration; Video S6: Flow pattern inside the bore for the WBSO configuration.

Author Contributions: Conceptualization, J.G.-T., R.M.-T. and R.G; methodology, J.G.-T., R.M.-T., C.A.R.-R. and R.G.; experimental tests, J.G.-T., R.M.-T. and F.C.-d.-l.-T.; PIV calculations, J.G.-T., F.C.-d.-l.-T. and R.G.; writing—original draft preparation, J.G.-T., R.G. and C.A.R.-R.; supervision, J.G.-T., F.C.-d.-l.-T. and R.G.; funding acquisition, J.G.-T., R.G., F.C.-d.-l.-T., C.A.R.-R. and R.M.-T. All authors have read and agreed to the published version of the manuscript.

Funding: This work was supported by Universidad Autonoma Metropolitana, grant number 22703022.

Data Availability Statement: Data are contained within the article and Supplementary Materials.

Acknowledgments: The reconstruction of the fluid velocity field was carried out using the PIVlab software. The hydrodynamic simulations were made with publicly available GPUSPH v5.0 code www.gpusph.org (accessed on 5 June 2023). The authors acknowledge anonymous reviewers' comments and subjections, which improve the manuscript structure and results presentation.

Conflicts of Interest: The authors declare no conflicts of interest.

Nomenclature

CCC	Conventional continuous casting
CO_2	Carbon dioxide
ESP	Endless strip production
FB	Flat-bottom SEN
FBMO	Flat-bottom SEN with moderate obstruction
FBNO	Flat-bottom SEN with no obstruction
FBSO	Flat-bottom SEN with severe obstruction
NE	Northeast
NW	Northwest
PIV	Particle image velocimetry
PLA	Polylactic acid
PSD	Power spectral density
PVC	Polyvinyl chloride
SE	Southeast
SEN	Submerged entry nozzle
SGV	Sliding-gate valve
SPH	Smoothed particle hydrodynamics
SR	Stopper rod

SW	Southwest
TSC	Thin slab caster
WB	Well-bottom SEN
WBMO	Well-bottom SEN with moderate obstruction
WBNO	Well-bottom SEN with no obstruction
WBSO	Well-bottom SEN with severe obstruction

References

1. Birat, J.-P. Society, Materials, and the Environment: The Case of Steel. *Metals* **2020**, *10*, 331. [CrossRef]
2. Holappa, L. A General Vision for Reduction of Energy Consumption and CO_2 Emissions from the Steel Industry. *Metals* **2** *10*, 1117. [CrossRef]
3. Holappa, L. Challenges and Prospects of Steelmaking towards the Year 2050. *Metals* **2021**, *11*, 1978. [CrossRef]
4. Raabe, D. The Materials Science behind Sustainable Metals and Alloys. *Chem. Rev.* **2023**, *123*, 2436–2608. [CrossRef]
5. Mousa, E.; Wang, C.; Riesbeck, J.; Larsson, M. Biomass Applications in Iron and Steel Industry: An Overview of Challenges Opportunities. *Renew. Sustain. Energy Rev.* **2016**, *65*, 1247–1266. [CrossRef]
6. Cemernek, D.; Cemernek, S.; Gursch, H.; Pandeshwar, A.; Leitner, T.; Berger, M.; Klösch, G.; Kern, R. Machine Learnin Continuous Casting of Steel: A State-of-the-Art Survey. *J. Intell. Manuf.* **2022**, *33*, 1561–1579. [CrossRef]
7. Merten, D.C.; Hütt, M.-T.; Uygun, Y. Effect of Slab Width on Choice of Appropriate Casting Speed in Steel Production. *J. Iron Res. Int.* **2022**, *29*, 71–79. [CrossRef]
8. Guthrie, R.I.L.; Isac, M.M. Continuous Casting Practices for Steel: Past, Present and Future. *Metals* **2022**, *12*, 862. [CrossRef]
9. Wang, Y.; Zhang, L. Transient Fluid Flow Phenomena during Continuous Casting: Part I—Cast Start. *ISIJ Int.* **2010**, *50*, 1777–1 [CrossRef]
10. Zhang, Q.-Y.; Wang, X.-H. Numerical Simulation of Influence of Casting Speed Variation on Surface Fluctuation of Molten in Mold. *J. Iron Steel Res. Int.* **2010**, *17*, 15–19. [CrossRef]
11. Kubo, N.; Kubota, J.; Ishii, T. Simulation of Sliding Nozzle Gate Movements for Steel Continuous Casting. *ISIJ Int.* **2001** 1221–1228. [CrossRef]
12. Kalter, R.; Tummers, M.J.; Wefers Bettink, J.B.; Righolt, B.W.; Kenjereš, S.; Kleijn, C.R. Aspect Ratio Effects on Fluid F Fluctuations in Rectangular Cavities. *Metall. Mater. Trans. B* **2014**, *45*, 2186–2193. [CrossRef]
13. Du, F.; Li, T.; Zeng, Y.; Zhang, K. Influence of Nozzle Design on Flow Characteristic in the Continuous Casting Machi *Coatings* **2022**, *12*, 631. [CrossRef]
14. Sambasivam, R. Clogging Resistant Submerged Entry Nozzle Design through Mathematical Modelling. *Ironmak. Steelmak.* *33*, 439–453. [CrossRef]
15. Chaudhary, R.; Lee, G.-G.; Thomas, B.G.; Kim, S.-H. Transient Mold Fluid Flow with Well- and Mountain-Bottom Nozzl Continuous Casting of Steel. *Metall. Mater. Trans. B* **2008**, *39*, 870–884. [CrossRef]
16. Chatterjee, D. CFD Model Study of a New Four-Port Submerged Entry Nozzle for Decreasing the Turbulence in Slab Cas Mold. *ISRN Metall.* **2013**, *2013*, 981597. [CrossRef]
17. Srinivas, P.S.; Singh, A.; Korath, J.M.; Jana, A.K. A Water-Model Experimental Study of Vortex Characteristics Due to No Clogging in Slab Caster Mould. *Ironmak. Steelmak.* **2017**, *44*, 473–485. [CrossRef]
18. Cho, S.-M.; Thomas, B.G. Electromagnetic Forces in Continuous Casting of Steel Slabs. *Metals* **2019**, *9*, 471. [CrossRef]
19. Bao, Y.; Li, Z.; Zhang, L.; Wu, J.; Ma, D.; Jia, F. Asymmetric Flow Control in a Slab Mold through a New Type of Electromag Field Arrangement. *Processes* **2021**, *9*, 1988. [CrossRef]
20. Li, Z.; Zhang, L.; Bao, Y.; Ma, D.; Wang, E. Influence of the Vertical Pole Parameters on Molten Steel Flow and Meniscus Beha in a FAC-EMBr Controlled Mold. *Metall. Mater. Trans. B* **2022**, *53*, 938–953. [CrossRef]
21. Schurmann, D.; Glavinić, I.; Willers, B.; Timmel, K.; Eckert, S. Impact of the Electromagnetic Brake Position on the Flow Stru in a Slab Continuous Casting Mold: An Experimental Parameter Study. *Metall. Mater. Trans. B* **2020**, *51*, 61–78. [CrossRef]
22. Kharicha, A.; Vakhrushev, A.; Karimi-Sibaki, E.; Wu, M.; Ludwig, A. Reverse Flows and Flattening of a Submerged Jet unde Action of a Transverse Magnetic Field. *Phys. Rev. Fluids* **2021**, *6*, 123701. [CrossRef]
23. Vakhrushev, A.; Kharicha, A.; Karimi-Sibaki, E.; Wu, M.; Ludwig, A.; Nitzl, G.; Tang, Y.; Hackl, G.; Watzinger, J.; Ecke Generation of Reverse Meniscus Flow by Applying an Electromagnetic Brake. *Metall. Mater. Trans. B* **2021**, *52*, 3193– [CrossRef]
24. Zhang, X.-W.; Jin, X.-L.; Wang, Y.; Deng, K.; Ren, Z.-M. Comparison of Standard k-ε Model and RSM on Three Dimens Turbulent Flow in the SEN of Slab Continuous Caster Controlled by Slide Gate. *ISIJ Int.* **2011**, *51*, 581–587. [CrossRef]
25. Gursoy, K.A.; Yavuz, M.M. Effect of Flow Rate Controllers and Their Opening Levels on Liquid Steel Flow in Continuous Ca Mold. *ISIJ Int.* **2016**, *56*, 554–563. [CrossRef]
26. Thumfart, M.; Hackl, G.; Fellner, W. Water Model Experiments on the Influence of Phase Distribution in the Submerged E Nozzle Considering Varying Operating Conditions. *Steel Res. Int.* **2022**, *93*, 2100824. [CrossRef]
27. Bai, H.; Thomas, B.G. Turbulent Flow of Liquid Steel and Argon Bubbles in Slide-Gate Tundish Nozzles: Part II. Effe Operation Conditions and Nozzle Design. *Metall. Mater. Trans. B* **2001**, *32*, 269–284. [CrossRef]

Bai, H.; Thomas, B.G. Turbulent Flow of Liquid Steel and Argon Bubbles in Slide-Gate Tundish Nozzles: Part I. Model Development and Validation. *Metall. Mater. Trans. B* **2001**, *32*, 253–267. [CrossRef]
Szekely, J.; Yadoya, R.T. The Physical and Mathematical Modeling of the Flow Field in the Mold Region in Continuous Casting Systems: Part I. Model Studies with Aqueous Systems. *Metall. Trans.* **1972**, *3*, 2673–2680. [CrossRef]
Li, G.; Tu, L.; Wang, Q.; Zhang, X.; He, S. Fluid Flow in Continuous Casting Mold for Ultra-Wide Slab. *Materials* **2023**, *16*, 1135. [CrossRef]
Mahapatra, R.B.; Brimacombe, J.K.; Samarasekera, I.V.; Walker, N.; Paterson, E.A.; Young, J.D. Mold Behavior and Its Influence on Quality in the Continuous Casting of Steel Slabs: Part I. Industrial Trials, Mold Temperature Measurements, and Mathematical Modeling. *Metall. Trans. B* **1991**, *22*, 861–874. [CrossRef]
Shen, J.L.; Chen, D.F.; Xie, X.; Zhang, L.L.; Dong, Z.H.; Long, M.J.; Ruan, X.B. Influences of SEN Structures on Flow Characters, Temperature Field and Shell Distribution in 420 Mm Continuous Casting Mould. *Ironmak. Steelmak.* **2013**, *40*, 263–275. [CrossRef]
Cai, C.; Shen, M.; Ji, K.; Zhang, Z.; Liu, Y. Research on the Influence of the Inner Wall Structure of the Continuous Casting Submerged Nozzle on the Stream of Molten Steel. *Trans. Indian Inst. Met.* **2022**, *75*, 613–624. [CrossRef]
Zhang, L.; Yang, S.; Cai, K.; Li, J.; Wan, X.; Thomas, B.G. Investigation of Fluid Flow and Steel Cleanliness in the Continuous Casting Strand. *Metall. Mater. Trans. B* **2007**, *38*, 63–83. [CrossRef]
Najjar, F.M.; Thomas, B.G.; Hershey, D.E. Numerical Study of Steady Turbulent Flow through Bifurcated Nozzles in Continuous Casting. *Metall. Mater. Trans. B* **1995**, *26*, 749–765. [CrossRef]
Gupta, D.; Lahiri, A.K. Water Modelling Study of the Jet Characteristics in a Continuous Casting Mould. *Steel Res. Int.* **1992**, *63*, 201–204. [CrossRef]
Zhang, X.-G.; Zhang, W.-X.; Jin, J.-Z.; Evans, J.W. Flow of Steel in Mold Region During Continuous Casting. *J. Iron Steel Res. Int.* **2007**, *14*, 30–35. [CrossRef]
Mohammadi-Ghaleni, M.; Asle Zaeem, M.; Smith, J.D.; O'Malley, R. Computational Fluid Dynamics Study of Molten Steel Flow Patterns and Particle–Wall Interactions Inside a Slide-Gate Nozzle by a Hybrid Turbulent Model. *Metall. Mater. Trans. B* **2016**, *47*, 3056–3065. [CrossRef]
Lu, H.; Li, B.; Li, J.; Zhong, Y.; Ren, Z.; Lei, Z. Numerical Simulation of In-Mold Electromagnetic Stirring on Slide Gate Caused Bias Flow and Solidification in Slab Continuous Casting. *ISIJ Int.* **2021**, *61*, 1860–1871. [CrossRef]
Yang, H.; Olia, H.; Thomas, B.G. Modeling Air Aspiration in Steel Continuous Casting Slide-Gate Nozzles. *Metals* **2021**, *11*, 116. [CrossRef]
Chen, K.K.; Rowley, C.W.; Stone, H.A. Vortex Breakdown, Linear Global Instability and Sensitivity of Pipe Bifurcation Flows. *J. Fluid Mech.* **2017**, *815*, 257–294. [CrossRef]
Chen, K.K.; Rowley, C.W.; Stone, H.A. Vortex Dynamics in a Pipe T-Junction: Recirculation and Sensitivity. *Phys. Fluids* **2015**, *27*, 034107. [CrossRef]
Real, C.; Miranda, R.; Vilchis, C.; Barron, M.; Hoyos, L.; Gonzalez, J. Transient Internal Flow Characterization of a Bifurcated Submerged Entry Nozzle. *ISIJ Int.* **2006**, *46*, 1183–1191. [CrossRef]
Real-Ramirez, C.A.; Carvajal-Mariscal, I.; Sanchez-Silva, F.; Cervantes-de-la-Torre, F.; Diaz-Montes, J.; Gonzalez-Trejo, J. Three-Dimensional Flow Behavior Inside the Submerged Entry Nozzle. *Metall. Mater. Trans. B* **2018**, *49*, 1644–1657. [CrossRef]
Gonzalez-Trejo, J.; Real-Ramirez, C.A.; Miranda-Tello, J.R.; Gabbasov, R.; Carvajal-Mariscal, I.; Sanchez-Silva, F.; Cervantes-de-la-Torre, F. Influence of the Submerged Entry Nozzle's Bottom Well on the Characteristics of Its Exit Jets. *Metals* **2021**, *11*, 398. [CrossRef]
Gonzalez-Trejo, J.; Real-Ramirez, C.A.; Carvajal-Mariscal, I.; Sanchez-Silva, F.; Cervantes-De-La-Torre, F.; Miranda-Tello, R.; Gabbasov, R. Hydrodynamic Analysis of the Flow inside the Submerged Entry Nozzle. *Math. Probl. Eng.* **2020**, *2020*, 6267472. [CrossRef]
Javurek, M.; Wincor, R. Bubbly Mold Flow in Continuous Casting: Comparison of Numerical Flow Simulations with Water Model Measurements. *Steel Res. Int.* **2020**, *91*, 2000415. [CrossRef]
American Water Works Association. *ANSI/AWWA C701-15: Cold-Water Meters—Turbine Type, for Customer Service*; American Water Works Association: Denver, CO, USA, 2015.
Real-Ramirez, C.A.; Carvajal-Mariscal, I.; Gonzalez-Trejo, J.; Miranda-Tello, R.; Gabbasov, R.; Sanchez-Silva, F.; Cervantes-de-la-Torre, F. Visualization and Measurement of Turbulent Flow inside a SEN and off the Ports. *Rev. Mex. Fis.* **2021**, *67*, 1–10. [CrossRef]
Hérault, A.; Bilotta, G.; Dalrymple, R.A. SPH on GPU with CUDA. *J. Hydraul. Res.* **2010**, *48*, 74–79. [CrossRef]
Gabbasov, R.; González-Trejo, J.; Real-Ramírez, C.A.; Molina, M.M.; la Torre, F.C. Evaluation of GPUSPH Code for Simulations of Fluid Injection Through Submerged Entry Nozzle. In Proceedings of the 10th International Conference on Supercomputing in Mexico, Monterrey, Mexico, 25–29 March 2019; Springer International Publishing: Cham, Switzerland, 2019; pp. 218–226.

fluids

Review

Fluid Flow in Helically Coiled Pipes

Leonardo Di G. Sigalotti [1,*], Carlos E. Alvarado-Rodríguez [2,3] and Otto Rendón [1]

1 Departamento de Ciencias Básicas, Universidad Autónoma Metropolitana-Azcapotzalco (UAM-A), Av. San Pablo 420, Colonia Nueva el Rosario, Alcaldía Azcapotzalco, Ciudad de México 02128, Mexico; ottorendon@gmail.com
2 Dirección de Cátedras Consejo Nacional de Humanidades, Ciencias y Tecnologías (CONAHCYT), Av. Insurgentes Sur 1582, Crédito Constructor, Benito Juárez, Ciudad de México 03940, Mexico; carlos.alvarado@conacyt.mx
3 Departamento de Ingeniería Química, División de Ciencias Naturales y Exactas (DCNyE), Universidad de Guanajuato, Noria Alta S/N, Guanajuato 36000, Mexico
* Correspondence: leonardo.sigalotti@gmail.com; Tel.: +52-55-21209913

Abstract: Helically coiled pipes are widely used in many industrial and engineering applications because of their compactness, larger heat transfer area per unit volume and higher efficiency in heat and mass transfer compared to other pipe geometries. They are commonly encountered in heat exchangers, steam generators in power plants and chemical reactors. The most notable feature of flow in helical pipes is the secondary flow (i.e., the cross-sectional circulatory motion) caused by centrifugal forces due to the curvature. Other important features are the stabilization effects of turbulent flow and the higher Reynolds number at which the transition from a laminar to a turbulent state occurs compared to straight pipes. A survey of the open literature on helical pipe flows shows that a good deal of experimental and theoretical work has been conducted to derive appropriate correlations to predict frictional pressure losses under laminar and turbulent conditions as well as to study the dependence of the flow characteristics and heat transfer capabilities on the Reynolds number, the Nusselt number and the geometrical parameters of the helical pipe. Despite the progress made so far in understanding the flow and heat transfer characteristics of helical pipe flow, there is still much work to be completed to address the more complex problem of multiphase flows and the impact of pipe deformation and corrugation on single- and multiphase flow. The aim of this paper is to provide a review on the state-of-the-art experimental and theoretical research concerning the flow in helically coiled pipes.

Keywords: laminar flow; turbulent flow; helical coil; secondary flow; heat transfer; pressure loss; friction factor; flow characteristics

1. Introduction

Although pipes and ducts have been used to transport water since the construction of the first aqueducts by the Romans during the fourth century BC, the first scientific studies began much later, from the year 1839, when Hagen [1] and then Poiseuille [2] carried out the first experiments on water flow in straight tubes of various sizes to determine pressure losses. Later on, Darcy [3] studied the effects of pipe roughness on pressure drop, and Reynolds [4] observed that the transition from laminar to turbulent flow in straight pipes occurs at a critical dimensionless parameter, known as the critical Reynolds number. In particular, the Reynolds number, defined as $\mathrm{Re} = vD/\nu$, where v is the mean flow velocity, D is the pipe diameter and ν is the kinematic viscosity, is commonly used to measure the relationship between inertial and viscous forces in the fluid and serves to indicate whether the flow is laminar or turbulent.

In many engineering applications and industrial processes, the transportation of liquids and gases through pipeline systems may require redirection of the flow by means of bends of various angles and sharpnesses. Studies of flow through curved tubes with different cross-sections date back to Boussinesq [5], who showed that, for laminar flow in a channel with a rectangular cross-section, secondary flow develops across a bend in the form of two symmetrical vortices. An explanation of this behavior was provided by Thomson in 1876 [6,7], who claimed that the curvature balance between pressure and centrifugal forces in a river bend induces an imbalance in fluid motion near the bottom, leading to an inward secondary flow there. However, it was not until the beginning of the twentieth century when the experiments of Williams et al. [8] showed that, across a curved pipe section, the maximum flow velocity always occurs towards the outer wall at the outlet of the bend, while, a bit later, Eustice [9,10] and White [11] demonstrated experimentally that the pressure drop is greater in curved pipes than in straight ones and that the curvature stabilizes the flow because the transitional Re number increases substantially compared to straight pipes. As suggested by Kalpakli Vester et al. [12], in their comprehensive review on turbulent flow in curved pipes, the most notable and well-known figure in curved-pipe-flow research is William R. Dean, who studied by analytical means the laminar flow in curved pipes with circular cross-sections and small curvature ratios, $\gamma = R/R_c$ [13,14], where R is the pipe radius and R_c is the curvature radius. In particular, he found that an important parameter was the square of the Dean number, $\mathrm{De} = \sqrt{\gamma}\mathrm{Re}$, and that, when projected on the cross-stream plane, the cross-flow velocity-field pattern can be identified as two counter-rotating vortex cells, which are today called Dean vortices in honor of his work (Dean vortices refer to small-amplitude laminar flow patterns. However, similar vortices are also encountered in turbulent flows, which are also called Dean vortices).

A type of curved pipes that have caught the attention of many researchers due to their particular geometry and its countless applications in many industrial situations are the helically coiled pipes. Due to their compact size, ease of manufacturing and high efficiency in heat and mass transfer, these pipes are widely used as heat exchangers and steam generators in nuclear power plants [15–18]. Helical pipes are also used in refrigeration systems [19], anaerobic digesters [20], fouling and clogging reduction in filtration membranes [21], mass transfer enhancement in catalytic reactors [22], mixing efficiency and homogenization [23] as well as in many other devices and applications. Motivated by their various industrial applications and the complex cross-sectional motion that takes place due to their curvature and centrifugal forces induced on the flow, experimental and theoretical research on helical coil pipes has flourished in the last few decades. A survey of work on helical tubes in the open literature shows that there are several experimental and theoretical publications on flow and heat transfer characteristics under laminar and turbulent flow conditions. With the exception of a few existing reviews examining heat transfer in helically coiled tubes [24,25], most overviews on helical pipe research have been included in reviews devoted to flow in curved pipes in general [12,26–29]. It is frequently mentioned that, while the literature on laminar and heat transfer in curved pipes, and, in particular, in helically coiled pipes, is quite extensive, studies of turbulent flow in such streamline curvatures are much less abundant. However, Kalpakli Vester et al. [12] mentioned that there is a great deal of work on turbulence in curve ducts that is not being covered by the available literature.

The experimental literature on helical pipe flow is quite varied. The transition from laminar to turbulent flow was first studied experimentally by White [11], who observed that the transition to turbulent flow occurs at much higher critical Reynolds numbers compared to flow in straight tubes, while stabilization effects of turbulent flow in helically coiled pipes was first recognized by Taylor [30] and then later on by several other authors [31–33]. In particular, one of the most important experimental studies on flow stabilization through helical pipes was reported by Sreenivasan and Strykowski [33], who found that the turbulent flow that conveys from a straight pipe and becomes laminar when passing through the coiled section can persist in a straight pipe for long when leaving the coiled section. Other later experimental works have dealt with studies regarding the geometrical coil effects on pressure drop and heat transfer [34–36]. More recently, the effects of coil geometry on incompressible laminar flow were studied by De Amicis et al. [37], while investigations on the turbulent forced convection flow and the laminar flow friction factor in helical pipes were reported by Rakhsha et al. [38] and Abushammala et al. [39], respectively.

In comparison to experimental research, numerical papers on helically coiled flow appear to be much more numerous. Most of this work has been oriented to study the prediction of laminar flow and heat transfer [40–44], turbulent flow [17,45,46], entropy generation [47], pulsating flow [48] and flow characteristics [49–51]. Investigations on multiphase flow in helical pipes are by far much more scarce (see, for instance, Colombo et al. [52] and references therein). On the other hand, analytical and semi-analytical works based on perturbation methods [53,54], asymptotic analysis [55], entropy generation analysis [56] as well as physical bounds on the flow rate and friction factor in pressure-driven flows through helical pipes using a background method formulation [57] have also been reported in the open literature.

In this paper, we perform an overview of the experimental, semi-analytical and numerical work on flow and heat transfer through helically coiled pipes. The review is organized as follows. The basic parameters and definitions that characterize helical pipes are briefly described in Section 2. Section 3 deals with an overview of experimental results on helical pipe flows in general, and Section 4 contains a review of theoretically derived results, which has been divided into analytical and semi-analytical studies and numerical simulations of laminar flow, turbulent flow and heat transfer. The section ends with an overview of flow and heat transfer in corrugated and twisted helical pipes. Section 5 deals with results regarding visualization and entropy generation analysis of helical pipe flows, while Section 6 provides a brief account on two-phase flows in helically coiled pipes. The review ends with a brief survey about helical coils in magnetohydrodynamics in Section 7 and the concluding remarks in Section 8.

2. Geometrical Parameters of a Helically Coiled Pipe

A schematic view of a typical helical pipe is shown in Figure 1. The main parameters characterizing the geometry of helical pipes are the inner radius R, the coil radius (also known as the pitch circle radius) R_c, measured between the center of the pipe and the axis of the coil, the coil pitch h, defined as the distance between two adjacent turns, the helix angle α, which is the angle between a coil turn, and the plane perpendicular to the axis of the coil. While these parameters are often used to define the geometry of typical helical pipes, in many other places, the curvature ratio is defined as the ratio of pipe radius to coil radius, $\gamma = R/R_c$, and the ratio of pitch to developed length of one turn, $\beta = h/2\pi R_c$, which is customarily called the dimensionless pitch; these are often used to characterize the geometry of helical coils.

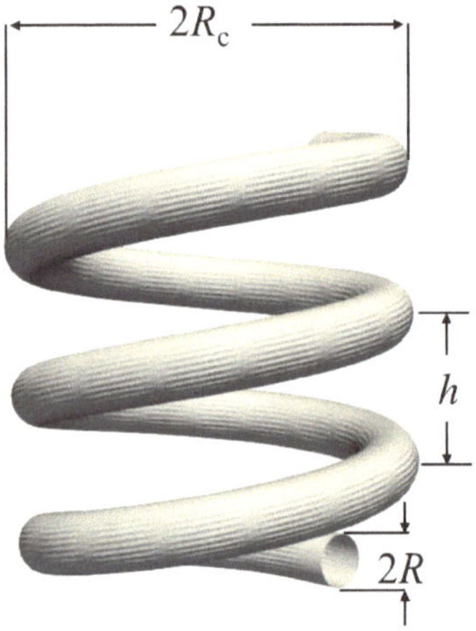

Figure 1. Schematic representation of a helically coiled pipe and its parametric definitions. Figure adapted from Rakhsha et al. [38].

Similar to other types of curved pipes and ducts, the most important dimensionless number that is used to characterize the flow in helical pipes is the Dean number [13,14] provided by

$$\mathrm{De} = \sqrt{\gamma}\mathrm{Re}, \tag{1}$$

which is based on the curvature ratio and the Reynolds number

$$\mathrm{Re} = \frac{vD}{\nu}, \tag{2}$$

where v is the mean flow (or bulk) velocity, $D = 2R$ is the inner pipe diameter and ν is the kinematic viscosity. A further relevant dimensionless parameter is the so-called Fanning friction factor F, defined as

$$F = -\frac{R}{\rho v^2}\frac{dp}{ds}, \tag{3}$$

where ρ is the fluid density and dp/ds is the applied pressure gradient along the pipe. In relation (3), the bulk velocity is often defined as

$$v = \frac{\langle Q \rangle}{\pi R^2}, \tag{4}$$

where $\langle Q \rangle$ is the long-time average of the dimensional volumetric flow rate and $Q^\star$ is a dimensionless volumetric flow rate [57], provided by

$$Q^\star = \frac{1}{R^2}\left[-\frac{\rho}{(dp/ds)R}\right]^{1/2}\langle Q \rangle. \tag{5}$$

It is well-known that, when a fluid flows through a pipe, the interaction of the fluid with the pipe wall causes friction, which slows down the fluid motion and decreases the pressure along the pipe. This way, the Fanning friction factor is used to quantify the pressure losses in a pipe, and its dependence on the Reynolds number has been used as an indicator of whether the flow is laminar, transitional or turbulent [12]. Another quantity of interest is the Darcy–Weisbach factor, defined as $F_D = 4F$, i.e., four times the Fanning friction factor. Similar to the Fanning factor, the Darcy–Weisbach friction factor is also used to describe friction losses in pipe flow as well as in open-channel flows.

3. Overview of Experimental Work

3.1. Earlier Observations

The earliest experimental work documented on curved pipes dates back to 1855 [58]. This work, authored by the German mathematician and engineer J. L. Weisbach, provides the first experimental determinations of pressure losses through a sharp-bent pipe. Later on, in 1876, Thomson [6,7] was the first to report experimental observations of the onset of secondary flow in a channel bend using a small laboratory model to mimic the windings of rivers. He observed the formation of vortices near the bottom of the bend and explained such inward motion as the result of the curvature balance between the pressure and centrifugal forces acting on the bulk flow. However, the onset of secondary flows in curved pipes occurs in a different manner, as described by Thomson from his laboratory experiments in a channel, where the fluid flows under the presence of an upper free surface. In fact, it was not until Williams et al.'s [8] experimental work of water flow in bends in 1902 that it was recognized that the maximum mean velocity in a pipe bend of circular cross-section always occurs towards the outer pipe wall close to the bend exit. Further experiments on water flow in curved streamlines were performed by Eustice [9,10], who found that the pressure losses are greater than in straight pipes and that, compared with the latter, the pipe curvature plays a role in flow stabilization against the transition to turbulence. This was confirmed almost twenty years later by White's experiments [11], who showed that the critical Reynolds number at which transition to turbulence occurs is much higher in curved than in straight pipes and ducts.

Contemporarily to White [11], Taylor [30] performed one of the first experiments on flow through a helical glass tube. In particular, he studied the criterion for turbulence by introducing a colored fluid through a small hole in the glass helix. By varying the mean flow velocity through the pipe, he confirmed White's findings that turbulence in curved pipes can be maintained with a higher flow velocity compared to straight pipes. For a helical pipe of coil diameter 18 times that of the pipe, Taylor observed that laminar motion was maintained up to Re $= 5830$, even in those cases when the flow was highly turbulent at the entrance of the helix. This transitional Reynolds number was reported by Taylor to be about 2.8 times that required in a straight pipe of the same circular cross-sectional diameter. Further earlier experimental measurements of mean velocity and pressure by Adler [59] and Wattendorf [60] were inspired by Dean's two seminal papers [13,14] on laminar flow through curved conduits of small curvature. For laminar and turbulent water flow in curved pipes of small curvature ratios ($0.005 \leq \gamma \leq 0.02$), Adler [59] investigated the structure of the cross-flow pattern, which was found to consist of two symmetric counter-rotating vortices similar to the vortex cells described analytically by Dean [14]. On the other hand, Wattendorf [60] performed experiments on fully developed turbulent flow through a curved channel of constant curvature and cross-section. He found that instability and increased mixing occur towards the outer walls of the curved channel, while a more stable flow and decreased mixing were both observed at the inner wall. Although most of these earlier experiments have actually dealt with flow through curved streamlines in pipe bends and elbows, many of the flow features observed and discoveries made from these previous measurements also apply to helically coiled pipes.

3.2. Flow Stabilization in Helical Pipes

After Taylor's [30] work, experimental studies on flow in helically coiled pipes were resumed with the works of Viswanath et al. [31] and Narasimha and Sreenivasan [32] in the late 1970s. An interesting and spectacular phenomenon that occurs in helically coiled pipes is the laminarization of turbulent flow. As was outlined by Viswanath et al. [31], the reversion from turbulent to a laminar state was many times greeted with incredulity since this would imply moving from a state of disorder to one of order, contradicting the principles of thermodynamics. However, Viswanath et al. [31] argued that such disbeliefs were of course not valid because the turbulent flows claimed to be reverting into laminar were by no means closed systems. Therefore, laminarization of the turbulent flow across the helical coil does not violate the second law of thermodynamics. After conveying a turbulent flow from an initial straight section of about 20 cm long into a helical pipe curled around a cylinder of 11 cm diameter, they observed laminarization of the flow when the fluid was passing across the fourth coil. The laminar state was maintained further downstream until the flow left the helical tube and entered a straight section, where it became turbulent again.

Further experiments on turbulent flow through a helically coiled pipe by Narasimha and Sreenivasan [32] confirmed the observations of Viswanath et al. [31]. They argued that turbulent fluctuations of negligible effect can still survive in the laminar flow as inherited from its previous history, thereby suggesting that such flow might be better called quasi-laminar. Despite these detailed experimental observations, little was known until then about the phenomenon. It was not until the pioneering work reported by Sreenivasan and Strykowski [33] that some light was shed on the mechanisms responsible for flow laminarization. They faced the problem by asking the following questions, which we copy literally here: (a) *For a given turbulent pipe, can one always set up a suitable helical coil which inevitably leads to laminarization?* (b) *Alternatively, for a given helical coil, what is the maximum flow Reynolds number for which laminarization is possible?* (c) *What is exactly the role of the tightness of the coil, the number of turns in the coil, etc.?* and (d) *How precisely does the laminarized flow returns to a turbulent state when downstream of the coil the flow is allowed to develop in another long straight section?*

To try to answer the above questions, Sreenivasan and Strykowski [33] performed a similar experiment to Narasimha and Sreenivasan [32] in which the set-up consisted of an upstream straight long pipe of standard inlet, followed by a helically coiled section connected to a downstream straight long pipe, as shown schematically in Figure 2. They considered two set-ups differing in the coil radius ($R_c = 16.51$ cm their set-up I, $R_c = 5.47$ their set-up II), the number of turns (3 their set-up I, 20.5 their set-up II), the inner pipe diameter ($2R = 1.905$ cm, their set-up I, $2R = 0.635$ cm, their set-up II) and the lengths of the upstream (L_1) and downstream (L_2) straight pipe sections ($L_1/2R = 144$ and $L_2/2R = 162$, their set-up I; $L_1/2R = 173$ and $L_2/2R = 937$, their set-up II). In the upstream straight section, they inferred maximum values of Re for which the flow remains laminar to be 2050 for set-up I and 2400 for set-up II, and the lowest values of Re for which the flow becomes fully turbulent to be 2800 for set-up I and 3300 for set-up II. In both cases, they observed the reversion process from turbulent to laminar in the coil section to be much more complex, with clear differences between transition near the inner and outer walls of the coil being evident until about 3 turns. The authors also observed that all critical Reynolds numbers increase as the flow moves through the first 3 turns. This behavior is shown in the left frame of Figure 3, where the upper critical value of Re near the outer wall, the so-called liberal estimate of the lower critical Reynolds number, corresponding to the first appearance of turbulence everywhere at the specified cross-section, and a conservative estimate of the lower critical Reynolds number, corresponding to the first burst near the outer wall, are depicted as functions of the number of turns for the set-up II experiment. The conservative lower critical Reynolds number corresponds to the maximum value of Re for which complete laminarization in the coil is possible. The right frame of Figure 3 shows the dependence of the asymptotic critical Reynolds numbers, as measured at the end of the twentieth coil for the set-up II experiment, on the radius ratio (i.e., the ratio of the inner pipe radius ($2R = 0.635$ cm) to the coil radius, R/R_c). Both lower critical Re curves grow for small radius ratios, reach a maximum value and then decay for larger radius ratios, while the upper critical Re curve increases monotonically. Therefore, complete laminarization is possible for lower Re values of $\approx$5200, corresponding to a radius ratio of about 0.04. Downstream of the coil, all critical Reynolds numbers were found to drop within a distance from the coil exit of about 100 pipe diameters, reaching asymptotically critical Re values of $\approx$5200 at larger distances much greater than those appropriate to the straight section upstream of the helical coil.

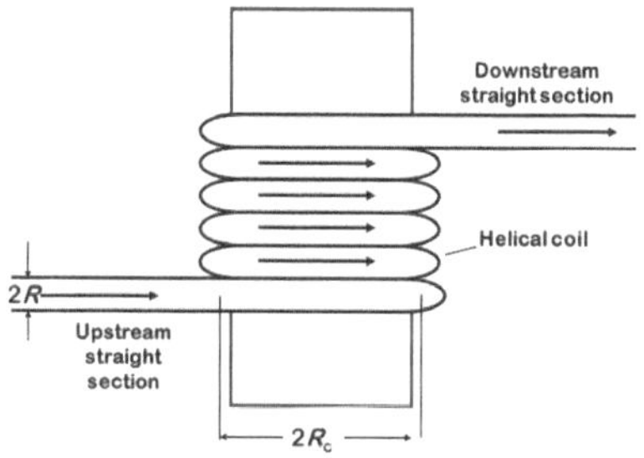

Figure 2. Schematic representation of the set-up used by Sreenivasan and Strykowski in their experimental work on flow stabilization. Figure adapted from Sreenivasan and Strykowski [33].

Similar results about the laminarization of turbulent flow in curved and helical pipes were also obtained experimentally by Kurokawa et al. [61] for low-Reynolds turbulent flow using smoke visualization and velocity measurements by means of hot-film anemometry. They also confirmed that the laminar flow in the downstream straight section is at a higher Re value compared to that in the upstream section. Further experiments on flow in helical pipes were carried out by Webster and Humphrey [62,63], who found that periodic low-frequency instabilities appeared at Re = 5000 for a helical coil with a curvature ratio of 0.054. In Ref. [63], these authors report flow visualizations for Re values between 3800 and 8650 (corresponding to Dean numbers in the interval $890 < \mathrm{De} < 2030$). By means of computer simulations of the experimental set-up at $\mathrm{Re} = 5480$ ($\mathrm{De} = 1280$), a rather complex interaction was found between the centrifugal force due to the curvature and the cross-stream velocity, thereby explaining the mechanism of the traveling wave instability observed in their experiments.

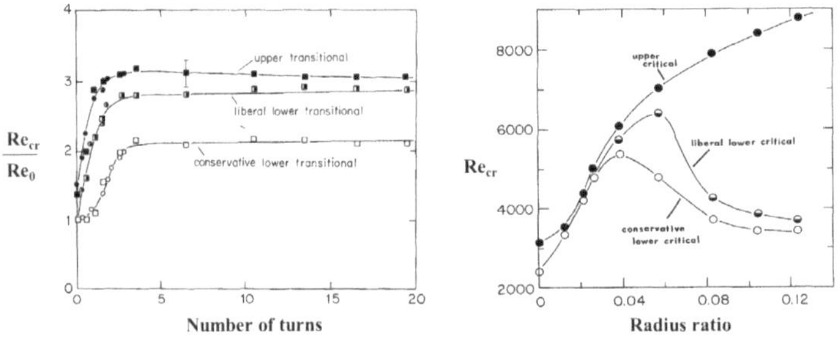

Figure 3. (**Left**) Variation in the critical Reynolds number, Re_{cr}, normalized to the lower critical value, Re_0, just before entering the coil helix for a radius ratio of 0.058 (circles: their set-up I; squares: their set-up II). (**Right**) Asymptotic dependence of Re_{cr} in the coil section as measured at the end of the 20th coil on the radius ratio for their set-up II. Figures taken from Sreenivasan and Strykowski [33].

3.3. Pressure Drop

A characteristic feature that is always present in helical tubes is the effect of centrifugal forces on the flow, as was first noticed by Thomson [6]. Almost 60 years later, using a boundary layer approximation, Adler [59] found that the pressure drop in a curved pipe is proportional to the square root of the Dean number. This relation was further verified numerically by Dennis and Ng [64]. For a helical pipe with a radius ratio $\gamma = 0.0157$, the experimental measurements of the product between the Fanning friction factor and the Reynolds number, $F\mathrm{Re}$, as a function of the Dean number performed by Ramshankar and Sreenivasan [65], resulted in a variation between $\mathrm{De}^{1/4}$ and $\mathrm{De}^{1/2}$, while their $F\mathrm{Re}$ data for $\gamma = 0.056$ confirmed the square root relation. Most studies reported in the literature on pressure losses in helical pipes usually refer to flow in the limiting case of a zero pitch ($h = 0$) corresponding to toroidal pipes. However, such studies will not be reviewed here since only helical pipes of finite pitch are of actual practical industrial and technological significance (however, most experimental work of flow through helically coiled pipes focused on helical coils having a small pitch).

Pressure losses of incompressible laminar flow in helically coiled pipes of finite pitch were studied theoretically by many authors (see, for instance, Refs. [53,66–71]). In particular, Liu and Masliyah [71] demonstrated numerically that the flow in helical pipes is governed by three parameters: the generalized curvature ratio, defined as

$$\gamma' = \frac{\gamma}{1 + (\gamma h/2\pi R)^2}, \tag{6}$$

the Dean number, $\mathrm{De} = \sqrt{\gamma'}\mathrm{Re}$, and the Germano number, $\mathrm{Gn} = \eta\mathrm{Re}$, where η is the torsion of the helix provided by

$$\eta = \frac{\gamma^2 h/2\pi R}{1 + (\gamma h/2\pi R)^2}. \tag{7}$$

Note that, for a toroidal pipe with $h = 0$, $\gamma' = \gamma = R/R_c$ and the torsion vanishes (i.e., $\eta = 0$). At high values of De, the flow parameter

$$\lambda = \frac{\text{Gn}}{\text{De}^{3/2}} = \frac{\eta}{(\gamma'\text{De})^{1/2}} \quad (8)$$

was derived for the transition from two- to one-vortex flow [71]. Therefore, helical flow is governed by γ', De and Gn, and it is precisely through Gn that the torsion effects come into play. For $\gamma' \ll 1$, the important parameters will be only De and Gn, and, when $\eta \to 0$ (i.e., $\text{Gn} \to 0$), the only relevant parameter will be De. It is important to mention that, for low Dean flows (i.e., $\text{De} < 20$), the parameter governing the flow pattern transition from two- to one-vortex flow is [71]

$$\lambda' = \frac{\text{Gn}}{\text{De}^2} = \frac{\eta}{\gamma'\text{Re}}. \quad (9)$$

There is fairly good agreement that the transition to turbulence in helical pipes occurs at high values of Re. As was observed by White [11] and then confirmed by Taylor [30], the sudden increase in $F\text{Re}$, defined as [36]

$$F\text{Re} = \frac{R\text{Re}}{\rho v^2}\frac{\Delta p}{\Delta s}, \quad (10)$$

where Δs is a length section along which Δp is measured, when plotted against De, establishes a criterion for the onset of turbulence in helically coiled pipes. According to Taylor [30], the flow becomes unsteady when De is only about 20% of the critical value, De_{cr}, required for the flow to become fully turbulent. The transition from laminar to turbulent flow corresponds to the point where $F\text{Re}$ suddenly increases. Several correlations for predicting the critical Re value in helical pipes have been reported in the literature. The best-known correlations are those provided by Kubair and Varrier [72],

$$\text{Re}_{\text{cr}} = 20{,}000\gamma'^{0.32}, \quad (11)$$

valid for $0.0005 < \gamma' < 0.1$, Ito [73],

$$\text{Re}_{\text{cr}} = 12{,}730\gamma'^{0.2}, \quad (12)$$

valid for $0.001165 < \gamma' < 0.0667$, Srinivasan et al. [74],

$$\text{Re}_{\text{cr}} = 2100(1 + 12\sqrt{\gamma'}), \quad (13)$$

valid for $\gamma' < 0.1$ and Ward-Smith [75],

$$\text{Re}_{\text{cr}} = 2300(1 + 10\sqrt{\gamma'}), \quad (14)$$

valid for $\gamma' < 0.1$. Among them, the most widely used are Ito's and Srinivasan et al.'s correlations. While Ito's correlation fails in the limit when $\gamma' \to 0$, Srinivasan et al.'s correlation states that an increase in the flow velocity for which the flow remains laminar is proportional to the strength of the secondary flow [36].

On the other hand, correlations for the pressure loss in terms of De were also reported in the literature for helical pipes with small pitch. In particular, Dean [13,14] provided a solution for fully developed laminar flow along a torus (for $\gamma \to 0$) by perturbing the solution for Poiseuille flow in a straight pipe, which in terms of the friction factor ratio can be written as

$$\frac{16}{F\text{Re}} = 1 - 0.03058\left(\frac{\text{De}^2}{288}\right)^2 + 0.00725\left(\frac{\text{De}^2}{288}\right)^4. \quad (15)$$

However, the first of these correlations for laminar flow was developed experimentally by White [11], which reads as follows

$$\frac{16}{F\mathrm{Re}} = 1 - \left[1 - \left(\frac{11.6}{\mathrm{De}}\right)^{0.45}\right]^{1/0.45}. \tag{16}$$

This correlation is valid for $11.6 < \mathrm{De} < 2000$ and $\gamma \leq 0.066$. Later on, White [76] developed a further correlation for turbulent flow in helical pipes of the form

$$F\mathrm{Re} = 0.08\mathrm{Re}^{-1/4} + 0.012\sqrt{\gamma}, \tag{17}$$

which is valid for Reynolds numbers between 15,000 and 100,000. However, none of these correlations incorporate the torsional effects so that $\gamma = \gamma' = R/R_c$. For large De values, Adler [59] provided the relation (in this and in some other correlations that follow below, the friction factor F is normalized with the calibrated friction factor for laminar flow in smooth straight pipes [77]), namely $F_s = 16/\mathrm{Re}$. In comparison, for turbulent flow in straight pipes, the following definition is used:

$$F_s = 0.0014 + \frac{0.125}{\mathrm{Re}^{0.32}}, \tag{18}$$

for the interval $3000 < \mathrm{Re} < 3 \times 10^6$.),

$$\frac{F\mathrm{Re}}{16} = 0.1064\sqrt{\mathrm{De}}, \tag{19}$$

while Prandtl [78] ended up with the correlation

$$\frac{F\mathrm{Re}}{16} = 0.37(0.5\mathrm{De})^{0.36} \tag{20}$$

for laminar flows with $40 < \mathrm{De} < 2000$. Later on, Hasson [79], based on White's correlation (15), reported the form

$$\frac{F\mathrm{Re}}{16} = 0.556 + 0.0969\sqrt{\mathrm{De}} \tag{21}$$

for $22 < \mathrm{De} < 2000$ and $\gamma \leq 0.066$, while Topakoğlu [80] extended the validity of Equation (15) to finite values of the curvature ratio, obtaining the relation

$$\frac{16}{F\mathrm{Re}} = 1 - 0.03058\left(\frac{\mathrm{De}^2}{288}\right)^2 - 0.1833\gamma\left(\frac{\mathrm{De}^2}{288}\right) + \frac{\gamma^2}{48}. \tag{22}$$

On the other hand, Ito [73] improved Adler's [59] correlation provided by Equation (19) to obtain

$$\frac{F\mathrm{Re}}{16} = 0.1033\sqrt{\mathrm{De}}\left[\left(1 + \frac{1.729}{\mathrm{De}}\right)^{1/2} - \left(\frac{1.729}{\mathrm{De}}\right)^{1/2}\right]^{-3}. \tag{23}$$

For low De numbers, Van Dyke [81] developed the further correlation

$$\frac{F\mathrm{Re}}{16} = 0.47136\mathrm{De}^{1/4}, \tag{24}$$

which is valid only for the interval $20 < \mathrm{De} < 200$. Other correlations that have often been used in comparison with experimental measurements have been proposed by Barua [82],

$$\frac{F\mathrm{Re}}{16} = 0.509 + 0.0918\sqrt{\mathrm{De}}, \tag{25}$$

for large De, and by Mori and Nakayama [83],

$$\frac{F\mathrm{Re}}{16} = \frac{0.1080\mathrm{De}}{\sqrt{\mathrm{De}} - 3.253}, \tag{26}$$

which was experimentally verified for $13.5 < \mathrm{De} < 2000$.

A more accurate correlation valid for $\mathrm{De} \leq 5000$ that works equally well for small and finite pitch (i.e., for $0 < \gamma' < 1$) and incorporates the effects of torsion with $0 \leq \eta < 0.1\sqrt{\gamma'\mathrm{De}}$ was derived by Liu [84] and Liu and Masliyah [71] by means of numerical solutions of the Navier–Stokes equations to be

$$\begin{aligned} F\mathrm{Re} &= \left[16 + \left(0.378\sqrt{\mathrm{Re}} + \frac{12.1}{\sqrt{\gamma'\mathrm{De}}}\right)\eta^2\right] \\ &\times \left[1 + \frac{(0.0908 + 0.0233\sqrt{\gamma'})\sqrt{\mathrm{De}} - 0.132\sqrt{\gamma'} + 0.37\gamma' - 0.2}{1 + 49/\mathrm{De}}\right]. \end{aligned} \tag{27}$$

This equation was found to agree with Hasson's correlation (19) for small pitch and torsion.

The pressure drop of fully developed incompressible laminar water flow in helical pipes of both small and large pitch was investigated experimentally by Liu et al. [36]. The left frame of Figure 4 shows the normalized pressure drop measurements for coiled pipes with negligible torsion ($\eta < 0.0021$), small pitch ($h = 3R$) and $\gamma = 0.0213$ (up-pointing triangles), $\gamma = 0.0475$ (down-pointing triangles) and $\gamma = 0.0664$ (squares) as compared with Liu and Masliyah's [71] (Equation (27)) correlation for $\gamma = 0.0213$ (dotted line), $\gamma = 0.0475$ (solid line) and $\gamma = 0.0664$ (dashed line). The curves (a) and (b) correspond to Hasson's [79] (Equation (21)) and Van Dyke's [81] (Equation (24)) correlations, respectively. The measured $\mathrm{De}_{\mathrm{cr}}$ values indicating the onset of turbulence were found to agree fairly well with Ito's [73] (Equation (12)) and Srinivasan et al.'s [74] (Equation (13)) correlations for prediction of the critical Re values. It is clear from the left plot of Figure 4 that, with the exception of Van Dyke's correlation (24), the pressure drop predictions based on correlations (21) and (27) are in very good agreement with Liu et al.'s [36] experimental data for small helical pitch. Moreover, the right frame of Figure 4 shows the experimental $F\mathrm{Re}$ measurements for various helical pipes of finite pitch and $\gamma = R/R_c = 0.719$, i.e., $h = 359R$, $\gamma' = 0.000403$, $\eta = 0.017$ (squares); $h = 179R$, $\gamma' = 0.00171$, $\eta = 0.035$ (diamonds); $h = 89.2R$, $\gamma' = 0.00683$, $\eta = 0.0698$ (up-pointing triangles) and $h = 44R$, $\gamma' = 0.00273$, $\eta = 0.1374$ (down-pointing triangles), as compared with Liu and Masliyah's [71] correlation: solid line for square data, double-dotted dashed for diamond data, dashed line for up-pointing triangle data and dotted-dashed for down-pointing triangle data. The curves (a) and (b) correspond to Hasson's [79] and Van Dyke's [81] correlations, respectively. The scatter of experimental data from the mainstream are indicative of the onset of turbulence.

A complete and exhaustive list of pressure-drop correlations can be found in Ali [85] and Gupta et al. [86]. In particular, the former author derived by means of experimental measurements generalized pressure-drop correlations of the form

$$\mathrm{Eu}\left[\frac{(2R)^{0.85}D_{\mathrm{eq}}}{L_c}\right] = \alpha'\mathrm{Re}^{-\beta'}, \tag{28}$$

where Eu is the Euler number provided by

$$\mathrm{Eu} = \frac{\Delta p}{2\rho v^2}, \tag{29}$$

where Δp is the pressure drop, ρ is the fluid density, v is the average velocity, D_{eq} is the equivalent coil diameter defined as

$$D_{\mathrm{eq}} = \frac{1}{\pi}\sqrt{h^2 + 4\pi^2 R^2} \tag{30}$$

and L_c is the length of the coil portion of the pipe. In Equation (28), α' and β' are constants that depend on whether the flow regime is low laminar, laminar, mixed or turbulent. For instance, Ali [85] obtained values of α' and β' from straight-line fits to his experimental data provided by (α', β') =(38, 1) for the low-laminar regime, (5.25, 2/3) for the laminar regime, (0.31, 1/3) for the mixed regime and (0.045, 1/8) for the turbulent state (see his Figure 5). He also showed that Equation (28) fits the experimental data very well for a different set of (α', β') values for the Re intervals: Re $<$ 500 (low laminar), 500 $<$ Re $<$ 6300 (laminar), 6300 $<$ Re $<$ 10,000 (mixed) and Re $>$ 10,000 (fully turbulent). In a more recent work, Gupta et al. [86] reported experimental observations on pressure drop measurements for fully developed laminar flow in helical pipes of varying coil pitch ($8.3 \leq h/2R \leq 66.7$) and coil radius ($11.7 \leq R_c/R \leq 105.48$). Their parametric study demonstrated that the coil friction factor, F, depends on these geometrical parameters and that it can be predicted by the following correlation in terms of the Germano number

$$\frac{F\mathrm{Re}}{16} = \begin{cases} 1 + 0.803\mathrm{Gn}^{0.227} & \textit{for}\ \ \mathrm{Gn} \leq 70, \\ 1 + 0.525\mathrm{Gn}^{0.525} & \textit{for}\ \ \mathrm{Gn} > 70, \end{cases}$$

which performs better under laminar flow conditions than other correlations in terms of the Dean number and predicts the friction factor data on coils available in the open literature to within $\pm$15%.

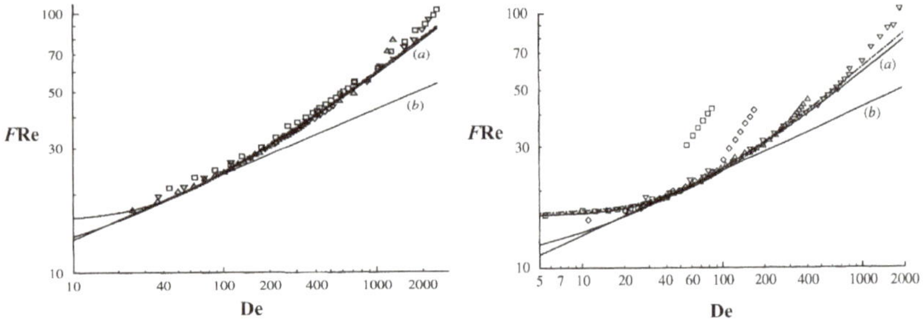

Figure 4. (**Left**) Experimental pressure drop measurements for flow in helical pipes of negligible torsion (η $<$ 0.0021), small pitch (h = 3R) and varying curvature ratios as compared with correlations (21), (24) and (27). (**Right**) Same as before but for helical pipes of finite pitch and varying torsion and curvature ratios. For details of the symbols, see the text above. Figure taken from Liu et al. [36].

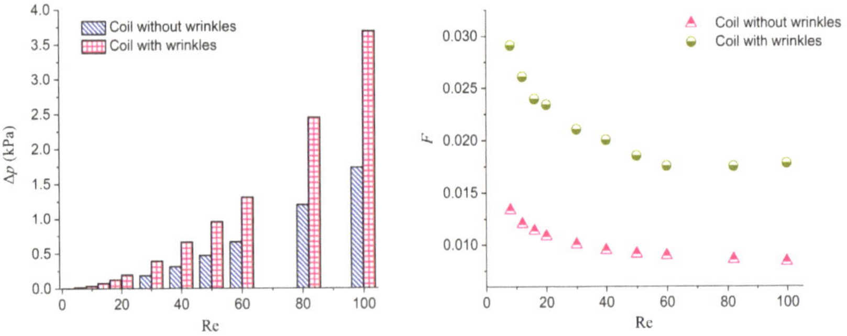

Figure 5. Pressure drop (**left**) and friction factor (**right**) as a function of the Reynolds number for flow across helical pipes with and without wrinkles. Figure taken from Periasamy et al. [87].

Most experimental work on pressure losses in helical pipes is based on smooth pipe flows. However, it is well-known that pipe roughness has important effects on the flow behavior under turbulent conditions. Experiments on water flow in rough pipes were performed by Das [35], who developed by means of multivariable linear regression analysis the following correlation

$$F - F_s = 17.5782\mathrm{Re}^{-0.3137\pm0.0364}\gamma^{0.3621\pm0.0454}\left(\frac{e}{2R}\right)^{0.6885\pm0.0758}, \tag{31}$$

where F_s refers to Mishra and Gupta's [88] correlation for turbulent flow in smooth pipes and e is the roughness height. When plotted against the experimental data, Equation (31) complies with a coefficient correlation of 0.9715 (see Das' [35] Figure 3). On the other hand, when helical coils are constructed by means of a rolling process, they may result in geometrical irregularities and imperfections, such as wrinkles and ovality. The effects of these flaws on the flow hydrodynamics were recently studied by Periasamy et al. [87]. The presence of wrinkles in the helical coil has the effect of increasing the equivalent surface roughness. In fact, in their experiments, the effects of wrinkles were assessed by measuring the friction factor and comparing it for coils without wrinkles. The pressure drop as a function of Re based on their experimental data is shown in the left frame of Figure 5, while the right plot depicts the friction factor for coils with and without wrinkles. In particular, at higher Re values, the wrinkles contribute significantly to the pressure drop across the coil, and therefore the presence of wrinkles increases the friction factor compared to the case of smooth coils.

3.4. Heat Transfer

Helically coiled pipes are also used in a wide variety of industrial and technological applications because of their very good heat transfer performance. In fact, many industries, including the nuclear, chemical and food industries, use helical heat exchanger tubes for heating of evaporating flows and refrigeration of condensing flows [34,37,89]. In particular, Austen and Soliman [34] experimentally studied the influence of pitch on pressure drop and heat transfer characteristics for a uniform input heat flux. They compared their experimentally fully developed friction factor for isothermal flow with Mishra and Gupta's [88] correlation, finding a 90% agreement. For variations in the tube-wall temperature, they also observed a rapid development of the temperature field within a short distance from the coil inlet, followed by oscillations of decreasing amplitude until the temperature field becomes fully developed. The amplitude of the oscillations was observed to increase in flows with increasing Re values and was attributed to the strength of the secondary flow arising from the action of centrifugal forces. They also concluded that, owing to free convection, pitch effects are more important at low Re values and that they gradually disappear as long as Re increases. By calculating the local average Nusselt number, provided by

$$\langle \mathrm{Nu} \rangle = \frac{2Rq}{k(\bar{T}_{\mathrm{w}} - T_b)}, \tag{32}$$

at each temperature-measuring station along the coil, where q is the heat flux at the inner tube surface, k is the thermal conductivity of distilled water, which was used as the working fluid, $\bar{T}_{\mathrm{w}}$ is the inner wall temperature and T_b is the bulk temperature; they observed a significant enhancement in $\langle \mathrm{Nu} \rangle$ due to increasing pitch up to a certain Re value, beyond which the pitch has no effect. For fully developed Nu, their experimental measurements were found to fit, within ±20% error, the correlation of Nu versus De proposed by Manlapaz and Churchill [90], namely

$$\mathrm{Nu} = \left\{ \left[\frac{48}{11} + \frac{51/11}{[1 - 1342/(\mathrm{Pr}\mathrm{De}^2)]^2} \right]^3 + 1.816\left(\frac{\mathrm{De}}{1 + 1.15/\mathrm{Pr}} \right)^{3/2} \right\}^{1/3}. \tag{33}$$

Other earlier known Nusselt-number correlations for laminar convection in helically coiled pipes are those developed by Seban and McLaughlin [91], provided by the expression

$$\mathrm{Nu} = 0.0325(F\mathrm{Re})^2\mathrm{Pr}^{1/3}, \tag{34}$$

which is valid for $12 < \mathrm{Re} < 5600$, $100 < \mathrm{Pr} < 657$ and $0.010 < \gamma < 0.059$; Dravid et al. [92], provided by

$$\mathrm{Nu} = \left(0.76 + 0.65\sqrt{\mathrm{De}}\right)\mathrm{Pr}^{0.175}, \tag{35}$$

which is valid for $50 < \mathrm{De} < 2000$, $5 < \mathrm{Pr} < 175$ and $\gamma = 0.055$ and Xin and Ebadian [93], which reads as

$$\mathrm{Nu} = \left(2.153 + 0.318\mathrm{De}^{0.643}\right)\mathrm{Pr}^{0.177}, \tag{36}$$

valid for $20 < \mathrm{De} < 2000$, $0.70 < \mathrm{Pr} < 175$ and $0.027 < \gamma < 0.080$.

More recent experimental measurements of the friction factor for laminar flow in helical pipes were reported by De Amicis et al. [37], who also compared their experimental data with numerical simulations using different CFD tools. The experimental measurements correspond to a test facility built at the SIET laboratories in Piacenza, Italy, which reproduces the helically coiled Steam Generator of the IRIS nuclear reactor [16]. The left frame of Figure 6 shows their measured Darcy friction factors for varying Re in the laminar regime, i.e., for $\mathrm{Re} \lesssim 3200$, where they are compared with Ito's [73] correlation. The predicted value of $\mathrm{Re} \approx 3200$ marks a first discontinuity and initiates a regime with lower friction factor up to $\mathrm{Re} \approx 5000$. This trend agrees very well with the predictions by Cioncolini and Santini [94] for medium-curvature coils in the range $3200 \lesssim \mathrm{Re} \lesssim 5000$. A second discontinuity occurs at about $\mathrm{Re} = 5000$, which marks the onset of turbulence. The right plot of Figure 6 shows the dependence of the Darcy friction factor on Re in the range $1750 < \mathrm{Re} < 5250$ for the SIET duct as compared with several correlations and numerical results from different CFD tools. The errors between the numerical predictions and the experimental data were all reported to be within 5%.

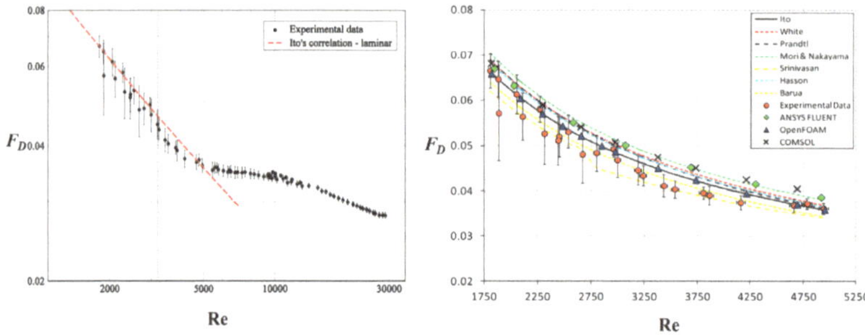

Figure 6. (**Left**) Darcy friction factor as a function of the Reynolds number for the experimental helical coil operated at SIET laboratories. (**Right**) Comparison of the experimental Darcy friction factor with Ito's [73], White's [11], Prandtl's [78], Mori and Nakayama's [83], Srinivasan et al.'s [74], Hasson's [79] and Barua's [82] correlations. The experimental data are also compared with model simulations performed with different CFD tools. Figures taken from De Amicis et al. [37].

The pressure drop and convective heat transfer of a CuO nanofluid flow in a helical pipe at constant wall temperature was further investigated by Rakhsha et al. [38]. In particular, they obtained by experimental means the friction factor and the Nusselt number for both water and the CuO nanofluid flow. Based on their experimental results, the following correlations were proposed:

$$F = 0.38\mathrm{Re}^{-0.216}\gamma^{0.1}(1+\phi)^{0.19}, \tag{37}$$

and

$$\mathrm{Nu} = 0.061\mathrm{Re}^{0.77}\mathrm{Pr}^{0.4}(1+\phi)^{0.22}, \tag{38}$$

where ϕ is the concentration of nanofluid. These correlations were found to be accurate enough for any single-phase flow and the CuO nanofluid for $10{,}000 < \mathrm{Re} < 90{,}000$, $4 < \mathrm{Pr} < 5$, $0.04 < \gamma < 0.142$ and $0 < \phi < 1$. Experimental observations of the uneven circumferential heat transfer induced by the secondary flow as well as pressure drop and heat transfer characteristics of helical pipes were very recently reported by Zheng et al. [95]. Their results indicate that the coil diameter is responsible for the pressure drop and nonuniform circumferential heat transfer, while the lift angle plays a minor role. Based on the experimental pressure data, Zheng et al. [95] proposed the following correlation for single-phase flow:

$$F = \frac{0.0791}{\mathrm{Re}^{0.25}} + \frac{81858}{\mathrm{Re}^{1.54}}\left(\frac{R}{R_c}\right)^{0.48}, \tag{39}$$

where $R_c = R_i(1+\tan\alpha)$, R_i is the coil radius and α is the lift angle. As shown in their Figure 11, the empirical correlations proposed by Ito [96] and Srinivasan et al. [74] were found to underestimate the experimental data for $F > 0.01$, with maximum errors of about 80%. However, a better agreement was found when comparing the experimental pressure drops for two-phase flow with the values predicated on the empirical correlations proposed by Ju et al. [97], Hardik and Prabhu [98] and Xiao et al. [99] (see Zheng et al.'s [95] Figure 12).

It is well-known that helically coiled tubes have received much attention because of their application in refrigeration, air-conditioning systems, heat recovery processes and, in particular, as efficient heat exchangers. They are used as passive heat transfer augmentation techniques in a wide range of industrial applications [24]. Experimental investigations of helical heat exchangers have mainly focused on forced convection flows under turbulent conditions [100–103]. In particular, Ghorbani et al. [102] experimentally investigated the mixed convection in helical coiled heat exchangers for various Reynolds numbers, Rayleigh numbers, tube-to-coil diameter ratios and coil pitches for both laminar and turbulent flow. Their results demonstrated that, for mass flow rates of tube side to shell side greater than unity, quadratic temperature profiles were obtained from bottom to top of the heat exchanger. Pawar and Sunnapwar [103] investigated steady state convection in vertical helical tubes for laminar flow. They developed an innovative approach to correlate the Nu number with the dimensionless M number for Newtonian fluids and proposed the following correlation for laminar convection:

$$\mathrm{Nu} = 0.02198\mathrm{Re}^{0.9314}\mathrm{Pr}^{0.4}\gamma^{0.391}, \tag{40}$$

which is valid for $3166 < \mathrm{Re} < 9658$, $3.80 < \mathrm{Pr} < 4.80$ and $0.055 < \gamma < 0.0757$. Other correlations for laminar convection in helical tubes were developed experimentally by Pimenta and Campos [104] and more recently by Hardik et al. [105] to be

$$\mathrm{Nu} = \left(0.5\mathrm{De}^{0.481} - 0.465\right)\mathrm{Pr}^{0.367}, \tag{41}$$

valid for $91 < \mathrm{Re} < 6293$, $10 < \mathrm{Pr} < 353$ and $\gamma = 0.026$ and

$$\mathrm{Nu} = 0.0456\mathrm{Re}^{0.8}\mathrm{Pr}^{0.4}\gamma^{0.16}, \tag{42}$$

valid for $1700 < \mathrm{Re} < 14{,}000$, $3 < \mathrm{Pr} < 6$ and $0.015 < \gamma < 0.076$, respectively. A more complete list of Nusselt correlations for laminar convective flows in helical coils can be found in Refs. [106–108]. In particular, Zhao et al. [107] obtained by regression analysis of experimental data in the literature the correlation

$$\mathrm{Nu} = 0.0254F\mathrm{Re}^{1.197}\mathrm{Pr}^{0.159}, \tag{43}$$

for $200 < \mathrm{Re} < 8000$, $3 < \mathrm{Pr} < 175$ and $0.015 < \gamma < 0.077$. Figure 7 compares this expression with Austen and Soliman's [34], Manlapaz and Churchill's [90] (Equation (33)), Dravid et al.'s [92] (Equation (35)), Xin and Ebadian's [93] (Equation (36)), Hardik et al.'s [105] (Equation (42)) and Aly et al.'s [109] correlations for varied Pr values and curvature ratios. The predictions from Equation (36) are closer to those from Equation (43) than all other correlations.

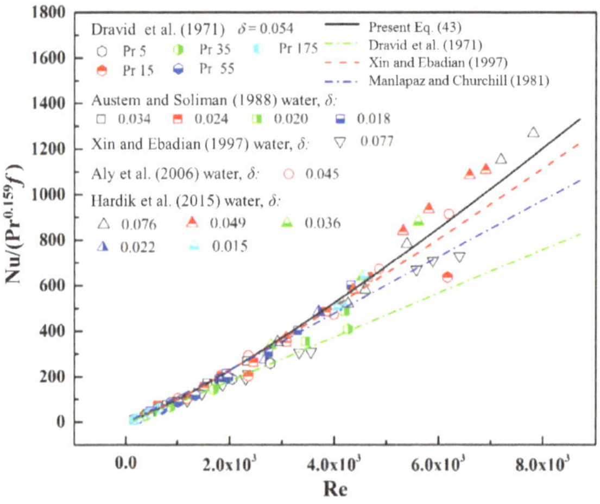

Figure 7. Nusselt number as a function of Reynolds number for laminar convection in helically coiled pipes. Equation (43) is compared with Austen and Soliman's [34], Manlapaz and Churchill's [90], Dravid et al.'s [92], Xin and Ebadian [93], Hardik et al.'s [105] and Aly et al.'s [109] experimental correlations. Figure taken from Zhao et al. [107].

An experimental analysis of heat transfer enhancement in shell and coiled heat exchangers of 10 turns and equipped with copper tubes was performed by Jamshidi et al. [110], while Hashemi and Behabadi [111] performed experimental observations of the pressure drop and heat transfer characteristics of CuO-based oil nanofluid flow for $\mathrm{Re} \sim 10$–150 in a horizontal helical copper tube. Recently, Ayuob et al. [108] developed further Nusselt-number correlations for helical-coil-based energy storage integrated with solar water heating systems. They developed a number of Nu correlations in terms of Re, De and M from 54 simulations, which were conducted for a 50% water/glycol mixture flow in helical coils of varying inner pipe diameter, coil diameter and coil pitch. Using the MatLAB 2018 curve fitting tool, they derived the following correlations:

$$\mathrm{Nu} = 0.43296\mathrm{Re}^{0.44564}\mathrm{Pr}^{0.4}, \tag{44}$$

for $56.045 \leq \mathrm{Re} \leq 382.63$, $74.135 \leq \mathrm{Pr} \leq 122.09$ and $0.09 \leq \gamma \leq 0.184$;

$$\mathrm{Nu} = 0.7396\mathrm{De}^{0.4282}\mathrm{Pr}^{0.4}, \tag{45}$$

for $19.005 \leq \mathrm{De} \leq 128.45$, $74.135 \leq \mathrm{Pr} \leq 122.09$ and $0.09 \leq \gamma \leq 0.184$ and

$$\mathrm{Nu} = 0.175\mathrm{M}^{0.6364}\mathrm{Pr}^{0.4}, \tag{46}$$

for $68.615 \leq \mathrm{M} \leq 266.834$ and $74.135 \leq \mathrm{Pr} \leq 122.09$. However, as was claimed by Ayuob et al. [108], these correlations produce good results when the flow rate is variable for a constant value of the curvature ratio. In order to allow for constant and variable flow rates and for constant and variable values of the coil curvature, they introduced a dependence on the curvature ratio, ending up with the correlation

$$\mathrm{Nu} = 0.1868M^{0.6958}\gamma^{0.1703}\mathrm{Pr}^{0.4}, \tag{47}$$

which is valid for the same intervals of M and Pr as for Equation (46) and $0.09 \leq \gamma \leq 0.184$. Further experimental investigations on helically coiled heat exchangers were performed by Xin and Ebadian [93], Pawar and Sunnapwar [112], Kumbhare et al. [113] and Pimenta and Campos [104], among others. In particular, the latter authors derived a global correlation for the Nu number in terms of Péclet, Dean and Weissenberg numbers, which works well for both Newtonian and non-Newtonian fluids.

Nusselt-number correlations for turbulent convection in helically coiled pipes have also been reported in the literature. Under turbulent conditions, the use of constant wall temperature or constant heat flux in the experiments produces similar heat transfer coefficients. Most of these experiments were conducted using either air or water as the working fluid and varied Re-, Pr- and γ values. One of the first experimentally developed correlations, if not the first, for turbulent convective flows in helical coils was reported in 1925 by Jeschke [114]. This correlation has the form

$$\mathrm{Nu} = (0.039 + 0138\gamma)(\mathrm{RePr})^{0.76} \tag{48}$$

and is valid for $\mathrm{Re} < 1.5 \times 10^5$, $0.050 < \gamma < 0.15$ and Pr of air. The exponent of the Prandtl number in most modern correlations for turbulent convection in helical tubes is 0.4, which is also appropriate for straight pipes. In contrast to many correlations for laminar convection, as is the case in Equations (38), (40), (42) and (44) to (47), some correlations for turbulent convection do not include the curvature ratio. An exception to this rule are the correlations developed by Rogers and Mayhew [115] provided by

$$\mathrm{Nu} = 0.023\mathrm{Re}^{0.85}\mathrm{Pr}^{0.4}\gamma^{0.1}, \tag{49}$$

valid for $10^4 < \mathrm{Re} < 10^5$, $0.05 < \gamma < 0.10$ and Pr for water; those derived by Mori and Nakayama [116] provided by the expressions

$$\mathrm{Nu} = \frac{1}{41}\mathrm{Re}^{5/6}\gamma^{1/12}\mathrm{Pr}^{0.4}\left[1 + \frac{0.061}{(\mathrm{Re}\gamma^{2.5})^{1/6}}\right], \tag{50}$$

valid for $\mathrm{Pr} > 1$ and $\mathrm{Re}\gamma^{2.5} > 0.4$ and

$$\mathrm{Nu} = \frac{\mathrm{Re}^{4/5}\gamma^{0.1}\mathrm{Pr}}{26.2(\mathrm{Pr}^{2/3} - 0.074)}\left[1 + \frac{0.098}{(\mathrm{Re}\gamma^{2})^{1/3}}\right] \tag{51}$$

for $\mathrm{Pr} = 0.7$ and $\mathrm{Re}\gamma^2 > 0.1$; the one by Gnielinski [117] provided by

$$\mathrm{Nu} = \frac{(F/8)\mathrm{RePr}}{1 + 12.7\sqrt{F/8}(\mathrm{Pr}^{2/3} - 1)}\left(\frac{\mathrm{Pr}}{\mathrm{Pr_w}}\right)^{0.14} \tag{52}$$

for $\mathrm{Re} > 2.2 \times 10^4$ and $0.714 < \mathrm{Pr} < 6.0$, where the friction factor is defined by the expression

$$F = \left[\frac{0.3164}{\mathrm{Re}^{0.25}} + 0.03\gamma^{1/2}\right]\left(\frac{\mu_w}{\mu_b}\right)^{0.27}, \tag{53}$$

and the correlation by Xin and Ebadian [93], which obeys the form

$$\mathrm{Nu} = 0.0062\mathrm{Re}^{0.92}\mathrm{Pr}^{0.4}(1 + 3455\gamma) \tag{54}$$

and is valid for $5 \times 10^3 < \mathrm{Re} < 10^5$, $0.70 < \mathrm{Pr} < 5.0$ and $0.027 < \gamma < 0.080$.

Nusselt correlations for turbulent convection in helical coils that do not include the curvature ratio are the one developed by Bai et al. [118] provided by

$$\mathrm{Nu} = 0.328\mathrm{Re}^{0.58}\mathrm{Pr}^{0.4}\left(\frac{\mu_w}{\mu_b}\right)^{0.11}, \tag{55}$$

valid for $4.5 \times 10^4 < \mathrm{Re} < 10^5$, Pr of water and $\gamma = 0.043$, and that derived by Mandal and Nigam [101], which has the form

$$\mathrm{Nu} = 0.55\mathrm{De}^{0.637}\mathrm{Pr}^{0.4}, \tag{56}$$

valid for $1.4 \times 10^4 < \mathrm{Re} < 8.6 \times 10^4$, $\mathrm{Pr} = 0.70$ and $\gamma = 0.033$. Using regression analysis of the conventional correlations provided by Equations (48)–(56), Zhao et al. [107] derived the further correlation

$$\mathrm{Nu} = 0.040F\mathrm{Re}^{1.13}\gamma^{0.077}\mathrm{Pr}^{0.4}, \tag{57}$$

where F is replaced by Ito's [96] friction factor for turbulent flow. Equation (57) works well in the intervals $9.7 \times 10^3 < \mathrm{Re} < 1.4 \times 10^5$, $0.7 < \mathrm{Pr} < 6$ and $0.012 < \gamma < 0.177$. Figure 8 compares Zhao et al.'s [107] correlation provided by Equation (57) with Rogers and Mayhew's [115] (Equation (49)), Schmidt's [119], Gnielinski's [117] (Equation (52)), Xin and Ebadian's [93] (Equation (54)), Aly et al.'s [109] and Hardik et al.'s [105] correlations. The curvature ratios are set as 0.012 and 0.177, which are the minimum and maximum of the experimental data. Equation (57) predicts the experimental data satisfactorily well with a wide range of curvature ratios.

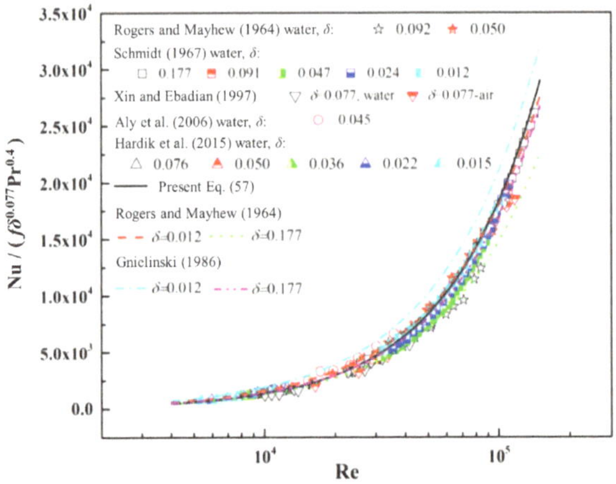

Figure 8. Nusselt number as a function of Reynolds number for turbulent convection in helically coiled pipes. Equation (57) is compared with Rogers and Mayhew's [115], Schmidt's [119], Gnielinski's [117], Xin and Ebadian's [93], Aly et al.'s [109] and Hardik et al.'s [105] experimental correlations. Figure taken from Zhao et al. [107].

3.5. Non-Newtonian Fluid Flow

Although most of the fluid flows encountered in processing applications are actually non-Newtonian, there are relatively fewer experimental studies of non-Newtonian fluid flows through curved and helically coiled pipes compared to the Newtonian case. (Non-Newtonian fluids are distinguished from Newtonian ones in that the former do not obey Newton's law of viscosity. Under shear effects, the viscosity of a non-Newtonian fluid can either increase or decrease depending on the fluid properties. Those fluids for which the viscosity increases under shear are called *dilatant*. Typical examples are quicksand and silly putty. In contrast, if the viscosity decreases under shear, the fluid behaves as a *pseudoplastic*. This is the case of the well-known ketchup. When the viscosity increases under shear in a time-dependent fashion, the fluid is called *rheopectic*, as is the case of many creams. Finally, if under shear the viscosity decreases in a time-dependent fashion, the fluid is called *thixotropic*. Examples of these fluids are paints, glues and asphalt.). Typical examples of non-Newtonian fluids encountered in the industry are elastoviscous liquids, plastics, polymeric melts, pharmaceuticals and multiphase mixtures in general, such as emulsions, foams and other compositional fluids. Earlier attempts to investigate such flows in curved pipes and helical coils can be found in Refs. [120–123]. In particular, Mashelkar and Devarajan [122] studied the effects of the curvature ratio on pressure drop and proposed the following correlation for laminar flow:

$$F\mathrm{Re} = 1 + 0.026\mathrm{De}'^{0.675}, \tag{58}$$

where De' is the generalized Dean number (the generalized Reynolds number, Re', was introduced by Madlener et al. [124] to describe the flow of non-Newtonian fluids in ducts and pipes. It is defined as

$$\mathrm{Re}' = \frac{\rho D^n v^{2-n}}{8^{n-1}K[(3n+1)/(4n)]^n}, \tag{59}$$

where D is the duct diameter, n is the global exponential factor (or consistency index) and K is the prefactor of power-law (or the behavior index) of the fluid. The generalized Dean number, De', is defined in terms of Re' as $\mathrm{De}' = \sqrt{\gamma}\mathrm{Re}'$). Correlation (58) is valid for $10 \leq \mathrm{De}' \leq 2300$. In more recent times, Krishna [125] experimentally studied the pressure drop in single-phase non-Newtonian fluids in helical coils with five different helix angles using carboxy methyl cellulose (CMC) as the working fluid. It was found that the effects of helix angle on pressure drop are not significant in low-generalized-Dean-number flows and in flows under turbulent conditions. However, the helix angle was found to become significant under laminar flow conditions for moderate and high generalized Dean numbers. Also, the same author proposed the following correlation for laminar flow with helix angle

$$F\mathrm{Re} = 0.015\mathrm{De}'^{0.75} + \sin^{0.25}\alpha, \tag{60}$$

and for turbulent flow with no helix angle as

$$F\mathrm{Re} = 6.2\mathrm{De}'^{-0.2}. \tag{61}$$

These predicted values were found to be in fairly good agreement with the experimental measurements with root-mean-square errors of $\sim$24% for laminar flow and $\sim$16% for turbulent flow.

Recent experimental pressure drop investigations of yield power law (YPL) fluids were reported by Gul et al. [126]. In particular, they tested a total number of 20 polymer-based fluids across two helical pipe sections differing in their size (see their Table 1). Figure 9 shows the experimentally obtained friction factor, $F\mathrm{Re}$, as a function of the Dean number for small and large helical pipe data and YPL fluids as compared with literature correlations for non-Newtonian fluids and Gul et al.'s [126] correlation, provided by

$$F\mathrm{Re} = \left(1 + \frac{a\mathrm{De}^b}{70 + \mathrm{De}}\right), \tag{62}$$

with $a = 0.008$ and $b = 1.78$. This correlation has the same mathematical form of that derived by Hart et al. [127] for Newtonian fluids, where $a = 0.09$ and $b = 1.5$. It is clear from the above figure that existing literature correlations for non-Newtonian fluids are overestimating the experimental predictions for YPL fluids, while Equation (62) performs much better in reproducing the experimental measurements. Therefore, previous correlations derived for non-Newtonian fluids cannot be used to predict the friction factor of YPL fluids.

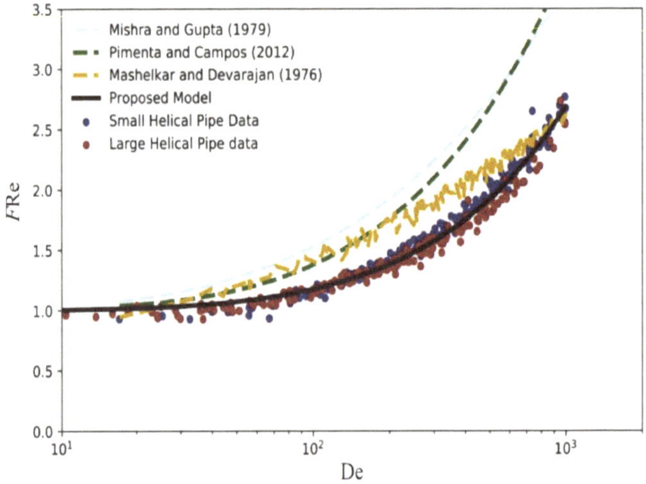

Figure 9. Experimental measurements of the friction factor for yield power-law (YPL) fluids as functions of the Dean number. The experimental data are compared with Mishra and Gupta's [88], Pimenta and Campos' [128] and Mashelkar and Devarajan's [122] correlations for non-Newtonian fluids and relation (62) for the developed model for YPL fluids. Figure taken from Gul et al. [126].

4. Overview of Theoretical Work

The theoretical work on flow through helically coiled pipes can be divided into two main groups, namely the group dealing with analytical and semi-analytical methods for solving the Navier–Stokes equations under certain assumptions and simplifications, and the group of numerical simulations, where the Navier–Stokes equations are solved with the aid of numerical methods for prescribed initial and boundary conditions.

4.1. Analytical and Semi-Analytical Approaches

The first theoretical analysis describing the fully developed laminar flow of an incompressible Newtonian flow in a helical pipe was reported by Murata et al. [53]. They wrote the steady-state Navier–Stokes equations in curvilinear coordinates appropriate for a circular helix and considered the limiting case when $\gamma = R/R_c \ll 1$. Under this assumption, the equations of motion and continuity were reduced to a simpler form by neglecting terms of higher order in γ. These equations were finally solved by means of two distinct methods: a perturbation analysis applied to the case when the characteristic number

$$\mathcal{D} = \frac{1}{\rho\nu}\left(-\frac{\partial p}{\partial s}\right)R^3\left(\frac{2R}{R_c}\cos^2\alpha\right)^{1/2}, \tag{63}$$

where ν is the kinematic viscosity, ρ is the fluid density and α is the helix angle, and which plays the role of the Dean number in a toroidally curved pipe, is assumed to vanish (i.e., $\mathcal{D} \ll 1$). In the second place, the equations were solved numerically for the case when $\mathcal{D}$ remains finite. When $\mathcal{D}$ is sufficiently large, the fluid in the coil is subjected to two forces, a Coriolis force due to torsion of the centerline and a centrifugal force due to the coil curvature. Under these conditions, their solution was able to predict the structure of the secondary flow and the distribution of the cross-sectional velocity component for $\mathcal{D} = 500$ and $\alpha = 60^\circ$. Figure 10 displays a schematic drawing of cross-sectional streamlines showing the secondary flow pattern that arises in curved pipes. The pattern consists of two counter-rotating vortex cells whose nature depends on the Dean number. McConalogue and Srivastava [129] numerically solved the governing differential flow equations by means of a Fourier-series expansion with respect to the polar angle in the cross-sectional plane of a tube for fully developed flow of an incompressible fluid along a curved tube and Dean numbers between 16.97 and 106.07. They found that the secondary flow becomes evident at De $\approx$ 106.07.

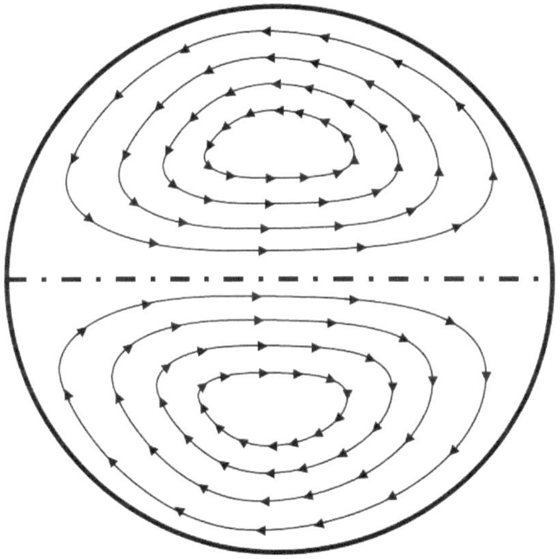

Figure 10. Schematic drawing of the secondary flow that circulates cross-sectionally in a helically coiled pipe.

A few more studies on perturbation methods applied to helical circular pipes with finite pitch can be found in the literature. For example, Wang [66] provided first-order solutions for the flow using helical coordinates and found that torsion has a first-order effect on the flow. Germano [67] investigated the effects of torsion on the flow and, using an orthogonal system, obtained first-order solutions for the secondary flow and, in contrast to Wang [66], predicted that torsion indeed has a second-order effect on the flow. The effect of torsion was further studied by Kao [68] and Chen and Jan [130], both finding that torsion induces a rotation of the secondary vortices and the maximum axial velocity. In an attempt to provide more accurate solutions, Xie [131] solved the Navier–Stokes equations without simplifications in a helical system and obtained second-order flow solutions. He predicted a turning of the secondary flow as an effect of torsion. Later on, Bolinder [132] employed a series expansion method to determine the first-order terms in curvature γ and torsion η for laminar flow in helical conduits of square and rectangular cross-sectional area. He concluded that flow in a helical pipe with finite pitch or torsion to the first order can be obtained as a superposition of flow in a toroidal tube and a straight twisted duct. He also found that, for small Re, the secondary flow in helical ducts of square and rectangular sections is dominated by torsional effects, while, for higher Re, it is dominated by the effects of coil curvature. A third perturbation solution for flow in helical circular pipes was obtained by Jinsuo and Banzhao [54]. They discussed in detail the first-, second- and third-order effects of curvature and torsion on the secondary flow and axial velocity, finding that the first-order effect of curvature is to induce a secondary flow in the form of two counter-rotating vortices and to drive the maximum axial velocity towards the outer wall of the bend, while a second-order effect of curvature is to push the two vortices to the outer bend. Moreover, they found that the combined second- and third-order effects of curvature and torsion were those of enlarging the lower vortex cell at the expense of the upper one.

Marušić-Paloka and Pažanin [55] developed an asymptotic expansion of the solution of the Navier–Stokes equations in terms of the pipe thickness for the case when the curvature is of order one and the helix torsion is of the same order of the pipe thickness. In contrast, previous analyses by Wang [66] and Germano [67] have considered the case when the torsion and curvature are small and of the same order. A rigorous treatment of flow in helical pipes when both the curvature and torsion are of order one has been previously provided by Marušić-Paloka [133]. The asymptotic analysis was shown to provide convergence results and the error estimate for the approximation was proved as the pipe thickness tends to zero. On the other hand, it has long been argued that a crucial point in the study of turbulent flows through curved pipes is to determine as accurately as possible the dependence of the flow rate and friction factor on the pressure difference between the ends of the pipe and on the geometrical parameters, such as helix torsion and coil curvature. For instance, Tuttle [70] demonstrated that a small torsion produces a second-order decrease in the flow rate. However, for finite curvature or torsion, no analytical solution to this question exists for steady flow in helical pipes. In fact, the dependence of flow rate and friction factor on model parameters for flow in helical pipes appears to be a very hard task. A step forward in clearing up this problem was recently provided by Kumar [57], who derived a rigorous lower bound on the volume flow rate in a helical pipe as driven by a pressure difference in the limit of $\mathrm{Re} \gg 1$ using the background method. He also derived an upper bound for the friction factor. In particular, using Kumar's notation $a = 1/\gamma = R_c/R$ and $b = h/(2\pi R)$, the dimensionless curvature, κ, and helix torsion, τ, are defined according to

$$\kappa = \frac{a}{a^2 + b^2}, \qquad \tau = \frac{b}{a^2 + b^2}, \tag{64}$$

so that for $\tau \ll 1$, the lower bound for the flow rate, Q, is provided by

$$\sqrt{\frac{32\pi^2}{27}}\left(1 + 3\kappa^2 + \frac{3}{8}\kappa^4\right)^{-1/2}\left[1 - \frac{3(2+\kappa^2)\tau^2}{8 + 24\kappa^2 + 3\kappa^4}\right], \tag{65}$$

while the upper bound on the friction factor obeys the form

$$\frac{27}{8}\left(1 + 3\kappa^2 + \frac{3}{8}\kappa^4\right)\left[1 + \frac{6(2+\kappa^2)\tau^2}{8 + 24\kappa^2 + 3\kappa^4}\right]. \tag{66}$$

As was stated by Kumar [57] himself, the above bounds are also valid for toroidal and straight pipes as limiting cases.

4.2. Numerical Simulations: Laminar Flow

Numerical simulations based on solutions of the Navier–Stokes equations to predict the flow in helical pipes began to appear in the early 1970s. One of the first efforts to predict the velocity and temperature fields in helical pipes was reported in 1974 by Patankar et al. [40]. They solved the Navier–Stokes equations in cylindrical coordinates using finite-difference methods. Their numerical results for the axial velocity profiles effectively reproduced the experimental data from Adler [59] (for $\mathrm{De} = 372$, $\gamma = 0.01$) and Mori and Nakayama [83] (for $\mathrm{De} = 442.7$ and 632.4, $\gamma = 0.025$). Figure 11 shows the axial velocity profiles for various De values as compared with a straight pipe in the $\theta = 0$ (left plot) and $\theta = 90^\circ$ planes (right plot). The numerically obtained friction factor for fully developed flow was also found to match Ito's [73] experimental measurements reasonably well. However, their numerical temperature profile along the $\theta = 0$ plane did not reproduce the experimental profile that was reported by Mori and Nakayama [83] in the inside region (see their Figure 11).

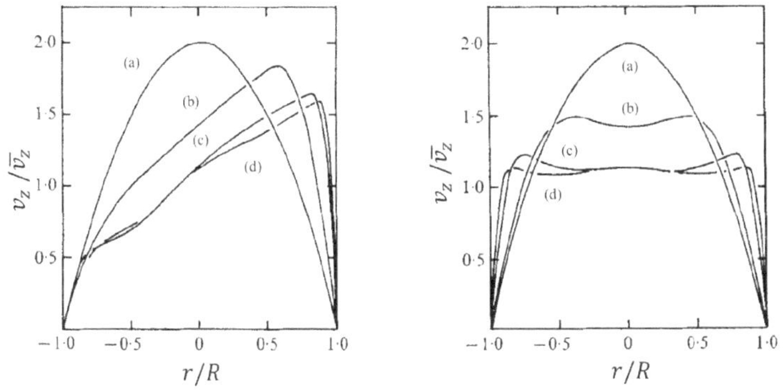

Figure 11. Axial velocity profiles of fully developed laminar flow in a helically coiled pipe for different Dean numbers along (**left**) a horizontal ($\theta = 0$) and (**right**) a vertical plane ($\theta = 90°$). The profiles for (b) De = 60, (c) De = 500 and (d) De = 1200 are compared with (a) the Poiseuille flow along a straight pipe. Figure taken from Patankar et al. [40].

In 1980, Manlapaz and Churchill [41] reported for the first time simulations of steady, fully developed laminar flow in helical coils of finite pitch. They solved the hydrodymanic equations for flow through a helical pipe of circular cross-section by expressing them in terms of the stream function and vorticity and using a finite-difference discretization. They simulated upward flow motion along the coil and found that a finite pitch has the effect of increasing the fluid movement in the upper half of the tube at the expense of fluid motion in the lower half. They also found that the mainstream (axial) and cross-sectional (secondary) flow velocity increases, with the upper vortex cell occupying more than half of the pipe cross-sectional area. However, these results were inferred to change only slightly for varying ratios of the pitch to coil radius, h/R_c, even when $h/R_c \to 1$. By trial and error, these authors developed a new correlation for the friction factor, namely

$$\frac{F\mathrm{Re}}{16} = \left[\left(1 - \frac{0.18}{\sqrt{1 + (35/\mathrm{De})^2}}\right)^m + \frac{\mathrm{De}}{88.33}\right]^{1/3}, \tag{67}$$

where, in general, the experimental data are fairly well represented for $m = 1$, while better representations of the experimental data for $\mathrm{De} < 20$ are obtained with $m = 2$, for $20 < \mathrm{De} < 40$ with $m = 1$ and for $\mathrm{De} > 40$ with $m = 0$. If the effects of large curvature ratios are added, Manlapaz and Churchill [41] suggested the following modified form

$$\frac{F\mathrm{Re}}{16} = \left[\left(1 - \frac{0.18}{\sqrt{1 + (35/\mathrm{De})^2}}\right)^m + \left(1 + \frac{R}{3R_c}\right)^2 \frac{\mathrm{De}}{88.33}\right]^{1/3}, \tag{68}$$

from fitting to the experimental data of Schmidt [119] and the calculated correlations of Austin and Seader [134] and Tarbell and Samuels [135]. The generalization of the above correlations for finite pitch can be obtained from Equation (68) by replacing the Dean number with the helical number, defined as

$$\mathrm{He} = \sqrt{\gamma}\mathrm{De}, \tag{69}$$

after fitting to the experimental data of Mishra and Gupta [88]. Further numerical simulations of time-dependent laminar flow in helical pipes of rectangular cross-section were performed by Wang and Andrews [42] by solving the Navier–Stokes equations written in the helical coordinate system described by Huang and Gu [136], which, apart from being slightly non-orthogonal, are more appropriate for helical ducts. In particular, Wang and Andrews [42] investigated the dependence of the fully developed laminar flow on pressure gradient and the dimensionless curvature, D_h/R_c, and torsion, h/R_c, where $D_h = 4bc/(b+c)$ is the hydraulic diameter and b and c are the half-width and half-height of the rectangular cross-section. They found that the relative friction factor increases with the pitch ratio and the pressure gradient. When $h/R_c = 10$, the secondary flow causes the transition from a two-vortex system to a single vortex. However, the pressure gradient appears to have a greater influence on both the secondary flow pattern and the flow resistance. For example, as displayed in Figure 12, four vortices formed in the cross-sectional plane when the pressure gradient, defined as $\partial(p/\rho)/\partial\theta$ (where p is pressure, ρ is density and θ the coordinate of the helix), was set to 2300. Other authors, such as, for instance, Choi and Park [137], performed numerical calculations of the steady laminar flow in a helical pipe to explore the evolution of the secondary flow and the dependence of the flow characteristics with the radius ratio, finding that the complex interactions between the viscous and centrifugal forces may impede the full development of the laminar flow at the entrance of the coil when the radius ratio is larger than a certain value.

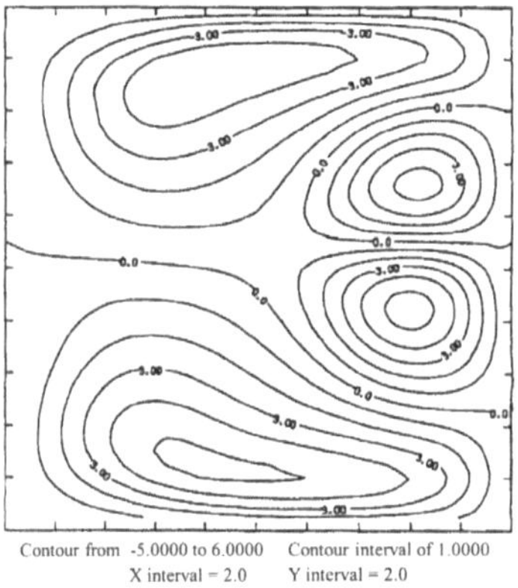

Figure 12. Contour lines showing the structure of the secondary flow consisting of four vortices occupying the cross-sectional plane for flow along a helical duct of square cross-section, pitch $h = R_c$ and pressure gradient equal to 2300. Figure taken from Wang and Andrews [42].

More recent numerical simulations of laminar flow in helical pipes were reported by De Amicis et al. [37] and Ahmadloo et al. [44]. The former authors employed different fuid-dynamic codes based on commercial software, such as FLUENT, OpenFOAM and COMSOL Multiphysics, to predict the numerically obtained Darcy friction factor with experimental measurements and existing correlations in the literature (see Figure 6). Variations in the coil geometry were found to affect the friction factor as well as the emergence of the secondary flow and the deformation of the axial flow. On the other hand, Ahmadloo et al. [44] simulated the flow of water through a hollow helical duct for Reynolds numbers between 703.2 and 1687.7, using the SIMPLEC algorithm for solving the Navier–Stokes equations. A major finding from this study was that the friction factor decreases as the tendency to turbulence increases. CFD simulations with the aid of ANSYS FLUENT 16.0 were further reported by Abushammala et al. [39] to evaluate the laminar flow friction factor in highly curved helical pipes, i.e., in helical pipes of low pitches and relatively low helical radii. As these authors mentioned in their paper, the difficulty to manufacture highly curved helical pipes has led to a complete lack of data on the friction factor in such geometries. Almost all correlation studies for predicting the friction factor of fully developed laminar flows in helical pipes have relied on the use of the Dean number as provided by Equation (1) to account for both flow and geometry effects, except perhaps the solution provided by Mishra and Gupta [88], defined as

$$\frac{F\text{Re}}{16} = 1 + 0.033(\log_{10}\text{De}^{\star}), \tag{70}$$

where the Dean number, De*, is provided by the alternative form

$$\text{De}^{\star} = \text{Re}\sqrt{\frac{\gamma}{1+\beta^2}}, \tag{71}$$

which, unlike Equation (1), now accounts for the effects of the helix pitch through the parameter $\beta = h/(2\pi R_c)$. In the limit of straight pipe flows, the Dean number provided by Equation (71) vanishes identically since in such flows there are no Dean vortices and centrifugal forces. Moreover, it tends to infinity as $R_c \to 0$, which is consistent with the idealization of Dean vortices of infinite intensity. Therefore, as R_c and h become increasingly small, the flow in such helical pipes will be characterized by more intense Dean vortices and higher pressure drops. Abushammala et al. [39] performed more than 150 simulations for $1.25 \le h/(2R) \le 15$, $0.05 \le 1/(2\gamma) \le 10$ and $10 \le \text{Re} \le 2000$ to develop an accurate prediction of the local friction factor for highly curved helical pipes. Using a regression model for FRe, they obtained the following expression as the best fit of the CFD data

$$F\text{Re} = \frac{64}{\text{Re}} + p_1\mathcal{B}\left(\frac{\mathcal{B}}{\text{Re}}\right)^{p_2}\left(2\gamma + \frac{1}{2\gamma}\right)^{p_3}\exp\left[-p_4\mathcal{B}\left(\frac{h}{2R}\right)\left(\frac{1}{2\gamma}\right)^{-p_5}\right], \tag{72}$$

where

$$\mathcal{B} = \left[\left(\frac{1}{2\gamma}\right)^{-p_6}\left(1+\beta^2\right)\right]^{-p_7}. \tag{73}$$

The quantities p_i, with $i = 1,2,3,4,5,6$ and 7 are regression parameters, which are determined using an optimization procedure that minimizes the deviations of the correlation outputs from the CFD data. Optimized values are listed in Table 3 of Abushammala et al. [39] along with the Re values ranges for which they are valid. Figure 13 shows a parity diagram that compares the correlation predictions against the CFD and experimental data. The graph shows that Equations (72) and (73) fit the FRe data within an error margin of 10%.

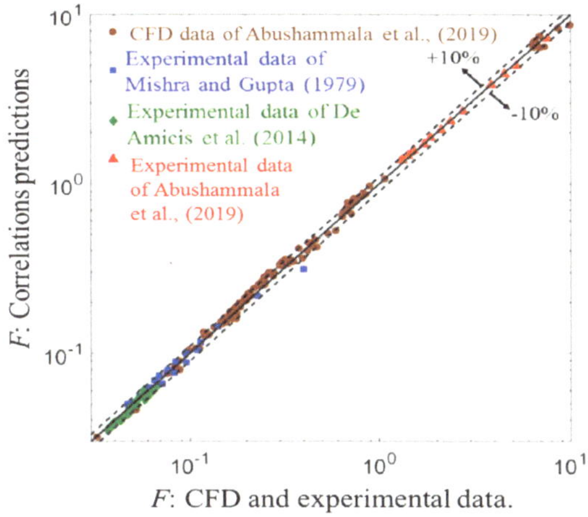

Figure 13. Parity diagram showing the comparison of Mishra and Gupta's [88] and De Amicis et al.'s [37] experimental correlations with Abushammala et al's [39] experimental and CFD data. Figure taken from Abushammala et al. [39].

4.3. Numerical Simulations: Turbulent Flow and Heat Transfer

One main feature of flow in helically coiled pipes is that the transition from a laminar to a turbulent state occurs at critical Reynolds numbers higher than in straight pipes. The dependence of the critical Reynolds number on the curvature ratio, $\gamma = R/R_c$, can be estimated using the correlations for turbulent flows provided by Ito [96], Schmidt [119], Srinivasan et al. [138] and Janssen and Hoogendoorn [139]. These correlations are plotted in Figure 14 for $0 < \gamma \leq 0.25$. Although all these correlations approximately converge for $\gamma \lesssim 0.06$, only the correlations developed by Ito and Schmidt predict approximately the same value of $\mathrm{Re_{cr}}$. The other two correlations predict values of $\mathrm{Re_{cr}}$ that are higher at comparable values of $\gamma \gtrsim 0.06$.

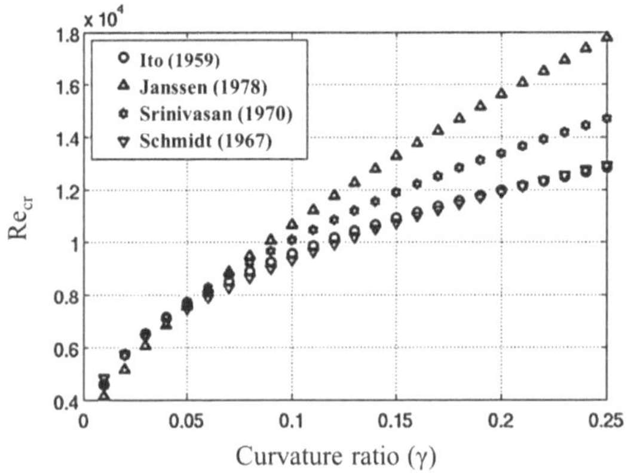

Figure 14. Estimated critical Reynolds number as a function of the curvature ratio according to the correlations for turbulent flow developed by Ito [96], Schmidt [119], Srinivasan et al. [138] and Janssen and Hoogendoorn [139]. Figure taken from Jayakumar et al. [43].

Heat transfer in turbulent flows along helical coils has been studied numerically by a number of authors since the late 1960s. For instance, Mori and Nakayama [140] performed calculations of forced convective heat transfer in helical turbulent flows under constant wall heat flux boundary conditions. In a separate paper, they theoretically investigated heat transfer under uniform temperature wall boundary conditions [116]. However, true numerical simulations of turbulent flow and convective heat transfer in helical pipes began to appear in the open literature in the late 1990s. Turbulent forced convection in a helical pipe of circular cross-section with finite coil pitch was simulated by Yang and Ebadian [141]. They solved the time-averaged momentum and energy equations using a control-volume finite element method coupled to the $\kappa - \epsilon$ standard two-equation turbulence model with the aid of the FLUENT/UNS code. They found that, as the coil pitch increases, the cross-sectional temperature distribution becomes asymmetric and the torsional effects on heat transfer are reduced for increased Prandtl numbers. Using the same numerical model, Lin and Ebadian [142] studied three-dimensional turbulent developing convective heat transfer in helical pipes for $2.5 \times 10^4 \lesssim \mathrm{Re} \lesssim 1.0 \times 10^5$, coil pitches in the interval between 0 and 0.6 and curvature ratios of 0.025–0.050. They examined the development of the thermal conductivity, temperature fields as well as the local and average Nusselt numbers, finding that these parameters exert rather complex effects on the developing thermal fields and heat transfer in helical pipes. Using the same numerical strategy of Lin and Ebadian [142], this time coupled with the renormalization group $\kappa - \epsilon$ turbulence model, Li et al. [143] investigated the three-dimensional turbulent flow and heat transfer at the entrance of a curved pipe. They found that, at high Grashof numbers, up to three vortices formed the structure of the developing secondary flow.

On the other hand, chaotic heat transfer in heat exchanger designs at Reynolds numbers from 30 to 30,000 and varied Prandtl numbers was studied by Chagny et al. [144], while simulations of turbulent flow and heat transfer to study pressure drop in tube-in-tube heat exchangers were performed by Kumar et al. [145] using the FLUENT 6.0 code. CFD simulations were also employed by Jayakumar et al. [146] to perform estimations of heat transfer in helically coiled heat exchangers. A CFD analysis of the detailed characteristics of fluid flow and heat transfer in helical tubes was reported by Jayakumar et al. [43]. They carried out simulations for vertically oriented helical pipes with varied geometrical parameters. Among the most relevant results, these authors found that (a) fluctuations in the heat transfer rates are caused by flow oscillations inside the tube, (b) the use of either a constant wall temperature or a constant wall heat flux does not affect the velocity profiles, while different temperature profiles will result and (c) the effects of torsion induced by a finite pitch cause oscillations in the Nusselt number, while the average Nusselt number is not affected. Figure 15 shows velocity, turbulent kinetic energy and turbulent intensity contours at various cross-sectional planes along the helical pipe for one of their model simulations using constant wall temperature boundary conditions. A correlation based on their CFD data was also derived for estimation of the Nusselt number, namely

$$\mathrm{Nu} = 0.116\mathrm{Re}^{0.71}\mathrm{Pr}^{0.4}\gamma^{0.11}, \tag{74}$$

valid for $14{,}000 < \mathrm{Re} < 70{,}000$, $3000 < \mathrm{De} < 22{,}000$, $3 < \mathrm{Pr} < 5$ and $0.05 < \gamma < 0.2$. As shown in Figure 16, this correlation closely follows the predictions of Mori and Nakayama [116] and Rogers and Mayhew [115] for a uniform wall temperature boundary condition. A similar plot was also obtained for a constant wall heat flux boundary condition (see Jayakumar et al.'s [43] Figure 21).

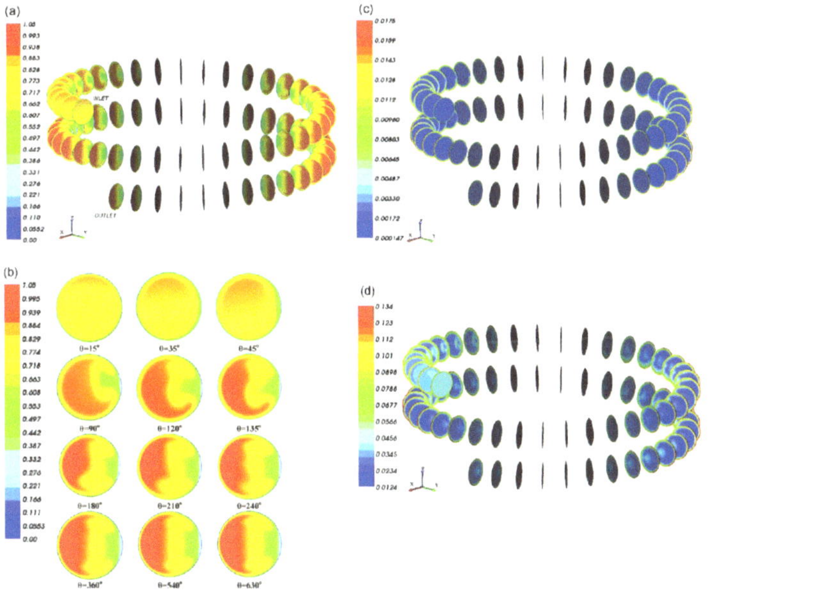

Figure 15. (**a**,**b**) Velocity, (**c**) turbulent kinetic energy and (**d**) turbulent intensity contour plots at various cross-sectional planes along the length of a helically coiled pipe of inner radius $R = 10$ mm, coil pitch $h = 30$ mm and pitch circle diameter of 200 mm. The CFD results correspond to hot water at 330 K and velocity of 0.8 m s^{-1} entering the helical coil at the top for uniform pipe wall temperature boundary conditions. Figure taken from Jayakumar et al. [43].

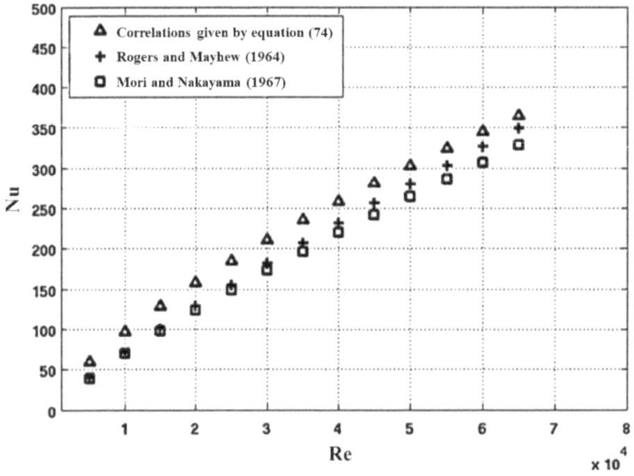

Figure 16. Diagram showing the Nusselt number as a function of the Reynolds number as predicted by Equation (74) compared with the correlations of Rogers and Mayhew [115] and Mori and Nakayama [116]. Figure taken from Jayakumar et al. [43].

Further predictions of turbulent flow and heat transfer in helical pipes were reported by Di Piazza and Ciofalo [17]. They solved the governing equations using the general purpose code ANSYS CFX 11 coupled with three different turbulence models, namely the $\kappa-\epsilon$, the Shear Stress Transport (SST) $\kappa-\omega$ and the Reynolds Stress (RSM$-\omega$) models. Simulation results with these models were compared with Direct Numerical Simulations (DNS) and experimental pressure loss and heat transfer data. In particular, they found that the $\kappa-\epsilon$ turbulence model provided unsatisfactory results, while results from the RSM$-\omega$ model were in good agreement with Ito's [96] and the experimental data of Cioncolini and Santini [94] for pressure losses in fully developed turbulent flows (with Re $>$ 14,000) and pipes of different curvature ratios $\gamma = R/R_c$. Di Piazza and Ciofalo [17] compared the experimental and computational results for the Darcy–Weisbach friction factor versus Re for the case when $\gamma = 9.64 \times 10^{-3}$ and 0.143 (their Figures 7 and 8), finding that Ito's correlations are in excellent agreement with the experimental data in the laminar and turbulent regime. With the aid of the CFD package FLUENT, Colombo et al. [45] performed further simulations to assess the capability of different turbulence models to predict available experimental data on pressure drop and wall shear stress for fully developed turbulent flow in helical pipes. They tested five different turbulence models and used two different meshes depending on whether the wall function approach or the enhanced wall treatment was implemented. Grid sizes provided by 605×280 and 1125×240 elements were employed with the wall function approach, while meshes consisting of 3125×280 and 4500×240 were used with the wall-enhanced treatment in order to obtain grid-independent solutions. They concluded that the Realizable $\kappa-\epsilon$ model provided the lowest deviations from the experimental measurements.

The effects of curvature and torsion on turbulent flow and heat transfer in helically coiled pipes were studied next by Ciofalo et al. [147] by means of DNS using highly resolved finite-volume methods. The computational grid was hexahedral and multi-block-structured, with 7.86 million nodes covering the entire pipe for $\gamma = 0.3$ and 23.6 million nodes for $\gamma = 0.1$. Geometric refinement was introduced close to the pipe wall to increase the convergence rate, with a consecutive cell-size ratio of $\sim$1.025 in the radial direction. For 23.6 million nodes, the overall CPU time required was close to 5×10^8 core-seconds. They introduced a Reynolds number, defined in terms of the friction velocity $v_\tau = \sqrt{\langle \bar{\tau}_w \rangle / \rho}$ and based on the time- and circumferentially averaged wall shear stress $\langle \bar{\tau}_w \rangle$ as $\mathrm{Re}_\tau = v_\tau R/\nu$. For $\mathrm{Re}_\tau = 400$, $\gamma = 0.1$ and 0.3 and torsion ratios $h/R_c = 2\pi\beta = 0$ and 0.3, they found that the effects of curvature on the flow cannot be neglected; i.e., as γ is increased from 0.1 to 0.3, both the friction coefficient and the Nusselt number increase, causing the secondary flow to become more intense. Also, with increasing curvature, the fluctuations in the axial velocity decrease and Re_τ increases. In contrast, torsional effects were found to have only a minor effect, at least when h/R_c is increased from 0 (torus) to 0.3. Turbulent flow characteristics through helical pipes were also studied by Tang et al. [49] for different turbulence models using the FLUENT code. They generated the computational grid using the ICEM CFD tool and obtained mesh-independent solutions for the mainstream axial velocity using $\approx$0.992 million nodes by setting the convergence criterion to 10^{-5}. It was found that the maximum velocity along the coil increases gradually and causes unsteady flow behavior because of large cross-sectional gradient fields. As the pressure decreases along the coil, the large pressure differences generated squeeze the flow and give rise to centrifugal forces.

Numerical investigations of turbulent forced convective flow of a CuO nanofluid in helical tubes were performed by Rakhsha et al. [38] using the OpenFOAM software with uniform wall temperature boundary conditions. Their simulations predicted a 6–7% increase in the convective heat transfer and a 9–10% increase in the pressure drop compared to the experimental results of a 16–17% increase in the coefficient of heat transfer and a 14–16% increase in the pressure losses for different pipe geometries and Re values. The top two rows of Figure 17 depict flow velocity intensity plots at different cross-sectional planes along the helix, while the bottom two rows show temperature intensity plots at the same pipe stations. It is clear from these plots that fully developed hydrodynamical and thermal conditions are achieved by the flow at the outlet of the coil after two turns. In a more recent study, Faraj et al. [46] simulated, using the ANSYS FLUENT solver, the effects of varying the coil pitch in the turbulent flow regime. They obtained grid-independent solutions with minimum computer resources using a five-domain O-H grid method "butterfly topology" with 313,823 and 597,600 cells. In particular, these authors considered helical pipes of the same inner diameter ($D = 0.005$ m) and coil diameter ($D_c = 2R_c = 0.04$ m) and varying coil pitches (i.e., $h = 0.01$, 0.05 and 0.25 m). When the pitch size is increased, the turbulent fluctuations are damped out and the emergence of the secondary flow is delayed. However, based on their CFD simulations, they concluded that more accurate results are obtained when using the STD ($\kappa - \omega$) turbulence model than when using the STD ($\kappa - \epsilon$) model and that reduction in the coil friction factor is largely due to the effects of the Dean number and, to a much minor extent, to the increment of the pitch size. In passing, it is worth mentioning the work by Demagh et al. [50], who performed a comparative numerical study on pressure drop in helically coiled and longitudinally C-shaped pipes. However, the latter pipes have been much less studied mainly due to their limited use in the industry.

4.4. Flow and Heat Transfer in Corrugated and Twisted Helical Pipes

Enhancement regarding heat transfer rates in helically coiled pipes is of great interest in the industry and in many engineering applications. As was commented by Li et al. [148], there are two different methods to enhance the rate of heat transfer in helical coils, namely the active and the passive methods. While the active method requires the application of external forces, the passive concept relies on the addition of fluid additives or particular surface geometries, as may be the case regarding corrugations in the pipe surface. However, helical pipes with surface wall corrugations have received comparatively less attention compared to smooth helical pipes owing to the relatively high cost and difficulty in fabrication. In relation to corrugated pipes, Yildiz et al. [149] studied the heat transfer characteristics in a helical pipe constructed with spring-shaped wires of varying pitch inside the pipe. On the other hand, Zachár [150] performed numerical simulations of flow through a helical pipe with a spiral corrugation on the outer wall, which produced a helical rib on the inner wall. This gives rise to a swirling motion of the fluid. Zachár found that, due to this additional swirling motion, the heat transfer rate in the inner wall of the pipe exhibited an 80–100% increase compared to smooth heat exchangers, while the pressure drop was from 10 to 600% larger.

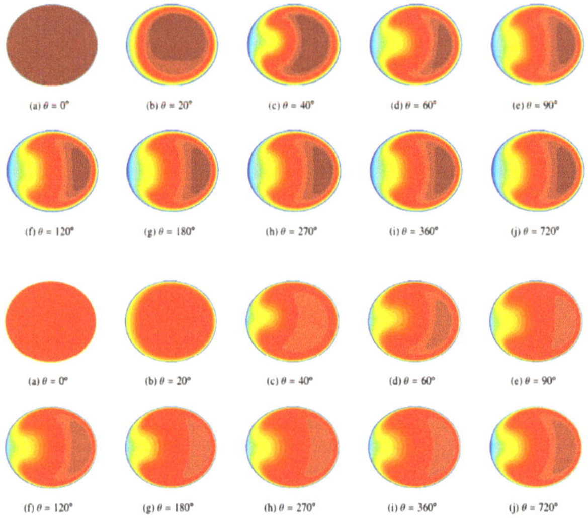

Figure 17. Cross-sectional velocity (first two rows) and temperature (last two rows) intensity plots along the helical pipe length for Re = 13,000 and curvature ratio $\gamma = R/R_c = 0.032$. Figure taken from Rakhsha et al. [38].

Li et al. [148] performed further numerical simulations to investigate the turbulent flow and heat transfer in helical pipes, this time with spiral corrugations in the inner wall, as a further heat transfer enhancement method. Figure 18 shows the spirally corrugated helical pipe model employed in Li et al.'s [148] simulations. They considered three pipe models, all with $R_c = 30$ mm, inner diameter $2R = 10$ mm, coil pitch $h = 20$ mm, differing only in the pitch of the spiral corrugation, which was $h' = 18.95$ mm (their Tube I), 7.59 mm (their Tube II) and 5.41 mm (their Tube III). Figure 19 shows axial velocity intensity plots (left) and secondary flow patterns (right) generated for the three corrugated models as compared with a smooth helical pipe for turbulent flow at Re = 22,000. The saddle-shaped axial velocity formed in the smooth pipe is destroyed by the spiral corrugation, while the two counter-rotating vortices are present in all models. However, their centers change with different position of corrugation on the cross-sectional plane.

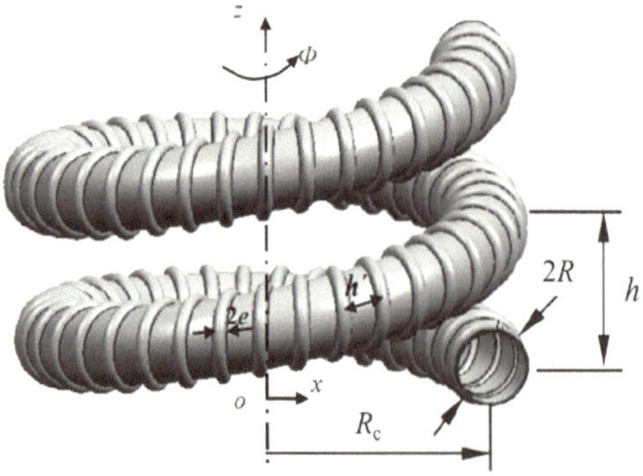

Figure 18. Drawing of a helically coiled pipe with a spiral corrugation of semicircular cross-section. The pitch of the spiral corrugation is h' and e is its depth. The angle Φ corresponds to the rotation angle of an equivalent smooth helical pipe along the helical line. Figure taken from Li et al. [148].

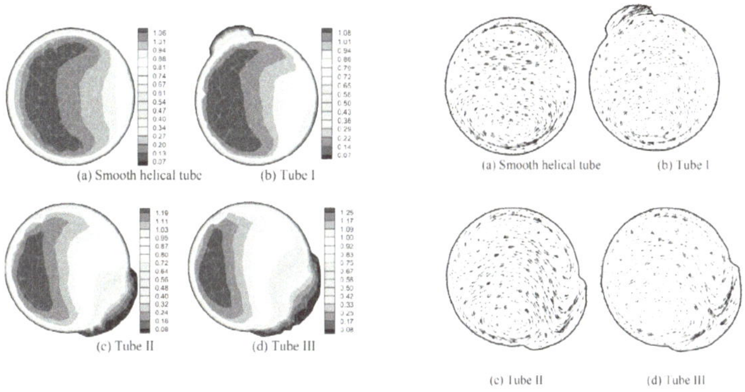

Figure 19. Comparison of cross-sectional velocity contour plots (**left**) and secondary flow patterns (**right**) for the smooth and spirally corrugated (Tubes I, II and III) helical pipe flow simulations of Li et al. [148]. Figure taken from Li et al. [148].

In a more recent work, Wang et al. [51] studied by means of numerical simulations the flow and heat transfer characteristics of a twisted helical pipe of elliptical cross-section for $500 \leq \text{Re} \leq 3000$. The physical details of their twisted helical pipe are provided in Figure 20. They considered the flow of water and oil through twisted helical pipes of helix diameter $D = 90$ mm, screw pitch $h = 30$ mm, twist pitches in the interval $35 \leq p' \leq 65$ mm and lengths of the semi-major axis a' between 4.4 and 5.6 mm. Lower values of p' and a' were found to favor higher fluid mixing accompanied by larger temperature gradients near the pipe wall, with the consequent effect of inducing large friction resistance and enhanced heat transfer. However, compared to a reference model consisting of a smooth helical pipe of circular cross-section, they reported improvements in the heat transfer performance, which varied from factors of 1.04 to 1.21 when changing the semi-major axis, while the thermal performance improved by factors of 1.02–1.25 for different twist pitch lengths when $\text{Re} = 1000$ and by factors of 1.16–1.29 when $\text{Re} = 3000$.

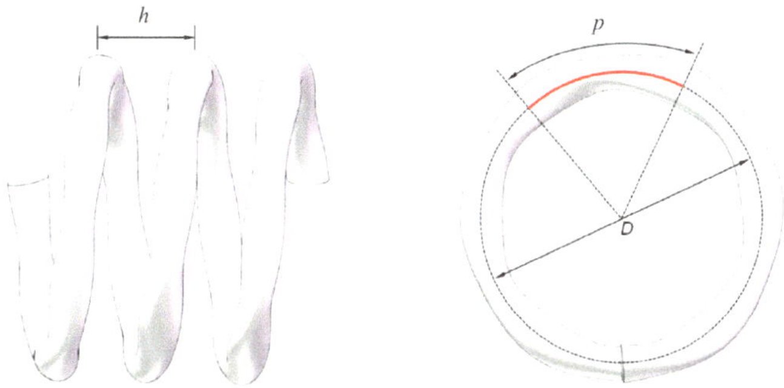

Figure 20. Physical model of the twisted helically coiled pipes of elliptical cross-section used in the CFD simulations of Wang et al. [51]. The various geometrical parameters are defined in the text above. Figure taken from Wang et al. [51].

Figure 21 is illustrative of a comparison of the streamlines, velocity vectors and temperature distributions between the smooth and the twisted pipes. In particular, this figure corresponds to $p' = 45$ mm, $a' = 5.2$ mm and $\text{Re} = 1500$. The streamlines in the corrugated pipe appear highly disordered compared to the smooth pipe, while the secondary flow pattern generated consists of two enhanced vortices, which increases the mixing within the pipe with a consequent increase in the thermal performance. Figure 22 provides details of the temperature field along the smooth and twisted pipes for $\text{Re} = 1500$.

As was outlined by Wang et al. [51], the overall temperature of the twisted pipe is higher than that of the smooth pipe for a comparable cross-sectional perimeter. These authors derived by means of multiple linear regression analysis correlations for the Nusselt number and the friction factor as functions of the Reynolds number, which obey the expressions

$$F = 10.93348\mathrm{Re}^{-0.56554}\mathrm{Pr}^{-0.00255}\left(\frac{a'}{b'}\right)^{-0.24335}\left(\frac{p'}{d}\right)^{-0.25628}, \quad (75)$$

$$\mathrm{Nu} = 0.66275\mathrm{Re}^{0.50508}\mathrm{Pr}^{0.32743}\left(\frac{a'}{b'}\right)^{-0.19620}\left(\frac{p'}{d}\right)^{-0.28430}, \quad (76)$$

where b' is the semi-minor axis of the elliptical cross-section and d is the diameter of a circle having the same perimeter of the elliptical cross-section. In their Figure 16, they compare the Nusselt number and the friction factor as obtained from the simulated data with literature correlations for the Nusselt number developed by Xin and Ebadian [93] and Salimpour [151] and for the friction factor developed by Ito [96] and Yanase et al. [152], finding deviations between the predicted and calculated values within 10%.

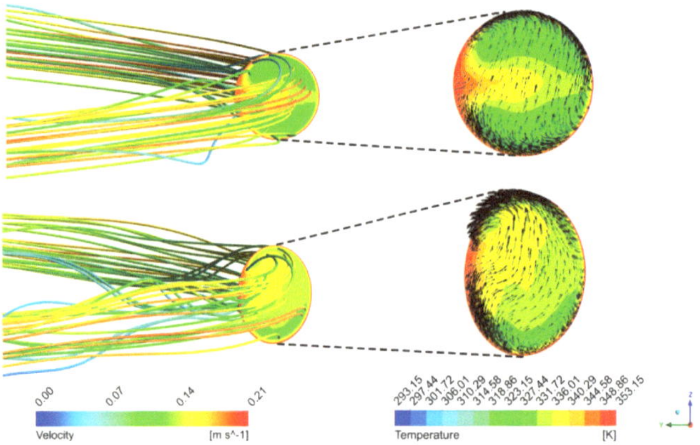

Figure 21. Comparison of the streamlines, cross-sectional velocity vectors and temperature distributions between a smooth helical pipe of circular cross-section and a twisted helical tube of elliptical cross-section for Re = 1500. Figure taken from Wang et al. [51].

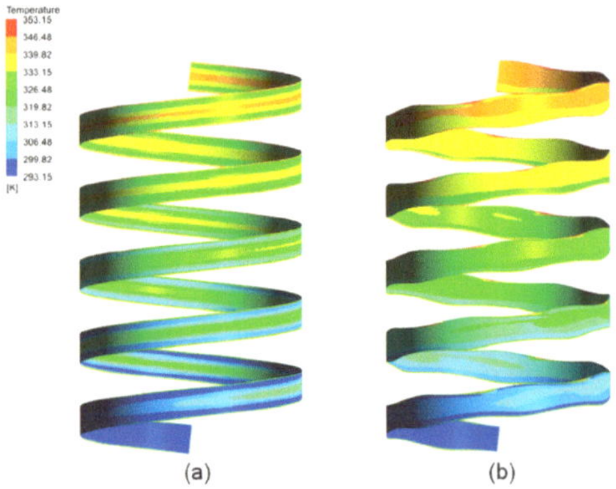

Figure 22. Comparison of the temperature field between (**a**) the smooth and (**b**) the twisted helical pipes for the same flow of Figure 21. Figure taken from Wang et al. [51].

The research regarding cost-effective, reliable and efficient novel devices to manage the heat flux problem is growing exponentially. The wider range of applications of such management systems imposes a strong demand that is attracting many scientists and engineers. In this line, the recent work by Adhikari and Maharjan [48] represents one such effort towards the improvement in design and capabilities of heat pipes. In particular, they performed CFD simulations of helically coiled closed-loop pulsating heat pipes on the basis of the experiments conducted by Pachghare and Mahalle [153]. They found that thermal resistance in such systems is less than in more conventional helical exchangers. However, since this area of research is relatively new, more work has to be developed before the implementation of this technology in heat exchangers and thermal management systems. Also, CFD analyses of helically coiled tube-in-tube heat exchangers have recently been carried out by Vijaya Kumar Reddy et al. [154].

5. Other Investigation Aspects of Helical Coiled Flows

5.1. Visualization of Helical Pipe Flow

The structure of internal fluid flows in curved pipes with a secondary flow induced by centrifugal, buoyancy and Coriolis forces forms a class of technological problems of relevance to many industrial and engineering applications. In spite of this, relatively little experimental work exists in the literature on the visualization of such flows. In fact, currently, most visualization work on secondary flow in helical tubes and ducts relies on the analysis of CFD data with the aid of specialized graphing software. Recently, "virtual reality" is being used as a power tool for the visualization of CFD flow simulations [155].

Visualization of secondary flow structure in helical pipes was investigated by Liou et al. [156] using a narrow laser light sheet for smoke illumination and laser Doppler velocimetry (LDV) techniques for measurement of the velocity field. Their flow visualization results showed good agreement with the CFD simulations of Wang [66] and Chen and Fan [157] for varying Re values between 35 and 330 and torsion-to-curvature ratios from 0.06 to 5.55. The flow visualization photographs allowed for detailed documentation of the secondary flow structure and revealed that the deformation of the symmetric two-vortex structure into a single circulating vortex increases as the torsion-to-curvature ratio also increases. Further visualization studies of the relaminarization phenomena in bends and helically coiled pipes were carried out by Kurokawa et al. [61] using a hot-film anemometer. They measured the stabilization effect in helical coils for fully developed air turbulent flow at the entrance of the coil and the re-transition of the flow from a laminar to a turbulent state in the downstream straight section after the exit from the coil. Photographs of the time-mean streamwise velocity and axial turbulence intensity field were taken for flow through helical pipes of 1, 2 and 5 turns, inner pipe diameter of 37.5 mm, curvature ratio $\gamma = 0.049$ and downstream straight pipe length equal to 30 times the inner pipe diameter. The relaminarization phenomenon was interpreted in terms of the turbulence intensity together with the behavior of the velocity fluctuations, suggesting that the redistribution of the turbulence level in the downstream straight section is caused by transport processes of the turbulent kinetic energy.

An analysis of the fluid particle trajectories and experimental visualization of the secondary flow in helical pipes was reported by Yamamoto et al. [158]. Calculation of the trajectory of fluid particles was performed by expressing the position vector of particles in a cross-sectional plane using Germano's [67] coordinate system and by transforming the velocity components to Cartesian coordinates (e.g., see their Equations (13) to (21)). Successive repetition of the method yields the fluid particle trajectories. Their visualization results confirmed those previously found by Liou [156] that a two-vortex pattern formed at low torsional effects becomes a single-vortex pattern at high torsional effects. Figure 23 shows a sequence of photographs of the secondary flow at increasing Reynolds number when the torsion parameter $\beta_0 = 0.48$, where

$$\beta_0 = \frac{\lambda}{\sqrt{2\kappa}}, \tag{77}$$

and $\lambda \propto \tau/\kappa$ is the torsion to curvature ratio. Here, κ and τ are provided by relations (64). At Re = 42, the secondary flow consists of a single circulatory vortex with an approximate center in the centerline of the helical pipe. As Re increases to 142, the centrifugal force due to the helicoidal curvature also increases, leading to the formation of a second vortex near the right-hand corner. At even higher Re values, the two-vortex pattern becomes clear, appearing to rotate in the clockwise direction relative to the pipe centerline. The last two pictures in the right-hand column depict the fluid particle trajectories in the cross-sectional plane at comparable Re values of the photographs at Re = 327 and 861, respectively. As β_0 is increased to 1.60 (see their Figure 11), only a single vortex is visible at all Reynolds numbers between 400 and 1468, confirming that, at increased torsion, the secondary flow pattern undergoes a transition from two vortices to one vortex.

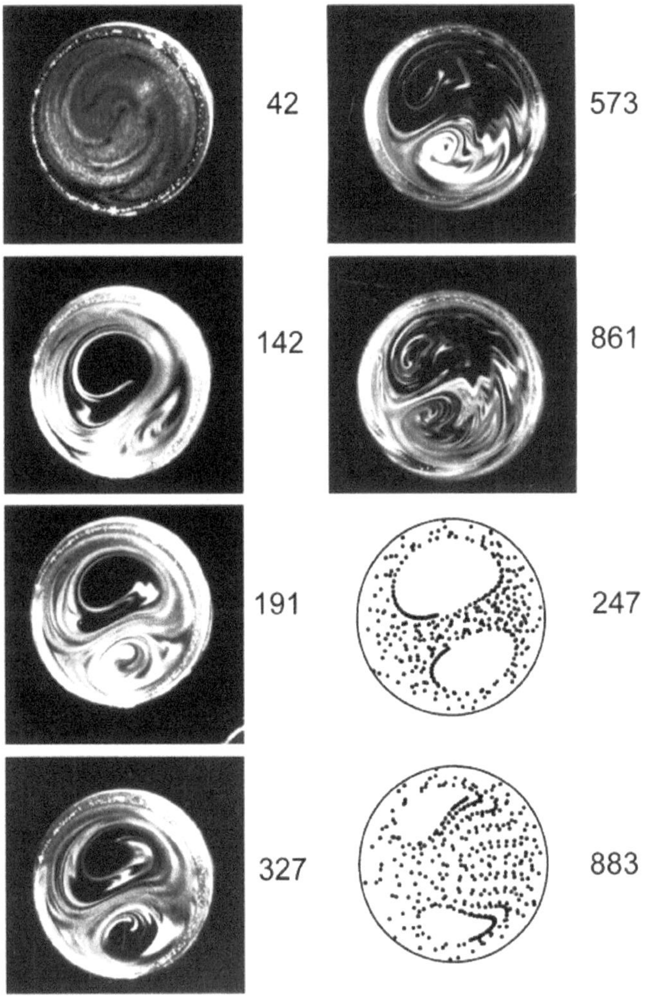

Figure 23. Photographic visualization of the cross-sectional secondary flow pattern through a helically coiled pipe for the torsion parameter $\beta_0 = 0.48$. The number next to each photograph indicates the Reynolds number. The last two pictures in the right column depict the cross-sectional trajectories of fluid particles after 10-pitch from the initial position. Figure taken from Yamamoto et al. [158].

5.2. Entropy Generation of Helical Pipe Flow

Irreversible processes associated with fluid flow in pipes are mainly due to fluid friction and heat transfer. For example, the temperature differences between the flowing fluid and the pipe wall are sources of thermal irreversibilities, while the viscous friction between fluid elements causes, on the other hand, friction losses. A study of entropy generation in straight pipe flows under uniform wall temperature conditions was first reported by Şahin [159]. Further studies on curved pipes and injunctions were reported by Ko [160] and Sanchez et al. [161], respectively. Entropy generation in helical pipe flows has instead been analyzed by Shokouhmand and Salimpour [162], Satapathy [163], Bahiraei et al. [164], Ahadi and Abbassi [165], Dizaji et al. [166], Kurnia et al. [47], Huminic and Huminic [167] and more recently by Pendyala et al. [168] and Prattipati et al. [56]. Evidently, in the last 10 or more years, there has been an ever-increasing interest to evaluate the thermal performance of helically coiled pipes (and other systems) using the second law of thermodynamics [169]. For example, Ahadi and Abbasi [165] estimated the entropy generation of laminar flow of water with temperature-dependent properties in helical pipes by analytical means, finding that the rates of entropy generation depend on the combined effects of length and heat flux of the coil. On the other hand, the dependence of exergy losses on the flow, thermodynamic and geometrical characteristics of helical coils was studied experimentally by Dizaji et al. [166], concluding that the Reynolds number and the temperature are likely to affect the exergy losses.

In particular, Kurnia et al. [47] evaluated the thermal performance and the entropy generation for laminar air flow in helical pipes of circular, elliptical and square cross-sections. For the sake of comparison, they also considered straight pipes with the same cross-sections as helical tubes. In general, the rate of entropy generation per unit volume, S_g, is the sum of the contributions of viscous dissipation, heat transfer, mass transfer and chemical reactions. However, in studies of pipe flow, only the viscous dissipation and heat transfer contributions, S_μ and S_h, respectively, are of relevance in most cases. Hence,

$$S_g = S_\mu + S_h = \nabla \cdot \mathbf{f}, \tag{78}$$

where **f** is the entropy flux and

$$S_\mu = -\frac{1}{T}\mathbb{T} : \nabla \mathbf{v}, \tag{79}$$

$$S_h = \frac{1}{T^2}\nabla \cdot (k\nabla T). \tag{80}$$

Here, T is the temperature, $\mathbb{T}$ is the viscous stress tensor, k is the thermal conductivity, $\mathbf{v}$ is the fluid velocity vector and the symbol ":" means double dot product.

Equation (78) is the formulation of the second law of thermodynamics within the framework of continuum theory and complies with the entropy balance in an open system, as is indeed required to evaluate the entropy generation in a tube. Kurnia et al. [47] studied the thermal performance of helical tubes in terms of a mixed mean temperature along the tube, T_{mean}, the Nusselt number, defined as

$$\text{Nu} = \frac{2Rq_{\text{w}}}{k(T_{\text{w}} - T_{\text{mean}})}, \tag{81}$$

where q_{w} is the wall heat flux, T_{w} is the wall temperature and the figure of merit (FoM) provided by

$$\text{FoM} = \frac{\dot{Q}_T}{P_{\text{pump}}}, \tag{82}$$

where $\dot{Q}_T$ is the total heat transferred from the pipe wall to the working fluid and P_{pump} is the pumping power. The interested reader is referred to Kurnia et al.'s [47] study for more details about the expressions used for $\dot{Q}_T$ and P_{pump}. The entropy generation rate per unit volume, $\dot{S}_g$, is then calculated as the integral of S_g over the entire fluid volume. Figures 24 and 25 compare the axial velocity and temperature contours between helical coiled and straight pipes of different cross-sections. Secondary flow near the outer wall is always present in all helical pipes due to curvature effects compared to the straight pipes, where, in all cases, the peak velocity is shifted below the middle of the pipe due to gravitational effects. Because of its elongated shape, the helical coil of an elliptical cross-section favors the formation of a two-vortex structure compared to the other two cases where only a single vortex is formed. Figure 26 shows the contours of total entropy generation for the same models of Figures 24 and 25. Compared to the straight pipes, heat transfer is more efficient in the helical tubes, as is reflected by their lower entropy generation. An important result form these calculations is that entropy generation from heat transfer is about two orders of magnitude higher than from viscous dissipation.

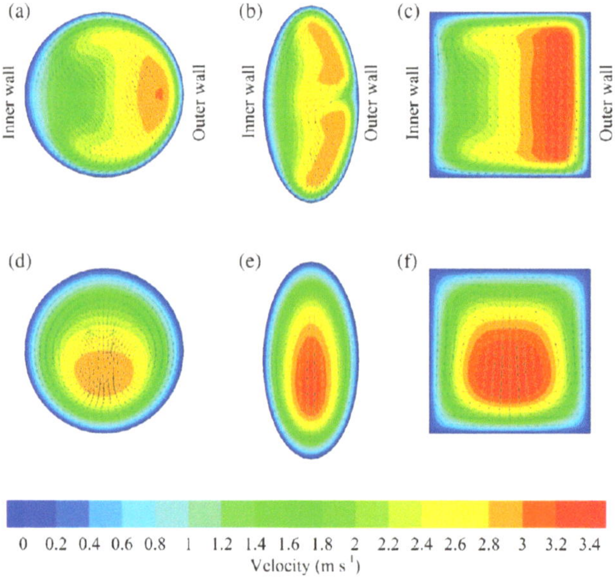

Figure 24. Cross-sectional axial velocity contours and velocity vectors for airflow along a helical pipe of (**a**) circular, (**b**) elliptical and (**c**) square cross-section. The figures in (**d–f**) correspond to the same flow along a straight pipe of circular, elliptical and square cross-section. In all cases, the pipe wall temperature is $T_w = 423.15$ K, Re $= 1000$ and the pipe length is 25 cm. Figure taken from Kurnia et al. [47].

In a more recent work, Prattipati et al. [56] analytically investigated the entropy generation for fully developed laminar flow of a highly viscous fluid in a helically coiled pipe under uniform wall-temperature boundary conditions. They found that, for glycerol as the working fluid, frictional effects produce large irreversibilities compared to lighter fluids, as is the case in water. Also, for highly viscous fluids, the exponential temperature dependence of the viscosity, namely

$$\mu(T) = \mu_{\text{ref}}(T/T_{\text{ref}})^A \exp\left[\frac{B}{T_{\text{ref}}}\left(\frac{T}{T_{\text{ref}}} - 1\right)\right], \tag{83}$$

where T_{ref} is a reference temperature and A and B are fluid-dependent constant parameters, provides a more accurate model. In fact, the thermodynamic potential of improvement analysis reveals that, for heating, up to 35% of total exergy destruction can be avoided based on Equation (83) against 20–25% based on the constant viscosity model. The amount of avoidable exergy destruction is an important parameter together with the avoidable investment cost analysis for the design of cost-effective energy systems.

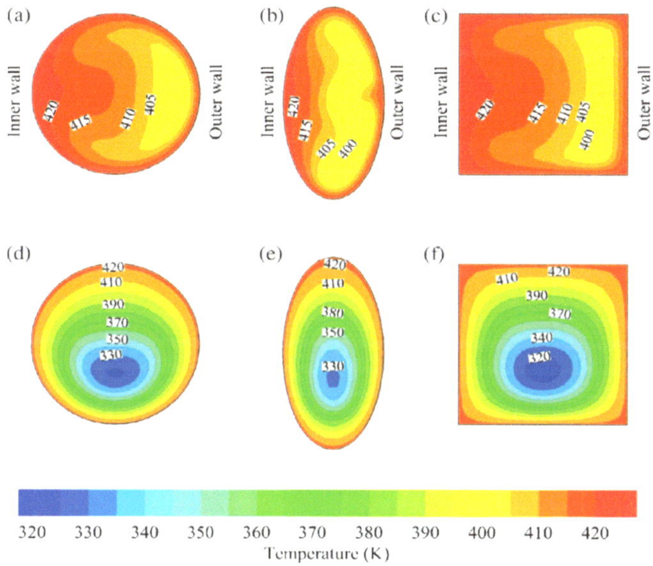

Figure 25. Temperature distribution for the same pipe models and parameters of Figure 24. The figures in (**a–c**) shows the temperature maps in helical pipes of different cross-sections, while the figures in (**d–f**) show the temperature maps for the same flow along straight pipes. The numbers indicate the temperature in kelvin. Figure taken from Kurnia et al. [47].

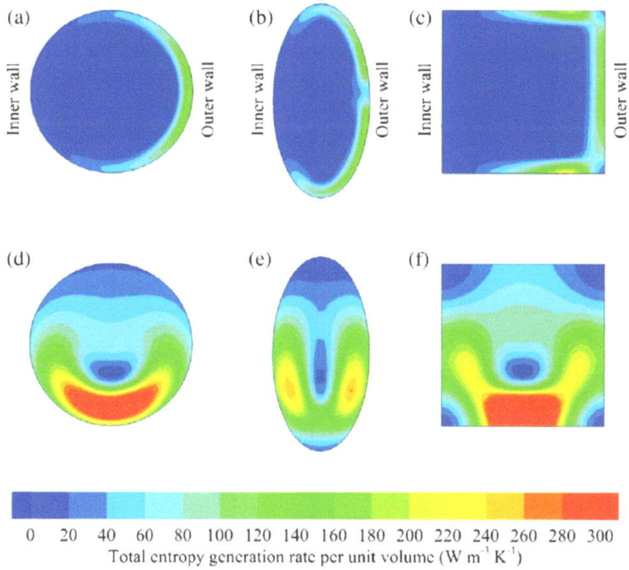

Figure 26. Contours of total entropy generation for the same models and parameters of Figures 24 and 25. The figures in (**a–c**) shows the total entropy generation maps in helical pipes of different cross-sections, while the figures in (**d–f**) show the total entropy generation maps for the same flow along straight pipes. Figure taken from Kurnia et al. [47].

6. Two-Phase Flow in Helically Coiled Pipes

One of the first experimental studies of two-phase flow in helical pipes dates back to 1965 [170]. In general, the liquid–gas flow in helical pipes is characterized by the increase in pressure drop when the liquid is introduced into the gas flow and the volume fraction occupied by the liquid in the pipe. In particular, Rippel et al. [170] experimentally studied the pressure drop, the liquid holdup and the axial liquid mixing in a coiled tube. They found that the pressure drop in a downward helical tube can be predicted by Lockhart and Martinelli's [171] correlation, as was derived from horizontal flow data. They also obtained two-phase frictional pressure-drop correlations for annular, bubble, slug and stratified flow patterns. Over the years, two-phase flows in helically coiled pipes have been studied experimentally by a number of authors [172–180].

In spite of the more or less extensive experimental investigations of two-phase flows in helically coiled pipes, only a limited number of CFD simulation studies are indeed available in the open literature. In particular, the description of multiphase flows is generally a complex subject because the flow pattern as well as the volume fractions occupied by the phases are continuously changing during the flow. The numerical treatment requires to track the interfaces in a stable manner and describe the exchanges of mass, momentum and energy between adjacent phases. In addition, different phases may flow with different velocities and not be in thermal equilibrium. Numerical simulations of gas–liquid flows in helically coiled pipes were conducted by Colombo et al. [52] and more recently by Zhou et al. [181] and Sun et al. [182]. The former authors carried out CFD simulations of air–water flow in a helical pipe with the aid of the finite-volume ANSYS FLUENT 14.0 code. Centrifugal forces were observed to push the water, which is the heavier phase, towards the outer pipe wall, while air, which is the lighter phase, concentrated towards the inner wall and flowed faster than water. Therefore, the mainstream peak velocity of the air–water flow was shifted near the inner pipe wall. On the other hand, cross-sectional recirculation flow in the form of vortices is also observed much in the same way as in single-phase flows. The results for the frictional pressure drop and void fraction were found to reproduce the experimental data provided by Akagawa et al. [173], with mean absolute percentage errors of 4.5% and 12.3%, respectively. As these authors argued, part of the discrepancy with the experimental data can be attributed to limitations in the CFD model. For instance, a drawback of many numerical simulations with commercial codes is the difficulty in correctly describing the phase separation and stratification of multiphase flows in helically coiled pipes due to the simultaneous effects of gravitational and centrifugal forces.

More recently, Zhou et al. [181] performed CFD simulations of two-phase flows in a helical gas–liquid separator of a square cross-section. They investigated the effects of mass flux, curvature and helix angle on pressure drop at different inlet velocities. They found that varying the helix angle has only very little effect on the pressure drop (see their Figure 5), while the effect of curvature appears to be more prominent. As depicted in their Figure 6, for values of the curvature ratio in the interval $0.10 \leq \gamma \leq 0.42$, the pressure losses were always observed to increase with increasing mass flux and curvature ratio (see their Figure 6). As a consequence of increasing the curvature, the separation of the liquid phase from the gas phase is accelerated due to the stronger centrifugal forces.

Further numerical simulations of air–water flow in coiled tubing were recently reported by Sun et al. [182] using the commercial CFD Fluent 19.0 tool coupled to a standard κ-ϵ turbulence model. They studied the dependence of frictional pressure loss on the void fraction, curvature ratio and fluid inlet velocity for an air–water mixture flowing along a coiled tube wound on a spool, as shown schematically in Figure 27 for curvature ratios in the range $0.010 \leq \gamma \leq 0.076$, coil diameters between 0.5 and 82 in and pitches of 0.435, 0.810 and 1.532 in. The simulations were validated for flows with Reynolds numbers between 5000 and 230,000 against Srinivasan et al.'s [138] friction factor correlation for turbulent flow. The maximum average error and standard deviation between simulation and experiments were 2.14% and 0.006, respectively. They found that the functional dependence of the frictional pressure gradient on the void fraction defines a parabolic curve, with the highest pressure losses occurring for the case when $h = 1.532$ in and $2R_c = 82$ in. Independently of the coil geometry, the friction factor peaks at a void fraction of 0.8. This value is, however, slightly larger than those predicted by the empirical correlations for steam–water flow developed by Hardik and Prabhu [98] and Guo et al. [183] and that calculated by Zhao et al. [184] for turbulent flow in a rough helical pipe. On the other hand, the pressure losses were found to increase with the curvature and void fraction, a result that is consistent with previous simulations [52,181].

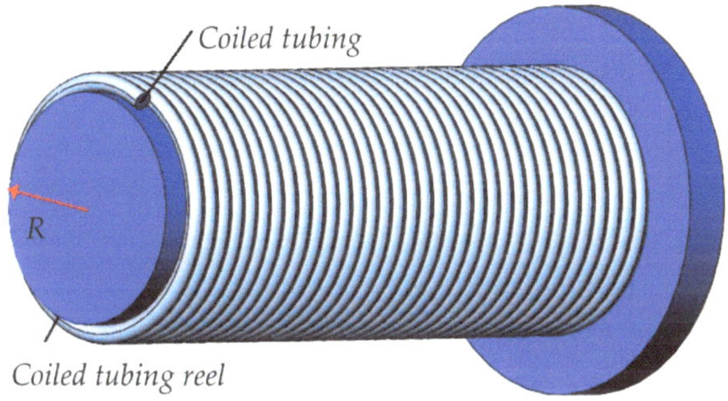

Figure 27. Schematic drawing showing a helically coiled tube wound on a spool. Figure taken from Sun et al. [182].

Sun et al. [182] also studied the influence of secondary flow intensity on the friction factor using the Dean number for two-phase flow defined as

$$\mathrm{De_{tp}} = \sqrt{\gamma}\mathrm{Re_{tp}}, \tag{84}$$

where $\mathrm{Re_{tp}}$ is the Reynolds number for two-phase flow defined by

$$\mathrm{Re_{tp}} = \mathrm{Re_l} + \mathrm{Re_g}\left(\frac{\mu_g}{\mu_l}\right)\left(\frac{\rho_l}{\rho_g}\right)^{1/2}. \tag{85}$$

In the above expression, μ_l, μ_g, ρ_l and ρ_g are, respectively, the liquid viscosity, the gas viscosity, the liquid density and the gas density. As for single-phase flow, the frictional pressure gradient increases with increasing Dean number, $\mathrm{De_{tp}}$. These authors were also able to develop a frictional pressure-drop correlation for gas–liquid two-phase flow, which reads as follows

$$\frac{\Delta p_{ftp}}{\Delta p_l} = 1 + \phi\left[\left(\frac{\rho_l}{\rho_g}\right)^{1.25}\left(\frac{\mu_g}{\mu_l}\right)^{0.25}\right], \tag{86}$$

where

$$\phi = 2.35\gamma^{0.75}\left(\frac{v}{100}\right)^{0.33}(1-\alpha)^{0-3} + \alpha^{2.5}, \tag{87}$$

with

$$\Delta p_l = f_l \frac{L}{h}\frac{v_l^2}{2} \tag{88}$$

being the frictional pressure drop of single-phase flow (gas or liquid), L the pipe length, v_l the mean axial velocity of single-phase flow,

$$f_l = \frac{1}{4}\sqrt{\gamma}\left[0.029 + 0.304\left(\gamma^2\mathrm{Re}\right)^{-0.25}\right], \tag{89}$$

the friction factor of single-phase fluid flowing in a spiral pipe and Re, the Reynolds number of single-phase flow. In Equation (87), v is the inlet velocity and α is the gas void fraction. The parity plot in Figure 28 shows the simulated pressure gradient as a function of the calculated pressure gradient, $\Delta p_{f\text{tp}}$, provided by Equation (86). The simulated data follow the trend of the calculated data within a margin of error of 20%. Sun et al. [182] suggested that a possible cause for the observed error is that there are no models available to accurately predict two-phase flow parameters.

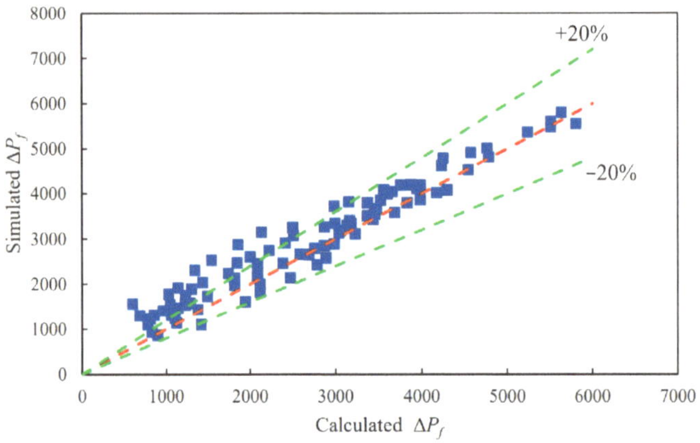

Figure 28. Parity plot showing the simulated frictional pressure loss as a function of the calculated data provided by Equation (86) for air–water two-phase flow in a helical tube, as shown schematically in Figure 27. Figure taken from Sun et al. [182].

7. Helical Flows in Magnetohydrodynamics (MHD)

As was pointed out by Pouquet and Yokoi [185] in their recent review on helical fluid and MHD turbulence, the first discussions about helical structures in turbulent flows occurred in the context of magnetic fields, which are ubiquitous in the universe. Helicity is a topological property of the flows and fields, through links, knots, twists and writhes and their entanglement [186,187]. Early studies on helical flows in MHD have mainly focused on the issue of stability. For instance, the stability of the steady non-dissipative helical flow of an electrically conducting fluid in the presence of an axial magnetic field and current was studied by Howard and Gupta [188]. They found that such a flow, consisting of an azimuthal and an axial velocity component, would be stable against axisymmetric perturbations if the Richardson number, Ri, based on the azimuthal velocity, the circular magnetic field and the shear in the axial flow was greater than $1/4$ everywhere in the flow. Later on, Agrawal [189] derived a sufficient condition for the stability of this type of flow. On the other hand, the hydromagnetic stability of a steady non-dissipative MHD helical flow of a fluid permeated by a helical magnetic field against non-axisymmetric disturbances was further studied by Ganguly and Gupta [190]. The stability of MHD helical flows with respect to non-axisymmetric perturbations is important in problems of controlled thermonuclear reactions. Moreover, equilibrium helical flows also have an impact on the stability properties of low-shear tokamak plasmas [191].

It is well-known that, like vorticity, magnetic induction is an axial vector, and, therefore, it is not surprising that kinetic helicity could be responsible for the growth in large-scale magnetic fields. This problem has been studied in terms of the so-called α-dynamos [192,193]. In particular, dynamo theory deals with the generation of magnetic fields by electrically conducting fluid flows. On the other hand, the Riga dynamo experiment is a laboratory experiment designed to study the self-excitation of the magnetic field in a single helical flow [194]. Therefore, the trend was to tune the flows to have a well-marked helicity to enforce the generation of magnetic fields. In fact, an exponentially growing eigenmode was observed for the first time by the end of 1999 [195]. Since then, there have been many experimental campaigns, which have provided a plethora of data on the kinematic and saturated regime. A comprehensive overview regarding these experimental campaigns and the main results of the Riga dynamo experiments have recently been reported by Gailitis et al. [196]. Important results related to magnetic instabilities have been the experimental demonstration of the helical [197] and the current-driven Taylor instability [198]. However, a two-scale analysis performed by Gilbert et al. [199] showed that helicity is not necessary for the associated dynamo instability, and the lack of parity-invariance in the velocity field is sufficient for the dynamo action. In compliance with this point, Andrievsky et al. [200] recently provided numerical evidence that vanishing velocity helicity does not prevent steady flows from generating small-scale magnetic fields and that large-scale magnetic fields can be generated by the α-effect or the negative diffusivity mechanisms. Therefore, the kinematic generation of magnetic fields does not necessarily require the production of helical flows. However, these findings do not preclude the fact that helicity also plays a role in magnetic field generation, as has been demonstrated by the Riga experiments [196].

8. Concluding Remarks

In this paper, we have reviewed past and recent experimental and theoretical work dealing with flow through helically coiled pipes. Over the years, there has been growing interest in this type of systems due to their wide range of applications in the industry. Unlike other pipe geometries, helically coiled pipes can accommodate a larger heat transfer area per unit volume, exhibit higher efficiency in heat and mass transfer and provide small residence time distributions. In addition, due to their compactness, they are mostly used as heat exchangers and steam generators in power plants.

The most relevant feature of helical pipe flows is the secondary flow field, i.e., the cross-sectional circulatory flow that overlaps the main helical flow, caused by the centrifugal forces that originate from the pipe curvature. As the flow rate increases, the intensity of the circulatory flow in the form of either a couple of counter-rotating vortices or a single vortex also increases. The secondary flow has the effect of stabilizing the flow so that laminar flow can persist longer compared to other conventional pipe geometries. This has the immediate implication that the critical Reynolds number at which the flow experiences a transition from a laminar to a turbulent state occurs at much higher values than, for example, in straight tubes.

A survey of the open literature on experimental and theoretical investigations of the flow and heat transfer characteristics in helical pipes shows the existence of a large number of papers. Most work on laminar flow has mainly focused on studying pressure losses for different flow rates and helical pipe geometries and deriving predictive correlations of the friction factor coefficient as a function of the Reynolds and/or Dean number under laminar and turbulent flow conditions. In the present review, the discussion has been divided into three main parts. The first part deals with an overview of the more relevant results from the experimental research, while the second part is devoted to a brief discussion on analytically and semi-analytically derived results. The third part overviews the results for laminar and turbulent flows from computational fluid dynamics (CFD) simulations. A short review on the investigation of heat transfer enhancement in corrugated and twisted helical pipes has also been added to the CFD part. Other aspects of the research regarding flow in helical pipes, such as flow visualization and entropy generation due to viscous dissipation and heat transfer, were discussed in a separate section. Although significant progress has been achieved in understanding the complex flow interactions that occur in a helical pipe, there still remains much work to be completed to address the effects of pipe corrugations and deformations on the flow, particularly for the case of randomly spaced corrugations and surface ribs. On the side of multiphase flows, nearly all the research has focused on two-phase flows in helical pipes. Moreover, these studies are mostly on air–water flows, which are different from the helical pipe flows that operate in the environment of the oil and gas industry. Also, the geometrical parameters of the coil pipes employed in most experimental and numerical studies differ from the actual operating conditions in heat transfer areas. In general, several important issues concerning complex thermal hydraulic mechanisms in nuclear reactors and other industrial devices still remain to be solved. However, some of these issues are closer than ever to be at least partially solved owing to the more and more powerful computational resources that are becoming available today.

Author Contributions: L.D.G.S. was responsible for writing—original draft preparation and for writing—review and editing, project administration and funding acquisition. C.E.A.-R. was responsible for writing—review and editing and for organizing the figures and permissions. O.R. organized the reviewed literature. All authors have read and agreed to the published version of the manuscript.

Funding: This research was funded by the European Union's Horizon 2020 Programme under the ENERXICO Project grant number 828947 and by the Mexican CONAHCYT-SENER-Hidrocarburos under grant number B-S-69926 and by CONAHCYT under project number 368.

Institutional Review Board Statement: Not applicable.

Informed Consent Statement: Not applicable.

Data Availability Statement: This study did not report any data.

Acknowledgments: One of us (C.E.A.-R.) thanks CONAHCYT for financial support from Project No. 368. C.E.A.-R. is a research fellow commissioned to the University of Guanajuato (under Project No. 368).

Conflicts of Interest: The authors declare no conflict of interest. The funders had no role in the design of the study; in the collection, analyses or interpretation of data; in the writing of the manuscript or in the decision to publish the results.

Nomenclature

a	Constant factor
a'	Semi-major axis of elliptical cross-section (m)
b	Constant factor
b'	Semi-minor axis of elliptical cross-section (m)
$\mathcal{D}$	Characteristic number (dimensionless)
d	Diameter of circular cross-section (m)
D	Pipe inner diameter (m)
D_c	Coil diameter (m)
De	Dean number (dimensionless)
De′	Generalized Dean number (dimensionless)
D_{eq}	Equivalent coil diameter (m)
e	Roughness height (mm)
Eu	Euler number (dimensionless)
$\mathbf{f}$	Entropy flux vector (W m^{-2} K^{-1})
F	Fanning friction factor (dimensionless)
F_D	Darcy–Weisbach friction factor (dimensionless)
FoM	Figure of merit
F_s	Friction factor for laminar flow (dimensionless)
Gn	Germano number (dimensionless)
h	Coil pitch (m)
h'	Pitch of spiral corrugation (mm)
K	Behavior index
k	Thermal conductivity (W m^{-1} K^{-1})
L	Straight pipe section (m)
L_c	Length of coil portion (m)
n	Consistency index
Nu	Nusselt number (dimensionless)
p	Pressure (Pa)
p'	Twist pitch (mm)
p_i	Regression parameters
P_{pump}	Pumping power (W)

Pr	Prandtl number (dimensionless)
q	Heat flux (W m^{-2})
Q	Volumetric flow rate (m^3 s^{-1})
$\dot{Q}_T$	Total heat transfer rate (W)
R	Pipe inner radius (m)
R_c	Helical coil radius (m)
Re	Reynolds number (dimensionless)
Re$'$	Generalized Reynolds number (dimensionless)
Re$_{cr}$	Critical Reynolds number (dimensionless)
Re$_\tau$	Frictional Reynolds number (dimensionless)
S	Entropy generation rate per unit volume (W m^{-3} K^{-1})
$\mathbb{T}$	Viscous stress tensor (N m^{-2})
T_b	Bulk temperature (K)
T_{mean}	Mean temperature (K)
$\bar{T}_{\text{w}}$	Inner wall temperature (K)
v	Mean flow velocity (m s^{-1})
$\mathbf{v}$	Velocity vector (m s^{-1})
v_τ	Friction velocity (m s^{-1})
Δp	Differential pressure (Pa)
Δs	Section length (m)
$\bar{\tau}_{\text{w}}$	Averaged wall shear stress (kg m^{-1} s^{-2})
λ	Ratio of torsion to curvature ratio (dimensionless)
β_0	Torsion parameter (dimensionless)
∇	Nabla operator (m^{-1})
Greek letters	
ν	Kinematic viscosity (m^2 s^{-1})
γ	Curvature ratio (dimensionless)
α	Helix angle, lift angle
β	Ratio of pitch to length of one helical turn (dimensionless)
ρ	Density (kg m^{-3})
γ'	Generalized curvature ratio (dimensionless)
η	Torsion of the helix (dimensionless)
λ'	Flow pattern transition parameter (dimensionless)
α'	Constant
β'	Constant
ϕ	Concentration (dimensionless)
κ	Dimensionless curvature
τ	Dimensionless helix torsion
Φ	Rotation angle
θ	Angle
μ	Dynamic viscosity (kg m^{-1} s^{-1})
Subscripts	
c	Curvature, coil
D	Darcy
cr	Critical
0	Initial, lower
eq	Equivalent
w	Wall
b	Bulk
i	Integer index
τ	Shear stress
ref	Reference
g	Gas, global
l	Liquid
tp	Two-phase
μ	Viscous
h	Heat transfer

References

1. Hagen, G. Über die Bewengung des Wassers in engen zylindrischen Röhr. *Poggendorffs Ann.* **1839**, *46*, 423–442.
2. Poiseuille, J.L.M. Recherches expérimentales sur le mouvement del liquides dans les tubes de trés-petits diamètres. *Con Rendus* **1842**, *11*, 961–967.
3. Darcy, H. *Recherches Expérimentales Relatives au Mouvement de l'Eau dans les Tuyaux*; Mallet-Bachelier: Paris, France, 1857.
4. Reynolds, O. An experimental investigation of the circumstances which determine whether the motion of water should be d or sinuous, and of the law of resistance in parallel channels. *Proc. R. Soc. Lond.* **1883**, *11*, 84–89.
5. Boussinesq, M.J. Mémoire sur l'influence des frottements dans le mouvement réguliers des fluides. *J. Math. Pures Appl.* **186** 377–424.
6. Thomson, J. On the origin of windings of rivers in alluvial plains with remarks on the flow of water round bends in pipes. *R. Soc. Lond.* **1876**, *25*, 5–8.
7. Thomson, J. Experimental demonstration in respect to the origin of windings of rivers in alluvial plains, and to the mode of of water round bends of pipes. *Proc. R. Soc. Lond.* **1877**, *26*, 356–357.
8. Williams, G.S.; Hubbell, C.W.; Fenkell, G.H. Experiments at Detroit, Mich.; on the effect of curvature upon the flow of wat pipes. *Trans. Ofthe Am. Soc. Civ. Eng.* **1902**, *47*, 1–196. [CrossRef]
9. Eustice, J. Flow of water in curved pipes. *Proc. R. Soc. A* **1910**, *84*, 107–118.
10. Eustice, J. Experiments on stream-line motion in curved pipes. *Proc. R. Soc. A* **1911**, *85*, 119–131.
11. White, C.M. Streamline flow through curved pipes. *Proc. R. Soc. A* **1929**, *123*, 645–663.
12. Kalpakli Vester, A.; Örlü, R.; Alfredsson, P.H. Turbulent flows in curved pipes: Recent advances in experiments and simula *Appl. Mech.* **2016**, *68*, 050802. [CrossRef]
13. Dean, W.R. Note on the motion of fluid in a curved pipe. *Philos. Mag.* **1927**, *4*, 208–223. [CrossRef]
14. Dean, W.R. The stream-line motion of fluid in a curved pipe. *Philos. Mag.* **1928**, *5*, 671–695. [CrossRef]
15. Prabhanjan, G.S.V.; Raghavan, G.; Rennie, T.J. Comparison of heat transfer rates between a straight tube heat exchanger a helically coiled heat exchanger. *Int. Commun. Heat Mass Transf.* **2002**, *29*, 185–191. [CrossRef]
16. Carelli, M.D.; Conway, L.E.; Oriani, L.; Petrovič, B.; Lombardi, C.V.; Ricotti, M.E.; Barroso, A.C.O.; Collado, J.M.; Cinot Todreas, N.E.; et al. The design and safety features of the IRIS reactor. *Nucl. Des.* **2004**, *230*, 151–167. [CrossRef]
17. Di Piazza, I.; Ciofalo, M. Numerical prediction of turbulent flow and heat transfer in helically coiled pipes. *Int. J. Therm. Sci.* *49*, 653–663. [CrossRef]
18. Pioro, I.L. *Handbook of Generation IV Nuclear Reactors*; Woodhead Publishing Series in Energy: Thorston, UK, 2016.
19. Gill, J.; Singh, J. Use of artificial neural network approach for depicting mass flow rate of R134a/LPG refrigerant through str and helical coiled adiabatic capillary tubes of vapor compression refrigeration system. *Int. Refrig.* **2018**, *86*, 228–238. [Cross
20. Liu, Y.; Chen, Y.; Zhou, Y.; Wang, D.; Wang, Y.; Wang, D. Experimental research on the thermal performance of PEX helica pipes for heating the biogas digester. *Appl. Therm. Eng.* **2019**, *147*, 167–176. [CrossRef]
21. Moll, R.; Veyret, D.; Charbit, F.; Moulin, P. Dean vortices applied to membrane process: Part I. Experimental approach. *J. M Sci.* **2007**, *288*, 307–320. [CrossRef]
22. Abdel-Aziz, M.H.; Mansour, L.A.S.; Sedahmed, G.H. Study of the rate of liquid-solid mass transfer controlled processes in h tubes under turbulent flow conditions. *Chem. Eng. Process. Process Intensif.* **2010**, *49*, 643–648. [CrossRef]
23. Mansour, M.; Liu, Z.; Janiga, G.; Nigam, K.D.; Sundmacher, K.; Thévenin, D.; Zähringer, K. Numerical study of liquid-li mixing in helical pipes. *Chem. Eng. Sci.* **2017**, *172*, 250–261. [CrossRef]
24. Andhare, A.M.; Kriplani, V.M.; Modak, J.P. Heat transfer studies in helically coiled tube: A review. *Int. J. Res. Mech.* **2014**, *2*, 7
25. Pawar, Y.; Zare, A.; Sarode, A. Helically coiled tube with different geometry and curvature ratios on convective heat transf review. *Int. Innov. Res. Adv. Eng.* **2016**, *3*, 19–23.
26. Berger, S.A.; Talbot, L.; Yao, L.S. Flow in curved pipes. *Annu. Rev. Fluid Mech.* **1983**, *15*, 461–512. [CrossRef]
27. Ito, H. Flow in curved pipes. *Bull. JMSE* **1987**, *30*, 543–552. [CrossRef]
28. Naphon, P.; Wongwises, S. A review of flow and heat transfer characteristics in curved tubes. *Renew. Sustain. Energy Rev.* **200** 463–490. [CrossRef]
29. Vashisth, S.; Kumar, V.; Nigam, K.D.P. A review on the potential applications of curved geometries in process industry. *Ind. Chem. Res.* **2008**, *47*, 3291–3337. [CrossRef]
30. Taylor, G.I. The criterion for turbulence in curved pipes. *Proc. R. Soc. Lond. A* **1929**, *124*, 243–249.
31. Viswanath, P.R.; Narasimha, R.; Prabhu, A. Visualization of relaminarizing flows. *J. Indian Inst. Sci.* **1978**, *60*, 159–165.
32. Narasimha, R.; Sreenivasan, K.R. Relaminarization of fluid flows. *Adv. Appl. Mech.* **1979**, *19*, 221–309.
33. Sreenivasan, K.R.; Strykowski, P.J. Stabilization effects in flow through helically coiled pipes. *Exp. Fluids* **1983**, *1*, 31–36. [Cros
34. Austen, D.S.; Soliman, H.M. Laminar flow and heat transfer in helically coiled tubes with substantial pitch. *Exp. Therm. Flui* **1988**, *1*, 183–194. [CrossRef]
35. Das, S.K. Water flow through helical coils in turbulent conditions. *Can. J. Chem. Eng.* **1993**, *71*, 971–973. [CrossRef]
36. Liu, S.; Atacan, A.; Nasr-El-Din, H.A.; Masliyah, J.H. An experimental study of pressure drop in helical pipes. *Proc. R. Soc. A* **1994**, *444*, 307–316.
37. De Amicis, J.; Cammi, A.; Colombo, L.P.M.; Colombo, M. Experimental and numerical study of the laminar flow in heli coiled pipes. *Prog. Nucl. Energy* **2014**, *76*, 206–215. [CrossRef]

Rakhsha, M.; Akbaridoust, F.; Abbassi, A.; Saffar-Avval, M. Experimental and numerical investigations of turbulent forced convection flow of nano-fluid in helical coiled tubes at constant surface temperature. *Powder Technol.* **2015**, *283*, 178–189. [CrossRef]
Abushammala, O.; Hreiz, R.; Lemaître, C.; Favre, É. Laminar flow friction factor in highly curved helical pipes: Numerical investigation, predictive correlation and experimental validation using a 3D-printed model. *Chem. Sci.* **2019**, *207*, 1030–1039. [CrossRef]
Patankar, S.V.; Pratap, V.S.; Spalding, D.B. Prediction of laminar flow and heat transfer in helically coiled pipes. *J. Fluid Mech.* **1974**, *62*, 539–551. [CrossRef]
Manlapaz, R.L.; Churchill, S.W. Fully developed laminar flow in a helically coiled tube of finite pitch. *Chem. Eng. Commun.* **1980**, *7*, 57–78. [CrossRef]
Wang, J.-W.; Andrews, J.R.G. Numerical simulation of flow in helical ducts. *AIChE J.* **1995**, *41*, 1071–1080. [CrossRef]
Jayakumar, J.S.; Mahajani, S.M.; Mandal, J.C.; Iyer, K.N.; Vijayan, P.K. CFD analysis of single-phase flows inside helically coiled tubes. *Comput. Chem. Eng.* **2010**, *34*, 430–446. [CrossRef]
Ahmadloo, E.; Sobhanifar, N.; Hosseini, F.S. Computational fluid dynamics study on water flow in a hollow helical pipe. *Open J. Fluid Dyn.* **2014**, *4*, 133–139. [CrossRef]
Colombo, M.; Cammi, A.; Ricotti, M.E. Assessment of different turbulence models in helically coiled pipes through comparison with experimental data. In Proceedings of the 2012 20th International Conference on Nuclear Energy Collocated with the ASME 2012 Power Conference, Anaheim, California, USA, 30 July–3 August 2012; Paper No.: ICONE20-Power2012-54546, pp. 273–283.
Faraj, A.F.; Azzawi, I.D.J.; Yahya, S.G. Pitch variations study on helically coiled pipe in turbulent flow region using CFD. *Int. J. Heat Technol.* **2020**, *38*, 775–784. [CrossRef]
Kurnia, J.C.; Sasmito, A.P.; Shamim, T.; Mujumdar, A.S. Numerical investigation of heat transfer and entropy generation of laminar flow in helical tubes with various cross sections. *Appl. Therm. Eng.* **2016**, *102*, 849–860. [CrossRef]
Adhikari, B.; Maharjan, S. Numerical simulation of helically coiled closed loop pulsating heat pipe. *Int. J. Eng. Manag.* **2019**, *9*, 206–212. [CrossRef]
Tang, L.; Tang, Y.; Parameswaran, S. A numerical study of flow characteristcs in a helical pipe. *Adv. Mech. Eng.* **2016**, *8*, 1–8. [CrossRef]
Demagh, Y.; Bitam, E.; Bordja, L. Comparative numerical study on pressure drop in helically coiled and longitudinally C-shaped pipes. *SN Appl. Sci.* **2020**, *2*, 1570. [CrossRef]
Wang, J.; Liu, Y.; Ding, R. Analysis of heat transfer and flow characteristics of a helically coiled tube with twisted elliptical in a low Reynolds number flow. *Processes* **2022**, *10*, 2229. [CrossRef]
Colombo, M.; Cammi, A.; Guédon, G.R.; Inzoli, F.; Ricotti, M.E. CFD study of an air-water flow inside helically coiled pipes. *Prog. Nucl. Energy* **2015**, *85*, 462–472. [CrossRef]
Murata, S.; Miyake, Y.; Inaba, T.; Ogata, H. Laminar flow in a helically coiled pipe. *Bull. JSME* **1981**, *24*, 355–362. [CrossRef]
Zhang, J.; Zhang, B. Fluid flow in a helical pipe. *Acta Mech. Sin.* **1999**, *15*, 299–312.
Marušić-Paloka, E.; Pažanin, I. Fluid flow through a helical pipe. *Z. Angew. Math. Phys.* **2007**, *58*, 81–99. [CrossRef]
Prattipati, R.; Narla, V.K.; Pendyala, S. Effect of viscosity on entropy generation for laminar flow in helical pipes. *J. Therm.* **2021**, *7*, 1100–1109. [CrossRef]
Kumar, A. Pressure-driven flows in helical pipes: Bounds on flow rate and friction factor. *J. Fluid Mech.* **2020**, *904*, A5. [CrossRef]
Weisbach, J.L. *Die Experimental-Hydraulik*; Kessinger's Legacy Reprints: Whitefish, MN, USA, 1855.
Adler, M. Strömung in gekrümmten Rohren. *Z. Angew. Math. Mech.* **1934**, *14*, 257–275. [CrossRef]
Wattendorf, F.L. A study of the effect of curvature on fully developed turbulent flow. *Proc. R. Soc. A* **1935**, *148*, 565–598.
Kurokawa, M.; Cheng, K.C.; Shi, L. Flow visualization of relaminarization phenomena in curved pipes and related measurements. *J. Vis.* **1998**, *1*, 9–28. [CrossRef]
Webster, D.R.; Humphrey, J.A.C. Experimental observations of flow instability in a helical coil (data bank contribution). *J. Fluids Eng.* **1993**, *115*, 436–443. [CrossRef]
Webster, D.R.; Humphrey, J.A.C. Traveling wave instability in helical coil flow. *Phys. Fluids* **1997**, *9*, 407–418. [CrossRef]
Dennis, S.C.R.; Ng, M. Dual solutions for steady laminar flow through a curved tube. *Q. J. Mech. Appl. Math.* **1982**, *35*, 305–324. [CrossRef]
Ramshankar, R.; Sreenivasan, K.R. A paradox concerning the extended Stokes series solution for the pressure drop in coiled pipes. *Phys. Fluids* **1988**, *31*, 1339–1347. [CrossRef]
Wang, C.Y. On the low-Reynolds-number flow in a helical pipe. *J. Fluid Mech.* **1981**, *108*, 185–194. [CrossRef]
Germano, M. On the effect of the torsion in helical pipe flow. *J. Fluid Mech.* **1982**, *125*, 1–8. [CrossRef]
Kao, H.C. Torsion effect on fully developed flow in a helical pipe. *J. Fluid Mech.* **1987**, *184*, 335–356. [CrossRef]
Germano, M. The Dean equations extended to a helical pipe flow. *J. Fluid Mech.* **1989**, *203*, 289–305. [CrossRef]
Tuttle, E.R. Laminar flow in twisted pipes. *J. Fluid Mech.* **1990**, *219*, 545–570. [CrossRef]
Liu, S.; Masliyah, J.H. Axially-invariant laminar flow in helical pipes with a finite pitch. *J. Fluid Mech.* **1993**, *251*, 315–353. [CrossRef]
Kubair, V.; Varrier, C.B.S. Pressure drop for liquid flow in helical coils. *Trans. Indian Inst. Chem. Eng.* **1961**, *14*, 93–97.
Ito, H. Laminar flow in curved pipes. *Z. Angew. Math. Mech.* **1969**, *11*, 653–663. [CrossRef]

74. Srinivasan, P.S.; Nandapurkar, S.S.; Holland, F.A. Pressure drop and heat transfer in coils. *Chem. Eng.* **1968**, *218*, 113–119.
75. Ward-Smith, A.J. *Internal Flow: The Fluid Dynamics of Flow in Pipes and Ducts*; Clarendon Press: Oxford, UK, 1980.
76. White, C.M. Fluid friction and its relation to heat transfer. *Trans. Inst. Chem. Eng.* **1932**, *10*, 66–86.
77. McCabe, W.L.; Smith, C.J.; Harriott, P. *Unit Operations of Chemical Engineering*; McGraw-Hill: New York, NY, USA, 1993.
78. Prandtl, L. *Führer durch die Strömungslehere: Grundlagen und Phänomene*; F. Vieweg: Braunschweig, Germany, 1949.
79. Hasson, D. Streamline flow resistance in coils. *Res. Corresp.* **1955**, *1*, S1.
80. Topakoğlu, H.C. Steady laminar flows of an incompressible viscous fluid in curved pipes. *J. Math. Mech.* **1967**, *16*, 1321–133
81. Van Dyke, M. Extended Stokes series: Laminar flow through a loosely coiled pipe. *J. Fluid Mech.* **1978**, *86*, 129–145. [CrossR
82. Barua, S.N. On secondary flow in stationary curved pipes. *Q. J. Mech. Appl. Math.* **1963**, *16*, 61–77. [CrossRef]
83. Mori, Y.; Nakayama, W. Study on forced convective heat transfer in curved pipes: (1st report, laminar region). *Int. J. Heat M Transf.* **1965**, *8*, 67–82. [CrossRef]
84. Liu, S. Laminar Flow and Heat Transfer in Helical Pipes with Finite Pitch. Ph.D. Thesis, University of Alberta, Edmonton, Canada, 1992.
85. Ali, S. Pressure drop correlations for flow through regular helical coil tubes. *Fluid Dyn. Res.* **2001**, *28*, 295–310. [CrossRef]
86. Gupta, R.; Wanchoo, R.K.; Jafar Ali, T.R.M. Laminar flow in helical coils: A parametric study. *Ind. Eng. Chem. Res.* **2011** 1150–1157. [CrossRef]
87. Periasamy, G.; Mouleeswaran, S.; Venugopal, P.R.; Perumal, C. Investigation of hydrodynamic flow characteristics in helical c with ovality and wrinkles. *J. Mech. Eng.* **2021**, *67*, 570–579. [CrossRef]
88. Mishra, P.; Gupta, S.N. Momentum transfer in curved pipes. 1. Newtonian fluids. *Ind. Eng. Chem. Process Des. Dev.* **1979** 130–137. [CrossRef]
89. Jensen, M.K.; Bergles, A.E. Critical heat flux in helical coiled tubes. *Trans. ASME* **1981**, *103*, 660–666. [CrossRef]
90. Manlapaz, R.L.; Churchill, S.W. Fully developed laminar convection from a helical coil. *Chem. Eng. Commun.* **1981**, *9*, 185– [CrossRef]
91. Seban, R.A.; McLaughlin, E.F. Heat transfer in tube coils with laminar and turbulent flow. *Int. J. Heat Mass Transf.* **1963**, *6*, 387– [CrossRef]
92. Dravid, A.N.; Smith, K.A.; Merrill, E.W.; Brian, P.L.T. Effect of secondary fluid motion on laminar flow heat transfer in helic coiled tubes. *AIChE J.* **1971**, *17*, 1114–1122. [CrossRef]
93. Xin, R.C.; Ebadian, M.A. The effects of Prandtl numbers on local and average convective heat transfer characteristics in he pipes. *J. Heat Transf.* **1997**, *119*, 467–473. [CrossRef]
94. Cioncolini, A.; Santini, L. An experimental investigation regarding the laminar and turbulent flow transition in helically co pipes. *Exp. Fluid Sci.* **2006**, *30*, 367–380. [CrossRef]
95. Zheng, X.; Lu, X.; Gao, Y.; Jin, D.; Hu, Y.; Hu, Y.; Mao, Y. Experimental study on friction pressure drop and circumferential transfer characteristics in helical tubes. *Front. Energy Res.* **2023**, *11*, 1204850. [CrossRef]
96. Ito, H. Friction factors for turbulent flow in curved pipes. *J. Basic Eng.* **1959**, *81*, 123–132. [CrossRef]
97. Ju, H.; Huang, Z.; Xu, Y.; Duan, B.; Yu, Y. Hydraulic performance of small bending radius helical coil-pipe. *J. Nucl. Sci. Tec* **2001**, *38*, 826–831. [CrossRef]
98. Hardik, B.K.; Prabhu, S.V. Boiling pressure drop and local heat transfer distribution of helical coils with water and low pres *Int. Therm. Sci.* **2017**, *114*, 44–63. [CrossRef]
99. Xiao, Y.; Hu, Z.; Chen, S.; Gu, H. Experimental study of two-phase frictional pressure drop of steam-water in helically co tubes with small coil diameters and high pressure. *Appl. Therm. Eng.* **2018**, *132*, 18–29. [CrossRef]
100. Rennie, T.J.; Raghavan, V.G.S. Experimental studies of a double-pipe helical heat exchanger. *Exp. Therm. Fluid Sci.* **2005** 919–924. [CrossRef]
101. Mandal, M.M.; Nigam, K.D.P. Experimental study on pressure drop and heat transfer of turbulent flow in tube helical exchanger. *Ind. Eng. Res.* **2009**, *48*, 9318–9324. [CrossRef]
102. Ghorbani, N.; Taherian, H.; Gorji, M.; Mirgolbabaei, H. An experimental study of thermal performance of shell-and-coil exchangers. *Int. Commun. Heat Mass Transf.* **2010**, *37*, 775–781. [CrossRef]
103. Pawar, S.S.; Sunnapwar, V.K. Studies of convective heat transfer through helical coils. *Heat Mass Transf.* **2013**, *49*, 1741– [CrossRef]
104. Pimenta, T.A.; Campos, L.M. Heat transfer coefficients from Newtonian and non-Newtonian fluids flowing in laminar regim a helical coil. *Int. J. Heat Mass Transf.* **2013**, *58*, 676–690. [CrossRef]
105. Hardik, B.K.; Baburajan, P.K.; Prabhu, S.V. Local heat transfer coefficient in helical coils with single phase flow. *Int. J. Heat Transf.* **2015**, *89*, 522–538. [CrossRef]
106. Kruthiventi, S.S.; Rasu, N.G.; Kruthiventi, S.S.; Rao, Y.V.H. Coiled tube heat exchangers—A review. *Int. J. Mech. Eng. Tec* **2018**, *9*, 895–904.
107. Zhao, H.; Li, X.; Wu, Y.; Wu, X. Friction factor and Nusselt number correlations for forced convection in helical tubes. *Int. J. Mass Transf.* **2020**, *155*, 119759. [CrossRef]
108. Ayuob, S.; Mahmood, M.; Ahmad, N.; Waqas, A.; Saeed, H. Development and validation of Nusselt number correlations helical coil based energy storage integrated with solar water heating systems. *J. Energy Storage* **2022**, *55*, 105777. [CrossRef]

Aly, W.I.; Inaba, H.; Haruki, N.; Horibe, A. Drag and heat transfer reduction phenomena of drag-reducing surfactant solutions in straight and helical pipes. *J. Heat Transf.* **2006**, *128*, 800–810. [CrossRef]
Jamshidi, N.; Farhadi, M.; Ganji, D.D.; Sedighi, K. Experimental analysis of heat transfer enhancement in shell and helical tube heat exchangers. *Appl. Therm. Eng.* **2013**, *51*, 644–652. [CrossRef]
Hashemi, S.M.; Behabadi, M.A.A. An empirical study on heat transfer and pressure drop characteristics of CuO-base oil nanofluid flow in a horizontal helically coiled tube under constant heat flux. *Int. Commun. Heat Mass Transf.* **2012**, *39*, 144–151. [CrossRef]
Pawar, S.S.; Sunnapwar, V.K. Experimental studies of heat transfer to Newtonian and non-Newtonian fluids in helical coils with laminar and turbulent flow. *Exp. Therm. Fluid Sci.* **2013**, *44*, 792–804. [CrossRef]
Kumbhare, B.P.; Purandare, P.S.; Mali, K.V. Experimental analysis of square and circular coil for heat recovery system. *Int. J. Sci.* **2012**, *2*, 318–327.
Jeschke, H. Wärmeübergang und Druckverlust in Rohrschlangen. *VDI Z.* **1925**, *69*, 24–28.
Rogers, G.F.C.; Mayhew, Y.R. Heat transfer and pressure loss in helically coiled tube with turbulent flow. *Int. J. Heat Mass Transf.* **1964**, *7*, 1207–1216. [CrossRef]
Mori, Y.; Nakayama, W. Study of forced convective heat transfer in curved pipes (3rd report, theoretical analysis under the condition of uniform wall temperature and practical formulae). *Int. J. Heat Mass Transf.* **1967**, *10*, 681–695. [CrossRef]
Gnielinski, V. Heat transfer and pressure drop in helically coiled tubes. In *International Heat Transfer Conference 8*; Digital Library, Bergel House Inc.: Kington, UK, 1986; pp. 2847–2854.
Bai, B.; Guo, L.; Feng, Z.; Chen, X. Turbulent heat transfer in a horizontal helically coiled tube. *Heat Transf.* **1999**, *28*, 395–403. [CrossRef]
Schmidt, E.F. Wärmeübergang und Druckverlust in Rohrschlangen. *Chem. Ing. Tech.* **1967**, *39*, 781–789. [CrossRef]
Jones, J.R. Flow of a non-Newtonian liquid in a curved pipe. *Q. J. Mech. Appl. Math.* **1960**, *13*, 428–443. [CrossRef]
Thomas, R.H.; Walters, K. On the flow of an elastico-viscous liquid in a curved pipe under a pressure gradient. *J. Fluid Mech.* **1963**, *16*, 228–242. [CrossRef]
Mashelkar, R.A.; Devarajan, G.V. Secondary flows of non-Newtonian fluids. Part I—Laminar boundary layer flow of a generalized non-Newtonian fluid in coiled tube. *Trans. Inst. Chem. Eng.* **1976**, *54*, 100–107.
Mujawar, B.A.; Rao, M.R. Flow on non-Newtonian fluids through helical coils. *Ind. Eng. Chem. Process Des. Dev.* **1978**, *17*, 22–27. [CrossRef]
Madlener, K.; Frey, B.; Ciezki, H.K. Generalized Reynolds number for non-Newtonian fluids. *Prog. Propuls. Phys.* **2009**, *1*, 237–250.
Krishna, B.S.V.S.R. Prediction of pressure drop in helical coil with single phase flow of non-Newtonian fluid. *Int. J. Appl. Res. Mech. Eng.* **2012**, *1*, 6. [CrossRef]
Gul, S.; Erge, O.; van Oort, E. Frictional pressure losses of non-Newtonian fluids in helical pipes: Applications for automated rheology measurements. *J. Nat. Gas Sci. Eng.* **2020**, *73*, 103042. [CrossRef]
Hart, J.; Ellenberger, J.; Hamersma, P.J. Single- and two-phase flow through helically coiled tubes. *Chem. Eng. Sci.* **1988**, *43*, 775–783. [CrossRef]
Pimenta, T.A.; Campos, J.B.I.M. Friction losses of Newtonian and non-Newtonian fluids flowing in laminar regime in a helical coil. *Exp. Therm. Fluid Sci.* **2012**, *36*, 194–204. [CrossRef]
McConalogue, D.J.; Srivastava, R.S. Motion of a fluid in a curved tube. *Proc. R. Soc. Lond. A* **1968**, *307*, 37–53.
Chen, W.H.; Jan, R. The characteristics of laminar flow in a helical circular pipe. *J. Fluid Mech.* **1992**, *244*, 241–256. [CrossRef]
Xie, G.D. Torsion effect on secondary flow in helical pipe. *Int. Heat Fluid Flow* **1990**, *11*, 114–119. [CrossRef]
Bolinder, C.J. First- and higher-order effects of curvature and torsion on the flow in a helical rectangular duct. *J. Fluid Mech.* **1996**, *314*, 113–138. [CrossRef]
Marušić-Paloka, E. The effects of flexion and torsion for a fluid flow through a curved pipe. *Appl. Math. Optim.* **2001**, *44*, 245–272. [CrossRef]
Austin, L.R.; Seader, J.D. Fully developed viscous flow in coiled circular pipes. *AIChE J.* **1973**, *19*, 85–94. [CrossRef]
Tarbell, J.M.; Samuels, M.R. Momentum and heat transfer in helical coils. *Chem. Eng. J.* **1973**, *5*, 117–127. [CrossRef]
Huang, W.; Gu, D. A study of secondary flow and fluid resistance in rectangular, helical coiled channel. *Int. Chem. Eng.* **1989**, *29*, 480–485.
Choi, H.K.; Park, S.O. Laminar entrance flow in curved annular ducts. *Int. J. Heat Fluid Flow* **1992**, *13*, 41–49.
Srinivasan, P.S.; Nandapurkar, S.S.; Holland, F.A. Friction factors for coils. *Trans. Inst. Chem. Eng.* **1970**, *48*, T156–T161.
Janssen, L.A.M.; Hoogendoorn, C.J. Laminar convective heat transfer in helical coiled tubes. *Int. J. Heat Mass Transf.* **1978**, *21*, 1197–1206. [CrossRef]
Mori, Y.; Nakayama, W. Study of forced convective heat transfer in curved pipes (2nd report, turbulent region). *Int. J. Heat Mass Transf.* **1967**, *10*, 37–59. [CrossRef]
Yang, G.; Ebadian, M.A. Turbulent forced convection in a helicoidal pipe with substantial pitch. *Int. J. Heat Mass Transf.* **1996**, *39*, 2015–2022. [CrossRef]
Lin, C.X.; Ebadian, M.A. Developing turbulent convective heat transfer in helical pipes. *Int. J. Heat Mass Transf.* **1997**, *40*, 3861–3873. [CrossRef]
Li, L.J.; Lin, C.X.; Ebadian, M.A. Turbulent mixed convective heat transfer in the entrance region of a curved pipe with uniform-wall temperature. *Int. J. Heat Mass Transf.* **1998**, *41*, 3793–3805. [CrossRef]

144. Chagny, C.; Castelain, C.; Peerhossaini, H. Chaotic heat transfer for heat exchanger design and comparison with a regular re for a large range of Reynolds numbers. *Appl. Therm. Eng.* **2000**, *20*, 1615–1648. [CrossRef]
145. Kumar, V.; Saini, S.; Sharma, M.; Nigam, K.D.P. Pressure drop and heat transfer in tube-in-tube helical heat exchanger. *Chem. Sci.* **2006**, *61*, 4403–4416. [CrossRef]
146. Jayakumar, J.S.; Mahajani, S.M.; Mandal, J.C.; Vijayan, P.K.; Bhoi, R. Experimental and CFD estimation of heat transfer in heli coiled heat exchangers. *Chem. Eng. Res. Des.* **2008**, *86*, 221–232. [CrossRef]
147. Ciofalo, M.; Di Liberto, M.; Marotta, G. On the influence of curvature and torsion on turbulence in helically coiled pipes. *J. Conf.* **2013**, *501*, 012025. [CrossRef]
148. Li, Y.; Wu, J.; Wang, H.; Kou, L.; Tian, X. Fluid flow and heat transfer characteristics in helical tubes cooperating with s corrugation. *Energy Procedia* **2012**, *17*, 791–800. [CrossRef]
149. Yildiz, C.; Biçer, Y.; Pehlivan, D. Heat transfer and pressure drop in a heat exchanger with a helical pipe containing inside spr *Energy Conserv. Manag.* **1997**, *38*, 619–624. [CrossRef]
150. Zachár, A. Analysis of coiled-tube heat exchangers to improve heat transfer rate with spirally corrugated wall. *Int. J. Heat Transf.* **2010**, *53*, 3928–3939. [CrossRef]
151. Salimpour, M.R. Heat transfer coefficients of shell and coiled tube heat exchangers. *Exp. Therm. Fluid Sci.* **2009**, *33*, 203- [CrossRef]
152. Yanase, S.; Goto, N.; Yamamoto, K. Dual solutions of the flow through a curved tube. *Fluid Dyn. Res.* **1989**, *5*, 191–201. [Cross
153. Pachghare, P.R.; Mahalle, A.M. Thermo-hydrodynamics of close loop pulsating heat pipe: An experimental study. *J. Mech Technol.* **2014**, *28*, 3387–3394. [CrossRef]
154. Vijaya Kumar Reddy, K.; Sudheer Prem Kumar, B.; Ravi, G.; Kakaraparthi, A.; Vijaya Rao, P. CFD analysis of a helically c tube in tube heat exchanger. *Mater. Today Proc.* **2017**, *4*, 2341–2349. [CrossRef]
155. Islami, S.B.; Wesolowski, M.; Revell, W.; Chen, X. Virtual reality visualization of CFD simulated blood flow in cerebral aneur treated with flow diverter stents. *Appl. Sci.* **2021**, *11*, 8082. [CrossRef]
156. Liou, T.M. Flow visualization and LDV measurement of fully developed laminar flow in helically coiled tubes. *Exp. Fluids* *13*, 332–338. [CrossRef]
157. Chen, W.H.; Fan, C.N. Finite element analysis of incompressible viscous flow in helical pipe. *Comput. Mech.* **1986**, *1*, 281- [CrossRef]
158. Yamamoto, K.; Aribowo, A.; Hayamizu, Y.; Hirose, T.; Kawahara, K. Visualization of the flow in a helical pipe. *Fluid Dyn.* **2002**, *30*, 251–267. [CrossRef]
159. Şahin, A.Z. A second law comparison for optimum shape of duct subjected to constant wall temperature and laminar flow. *Mass Transf.* **1998**, *33*, 425–430. [CrossRef]
160. Ko, T.H. A numerical study on entropy generation and optimization for laminar forced convection in a rectangular curved with longitudinal ribs. *Int. J. Therm. Sci.* **2006**, *45*, 1113–1125. [CrossRef]
161. Sanchez, M.; Henderson, A.W.; Papavassiliou, D.V.; Lemley, E.C. Entropy generation in laminar flow junctions. In Proceedin the ASME 2012 Fluids Engineering Division Summer Meeting Collocated with the ASME 2012 Heat Transfer Summer Confe and ASME 2012 10th International Conference on Nanochannels, Microchannels, and Minichannels, Rio Grande, Puerto USA, 8–12 July 2012; pp. 325–330.
162. Skokouhmand, H.; Salimpour, M.R. Entropy generation analysis of fully developed laminar forced convection in a helical with uniform wall temperature. *Heat Mass Transf.* **2007**, *44*, 213–220. [CrossRef]
163. Satapathy, A.K. Thermodynamic optimization of a coiled tube heat exchanger under constant wall heat flux condition. *E* **2009**, *34*, 1122–1126. [CrossRef]
164. Bahiraei, F.; Saray, R.K.; Salehzadeh, A. Investigation of potential of improvement of helical coils based on avoidable unavoidable exergy destruction concepts. *Energy* **2011**, *36*, 3113–3119. [CrossRef]
165. Ahadi, M.; Abbassi, A. Entropy generation analysis of laminar forced convection through uniformly heated helical considering effects of high length and heat flux and temperature dependence of thermophysical properties. *Energy* **201** 322–332. [CrossRef]
166. Dizaji, H.S.; Jafarmadar, S.; Hashemian, M. The effect of flow, thermodynamic and geometrical characteristics on exergy lo shell and coiled tube heat exchangers. *Energy* **2015**, *91*, 678–684. [CrossRef]
167. Huminic, G.; Huminic, A. Heat transfer and entropy generation analyses of nanofluids in helically coiled tube-in-tube exchangers. *Int. Commun. Heat Mass Transf.* **2016**, *71*, 118–125. [CrossRef]
168. Pendyala, S.; Narla, V.K.; Prattipati, R. Second law analysis for turbulent flow in helical pipes subject to variable viscosity. *Conf. Proc.* **2020**, *2246*, 020038.
169. Sciacovelli, A.; Verda, V.; Sciubba, E. Entropy generation analysis as a design tool—A review. *Renew. Sustain. Energy Rev.* **201** 1167–1181. [CrossRef]
170. Rippel, G.R.; Eidt, C.M.; Jordan, H.B. Two-phase flow in a coiled tube. *Ind. Eng. Chem. Process Des. Dev.* **1965**, *5*, 32–39. [Cros
171. Lockhart, R.W.; Martinelli, R.C. Proposed correlation of data for isothermal two-phase, two-component flow in pipes. *Chem. Prog.* **1949**, *45*, 38–48.
172. Owhadi, A.; Bell, K.J.; Crain, B., Jr. Forced convection boiling inside helically-coiled tubes. *Int. J. Heat Mass Transf.* **196** 1779–1793. [CrossRef]

. Akagawa, B.K.; Sakaguchi, T.; Ueda, M. Study on gas-liquid two-phase flow in helically coiled tubes. *Bull. JSME* **1971**, *14*, 564–571. [CrossRef]
. Unal, H.C. Determination of void fraction, incipient point of boiling, and initial point of net vapor generation in sodium-heated helically coiled steam generator tubes. *J. Heat Mass Transf.* **1978**, *100*, 268–274.
Czop, V.; Barbier, D.; Dong, S. Pressure drop, void fraction and shear stress measurements in an adiabatic two-phase flow in a coiled tube. *Nucl. Des.* **1994**, *149*, 323–333. [CrossRef]
Xin, R.C.; Awwad, A.; Dong, Z.F.; Ebadian, M.A. An experimental study of single-phase and two-phase flow pressure drop in annular helicoidal pipes. *Int. J. Heat Fluid Flow* **1997**, *18*, 482–488. [CrossRef]
. Zhao, L.; Guo, L. Bai, B.; Hou, Y.; Zhang, X. Convective boiling heat transfer and two-phase flow characteristics inside a small horizontal helically coiled tubing once through a steam generator. *Int. J. Heat Mass Transf.* **2003**, *46*, 4779–4788. [CrossRef]
Santini, L.; Cioncolini, A.; Lombardi, C.; Ricotti, M.E. Two-phase pressure drops in a helically coiled steam generator. *Int. J. Heat Mass Transf.* **2008**, *51*, 4926–4939. [CrossRef]
. Chung, Y.-J.; Kim, H.J.; Chung, B.-D.; Lee, W.-J.; Kim, M.-H. Thermo-hydraulic characteristics of the helically coiled tube and the condesate heat exchanger for SMART. *Ann. Nucl. Energy* **2013**, *55*, 49–54. [CrossRef]
. Chung, Y.-J.; Bae, K.-H.; Kim, K.K.; Lee, W.-J. Boiling heat transfer and dryout in helically coiled tubes under different pressure conditions. *Ann. Nucl. Energy* **2014**, *71*, 298–303. [CrossRef]
. Zhou, C.; Song, M.; Xiao, S.; Zhou, X. Two-phase simulation of the pressure loss in helical channel. *Vibroeng. Procedia* **2018**, *19*, 259–263. [CrossRef]
. Sun, S.; Liu, J.; Zhang, W.; Yi, T. Frictional pressure drop for gas-liquid two-phase flow in coiled tubing. *Energies* **2022**, *15*, 8969. [CrossRef]
. Guo, L.; Feng, Z.; Chen, X. An experimental investigation of the frictional pressure drop of steam–water two–phase flow in helical coils. *Int. J. Heat Mass Transf.* **2001**, *44*, 2601–2610. [CrossRef]
. Zhao, H.; Li, X.; Wu, X. New friction factor equations developed for turbulent flows in rough helical tubes. *Int. J. Heat Mass Transf.* **2016**, *95*, 525–534. [CrossRef]
. Pouquet, A.; Yokoi, N. Helical fluid and (Hall)-MHD turbulence: A brief review. *Philos. Trans. R. Soc. A* **2022**, *380*, 20210087. [CrossRef] [PubMed]
Berger, M.A.; Field, G.B. The topological properties of magnetic helicity. *J. Fluid Mech.* **1984**, *147*, 133–148. [CrossRef]
. Moffat, H.K.; Tsinober, A. Helicity in laminar and turbulent flows. *Annu. Fluid Mech.* **1992**, *24*, 281–312. [CrossRef]
. Howard, L.N.; Gupta, A.S. On the hydrodynamic and hydromagnetic stability of swirling flows. *J. Fluid Mech.* **1962**, *14*, 463–476. [CrossRef]
Agrawal, G.S. Rayleigh-Taylor instability with Hall-currents. *J. Phys. Soc. Jpn.* **1969**, *26*, 561–565 [CrossRef]
. Ganguly, K.; Gupta, A.S. On the hydromagnetic stability of helical flows. *J. Math. Anal. Appl.* **1985**, *106*, 26–40. [CrossRef]
. Brunetti, D.; Graves, J.P.; Lazzaro, E.; Mariani, A.; Nowak, S.; Cooper, W.A.; Wahlberg, C. Helical equilibrium magnetohydrodynamic flow effects on the stability properties of low-*n* ideal external-infernal modes in weak shear tokamak configurations. *Plasma Phys. Control. Fusion* **2019**, *61*, 064003. [CrossRef]
. Brandenburg, A.; Subramanian, K. Astrophysical magnetic fields and nonlinear dynamo theory. *Phys. Rep.* **2005**, *417*, 1–209. [CrossRef]
Tobias, S.M. The turbulent dynamo. *J. Fluid Mech.* **2021**, *912*, 1–76. [CrossRef] [PubMed]
. Gailitis, A.; Freibergs, Y. Nonuniform model of a helical dynamo. *Magnetohydrodynamics* **1980**, *16*, 116–121.
. Gailitis, A.; Lielausis, O.; Dement'ev, S.; Platacis, E.; Cifersons, A.; Gerbeth, G.; Gundrum, T.; Stefani, F.; Christen, M.; Hänel, H.; et al. Detection of a flow induced magnetic field eigenmode in the Riga dynamo facility. *Phys. Rev.* **2000**, *84*, 4365–4368.
Gailitis, A.; Gerbeth, G.; Gundrum, T.; Lielausis, O.; Lipsbergs, G.; Platacis, E.; Stefani, F. Self-excitation in a helical liquid metal flow: The Riga dynamo experiments. *J. Plasma Phys.* **2018**, *84*, 735840301. [CrossRef]
Stefani, F.; Gundrum, T.; Gerbeth, G.; Rüdiger, G.; Schultz, M.; Szklarski, J.; Hollerbach, R. Experimental evidence for magnetorotational instability in a Taylor-Couette flow under the influence of a helical magnetic field. *Phys. Lett.* **2006**, *97*, 184502. [CrossRef]
Seilmayer, M.; Stefani, F.; Gundrum, T.; Weier, T.; Gerbeth, G.; Gellert, M.; Rüdiger, G. Experimental evidence for a transient Taylor instability in a cylindrical liquid-metal column. *Phys. Rev. Lett.* **2012**, *108*, 244501. [CrossRef]
Gilbert, A.D.; Frisch, U.; Pouquet, A. Helicity is unnecessary for alpha effect dynamos, but it helps. *Geophys. Astrophys. Fluid Dyn.* **1988**, *42*, 151–161. [CrossRef]
Andrievsky, A.; Chertovskih, R.; Zheligovsky, V. Pointwise vanishing velocity helicity of a flow does not preclude magnetic field generation. *Phys. Rev. E* **2019**, *99*, 033204. [CrossRef]

fluids

Communication

Pipe Flow of Suspensions of Cellulose Nanocrystals

Saumay Kinra and Rajinder Pal *

Department of Chemical Engineering, University of Waterloo, Waterloo, ON N2L 3G1, Canada; s2kinra@uwaterloo.ca
* Correspondence: rpal@uwaterloo.ca; Tel.: +1-519-888-4567 (ext. 32985)

Abstract: The pipeline flow behavior of suspensions of cellulose nanocrystals (CNCs) was investigated over the CNC concentration range of 0.24 to 3.65 wt% in different diameter pipelines. The CNC suspensions were Newtonian below the CNC concentration of 1 wt%. At higher concentrations, the CNC suspensions were non-Newtonian power-law fluids. For Newtonian CNC suspensions, the experimental friction factor–Reynolds number data were obtained only in the turbulent regime, and the data followed the Blasius equation closely. For power-law CNC suspensions, the experimental data of friction factor–Reynolds number covered both laminar and turbulent regimes. The experimental data followed the friction factor–Reynolds number relationships for power-law fluids reasonably well.

Keywords: nanocrystals; nanocrystalline cellulose; pipe flow; pipeline; friction factor; pressure drop; flow behavior; Reynolds number; non-Newtonian; rheology

1. Introduction

Cellulose nanocrystals (CNCs) are promising low-cost nanomaterials with unique properties [1–13] such as high stiffness, high aspect ratio, high surface area, low density, non-toxicity, biodegradability, and renewability. They are produced from cellulose via sulfuric acid hydrolysis of amorphous portions of cellulose fibers. When dispersed in water, they carry a negative charge due to the presence of anionic half ester groups.

The potential applications of CNCs are many. CNCs can greatly improve the gas barrier properties of packaging films when they are added to the polymeric matrix (poly lactic acid) of packaging film. CNCs act as a lubricant in reducing the coefficient of friction between surfaces and surface wear due to alignment of nanocrystals. CNCs are also good dispersants for the suspension of particles in liquids. The high aspect ratio and surface charge make CNCs excellent rheology modifiers; they thicken liquids and impart shear-thinning properties to liquids [14]. The thickening of liquids is required in many applications. For example, the texture and mouth feel properties of many food products can be manipulated using thickeners such as CNCs. For thickening purposes, the CNC is normally used at high concentrations (>1 wt%). CNCs are also excellent stabilizers for oil/water emulsions. Emulsions can be stabilized with CNC concentration anywhere in the range of 0.1 to 1.0 wt%. CNC-stabilized emulsions have potential applications in the food, pharmaceutical, and cosmetics industries. CNCs are also finding applications in the fabrication of flexible and stretchable strain sensors [15–18], stretchable electroluminescent devices [19], flexible triboelectric nanogenerators [20], and recyclable/biodegradable packaging products [21].

However, systematic studies dealing with rheology and the pumping flow behavior of suspensions of CNCs are lacking, which inspires us to explore this topic. To our knowledge, no work has been published on the flow behavior of CNC suspensions in pipelines. A good understanding of the flow behavior of CNC suspensions in pipes is important from both fundamental and practical points of view. For example, knowledge of the friction factor vs. Reynolds number relationship is required for the design and operation of pipelines and related process equipment used in the formulation and transport of CNC suspensions.

The objective of this study is to systematically investigate the rheology and pipeline flow behavior of CNC suspensions over a broad range of CNC concentrations.

2. Background

The flow behavior of fluids in pipes is described in terms of friction factor–Reynolds number relationships. The friction factor (f) is defined as follows:

$$f = \frac{\tau_w}{\frac{1}{2}\rho V^2}, \tag{1}$$

where τ_w is the wall shear stress, ρ is fluid density, and V is the average fluid velocity in the pipe. For horizontal pipes, the wall shear stress is related to pressure drop as follows:

$$\tau_w = \frac{D\Delta P}{4L}, \tag{2}$$

where D the is pipe internal diameter, ΔP is the pressure drop over the length L of the pipe.

Thus, friction factor in pipe flow can be measured by measuring the pressure drop as a function of flow rate.

The Reynolds number for Newtonian fluids is defined as follows:

$$Re = \frac{\rho DV}{\eta}, \tag{3}$$

where η is the fluid viscosity. For non-Newtonian power-law fluids, the Reynolds number is defined as follows:

$$Re, n = 8\left[\frac{n}{6n+2}\right]^n \left[\frac{\rho V^{2-n} D^n}{K}\right] \tag{4}$$

where K and n are power-law constants, defined by the power-law model as follows:

$$\tau = K\dot{\gamma}^n, \tag{5}$$

where τ is the shear stress and $\dot{\gamma}$ is the shear rate. The power-law constants K and n are determined by fitting the power-law model to the shear stress vs. shear rate data obtained from viscometer measurements. Note that the Reynolds number for non-Newtonian fluids Re, n is also referred to as the generalized Reynolds number. For Newtonian fluids where $K = \eta$ and $n = 1$, Re, n reduces to the conventional Reynolds number Re.

2.1. Friction Factor vs. Reynolds Number for Newtonian Fluids

In laminar flow of Newtonian fluids, the friction factor is related to Reynolds number as follows:

$$f = \frac{16}{Re}. \tag{6}$$

The friction factor is independent of pipe roughness in laminar flow. However, in turbulent flow of Newtonian fluids, the friction factor is a function of both the Reynolds number and the relative roughness of the pipe (ϵ/D). When the pipe is a hydraulically smooth pipe $(\epsilon/D \to 0)$, the friction factor depends only on Re in the turbulent regime. The friction factor data for turbulent flow of Newtonian fluids in smooth pipes can be described accurately via the following semi-empirical equation, often referred to as the von Karman–Nikuradse equation:

$$1/\sqrt{f} = 4log_{10}\left(Re\sqrt{f}\right) - 0.40. \tag{7}$$

The von Karman–Nikuradse equation is not explicit in the friction factor. Several explicit f vs. Re relations are available in the literature. One of the popular ones is the following Blasius friction factor equation for turbulent flow of Newtonian fluids in smooth pipes:

$$f = 0.079/Re^{0.25}. \tag{8}$$

2.2. Friction Factor vs. Reynolds Number for Non-Newtonian Power-Law Fluids

For laminar flow of non-Newtonian power-law fluids in pipes, the friction factor is a function of the generalized Reynolds number Re,n, as shown below:

$$f = \frac{16}{Re,n}. \tag{9}$$

This is the same relationship as that of Newtonian fluids with the conventional Reynolds number Re replaced by the generalized Reynolds number Re,n.

The friction factor in turbulent flow of non-Newtonian power-law fluids in hydraulically smooth pipes is given by the following Dodge–Metzner equation [22]:

$$\frac{1}{\sqrt{f}} = \left(\frac{4}{n^{0.75}}\right) log_{10}\left[f^{(1-0.5n)} Re,n\right] - \frac{0.4}{n^{1.2}}. \tag{10}$$

In the special case of Newtonian fluids ($n = 1$, $K = \eta$), the Dodge–Metzner equation reduces to the von Karman–Nikuradse equation (Equation (7)).

The Dodge–Metzner equation (Equation (10)) is not explicit in f and has to be solved numerically. Dodge and Metzner [22] also proposed a Blasius-type equation explicit in f for non-Newtonian fluids as follows:

$$f = \frac{\alpha_n}{(Re,n)^{\beta_n}}, \tag{11}$$

where α_n and β_n are functions of n reported graphically [22]. Pal [23] proposed the following expressions α_n and β_n:

$$\alpha_n = 0.0077ln(n) + 0.078, \tag{12}$$

$$\beta_n = 0.25(n)^{-0.22}. \tag{13}$$

3. Materials and Methods

3.1. Materials

The CNCs used in this work were provided by CelluForce Inc., Windsor, ON, Canada, under the trade name of NCC NCV100-NASD90. They were produced via sulfuric acid hydrolysis of wood pulp followed by spray-drying. The nanocrystals were rod-shaped with a mean length of 76 nm and mean width of 3.4 nm. The surface area of CNCs was 500 m^2/g and the crystallinity was 88%. The atomic force microscopy (AFM) image of the nanocrystals is shown in Figure 1. The water used throughout the experiments was deionized.

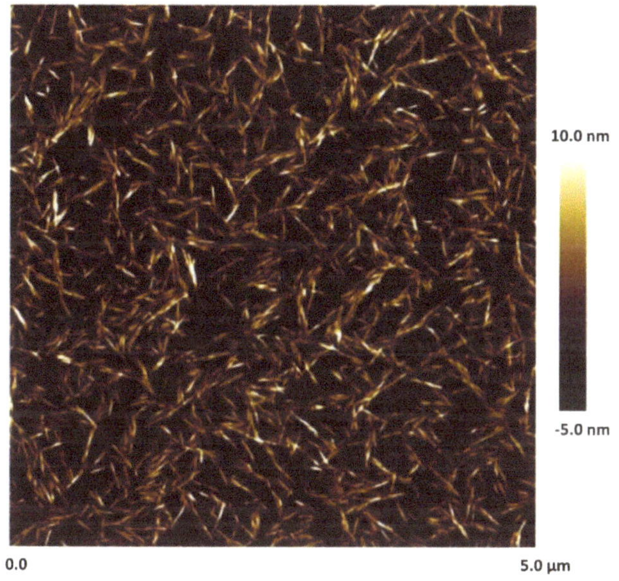

Figure 1. Atomic force microscopy (AFM) image of cellulose nanocrystals [14,24].

3.2. Flow Loop

The flow behavior of CNC suspensions was investigated in a closed-flow-loop system. The schematic diagram of the flow loop and the images of different portions of the flow loop are shown in Figures 2 and 3, respectively. The CNC suspension was prepared in a large, jacketed mixing tank present in the flow loop (see Figure 3a). The temperature inside the tank was maintained constant at 22 ± 0.5 °C by passing cold or hot water through the tank jacket with the help of a temperature controller. Two centrifugal pumps (low and high capacities) were installed in the loop. Three straight pipe test sections (seamless, hydraulically smooth) of stainless steel with different diameters were installed horizontally (see Figure 3c). The pressure taps in the pipe test sections were made by drilling small holes through the pipe walls. The pressure taps on the pipe test sections were placed far enough from the entrance of flow to the pipe to ensure fully developed flow in the test section where pressure drop measurements were made. Three pressure transducers of different pressure ranges (Rosemount and Cole–Parmer: 0–0.5, 0–5, 0–10 psi) were installed in the flow loop. The pressure transducers were configured in such a manner that a desired pressure transducer could be easily connected to any of the pressure taps in use (see Figure 3b). The loop was equipped with a computer data acquisition system (see Figure 3d) which consisted of an electronic board for input and output signals and a computer terminal to process signals and gather data using the LABVIEW software version 7.1.

Table 1 gives further details about the dimensions of the pipeline test sections installed in the flow loop.

Table 1. Dimensions of the pipeline test sections.

Nominal Diameter (inch)	Inside Diameter (mm)	Test Section Lengths (m)
0.5	9.45	1.22, 3.667
1.0	22.02	0.92, 3.048
1.5	34.80	1.52, 3.048

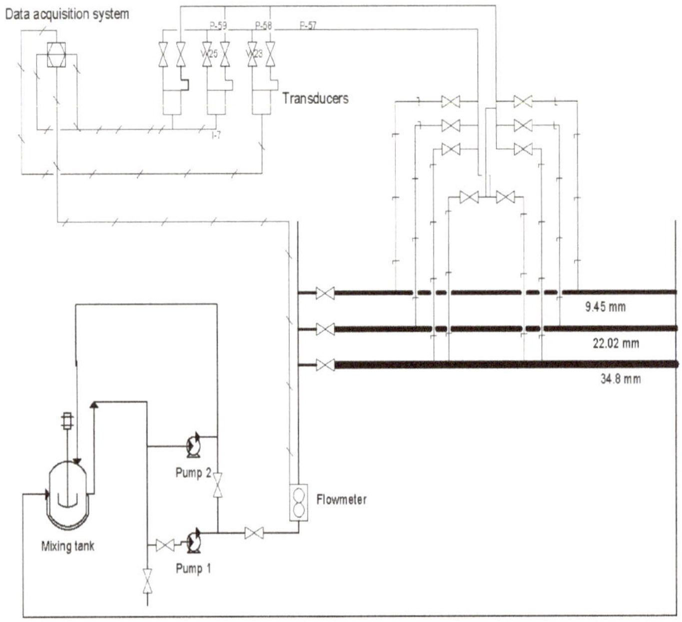

Figure 2. Schematic diagram of the experimental flow loop.

(a) (b)

(c) (d)

Figure 3. Images of different portions of the experimental flow loop: (**a**) mixing tank; (**b**) pressure drop measuring panel; (**c**) three different diameter pipeline test sections; (**d**) computer terminal of data acquisition system.

3.3. Viscometry

Fann and Haake co-axial cylinder-type viscometers were used for the rheological measurements. The relevant dimensions of the viscometers are given in Table 2. There were 12 speeds ranging from 0.9 to 600 rpm in the Fann viscometer where the inner cylinder was kept stationary, and the outer cylinder rotated. In the Haake viscometer, there were 30 speeds ranging from 0.01 to 512 rpm, and the inner cylinder rotated, whereas the outer cylinder was held stationary. The viscosity standards of known viscosities were used to calibrate the viscometers. The measurements were carried out at room temperature (22 ± 1 °C).

Table 2. Relevant dimensions of the viscometers.

Device	Inner Cylinder Radius, R_i	Outer Cylinder Radius, R_o	Length of Inner Cylinder	Gap-Width
Fann 35A/SR-12 viscometer	1.72 cm	1.84 cm	3.8 cm	0.12 cm
aake Roto-visco RV 12 with MV I	2.00 cm	2.1 cm	6.0 cm	0.10 cm

3.4. Preparation of CNC Suspensions

Stock solutions containing 10 wt% CNC in deionized water were first prepared in batches of approximately 4 kg in a benchtop variable-speed homogenizer (Gifford–Wood, model 1L). The mixture was sheared at high speed in the homogenizer for at least one hour. Figure 4 shows the preparation of the stock solution. The known amount of stock solution was then added to the known amount of deionized water in the flow loop tank to prepare the desired concentration of CNC suspension for the pipeline study. The suspension was thoroughly mixed in the flow loop tank with the help of an in-line mixer and pumping system for at least one hour before any pipeline data collection. Figure 5 shows the CNC suspension in the flow loop tank. To prepare a higher CNC concentration suspension, more stock solution (10 wt% CNC) was added to the existing lower CNC concentration suspension in the tank. The rheological and DLS (dynamic light scattering) measurements were carried out on CNC suspensions at each CNC concentration after collection of pipeline data in the flow loop.

Preparation of CNC suspension using Gifford-Wood homogenizer

10 wt% CNC stock solution

Figure 4. Preparation of CNC stock solution using benchtop homogenizer.

Figure 5. CNC suspension in the flow loop mixing tank.

3.5. Calibration of Pipeline Test-Sections

Deionized water was used to calibrate the pipeline test sections. The pressure-drop vs. flow rate data were collected over a broad range of flow rates. The pressure-drop vs. flow rate data were transformed into friction factor (f) vs. Reynolds number (Re) data. Figure 6 compares the predictions of the Blasius equation (Equation (8)) with experimental friction factor data obtained from three different diameter pipe test sections using deionized water. There is a reasonably good agreement between the experimental turbulent flow data and the prediction of the Blasius equation, indicating that the pipeline test sections were hydraulically smooth. Note that it was not possible to collect data in the laminar regime as the pressure drops were too small to be measured accurately using the available pressure transducers.

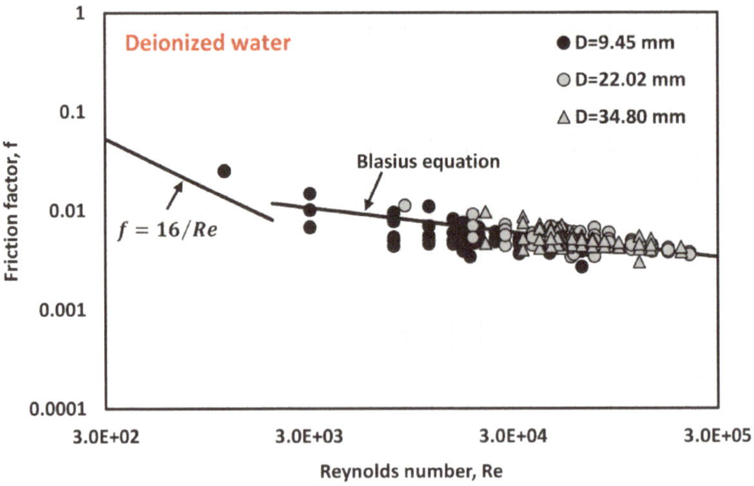

Figure 6. Friction factor vs. Reynolds number data for deionized water.

4. Results and Discussion

4.1. Particle Size Distribution of CNC Suspensions

The size distribution of CNC suspension was determined via DLS using a Zetasizer Nano ZS90 with a He-Ne laser operating at 633 nm frequency. The dispersant (water) properties were specified at 25 °C as follows: viscosity = 0.8872 mPa.s; and refractive index = 1.330. For the CNCs, the refractive index specified was 1.51. This value of CNC refractive index was available in the software of the instrument and agrees with the value reported in the literature [25]. For each CNC concentration, three DLS measurements were made, and the average values were calculated. Figure 7 shows the size distributions of CNC suspensions at different CNC concentrations. The average hydrodynamic diameter of CNC at different concentrations is shown in Figure 8. The average hydrodynamic diameter of CNC (Figure 8) decreases with the increase in CNC concentration initially and then levels off at high concentrations (>1 wt%) to approximately 10 nm. The decrease in average hydrodynamic diameter of CNC is probably due to interaction of nanocrystals at high concentrations. Note that the CNC suspensions were subjected to intense shear in the pumping system of the flow loop before the DLS measurements were made.

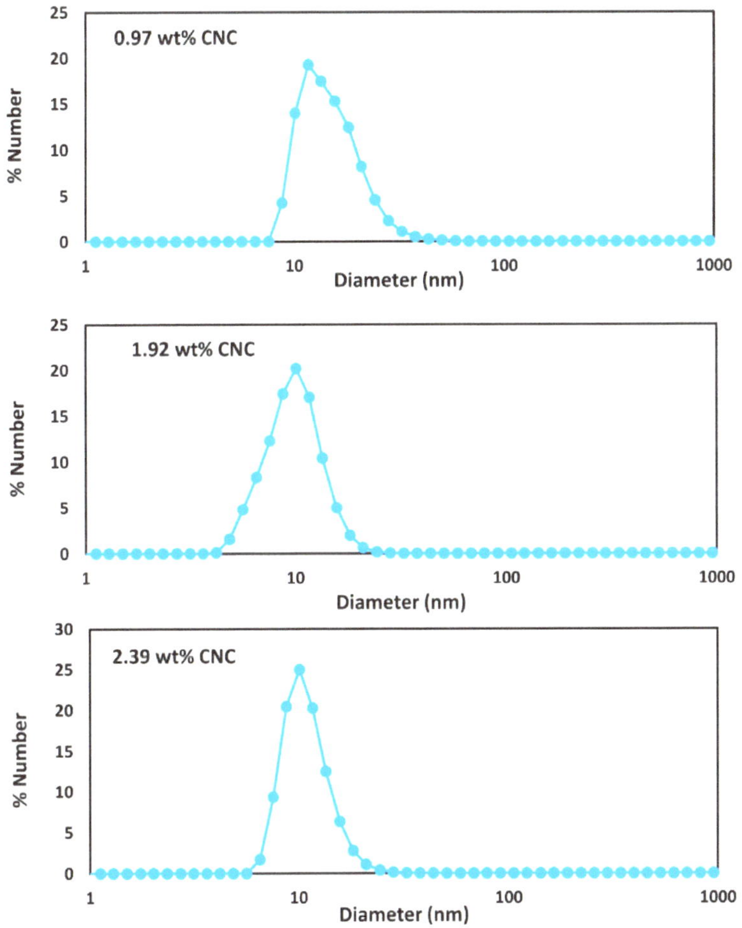

Figure 7. Size distributions of CNC suspensions at different CNC concentrations.

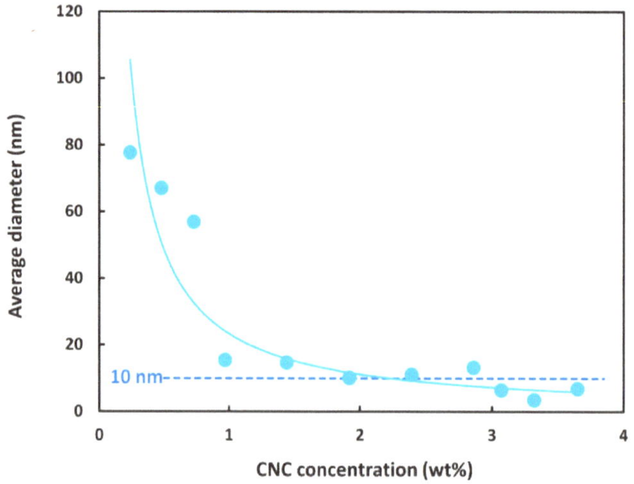

Figure 8. Average hydrodynamic diameter of CNC suspensions as a function of CNC concentration.

4.2. Rheology of CNC Suspensions

The rheology of CNC suspensions was measured at each concentration after collection of the pipeline data in the flow loop. Figure 9 shows the viscosity vs. shear rate plots of CNC suspensions at different CNC concentrations. The CNC suspensions are Newtonian at CNC concentrations lower than approximately 1 wt%; the viscosity is constant independent of the shear rate. At higher CNC concentrations, the suspensions become shear-thinning in that the viscosity decreases with the increase in shear rate. As the viscosity vs. shear rate plots are linear on a log-log scale, the CNC suspensions follow the power-law model, expressed in the form of Equation (5). The power-law model can be re-written as follows:

$$\eta = \tau / \dot{\gamma} = K\dot{\gamma}^{n-1}, \tag{14}$$

where η is the apparent shear viscosity. From the plots of η and $\dot{\gamma}$ data, the power-law constants can be determined via linear regression.

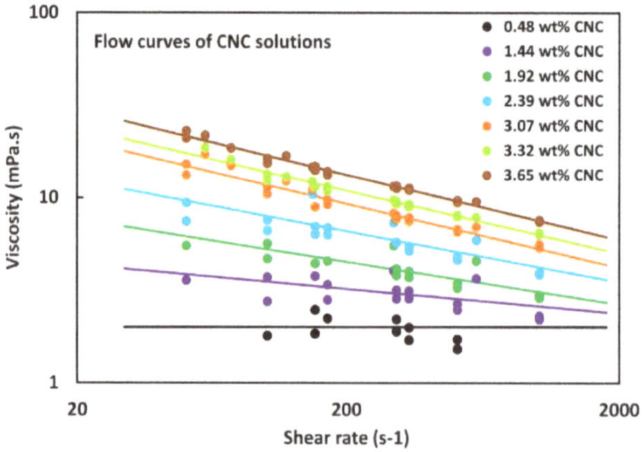

Figure 9. Viscosity vs. shear-rate plots of CNC suspensions at different CNC concentrations.

Figure 10 shows the plots of power-law constants (K and n) as a function of CNC concentration. The CNC suspensions are Newtonian ($n = 1$) at CNC concentrations below

1 wt%. At higher concentrations, the CNC suspensions are shear-thinning ($n < 1$) and the flow behavior index n decreases with the increase in CNC concentration. The consistency index (K) increases with the increase in CNC concentration.

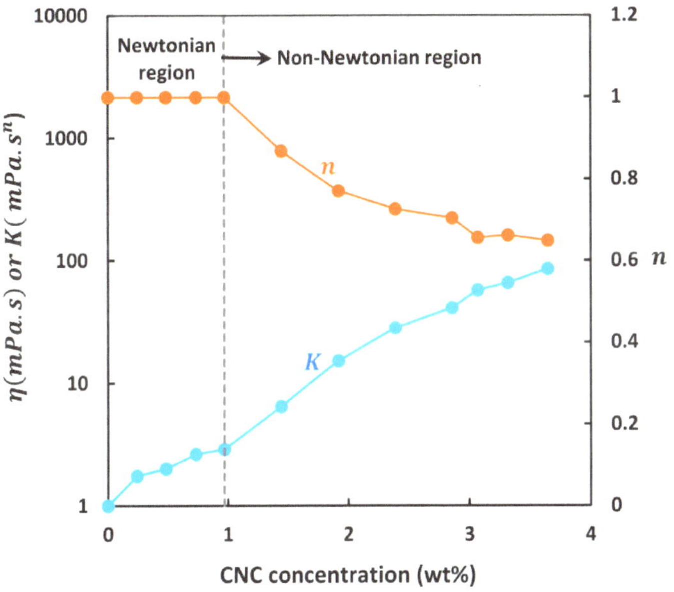

Figure 10. Variation of power-law constants (K and n) as a function of CNC concentration.

The regression analysis of the power-law constants gives the following relations:

$$K = 1.104exp(1.255C), \quad (15)$$

$$n = 1.0 \text{ when } C \leq 1\ wt\%;\ n = 0.9785C^{-0.332} \text{ when } C > 1\ wt\%, \quad (16)$$

where C is the concentration of CNC in wt%. The R-squared values are 0.97 for Equation (15) and 0.99 for Equation (16), respectively.

4.3. Pipeline Flow Behavior of CNC Suspensions

The pipeline experimental data for CNC suspensions obtained from different diameter pipes at different CNC concentrations are plotted in the form of friction factor vs. Reynolds number in Figures 11–16. For the Newtonian CNC suspensions (CNC concentration < 1 wt%), the conventional Reynolds number (Equation (3)) is used, and for the non-Newtonian CNC suspensions, the generalized Reynolds number (Equation (4)) is used. The experimental friction factor data obtained for Newtonian CNC suspensions from different diameter pipes (Figures 11 and 12) cover mainly the turbulent regime, and the data follow the Blasius equation (Equation (8)) closely. For non-Newtonian power-law CNC suspensions (CNC concentration > 1 wt%), the experimental data obtained from different diameter pipes (Figures 13–16) cover both laminar and turbulent regimes, and the data show satisfactory agreement with the corresponding equations for non-Newtonian power-law fluids (Equation (9) for laminar flow and the Dodge–Metzner equation Equation (11) for turbulent flow). Thus, it can be concluded that the CNC suspensions investigated in this study over the CNC concentration range of 0.24–3.65 wt% follow the usual pipeline flow equations for homogeneous Newtonian and non-Newtonian flows with averaged properties. Most of the experimental data points fall within ±30% of the values predicted by the equations.

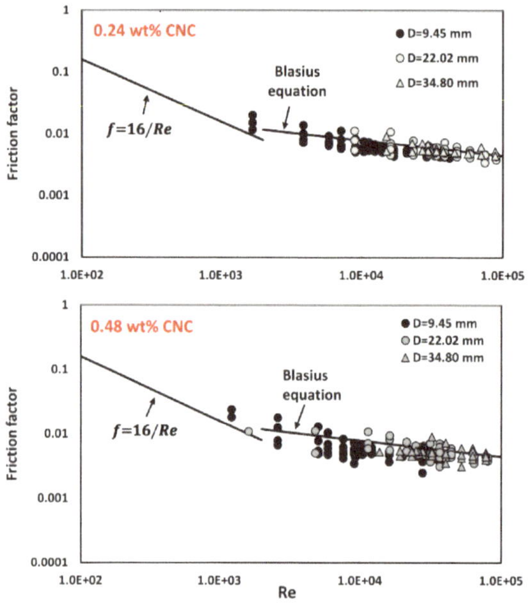

Figure 11. Friction factor vs. Reynolds number data for CNC suspensions at 0.24 and 0.48 wt% concentrations.

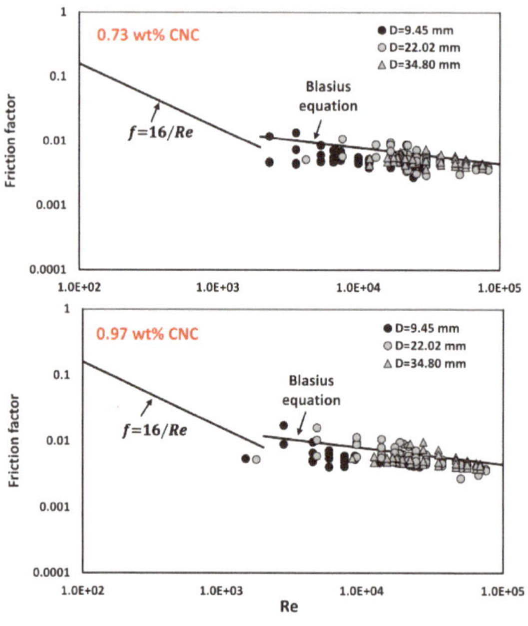

Figure 12. Friction factor vs. Reynolds number data for CNC suspensions at 0.73 and 0.97 wt% concentrations.

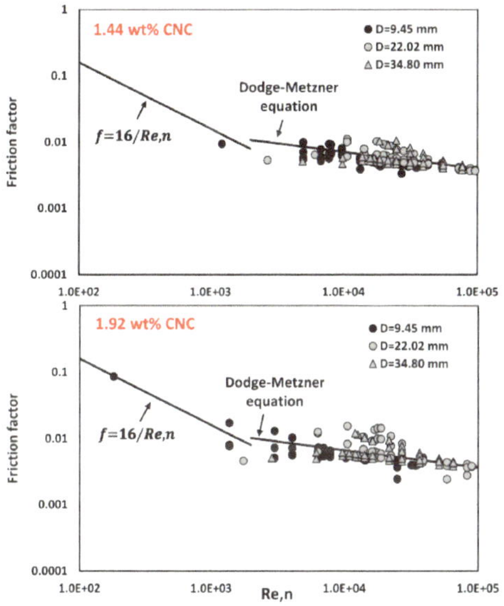

Figure 13. Friction factor vs. Reynolds number data for CNC suspensions at 1.44 and 1.92 wt% concentrations.

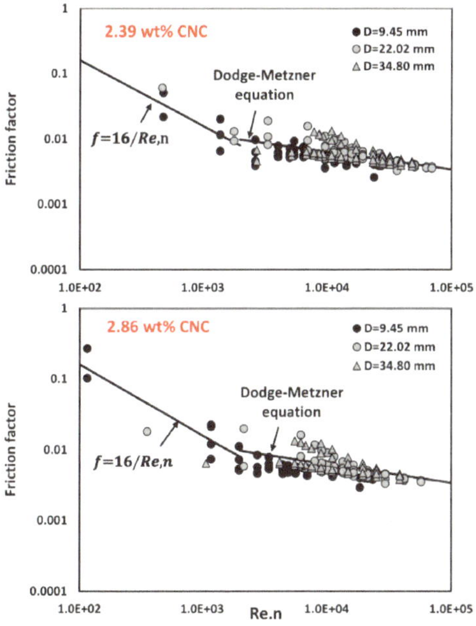

Figure 14. Friction factor vs. Reynolds number data for CNC suspensions at 2.39 and 2.86 wt% concentrations.

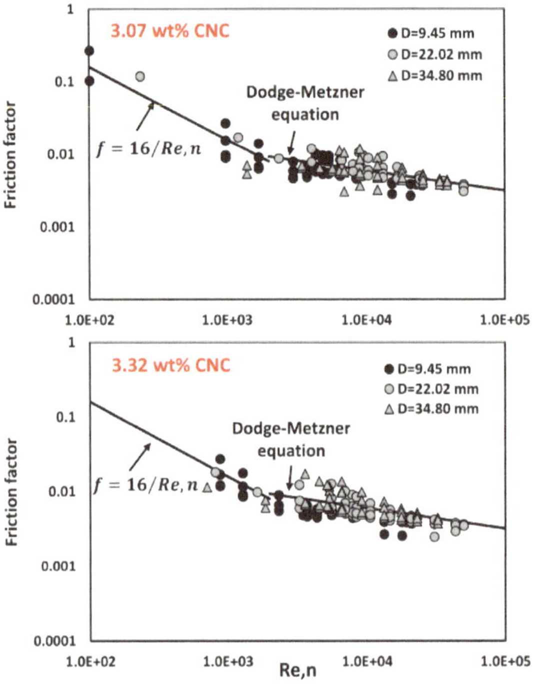

Figure 15. Friction factor vs. Reynolds number data for CNC suspensions at 3.07 and 3.32 wt% concentrations.

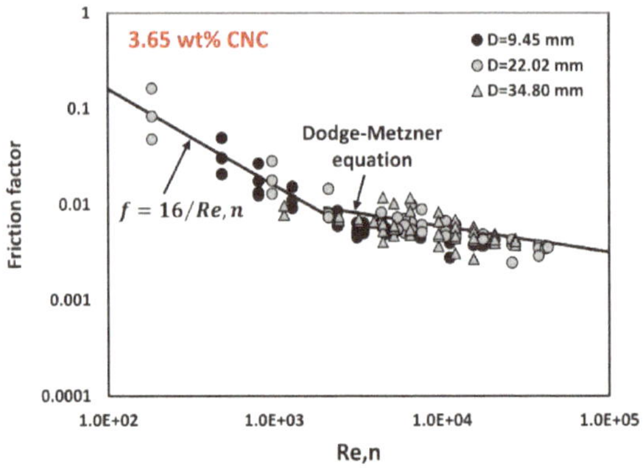

Figure 16. Friction factor vs. Reynolds number data for CNC suspension at 3.65 wt% concentration.

5. Conclusions

The laminar and turbulent flow behaviors of suspensions of cellulose nanocrystals (CNCs) were studied in three different diameter pipes. The CNC concentration varied from 0.24 to 3.65 wt%. At low concentrations of CNC (less than 1 wt%), the suspensions were Newtonian in nature. The CNC suspensions behaved as non-Newtonian pseudoplastic fluids at CNC concentrations above 1 wt%. The power-law model was able to describe the rheology of non-Newtonian CNC suspensions adequately. The pipeline data were analyzed in terms of friction factor vs. Reynolds number. For the non-Newtonian suspensions, the generalized Reynolds number was used. The experimental friction factor vs. Reynolds number data obtained for CNC suspensions were described reasonably well using the pipeline flow equations for homogeneous Newtonian and non-Newtonian flows with averaged properties.

Author Contributions: Conceptualization, R.P.; methodology, S.K. and R.P.; software, S.K.; validation, S.K. and R.P.; formal analysis, R.P.; investigation, S.K. and R.P.; resources, R.P.; data curation, S.K.; writing—original draft preparation, R.P.; writing—review and editing, R.P.; visualization, R.P.; supervision, R.P.; project administration, R.P.; funding acquisition, R.P. All authors have read and agreed to the published version of the manuscript.

Funding: This research was funded by the Discovery Grant awarded to R.P. by the Natural Sciences and Engineering Research Council of Canada.

Data Availability Statement: The data presented in this study are available on request from the corresponding author.

Conflicts of Interest: The authors declare no conflict of interest.

erences

Girard, M.; Vidal, D.; Bertrand, F.; Tavares, J.R.; Heuzey, M. Evidence-based guidelines for the ultrasonic dispersion of cellulose nanocrystals. *Ultrason. Sonochem.* **2021**, *71*, 105378. [CrossRef]

Shojaeiarani, J.; Bajwa, D.S.; Chanda, S. Cellulose nanocrystal-based composites: A review. *Compos. Part C Open Access* **2021**, *5*, 100164. [CrossRef]

Prathapan, R.; Thapa, R.; Garnier, G.; Tabor, R.F. Modulating the zeta potential of cellulose nanocrystals using salts and surfactants. *Colloids Surf. A Physicochem. Eng. Asp.* **2016**, *509*, 11–18. [CrossRef]

Lu, P.; Hsieh, Y. Preparation and properties of cellulose nanocrystals: Rods, spheres, and network. *Carbohydr. Polym.* **2010**, *82*, 329–336. [CrossRef]

Yang, X.; Biswas, S.K.; Han, J.; Tanpichai, S.; Li, M.; Chen, C.; Zhu, S.; Das, A.K.; Yano, H. Surface and interface engineering for nanocellulosic advanced materials. *Adv. Mater.* **2021**, *33*, 2002264. [CrossRef] [PubMed]

Aziz, T.; Ullah, A.; Fan, H.; Ullah, R.; Haq, F.; Khan, F.U.; Iqbal, M.; Wei, J. Cellulose nanocrystals applications in health, medicine, and catalysis. *J. Polym. Environ.* **2021**, *29*, 2062–2071. [CrossRef]

Dufresne, A. Nanocellulose processing properties and potential applications. *Curr. For. Rep.* **2019**, *5*, 76–89. [CrossRef]

Trache, D.; Hussin, M.H.; Haafiz, M.K.M.; Thakur, V.K. Recent progress in cellulose nanocrystals: Sources and production. *Nanoscale* **2017**, *9*, 1763–1786. [CrossRef]

Aziz, T.; Fan, H.; Zhang, X.; Haq, A.; Ullah, R.; Khan, F.U.; Iqbal, M. Advance study of cellulose nanocrystals properties and applications. *J. Polym. Environ.* **2020**, *28*, 1117–1128. [CrossRef]

Vanderfleet, O.M.; Cranston, E.D. Production routes to tailor the performance of cellulose nanocrystals. *Nat. Rev. Mater.* **2021**, *6*, 124–144. [CrossRef]

Zhang, H.; Dou, C.; Pal, L.; Hubbe, M.A. Review of electrically conductive composites and films containing cellulosic fibers or nanocellulose. *BioResources* **2019**, *14*, 7494–7542. [CrossRef]

Panchal, P.; Ogunsona, E.; Mekonnen, T. Trends in advanced functional material applications of nanocellulose. *Processes* **2019**, *10*, 1–27. [CrossRef]

Gupta, A.; Mekonnen, T.H. Cellulose nanocrystals enabled sustainable polycaprolactone based shape memory polyurethane bionanocomposites. *J. Colloid Interface Sci.* **2022**, *611*, 726–738. [CrossRef] [PubMed]

Cellulose Nanocrystals (CNC). Available online: https://celluforce.com/cellulose-nanocrystals-cnc/ (accessed on 26 February 2023).

Lu, Y.; Yue, Y.; Ding, Q.; Mei, C.; Xu, X.; Wu, Q.; Xiao, H.; Han, J. Self-recovery, fatigue-resistant, and multifunctional sensor assembled by a nanocellulose/carbon nanotube nanocomplex-mediated hydrogel. *Appl. Mater. Interfaces* **2021**, *13*, 50281–50297. [CrossRef] [PubMed]

Zhu, S.; Sun, H.; Lu, Y.; Wang, S.; Yue, Y.; Xu, X.; Mei, C.; Xiao, H.; Fu, Q.; Han, J. Inherently conductive poly(dimethylsiloxane) elastomers synergistically mediated by nanocellulose/carbon nanotube nanohybrids toward highly sensitive, stretchable, and durable strain sensors. *Appl. Mater. Interfaces* **2021**, *13*, 59142–59153. [CrossRef] [PubMed]

Zhou, J.; Yu, H.; Xu, X.; Han, F.; Lubineau, G. Ultrasensitive, stretchable strain sensors based on fragmented carbon nanotube papers. *Appl. Mater. Interfaces* **2017**, *9*, 4835–4842. [CrossRef] [PubMed]

Zhu, S.; Lu, Y.; Wang, S.; Sun, H.; Yue, Y.; Xu, X.; Mei, C.; Xiao, H.; Fu, Q.; Han, J. Interface design of stretchable and environment-tolerant strain tensors with hierarchical nanocellulose-supported graphene nanocomplexes. *Compos. Part A* **2023**, *164*, 107313. [CrossRef]

Sun, H.; Lu, Y.; Chen, Y.; Yue, Y.; Jiang, S.; Xu, X.; Mei, C.; Xiao, H.; Han, J. Flexible environment-tolerant electroluminescent devices based on nanocellulose-mediated transparent electrodes. *Carbohydr. Polym.* **2022**, *296*, 119891. [CrossRef] [PubMed]

20. Niu, Z.; Cheng, W.; Cao, M.; Wang, D.; Wang, Q.; Han, J.; Long, Y.; Han, G. Recent advances in cellulose-based flexible triboele nanogenerators. *Nano Energy* **2021**, *87*, 106175. [CrossRef]
21. Wang, J.; Euring, M.; Ostendorf, K.; Zhang, K. Biobased materials for food packaging. *J. Bioresour. Bioprod.* **2022**, *7*, [CrossRef]
22. Dodge, D.W.; Metzner, A.B. Turbulent flow of non-Newtonian systems. *AIChE J.* **1959**, *5*, 189–204. [CrossRef]
23. Pal, R. Entropy generation in flow of highly concentrated non-Newtonian emulsions in smooth tubes. *Entropy* **2014**, *16*, 5178– [CrossRef]
24. Kinra, S.; Pal, R. Rheology of Pickering emulsions stabilized and thickened by cellulose nanocrystals over broad ranges of oi nanocrystal concentrations. *Colloids Interfaces* **2023**, *7*, 36. [CrossRef]
25. Niskanen, I.; Suopajarvi, T.; Liimatainen, H.; Fabritius, T.; Heikkila, R.; Thungstrom, G. Determining the complex refractive i of cellulose nanocrystals by combination of Beer-Lambert and immersion matching methods. *J. Quant. Spectrosc. Radiat. T* **2019**, *235*, 1–6. [CrossRef]

fluids

icle

ill Role Effect on the Flow Characteristics (Experimental and egression Model Analytical)

midreza Abbaszadeh [1], Reza Norouzi [1], Veli Sume [2], Alban Kuriqi [3], Rasoul Daneshfaraz [1,*]
d John Abraham [4]

[1] Department of Civil Engineering, Faculty of Engineering, University of Maragheh, Maragheh 5518183111, Iran; abbaszadeh@stu.maragheh.ac.ir (H.A.); norouzi@maragheh.ac.ir (R.N.)
[2] Department of Civil Engineering, Faculty of Engineering and Architecture, Recep Tayyip Erdogan University, Rize 53100, Türkiye; veli.sume@erdogan.edu.tr
[3] Civil Engineering Research and Innovation for Sustainability, Instituto Superior Técnico, Universidade de Lisboa, 1049-001 Lisboa, Portugal; alban.kuriqi@tecnico.ulisboa.pt
[4] School of Engineering, University of St. Thomas, St. Paul, MN 33901, USA; jpabraham@stthomas.edu
* Correspondence: daneshfaraz@maragheh.ac.ir; Tel.: +98-9143202126

Abstract: This study investigates the effects of gate openings and different sill widths on the sluice gate's energy dissipation and discharge coefficient (C_d). The physical model of the sills includes rectangular sills of different dimensions. The results show that the gate opening size is inversely related to the C_d for a gate without a sill. In addition, increasing the gate opening size for a given discharge decreases the relative energy dissipation, and increasing the Froude number increases the relative energy dissipation. The results also show that the C_d and relative energy dissipation decrease when the width of the sill is decreased, thus increasing the total area of the flux flowing through the sluice gate and vice versa. According to the experimental results, the relative energy dissipation and the C_d of the sluice gate are larger for all sill widths than without the sill. Finally, non-linear polynomial relationships are presented based on dimensionless parameters for predicting the relative energy dissipation and outflow coefficient.

Keywords: gate; sill role; discharge coefficient; hydraulic jump

1. Introduction

The gates are structures where water flow is regulated and controlled based on the height of the gate openings from the lower surface. The most common type of structure is the sluice gate (a gate that moves in a vertical plane); flow accuracy is based on the energy loss and discharge coefficient (C_d). Designers often exercise extreme care when controlling and distributing water in irrigation networks to avoid wasting water.

Structures for river control, such as locks, should always be selected correctly and according to the conditions of the area in question so as not to have problems later. Multiple gates (e.g., double/triple) are used when the design height of the gate exceeds the design criteria [1]. Multiple gates are very expensive. Gate dimensions can be reduced through the use of a sill. The sill will reduce the gate structure's height and the force on the gate body. Therefore, a combination of gate and sill can be considered.

Henry [2] and Rajaratnam and Subramanya [3] were the first studies to determine the C_d value of sluice gates. Rajaratnam [4] studied the free flow in sluice gates and established an equation to estimate the C_d value. Swamee [5] determined the C_d of sluice gates subjected to free flow conditions; the relationship included the dependence of upstream depth and gate opening. Shivapur and Prakash [6] studied the sluice gates at different positions and established a relationship for C_d. Using Mathematica software, Nasehi Oskuyi and Salmasi [7] determined the C_d value of sluice gates. Their results agreed well with the results of Henry [2]. Daneshfaraz et al. [8] studied the edge shapes of sluice gates and their impact on flow characteristics using FLOW-3D. They found a flow contraction coefficient for sluice gates with sharp edges upward and downward, and round edges decrease when the sluice gate opening/specific energy upstream is less than 0.4 and increase for larger ratios. Salmasi et al. [9] evaluated the C_d of inclined gates using multiple machine intelligence models. Their study showed that the C_d value increases with increasing angle. In Salmasi and Abraham study [10], laboratory experiments were performed to quantify the C_d for oblique sluice gates. They showed that the sluice gate slope has an effect on the C_d; using a gate increases the C_d.

For a sill/gate combination, it is worth mentioning an experimental study on the shape and height of the sill below the sluice gate [11]. The results showed that the C_d increases when a sill is employed. Salmasi and Norouzi [12] showed that a circular sill increases the C_d value by at least 23–31%. Karami et al. [13] numerically investigated the effect of geometric sill shape on C_d; they found that the semicircular sill has a greater effect. Salmasi and Abraham [14] carried out experiments on sills. They found that a sill plays an effective role in increasing C_d. Ghorbani et al. [15] analyzed sluice gate C_d using the H_2O method and soft computing models. Lauria et al. [16] studied sluice gates for wide-crowned weirs. They found that it is possible to operate a weir so that viscous effects can be neglected.

The dissipation and discharge performance of hydraulic structures such as sills can affect the stability and strength of structures in the riverbed and channels. The structure must be efficient and economically viable when comparing and designing dissipator structures to reduce flow energy. In addition, a stilling basin requires increased construction time and cost, specialized components and materials, skilled labor, and accuracy in design and construction. In contrast, sill elements are simple and inexpensive.

In all of the above studies, various studies have been conducted on the effect of sills. In addition, there is a need to study the sill with different widths to prevent sediment accumulation upstream of the gate and under the sluice gate, as well as their effects on the hydraulic capacity, the corresponding C_d, and energy dissipation, which were studied in this research. This research intends to improve the design of hydraulic control structures. Due to the importance of the subject, the C_d and energy dissipation in the conditions without a sill, with a suppressed sill, and with an unsuppressed sill are investigated at various gate openings.

2. Materials and Methods

2.1. Experimental Equipment

Here, an experimental facility with a flow-controlling flume of a rectangular cross-section shape with 5 m length, 0.3 m width, and 0.5 m depth with transparent polymeric walls was used to conduct the experiments. The channel bottom slope could be modified but was set to horizontal during the experiments. A pump provided a flow of 900 L per minute to the flume, and a rotameter with a relative error of ±2% was installed on the flume to read the inlet flow. Stilling plates reduced the turbulence entering the reservoir. The point gauge (±1 mm) was used with a movable rail to measure water depth at four cross-section locations, and their average was calculated. Another gate was installed downstream to stabilize the hydraulic jump within the channel. Experiments were conducted in two modes with and without sills in different openings. This study conducted experiments with polyethylene sills, with a thickness and height of 0.05 m and 0.03 m, respectively. Various sill widths were employed (0.025, 0.05, 0.075, 0.10, 0.15, 0.20, 0.25, and 0.30 m) below the sluice gate. A schematic image of the sluice gate sill and experimental channel of the present study is shown in Figure 1. A total of 111 experiments were conducted in a discharge range of 150 to 750 L/min to investigate the energy dissipation and C_d of the vertical sluice gate. Figure 2 shows photographs of the physical experiment.

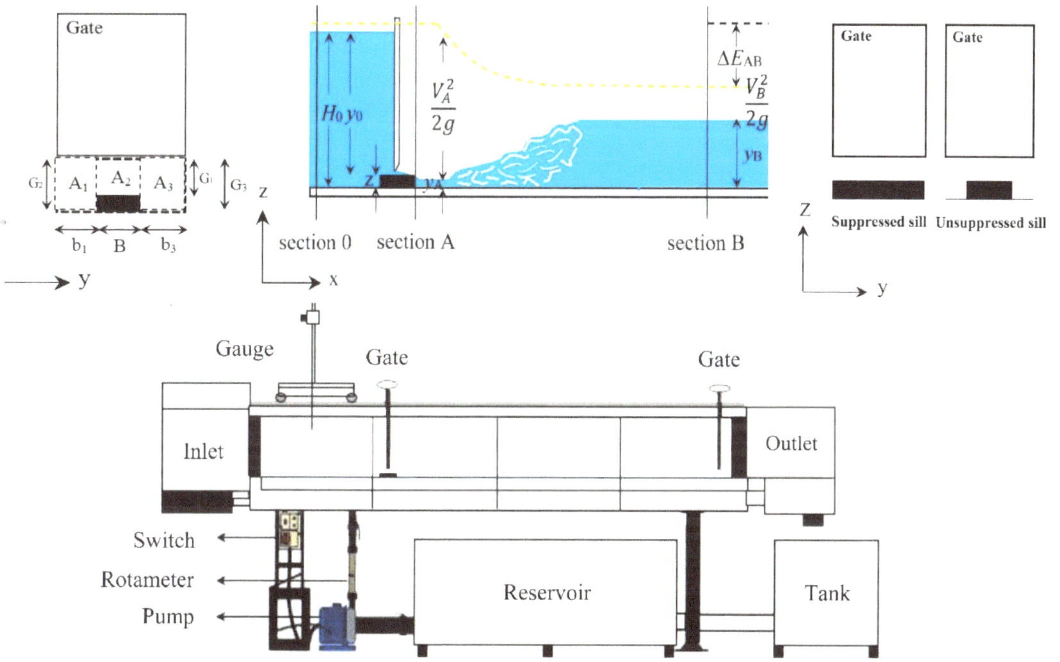

Figure 1. The experimental flume and hydraulic characteristics of flow.

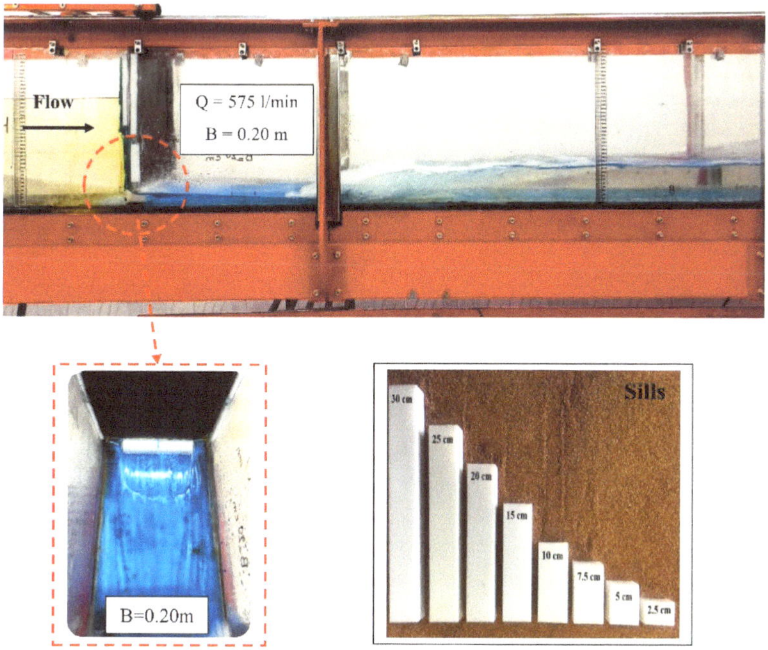

Figure 2. An example of the model.

2.2. Dimensional Analysis

Energy conservation/loss between sections A and B is calculated using the energy principle according to Equation (1):

$$\Delta E_{AB} = E_A - E_B = \left(y_A + \alpha_A \frac{V_A^2}{2g}\right) - \left(y_B + \alpha_B \frac{V_B^2}{2g}\right) \tag{1}$$

where E_A and E_B are the specific energies of water in sections A and B, respectively. y_A is the depth of water in section A or, in other words, the initial depth; y_B is the depth of water in section B or the following depth; V_A and V_B are the velocities averaged over depth in sections A and B, respectively; and g is the gravitational acceleration. In Equation (1), α is the correction factor for kinetic energy and is equal to

$$\alpha = \frac{\sum V_i^3 \times A_i}{V^3 \times A} \tag{2}$$

In Equation (2), V_i is the velocity in section i, A_i is the cross-sectional area of i, A is the total area of the section ($A = \sum A_i$), and V is the velocity averaged over depth in the entire section.

The parameters affecting energy dissipation are

$$f_1(Q, W, B, L, Z, E_A, E_B, y_A, y_B, g, \rho, \mu) = 0 \tag{3}$$

In Equation (3), Q is the discharge, W represents the channel width, B quantifies the sill width, L is the sill thickness, Z is the sill height, ρ is density, and μ is dynamic viscosity. Considering ρ, g, and y_A as iterative variables and using the π-Buckingham, Equation (4) emerges as

$$f_2\left(Fr_A, \frac{W}{y_A}, \frac{B}{y_A}, \frac{L}{y_A}, \frac{Z}{y_A}, \frac{E_A}{y_A}, \frac{E_B}{y_A}, \frac{y_B}{y_A}, Re_A\right) = 0 \tag{4}$$

In Equation (4), Fr_A and Re_A are the Froude and Reynolds numbers, respectively, in section A. Some of the parameters in the above relationship, such as channel width, thickness, and sill height, have assumed specific values and are not present in the research objectives, so the effects of these parameters have been ignored. In the present study, since the flow is turbulent, the Reynolds number can be ignored [17–19]. To make the parameters meaningful, the dimensional analysis of the present study was summarized and calculated in Equation (5) by dividing some of them by each other.

$$\frac{\Delta E_{AB}}{E_A}, \frac{\Delta E_{AB}}{E_B} = f_3\left(Fr_A, \frac{B}{y_A}, \frac{y_B}{y_A}\right) \tag{5}$$

The discharge rate below the sluice gate without sill (Equation (6)) and with sill (Equation (7)) can be calculated under free flow conditions:

$$Q = C_d W G_1 \sqrt{2gH_0} \tag{6}$$

$$Q = C_d W G_1 \sqrt{2g(H_0 - Z)} \tag{7}$$

where H_0 is the upstream water depth of the sluice gate, G_1 is the gate opening with suppressed sill and without sill, WG_1 is the flow area under the gate, and C_d is the discharge coefficient.

According to this, Equation (7) is modified to Equation (8) for the unsuppressed sill situation:

$$Q = C_d\left(\left(A_1\sqrt{2gH_0}\right) + \left(A_2\sqrt{2g(H_0 - Z)}\right) + \left(A_3\sqrt{2gH_0}\right)\right) \tag{8}$$

where A_1, A_3, and A_2 are the areas of the flow without the sill and above the unsuppressed sill, respectively (Figure 1).

The magnitude of the C_d in the condition without a sill depends on the upstream depth and the openings. The functional dependence is [5]

$$C_d = f_1(H_0, G_1) \tag{9}$$

For the sill situation, the most important parameters affecting the C_d are

$$f_1(C_d, A_1, A_2, A_3, H_0, B, Z, L, \rho, g, \mu) = 0 \tag{10}$$

With the same method, a dimensionless relation (11) can be presented:

$$f_2\left(C_d, \frac{A_1}{B^2}, \frac{A_2}{B^2}, \frac{A_3}{B^2}, \frac{H_0}{B}, \frac{Z}{B}, \frac{L}{B}, Re\right) = 0 \tag{11}$$

In the present study, considering that the sill is located in the flume's center, the flow's areas on both sides of the sill are equal to each other, so the combined area of the flow will be $A_{\text{total}} = 2A_1 + A_2$. Therefore, the parameters studied in the present study were presented as relation (12):

$$C_d = f_3\left(\frac{A_2}{2A_1}, \frac{Z}{B}, \frac{H_0}{B}\right) \tag{12}$$

According to Equation (13), for the condition without a sill, hydrodynamic force applied to the sluice gate can be calculated by writing the momentum equation between sections 0 and A.

$$\frac{1}{2}\gamma H_0^2 - \frac{1}{2}\gamma y_A^2 - R = \rho q(V_A - V_0) \tag{13}$$

Here, the symbol q represents the discharge per unit width of the channel, γ is the specific water weight, and R is the reaction force from the gate on the water, which is equal to the hydrodynamic force. The force on the gate is calculated by measuring the fluid depth in sections 0 and A, calculating the average velocity in these sections, and placing the values of γ and ρ in Equation (13).

2.3. Statistical Indicators

In the present study, equations are presented to estimate the ratio of energy dissipation upstream and downstream of the hydraulic jump and the C_d of the gate with and without a sill. For this purpose, the dependent parameters were considered a function of the independent parameters. The statistical indicators of absolute error (AE), percent relative error (RE %), root mean square error (RMSE), and coefficient of determination (R^2) were used to evaluate the equations:

$$AE = \left|\left(\frac{\Delta E_{AB}}{E_A}, \frac{\Delta E_{AB}}{E_B}, C_d\right)_{exp} - \left(\frac{\Delta E_{AB}}{E_A}, \frac{\Delta E_{AB}}{E_B}, C_d\right)_{cal}\right| \tag{14}$$

$$RE\% = \frac{AE}{\left(\frac{\Delta E_{AB}}{E_A}, \frac{\Delta E_{AB}}{E_B}, C_d\right)_{exp}} \times 100 \tag{15}$$

$$RMSE = \sqrt{\frac{\sum_{i=1}^{n}(AE)_i^2}{n}} \tag{16}$$

$$R^2 = 1 - \frac{SS_{Regression}}{SS_{Total}} \tag{17}$$

In the above equations, *exp* and *cal* represent the experimental and calculated values, and n is the total data. $SS_{\text{regression}}$ and SS_{total} represent the sum squared regression error and total squared error, respectively. The values of Equations (14)–(16) when close to the number zero and the values of the relation (17) when close to the number one indicate the high accuracy of the presented relations.

3. Results and Discussion

3.1. Energy Dissipation of Gate without Sill

Based on the dimensional analysis, the experimental results were evaluated by two dimensionless parameters of the energy dissipation ratio to the upstream and downstream ($\Delta E_{AB}/E_A$ and $\Delta E_{AB}/E_B$). One of the properties of the flow that is very important for understanding the flow behavior is the Froude number. Figure 3a,b shows the rate of change of these parameters at different apertures, where the horizontal axis is the dimensionless parameter Fr_A and the vertical axis is the energy dissipation ratio between sections A and B to the flow-specific energy in sections A and B. According to Figure 3a,b, it can be observed that as the Froude number increases, the ratio of energy dissipation upstream and downstream of the hydraulic jump increases. The depth of the hydraulic jump increases due to the reduction of the gate opening compared to large gate openings at different discharges, resulting in increased energy dissipation. To illustrate the results and provide better agreement with the data, the energy dissipations at different discharges and openings are shown in Figure 3c,d, respectively. The relative energy dissipation is lowest when the aperture is 0.04 m; decreasing the gate opening rate increases the relative energy dissipation. As the opening rate increases, the velocity of the flow that passes under the gate decreases, and, as a result, the initial depth of the flow increases, which decreases the specific energy in section A. The increase in depth results in a decrease in the following depth compared to the smaller openings, resulting in a decrease in specific energy in section B as in section A. As can be seen in Figure 3c,d, the relative energy dissipation at a constant flow is greater for an orifice of 0.01 m than for the orifices of 0.02 and 0.04 m, respectively. Thus, the average ratio of energy dissipation to upstream energy is 15.93% and 56% higher for an orifice of 0.01 m than for orifices of 0.02 and 0.04 m, respectively. For the downstream opening, this value is 41.32% and 83.27%, respectively.

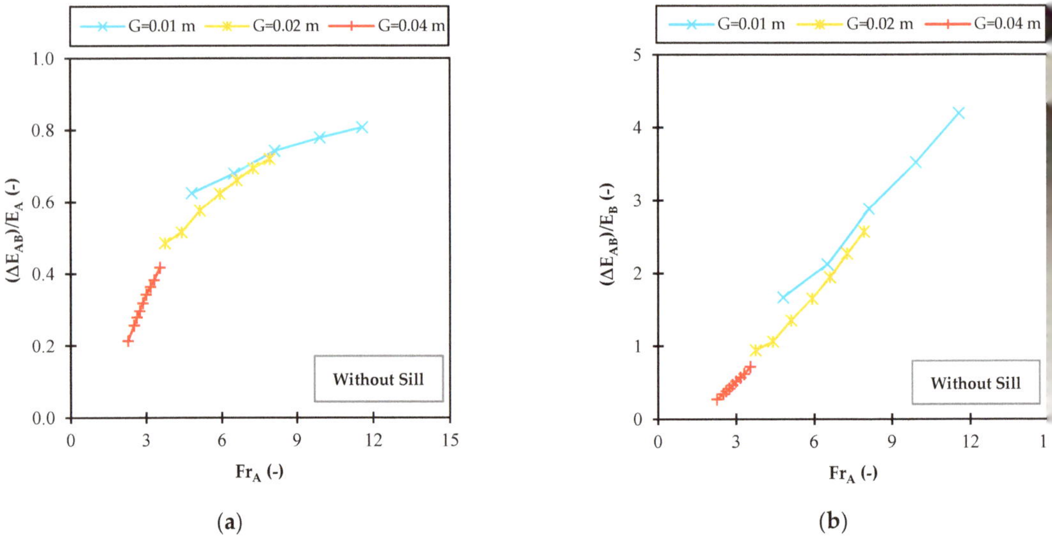

Figure 3. *Cont.*

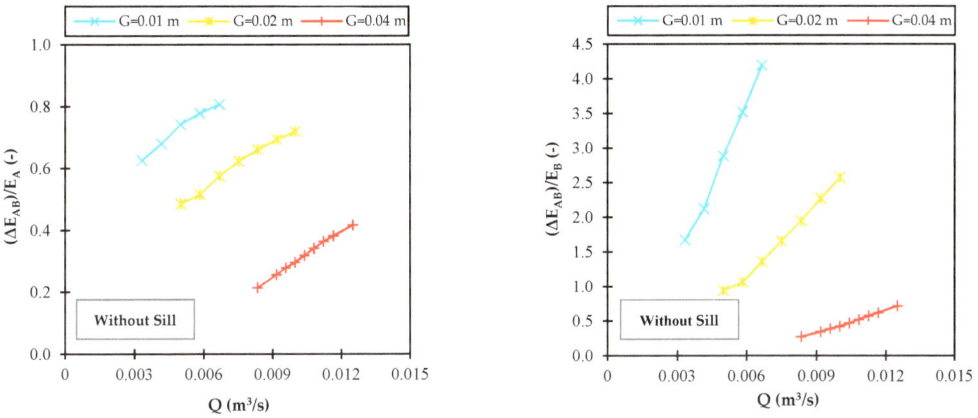

(c) (d)

Figure 3. (**a**,**b**) Changes in the relative energy dissipation against Froude number/ (**c**,**d**) Changes in the relative energy dissipation in different discharges.

3.2. C_d without Sill

Figure 4a shows that the vertical sluice C_d increases as the ratio of upstream water depth to the sluice opening (H_0/G_1) is increased. Moreover, the C_d decreases as the gate opening increases. In other words, the C_d is inversely related to the opening rate. A parameter that affects the C_d is the upstream water depth. If the sluice gate opening increases, the upstream water depth upstream decreases, and this factor will reduce the C_d at larger openings. If you decrease the gate opening, the flow converges, and the area below the gate decreases, increasing the C_d. As shown in Figure 4a, the maximum C_d value for the specific (H_0/G_1) is at an opening of 0.01 m and the lowest value at 0.04 m. Figure 4b shows the diagram of stage discharges for the different sluice openings. For a given discharge, the size of the gate opening is inversely related to the upstream water depth and decreases as the opening increases. Here, the C_d for an opening of 0.01 m is, on average, higher than that for the 0.02 and 0.04 m openings, namely, 7.75% and 16.51%, respectively, and a maximum of 16.62% and 28.9%, respectively.

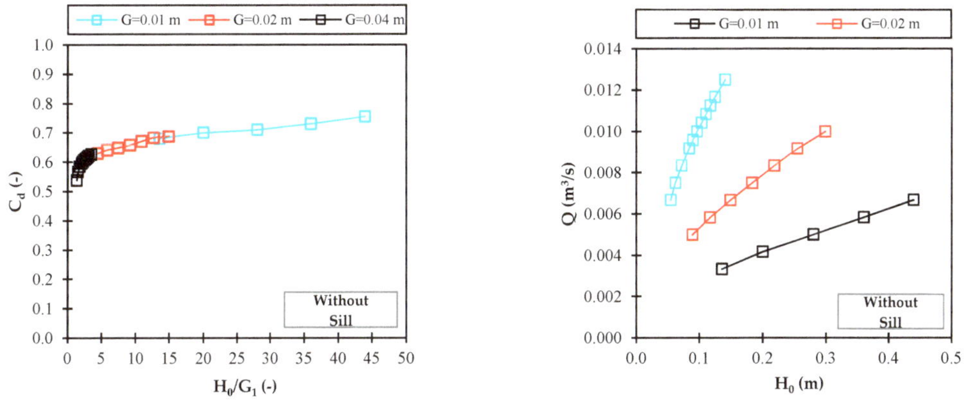

(a) (b)

Figure 4. (**a**) Variation of C_d versus H_0/G_1; (**b**) stage-discharge diagram at various openings.

Table 1 shows the magnitude of the hydrodynamic force acting on the lock at the various discharges and openings. The magnitude of the hydrodynamic force is calculated using Equation (12). Due to the rectangular cross-section, this amount is calculated for one meter of width, shown in Table 1. From Table 1, the hydrodynamic force on the gate increases as the discharge rate increases. Furthermore, the hydrodynamic force on the gate is inversely proportional to the opening for the same Q rate. This is due to increased water depth upstream, increasing the pressure and force on the sluice gate. For example, for an outflow of 600 L/min at an opening of 0.02 m, the water depth upstream is about 0.30 m, while the same outflow at an opening of 0.04 m can provide a water depth of 0.096 m upstream of the gate. This means that 35.61 and 0.93 kg/m act on the gate, respectively.

Table 1. The hydrodynamic force is applied to the sluice gate at different openings.

Gate Openings (m)					
0.01		**0.02**		**0.04**	
q (m^3/s·m)	R (kg/m)	q (m^3/s·m)	R (kg/m)	q (m^3/s·m)	R (kg/m)
0.0111	7.77	0.0167	1.96	0.0278	0.21
0.0139	17.53	0.0194	4.02	0.0306	0.49
0.0167	35.52	0.0222	7.36	0.0319	0.69
0.0194	59.62	0.025	11.90	0.0333	0.93
0.0222	89.92	0.0278	17.58	0.0347	1.27
-	-	0.0306	24.78	0.0361	1.61
-	-	0.0333	35.61	0.0375	1.96
-	-	-	-	0.0389	2.36
-	-	-	-	0.0417	3.58

3.3. Energy Dissipation of the Gate with Sill

Correction factors for kinetic energy were calculated. Table 2 shows the α-values in sections A and B. In addition, the values of specific energy in sections A and B are given in Table 3, with and without considering α.

Table 2. Values of α in sections A and B.

Q (L/min)	Sill widths (m)							
	0.025		0.05		0.075		0.10	
	α_A	α_B	α_A	α_B	α_A	α_B	α_A	α_B
450	-	-	-	-	1.024	1.002	1.045	1.003
500	-	-	1.021	1.001	1.018	1.005	1.040	1.006
550	1.022	1.001	1.013	1.002	1.015	1.008	1.030	1.009
575	1.019	1.002	1.009	1.009	1.007	1.025	1.015	1.018
600	1.010	1.008	1.003	1.030	1.005	1.038	1.005	1.038
625	1.008	1.020	1.002	1.065	1.002	1.065	1.001	1.062
650	1.006	1.050	1.001	1.075	1.001	1.080	1.001	1.095
675	1.001	1.075	1.000	1.095	1.001	1.098	1.001	1.100
700	1.001	1.090	1.000	1.100	1.000	1.105	1.001	1.108
750	1.001	1.100	1.000	1.105	1.000	1.130	1.000	1.119
Q (L/min)	Sill widths (m)							
	0.15		0.20		0.25		0.30	
	α_A	α_B	α_A	α_B	α_A	α_B	α_A	α_B
300	-	-	-	-	1.009	1.004	-	-
325	-	-	-	-	-	-	1.001	1.050
350	-	-	-	-	1.007	1.009	1.001	1.084

Table 2. *Cont.*

Q (L/min)	Sill widths (m)							
	0.15		0.20		0.25		0.30	
	α_A	α_B	α_A	α_B	α_A	α_B	α_A	α_B
375		-	-	-	1.005	1.030	1.000	1.100
400	-	-	-	-	1.001	1.075	-	-
450	-	-	1.020	1.002	1.000	1.098	-	-
500	1.030	1.002	1.015	1.005	1.000	1.107	-	-
550	1.028	1.004	1.012	1.009	-	-	-	-
575	1.028	1.006	1.007	1.020	-	-	-	-
600	1.015	1.008	1.003	1.055	-	-	-	-
625	1.010	1.010	1.001	1.085	-	-	-	-
650	1.008	1.020	1.000	1.140	-	-	-	-
675	1.001	1.055	-	-	-	-	-	-
700	1.001	1.085	-	-	-	-	-	-
750	1.000	1.130	-	-	-	-	-	-

Table 3. Values of E_A and E_B with and without considering α.

Q (L/min)	Sill Widths (m)											
	0.025						0.05					
	with α E_A (m)	without α E_A (m)	RE (%)	with α E_B (m)	without α E_B (m)	RE (%)	with α E_A (m)	without α E_A (m)	RE (%)	with α E_B (m)	without α E_B (m)	RE (%)
500	-	-	-	-	-	-	0.096	0.094	1.56	0.073	0.073	0.01
550	0.107	0.105	1.63	0.086	0.086	0.01	0.111	0.110	1.04	0.077	0.077	0.03
575	0.115	0.113	1.43	0.079	0.079	0.03	0.121	0.120	0.71	0.081	0.081	0.11
600	0.124	0.123	0.80	0.082	0.082	0.11	0.130	0.130	0.21	0.084	0.083	0.39
625	0.136	0.135	0.66	0.088	0.088	0.23	0.141	0.141	0.13	0.089	0.089	0.72
650	0.146	0.145	0.50	0.090	0.090	0.59	0.151	0.151	0.07	0.092	0.092	0.81
675	0.155	0.155	0.08	0.096	0.095	0.78	0.162	0.162	0.01	0.098	0.097	0.90
700	0.165	0.165	0.07	0.098	0.097	0.93	0.175	0.175	0.01	0.100	0.099	0.97
750	0.186	0.186	0.04	0.106	0.105	0.93	0.204	0.204	0.01	0.107	0.106	0.93

Q (L/min)	Sill widths (m)											
	0.075						0.10					
	with α E_A (m)	without α E_A (m)	RE (%)	with α E_B (m)	without α E_B (m)	RE (%)	with α E_A (m)	without α E_A (m)	RE (%)	with α E_B (m)	without α E_B (m)	RE (%)
450	0.088	0.086	1.75	0.069	0.069	0.07	0.099	0.095	3.41	0.069	0.069	0.04
500	0.104	0.102	1.39	0.076	0.076	0.08	0.118	0.114	3.18	0.077	0.077	0.07
550	0.123	0.122	1.22	0.083	0.083	0.08	0.134	0.131	2.46	0.083	0.083	0.09
575	0.137	0.136	0.59	0.089	0.089	0.09	0.148	0.146	1.27	0.089	0.089	0.16
600	0.151	0.150	0.39	0.093	0.092	0.09	0.165	0.164	0.44	0.093	0.093	0.32
625	0.164	0.164	0.13	0.095	0.094	0.09	0.182	0.182	0.09	0.097	0.096	0.50
650	0.179	0.179	0.09	0.101	0.100	0.10	0.197	0.197	0.07	0.102	0.101	0.72
675	0.193	0.193	0.07	0.103	0.102	0.10	0.213	0.213	0.07	0.105	0.105	0.72
700	0.207	0.207	0.01	0.107	0.107	0.11	0.230	0.230	0.05	0.109	0.109	0.75
750	0.247	0.247	0.01	0.117	0.116	0.12	0.266	0.266	0.01	0.118	0.117	0.74

Q (L/min)	Sill widths (m)											
	0.15						0.20					
	with α E_A (m)	without α E_A (m)	RE (%)	with α E_B (m)	without α E_B (m)	RE (%)	with α E_A (m)	without α E_A (m)	RE (%)	with α E_B (m)	without α E_B (m)	RE (%)
450	-	-	-	-	-	-	0.155	0.152	1.77	0.079	0.079	0.01
500	0.135	0.131	2.51	0.084	0.084	0.02	0.189	0.186	1.36	0.088	0.088	0.03
550	0.167	0.163	2.43	0.088	0.088	0.03	0.242	0.239	1.11	0.098	0.098	0.05
575	0.183	0.179	2.46	0.092	0.092	0.05	0.266	0.264	0.66	0.101	0.101	0.11
600	0.205	0.202	1.35	0.098	0.098	0.07	0.302	0.302	0.29	0.105	0.105	0.30
625	0.222	0.220	0.91	0.101	0.101	0.07	0.332	0.332	0.05	0.114	0.113	0.40
650	0.251	0.250	0.74	0.108	0.108	0.12	0.393	0.393	0.01	0.116	0.116	0.66
675	0.280	0.280	0.09	0.111	0.111	0.32	-	-	-	-	-	-
700	0.303	0.303	0.08	0.116	0.116	0.47	-	-	-	-	-	-
750	0.349	0.349	0.03	0.123	0.122	0.70	-	-	-	-	-	-

Table 3. *Cont.*

Q (L/min)	Sill widths (m)											
	0.25						0.30					
	with α E_A (m)	without α E_A (m)	RE (%)	with α E_B (m)	without α E_B (m)	RE (%)	with α E_A (m)	without α E_A (m)	RE (%)	with α E_B (m)	without α E_B (m)	RE (
300	0154	0.153	0.83	0.062	0.062	0.03	0.375	0.375	0.08	0.068	0.068	0.2
325	-	-	-	-	-	-	0.425	0.425	0.06	0.073	0.072	0.4
350	0.214	0.213	0.62	0.073	0.073	0.05	0.492	0.492	0.04	0.078	0.078	0.4
375	0.256	0.255	0.48	0.076	0.076	0.17	-	-	-	-	-	-
400	0.315	0.315	0.08	0.085	0.084	0.34	-	-	-	-	-	-
450	0.398	0.398	0.01	0.094	0.094	0.42	-	-	-	-	-	-
500	0.495	0.495	0.01	0.103	0.103	0.42	-	-	-	-	-	-

As you can see, the relative percentage error is small; therefore, α can be ignored. For channels with regular and straight cross-sections, the effect of the non-uniform velocity distribution on the composite velocity super elevation and momentum is small, especially compared to other uncertainties involved in the calculation. Therefore, the coefficients for energy and momentum are often assumed to be unity [20]. The value of α is higher in a laminar flow than in a turbulent one. This is due to the more uniform velocity distribution in a turbulent flow. In a turbulent flow in a regular cross-section channel, α rarely exceeds 1.15 (average). Since there is little information on these coefficients, α is assumed to be one when analyzing practical problems in regular cross-section channels. The values of α for typical channel sections [20–22] are given in Table 4. For turbulent flow in a straight duct with rectangular, trapezoidal, or circular cross-sections, α is usually less than 1.15 [23]. Therefore, it cannot be included in the calculations because its value is unknown and almost equal to one [24].

Table 4. Values of α for typical sections [20,24].

Types of Channel	α Values		
	Min	Mean	Max
Regular channels, flumes, Spillways	1.10	1.15	1.20
Natural channels	1.15	1.30	1.50
Rivers with ice cover	1.20	1.50	2.00
River valleys, over flooded	1.50	1.75	2.00

Figure 5a,b shows the relationship between the energy loss using a suppressed and an unsuppressed sill below the lock gate with the Froude number of Section A. Figure 5a,b shows that the relative energy dissipation increases with increasing Froude numbers with some tendency and a high correlation coefficient.

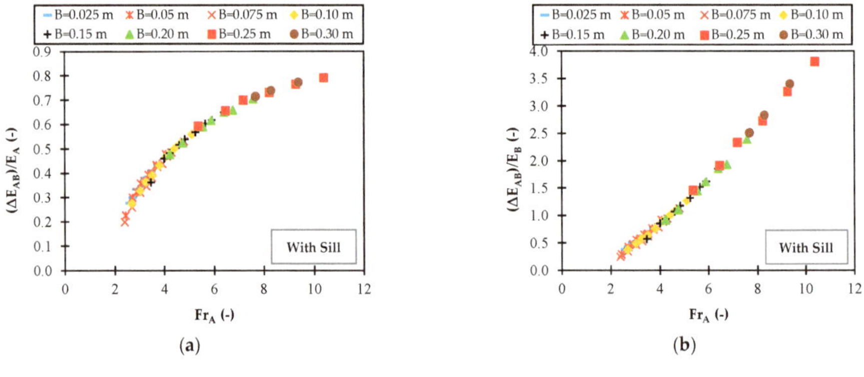

Figure 5. (**a**,**b**) Changes in the relative energy dissipation against Froude number.

Table 5 gives the sample's experimental discharges and the corresponding relative energy losses. At constant discharge, the energy decrease in the free classical hydraulic jump without the sill state is, in all cases, less than that of the hydraulic jump due to the use of the sill. In other words, the energy dissipation from a sill under the sluice gate is greater than without a sill. The reason is the change in the flow characteristics in the initial depth, the following depth, and the turbulent flows due to the use of the sill. In the case of a free classical hydraulic jump without a sill state, the energy loss is only due to the hydraulic jump.

Table 5. Comparison of the relative energy dissipation without and with sills in different widths.

B (m)		Without Sill G = 0.04	0.025	0.05	0.075	0.10	0.15	0.20	0.25	0.30
300	$\Delta E_{AB}/E_A$ (%)	-	-	-	-	-	-	-	59.3	71.5
350		-	-	-	-	-	-	-	65.7	77.3
400		-	-	-	-	-	-	-	73.2	-
450		-	-	-	19.9	27.4	-	47.8	76.5	-
500		21.5	-	22.6	25.9	32.8	36.3	52.5	79.2	-
550		25.8	27.7	29.9	32	36.5	46	59.2	-	-
600		29.7	33.5	35.8	38.3	43.2	51.6	65.1	-	-
650		34.3	38.1	39.4	44	48.9	56.9	70.6	-	-
300	$\Delta E_{AB}/E_B$ (%)	-	-	-	-	-	-	-	145.9	251.3
350		-	-	-	-	-	-	-	191.8	340.2
400		-	-	-	-	-	-	-	273.1	-
450		-	-	-	24.8	38.8	-	91.6	326.4	-
500		27.3	-	29.2	34.9	48.8	57	110.4	380.7	-
550		34.7	38.3	42.7	47	57.5	85.3	144.9	-	-
600		42.3	50.4	55.8	62.2	76.2	106.8	186.8	-	-
650		52.2	61.5	65	78.5	95.5	131.8	239.7	-	-

Separating the data for each sill with different discharge rates makes the relative energy dissipation for those with different widths visible. As the sill width increases, relative energy dissipation increases compared to the smaller width sill. In addition, the maximum relative energy dissipation for the same discharge is associated with the sill with a larger width. Therefore, if you increase the width of the sill and consequently decrease the opening of the gate and the total area of the flow passing through it, the flow becomes more directly under the gate, and flow separation occurs. In this mode, a jet of flow passes over the sill, and the wet perimeter of the sill downstream of the gate reaches its minimum. Moreover, by increasing the width of the sill, the initial depth is decreased, and the subsequent depth is increased, which is important for increasing energy dissipation. Figure 6 shows the images related to the jet's formation and the flow's release above the sill.

(a) (b)

Figure 6. Separation of the flow passing above the sill with width (**a**) 0.25 m; (**b**) 0.30 m.

The relative depth of the hydraulic jump (y_B/y_A) is a function of Fr_A. To study the effect of the sill below the gate on the subsequent flow depth, the plot of the relative depth of the hydraulic jump is shown in Figure 7. It can be observed that as the Froude number increases, the relative depth of the hydraulic jump linearly increases. The reason for this is the significant effect of the sill on increasing the sequent depth significantly on the jump depth increase. As the sill width increases, the jump depth is greater for the same discharge than for a sill with a smaller width.

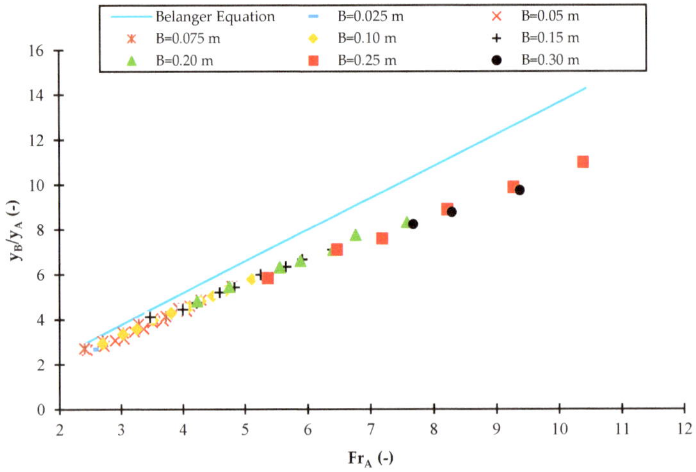

Figure 7. Changes in the relative depth of the hydraulic jump versus the initial Fr_A.

Both the magnitude and intensity of the hydraulic jump depend on the Froude number at the hydraulic jump in section A. As the Fr_A increases, the ratio between the following depth and the initial depth (y_B/y_A), i.e., the wave height (y_B-y_A), increases. The direct relationship of the energy output to the third power of the expression (y_B-y_A) causes the amount of energy output to be very sensitive to the intensity and strength of the jump. A comparison between the present results and those of [25] shows that applying the sill leads to a decrease in the following depth (Figure 7).

3.4. C_d with Sill

In Figure 8a, the C_d decreases with a decrease in the sill width. Thus, the sill with the smallest width has the smallest C_d. The reason for increasing the C_d is related to the even flow distribution across the gate. When the width of the sill below the gate increases, the sill acts as a barrier; downstream of the sill, the water above the sill is discharged all at once and uniformly. The return flow decreases to a minimum as the width increases, which increases the C_d. In addition, the C_d tends to increase as the ratio between the upstream depth and the width of the sill increases.

The rate of increase of the runoff coefficient decreases with increasing depth when the rate of the runoff coefficient is not affected by the increase in depth. Figure 8b shows the plot of the runoff coefficient as a function of Z/B. According to Figure 8b, the C_d increases with increasing runoff when the sill height is kept constant in all models and the sill width increases. Figure 8c shows the effect of the opening and the flow area under the gate. It is observed that by increasing the ratio of the flow area above the sill to the flow area on both sides of the sill, the C_d increases. Increasing the sill width, the A on both sides of the sill decreases, and, therefore, at the sill with a larger width, the A_{total} will be less than at the sill with a smaller width, which leads to an increase in C_d. A sill with a lower size below the gate increases the C_d compared to the mode without a sill. This increase is due to the reduction of the total area underneath the gate.

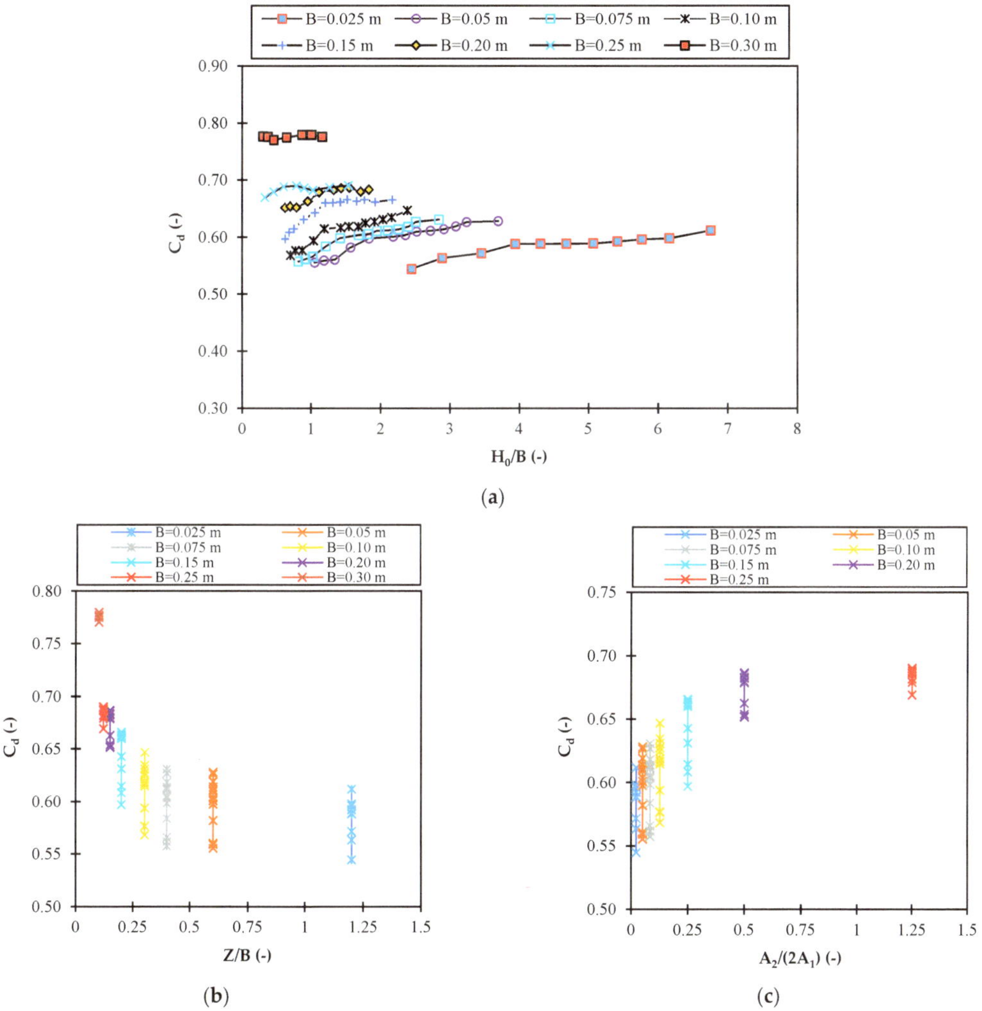

Figure 8. The C_d changes against the (**a**) upstream depth to sill width; (**b**) height to sill width; (**c**) flow area above the sill to flow area at the sill sides.

In Figure 9, the C_d was plotted against the H_0-Z/G_1 to find the best fit and compare the data. A comparison was made between the C_d without a sill and suppressed sills with the same opening (Figure 9). Figure 9 shows that a sill below the sluice gate increases the flow rate and improves the system performance compared to the without sill situation. At constant discharge, the upstream depth with a sill is less than without a sill. The presence of a sill that is the same width as the channel increases the discharge (at an opening of 0.01 m) by an average of 7.75%.

Table 6 lists some of the experimental observations with the corresponding C_d for the sample. For similar discharges, the C_d for the unsuppressed sill is higher than the no-sill condition, and this trend increases with increasing sill width. Therefore, unsuppressed sills can be considered and used because they increase flow efficiency and prevent sediment accumulation behind the gate.

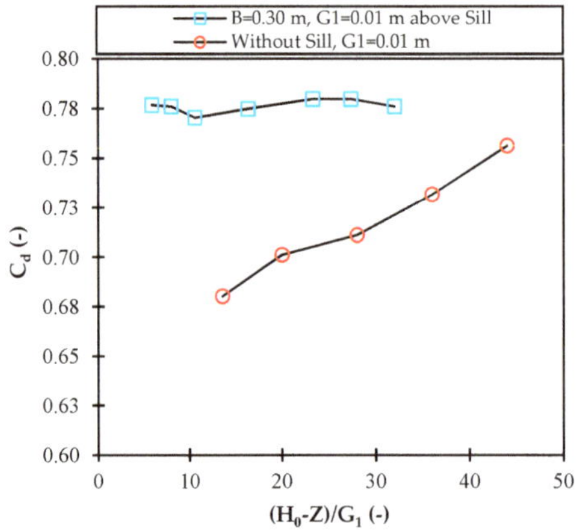

Figure 9. Comparison of C_d between without and with suppressed sill at the same opening.

Table 6. Comparison of C_d without and with sill state in various sizes (width).

	B (m)		Without Sill	0.025	0.025	0.075	0.10	0.15	0.20	0.25	0.3
Q (L/min)	350	C_d (-)	-	-	0.5554	0.5573	0.5683	0.5969	0.6515	0.6897	0.77
	375		-	-	0.5592	0.5617	0.5763	0.6083	0.6538	0.6860	0.77
	400		0.5377	0.5445	0.5604	0.5658	0.5769	0.6143	0.6520	0.6818	-
	450		0.5667	0.5675	0.5820	0.5838	0.5938	0.6310	0.6625	0.6868	-

This study established equations to predict the relative energy dissipation and C_d of the gate with and without sill conditions. First, the non-linear form of the proposed equations for relative energy dissipation as a function of the dimensionless parameters was determined. The proposed equations' general forms were considered Equation (18).

$$\frac{\Delta E_{AB}}{E_A}, \frac{\Delta E_{AB}}{E_B} = aFr_A{}^b + c\left(\frac{y_B}{y_A}\right)^d + e\left(\frac{B}{y_A}\right) \tag{18}$$

Using Solver in Excel and the regression technique, the equations were presented to obtain an appropriate form with the least error and a high correlation coefficient according to Equations (19) and (20):

$$\frac{\Delta E_{AB}}{E_A} = 0.3176Fr_A{}^{0.4233} - 0.8917\left(\frac{y_B}{y_A}\right)^{-1.4483} - 0.0005\left(\frac{B}{y_A}\right) \tag{19}$$

$$\frac{\Delta E_{AB}}{E_B} = 0.9334Fr_A{}^{0.8912} - 1.0722\left(\frac{y_B}{y_A}\right)^{0.5210} - 0.0039\left(\frac{B}{y_A}\right) \tag{20}$$

Figure 10a,c shows a comparison diagram of the calculated and experimental values of the relative energy dissipation. The results show that the tendency of changes in the energy dissipation ratio to the upstream and downstream parts of the experimental results agrees with the values obtained from the equations. The results of the statistical indicators are given in Table 7. Figure 10b,d examines the independent parameters y_B/y_A and the dependent parameters $\Delta E_{AB}/E_A$ and $\Delta E_{AB}/E_B$ to verify the accuracy of Equations (19) and (20). Figure 10b,d shows the graphs of the percent relative error against the effective dimensionless parameter y_B/y_A. In these figures, a large range of data lies within the relative error range of ±5%. This shows that the proposed equations have very good accuracy in predicting the relative energy dissipation.

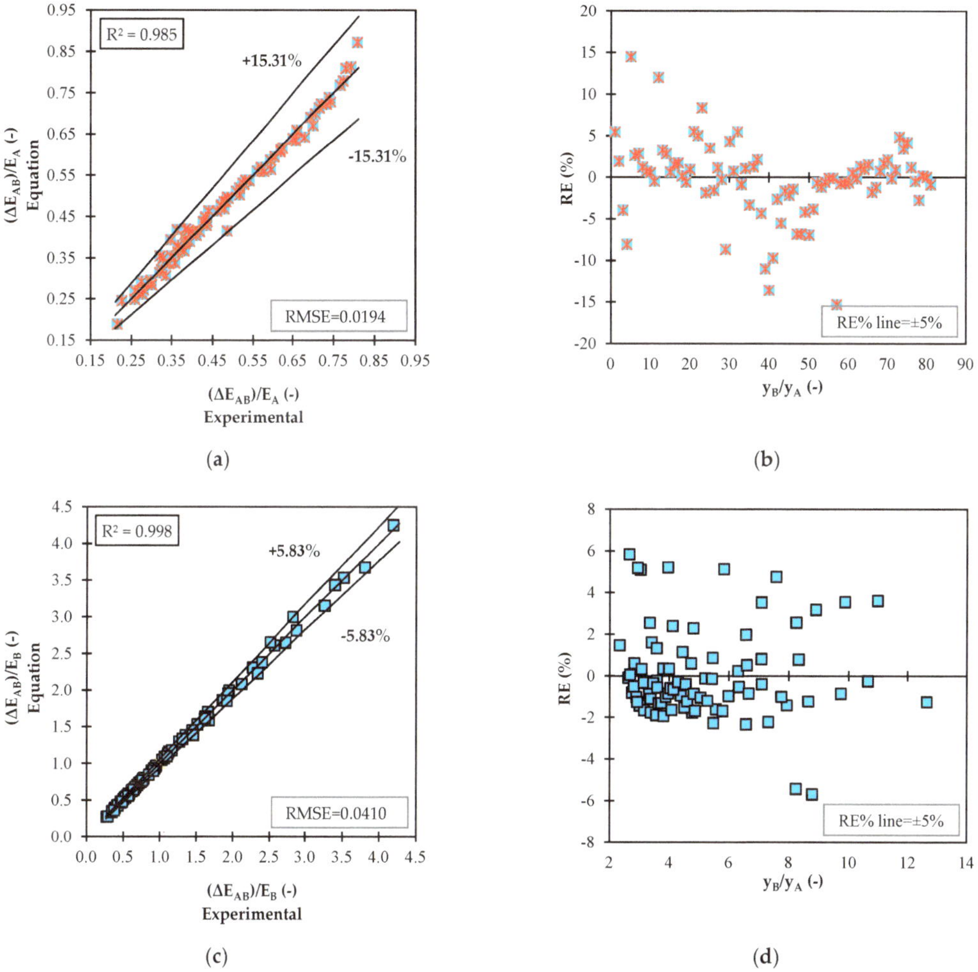

Figure 10. (**a**,**c**) Comparison of calculated and experimental values of the relative energy dissipation; (**b**,**d**) the percentage relative error dispersion.

Table 7. Results of statistical indicators comparing experimental results with Equations (18) and (19).

Mode	Mean AE (-)	Mean RE (%)	Max Relative Error (%)	Min Relative Error (%)	RMSE (-)	R^2
$\frac{\Delta E_{AB}}{E_A}$	0.0134	3.12	14.49	−15.31	0.0194	0.985
$\frac{\Delta E_{AB}}{E_B}$	0.0233	1.62	5.83	−5.7	0.0410	0.998

By combining the data from the different openings of the present study and using the regression technique with Solver in the Excel software, Equation (21) was obtained to estimate the C_d of the gate without the sill condition.

$$C_d = 2.7465\left(\frac{H_0}{G_1}\right)^{0.0177} - 2.1916 \quad (21)$$

Table 8 compares the C_d of the present study without the sill state with the results of the previous studies.

Table 8. Comparison of C_d with previous studies.

Gate	C_d (-)											
	Present Research (Integration of All Openings)			[4]			[26]			[6]		
	High	Low	Mean	High	Low	Mean	High	Low	Mean	High	Low	Me
Sluice gate	0.75	0.53	0.62	0.64	0.60	0.62	0.59	0.53	0.55	0.63	0.52	0.

Figure 11a shows that Equation (21) reasonably predicts the values of the runoff coefficient with a maximum percent relative error, a mean percent relative error, a mean absolute error, and a mean squared error of 2.81%, 0.97%, 0.0061, and 0.0072, respectively. In Figure 11b, by substituting the C_d obtained from the proposed Equation (21) into Equation (5), a comparison was made between the discharge rate obtained from the experimental results and Equation (5). In Figure 11b, it can be seen that a large area of the data is within the error range of ±1.5%. This shows that the formula is very accurate, such that more than 82% of the data have an error of less than ±1.5%.

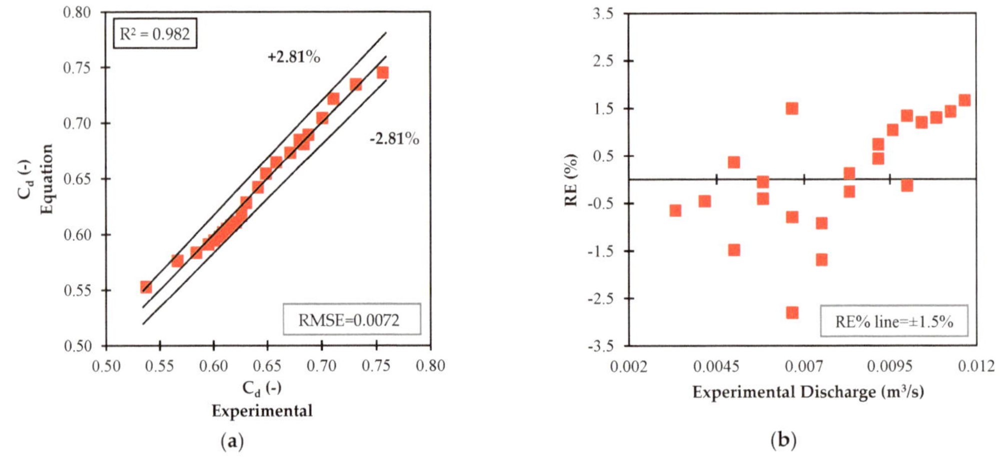

Figure 11. (**a**) Comparison diagram of calculated and experimental values of C_d; (**b**) percentage relative error versus experimental discharge.

Equation (22) can be used for suppressed and unsuppressed sill below the sluice gate. For the suppressed sill, $A_{total} = A_2$. One way to compare the experimental results with Equation (22) to determine its accuracy is to examine the magnitude of the difference between the C_d obtained from the experimental results and the C_d calculated using the predicted equation.

$$C_d = 0.1529 \times \left(\frac{A_{total}}{A_2}\right)^{-1.2093} + 0.6511\left(\frac{H_0 - Z}{B}\right)^{0.2565} \times \left(\frac{H_0}{B}\right)^{-0.2668} \quad (22)$$

Figure 12a shows the optimal trend of results between calculated and experimental values. According to Figure 12a, the maximum percent relative error is 4.92%. The mean percent relative error, mean absolute error, and root mean square error are 1.36%, 0.0087, and 0.0108, respectively. From Figure 12b, 94% of the data are within the error range of ±3%, indicating the high accuracy of the proposed equation.

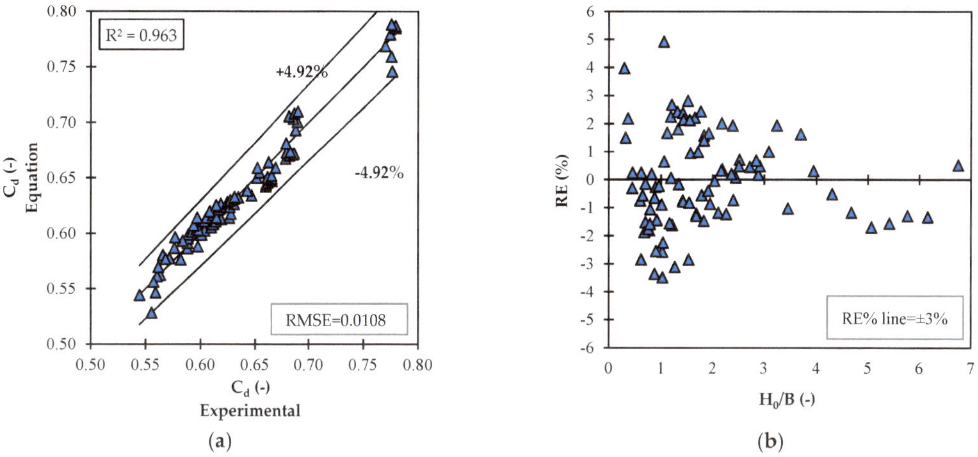

Figure 12. (**a**) Comparison diagram of calculated and experimental C_d values with sill in different widths; (**b**) dispersion of the percentage relative error.

4. Conclusions

The present study investigated energy dissipation and the C_d with and without sills below the lock gate. The results show that the relative energy dissipation without a sill and at different openings is inversely related to the gate openings. As the opening of the sluice gate increases, the relative energy dissipation decreases due to the increase in initial depth. As a result, a decrease in specific energy in section A and a decrease in exit depth and specific energy in section B can be observed. The flow of the gate without a sill decreases as the opening increases. The C_d of the sluice gate without a sill is most affected by the upstream flow depth and the opening. At constant discharge, as the opening increases, the upstream water depth of the sluice gate decreases, and the C_d tends to decrease in proportion to the lower opening of the sluice gate. The comparison of the sluice gates with different openings shows that the hydrodynamic force on the gate increases with a decrease in the number of openings for the same discharge rate. According to the results, in all cases where the sill is used under the sluice gate and at all discharge rates, the relative energy dissipation is greater than for the free classical hydraulic jump without a sill. The energy dissipation increases as the Fr_A increases. A comparison of the results for the C_d with sill and without sill shows that a sill under the sluice gate increases the C_d. In the present study, the general equation for discharge calculation was developed for an unsuppressed sill, and the calculations were performed based on the new equation of the present study, which can be used for unsuppressed symmetrical sills. The presence of a sill the same width as the channel below the sluice gate increases the C_d compared to the condition without a sill at a fixed opening. From the comparison of the rate of increase of the C_d, it can be concluded that the sill width parameter has the greatest influence on the C_d. Finally, non-linear polynomial regression relationships were determined to calculate the energy dissipation related to the upstream and downstream hydraulic jump. Non-linear regression equations were also established to predict the C_d.

Author Contributions: Conceptualization, H.A., R.N. and R.D.; methodology, H.A., R.N. and R.D.; formal analysis, H.A., R.N. and R.D.; investigation, H.A., R.N., V.S., A.K., R.D. and J.A.; data curation, H.A.; writing—original draft preparation, H.A.; writing—review and editing, H.A., R.N., V.S., A.K., R.D. and J.A.; supervision, R.D.; project administration, H.A. All authors have read and agreed to the published version of the manuscript.

Funding: This research did not receive external funding.

Data Availability Statement: Data are contained within the article.

Conflicts of Interest: The authors declare no conflict of interest.

References

1. Negm, A.M.; Alhamid, A.A.; El-Saiad, A.A. Submerged flow below sluice gate with sill. In Proceedings of the International Confer on Hydro-Science and Engineering Hydro-Science and Engineering ICHE98, Berlin, Germany, 31 August–3 September 1 University of Mississippi: Oxford, MS, USA, 1998. Advances in Hydro-Science and Engineering. Volume 3.
2. Henry, H.R. Discussion on Diffusion of submerged jets, by Albertson, M.L. et al. *Trans. Am. Soc. Civ. Eng.* **1950**, *115*, 687.
3. Rajaratnam, N.; Subramanya, K. Flow Equation for the Sluice Gate. *J. Irrig. Drain. Div.* **1967**, *93*, 167–186. [CrossRef]
4. Rajaratnam, N. Free Flow Immediately Below Sluice Gates. *J. Hydraul. Div.* **1977**, *103*, 345–351. [CrossRef]
5. Swamee, P.K. Sluice Gate Discharge Equations. *J. Irrig. Drain. Eng.* **1992**, *118*, 56–60. [CrossRef]
6. Shivapur, A.V.; Shesha Prakash, M.N. Inclined Sluice Gate for Flow Measurement. *ISH J. Hydraul. Eng.* **2005**, *11*, 46–56. [Cross
7. Nasehi Oskuyi, N.; Salmasi, F. Vertical Sluice Gate Discharge Coefficient. *J. Civ. Eng. Urban.* **2012**, *2*, 108–114.
8. Daneshfaraz, R.; Ghahramanzadeh, A.; Ghaderi, A.; Joudi, A.R.; Abraham, J. Investigation of the Effect of Edge Shape Characteristics of Flow Under Vertical Gates. *J. Am. Water Work. Assoc.* **2016**, *108*, E425–E432. [CrossRef]
9. Salmasi, F.; Nouri, M.; Sihag, P.; Abraham, J. Application of SVM, ANN, GRNN, RF, GP and RT Models for Predicting Discha Coefficients of Oblique Sluice Gates Using Experimental Data. *Water Supply* **2021**, *21*, 232–248. [CrossRef]
10. Salmasi, F.; Abraham, J. Expert System for Determining Discharge Coefficients for Inclined Slide Gates Using Genetic Progr ming. *J. Irrig. Drain. Eng.* **2020**, *146*, 06020013. [CrossRef]
11. Alhamid, A.A. Coefficient of Discharge for Free Flow Sluice Gates. *J. King Saud Univ.-Eng. Sci.* **1999**, *11*, 33–47. [CrossRef]
12. Salmasi, F.; Norouzi Sarkarabad, R. Investigation of different geometric shapes of sills on discharge coefficient of vertical sl gate. *Amirkabir J. Civ. Eng.* **2018**, *52*, 2.
13. Karami, S.; Heidari, M.M.; Adib Rad, M.H. Investigation of Free Flow Under the Sluice Gate with the Sill Using Flow-3D Mc *Iran. J. Sci. Technol. Trans. Civ. Eng.* **2020**, *44*, 317–324. [CrossRef]
14. Salmasi, F.; Abraham, J. Prediction of discharge coefficients for sluice gates equipped with different geometric sills under the using multiple non-linear regression (MNLR). *J. Hydrol.* **2020**, *597*, 125728. [CrossRef]
15. Ghorbani, M.A.; Salmasi, F.; Saggi, M.K.; Bhatia, A.S.; Kahya, E.; Norouzi, R. Deep learning under H_2O framework. A nc approach for quantitative analysis of discharge coefficient in sluice gates. *J. Hydroinformatics* **2020**, *22*, 1603–1619. [CrossRef]
16. Lauria, A.; Calomino, F.; Alfonsi, G.; D'Ippolito, A. Discharge Coefficients for Sluice Gates Set in Weirs at Different Upstr Wall Inclinations. *Water* **2020**, *12*, 245. [CrossRef]
17. Abbaspour, A.; Hosseinzadeh Dalir, A.; Farsadizadeh, D.; Sadraddini, A.A. Effect of Sinusoidal Corrugated Bed on Hydra Jump Characteristics. *J. Hydro-Environ. Res.* **2009**, *3*, 109–117. [CrossRef]
18. Murzyn, F.; Chanson, H. Experimental assessment of scale effects affecting two-phase flow properties in hydraulic jumps. *Fluids* **2008**, *45*, 513–521. [CrossRef]
19. Nasrabadi, M.; Mehri, Y.; Ghassemi, A.; Omid, M.H. Predicting Submerged Hydraulic Jump Characteristics Using Mach Learning Methods. *Water Supply* **2021**, *21*, 4180–4194. [CrossRef]
20. Chow, V.T. *Open-Channel Hydraulics*; McGraw-Hill Book Co.: New York, NY, USA, 1959.
21. Watts, F.J.; Simons, D.B.; Richardson, E.V. Variation of α and β values in Lined Open Channels. *J. Hydraul. Div. Am. Soc. Civ.* **1967**, *93*, 217–234, (see also Discussions: Vol. 94, **1968**, HY3, pp. 834–837; HY6, pp. 1560–1564; and vol. 95, **1969**, HY3, p. 1([CrossRef]
22. Temple, D.M. Velocity Distribution Coefficients for Grass-lined Channels. *J. Hydraul. Eng. Am. Soc. Civ. Eng.* **1986**, *12*, 193– [CrossRef]
23. Henderson, F.M. *Open Channel Flow*; MacMillan Publishing Co.: New York, NY, USA, 1966.
24. Chaudhry, M.H. *Open Channel Flow*, 2nd ed.; Springer: Berlin/Heidelberg, Germany, 2008.
25. Belanger, J.B.C.J. Essai sur la solution numerique de quelques problemes relatifs au movement permanent des eaux coura In *Test on the Numerical Solution of Some Problems Relating to the Permanent Movement of Running Waters*; Kessinger Publish Whitefish, MT, USA, 1828. (In French)
26. Hager, W.H. Underflow of Standard Sluice Gate. *Exp. Fluids* **1999**, *27*, 339–350. [CrossRef]

fluids MDPI

cle

fect of Serpentine Flow Field Channel Dimensions and ectrode Intrusion on Flow Hydrodynamics in an All-Iron edox Flow Battery

esh Basavegowda Krishnappa [1], S. Gowreesh Subramanya [2], Abhijit Deshpande [3] Bharatesh Chakravarthi [4,*]

1 Department of Mechanical Engineering, Jyothy Institute of Technology, Bengaluru 560052, Karnataka, India
2 Department of Mechanical Engineering, JSS Academy of Technical Education, Bengaluru 560059, Karnataka, India
3 Domain Expert, Powertrain CFD, Mercedes-Benz RD, Bengaluru 560066, Karnataka, India
4 School of Computing and Augmented Intelligence, Arizona State University, Tempe, AZ 85287, USA
* Correspondence: bshettah@asu.edu; Tel.: +1-602-716-1642

Abstract: This paper presents a study on flow hydrodynamics for single-channel serpentine flow field (SCSFF) and cross-split serpentine flow field configurations (CSSFF) for different geometric dimensions of channel and rib width ratios with electrode intrusion over varying compression ratios (CRs) in an all-iron redox flow battery. Pressure drops (Δp) measured experimentally across a cell active area of 131 cm^2 for different electrolyte flow rates were numerically validated. A computational fluid dynamics study was conducted for detailed flow analyses, velocity magnitude contours, flow distribution, and uniformity index for the intrusion effect of a graphite felt electrode bearing a thickness of 6 mm with a channel compressed to varying percentages of 50%, 60%, and 70%. Experimental pressure drops (Δp) over the numerical value resulted in the maximum error approximated to 4%, showing good agreement. It was also reported that the modified version of the cross-split serpentine flow field, model D, had the lowest pressure drop, Δp, of 2223.4 pa, with a maximum uniformity index at the electrode midplane of 0.827 for CR 50%, across the active cell area. The pressure drop (Δp) was predominantly higher for increased compression ratios, wherein intrusion phenomena led to changes in electrochemical activity; it was found that the velocity distribution was quite uniform for a volumetric uniformity index greater than 80% in the felt.

Keywords: iron redox flow battery; serpentine flow field; flow hydrodynamics; computational fluid dynamics; intrusion phenomenon; graphite felt electrode; uniformity index

1. Introduction

The current annual global energy generation capacity is estimated to be more than 20 TW (terawatt), and the energy consumption is estimated to be more than 15 TW. The major portion of contemporary energy needs is fulfilled by conventional energy sources, i.e., fossil fuels such as coal, natural gas, oil, etc., whereas the rate of energy consumption is increasing exponentially, and if it continues to grow at this pace, the predicted energy needs might double by 2050. Hence, there is a peak in demand for energy production, storage, and distribution. Environmental concerns over the use of non-renewable energy and their resource constraints, combined with energy security concerns, represent a launching pad to generate high-grade energy, i.e., electricity obtained from renewable energy sources. The energy obtained from solar power and wind, being intermittent in nature, poses a tough challenge for grid operators to store and retrieve. One such technology, which is ideal and also sustainable, is electrical energy storage systems (ESSs), which is considered to be a key enabler of smart grids or future grids. This technology might smoothen out the variable nature of renewable energy production and distribution, act as a bi-directional power regulator, offset the surplus of generated energy for future needs, facilitate effective energy storage, delivery, ensure improved grid reliability and utilization, and hence, represents a stable candidate for future electric grids. Many such energy storage technologies, such as mechanical, electrochemical (batteries), thermal, electrical, and hydrogen storage systems, already exist in the commercial domain. However, substantial research and development still needs to be conducted in the fields of material and technological advances to enhance electricity distribution, power backup range, duration of storage, and energy scale-up. These storage technologies are limited on the system-level usage suitability for required applications [1–4].

Research on electrochemical energy storage systems has been steadily growing since the flow battery concept evolved approximately four decades ago, and it is a promising agent for medium to large kilowatt-scale energy storage applications [5–7]. Redox flow battery (RFB) technology is well established and is gaining traction due to its suitable integration to achieve efficiency, scalability, rapid sensitivity, longer life cycle, less maintenance, low cost, flexibility in energy and power capacity, the least impact on environment, and as one of the many electrochemical energy storage (ESS) methods, particularly to store renewable energy. RFBs are the best alternative to Li-ion stationary systems and have been authenticated and standardized by the International Electrochemical Commission as grid storage systems [8,9].

RFBs represent many forms, developed as aqueous nature, based on their redox couples, including iron–chromium, bromine–polysulfide, quinone–bromine, zinc–bromine, and all-vanadium RFBs; single-metal-based, including all-iron, all-lead, and all-copper RFB systems; and non-aqueous forms, including all-uranium and all-neptunium RFBs dissolved in non-aqueous solvents. Vanadium-based batteries are well-established and commercially adopted flow batteries; however, they have certain operational limitations due to the inherent cross-contamination problem caused by the diffusion of different redox ions across the membrane, and low soluability [10,11].

We shifted our interest towards the initially developed iron-based RFBs: iron–chromium, iron–cadmium, zinc–iron, and iron–vanadium; these batteries are best suited for certain system-based applications. They persist with certain difficulties in improving system efficiency due to the inherent nature of redox couple activity of slow kinetic reactions, poor reversibility, and hydrogen evolution (side reaction). Cross-contamination results in self-discharge and a high operating temperature. Some oxidation forms are toxic in nature. Low solubility (limiting the energy density) and precipitation issues at about a 40 °C operating temperature lower the electrolyte utilization by blocking the effect due to electrodeposition, which essentially limits the energy capacity during charging. Dendrite formation can lead to short circuits and a high cost of vanadium-based species. Certain beneficial features of all-iron RFBs have emerged, including a high level of solubility, improved discharge energy density, operation stability with less precipitation even at increased electrolyte temperatures, non-toxic, environmentally friendly, low-cost redox species, and abundant earth metal [12,13]. The energy/power density of all-iron RFBs is reasonably high, with the least capital cost. To achieve this, a specific selection of key materials such as electrodes, electrolytes, and ion exchange membranes, in addition to an optimized flow field configuration, are the key components.

In an RFB, the positive and negative species of electrolyte are circulated through the cell stack, where charge and discharge take place before being returned to the external storage tank. The amount of energy stored depends on the volume of electrolytes, while the peak power density depends on the number and size of the cell stack, wherein both the power and energy stored can be widely varied independently. This feature indeed promotes RFBs as a very attractive alternative for kilowatt-scale energy storage applications [14].

Improvements in power density make RFBs a more competitive option for kilowatt-scale energy storage. The operating power density of an RFB is a function of the rate of electrochemical ionic activity at the electrode felt–electrolyte interface.

Inadequate electrolyte circulation limits the electrocatalytic activity, even though the proper selection of materials and porous media is realized.

The literature reports that the different channel and rib dimensions of a serpentine flow field should be clearly understood for their geometric dimensions, stability, and suitability over a selected cell size, on channel geometry, with dimensions varying about 1 to 2 mm in channel width and rib width occupying between 40% and 50% of the total cell area. The variation in channel dimension is reflected in larger cell sizes with a noticeable change in pressure drop, peak power density, and discharge energy density, thus recommending larger channels with reduced rib width to improve the overall performance of the cell [14,15]. In redox flow battery applications, the electrolyte is a liquid component that flows through a hydraulic diameter of the channel, whereas the results of pressure drop and flow distribution were also dependent on varied rib-to-channel width ratios, increased flow rate, flow circulation, length of flow path, and compression of the porous medium as additional parameters. Recent research and development has been performed to understand the flow hydrodynamics, flow channel interactions (interdigitated, spiral, and serpentine), electrodes, modified forms, and their properties, such as permeability, as a function of compression factors (intrusion effect), on overall battery performance [16–25].

Inherent properties such as permeability, porosity, and pore size of the electrode felt determine the level of diffusion and the drop-in pressure to be incurred for a given electrolyte discharge. Pressure drops (Δp) between adjacent serpentine flow channels possibly develop convective diffusion in the porous electrode, whereas the flow field (interdigitated) enables the electrolyte to flow along a defined path including the electrode. The increased pressure drop may lead to inadequate electrolyte distribution, resulting in decreased electrocatalytic activity at the electrode–electrolyte interface [26–28].

In addition, the cell-stack design parameters, such as torque applied to hold the cell assembly together to stop leaks, reduce stacking pressure, and decrease electrode compression, effectively determine the permeability. Hydrodynamic interactions are an active function of the cell size, design, and electrolyte circulation rate. One literature review identified a new flow field design, i.e., plug flow, later optimized to a short flow path to regulate the mass transport polarization behavior, which improves performance in redox flow battery systems [29–32].

A few studies have reported that the channel dimensions and electrode intrusion in interdigitated and conventional serpentine flow fields also lead to a pressure drop across the cell stack; their findings were based on understanding the hydrodynamics of the flow along with electrochemical performance studies on vanadium-based battery systems. Analysis of new flow field configurations, electrolyte flow dynamics in adjacent channel dimensions and under rib convection, and pressure drop parameters were addressed. Several significant studies have demonstrated that the serpentine flow channel configuration shows the highest energy efficiency with the least pressure drop, at different operating conditions, and predominantly enhances electrochemical activity in the flow cell battery application [33–36].

The development of a suitable flow field design can certainly reduce the cost of a redox flow battery. Starting from the interdigitate flow field design analysis, the channel and rib dimensions varied to investigate the impact on pressure drop, channel flow volume, flow uniformity, and parameters operating at different current densities. Design optimization is one component that can reduce the overall setup cost of the cell stack and also increase system performance.

Electrolyte flow distribution is an important factor that contributes to the performance of a redox flow battery, wherein the interdigitated and serpentine flow fields are simulated and studied closely for pressure drop parameters and computational fluid dynamics; the study revealed 'under the rib convection' for both flow field designs, but with a shorter residing time for the interdigitated flow field, showing superior electrochemical performance. The literatures quantify the simulation results of interdigitated and serpentine flow fields with details of channel passage and the dependence of pressure loss on cell size and flow field design, giving an understanding of the slow flow regions of mass transport behavior and the electrode parameters, which influence pressure drops. The most cost-effective way to build a redox flow battery is by optimizing flow field design, which leads to reduced stack area and increased power density [37–40].

The most significant way to recognize the influence of flow circulation and uniform distribution over the entire cell area for effective ionic activity is through design parameter changes such as charge and discharge energy capacity, peak power, and energy efficiency, which also depend on the stack size and electrolyte volume discharge. Furthermore, the main scope of this study focused on optimizing a modified version of serpentine flow field configurations at varying electrolyte flow rates to predominantly showcase the enhanced flow distribution and uniformity at the lowest possible pressure drop across the cell, and ultimately increase the electrochemical performance.

This paper reports an experimental study on pressure drop parameters for single and cross-split serpentine flow field configurations with the electrode intrusion effect as a function of the compression ratio at varying flow rates, with numerical validation. The flow hydrodynamic study was carried out using computational fluid dynamics (CFD) on modified versions of the cross-split serpentine flow field for different channel dimensions (rib-to-channel width ratios) with suitable porous media (graphite felt electrode) subjected to different compression ratios at varying electrolyte flow rates to analyze parameters such as pressure drop across the active cell area, velocity magnitude contours, flow circulation, and uniform distribution. The electrode–felt permeability values were obtained using a Tamayol–Bahrami correlation model [41]. The most suitable model for the electrode's planar fibrous microstructure was in close agreement with the rayon-based graphite felt material chosen in this study. Details of these studies and the results obtained are discussed below.

2. Materials and Methods

The systematic assembly of an all-iron redox flow battery (AIRFB) cell is depicted in Figure 1. The main components of AIRFB cells are graphite plates with flow channels, electrodes, anionic membrane, ferrous solution as an electrolyte, copper current collectors, gaskets, and end plates.

The chemical reactions in the battery are given by Equations (1)–(3) [37]

Positive electrode:

$$2Fe^{2+} \rightleftharpoons 2Fe^{3+} + 2e^{-} \quad E^{0} = 0.77 \text{ V} \tag{1}$$

Negative electrode:

$$Fe^{2+} + 2e^{-} \rightleftharpoons Fe^{0} \quad E^{0} = -0.44 \text{ V} \tag{2}$$

Overall:

$$3Fe^{2+} \rightleftharpoons Fe^{0} + 2Fe^{3+} \quad E^{0} = 1.21 \text{ V} \tag{3}$$

The AIRFB system has optimal power density and current capacity, whereas the stack is a single-cell assembly. During the operation, an electrolyte is constantly circulated using a peristaltic pump through the graphite plate flow channel from the respective electrolyte storage tank. The performance of the system was evaluated based on the columbic, voltaic, and energy efficiencies, energy density, and depth of discharge.

The models developed for this study had the same active cell area, 131 cm^2, with fixed inlet and outlet positions. Electrode graphite felt, a porous medium with a thickness of 6 mm, was specifically selected based on certain criteria such as electrical conductivity, surface area, pore size, pretreatment (thermal treatment), and electrochemical activity (cell resistance and cell efficiency). An electrolyte solution containing ferrous chloride tetrahydrate ($FeCl_2$) was proportionately mixed with 2 moles of ammonium (NH_4), 3.25 moles of chloride (Cl_2), and 0.3 moles of ascorbic acid ($C_6H_8O_6$) to maintain ideal pH conditions [37].

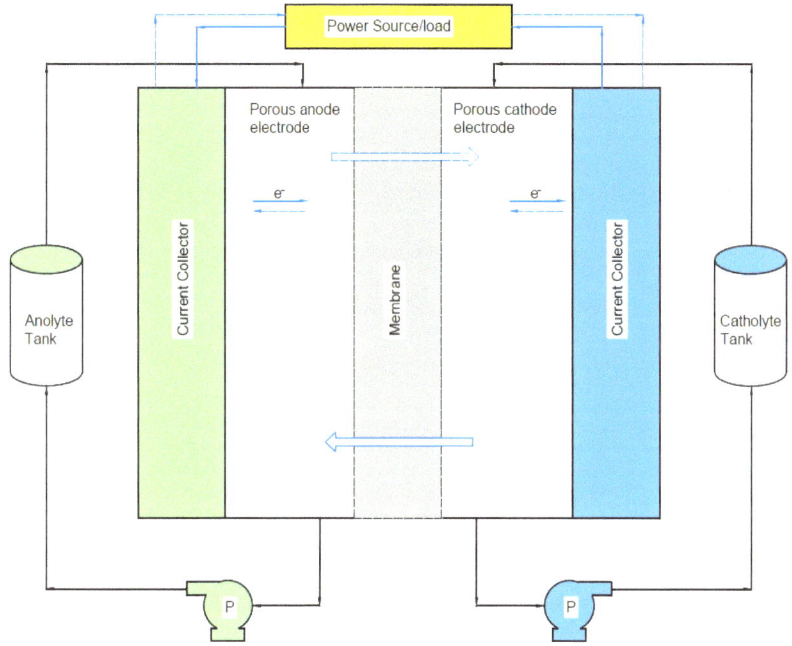

Figure 1. A Systematic Assembly of an All Iron Redox Flow Battery.

2.1. Flow Field without Felt Model

Details of the A, B, C, and D flow field models of cross-split serpentine flow field configurations with varying geometrical dimensions are presented in Table 1. These models were designed using SolidWorks Premium 2018 SP 4.0, developed by Dassault Systems. Models with graphite plates of 10 mm thickness, ET-10 (isostatic nature) grade, with the highest thermal conductivity had the lowest ash content compared with other commercially available grades, such as T-2, T-8, and EX-70.

Table 1. Geometric Parameters of the Flow Field Configurations.

odels	Width (mm)		Channel Depth (mm)	No of Channels		No. of Bends (N_b)	Total Flow Path Length (mm)	Active Area (mm^2)	Channel Hydraulic Diameter (mm)
	Channel	Rib		Horizontal	Vertical				
A	2	2	2	17	24	40	3037		2
B	2	2	3	17	24	40	3037		2.4
C	3	3	2	13	19	31	2364		2.4
D	3	3	3	13	19	31	2364	13,095	3

The graphite plates were subjected to CNC milling operations to generate engraved channels of the required dimensions, as shown in the CAD model depicted in Figure 2 for a precision flow path to ensure the uniform flow circulation of electrolyte solution over the entire cell active area to enhance the electro-kinetic activity at the electrode–electrolyte interface. The graphite plate used in the milling operation was purchased from IndianTech, Bengaluru, India.

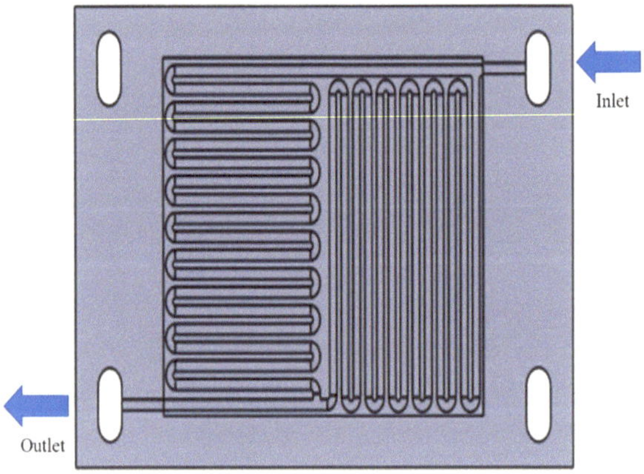

Figure 2. The 3 × 3 Cross Split Serpentine Flow Field Model (CSSFF).

2.2. Flow Field with Felt Model

The flow field integrated with graphite porous electrode felt with an original thickness (t) of 6 mm is shown in Figure 3. The graphite felt electrodes were purchased from Rayon Graphite Felt (AGFHT), USA. The anionic membrane (FUMASEP FAP-375PP) model and Nafion binder used therein were obtained from Fuel Cell Store, USA. The other essential battery components, such as epoxy endplates of 15 mm thickness, copper plates, and gaskets, were fabricated in-house for our investigation.

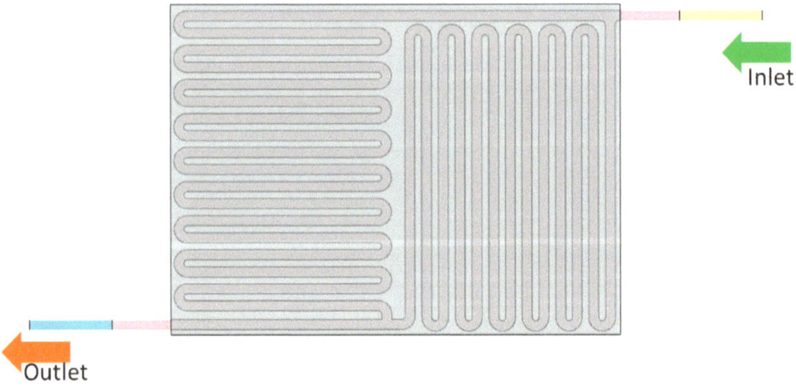

Figure 3. The 3 × 3 cross-split serpentine flow field with graphite felt model (CSSFF).

The flow characteristic analyses were carried out considering the felt channel intrusion factor at different compression ratios over the varying channel-rib geometric dimensions detailed in Table 1. Apart from the pressure drop effect caused by the non-uniformity of electrolyte flow circulation, the intrusion effect does play a vital role in the uniform distribution rate over the entire cell area. Establishing the highest ionic conductivity reaction rate for minimum electrode channel intrusion at different compression ratios resulted in a significant change in the pressure gradient over the entire active cell area, as reported by the measurements and CFD analysis [20]. A few studies have recommended an ideal electrode thickness for enhanced electrochemical performance [22]; however, a higher percentage of electrode compression will result in decreased porosity, which, in turn, decreases the rate of electrolyte circulation through the electrode and under the rib convection, thereby reducing the mass transport polarization [39].

2.3. Circuit Analogy Model

A hydraulic circuit model concept was developed corresponding to the flow field CAD model, to better analyze the electrolyte flow characteristics and resistance offered, as shown in Figure 4. Here, m represents the electrolyte mass flow rate; m_1 and m_2 are split mass flow, i.e., correlating to vertical and horizontal channels of the model, respectively; and R_1 and R_2 are resistance values corresponding to the vertical and horizontal halves of the model, respectively. Henceforth, the analysis considered the mass flow to be equivalent to the current flow, and the resistance was equivalent to flow deceleration due to skin friction and bend losses in the passage.

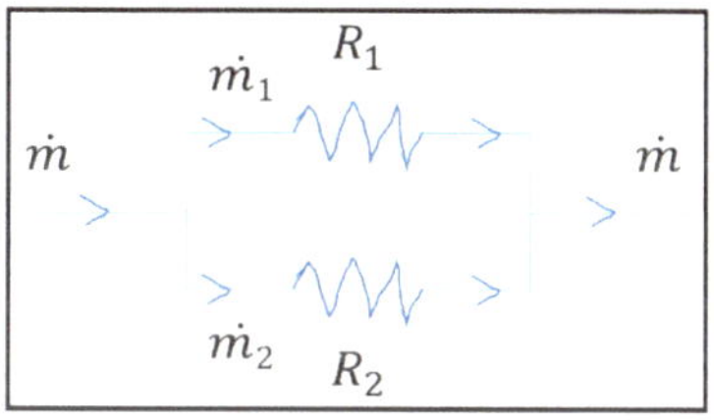

Figure 4. Cross Split Serpentine Flow Field (CSSFF) Circuit Analogy Model.

The assumptions made for the selected model were that the flow analysis was steady, laminar, incompressible in nature, and isothermal.

Pressure drops for cross-serpentine channel [14] are given by:

$$\Delta p = 0.5\rho u^2[4fL/D + N_b K_b] \tag{4}$$

where u is the average flow velocity, L is the straightened length along the channel path, D is the hydraulic diameter, f is the Fanning friction factor, N_b is the number of bends, and K_b is the bend loss coefficient.

The momentum conservation equation for flow through the porous substrate is given by:

$$\rho \frac{du}{dt} = \rho g - \frac{\partial \rho}{\partial x} + \mu \nabla^2 u + S_m \tag{5}$$

$$S_m = \Delta p/L = \alpha V + \beta V^2 \tag{6}$$

where α is the viscosity coefficient and β is the inertial resistance coefficient. Pressure drops in the porous substrate were determined using the source term Equation (6).

The source term was added to the momentum equation to account for viscous and inertial effects. Compression ratio and permeability equations are referenced from [25].

The compression ratio (CR) under the rib and channel is calculated by the equation:

$$CR_{rb} = 1 - \frac{t_c}{t} \tag{7a}$$

$$CR_{ch} = 1 - \frac{t_c + d}{t} \tag{7b}$$

where t, t_c, and d_{fi} are the original felt thickness, compressed felt thickness, and depth length of felt intrusion into the channel, respectively.

Similarly, permeability (K) was calculated corresponding to the compression ratio using the following equation from the Tamayol–Bahrami model [41]

$$k/d^2 = 0.012(1 - \phi)\,[\,\pi/4\phi^2 - 2\,(\pi/4\phi) + 1]\,[1 + 0.72\phi/(0.89 - \phi)^{0.54}] \tag{8}$$

where $\varphi = (1 - \varepsilon)$, ε is the porosity, K is the permeability, d is the fiber diameter, and ϕ is the solid volume fraction.

The volume uniformity index is as shown below. [37]

$$\varnothing = 1 - \sum c[vc - v]\ Vc\ /2[v] \sum c\ Vc \quad (9)$$

3. Experimental Study

Experimental investigation of a single-channel serpentine flow field (SCSFF), with an active cell area of 131 cm^2, i.e., 135 mm length $\times$ 97 mm width, wherein 17 parallel channels are aligned along the longer length of the rectangular cell. Notably, all are square channels with a 2 mm hydraulic diameter, each placed at an equal distance, as depicted in Figure 5. Geometrical details of the flow field along with the felt are as follows: channel width of 2 mm, rib width of 2 mm, channel depth of 2 mm, and Rayon-based graphite felt electrode (AGFHT) with a thickness of 6 mm and subjected to electrode compression (change in original thickness) to 60% and graphite plate (isostatic grade) with a thickness of 10 mm.

Figure 5. The 2 $\times$ 2 single-channel serpentine flow field with electrode felt (SCSFF) CFD flow field model.

The fabricated setup consisting of end plates on either side connected to electrolyte flow pipes on the top left and bottom right corners, representing entry and exit passages for electrolyte flow to separate analytic and catalytic tanks, respectively, is shown in Figure 6a. The pressure gradient across the active cell area was able to be measured using a U-tube manometer, as shown in Figure 6b. The two separate electrolyte tanks on either side were filled to a volume of 250 mL. The prepared solution contained iron species Fe^{2+}/Fe^{3+} and Fe^{2+}/Fe, acting as positive and negative electrolytes, respectively, as stated in Equations (1) and (2).

(**a**)

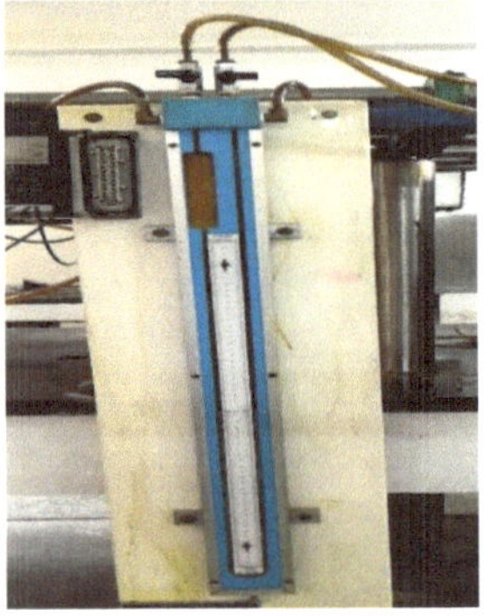

(**b**)

Figure 6. (**a**) An Experimental Set Up of Battery Stack. (**b**) U Tube Manometer to Measure Pressure Drop.

Experiments were conducted on a single-channel serpentine flow field (SCSFF) with electrode felt intrusion at CR 60% for varying electrolyte flow rates to determine the pressure drop, Δp, data using a U-tube manometer, and were compared with CFD data. The results presented in Table 2 show that the pressure drop values are close and approximate for both cases. The results clearly show that there is still scope for optimization of the flow field to reduce the pressure drop, Δp, to a great extent, improve the flow distribution and uniformity, and further enhance the electrochemical activity at the electrode–electrolyte interface. This eventually encouraged us to redesign and simulate modified versions of the serpentine flow field, as listed in Table 1.

Table 2. Comparison of CFD and Experiment pressure drop for 2 × 2 SCSFF.

oundary Condition	Flow Rate mL/min	Reynold's (Re)	CFD Pressure Drop p [Pa]	Exp Pressure Drop p [Pa]
1	30	180	4898.61	5100.00
2	60	360	11,188.90	11,600.00
3	90	540	17,772.72	18,550.00
4	120	720	24,647.79	25,750.00
5	150	899	31,815.35	33,250.00

4. CFD Analysis

4.1. Flow Field Model Analysis

Cross-split serpentine flow field models with different geometric dimensions were designed and simulated using commercially available software, i.e., Siemens Sim-Center *STAR CCM+* tool 15.02.009 *R*8 (double precision). Simulations carried out using a 3D unstructured mesh polyhedral type with prism cells in the order of 10 million generated for near-wall treatment [37] are depicted in Figure 7. Suitable boundary conditions were applied, with a laminar flow regime, isothermal process, and the electrode felt modeled as porous media to analyze the pressure gradient across the cell, velocity variation at different compression ratios, and electrolyte circulation at varying flow rates, to understand the uniform flow distribution pattern over the entire active cell area on the two half-cell regions, one on the positive half and the other on the negative half, in which each cell was integrated within the electrode and flow field domains. A sample model is depicted in Figure 3.

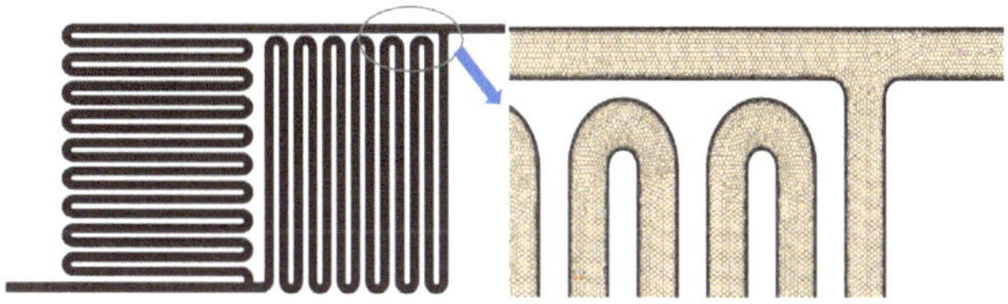

Figure 7. Illustration of Cross Split Serpentine Flow Field Polyhedral Mesh.

4.2. Flow Field with the Electrode Intrusion Model

Figure 8 shows the electrode felt intrusion with an uncompressed region into the channel and under-rib compression region, with electrolyte flow rates, Q_{ch} and Q_{pm}, flowing through the channel and porous electrode medium. The properties of the selected electrode were a plane permeability of 1.498×10^{-6} m^2, porosity of 0.80, and a fiber diameter of 0.0155 mm. The electrolyte had a viscosity of 0.0013897 Pa-s. Electrode intrusion into the channel is a strong function of compression ratios, which reduce the hydraulic diameter of the channel and thereby increase the mean effective flow velocity, resulting in an increased pressure drop. Equation (10) shows the calculation of the intrusion depth in terms of the compression ratio (CR) and the uncompressed thickness of the graphite felt.

$$\frac{d}{[t \cdot (1 - CR)]} = 0.67 - 0.058t\,(1 - CR) \quad (10)$$

The increase in electrode thickness would increase the pressure drop, Δp [25]. Intrusion depth values were approximately obtained from the above correlation for the study of different flow field geometries with the same materials and compression ratios. Different compression ratios resulted in different intrusion values and electrode compression for the given flow field, Model D, with channel and rib widths of 3 × 3 mm, increasing the compression ratio (CR) from 50% to 70%. The value of intrusion depth also increased, from 1.78 mm to 2.49 mm, as shown in Table 3. Thus, the pressure drop, Δp, tended to significantly increase, but had less influence on electrolyte circulation and distribution across the entire active cell area.

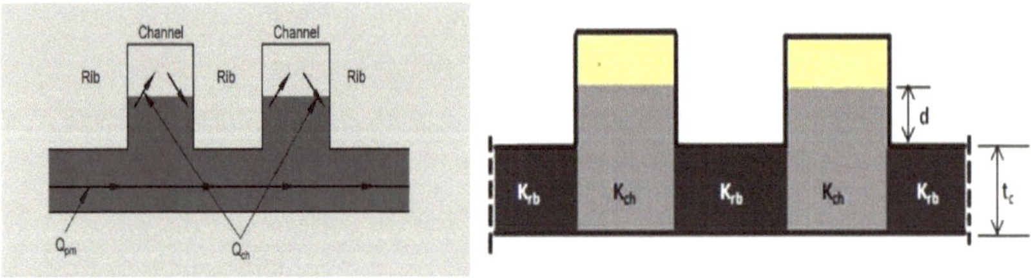

(**a**) (**b**)

Figure 8. (**a**) Graphite Electrode Felt Intrusion into Channels. (**b**) Geometry Modeled for CFD Analysis.

Table 3. Different Compression ratio (CR) corresponding intrusion value for 3 × 3 model.

Case	Graphite Felt Actual Thickness (mm)	CR 50%	CR 60%	CR 70%
Compressed value	6	3	2.4	1.8
Intrusion value		1.78	2.14	2.49

Compression of the porous electrode felt with a thickness of 6 mm into the channel with an electrode intrusion value differed for each compressed case from 50% to 70% of its original thickness, as shown schematically in Figure 9. Model D consisted of flow channels and electrode felt, whereas the reactant activity was higher in the positive electrolyte than in the negative electrolyte [34].

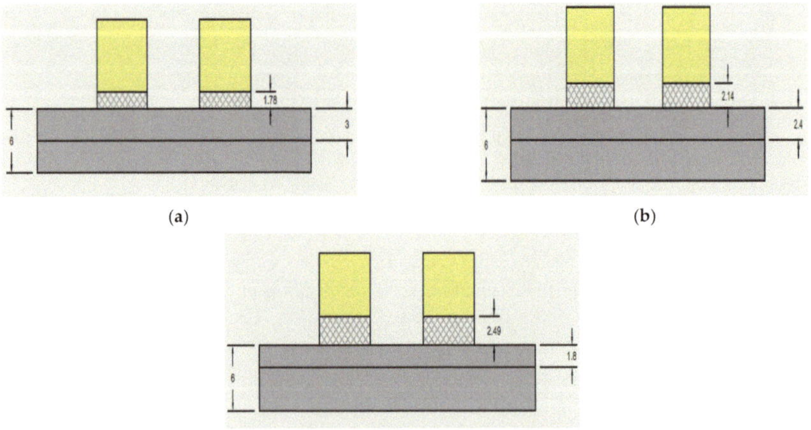

(a) (b) (c)

Figure 9. (**a**–**c**) are Schematic Representations of the Flow Field with Electrode Felt Intrusion at Varying Compression Ratios (50, 60 and 70%).

5. Results and Discussion

5.1. Numerical Software Validation

AIRFB (all-iron redox flow battery) systems were constructed using a single-cell active cell area of 131 cm^2. The experimental results of pressure drop, Δp, obtained for the above cell area were compared with those of numerically analyzed values. The pressure drop curves were derived based on the analysis results of a 2 × 2 single-channel serpentine flow field (SCSFF) with an intrusion effect for varying Reynold's numbers of 180, 360, 540, 720, and 899 at a 60% compression value, as depicted in Figure 10.

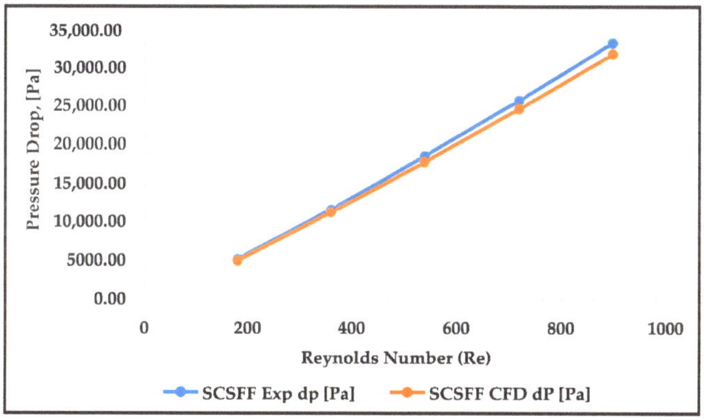

Figure 10. Comparison of CFD and Experiment Pressure Drop (Δp) for the Single Channel Serpentine Flow Field (SCSFF) for Different Reynold's Number.

To conclude, it was observed that the experimental and numerical results of pressure drop, Δp, were a linear function of Reynold's number, wherein both the results were in good agreement, as the maximum error is approximately less than 4%.

Figure 11a For the 2 × 2 SCSFF with an electrode intrusion, we observed a gradual decrease in the absolute total pressure from inlet to outlet over the entire active cell area, with the maximum value of 0.31 bar and approximately a 60% compression ratio (CR) for the flow rate of 150 mL/min. Figure 11b,c depict the general velocity magnitude pattern through the channel mid-plane and electrode felt mid-plane; the velocity flow behavior was almost same with the smallest velocity magnitude at the mid portion of the cell and higher velocity magnitude value at inlet and outlet flow regions. Subsequently, newly modeled 3 × 3 cross-split serpentine flow fields were subjected to CFD simulation to understand the better flow hydrodynamics characteristics. Table 4 depicts the experimental and CFD pressure drop values for Model D of the cross-split serpentine flow field (CSSFF).

Table 4. Compared experimental and CFD pressure drop values for Model D of the CSSFF at different CRs and for varying flow rates.

Flow Rates mL/min	Compression Ratio %	Experimental CSSFF Pressure Drop, Pa	CFD Model CSSFF Pressure Drop, Pa
30	50.00	1233	1002
	60.00	3128	2789
	70.00	12,450	11,890
90	50.00	1874	1560
	60.00	4840	4150
	70.00	18,300	17,780
150	50.00	2453	2223
	60.00	7350	6941
	70.00	26,130	24,679

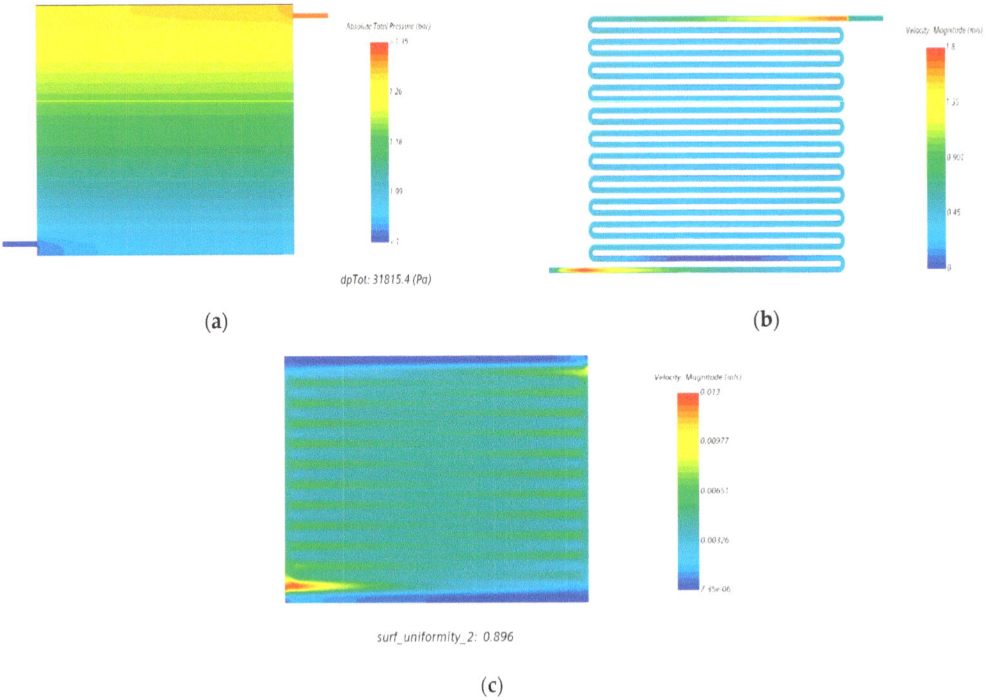

Figure 11. (**a**–**c**) 2 × 2 single serpentine flow field (SCSFF) absolute total pressure drop with electrode felt intrusion, predicted velocity magnitude at channel mid plane without electrode felt and with electrode felt mid plane 60% CR at 150 mL/min.

In Figure 12, the plotted line graphs represent the variation in pressure drop over an active cell area subjected to different CRs for varying flow rates. Figure 12a–c indicate that the pressure drop varied linearly for 50%, 60%, and 70% CRs, whereas there was a rapid increase in the pressure drop value at 70% CR for all the flow rates. The experimental pressure drop value reached a maximum of 26,130 Pa for the highest flow rate of 150 mL/min. The results demonstrate that linear variation showed good agreement for both the experimental and CFD values, with maximum error approximating 5%.

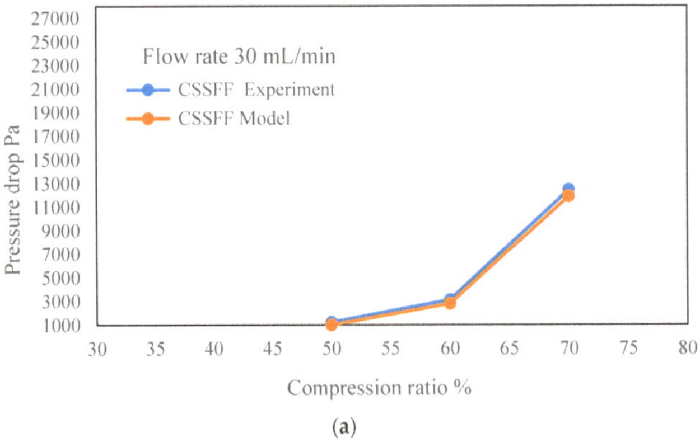

Figure 12. *Cont.*

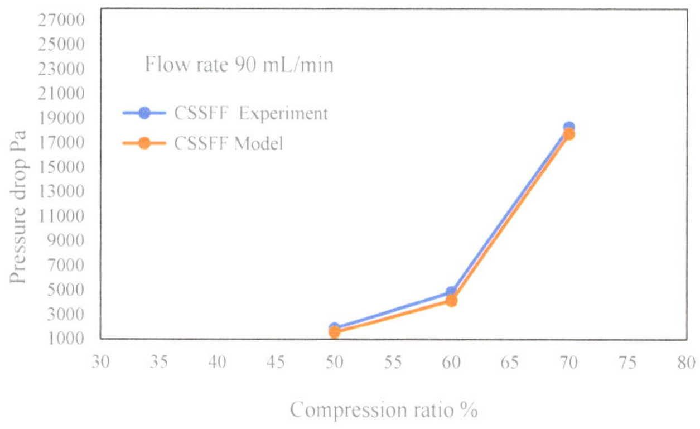

(b)

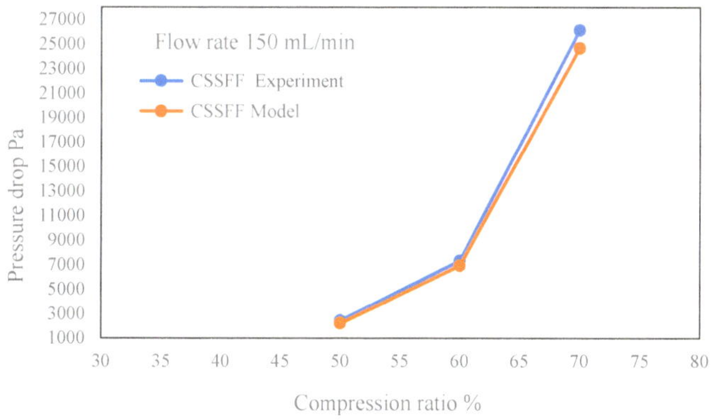

(c)

Figure 12. (**a–c**) Comparison of experimental and CFD pressure drop values for model D of CSSFF with an electrode intrusion at CR (50%, 60%, and 70%) for flow rates of 30, 90, and 150 mL/min.

5.2. Simulation Results

As observed in Figure 13a-c, the simulated pattern of Δp across the flow domain integrated with the electrode graphite felt with channel intrusion for different compression ratios was at a maximum flow rate of 150 mL/min. The rapid rise in the absolute pressure value was observed more in vertical channels than in horizontal channels, reaching relatively high levels at the right bottom corners and having a lower impact on flow pattern and distribution as the flow is laminar in nature. Meanwhile, the flow was well controlled by a peristaltic pump, which evenly produced pulsatile flow (not linear) in nature and supported the smooth flow and uniform distribution over an entire active cell area, thereby increasing the wettability factor. Hence, the higher the compression ratio, the higher the pressure drop, approximately 3.5 times greater for an individual case at different CRs. The asymmetric flow profiles in Figure 13a-c are due to the effect of the skin friction coefficient and self-weight of the fluid, which are at minimum values over the horizontal channels and slightly higher on the vertical channels represented in color contours.

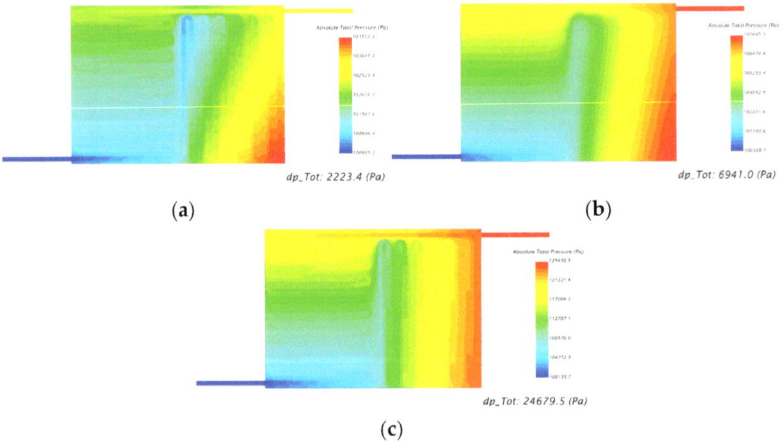

Figure 13. Predicted absolute pressure drop for Model D of the CSSFF with an electrode intrusion for a flow rate of 150mL/min at CRs: (**a**) 50%; (**b**) 60%; and (**c**) 70%.

As observed in Figure 14a–c, the velocity magnitude increased drastically at the channel inlet, split region, and junction point of the converging region of the channel exit, where the flow velocity magnitude through the channel with the above-mentioned point varied between the maximum range of 0.75 m/s and 1.5 m/s, while remaining the same in vertical and horizontal channels, i.e., the velocity magnitude remained at a minimum between the range of 0.05 and 0.75 m/s. Thus, electrolyte flow velocity contours visualize the smooth and uniform flow at the channel mid-plane for the highest flow rate of 150 mL/min.

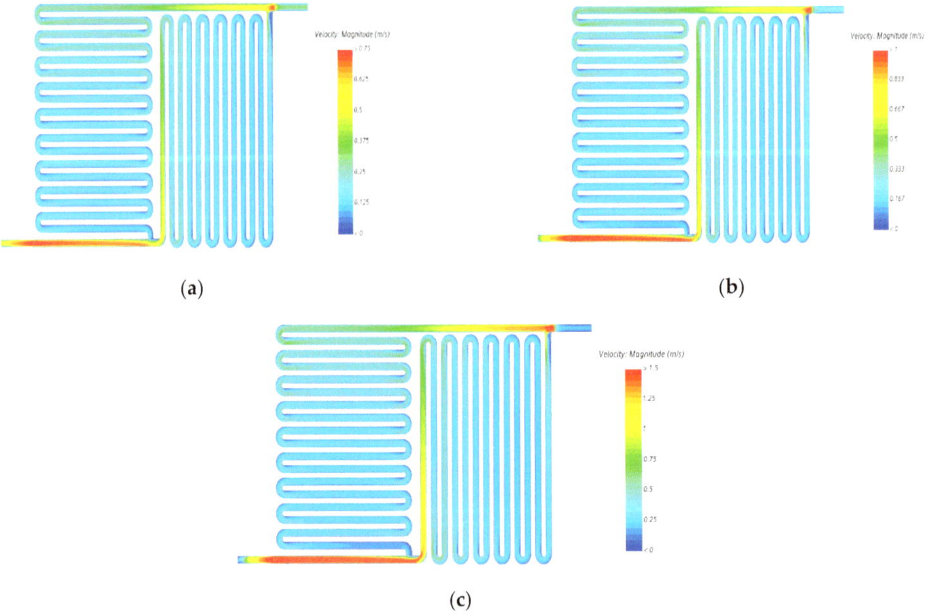

Figure 14. (**a**–**c**) Velocity magnitude at the mid-plane of Model D of the CSSFF channel for a flow rate of 150 mL/min.

Similar observations were made for three different cases, maintaining a constant maximum flow rate of 150 mL/min. We identified that the velocity magnitude pattern at the electrode mid-plane remained almost the same, but we found a higher velocity magnitude at the top portion of the felt region for the 70% compression ratio case, reaching up to 0.012 m/s, as shown in Figure 15c. However, for 50% and 60% CRs, the velocity magnitude through the electrode felt mid-plane exhibited a better flow distribution and maximum uniformity index of 0.827 and 0.820 for 50% and 60% CRs, respectively, as shown in Figure 15a,b.

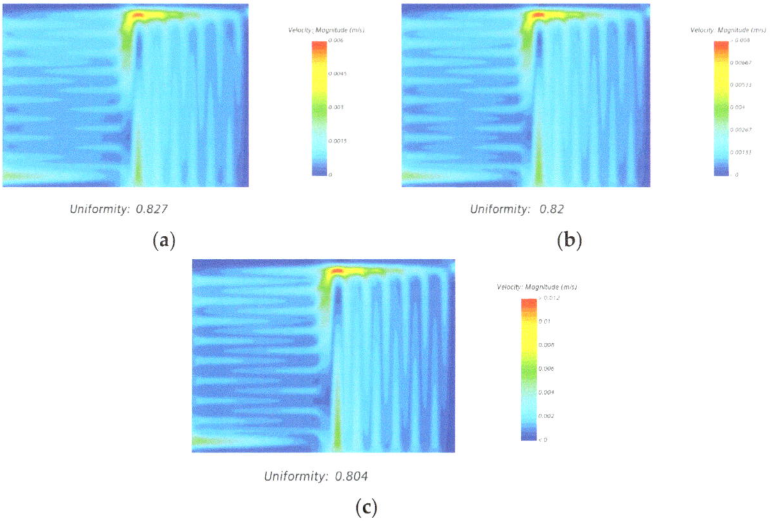

Figure 15. Predicted velocity magnitude at an electrode mid-plane for Model D of CSSFF with an electrode intrusion for a flow rate of 150 mL/min at CRs: (**a**) 50%; (**b**) 60; (**c**) 70%.

The minimum torque applied, equivalent to CR 50%, was required to hold the two halves of the cell tightly and uniformly to form the stack assembly, and also to prevent any leakages of the circulating electrolyte pumped from the external reservoir. To further study the electrode channel intrusion behavior on cell pressure drop, we considered two more CR values: 60% and 70%.

Table 5 presents a good understanding of the flow uniformity index, which is a predominant function of the compression ratio (CR), i.e., an increase in the CR value will gradually decrease the uniformity of flow distribution over an active cell area. This parametric variation, which was graphically projected and visualized, is depicted in Figure 16.

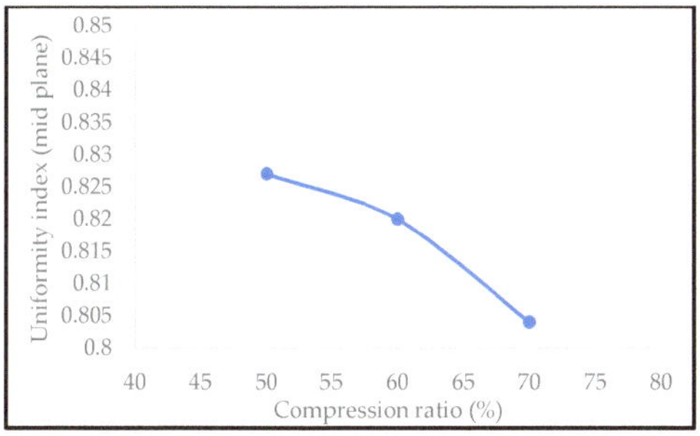

Figure 16. Uniformity index for Model D of CSSFF with an electrode intrusion at CRs of 50%, 60%, and 70% for a flow rate of 150 mL/min.

Table 5. Uniformity index values for different compression ratios.

Compression Ratio Percentage	Uniformity Index (Felt Mid)	Uniformity Index (Felt Volume)
50	0.827	0.768
60	0.820	0.749
70	0.804	0.721

The predicted simulation of volumetric flow distribution for each case visualized similar patterns to those depicted in Figure 17a–c, which show maximum volumetric flow magnitudes at the topmost portion of the mid-cell region and the bottom portion along the same line downward in the space between the vertical and horizontal channels, as well as at the channel exit region. These regions yielded the highest electrolyte concentration; however, the values shown in Table 5 suggest that the uniform volumetric flow distribution across an active cell area is a function of the compression ratio.

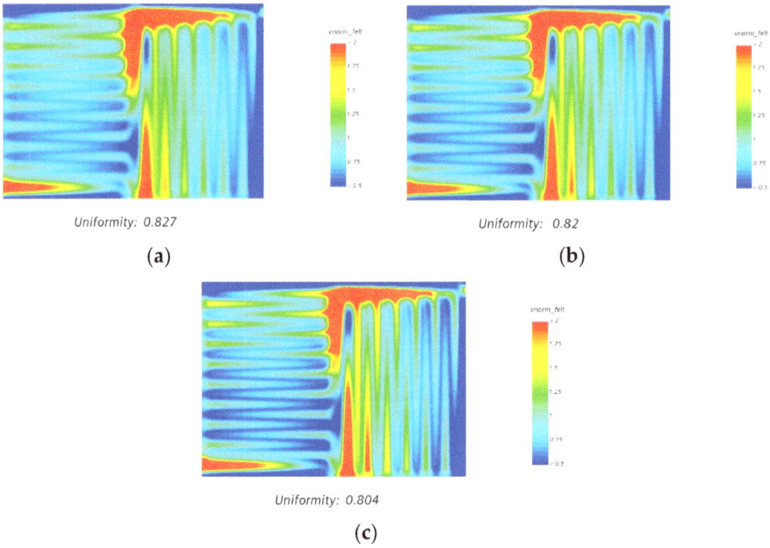

Figure 17. Predicted volumetric flow distribution at an electrode mid-plane for Model D of CSSFF with an electrode intrusion for a flow rate of 150mL/min at CRs: (**a**) 50%; (**b**) 60%; and (**c**) 70%.

6. Conclusions

An extensive study was conducted on the effect of flow hydrodynamics on a single and cross-split serpentine flow field for different geometrical configurations, i.e., channel-to-rib width ratios, over an active cell area of 131 cm^2. The parameters measured experimentally, such as cell pressure drop (Δp) through channels and with the presence of electrodes, were numerically validated using a CFD tool. The electrode felt channel intrusion behavior for both the flow fields, i.e., SCSFF and CSSFF at different CRs for various flow rates, was also numerically analyzed for flow velocity magnitude and flow distribution characteristics.

The following conclusions can be drawn from this study:

- A single-channel serpentine flow field (SCSFF) resulted in the highest pressure drop order of 31,815.35 Pa compared with a modified version of the cross-split serpentine flow field of Model D with 6941.12 Pa at CR 60% for a flow rate of 150 mL/min across an active cell area of 131 cm^2.
- The compression ratio (CR) was found to be a strong function of electrode felt channel intrusion, which resulted in a reduced effective hydraulic diameter of the channel, which, in turn, reduced the effective flow area, causing an increased mean flow velocity.

- We also noticed that a reduced effective flow area would significantly increase the pressure drop, Δp, which was demonstrated by the simulation results at compression ratios of 50%, 60%, and 70% for a maximum flow rate of 150 mL/min, as depicted in Figures 12 and 13.
- We observed that skin friction is a function of the Reynolds number and gradually increased due to a reduction in the effective hydraulic diameter, which meant the flow velocity had increased.
- We also observed that even with an increase in the volumetric flow uniformity index of more than 80%, the flow velocity distribution over electrode felt was relatively uniform at different compression ratios, as shown in Figure 15.
- We also noticed that the influence of an intrusion effect was marginal on the flow distribution and uniformity throughout the electrode felt region.
- The CSSFF design was found to be the better choice over SCSFF in terms of volumetric flow uniformity through electrode mid and end planes, and might also reduce the mass transport polarization behavior, establishing an ideal ionic activity rate.
- In this study, Model D, a modified version of CSSFF, was found to be an optimal design suitable for the defined active cell area of 131 cm^2, at different CRs, operating at a maximum flow rate of 150 mL/min.

Author Contributions: Conceptualization, R.B.K.; Formal analysis, R.B.K.; Methodology, R.B.K.; Investigation and software, R.B.K., A.D. and B.C.; Validation, R.B.K. and A.D.; Writing-original draft preparation, R.B.K.; Writing-review and editing, B.C.; Supervision, S.G.S. All authors have read and agreed to the published version of the manuscript.

Funding: This research received no external funding.

Data Availability Statement: Not applicable.

Acknowledgments: The facilities to conduct experiment was provided by Jyothy Institute of Technology, Fluid mechanics laboratory and relevant materials provided by Redox Flow Cell laboratory from CIIRC, Bengaluru, Karnataka, India.

Conflicts of Interest: The authors declare no conflict of interest.

erences

Yang, Z.; Liu, J.; Baskaran, S.; Imhoff, C.H. Enabling renewable energy and future grid—With advanced electricity storage. *Energy Storage Technol.* **2010**, *62*, 14–23. [CrossRef]

Dunn, B.; Kamath, H.; Tarascon, J.M. Electrical energy storage for the grid: A battery of choices. *Science* **2011**, *334*, 928–935. [CrossRef] [PubMed]

Yang, Z.; Zhang, J.; Kintner-Meyer, M.C.W.; Lu, X.; Choi, D.; Lemmon, J.P.; Liu, J. Electrochemical Energy Storage for Green Grid. *Chem. Rev. ACS Publ.* **2011**, *111*, 3577–3613. [CrossRef] [PubMed]

Emerging Technology News Customized Energy Solutions India Pvt. Ltd. Available online: https://etn.news/energy-storage/classification-of-energy-storage-technologies-an-overview (accessed on 21 September 2020).

Hossain, E.; Faruque, H.M.R.; Sunny, M.S.H.; Mohammad, N.; Nawar, N. A Comprehensive Review on Energy Storage Systems: Types, Comparison, Current Scenario, Applications, Barriers, and Potential Solutions, Policies, and Future Prospects. *Energies* **2020**, *13*, 3651. [CrossRef]

Skyllas-Kazacos, M.; Chakrabarti, M.H.; Hajimolana, S.A.; Mjalli, F.S.; Saleem, M. Progress in Flow Battery Research and Development. *J. Electrochem. Soc.* **2011**, *158*, 55–79. [CrossRef]

Ponce-de-León, C.; Frías-Ferrer, A.; González-Garcia, J.; Szánto, D.A.; Walsh, F.C. Redox flow cells for energy conversion. *J. Power Sources* **2006**, *160*, 716–732. [CrossRef]

Kumar, M.N.; Kumar, S.M.; Vijayakumar, G.C.; Kadirgama, K.; Samykano, M.; Venkatesh, K.; Murlidhara, H.B. Effect of Flow Field Geometry on Hydrodynamics of Flow in Redox Flow Battery. *Energy Eng. Tech. Sci. Press* **2021**, *119*, 201–217.

Arenas, L.F.; de León, C.P.; Walsh, F.C. Redox flow batteries for energy storage: Their promise, achievements and challenges. *Curr. Opin. Electrochem.* **2019**, *16*, 117–126. [CrossRef]

Di Noto, V.; Vezzu, K.; Crivellaro, G.; Pagot, G.; Sun, C.; Meda, L.; Zawodzinski, T.A. A general electrochemical formalism for vanadium redox flow batteries. *Electro. Chim. Acta* **2022**, *408*, 139937. [CrossRef]

Zhang, H.; Chen, N.; Luo, X. Investigations on physicochemical properties and electrochemical performance of graphite felt and carbon felt for iron-chromium redox flow battery. *Int. J. Energy Res.* **2020**, *44*, 3839–3853. [CrossRef]

12. Zhang, H.; Sun, C. Cost-effective iron-based aqueous redox flow batteries for large-scale energy storage application: A rev *J. Power Sources* **2021**, *493*, 229445. [CrossRef]
13. Weber, A.Z.; Mench, M.M.; Meyers, J.P.; Ross, P.N.; Gostick, J.T.; Liu, Q. Redox flow batteries: A review. *J. Appl. Electrochem.* 2 *41*, 1137–1164.
14. Gundlapalli, R.; Jayanti, S. Effect of channel dimensions of serpentine flow fields on the performance of a vanadium redox battery. *J. Energy Storage* **2019**, *23*, 148–158. [CrossRef]
15. Lisboa, K.M.; Marschewski, J.; Ebejer, N.; Ruch, P.; Cotta, R.M.; Michel, B.; Poulikakos, D. Mass transport enhancement in re flow batteries with corrugated fluidic networks. *J. Power Sources* **2017**, *359*, 322–331. [CrossRef]
16. Arenas-Martínez, L.F.; Ponce de León, C.; Walsh, F.C. Engineering aspects of the design, construction and performance of mod redox flow batteries for energy storage. *J. Energy Storage* **2017**, *11*, 119–153. [CrossRef]
17. Brown, L.D.; Tobias, P.; Neville, T.; Jervis, R.; Mason, T.J.; Shearing, P.R.; Brett, D.J.L. The effect of felt compression on performance and pressure drop of all-vanadium redox flow batteries. *J. Energy Storage* **2016**, *8*, 91–98. [CrossRef]
18. Chang, T.C.; Zhang, J.P.; Fuh, Y.K. Electrical, mechanical and morphological properties of compressed carbon felt electrode vanadium redox flow battery. *J. Power Sources* **2014**, *245*, 66–75. [CrossRef]
19. Jyothi Latha, T.; Jayanti, S. Ex-situ experimental studies of serpentine flow fields for redox flow battery applications. *J. P Sources* **2014**, *248*, 140–146. [CrossRef]
20. Darling, R.M.; Perry, M.L. The influence of electrode and channel configurations on flow battery performance. *J. Electro. C Soc.* **2014**, *161*, A1381–A1387. [CrossRef]
21. Xu, Q.; Zhao, T.S.; Zhang, C. Performance of a vanadium redox flow battery with and without flow fields. *Electro. Chem.* **2014**, *142*, 61–67. [CrossRef]
22. Aaron, D.S.; Liub, Q.; Tanga, Z.; Grimb, G.M.; Papandrewa, A.B.; Turhanb, A.; Zawodzinskia, T.A.; Mench, M.M. Dram performance gains in vanadium redox flow batteries through modified cell architecture. *J. Power Sources* **2012**, *206*, 450- [CrossRef]
23. Ke, X.; Prahl, J.M.; Alexander JI, D.; Savinell, R.F. Redox flow batteries with serpentine flow fields: Distributions of electro flow reactant penetration into the porous carbon electrodes and effects on performance. *J. Power Sources* **2018**, *384*, 295- [CrossRef]
24. Gerhardt, M.R.; Wong, A.A.; Aziz, M.J. The Effect of Interdigitated Channel and Land Dimensions on Flow Cell Performa *J. Electrochem. Soc.* **2018**, *165*, A2625–A2643. [CrossRef]
25. Kumar, S.; Jayanti, S. Effect of electrode intrusion on pressure drop and electrochemical performance of an all-vanadium re flow battery. *J. Power Sources* **2017**, *360*, 548–558. [CrossRef]
26. Kumar, S.; Jayanti, S. Effect of flow field on the performance of an all-vanadium redox flow battery. *J. Power Sources* **2016**, 782–787. [CrossRef]
27. Maharudrayya, S.; Jayanti, S. Flow distribution and pressure drop in parallel-channel configurations of planar fuel cells. *J. P Sources* **2004**, *144*, 94–106. [CrossRef]
28. Moro, F.; Trovo, A.; Bortolin, S.; Del Col, D.; Guarnieri, M. An alternative low-loss stack topology for vanadium redox battery: Comparative assessment. *J. Power Sources* **2017**, *340*, 229–241. [CrossRef]
29. Zheng, Q.; Xing, F.; Li, X.; Ning, G.; Zhang, H. Flow field design and optimization based on the mass transport polariza regulation in a flow-through type vanadium flow battery. *J. Power Sources* **2016**, *324*, 402–411. [CrossRef]
30. Zhou, X.L.; Zhao, T.S.; Zeng, Y.K.; An, L.; Wei, L. A highly permeable and enhanced surface area carbon-cloth electrode vanadium redox flow batteries. *J. Power Sources* **2016**, *329*, 247–254. [CrossRef]
31. Xu, Q.; Zhao, T.S.; Leung, P.K. Numerical investigations of flow field designs for vanadium redox flow batteries. *Appl. En* **2013**, *105*, 47–56. [CrossRef]
32. You, X.; Ye, Q.; Cheng, P. Scale-up of high power density redox flow batteries by introducing interdigitated flow fields. *Commun. Heat. Mass. Transf.* **2016**, *75*, 7–12. [CrossRef]
33. Prasad, K.B.S.; Jayanti, S. Effect of channel-to-channel cross flow on local flooding in serpentine flow fields. *J. Power Sources* *180*, 227–231. [CrossRef]
34. Xu, C.; Zhao, T.S. A new flow field design for polymer electrolyte-based fuel cells. *Electro. Chem. Commun.* **2007**, *9*, 497- [CrossRef]
35. Suresh, P.V.; Jayanti, S.; Deshpande, A.P.; Haridoss, P. An improved serpentine flow field with enhanced cross-flow for fue applications. *Int. J. Hydrogen Energy* **2011**, *36*, 6067–6072. [CrossRef]
36. Gundlapalli, R.; Jayanti, S. Performance characteristics of several variants of interdigitated flow fields for flow battery applica *J. Power Sources* **2020**, *467*, 228225. [CrossRef]
37. Rakesh, B.K.; Gowreesh, S.S.; Deshpande, A. Numerical investigation of hydrodynamics in a flow field and porous subs configuration for redox flow battery application. *J. Mines Met. Fuels* **2023**, *in press*.
38. Prumbohm, E.; Becker, M.; Flaischlen, S.; Wehinger, G.D.; Turek, T. Flow field designs developed by comprehensive CFD m decrease system costs of vanadium redox-flow batteries. *J. Flow Chem.* **2021**, *11*, 461–481. [CrossRef]
39. Jyothi Latha, T.; Jayanti, S. Hydrodynamic analysis of flow fields for redox flow battery applications. *J. Appl. Electro. Chem.* *44*, 995–1006. [CrossRef]

Knudsen, E.; Albertus, P.; Cho, K.T.; Weber, A.Z.; Kojic, A. Flow simulation and analysis of high-power flow batteries. *J. Power Sources* **2015**, *299*, 617–628. [CrossRef]
Tamayol, A.; McGregor, F.; Bahrami, M. Single phase through-plane permeability of carbon paper gas diffusion layers. *J. Power Sources* **2012**, *204*, 94–99. [CrossRef]

fluids

Article

Numerical Evaluation of the Flow within a Rhomboid Tessellated Pipe Network with a 3 × 3 Allometric Branch Pattern for the Inlet and Outlet

René Rodríguez-Rivera [1], Ignacio Carvajal-Mariscal [1,*], Hilario Terres-Peña [2], Mauricio De la Cruz-Ávila [3,*] and Jorge E. De León-Ruiz [4]

1 Instituto Politécnico Nacional, ESIME-UPALM, Mexico City 07738, Mexico; rivera_0710@hotmail.com
2 Departamento de Energía, Universidad Autónoma Metropolitana, San Pablo 180, Col. Reynosa Tamaulipas, Azcapotzalco, Mexico City 02200, Mexico
3 Centro de Investigación y de Estudios Avanzados, CINVESTAV, Instituto Politécnico Nacional 2508, San Pedro Zacatenco, Mexico City 07360, Mexico
4 Centro de Investigación en Materiales Avanzados, S.C., CIMAV, Miguel de Cervantes 120, Complejo Industrial Chihuahua, Chihuahua 31136, Mexico
* Correspondence: icarvajal@ipn.mx (I.C.-M.); mauriciodlca1@gmail.com (M.D.l.C.-A.)

Abstract: This study presents a comprehensive assessment of the hydrodynamic performance of a novel pipe network with tessellated geometry and allometric scales. Numerical simulations were used to evaluate flow behaviour and pressure drop. The comparison geometry featured a Parallel Pipe Pattern (PPP), while the proposed design employed a Rhombic Tessellation Pattern (RTP). Steady-state simulations were conducted under identical boundary conditions, examining water mass flows ranging from 0.01 to 0.06 kg/s. The results revealed RTP significant advantages over the PPP. The RTP, integrated with a fractal tree pattern, demonstrated remarkable capabilities in achieving uniform flow distribution and maintaining laminar flow regimes across the mass flow rates. Additionally, exhibited an average reduction in pressure drop of 92% resulting in improved efficiency. The Reynolds number at PPP inlet was 5.4 times higher than in the RTP, explaining the considerably higher pressure drop. At a mass flow rate of 0.06 kg/s, the PPP experienced a pressure drop of up to 3.43 kPa, while the RTP's pressure drop was only 0.350 kPa, highlighting a remarkable decrease of 91.5%. These findings underscore the RTP superior performance in minimizing pressure drop, making it suitable for accommodating higher mass flow rates, thus highlighting its exceptional engineering potential.

Keywords: hydrodynamic performance; allometric relation scales; rhombic tessellation; fractal pattern; numerical simulations; solar collector

1. Introduction

Solar collectors are utilized to harness clean, reliable, and cost-effective solar energy, meeting 50–80% of the demand for hot water [1]. An area of current interest in the investigation of flat solar collectors is their application as evaporators known as collector-evaporators. Collector-evaporators have been employed in Rankine organic cycles [2,3] and primarily in direct expansion heat pumps supported by solar energy (DX-SAHP) [4,5]. Several researchers have conducted both experimental and numerical studies to explore the characteristics and advantages of DX-SAHP systems, emphasizing the integration of a collector-evaporator and its potential for thermal energy generation [6–10].

In 2013, Amancio Moreno [11,12] conducted a study on a heat pump system that utilized a roll-bond collector-evaporator field to capture solar radiation. The research revealed that the energy consumption of the compressor was significantly affected by the pressure drop of the working fluid, R134a. Consequently, it was concluded that an investigation into modified geometric characteristics of the collector is crucial. Specifically, exploring channel size and optimizing the fluid entry from the supply line to the inlet of each manifold are key factors to consider in order to reduce pressure drop.

Various methodologies and approaches have been employed to enhance the efficiency and thermal performance of flat plate solar collectors. For instance, Abhishek et al. [13] conducted a compilation of studies utilizing Computational Fluid Dynamics (CFD) for the analysis of flat plate solar collectors. Additionally, investigations into collector-evaporators have explored diverse methods, such as the utilization of phase change materials for latent thermal energy storage [14], thermal behaviour analyses of collectors [7,14–19], and more recently, the implementation of pipes with varying geometries [7,17,19].

Xiaolin et al. [19] examined three types of collectors within the DX-SAHP system: the parallel-piping collector, T-fractal collector, and hexagonal tessellation collector. Their findings revealed that the collector utilizing a hexagonal tessellation demonstrated favourable performance, followed by the T-fractal collector and the parallel-piping collector.

Traditional solar collectors typically consist of metal tubes with various arrangements attached to an absorber plate. Among the collector configurations commonly found in the literature, the serpentine and parallel-pipe collectors are the most widely studied. In the serpentine configuration, a single continuous channel is formed by bending a pipe, while the parallel-pipe configuration consists of multiple parallel ducts interconnected by two cross channels. Numerous researchers have conducted numerical and experimental investigations on various flat collectors, focusing primarily on those with parallel-pipes in a serpentine configuration, as well as other specific patterns, to identify the key parameters that influence performance.

Solar collectors typically operate under specific conditions with a water mass flow rate ranging from 0.0011 to 0.066 kg/s at ambient temperatures [20–24]. Various studies have investigated collectors constructed from copper [25–32] or aluminium [25–28]. The collector areas examined in these studies range from 1.27 to 1.63 m^2, while the hydraulic diameter of the pipes varies between 7 and 12 mm [29,33–35].

The hydrodynamic results obtained in each study consistently demonstrated that the serpentine collector pattern exhibits a significantly pressure drop compared to the parallel-pipe collector. Primož et al. [17] conducted a numerical and experimental evaluation of three collectors with distinct design patterns: serpentine, parallel, and bionic. The serpentine and parallel collectors had an area of 0.47 m^2, while the bionic collector measured 0.45 m^2. The hydraulic diameter for all three collectors was 3.5 mm. In their investigation, a water mass flow rate of 0.013116 kg/s was considered, resulting in a pressure drop of 40 kPa for the serpentine collector, 2 kPa for the parallel collector, and 0.930 kPa for the bionic collector, respectively.

Aste et al. [34] investigated a solar collector featuring a parallel pipe configuration, measuring 1.3 $\times$ 1.2 m. The water mass flow rate was set at 0.066 kg/s, with an estimated pressure drop of 20 kPa. In a separate study, Buonomano et al. [35] examined a roll-bond solar collector integrated into a photovoltaic-thermal collector. The collector was constructed using aluminium and employed a parallel pipe configuration. It had a capacity of 0.9 litters, with dimensions of 0.992 $\times$ 1.644 m and an internal diameter of 8 mm. The water mass flow rate utilized in their study was 0.0902 kg/s.

Lari et al. [36] conducted a study on a solar collector that employed a parallel-serpentine hybrid pipe pattern using Computational Fluid Dynamics (CFD). The collector was constructed with a 1 mm thick stainless-steel material and featured a hydraulic diameter of 16.6 mm. It had a total area of 1.627 m^2 and operated with a water mass flow rate of 0.05 kg/s. Under these specific conditions, the calculated pressure drop was determined to be 7.125 kPa.

Extensive research has been conducted on solar collectors incorporating pipes with diverse geometric patterns. Traditional serpentine and parallel configurations are commonly studied, along with pipes featuring hexagonal or T-fractal tessellation arrangements [19]. The incorporation of fractal geometries in heat exchangers has also been examined by several authors [37–39], revealing significant improvements in heat transfer efficiency within compact designs, reduced energy consumption for fluid transport, and lower pressure drops across these geometries. Another related concept is that of constructive theories or allometric scales, which are characteristic of all organisms. Geoffrey et al. [40] presented a comprehensive model describing the transport of essential materials through fractal branching tubes that fill space. The model assumes the minimization of energy dissipation and that the terminal tubes, known as capillaries, have identical sizes. Although investigations into implementing the constructive theory in heat exchangers are relatively recent, the obtained results thus far [41–45] confirm the advantages of utilizing this approach.

Aim and Scope

This study introduces a novel 3D model of a pipe network featuring a distinctive geometry that is not commonly documented in the existing literature but shares dimensions with certain solar collector piping systems. The proposed geometry involves a pipe embedded within a plate resembling a solar collector, forming a rhombic tessellation arrangement within the mainframe. Recognizing the potential benefits of incorporating recursive patterns, a fractal tree pattern with trifurcation at the inlet and outlet of the pipe network was integrated. Allometric scales were utilized to determine the suitable diameters for the fractal tree, based on the pipe size in the channels of the piping pattern.

Given the significant cost associated with manufacturing a single device for experimental purposes, this study employs computational fluid dynamics to numerically evaluate the performance of the intricate geometry under investigation. The primary aim of this research is to gather valuable insights into the pressure drop and flow characteristics of the novel piping system. Such information can provide a solid foundation to justify the construction and application of this device in diverse thermodynamic systems that harness solar energy, including flat-bed solar collectors and solar concentrators, among others. By conducting this analysis, the study seeks to contribute to the advancement of solar energy utilization in various applications.

The simulation results obtained from the proposed model are compared with a pipe network of a conventional solar collector that incorporates parallel pipes. Both piping systems possess equivalent dimensions, the same area for the embedded pipe, identical capacity, and utilize the same working fluid properties. The focus of the comparison is solely based on the geometry of each piping system. The simulations were conducted to examine the hydrodynamic performance of each piping system, allowing for a comprehensive comparison of the results and the determination of whether the proposed design featuring a solar collector with rhombic tessellation offers significant advantages over the conventional parallel pipe configuration.

The research introduces advancement by presenting a comprehensive assessment of the hydrodynamic performance of a pipe network featuring a rhombic tessellation geometry with allometric scaling. This approach unveils a host of remarkable findings, showcasing the novel model's ability to achieve a uniform velocity distribution at identical mass flow rates. The result is a significantly reduced pressure drop compared to the traditional parallel pipe configuration, exceeding conventional expectations. Moreover, the study's novelty is further accentuated by the rhombic tessellation model's consistent maintenance of a laminar flow regime, even when subjected to an increased mass flow rate at the system's entrance. In stark contrast, the parallel pipe system repeatedly succumbs to turbulent flow in a majority of cases. These remarkable outcomes unequivocally underscore the unparallel superiority of the proposed rhomboid tessellation geometry, positioning it as a highly efficient alternative to the common parallel pipe configuration.

This research represents a pioneering endeavour, pushing the boundaries of current knowledge and offering a fresh perspective on the hydrodynamic performance of pipe networks. The innovative use of rhomboid tessellation coupled with allometric scaling brings forth a breakthrough that has the potential to reshape the engineering design.

2. Numerical Details

2.1. Case Study

This section presents the assessed proposed geometry and the numerical configuration utilized to simulate its operation. The computational model encompasses embedded piping arranged in a Rhombic Tessellation Pattern, RTP, incorporating allometric and fractal scales constrained to the 3 × 3-branched fractal tree geometry. The proposed model incorporates a fractal tree pattern with allometric relationships at the inlet and outlet of the numerical domain, allowing it to adapt to the dimensions of a real collector's embedded pipe. Figure 1 illustrates the proposed piping network, while Figure 2 presents detailed dimensions of the rhombic tessellation.

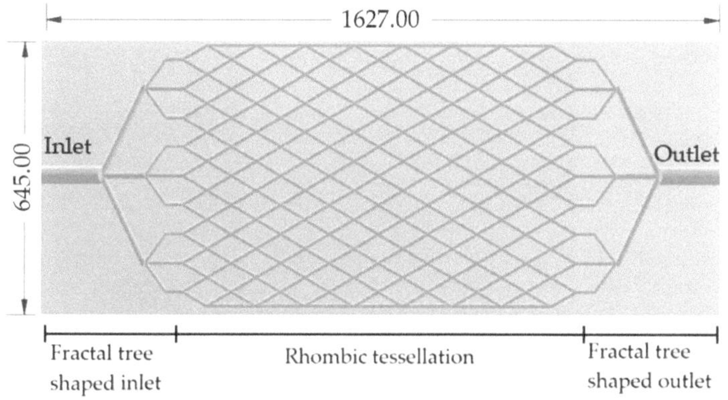

Figure 1. 3D model of the numerical domain with rhombic tessellation pattern, fractal tree inlet and outlet, and allometric scales (RTP), [mm].

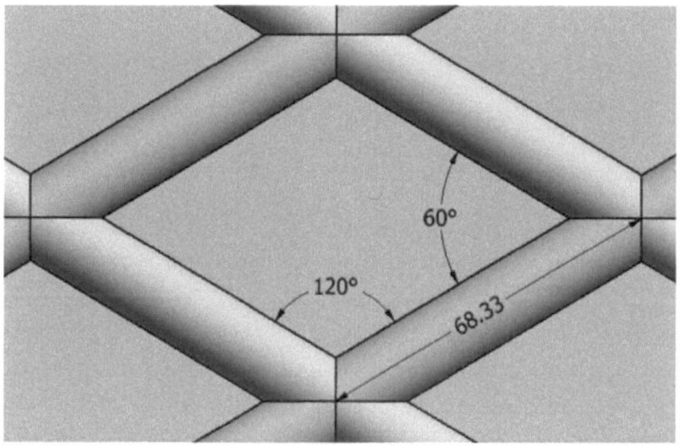

Figure 2. Detail of the rhombic tessellation construction that conform the piping network [mm].

The inner diameter of the pipe is 7.3 mm, which is equivalent to a 3/8-inch (nominal) copper pipe. This particular pipe size was selected based on its widespread usage in real collectors. It aligns with the existing literature where copper is commonly utilized for collectors' construction due to its availability, ease of handling, and excellent thermal properties.

2.2. Pipe Networking Inlet/Outlet Construction Conditions

The core principle of utilizing the fractal tree with trifurcation and allometric scales was implemented to minimize the energy consumption associated with fluid flow within the integrated pipe. The proposed fractal tree with trifurcation closely resembles those discussed in previous literature [40,43,46]. The generation of the self-similar fractal tree-like microchannel network follows these steps: (1) initially, a single microchannel is assigned at the 0-th branching level, characterized by a fixed diameter (d_0) and length (l_0); (2) starting from the 0-th branching level, each subsequent microchannel branches into N microchannels, maintaining an identical diameter and length at each subsequent branching level; (3) the diameter and length of each newly generated microchannel adhere to the scaling law expressed in Equations (1) and (2) [40]:

$$\beta_z = \frac{d_{z+1}}{d_z}, \tag{1}$$

$$\gamma_z = \frac{l_{z+1}}{l_z}, \tag{2}$$

where β is the scale of the diameter, γ is the length scale, and z is the branch.

The relationships for rigid pipe are utilized, and the scale factors for length and diameter in the fractal tree are defined by Equations (3) and (4), respectively [41,43,46].

$$\gamma_z = n^{-1/3}, \tag{3}$$

$$\beta_z = n^{-1/2}, \tag{4}$$

where n is the number of branches in the last branch, n = 9, as shown in Figure 3. The proposed fractal tree scheme is shown in Figure 3, and the diameter and length dimensions for the fractal tree input are shown in Table 1.

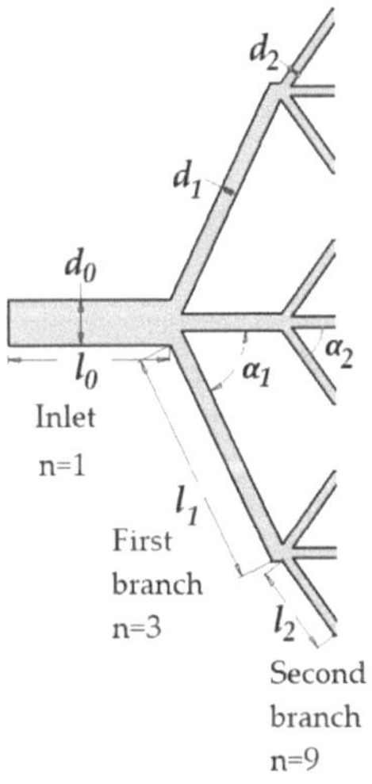

Figure 3. Manifold inlet with fractal tree form, $\alpha_1 = 64°$, $\alpha_2 = 53.7°$.

Table 1. Diameter and length dimensions for the fractal tree inlet.

	Diameter [mm]	Length [mm]
Inlet line	39.6	148
First Branch	13.2	229
Second Branch	7.3	130

2.3. *Pipe Networking Operation Conditions*

To evaluate the hydraulic behaviour of the proposed pipe network, a 3D model was developed. This model was based on a traditional solar collector with the same dimensions but with Parallel Pipes Pattern, PPP, and a constant diameter of 7.3 mm throughout. The 3D model of the conventional collector is depicted in Figure 4. The operation of both geometries was simulated to obtain their performance results under identical conditions. Table 2 presents the specific characteristics of each numerical domain.

Figure 4. 3D model of the parallel pipe pattern collector (PPP) [mm].

Table 2. Characteristics of each model.

	PPP	RTP
Material	Copper	Copper
Length [mm]	1627	1627
Width [mm]	645	645
Thickness [mm]	1	1
Area [m^2]	1.049	1.049
Pipe area [%]	20.81	20.96
Hydraulic diameter [mm]	7.3	39.6, 13.2, 7.3
Volume [m^3]	0.002	0.002

For simulations, liquid water was utilized at 20 °C, and its properties are shown in Table 3.

Table 3. Properties of liquid water for the simulation, at 20 °C.

Property	Value
Density, ρ [kg/m^3]	998.2
Viscosity, μ [$kg/(m{\cdot}s)$]	0.01003

A water mass flow ranging from 0.01 kg/s to 0.06 kg/s was applied at the inlet boundary to characterize the increase in pressure drop under different inlet mass flow rates with a constant increment of 0.01 kg/s, in order to obtain six different flows for evaluation [17,34,36]. The outlet condition for both domains was set at a pressure of 101.325 kPa. Simulations were conducted to observe the behaviour of both geometries under different water mass flow rates at a steady state.

2.4. Software and Computational Resource

The simulations were conducted using Autodesk® CFD, a commercial software with an academic license, which has shown good agreement with experimental data in previous CFD assessments [47,48]. Autodesk CFD utilizes the finite element method to convert the governing partial differential equations (PDEs) into a system of algebraic equations. This method employs polynomial shape functions that define the dependent variables over small areas or volumes called elements. These representations were then substituted into the governing PDEs and integrated over the elements using weighted functions that match the shape functions [49]. The outcome is a set of algebraic equations for the dependent variable at discrete points or nodes on each element.

The simulations were computed with a workstation that met the requirements for the software execution. The characteristics of the computational resources are a Workstation with an Intel i7-11800H, a 2.3 GHz 8 cores Processor, 24 GB of RAM memory, and Nvidia GeForce GTX 1650 for parallel computing.

2.5. Numerical Domain Details

Considering the dimensions of each piping network and the geometry of the embedded pipe of the real collector 3D model, a specific discretization strategy was employed for each numerical domain. Tetrahedral elements were chosen due to their suitability for capturing complex geometries effectively. Furthermore, refinement was implemented in regions adjacent to the walls of the numerical domain and in areas where the flow underwent division or experienced changes in direction. Figure 5 provides an example of the discretization using a mesh for the rhombic tessellation pipe networking. To enhance the treatment of the walls, the initial mesh length along the walls was set to 0.3 mm. Additionally, a no-slip boundary condition was applied to establish that the fluid velocity is zero at the walls of the numerical domain boundary.

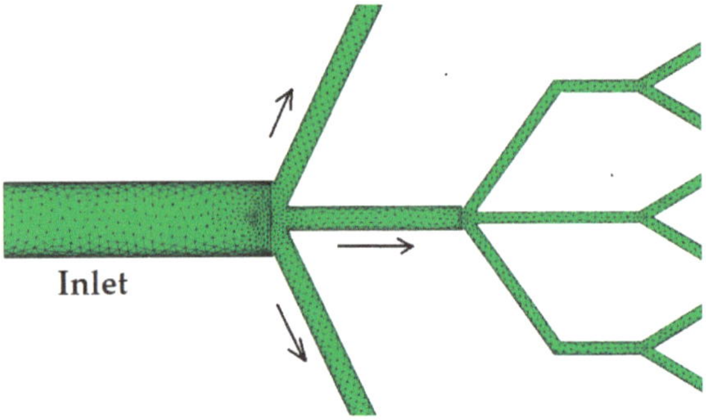

Figure 5. Example of the discretized model.

2.6. Numerical Models

In the Autodesk CFD software, the SIMPLE-R scheme was used for pressure-spatial discretization, which is a variant of the SIMPLE scheme (Semi-Implicit Method for Pressure Linked Equations). SIMPLE-R algorithm extracts a pressure field from a given velocity field, and convergence to the final solution can be much faster. The SIMPLE-R algorithm is described by Patankar [50], and it was used in other works [31,51–53] because it has shown that the convergence of velocity can be performed in a more synchronized and with good stability.

The resolution of the momentum transport equation in a 3D spatial discretization domain requires the definition of a numerical model, particularly for handling the advective terms. In this study, a streamline upwind approximation was employed to accurately represent the advection terms within the momentum equations. This approximation was preferred due to its ability to significantly reduce the numerical diffusion error compared to the conventional upwind method [54]. To ensure numerical stability, a modified Petrov-Galerkin advection scheme was implemented in the Autodesk CFD software, resulting in improved accuracy for incompressible flow in pipes.

2.7. Governing Equations

For the 3D numerical domain in steady state, without heat transfer and incompressible fluid, the governing equations are continuity and momentum given by the following expressions, respectively:

Continuity,

$$\frac{\partial u}{\partial x}+\frac{\partial v}{\partial y}+\frac{\partial w}{\partial z}=0, \tag{5}$$

Momentum in x, y and z directions,

$$\rho u\frac{\partial u}{\partial x}+\rho v\frac{\partial u}{\partial y}+\rho w\frac{\partial u}{\partial z}=-\frac{\partial p}{\partial x}+\mu\left[\frac{\partial^2 u}{\partial x^2}+\frac{\partial^2 u}{\partial y^2}+\frac{\partial^2 u}{\partial z^2}\right], \tag{6}$$

$$\rho u\frac{\partial v}{\partial x}+\rho v\frac{\partial v}{\partial y}+\rho w\frac{\partial v}{\partial z}=-\frac{\partial p}{\partial y}+\mu\left[\frac{\partial^2 v}{\partial x^2}+\frac{\partial^2 v}{\partial y^2}+\frac{\partial^2 v}{\partial z^2}\right], \tag{7}$$

$$\rho u\frac{\partial w}{\partial x}+\rho v\frac{\partial w}{\partial y}+\rho w\frac{\partial w}{\partial z}=-\frac{\partial p}{\partial z}+\mu\left[\frac{\partial^2 w}{\partial x^2}+\frac{\partial^2 w}{\partial y^2}+\frac{\partial^2 w}{\partial z^2}\right], \tag{8}$$

where ρ is the water density (kg/m^3), μ is the water viscosity ($kg/(m\cdot s)$), and p the static pressure of the water (Pa).

For the analytical calculation of the pressure drop (Pa) in each pipe network the following relation [55,56]:

$$\Delta p = f\frac{8L\dot{m}^2}{\rho\pi^2 d^5}, \tag{9}$$

where L is the length of the pipe (m), $\dot{m}$ is the mass flow of water (kg/s), d is the hydraulic diameter of the pipe (m) and f is the friction factor (dimensionless). This factor for laminar flow is calculated with the expression [56–58]:

$$f=\frac{64}{Re}, \tag{10}$$

and for turbulent flow, it is determined by the Colebrook expression [57,58]:

$$\frac{1}{\sqrt{f}}=-2.0\log\left(\frac{e/d}{3.7}+\frac{2.51}{Re\sqrt{f}}\right), \tag{11}$$

where e is the roughness of the pipe (m).

2.8. Turbulence Model

Since the collector with parallel pipes operates under a turbulent regime with mass flows exceeding 0.01 kg/s, the two-equation standard turbulence model (Equations (13) and (15)) was employed. This model is based on the Reynolds-Averaged Navier-Stokes (RANS) technique. The selected model offers numerical stability and computational efficiency, making it widely applied in industrial settings [17,59–62].

One of the distinguishing characteristics of two-equation turbulent models lies in their formulation and solution of two separate transport equations. The standard $k-\varepsilon$ turbulent model encompasses the turbulent kinetic energy, k, and the turbulent energy dissipation, ε, as the unknown variables, along with the time-averaged fluid velocities. In this model, the turbulent viscosity is calculated using the following equation:

$$\mu_t = C_\mu \rho\frac{k^2}{\varepsilon}. \tag{12}$$

The turbulent kinetic energy equation is described by the following expressions [59–61]:

$$\rho\frac{\partial k}{\partial t}+\rho\overline{u_x}\frac{\partial k}{\partial x}+\rho\overline{u_y}\frac{\partial k}{\partial y}+\rho\overline{u_z}\frac{\partial k}{\partial z}=\\ \frac{\partial}{\partial x}\left[\left(\mu+\frac{\mu_t}{\sigma_k}\right)\frac{\partial k}{\partial x}\right]+\frac{\partial}{\partial y}\left[\left(\mu+\frac{\mu_t}{\sigma_k}\right)\frac{\partial k}{\partial y}\right]+\frac{\partial}{\partial z}\left[\left(\mu+\frac{\mu_t}{\sigma_k}\right)\frac{\partial k}{\partial z}\right]+G_k-\rho\varepsilon\,, \tag{13}$$

$$G_k=2\mu_t\left[\left(\frac{\partial\overline{u_x}}{\partial x}\right)^2+\left(\frac{\partial\overline{u_y}}{\partial y}\right)^2+\left(\frac{\partial\overline{u_z}}{\partial z}\right)^2\right]+\mu_t\left(\frac{\partial\overline{u_x}}{\partial y}+\frac{\partial\overline{u_y}}{\partial x}\right)^2+\mu_t\left(\frac{\partial\overline{u_x}}{\partial z}+\frac{\partial\overline{u_z}}{\partial x}\right)^2\\ +\mu_t\left(\frac{\partial\overline{u_z}}{\partial y}+\frac{\partial\overline{u_y}}{\partial z}\right)^2. \tag{14}$$

The turbulent energy dissipation equation is [59–61]:

$$\rho\frac{\partial \varepsilon}{\partial t}+\rho\overline{u_x}\frac{\partial \varepsilon}{\partial x}+\rho\overline{u_y}\frac{\partial \varepsilon}{\partial y}+\rho\overline{u_z}\frac{\partial \varepsilon}{\partial z}=\\ \frac{\partial}{\partial x}\left[\left(\mu+\frac{\mu_t}{\sigma_\varepsilon}\right)\frac{\partial \varepsilon}{\partial x}\right]+\frac{\partial}{\partial y}\left[\left(\mu+\frac{\mu_t}{\sigma_\varepsilon}\right)\frac{\partial \varepsilon}{\partial y}\right]+\frac{\partial}{\partial z}\left[\left(\mu+\frac{\mu_t}{\sigma_\varepsilon}\right)\frac{\partial \varepsilon}{\partial z}\right]+C_{\varepsilon 1}\frac{\varepsilon}{k}G_k-C_{\varepsilon 2}\rho\frac{\varepsilon^2}{k}, \tag{15}$$

where μ_t is turbulent viscosity (m^2/s), k is turbulent kinetic energy (J/kg), ε is turbulent kinetic dissipation rate (W/kg), $\overline{u}$ is average velocity (m/s), and the constants values are [63] $C_\mu = 0.09$, $\sigma_k = 1.0$, $\sigma_\varepsilon = 1.3$, $C_{\varepsilon 1} = 1.44$, and $C_{\varepsilon 2} = 1.92$.

3. Sensitivity Analysis

Five meshes were generated to ensure the independence of the numerical results from the mesh employed, using a water mass flow rate of 0.01 kg/s for each 3D model. Table 4 provides details of the meshes created for each geometry, while Figure 6 illustrates the corresponding pressure drop values obtained with each mesh.

Table 4. Mesh sensitivity analysis.

	Mesh 1	Mesh 2	Mesh 3	Mesh 4	Mesh 5	$\Delta P_{analytic}$
			Pipe networking with rhombic tessellation			
Number of nodes	215,936	360,480	661,595	728,324	1,020,862	
Number of elements	648,909	1,186,953	2,478,962	2,796,240	4,102,085	
Pressure drop [Pa]	27.8	24.6	22.3	21.9	21.8	22.49
			Pipe networking with parallel pipe			
Number of nodes	252,426	671,693	932,002	990,800	1,195,763	
Number of elements	611,386	1,829,540	2,655,701	2,828,856	3,389,378	
Pressure drop [Pa]	210.8	179.3	151.3	150.6	150.1	147.9

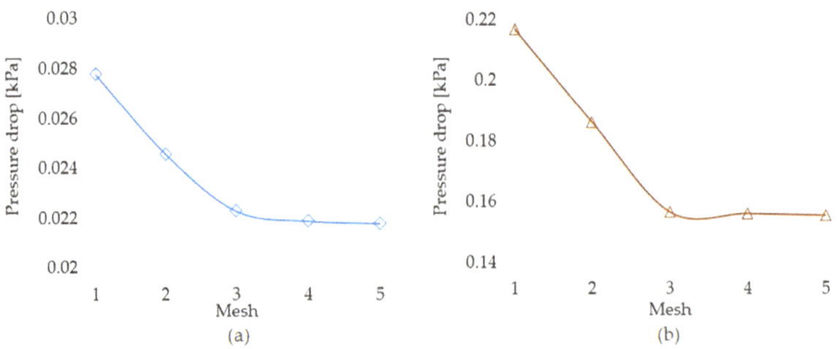

Figure 6. Sensitivity analysis for both numerical domains (**a**) Rhombic Tessellation Pattern, and (**b**) Parallel Pipe Pattern.

The mesh sensitivity analysis for the RTP reveals that mesh 3 causes a relative error of 0.8% in the pressure drop calculation compared to the analytical result, which is considered acceptable and congruent with the findings in the literature [17,31,32] for this type of simulation. However, as the number of nodes and elements increases in meshes 4 and 5, the convergence of the pressure drop deviates by 2.3%, and the error in the pressure drop calculation rises to 3%. Additionally, mesh 5 has 1,623,123 more elements than mesh 3, resulting in increased computational resources and time for the solution. Therefore, mesh 3 was chosen as the most affordable mesh for simulating the pipe network with rhombic tessellation. It offers the lowest relative error in the pressure drop calculation compared to the analytical value and requires fewer computing resources.

Regarding the meshes utilized for the PPP, the pressure drop calculated with mesh 5 closely matched the analytical value, with an error of 1.48%. The pressure drop results of meshes 4 and 5 exhibit only a 0.46% difference. However, mesh 5 comprises an additional 560,522 elements compared to mesh 4, leading to increased computational resources and processing time. With mesh 4, the error in the pressure drop calculation was 1.8% in comparison to the analytical result, representing only a 0.32% increase compared to mesh 5. Consequently, mesh 4 was selected for the PPP due to its minimal error percentage and shorter processing time compared to the finer mesh.

With the study of mesh independence, the number of nodes and elements in each pipe networking was defined. The PPP yielded 990,800 nodes and 2,828,856 elements, while the RTP resulted in 661,595 nodes and 2,478,962 elements.

4. Results

4.1. Velocity Results

Figures 7 and 8 depict the water velocity distribution in each piping model when a water flow rate of 0.03 kg/s is supplied. Upon comparing the figures, noticeable disparities in the velocity magnitude are observed. It is crucial to note that the simulation was conducted under steady-state conditions, assuming that the pipe network was fully filled with water.

Figure 7. Velocity distribution for PPP with 0.03 kg/s of water.

Figure 7 illustrates the distribution of water mass flow within the parallel pipes. The highest mass flow occurs in the central pipe, while the pipes farther away from the centre line experience a decrease in mass flow. This non-uniform distribution of mass flow through the network pipes results in varying velocity magnitudes, as indicated by the scale in Figure 7. In the PPP, the water attains a velocity magnitude of up to 1.0 m/s, primarily in the inlet and outlet lines of the numerical domain. This behaviour can be attributed to the pipe diameter size of 7.3 mm. As the water flows into the parallel pipe channels, where the flow is divided, its velocity gradually decreases, reaching its highest value close to 0.4 m/s.

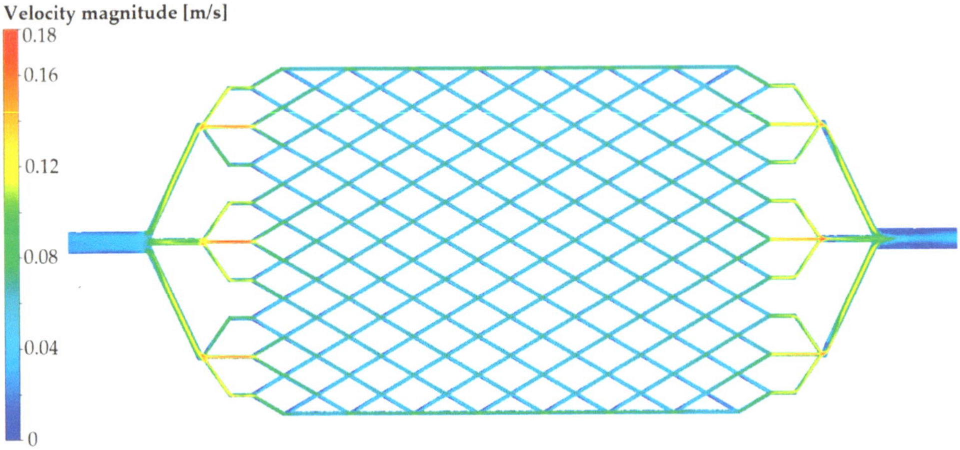

Figure 8. Velocity distribution for the RTP with 0.03 kg/s of water.

Figure 8 displays the velocity distribution in the RTP. The highest velocity is observed in the second branch of the fractal tree at the inlet and outlet, reaching a value of approximately 0.17 m/s. This magnitude represents 17% of the velocity magnitude obtained in the PPP. Within the embedded pipe of the RTP, characterized by its rhombic tessellation, the water maintains a uniform velocity of around 0.06 m/s throughout the entire rhombus section, as shown in Figure 8. The scale provided in the figure indicates the uniformity of velocity in the RTP for the considered angles in the tree fractal branches. This uniformity is achieved as the flow is divided into branches until it enters the rhombic tessellation. The uniform velocity distribution and lower velocity values in the RTP contribute to a reduced pressure drop. It is worth noting that the velocity distribution in the RTP differs from that of the PPP, where the maximum velocity is not located at the inlet or outlet of the numerical domain. The implementation of the fractal tree pattern at the piping entrance and exit, combined with the use of allometric relationships, has proven to be advantageous.

An exceedingly significant finding that emerged from the comparison of the two geometries is the consistent observation of laminar flow regime in RTP, irrespective of the defined mass flows as boundary conditions. This discovery carries immense importance as it highlights the unique hydraulic behaviour of the piping system. Specifically, at the input section of the tree fractal, where the highest mass flow rate of 0.06 kg/s was applied, the Reynolds number was calculated to be 1923.4. This confirmation of laminar flow at relatively higher mass flows further emphasizes the effectiveness and efficiency of the proposed design. This behaviour of the RTP is mainly attributed to the fractal tree pattern and the allometric relationships employed in constructing the inlet/outlet section. The different lengths and diameters of the fractal tree branches were adapted to the embedded pipe of the rhombic tessellation. Table 5 shows the Reynolds number values at the inlet line of both geometries. In particular, the Reynolds number in the inlet line of the PPP was 5.4 times higher than in the RTP. This difference may explain why the pressure drop in the PPP is considerably higher than in the RTP.

4.2. Pressure Drop Results

The investigation of pressure distribution results within each manifold of various mass flow rates constitutes a significant contribution of this study. Figures 9 and 10 showcase the water pressure distribution in each piping network under a mass flow rate of 0.03 kg/s. Notably, Figure 9 demonstrates a pressure drop of 1.175 kPa in the PPP, whereas Figure 10 reveals a significantly lower pressure drop of 0.1104 kPa in the RTP for the same mass flow rate. It is worth emphasizing that, in comparison to the PPP, the RTP exhibits a substantially reduced pressure drop along its surface, as clearly depicted in Figures 9 and 10, respectively. This discrepancy underscores the advantage of the RTP design in mitigating high-pressure drops, which can significantly impact the overall efficiency and operational cost of solar-assisted heat pump systems.

Table 5. Reynolds number in the inlet/outlet line of both geometries for each mass flow.

$\dot{m}$ [kg/s]	RTP	PPP
0.01	320.6	1738.9
0.02	641.1	3477.9
0.03	961.7	5216.8
0.04	1282.3	6955.8
0.05	1602.8	8694.7
0.06	1923.4	10,433.7

Figure 9. Static pressure for PPP with 0.03 kg/s of water.

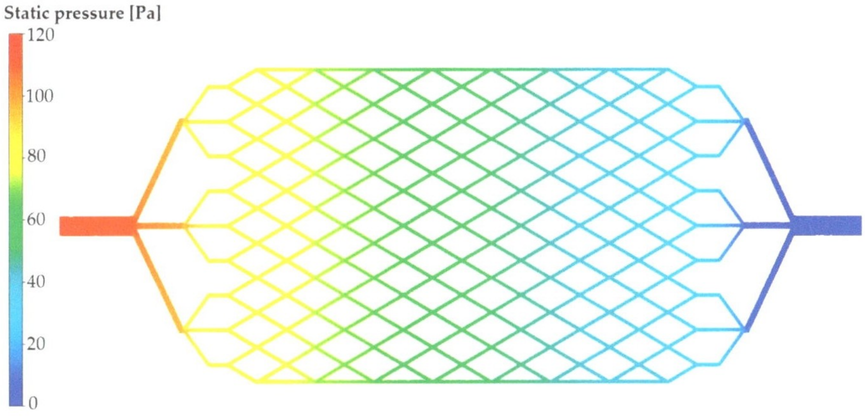

Figure 10. Static pressure for the RTP with 0.03 kg/s of water.

The pressure drop observed in the RTP amounts to a mere 8% of the pressure drop measured in the PPP. This remarkable reduction in pressure drop can be attributed to the implementation of allometric scales within the fractal tree design. The primary objective of incorporating these concepts is to minimize the energy consumption associated with fluid flow through the conduits. By adapting the dimensions of the fractal tree using allometric relationships, a more efficient and energy-saving system could be achieved, thereby enhancing the overall performance of the collector.

Figure 11 illustrates a compelling comparison of pressure drop between the RTP and PPP. It is highlighted that the piping with rhombic tessellation exhibits a remarkably smaller pressure drop when compared to the PPP design commonly encountered in the market. The figure serves to emphasize the significant advantage offered by the proposed piping networking model. The RTP demonstrates an average reduction in pressure drop of 92% in comparison to the PPP.

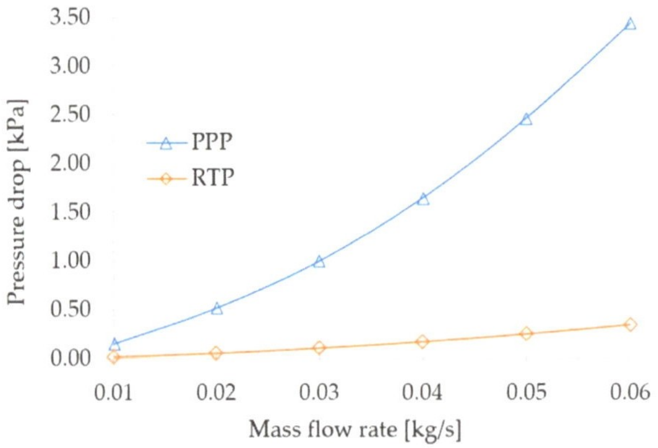

Figure 11. Pressure drop of both pipe network model with each mass flow of water simulated.

5. Discussion

The primary objective of this study was to analyse the internal flow characteristics of two different geometries: one with a PPP and the other with an RTP. Both PPP and RTP manifolds were constructed to have equivalent dimensions, including manifold plate area, percentage of area occupied by embedded tubes, and manifold capacity.

This study specifically examined the hydrodynamics of the observed behaviour in both geometries, without considering energy-related aspects such as heat transfer or phase change. The exclusion of the energy equation solution was due to its high computational demand and for not being a specific objective for this particular study. Additionally, convective phenomena were not taken into account in the analysis of each simulation, as there were no temperature gradients present. Therefore, the advective phenomenon played a crucial role in the transportation of fluid properties, such as mass and momentum, as the fluid flowed through the pipes.

The velocity distribution within the pipe network provides insights into the fluid behaviour and the impact of geometry on flow dynamics. In the PPP configuration, the fluid velocity was found to be highest near the inlet and outlet sections, reaching a maximum of 1.0 m/s. This high velocity is primarily influenced by the geometric arrangement of the parallel distribution tubes, which promotes uneven flow distribution. As the fluid entered the piping system, it gradually traversed through the parallel tubes, resulting in a decrease in flow rate as it reached the tubes located farther away on the sides from the inlet.

When the fluid reaches the outlet end, it encountered an abrupt change in direction due to the perpendicular placement of the tube leading to the outlet, resulting in what can be considered a "blocking" effect creating a zone of partial stagnation. Consequently, the central tube becomes the main pathway for fluid transport available, efficiently carrying it from the inlet to the outlet. As a result, the velocity of the fluid in the side tubes sharply decreases, approaching near-zero values, as the central tube adequately handles the fluid flow across the numerical domain. It is well-established that an increase in fluid velocity corresponds to a proportional pressure drop. In the case of the PPP, the observed pressure drop can be attributed to the flow restriction imposed by the geometry of the system and the higher velocities experienced by the water in the lateral tubes.

However, a notable difference is observed when analysing the RTP geometry. Particularly, the branching pattern from the inlet allows the fluid to irrigate each tube, traversing through each pathway. As a result, the velocity magnitude, as analysed through contour plots, appears more homogeneous and balanced.

It is observed in Figure 12 that, in the second trifurcation, a non-uniform distribution of flow is developed, as evidenced by distinct velocity profiles in each branch. Notably, the central tube within each branch exhibits a higher mass flow rate, possibly due to interference caused by branch 3, potentially inducing a suction effect. However, owing to the steep angle of branch 3, the fluid is unable to follow a curved trajectory. This behaviour is more clearly presented by the use of streamlines in Figure 12b. Consequently, a portion of the fluid is redirected towards branch 3, another portion towards branch 1, and the largest quantity towards the central branch 2. This symmetrical flow distribution pattern is observed in the remaining branches as well. The tessellation directly influences this behaviour for two primary reasons.

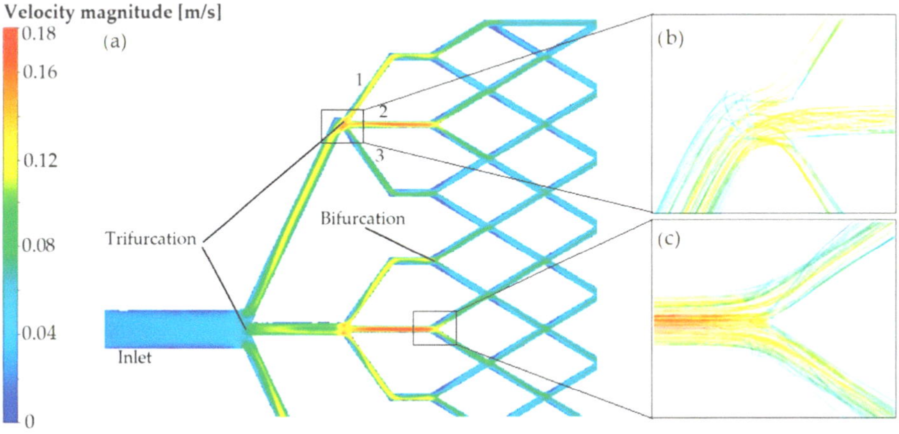

Figure 12. (**a**) Detail of branching pattern over the inlet velocity magnitude contour. (**b**) trifurcation and (**c**) bifurcation streamlines close up.

First, immediate trifurcation after the fluid enters causes a decrease in velocity, which is compensated by the reduction in diameter in that branch section. Subsequently, the fluid path trifurcates again, further compensating for the velocity magnitude through diameter reduction. In other words, the fluid velocity decreases due to diversion but increases as the diameter decreases. This phenomenon is reminiscent of the behaviour observed in Venturi tubes.

Secondly, as the fluid flows through the pipe with the rhombic pattern, there are as many stagnation zones as there are rhombic in the geometry pattern as seen in Figure 12c. This contributes to a homogenization of velocity throughout the entire pipe. Consequently, any pressure variation that may have occurred is recovered through the reunification of the branches. This behaviour is analogous to a bank of tubes exhibiting similar characteristics. As water is divided into the pipe channels, its velocity decreases due to the increased cross-sectional area.

In contrast, the RTP configuration exhibits a significantly lower pressure drop due to the more uniform velocity distribution and reduced flow opposition facilitated by the fractal geometry and rhombic tessellation. The fluid flow is more evenly distributed along the branches of the fractal tree and the embedded pipes, resulting in a reduced pressure drop compared to the PPP.

The fractal and rhombic pattern within the RTP geometry promotes smoother flow patterns, minimizing disruptions and flow restrictions. This leads to a more efficient transfer of fluid momentum and reduces energy losses due to friction. As a result, the pressure drop in the RTP configuration is significantly mitigated compared to the PPP.

The observed differences in pressure drop between the PPP and RTP highlight the influence of geometric design on flow opposition. The fractal geometry and rhombic tessellation in the RTP contribute to a more favourable flow distribution and reduced pressure drop, making it a promising configuration for applications where minimizing energy losses and flow opposition are crucial factors. Furthermore, this study revealed that for mass flows greater than 0.01 kg/s, both PPP and RTP configurations exhibited a turbulent flow regime at the inlet and outlet sections, resulting in higher water velocities and significant pressure drops.

For the PPP configuration, the pressure drop reached up to 3.43 kPa for a mass flow rate of 0.06 kg/s. In contrast, the RTP experienced a much lower pressure drop, measuring only 0.350 kPa for the same inlet mass flow rate. This remarkable decrease of 91.5% in pressure drop highlights the enhanced performance of the RTP configuration in reducing flow resistance compared to the PPP.

These findings demonstrate the improved performance of the RTP in terms of minimizing pressure drop, indicating its capacity to effectively accommodate higher mass flow rates while maintaining lower flow opposition highlighting its exceptional design and engineering potential. The allometric scaling, influenced by the proportion of the channel size through which the fluid flows, plays a crucial role in achieving this outcome. As the fluid traverses through the tessellation conduits, it experiences smoother displacement due to the direct influence of diameter. This characteristic is derived from Bernoulli's equation, which states that a proportional and consistent reduction in velocity results in a gradual pressure drop.

The observed results from both geometries revealed a noteworthy finding. The RTP consistently maintained laminar flow regime for all defined mass flows at the inlet. Preserving laminar flow, known for its smooth and streamlined characteristics, is highly desirable as it ensures more efficient operation and mitigates disadvantages associated with turbulence.

6. Conclusions

This study utilized computational fluid dynamics (CFD) to conduct a numerical assessment of the hydrodynamic behaviour of two novel 3D pipe networking geometries featuring distinct embedded pipe configurations. The first geometry employed a parallel pipe pattern (PPP), while the second utilized a rhombic tessellation pattern (RTP). Both configurations shared equivalent dimensions, differing solely in the geometric arrangement of the embedded pipes. Steady-state simulations were conducted on both models, applying identical boundary conditions and varying water mass flows within the range of 0.01 to 0.06 kg/s at a temperature of 20 °C. The obtained results included velocity distribution profiles and pressure drop measurements within each piping configuration, encompassing the entire range of mass flows considered.

By integrating the fractal tree pattern and the allometric relationship at the inlet and outlet sections of the RTP, a uniform flow distribution was achieved. The flow regime observed in the RTP remained laminar for all six defined mass flows. This unique characteristic of the pipe network was attributed to the carefully designed sizing of the fractal tree pattern and the incorporation of allometric relationships.

The implementation of the rhombic tessellation pattern enabled a homogeneous flow distribution within the piping system, leading to a uniform velocity magnitude that was lower compared to the water velocity in the parallel channels of the PPP. This uniform velocity distribution in the RTP contributed to a considerable reduction in the average pressure drop at the same water mass flow rate.

The geometry and size of the pipe networking play a crucial role in the hydrodynamics development. Conventional configurations, such as serpentine or parallel patterns, often result in higher pressure drops. To address this limitation, alternative geometries based on construction laws, such as allometric scales, have been proposed to enhance the performance of flat solar collectors. The current study evaluated the performance of the RTP, which incorporates a different geometry, and demonstrated its potential for improving the hydrodynamic characteristics of flat solar collectors.

The reduction in pressure drop observed in this study holds significant advantages for systems utilizing solar collectors' pipe complex configurations. Therefore, the results of this study serve as a diagnostic tool to estimate the performance of the device under the specified conditions and highlight the potential applications of the RTP geometry in various industrial activities. The findings offer valuable insights into the feasibility and benefits of incorporating the RTP design in practical applications.

Finally, the hydrodynamic outcomes presented in this study, resulting from the geometric characteristics of the RTP, hold significant potential for various industrial applications involving fluid transport. These outcomes include the potential for reducing operating costs and enhancing efficiency in fluid distribution. The unique geometric features of the RTP offer promising advantages that can positively impact multiple industrial activities.

Author Contributions: Conceptualization, I.C.-M. and J.E.D.L.-R.; methodology, R.R.-R., H.T.-P. and M.D.l.C.-Á.; software, R.R.-R. and M.D.l.C.-Á.; validation, R.R.-R., H.T.-P. and M.D.l.C.-Á.; formal analysis, I.C.-M., R.R.-R., J.E.D.L.-R. and M.D.l.C.-Á.; investigation, I.C.-M., R.R.-R., J.E.D.L.-R., H.T.-P. and M.D.l.C.-Á.; resources, I.C.-M. and H.T.-P.; data curation, R.R.-R. and M.D.l.C.-Á.; writing—original draft preparation, R.R.-R., H.T.-P. and M.D.l.C.-Á.; writing—review and editing, R.R.-R., H.T.-P. and M.D.l.C.-Á.; visualization, I.C.-M.; supervision, I.C.-M. and H.T.-P.; project administration, I.C.-M. and H.T.-P.; funding acquisition, I.C.-M. and H.T.-P. All authors have read and agreed to the published version of the manuscript.

Funding: This research was funded by the Instituto Politécnico Nacional and the Consejo Nacional de Humanidades, Ciencia y Tecnología, México.

Data Availability Statement: All data is within the document.

Acknowledgments: The authors of this paper are particularly grateful to Moreno-Rodríguez. from the Carlos III University of Madrid for the contributions made and the information provided.

Conflicts of Interest: The authors declare no conflict of interest.

erences

Sumair, F.A.; Mohammad, K.; Mahesh, V.R.; Arshid, N.; Abdul, K.R.; Nabisab, M.M. Recent progress in solar water heaters and solar collectors: A comprehensive review. *Therm. Sci. Eng. Prog.* **2021**, *25*, 100981.
Evangelos, B.; Christos, T.; Zafar, S. Investigation and optimization of a solar-assisted pumped thermal energy storage system with flat plate collectors. *Energy Convers. Manag.* **2021**, *237*, 114137.
Qureshi, I.A.; Waqas, A.; Ali, M.; Mehmood, A.; Javed, A. Performance evaluation of ORC system using evacuated flat plate Photovoltaic-Thermal collector as an evaporator. *Sol. Energy* **2021**, *230*, 859–873. [CrossRef]
Sun, X.; Dai, Y.; Novakovic, V.; Wu, J.; Wang, R. Performance comparison of direct expansion solar-assisted heat pump and conventional air source heat pump for domestic hot water. *Energy Procedia* **2015**, *70*, 394–401. [CrossRef]
Li, Y.W.; Wang, R.Z.; Wu, J.Y.; Xu, Y.X. Experimental performance analysis on a direct- expansion solar-assisted heat pump water heater. *Appl. Therm. Eng.* **2007**, *27*, 2858–2868. [CrossRef]
Sajid, A.; Yuan, Y.; Hassan, A.; Zhou, J.; Zeng, C.; Yu, M.; Emmanuel, B. Experimental and numerical investigation on a solar direct-expansion heat pump system employing PV/T & solar thermal collector as evaporator. *Energy* **2022**, *254*, 124312.
Yao, J.; Liu, W.; Zhao, Y.; Dai, Y.; Zhu, J.; Novakovic, V. Two-phase flow investigation in channel design of the roll-bond cooling component for solar assisted PVT heat pump application. *Energy Convers. Manag.* **2021**, *235*, 113988. [CrossRef]
Yao, J.; Zheng, S.; Chen, D.; Dai, Y.; Huang, M. Performance improvement of vapor-injection heat pump system by employing PVT collector/evaporator for residential heating in cold climate region. *Energy* **2021**, *219*, 119636. [CrossRef]
Jorge, L.R.; Ignacio, C.M. Mathematical Thermal Modelling of a Direct-Expansion Solar-Assisted Heat Pump Using Multi-Objective Optimization Based on the Energy Demand. *Energies* **2018**, *11*, 1773.
Jorge, L.R.; Ignacio, C.M. Thermal capacity: Additional relative efficiency to assess the overall performance of heat pump-based heating systems. *Appl. Therm. Eng.* **2019**, *159*, 113841.

11. Amancio, M.R.; Arturo, G.G.; Marcelo, I.; Nestor, G.H. Theoretical model and experimental validation of a direct-expansion s assisted heat pump for domestic hot water applications. *Energy* **2012**, *45*, 704–715.
12. Amancio, M.R.; Arturo, G.G.; Marcelo, I.; Nestor, G.H. Experimental validation of a theoretical model for a direct-expan solar-assisted heat pump applied to heating. *Energy* **2013**, *60*, 242–253.
13. Abhishek, T.; Sushil, K.; Pawan, K.; Sanjeev, K.; Bhardwaj, A.K. A review on the simulation/CFD based studies on the the augmentation of flat plate solar collectors. *Mater. Today Proc.* **2021**, *46*, 8578–8585.
14. Badiei, Z.; Eslami, M.; Jafarpur, K. Performance improvements in solar flat plate collectors by integrating with phase ch materials and fins: A CFD modeling. *Energy* **2020**, *192*, 116719. [CrossRef]
15. Mohammad, A.; Ben, H.; Andrew, H.; Dominic, C. Determining the Effect of Inlet Flow Conditions on the Thermal Efficiency Flat Plate Solar Collector. *Fluids* **2018**, *3*, 67.
16. Gunjo, D.G.; Mahanta, P.; Robi, P.S. Exergy and energy analysis of a novel type solar collector under steady state condi Experimental and CFD análisis. *Renew. Energy* **2017**, *114*, 655–669. [CrossRef]
17. Primož, P.; Urban, T.; Nada, P.; Boris, V.; Uroš, F.; Andrej, K. Numerical and experimental investigation of the energy and ex performance of solar thermal, photovoltaic and photovoltaic-thermal modules based on roll-bond heat exchangers. *En Convers. Manag.* **2020**, *210*, 112674.
18. Kasuba, S.; Suresh, A.; Kishen, K.R. Experimental and computational analysis of radiator and evaporator. *Mater. Today Proc.* 2, 2277–2290.
19. Sun, X.; Wu, J.; Dai, Y.; Wang, R. Experimental study on roll-bond collector/evaporator with optimized channel used in d expansion solar assisted heat pump water heating system. *Appl. Therm. Eng.* **2014**, *66*, 571–579. [CrossRef]
20. Aste, N.; Claudio, D.P.; Fabrizio, L. Water flat plate PV–thermal collectors: A review. *Sol. Energy* **2014**, *102*, 98–115.
21. Miglioli, A.; Aste, N.; Del Pero, C.; Leonforte, F. Photovoltaic-thermal solar-assisted heat pump systems for building applicat Integration and design methods. *Energy Built Environ.* **2023**, *4*, 39–56.
22. Aste, N.; Claudio, D.P.; Fabrizio, L. Thermal-electrical optimization of the configuration a liquid PVT collector. *Energy Proc* **2012**, *30*, 1–7. [CrossRef]
23. Al-Shamani, A.N.; Sopian, K.; Mat, S.; Hasan, H.A.; Abed, A.M.; Ruslan, M.H. Experimental studies of rectangular tube abs photovoltaic thermal collector with various types of nanofluids under the tropical climate conditions. *Energy Convers. M* **2016**, *124*, 528–542. [CrossRef]
24. Dupeyrat, P.; Ménézo, C.; Rommel, M.; Henning, H.M. Efficient single glazed flat plate photovoltaic–thermal hybrid collecto domestic hot water system. *Sol. Energy* **2011**, *85*, 1457–1468. [CrossRef]
25. Huide, F.; Xuxin, Z.; Lei, M.; Tao, Z.; Qixing, W.; Hongyuan, S. A comparative study on three types of solar utilization technolo for buildings: Photovoltaic, solar thermal and hybrid photovoltaic/thermal systems. *Energy Convers. Manag.* **2017**, *140*, [CrossRef]
26. Del Col, D.; Padovan, A.; Bortolato, M.; Dai Prè, M.; Zambolin, E. Thermal performance of flat plate solar collectors sheet-and-tube and roll-bond absorbers. *Energy* **2013**, *58*, 258–269. [CrossRef]
27. Swapnil, D.; Andrew, A.O. Testing of two different types of photovoltaic–thermal (PVT) modules with heat flow pattern u tropical climatic conditions. *Energy Sustain. Dev.* **2013**, *17*, 1–12.
28. Guarracino, I.; Mellor, A.; Ekins-Daukes, N.J.; Markides, C.N. Dynamic coupled thermal-and-electrical modelling of sheet- tube hybrid photovoltaic/thermal (PVT) collectors. *Appl. Therm. Eng.* **2016**, *101*, 778–795. [CrossRef]
29. Santbergen, R.; Rindt, C.M.; Zondag, H.A.; Van Zolingen, R.C. Detailed analysis of the energy yield of systems with cov sheet-and-tube PVT collectors. *Sol. Energy* **2010**, *84*, 867–878. [CrossRef]
30. Touafek, K.; Khelifa, A.; Adouane, M. Theoretical and experimental study of sheet and tubes hybrid PVT collector. *Energy Con Manag.* **2014**, *80*, 71–77. [CrossRef]
31. Hosseinzadeh, M.; Salari, A.; Sardarabadi, M.; Passandideh-Fard, M. Optimization and parametric analysis of a nanofluid b photovoltaic thermal system: 3D numerical model with experimental validation. *Energy Convers. Manag.* **2018**, *160*, 93–108.
32. Herrando, M.; Ramos, A.; Zabalza, I.; Markides, C.N. A comprehensive assessment of alternative absorber-exchanger design hybrid PVT-water collectors. *Appl. Energy* **2019**, *235*, 1583–1602. [CrossRef]
33. Fudholi, A.; Sopian, K.; Yazdi, M.H.; Ruslan, M.H.; Ibrahim, A.; Kazem, H.A. Performance analysis of photovoltaic thermal (I water collectors. *Energy Convers. Manag.* **2014**, *78*, 641–651. [CrossRef]
34. Aste, N.; Fabrizio, L.; Claudio, D.P. Design, modeling and performance monitoring of a photovoltaic–thermal (PVT) w collector. *Sol. Energy* **2015**, *112*, 85–99. [CrossRef]
35. Buonomano, A.; Francesco, C.; Maria, V. Design, simulation and experimental investigation of a solar system based on PV pa and PVT collectors. *Energies* **2016**, *9*, 497. [CrossRef]
36. Lari, M.O.; Ahmet, Z.S. Design, performance and economic analysis of a nanofluid-based photovoltaic/thermal system residential applications. *Energy Convers. Manag.* **2017**, *149*, 467–484. [CrossRef]
37. Yu, X.F.; Zhang, C.P.; Teng, J.T.; Huang, S.Y.; Jin, S.P.; Lian, Y.F.; Cheng, C.H.; Xu, T.T.; Chu, J.C.; Chang, Y.J.; et al. A study on hydraulic and thermal characteristics in fractal tree-like microchannels by numerical and experimental methods. *Int. J. Heat M Transf.* **2012**, *55*, 7499–7507. [CrossRef]
38. Wang, G.; Gu, Y.; Zhao, L.; Xuan, J.; Zeng, G.; Tang, Z.; Sun, Y. Experimental and numerical investigation of fractal-tree-like exchanger manufactured by 3D printing. *Chem. Eng. Sci.* **2019**, *195*, 250–261. [CrossRef]

Zhuang, D.; Yang, Y.; Ding, G.; Du, X.; Hu, Z. Optimization of Microchannel Heat Sink with Rhombus Fractal-like Units for Electronic Chip Cooling. *Int. J. Refrig.* **2020**, *116*, 108–118. [CrossRef]
Jing, D.; He, L.; Wang, X. Optimization analysis of fractal tree-like microchannel network for electroviscous flow to realize minimum hydraulic resistance. *Int. J. Heat Mass Transf.* **2018**, *125*, 749–755. [CrossRef]
Geoffrey, W.; James, B.; Brian, E. A general model for the origin of allometric scaling laws in biology. *Science* **1997**, *276*, 122–126.
Kittinan, B.; Mehrdad, M.; Javad, M.N.; Rasool, A.; Omid, M.; Ahmet, S.D.; Ho, S.A.; Somchai, W. Prediction of battery thermal behaviour in the presence of a constructal theory-based heat pipe (CBHP): A multiphysics model and pattern-based machine learning approach. *J. Energy Storage* **2022**, *48*, 103963.
Bejan, A.; Lorente, S. Constructal theory of generation of configuration in nature and engineering. *J. Appl. Phys.* **2006**, *100*, 5. [CrossRef]
Bejan, A. Constructal-theory network of conducting paths for cooling a heat generating volume. *Int. J. Heat Mass Transf.* **1997**, *40*, 799–816. [CrossRef]
Kittipong, S.; Mehrdad, M.; Jatuporn, K.; Ahmet, S.D.; Ho, S.A.; Omid, M.; Somchai, W. Novel design of a liquid-cooled heat sink for a high performance processor based on constructal theory: A numerical and experimental approach. *Alex. Eng. J.* **2022**, *61*, 10341–10358.
Tesař, V. Bifurcating channels supplying "numbered-up" microreactors. *Chem. Eng. Res. Des.* **2011**, *89*, 2507–2520. [CrossRef]
Johansson, E.; Moohammed, W.Y. Wind comfort and solar access in a coastal development in Malmö, Sweden. *Urban Clim.* **2020**, *33*, 100645. [CrossRef]
Nguyen, T.D.; Ha, M.B. Computational fluid dynamic model for smoke control of building basement. *Case Stud. Chem. Environ. Eng.* **2023**, *7*, 100318. [CrossRef]
Moaveni, S. *Finite Element Analysis Theory and Application with ANSYS*, 2nd ed.; Pearson Education: Hoboken, NJ, USA, 2011; pp. 5–8.
Patankar, S.V. *Numerical Heat Transfer and Fluid Flow*; Hemisphere Publishing Corporation: New York, NY, USA, 1980.
Walter, H. Dynamic simulation of natural circulation steam generators with the use of finite-volume-algorithms—A comparison of four algorithms. *Simul. Model. Pract. Theory* **2007**, *15*, 565–588. [CrossRef]
Nelson, O.M.; Juan, I.J.; Roberto, C.C. An approach to accelerate the convergence of SIMPLER algorithm for convection-diffusion problems of fluid flow with heat transfer and phase change. *Int. Commun. Heat Mass Transf.* **2021**, *129*, 105715.
Yin, R.; Chow, W.K. Comparison of four algorithms for solving pressure velocity linked equations in simulating atrium fire. *Int. J. Archit. Sci.* **2003**, *4*, 24–35.
Schnipke, R.J. *A Streamline Upwind Finite-Element Method for Laminar and Turbulent Flow*; University of Virginia: Charlottesville, VA, USA, 1986.
Garg, H.; Agarwal, R. Some aspects of a PV/T collector/forced circulation flat plate solar water heater with solar cells. *Energy Convers. Manag.* **1995**, *36*, 87–99. [CrossRef]
White, F.M. *Fluid Mechanics*, 5th ed.; McGraw-Hill Book Company: Boston, MA, USA, 2003.
Colebrook, C.F.; Blench, T.; Chatley, H.; Essex, E.H.; Finniecome, J.R.; Lacey, G.; Macdonald, G. Correspondence. turbulent flow in pipes, with particular reference to the transition region between the smooth and rough pipe laws. (includes plates). *J. Inst. Civ. Eng.* **1939**, *12*, 393–422. [CrossRef]
Fox, R.W.; McDonald, A.T.; Mitchell, J.W. *Fox and McDonald's Introduction to Fluid Mechanics*; John Wiley & Sons: Hoboken, NJ, USA, 2020.
Gabriela, L.; Andrew, K.; Amir, K. Experimental Techniques against RANS Method in a Fully Developed Turbulent Pipe Flow: Evolution of Experimental and Computational Methods for the Study of Turbulence. *Fluids* **2022**, *7*, 78.
Milad, A.; Paola, G.; David, V.; Carlo, G. Numerical Study of Flow Downstream a Step with a Cylinder Part 1: Validation of the Numerical Simulations. *Fluids* **2023**, *8*, 55.
Yoon, G.H. Topology optimization method with finite elements based on the k-ε turbulence model. *Comput. Methods Appl. Mech. Eng.* **2020**, *361*, 112784. [CrossRef]
Brice, R.; Jonas, K.J.; Svenn, K.H.; Wiebke, B.M. Analysis of Cold Air Recirculation in the Evaporators of Large-Scale Air-Source Heat Pumps Using CFD Simulations. *Fluids* **2020**, *5*, 186.
Launder, B.; Spalding, D. *Mathematical Models of Turbulence*; Academic Press: London, UK, 1972.

MDPI AG
Grosspeteranlage 5
4052 Basel
Switzerland
Tel.: +41 61 683 77 34

Fluids Editorial Office
E-mail: fluids@mdpi.com
www.mdpi.com/journal/fluids

www.ingramcontent.com/pod-product-compliance
Ingram Content Group UK Ltd.
Pitfield, Milton Keynes, MK11 3LW, UK
UKHW061013121026
15625UKWH00069B/606
9783725844364